AI-Enhanced Hyper-Personalization for Customer Experience in the Service Industry

Maria Antónia Rodrigues
CEOS.PP, School of Business Sciences of Porto, Technical University of Porto, Portugal

Maria Amélia Carvalho
https://orcid.org/0000-0002-9075-1793
University of Maia, Portugal & CEOS.PP, School of Business Sciences of Porto, Technical University of Porto, Portugal

Didar Büyüker Isler
Süleyman Demirel University, Turkey

IGI Global
Scientific Publishing
Publishing Tomorrow's Research Today

Vice President of Editorial Melissa Wagner
Director of Acquisitions Mikaela Felty
Director of Book Development Jocelynn Hessler
Production Manager Mike Brehm
Cover Design Jose Rosado

Published in the United States of America by
IGI Global Scientific Publishing
701 East Chocolate Avenue
Hershey, PA, 17033, USA
Tel: 717-533-8845 | Fax: 717-533-7115
Website: https://www.igi-global.com E-mail: cust@igi-global.com

Library of Congress Cataloging-in-Publication Data

Names: Rodrigues, Maria Antonia, 1977- editor | Carvalho, Maria Amélia Machado, 1989- editor | Isler, Didar, 1979- editor
Title: AI-enhanced hyper-personalization for customer experience in the service industry / [edited by] Maria Rodrigues, Maria Amélia Machado Carvalho, Didar Isler.
Description: Hershey, PA : IGI Global Scientific Publishing, [2027] | Includes bibliographical references and index. | Summary: "This book explores how AI technologies redefine the consumer experience in service environments. It integrates insights from marketing, service operations, information systems, and AI research, offering both conceptual clarity and managerial guidance"-- Provided by publisher.
Identifiers: LCCN 2026014691 (print) | LCCN 2026014692 (ebook) | ISBN 9798337391595 hardcover | ISBN 9798337391601 paperback | ISBN 9798337391618 ebook
Subjects: LCSH: Customer services--Technological innovations | Artificial intelligence--Business applications
Classification: LCC HF5415.5 .A388 2026 (print) | LCC HF5415.5 (ebook) | DDC 658.8/1201--dc23/eng/20260522
LC record available at https://lccn.loc.gov/2026014691
LC ebook record available at https://lccn.loc.gov/2026014692

British Cataloguing in Publication Data
A Cataloguing in Publication record for this book is available from the British Library.

Table of Contents

Detailed Table of Contents

trust. Adopting a qualitative case study approach, the chapter analyzes Netflix and Amazon as leading examples of AI-enabled personalization. The findings suggest that while hyper-personalization enhances perceived relevance, engagement, and satisfaction, trust is not an automatic outcome and is contingent upon transparency, perceived fairness, and data governance practices. The chapter contributes by conceptualizing the personalization–trust paradox and offers actionable insights for designing responsible AI-driven consumer experiences.

AI-driven hyper-personalization is transforming service encounters by tailoring information, offers, and interactions to individual consumers in real time. Across retail, banking, healthcare, and hospitality, providers increasingly rely on predictive models, recommender systems, automated decision tools, and conversational interfaces to adapt service content at the level of the single customer. Yet the rapid expansion of algorithmic personalization has not been matched by a comparable growth in consumer trust, and this widening gap raises a central question for service marketing: when does AI-enabled personalization deepen durable loyalty, and when does it produce shallow, fragile, or actively eroding relationships?

The use of Artificial Intelligence (AI) has revolutionized the delivery of services by providing efficient, tailored, and automated customer services. As AI-based services like chatbots, virtual assistants, and recommendation systems continue to gain more popularity, it is necessary to understand consumer behavior. This chapter will discuss how the trust and customer satisfaction contribute to consumer loyalty in AI-based services. According to the Stimulus-Organism-Response (S-O-R) model (Mehrabian and Russell, 1974) and the relationship marketing model (Morgan and Hunt, 1994), trust is an antecedent, customer satisfaction a mediator variable, and consumer loyalty is an outcome. Reliability and security lead to trust which lessens

This study examines the role of AI-powered hyper-personalization in transforming service experience design within hospitality and tourism. Using a mixed-method approach, it analyzes its impact on service quality, guest satisfaction, emotional engagement, and loyalty. The findings indicate that AI-driven personalization enhances both cognitive and emotional outcomes, while the balance between human interaction and automation, along with ethical AI governance, significantly strengthens trust and overall service effectiveness.

The technological aspect of the hospitality industry has experienced rapid change, transforming how companies engage with their consumers. Nonetheless, cultural beliefs and the different consumer demographics are important in determining the success of technology adoption. This chapter explains the complex relationships among culture and diversity, technology adoption in business, and consumer engagement in the hospitality industry. The research question is to identify whether and how cultural perceptions, language, digital literacy, and socio-emographic factors affect the usage of hospitality technologies, such as self-service kiosks, mobile applications, artificial intelligence chatbots, and digital concierge services, the level of trust in them, and satisfaction with their use. The chapter provides prudent advice to hospitality managers eager to address the needs of this diverse consumer base through bargaining in global markets.

The trend toward the widespread use of mobile technologies during tourist stays raises questions about the appropriateness and effectiveness of such practices in terms of tourist experiences and satisfaction with their stay in a given destination. Tourists are enthusiastic about the widespread use of various mobile technologies to prepare, carry out, and remember their trips, and their reasons for doing so are many and varied. To what extent does the use of m-tourism services, particularly mobile services for guidance, organization, and localized information search, promote the development of the quality of tourist experiences, and thus improve the overall perceived value of their stay? From a practical standpoint, we aim to inform tourism professionals about the characteristics their mobile services should have in order to improve the tourist experience and thus maximize customer satisfaction.

The airline industry is changing through Artificial Intelligence (AI) and its role in enhancing customer interactions and efficiency within the industry. The report goes into how chatbots, virtual assistants and predictive sentiment analysis are being deployed by airlines to provide better passenger experience, make well-informed decisions, and reduce business expenses. Using secondary data, the study's authors investigated AI's efficacy in the aviation sector. Mostly, airline companies concentrated on the AI applications to offer hyper-personalized services to customers such as improved in-flight entertainment, simplified security checks, more enjoyable booking experience, and expedited customer complaints and problems resolutions. At a more practical level, AI enhances flight scheduling, predictive maintenance, cost management, route planning and safety. Artificially intelligent-based baggage handling solutions can facilitate operations, streamline revenues, and decrease wait times, as they streamline the work of the staff.

Preface

Artificial intelligence is changing the way service organizations understand, engage with and create value for their customers. Advances in artificial intelligence, machine learning, predictive analytics, natural language processing, recommendation systems and real-time data analysis have increasingly enabled services and interactions to be tailored to the preferences, behaviors, circumstances and expectations of individual customers.

This change is the rise of hyper-personalization as one of the most important trends in modern service management and customer experience. Traditional personalization relies on static customer profiles or historical data. AI-powered hyper-personalization can evaluate data, recognize trends, predict needs and adapt interactions in real time.

For service organizations, these capabilities provide significant opportunities. Services are often characterized by interaction, heterogeneity, uncertainty and the need to understand customers at different points in their journeys. AI offers new ways of handling this complexity. Predictive systems can help organizations to anticipate behavior, recommendation engines can improve the relevance of service offerings, chatbots and virtual assistants can provide immediate and increasingly individualized support, and behavioral analytics can help organizations to understand changing customer expectations across multiple touchpoints.

Customer experience has become an important source of differentiation in service markets. When AI is used, hyper-personalization can reduce customer effort, increase relevance, improve responsiveness, strengthen engagement, and contribute to satisfaction and loyalty. For organizations it helps in designing services around individual needs rather than expecting customers to adapt to standardized service processes.

At the same time, the used of individualized and data-intensive services introduces questions that cannot be addressed by technology alone. The greater the ability of organizations to know, predict, and respond to customers, the greater the need to consider how that knowledge is obtained and used. Consumers may like a service that can predict their preferences but may not like the amount of personal information required to make that prediction possible. They may like the efficiency of automated help but also want human judgment applied when a conversation gets complex or sensitive. They may like relevant recommendations but be confused as to why a specific recommendation was made.

These tensions make AI-enhanced hyper-personalization a particularly important area of inquiry for the service industry. The central issue is not simply whether artificial intelligence can enable greater personalization, but what kind of personalization creates value, under what conditions customers respond positively to it, and how organizations can combine technological intelligence with ethic, privacy, responsibility, and meaningful customer relationships.

Service interactions have always depended on knowledge of the customer. What has changed is the scale, speed, and depth at which knowledge can now be developed and applied. The traditional logic of market segmentation is being challenged. Segmentation remains useful for understanding consumers, but AI increasingly allows organizations to move beyond fixed categories toward individualized and context-sensitive interactions. A customer may no longer be treated primarily as a member of a demographic or behavioral segment. Instead, systems can respond to the individual according to a combination of previous behavior, current circumstances, channel, location, timing, preferences, and predicted intentions.

This development has implications throughout the customer journey. Before a service encounter, AI may support targeting, prediction, and recommendation. During the encounter, intelligent systems may personalize communication, content, prices, interfaces, or support. Following the interaction, AI can interpret feedback and behavioral information to refine future experiences. Personalization therefore becomes an ongoing process rather than a discrete marketing action.

At the same time, customer experience is not created by algorithms in isolation. It emerges through interactions among customers, technologies, employees, organizational processes, service environments, and other actors. This makes the human dimension of AI-enhanced service particularly important. Greater accuracy or efficiency does not necessarily produce greater satisfaction, just as increased personalization does not automatically create greater trust or loyalty. The way customers perceive and interpret AI-mediated interactions remains fundamental.

Responsibility means that organizations need to recognize these trade-offs, not make them secondary considerations in hyper-personalization. The service context further complicates this challenge, because the appropriate balance between personalization, automation and human involvement is not likely to be the same across industries. An AI-assisted decision in financial services is not the same as a personalized recommendation in entertainment. An AI system involved in healthcare, education or financial decision-making creates different expectations than a virtual assistant answering a mundane travel question. Cultural and demographic differences can also influence consumers' responses to digital technologies, privacy practices, automation and personalized interactions.

The diversity of contexts is one reason why the study of AI-enhanced hyper-personalization benefits from a multidisciplinary approach. Marketing and customer experience perspectives are essential, but so too are service theory, information systems, technology adoption, consumer behavior, ethics, and artificial intelligence. AI-Enhanced Hyper-Personalization for Customer Experience in the Service Industry brings these perspectives together.

The book examines the technological capabilities that make hyper-personalization possible, the mechanisms through which value and customer experience are affected, the role of trust, satisfaction, loyalty and adoption, the ethical challenges created by extensive personalization, and the application of these developments across different service industries and digital environments.

The book combines conceptual contributions, empirical studies, systematic reviews, mixed-method research, predictive modeling, case studies, and sector-specific analyses.

This book is an important academic resource for graduate and doctoral students, customer experience strategists, marketing analysts, service designers, digital transformation leaders, product managers, policymakers, and more. The book provides insights into how AI-enabled personalization can be designed and managed across different service contexts. Professionals concerned with data strategy, responsible AI, digital services, customer engagement, and technology adoption may also find the volume useful in understanding the broader implications of increasingly personalized service systems.

ORGANIZATION OF THE BOOK

The book is organized into sixteen chapters. The first four chapters establishes the conceptual, technological, and analytical foundations of AI-enhanced hyper-personalization. The following four chapters examines the relational and ethical conditions that influence customer responses, with particular attention to trust, satisfaction, loyalty, privacy, and responsible AI. The two subsequent chapters focuses on intelligent interfaces and emerging digital environments through which personalized experiences increasingly take place. The last six chapters moves into specific service industries and demonstrates how AI-enhanced personalization and customer experience are shaped by particular sectoral and cultural contexts.

Chapter 1, "AI-Driven Hyper-Personalisation in the Service Industry: Post-Segmentation Marketing," introduces the shift from traditional segmentation-based approaches toward a post-segmentation marketing paradigm. Drawing on Service-Dominant Logic, the Stimulus-Organism-Response framework, and dynamic capabilities, the chapter examines how AI-based technologies enable real-time personalized service interactions and how these influence customer experience, satisfaction, engagement, and loyalty. As the opening chapter, it establishes the central transition addressed throughout the book: from managing customer groups toward increasingly individualized service relationships.

Chapter 2, "Predictive Analytics and AI as Drivers of Personalized Consumer Experience in Digital Service Ecosystems," examines the analytical capabilities that make this transition possible. The chapter considers how machine learning, behavioral analytics, and real-time analytics support predictive and prescriptive approaches to customer experience. It discusses applications such as behavioral prediction and personalization algorithms across different service settings while also acknowledging challenges related to privacy, algorithmic bias, transparency, and organizational preparedness. The chapter demonstrates why data analysis is no longer simply a supporting activity but an integral component of contemporary service experience design.

Chapter 3, "Value Co-Creation in AI-Driven Services: Hyper-Personalization, Distributed Agency, and Consumer Experience," extends the discussion from prediction to value creation. Integrating Service-Dominant Logic, Actor-Network Theory, and post-phenomenological perspectives, the chapter explores how AI redistributes agency within service ecosystems and mediates the customer experience. It develops mechanisms involving distributed agency, experiential mediation, resource reconfiguration, and relational tension and recognizes that hyper-personalization may contribute to both value co-creation and value co-destruction. The chapter is particularly important in positioning AI as a participant in the service system rather than simply as an organizational tool.

Chapter 4, "From Segmentation to Hyper-Personalization – Case Studies on Consumer Experience and Trust in AI-Based Service Ecosystems," illustrates the movement from broad segmentation toward individualized experiences through the cases of Netflix and Amazon. The analysis shows how AI-enabled personalization can increase relevance, engagement, and satisfaction, but also demonstrates that trust cannot be taken for granted. Transparency, perceived fairness, and data governance influence whether personalization strengthens the customer relationship.

Chapter 5, "The Trust-Loyalty Nexus in AI-Mediated Hyper-Personalized Services: Transparency, Authenticity, and Vulnerability," examines the conditions under which AI-enabled personalization can strengthen or weaken customer relationships. The chapter places trust at the center of the relationship between hyper-personalization and loyalty and considers transparency, explainability, authenticity, vulnerability, privacy, and governance. Its contribution is particularly valuable because it challenges the assumption that greater personalization naturally produces stronger relationships. Instead, the effects of personalization depend on how consumers interpret the organization, technology, and use of their data.

Chapter 6, "Understanding Consumer Loyalty in AI-Based Services: The Roles of Trust and Satisfaction," develops the relationship between AI-enabled services and loyalty through the Stimulus-Organism-Response model and relationship marketing. The chapter considers trust as an important antecedent, satisfaction as a key mechanism, and loyalty as a relational outcome. Reliability, security, service quality, and personalization are discussed as important elements shaping these responses. The contribution reinforces the view that successful AI-based service cannot be assessed only through functional efficiency but should also be evaluated through customers' relational and experiential responses.

Chapter 7, "AI-Based Services and Consumer Loyalty: A Trust–Satisfaction Perspective," further investigates these relationships by conceptualizing AI service quality through dimensions such as reliability, responsiveness, accuracy, personalization, and transparency. Trust and satisfaction are positioned as mediating mechanisms linking AI service quality with loyalty. Through its proposed quantitative approach, the chapter provides a structured basis for examining how specific characteristics of AI-enabled services can contribute to stronger customer relationships.

Chapter 8, "Convenience versus Privacy: Navigating Ethical Trade-Offs in AI-Based Services," addresses a central tension in hyper-personalized customer experience. Consumers increasingly value personalized and convenient services while simultaneously becoming more concerned about how organizations collect, process, and use personal information. Drawing on a systematic review of the literature, the chapter examines privacy, algorithmic bias, transparency, explainability, accountability, and consumer autonomy. It shows that the advantages of personalization may be undermined when data collection is perceived as excessive or AI-supported decisions are difficult to understand. The chapter consequently emphasizes responsible AI governance, privacy-by-design, explainable AI, human oversight, and meaningful consumer control as important elements in reconciling personalization with privacy and long-term trust.

Chapter 9, "AI-Driven Chatbots and Virtual Assistants: Transforming Customer Engagement in the Digital Era," examines the growing importance of conversational AI in customer service and engagement. The chapter discusses how natural language processing, machine learning, and predictive analytics enable chatbots and virtual assistants to provide immediate support, automate interactions, personalize responses, and contribute to predictions of future customer behavior. By considering customer interaction, operational efficiency, retention, omnichannel integration, brand loyalty, and AI ethics, the chapter illustrates the dual role of conversational technologies as both service delivery mechanisms and personalized customer interfaces.

Chapter 10, "Consumer Experience in Metaverse Environments," expands the discussion into immersive digital settings. Drawing on perspectives from the experience economy, experiential marketing, and immersive technologies, the chapter examines how presence, flow, interactivity, social presence, and avatar-mediated interaction shape consumer experience. Artificial intelligence adds a further layer by enabling adaptive and personalized experiences within these environments. The chapter therefore shows how hyper-personalization may evolve as customer experiences increasingly take place within interactive, immersive, and technologically mediated service spaces.

Chapter 11, "From Data to Delight: AI-Powered Hyper-Personalization in Service Experience Design – Conceptual and Managerial Perspectives," focuses on hospitality and tourism and examines how AI-supported hyper-personalization influences service quality, guest satisfaction, emotional engagement, and loyalty. The chapter also addresses the relationship between automation and human interaction and recognizes ethical AI governance as an important condition for effective service design. Its contribution highlights that personalized guest experience depends not only on the sophistication of AI technologies but also on how those technologies are integrated with human service.

Chapter 12, "The Role of Culture and Diversity in Technology Adoption on Consumer Engagement in Hospitality," introduces cultural and demographic variation into the analysis of technology-mediated service. The chapter explores how cultural perceptions, language, digital literacy, and socio-demographic characteristics affect customer engagement with self-service kiosks, mobile applications, AI chatbots, and digital concierge services. By connecting these factors with trust and satisfaction, the chapter reminds service organizations that customer responses to technological personalization cannot be assumed to be universal. Designing inclusive customer experiences requires sensitivity to the characteristics of different consumer groups and markets.

Chapter 13, "Hyper-Personalized M-Tourism Services and Customer Experience Value: An AI-Enhanced Analytical Model," considers the increasingly important role of mobile services throughout the tourism experience. It examines how mobile technologies used for guidance, organization, and localized information can influence the quality and perceived value of tourist experiences. The chapter has particular managerial relevance because it connects the characteristics of mobile tourism services with customer satisfaction and provides insights for tourism organizations seeking to make mobile interactions more useful and contextually relevant.

Chapter 14, "The Transformative Applications of Artificial Intelligence in Airlines: Enhancing Passenger Experience and Operations," examines AI in the airline industry from both customer-facing and operational perspectives. Applications include chatbots, virtual assistants, predictive sentiment analysis, personalized in-flight entertainment, booking support, security processes, and complaint resolution, alongside operational uses such as scheduling, maintenance, route planning, baggage handling, and cost management. The chapter demonstrates that customer experience is closely connected with the quality and efficiency of the systems operating behind the customer interface and that AI can create value simultaneously across both dimensions.

Chapter 15, "AI-Enhanced Hyper-Personalization and Its Impact on Customer Experience Excellence in the Food & Beverage Service Industry," investigates hyper-personalization in restaurants, cafés, and quick-service environments. Grounded in Service-Dominant Logic and customer experience theory, the chapter examines how recommendation systems, predictive analytics, and intelligent customer interfaces may contribute to experiential value, emotional engagement, customer experience excellence, and loyalty. Its sequential mixed-method design brings together customer and managerial perspectives and provides insight into how personalization is being incorporated into highly competitive and experience-oriented service environments.

Chapter 16, "AI-Driven Assessment Design in Higher Education: Enhancing Personalization, Academic Integrity, and Learning Outcomes," concludes the book by extending the discussion of AI-enabled personalization to higher education as a service environment. The chapter considers how machine learning, natural language processing, and learning analytics can support adaptive assessment, automated feedback, and real-time performance monitoring. By addressing personalization alongside academic integrity and learning outcomes, the chapter illustrates how the principles underlying AI-enhanced individualized experiences can extend beyond conventional commercial customer interactions. Its placement as the final chapter also highlights the wider implications of intelligent personalization for service systems in which individual needs, responsible technology use, and experience quality must be balanced.

The chapters brought together in *AI-Enhanced Hyper-Personalization for Customer Experience in the Service Industry* illustrate a service landscape in which personalization is becoming more intelligent, dynamic, predictive, and embedded in the customer journey. Artificial intelligence enables organizations to move beyond conventional segmentation and respond to individuals with a degree of precision and immediacy that would previously have been difficult to achieve.

Yet the book also demonstrates that technological capability alone does not determine the quality of the customer experience. The ability to predict customer behavior does not guarantee that a recommendation will be welcomed. The capacity to collect more customer information does not mean that doing so will strengthen the relationship. Automation may improve responsiveness while simultaneously reducing an element of human interaction that customers value. Hyper-personalization can increase relevance while also creating concerns about privacy and control. For this, the future of AI-enhanced customer experience depends on the relationship between technological intelligence and responsible service design. One of the principal contributions of this book is therefore to bring these dimensions together. Rather than examining artificial intelligence simply as a set of technologies, the chapters consider AI within the wider service ecosystem.

For researchers, these contributions identify a field in which many important questions remain open. Future research will need to examine how different degrees of personalization influence customer responses, when customers consider personalization useful rather than intrusive, how transparency and explainability affect trust, and how these relationships vary across technologies, industries, cultures, and stages of the customer journey.

For managers, the message emerging from the volume is equally significant. Effective hyper-personalization should not be understood simply as the ability to know more about customers or automate more aspects of the service process. It requires deciding what information is appropriate to use, which aspects of an interaction benefit from personalization, where automation adds value, when human judgment remains essential, and how customers can maintain confidence and meaningful control over their interactions with intelligent systems.

It is our hope that this book will contribute to this discussion by providing researchers, students, managers, and professionals with conceptual perspectives, empirical evidence, methodological approaches, and practical insights into the changing relationship between artificial intelligence, hyper-personalization, and customer experience. As AI becomes increasingly embedded in service encounters, understanding this relationship will be essential to designing the next generation of customer experiences.

Maria Antónia Rodrigues

CEOS.PP, School of Business Sciences of Porto, Technical University of Porto, Portugal

Maria Amélia Carvalho

University of Maia, Portugal & CEOS.PP, School of Business Sciences of Porto, Technical University of Porto, Portugal

Didar Buyuker

Business Administration Department, Suleyman Demirel University, Türkiye

Acknowledgment

The editors would like to acknowledge the support of the researchers and the IGI Global editorial team involved in this project. Among the editors, authors, and reviewers, ninety researchers participated and committed to the book.

Forty-five authors from diverse countries and continents contributed to the book. The editors would like to thank each of the authors for their contributions.

The chapters were reviewed by forty-two reviewers, whose valuable work helped enrich and improve the final result of the book. Therefore, we are grateful for the support of the reviwers who contributed to the review process of each chapter.

The editors also appreciate IGI Global's support throughout the process.

The editors gratefully acknowledge financial support from FCT – Fundação para a Ciência e a Tecnologia, I.P., under the project UID/05422/2025: Centre for Organisational and Social Studies of the Technical University of Porto (CEOS.PP).

Chapter 1

AI-Driven Hyper-Personalisation in the Service Industry: Post-Segmentation Marketing

Piali Haldar
http://orcid.org/0000-0003-4729-6964
Brainware University, Kolkata, India

Dev Kumar Mandal
http://orcid.org/0009-0005-3740-6885
Brainware University, Kolkata, India

ABSTRACT

The times are different now. The era in which the business operated using traditional marketing practices to extend its operations has changed, and hyper-personalized AI customer interactions are the order of the day. This paper presents a Post-Segmentation Marketing Paradigm and proves the AI Hyper-Personalisation model (AI HP), with integration of Service-Dominant Logic, SOR, and dynamic capabilities. The study adopted a mixed-method design with PLS-SEM to examine how AI-based technologies advance personalized service and consequently enhance users' experience, customer satisfaction, engagement, and loyalty. The results reveal that the days of segmentation are arguably behind us, and revising one's opinions on an earlier argument that segmentation was actually slowly phasing out is there to be seen. Real-time AI-driven interaction design is presented as the replacement of traditional segmentation, and more importantly, the new sexy AI app family introduction cycle has some of those inevitable challenges, which are trust and privacy.

DOI: 10.4018/979-8-3373-9159-5.ch001

1. INTRODUCTION

In the service industry, the separation, concentration on certain groups, and convenient location have always relied heavily on segmentation, targeting, and positioning (STP) as the basis of marketing strategy since time immemorial. It rests on the belief that, across different types of convenient demographics, psychographics, or behavioural segments, people can be grouped into relatively equal piles, while segmentation helps businesses create products and services that meet the needs of a given section of the audience (Philip Kotler & Keller, 2015). The rise of IT and the present business environment, with an emphasis on AI, has largely expanded these traditional constraints. According to the latest trend, technologically dominant services are built around data availability and its usage, interconnected platform operations, and real-time assessment, which has made the conventional segmentation irrelevant in the current reality, as it fails to take into account the context of consumer experience and their different behaviours (Olayinka, 2021).

AI helpers have changed the marketing industry significantly. Service industries can extend their customer limits comfortably from historic and general customer groupings to tailored products for each customer (Heskett, 1990). For instance, robotic marketing or machine learning for specific customers rather than marketing to customer groups (Boddu et al., 2022). Indeed, there is, or was, hyper-personalization, which involves targeting at an individual service level or at a particular target market category, based on the information or signal sources that include the actions of the individual, the event, and the time, and the predictive forecasts. Hence, the expectation is that the core proposition within any service offering, what can a service provider do or how far can the customer be gotten, is modifiable based on marketing need: it begins with the marketer thinking who the right customer is first; then, she goes on to ask where are the customer and how best the service provider's capabilities can be marshalled to deliver the intended product such that both the company and the customer are satisfied.

This structural turn does not just mean a move on, but a change in the very idea of what marketing is understood as, from dividing, cutting into, and dividing again, towards what could be termed something like post-dividing marketing. Given this new shift, traditional appreciation of consistent customer segments is substituted by rather dynamic, ever-changing profiles of individual clients that are woven from massive data and updated without any delay (Sandra, 2024; Sarkar, 2019). Service delivery is, at the present time, no longer a routine affair devoid of variability, but instead involves tailor-made and intelligent designs created by the AI procedures. For example, more and more AI-powered recommendation engines, chatbots, and proactive service tools are being adopted by digital platforms in the fields of banking, hospitality, and healthcare to customize user experiences to an entirely new and deeper level than before (Huang & Rust, 2021). These changes also cause difficulties in the traditional understanding of segmentation, involving a reconsideration of how customer experience is addressed and managed in the context of services.

Instead of enhancing segmentation, AI ensures that this traditional marketing tool is no longer used as a result of its use for the purpose of individual or continuous experience management. In such an environment, the concept of user experience is better understood as an ever-changing and unfolding concept that would arise as an immersive interaction between human subjects and intelligent machines. This is consistent with the concept of service logic, which suggests that value should be seen more as created by interaction among the service provider and the service consumer and less as contained in the product or the service itself (Vargo & Lusch, 2008). Meeting the perspective of interaction creation of value, AI techniques allow further application of SDL principles in digital realities, taking faster and more individualized developments with the aim of value creation.

In the chapter, the SOR model, together with SDL and its principles, is used to illustrate how AI applications can serve as external stimuli that affect an individual's internal states, leading to behavioural change. This model can be used to study customer behaviour in AI-prompted scenarios, enabled by stimuli like AI services. For example, perception of trust, satisfaction, and other positive outcomes influence their behaviour, which will keep a member or even encourage him/her to recommend others. Particularly, the SOR model will also need to explain the dynamics of the AI systems and the various types that are accommodative and change based on their use.

Finally, the paragraph mentions the principles of Dynamic capabilities that focus attention on how the control of several resources is achieved to change an environment (Teece, 2018). The capabilities offered that way can be considered dynamic capabilities, which make available provision for firms to sense, seize, and transform possibilities in the landscape of the service sector. Through AI, firms have the potential to align their service portfolios over time with the demands of individual customers, which ultimately contributes to active engagement in highly uncertain and complex business landscapes.

An important aspect of AI-based personalization mechanisms is in the context of trust and privacy. Even though custom services tend to add value and satisfaction by enhancing what is relevant, there are shortfalls through concerns of how personal data is used, data and surveillance, and in deploying software algorithmically, opaque service provision. The paradox involved within this process is that the concept of personalization tends to conflict with concerns over the use of personal possessions or information of properties (Awad & Krishnan, 2006). Trust in AI systems and their perceived transparency have significant implications in striking this balance, dictating consumer response to the experiences overly tailored to them. Thus, any comprehensive model of marketing after segmentation should consider these intervening variables.

Within this framework, the AI Hyper-Personalization Experience Model (AI-HPEM or the model) is developed in this section with the purpose of illustrating the influence of AI on the customer experience management of the service industry. The model considers the outsourced AI capabilities as key facets of the system that encompass personalization mechanisms, and, in turn, influence customer experience in terms of scores on satisfaction, emotions, value-added, loyalty, and more. However, this 'background' is a bit complicated; the development of the model aims at accommodating two potential rationalities. Thus, this framework incorporates two levels, using different theories that would tackle the transitional nature of marketing.

The value in this chapter is that it possesses significant importance for the development of the subject, its application, and its effect on society. Theoretically, it takes the knowledge of post-segmentation marketing to another level by attempting to reflect on the use of AI in transforming services in a new way. Practically, it shares ideas on the potential usage of AI by service organizations to gain competitive advantages and leans on the interaction design, data stack, and welfare ideal. Regarding policy frameworks, there are compelling reasons to implement regulations that address emerging AI economies, focusing on data sovereignty, algorithm oversight, and protecting user safety.

As shown earlier, the service industry is now the latest ellipses of the IMP as we know it, a new period, an AI-led era, where it is necessary to apply new visions of marketing purchased ideas. Transitioning from segmenting to hyper-customization accounts for a key shift in the way customer values and experiences are perceived and created. In building and empirically validating the AI-HPEM, the goal of this chapter is to develop a broader perspective on this metamorphosis and how it relates to service market practices in the years to come.

2. LITERATURE REVIEW

2.1 Traditional Segmentation Models and Their Limitations

Ever since market segmentation was introduced as a marketing strategy, it has afforded marketers the ability to focus on specific market segments that are more united and offer services designed to help those segments secure value (Smith, 1956). In real market situations, though, the circumstances have been such that the most predominant segmentation strategies in use recently are hardly ever the first four, which are demographic, geographic, needs-based, and attitudinal segmentation (Kotler and Keller, 2015).

Yet, from the perspective of digitally mediated service delivery, these principles are, to an even greater extent, questioned. The dynamic, situational, and more often than not connected to real-time responses made across many digital communication points, consumer behaviour in modern times has evolved; the so-called era of Web 3.0 has become far too contextual and perspective-dependent (Wedel & Kannan, 2016). Instead of static and empirical data, the traditional segmentations were more effective in framing approaches to marketing. Segmentation is, in essence, abstract in that individuals are identified within distinct units where attributes of the group are considered more important, thus losing its descriptive and experiential richness in the process (Dolnicar et al., 2018).

A second limitation of segmentation is that it does not take into account the inability to adapt to sudden changes in customer preferences, especially in fast-paced industries (Sandra, 2024). Such industries include but are not limited to tourism, finance, and healthcare. Often, the requirements of the same customer may vary in different situations, over time, and depending on the client's current mood. Rigid segmentation cannot be adjusted to these changes, leading to the inability to satisfy the customer with the services expected, a situation highlighted by Rust (2020). This realisation paves the way for the assertion that modern, informed consumers do merit more creative approaches than segmentation in this regard, which is more evident when it comes to service design and its customization.

2.2 Distinguishing Post-Segmentation from Micro-Segmentation

The concepts of micro-segmentation and post-segmentation marketing are often mistaken for each other; however, their meanings are quite different and represent different theoretical paradigms. Micro-segmentation is one such sophisticated form of segment identification that uses detailed variables like demographic, psychographic, behaviouristic, and transaction-oriented factors to identify even smaller and more uniform groups of customers (Wedel & Kannan, 2016). Only that this time, the focal unit of attention is still the customer segment, but then the weighing of such segments goes further and ever into narrower confines. Therefore, the marketing options that are derived and implemented remain more focused on the common collective segmental trends rather than the unique traits of a single customer, as discussed in Table 1

One of the primary reasons why this is important in services marketing is because services involve interpersonal interaction where the needs of the customers along with their emotions, expectations, and situational context change over time on a frequent basis. Even though the process of micro-segmentation increases efficiency of the target audience identification within the traditional STP, it does not suffice until segmentation is amended to its very core perspective at the emergence of post-segmentation customer experience management, which is based on dynamic and interactive engagement with the customer through creation of individual experiences for every interaction through use of continuous AI technologies. Hence, it is important to comprehend the concept of hyper-personalization not as the last step of segmentation but rather as the primary one within the context of the post-segmentation age.

Table 1. Comparison between Traditional Segmentation, Micro-Segmentation, and Post-Segmentation Marketing

Dimension	Traditional Segmentation	Micro-Segmentation	Post-Segmentation Marketing
Unit of Analysis	Large customer groups	Small customer groups	Individual customer
Customer Classification	Static	Fine-grained	Dynamic and continuous
Data Source	Historical	Historical + Behavioural	Real-time AI-driven data
Decision Logic	Rule-based	Data-enhanced	AI-driven adaptive decisions
Personalization	Low	Moderate	Hyper-personalized
Experience Design	Segment level	Micro-group level	Individual level
Technology	CRM	Analytics	AI, Machine Learning, Predictive Analytics
Strategic Goal	Targeting	Precision Targeting	Individual Experience Orchestration

2.3 Artificial Intelligence in Service Systems

Various industries are the beneficiaries of AI-powered technologies, which have become a force for change in them through the creation of value and customer involvement through AI (Chowdhury, 2024). Utilizing AI and other technologies such as machine learning, natural language processing, computer vision, and deep learning, businesses help to process huge amounts of structured and unstructured information to come up with actionable takeaways (Davenport et al., 2020). The other benefits of such applications stem from their capacity to allow for on-the-spot course of action as well as miracles, like automation and customization on massive levels.

AI is widely utilized within service sectors through texting bots, virtual assistants, recommendation algorithms, and proactive service delivery structures (Inavolu,

2024). These mechanisms are put in place to reduce operational costs and enrich customer experience by fostering appropriate, timely, relevant, and purpose-driven interactions (Huang & Rust, 2021). Having made productivity progress in the control of service delivery, AI, on a more conceptual level, conducts a revolution in the whole process of service provision by invigorating the infusion suffering service systems. Such systems can be described as they can learn from experience, modify themselves according to the dynamics of the environment, and optimize service operations and disciplines all by themselves (Wirtz et al., 2018). In the picture that is drawn, there are no such things as service encounters that are liable to stay the same between two points, which are characterized by the presence of continuous feedback loops between the client and the system.

While these advances are impressive, emphasis on leveraging AI into service delivery infrastructure makes it complex and raises questions on transparency, accountability, and ethical concerns (Dutta, 2024). The application of algorithms to make decisions is, in many cases, done in a very non-transparent way, such that it can be a challenge to lay out its functionality to the public. Such opacity poses significant threats, such as erosion of trust and growth in the consumer base that is using AI-enabled services (Pasquale, 2015).

2.4 Emergence of Hyper-Personalization

Hyper-personalization, the next level of personalization facilitated by AI and big data analytics, can be referred to as hyper-personalization (Tiwari, 2024). Unlike traditional personalization that is often reliant on static rules and/or limited customer information, hyper-personalization goes further by incorporating real-time data, predictions, and inferences relevantly (Arora et al., 2008; Wedel & Kannan, 2016). Hyper-personalized service involves the process of continuously observing the reactions of customers to the service and its improvements so as to determine their habits and desires (Guendonz, 2024; Rane et al., 2023). These findings are then applied to customize the services further so that they can be useful in the indicated areas. For example, some applications of predictive services, such as recommendations delivered by AI, are present in streaming platforms that suggest what content viewers may enjoy based on past views, and in banking applications, which offer customers advice related to their transactions.

The power of hyper-targeting algorithms is that they provide not only the supply that is deficient in users, but they also provide support for maintaining structure and level of close attention (Bleier & Eisenbeiss, 2015). This widespread adoption of personalized marketing in an unlimited context has led to the emergence of the concept of the personalization-privacy paradox (Awad & Krishnan, 2006). Most people will enjoy the benefits of custom-tailored institutions while having fears about the collection, storage, and use of their details. This conflict calls for maintaining high levels of trust and openness in service provision, enhanced by artificial intelligence.

2.5 Customer Experience in the Digital Age

Today, customer satisfaction has undoubtedly become a major buzzword in relation to cognitive, emotional, and behavioural perceptions of customers of services (Lemon & Verhoef, 2016). AI-based hyper-personalization systems can be useful in improving CX as they can provide the right information at the right time (Tiwari, 2024; Sigh & Kaunert, 2024). By using information, businesses can address consumers' requirements in advance, customize communication, and enable customers to shop through all available channels in a seamless manner (Verhoef et al., 2022). Such developments reflect the general tendency of the dominating experience-based approach in marketing, where primary attention is paid to building particularly valuable and strong interpersonal relationships, and not delusions or confusion about what must be done with a given service or product.

By including AI in CX project work, people's participation in providing services has emerged as an issue of significance. It has its advantages in that it promotes efficiency and personalization in interactions, but it may interfere with the human intervention that is essential for emotional bonding with clients (Huang & Rust, 2021). Thus, firms have to find ways of managing the balance between machines and man in improving the efficiencies of the CX.

2.6 Algorithmic Bias and Ethical Challenges in AI-Driven Personalization

Implementing AI-based personalization techniques presents numerous opportunities to enhance customer satisfaction. Algorithmic biases reflect a situation where the AI work systems are such that individuals or groups are systematically left out due to prejudice in the data sets, bias within the model, which is prevalent in the predictive model and sometimes a result of societal imbalances across consumer populations (Mehrabi et al., 2021). Given that the AI arrangement is usually premised on predicting customers based on their behaviours, blockchain models further provide a superb operational platform for machine learning management tools that arrest such patterns from deepening.

In service industries, cases of algorithmic bias can be incredibly disadvantageous to client satisfaction by means of reducing product choice, neglecting to value opinions of small groups, generating price discrepancies, or even leading to discrimination induced by stereotypical consumption models. Instead of providing better matching, faulty algorithms can always end up adding a certain degree of uncertainty and discouragement, especially in cases when the relation is based on trust and the will to buy any recommended items (Martin, 2019). Critical to this is the importance of assuring that, even as an underlying mechanism, personalization is continuously and flexibly used to enhance customer value without disrupting customer self-sufficiency, sociability, and fairness. This is why segmentation cannot solve the entire puzzle because it is equally important how and for what purposes these algorithms are used.

2.7 Theoretical Foundations

This research examines post-segment marketing in practice as branded marketing done in sections post a certain period of time due to AI technology and inclusivity and tailoring of customer-centric interactions locally/group specific approach rather than the blanket allotment of customers over the broad segments. Market, however, retargeting does not consider a client as a constituent of a predetermined number of segments, but as a single person whose preferences change severally to a certain extent.

Service-Dominant Logic (SDL) places the value creation in the course of interaction between the provider and the customer, as the most predominant factor for business. Such an interaction is managed by the engaging system in the case of an intelligent load. The Stimulus–Organism–Response (SOR) model of consumer psychology, which explains how outside forces (such as AI-driven personalization) cause stress and feelings with regard to cognitive and emotional response to the environment (Mehrabian & Russell, 1974). Here, the AI use causes the behaviour and experience of the heat.

Highly dynamic markets require organizations to quickly adjust to these changes. This need is very well illustrated by the Dynamic Capabilities Theory developed by Teece (2018). Dynamic capabilities can be classified as artificial intelligence, where certain abilities of an organization help it to pick up on customer needs, take advantage of opportunities, and change the service delivery process.

Lastly, users of AI systems generally have concerns about the privacy of their personal data (Awad & Krishnan, 2006). However, according to the Personalisation-Privacy Paradox as characterized in this study, there are times when consumers will avoid personalized technologies because they fear privacy intrusion. The current study also addresses this perspective regarding the moderating effect of trust and privacy in the context of artificial intelligence use in service delivery.

2.8 Research Gap

Given the vast body of literature that elucidates artificial intelligence, personalization, and the customer experience, several research gaps exist. While many studies view personalization as simply another layer for targeting, rather than as a replacement, the scope of changes after segmentation has been most often left unaddressed. Thirdly, no universal frameworks have been designed to calibrate the technological abilities as well as psychological and experiential zones with the particular needs of AI-driven services. Lastly, very few examples exist of empirical studies on the mediation or moderation effects in the context of a hyper-personalized service delivery environment.

In this chapter, these gaps are addressed with the help of a new research model that incorporates AI capabilities, mechanisms for hyper-personalization as well as customer experience outcomes, and explains them within the post-segmenting paradigm. Furthermore, all these constructs and hypotheses have been assessed through quantitative research by using structured interviews and quantitative statistical analyses, such as PLS-SEM. In this way, we intend to contribute to both theoretical development in the field of AI-based service delivery and how it functions, and to the empirical advancement of research in this area.

3. CONCEPTUAL FRAMEWORK AND MODEL DEVELOPMENT

The traditional approach to market segmentation is no longer enough with the recent introduction of AI hyper-personalization. This means that there needs to be a change in the understanding and handling of customer experiences in various service ecosystems. Consequentially, this unit aims to fill in this research gap and puts forth an AI-Driven Hyper-Personalization Experience Model (AI-HPEM), which is a comprehensive model that showcases the process by which AI augmentations enhance service interactions to build a customer experience that is tailored, responsive, and dynamic. It's a complex system that relates the intermediary movement of the mouse, the path of the gaze of the eyes, pressing down of buttons, and the configuration of services in a company.

Consequently, this research specifies post-segment marketing in practical terms as an AI-driven brand marketing campaign which entails the regional or subdivision customization of customer interactions in a system view rather than the establishment of broad customer segments. Post-segmentation marketing, on the other hand, does not regard a customer as part of a segmented group of a certain size but as an individual who is a constantly changing decision-crunching element.

Figure 1. AI-Driven Hyper-Personalization Experience Model (AI-HPEM)

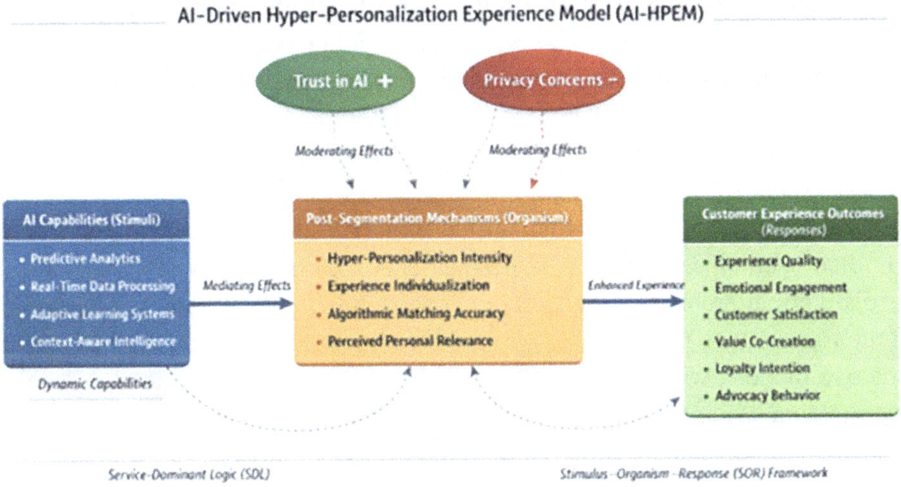

Source: Author's own work

In Figure 1 of the proposed model, artificial intelligence capabilities describe the different ways in which one can produce a customer experience. These AI capabilities include experience in the use of technology, visualization, processing of data in real-time, continuous monitoring of situation changes, and profile-based data processing. AI enables an organization to pore through a big mass of customer data and provide recommendations that will be useful for a particular service, and that will depend on the current context of the customer (Davenport et al., 2020). In the context of Dynamic Capabilities, the capability endowed by AI-based technological intelligence allows firms to sense and identify this need, take such an opportunity, and create or adjust their service provision as and when such behaviour changes (Teece, 2018). Therefore, it is not surprising that AI is portrayed as a business tool in the service sector that helps to create service ecosystems going well beyond mass customization to every individual.

3.1 Transformation Mechanism from AI Capabilities to Hyper-Personalization

In the framework of AI-HPEM, also known as AI-Driven Hyper-Personalization Experience Model, the effect of AI on hyper-personalization is seen as more than a direct effect but rather as the cause and effect between the 'media' of the effect and hyper-personalization. That is, it is the set of AI capabilities, including predictive intelligence, machine learning, real-time analytics, adaptive learning, neurolinguistics, and context-aware computing, among others, that do not automatically create

AI capabilities—including predictive intelligence, machine learning, real-time data analysis, and personalized services- but are created traditionally and accumulated and processed continuously. Such capabilities operate at their potential within the confines of individual systems, whereas different customers spread across networks generate a lot of data, which calls for the creation of data algorithms to optimize learning-based AI, to identify behavioural sequences and predict future taste/style trends and their disparities, to handle environmental changes, and to keep consumer tendencies up-to-date without any lag (Davenport et al., 2020).

In line with this argument, hyper-personalization is achieved by following four distinct patterns: the process of collecting more and more data from clients and the transactions they make, web analytics integration based on AI to produce predictive models, which then decide how to act upon the data gathered, levels of customization while making the service content and behaviour adapt in real time, and improving the design. Moreover, there is a further component of this process: the one that calls for getting feedback to correct the assumptions that AI makes in the course of recommendations, thanks to the customers. These several stages are how the computer capabilities become customer-focused.

Consequently, in terms of the Scheme as well, which basically relates the AI capacities as being the facilitation resources and the coefficient of hyper-personalization as representing the means of deploying these resources towards creating imperatively hyper-customer experiences, one may infer that this effort in place in the company walks in the shadow of the Dynamic Capabilities theory by suggesting that no competitive advantage can be realized from owning AI except the effective use of the existing AI to re-arrange customer experiences on a recurrent basis (Teece, 2018).

These mediating variables can be understood in terms of the "organism" frame, i.e., the end-user's comprehension in their interactions with artificial intelligence triggers (Mehrabian and Russell, 1974). For that matter, help systems that keep in view the SOR model of users' reactions, the well-accepted signals, which serve as feedback notifications. When the AI recommends precise, contextually accurate, and helpful suggestions, the level of relevancy assigned to the content while using it increases. What this implies is a shift from the standard form of service provision to the customization of experiences, all under the concept of SDL, which holds interactivity as value (Vargo and Lusch, 2008).

In our model, it was necessary to introduce additional factors, and above all, trust in AI and privacy concerns. They show how the other variables, such as moderating factors, shape and determine to what extent the hype model drivers lead further on to a customer output. Without credence in AI, all efforts to foster personalization will go down the drain, as there will be fear and doubt in human cognitive operations. Similarly, any efforts or campaigns to enhance personalization can backfire and repel consumers as people may view personalization as intrusive (Blythe et al,

2018). The dependent variables in the model represent key customer experience outcomes, which consist of customer experience quality, emotional engagement, customer satisfaction, perceived value co-creation, loyalty intention, and advocacy behaviour. These outcomes establish both cognitive and emotional dimensions of customer experience, which is in line with present CX literature (Lemon & Verhoef, 2016). The model asserts that by offering more targeted, timely, and appropriate interactions, hyper-personalization will improve customer relationships and all future interactions, thereby leading to increases in these outcomes.

3.2 Research Objectives

1. To explore the boundaries of traditional division models in the field of services operated by artificial intelligence.
2. To suggest ways of extending effective post-segmentation marketing strategies through the adoption of AI-based ultra-segmentation.
3. To check the influence of AI features on the quality of individual-oriented services.
4. To investigate the indirect effects and conditions of AI personalization.
5. To examine mediating and moderating mechanisms in AI-driven personalization.

3.3 Hypotheses Development

The increasing necessity to go towards AI-enhanced hyper-personalization in the service industry calls for an organized analysis of the bonds between technical capacities, experience drivers, and service results. In full support of the Modified-SOR Model, Service-Dominant Logic (SDL), and Dynamic Capabilities Theory, this chapter advances ideas for the association between AI capabilities (external), systems of hyper-customization (mediating or linking), and impacts of customer experience (end or consequence), where trust and privacy are identified as legitimating factors.

AI usage within businesses is trending upwards, whereby these AI technologies, like prediction, real-time analysis, or adaptive learning, simplify the processing of customer data, leading to very useful service interactions. These augmentations to customers change from general supplies to one-on-one quests for experience. Previous scholars claim that AI-based analytics improves the level of tailored experiences and relevance between the consumer and the produced products. It is, therefore, anticipated that AI developments should result in higher levels of aggressive degrees of personalized marketing, termed hyper-personalization.

H1: AI capabilities positively influence hyper-personalization intensity.

In the case of hyper-personalization, where one-to-one spaces are targeted towards a specific consumer in a very specific and pinpoint manner, there is a perception of a more effective experience created for consumers. BMC has been entrenched by Wedel and Kannan, R. (2016) whereby services are related to customer loyalty and assisted by the individual consumer. This makes a link with the SOR model, where the understanding of contrasted aspects serves as a motivating factor toward HEs and, consequently, to the attainment of the goals.

H2: Hyper-personalization intensity positively affects customer experience quality.

The interrelation involving the complexity of AI tools and customer satisfaction is not self-evident, for actions are borne more by the very craft of customization. Innovations in AI help in offering customized services to each individual, thereby enhancing the benefits and the happiness. This mediating function corresponds to the shift from technology-centred processes to experiential outcomes.

H3: Experience individualization mediates the relationship between AI capabilities and customer satisfaction.

The reason why trust in AI is crucial to people in their attitude to hyper-personalized services is that when clients have confidence that the AI system is dependable, consistent, and just, chances are that they react positively towards the personalized marketing stimuli (Huang & Rust, 2021). This trust does away with the need for speculative behaviour and increases the levels of emotional commitment, which enhances personalization expectations.

H4: Trust in AI positively moderates the relationship between hyper-personalization and emotional engagement.

However, the issue of privacy cannot be oversimplified because it also poses a threat to the acceptability and deployment of hyper-personalization technology. The very nature of personalization, together with the related data security concerns, sets up a paradox in that recipients may find it paradoxical that they both demand personalization on one hand, and yet are concerned about how their personal data is used, stating therein what is referred to as the personalization–privacy paradox (Awad et al., 2006). It is likely that as the level of trust evoked by the engagement decreases, the level of trust in the data collection and its use will also decrease, thus having a negative impact on behavioural outcomes like loyalty.

H5: Privacy concerns negatively moderate the relationship between hyper-personalization and loyalty intention.

The grade of the customer experience is essential in determining the creation of value in service contexts. According to Service Dominant Logic (SDL), value is comprehended to be generated only on the consumption of the outcome and through the interaction between firms and consumers (Vargo & Lusch, 2008). High-quality, even perfect at times, personalized experiences help customers in no small way in enhancing their role in the process of value addition.

H6: Customer experience quality positively influences perceived value co-creation.

There is a glimmer of hope that the other party, or the vested stakeholders, reciprocate the goodwill, and hence, there is a possibility of, without question, showing dedication, loyalty, and even higher levels of empowerment. If customers feel the ability to influence what they are offered positively, they tend to argue that there is improved satisfaction with positive effects. Likely, customers who feel able to influence how their products or services are given, as everyone is poor, have very low feelings of affection towards the sugar Mamma (Lemon & Verhoef, 2016).

H7: Perceived value co-creation positively influences loyalty intention and advocacy behaviour.

4. RESEARCH METHODOLOGY

To fully assess the move from customer segmentation approaches to those of AI-personalized marketing, the chapter introduces a combined qualitative and quantitative research design, which is suited to the examination of system sales in the retail sector. The primary information is collected directly from clients in several sectors usually referred to as high-tech services, such as banking, hotels, medical, e-businesses, and other online market/platforms where both products and services are present. The next step, the quantitative phase template, is a questionnaire that consists of several constructs. These include AI capabilities, hyper-personalization, customer experience, affinity, and privacy worries, which are rated using the following five-point Likert scale.

To achieve an equal number of informants from different age and occupation groups by the use of the quota sampling technique. This is because the number of respondents, within the normal range of between 300 and 500 respondents, is considered to suffice for structural equation modelling. About the qualitative dimension, semi-structured interviews will be conducted with some of the respondents as well as stakeholders in the industry to enable an in-depth, comprehensive understanding of the issues. In addition to the content and criterion validity of the constructs, we made use of validated scales, most of which had been taken from previous studies. To maintain consistency of the proposed AI-Driven Hyper-Personalization Experience Model (AI-HPEM), the method involves each element being measured according to recognized scales developed from references. The survey observes that all structures are assessed with the aid of reflective tools, and one such tool is a five-point scale graded from 1 to 5, Strongly Disagree to Strongly Agree. The content of the above items is written appropriately for AI and is focused on AI in industries that render services. Table 2 clarifies the research criteria, as well as its methodological and literature framework.

Table 2. Summary of Variables and Measurement Scales

Construct	Operational Definition	Source
AI Capabilities (Independent Variable)	The organization's ability to use AI technologies for prediction, learning, automation, and decision-making in service delivery.	Davenport et al. (2020); Huang & Rust (2020)
Hyper-Personalization Intensity (Mediator)	The extent to which AI dynamically personalizes services based on individual real-time behavioural and contextual information.	Wedel & Kannan (2016); Bleier & Eisenbeiss (2015)
Customer Experience Quality (Dependent Variable)	Customer evaluation of the overall quality of AI-enabled service interactions.	Lemon & Verhoef (2016)
Trust in AI (Moderator)	Customer confidence in the reliability, fairness, and transparency of AI-driven decisions.	Huang & Rust (2021)
Privacy Concerns (Moderator)	Customer concerns regarding the collection and use of personal information by AI systems.	Awad & Krishnan (2006)
Value Co-Creation (Dependent Variable)	Customer perception of jointly creating value with the service provider through AI-enabled interactions.	Vargo & Lusch (2008)
Loyalty Intention (Dependent Variable)	Customer willingness to continue using and recommending AI-enabled services.	Zeithaml, Berry, & Parasuraman (1996)

The gathered statistical data, which is included in the study, will be analysed by way of Partial Least Squares analysis.

Table 3. Reliability and Convergent Validity

Construct	Cronbach's Alpha	Composite Reliability (CR)	AVE
AI Capabilities	0.89	0.92	0.65
Hyper-Personalization	0.91	0.93	0.68
Customer Experience Quality	0.88	0.91	0.64
Trust in AI	0.86	0.90	0.62
Privacy Concerns	0.84	0.89	0.60
Value Co-Creation	0.87	0.91	0.63
Loyalty Intention	0.90	0.93	0.69

From the results in Table 3, it is possible to note that the Cronbach's alpha values for the independent variables are above 0.70, which indicates that the internal consistency measures in the study are strong. There is also no issue of multicollinearity as the evolution of scores is acceptable. In addition, the AVE's (Average Variance Extracted) are more than 0.50, affirming but one concern: convergent validity. Therefore, the measurement model is considered sufficient for subsequent evaluations.

Table 4. Discriminant Validity (Fornell-Larcker Criterion)

Construct	AI Cap	HP	CX	Trust	Privacy	VCC	Loyalty
AI Capabilities	0.81						
Hyper-Personalization	0.65	0.82					
Customer Experience (CX)	0.60	0.70	0.80				
Trust in AI	0.58	0.66	0.69	0.79			
Privacy Concerns	-0.40	-0.45	-0.42	-0.50	0.77		
Value Co-Creation	0.55	0.68	0.72	0.65	-0.38	0.79	
Loyalty Intention	0.57	0.69	0.74	0.67	-0.41	0.76	0.83

According to Table 4, the criteria of Fornell-Larcker substantiate determinable reliability. It was found that the square root of AVE (on the diagonal) was larger than the importance of the variables. This implies that the constructs estimated are separable and describe separate aspects of the entity. This being the case, the constructs are mutually orthogonal and do not weigh each other.

Table 5. Structural Model Path Coefficients

Hypothesis	Path Relationship	Beta (β)	t-value	p-value	Result
H1	AI Capabilities → Hyper-Personalization	0.72	12.45	0.000	Supported
H2	Hyper-Personalization → CX Quality	0.68	10.32	0.000	Supported
H3	AI Capabilities → CX (via HP)	0.55	8.90	0.000	Supported
H4	HP × Trust → Emotional Engagement	0.30	5.21	0.000	Supported
H5	HP × Privacy → Loyalty	-0.25	4.75	0.000	Supported
H6	CX Quality → Value Co-Creation	0.70	11.10	0.000	Supported
H7	Value Co-Creation → Loyalty	0.75	13.25	0.000	Supported

The results of the Structural model that are presented in Table 5 reveal that all hypothesized paths are significantly related to each other ($p < 0.05$). Enhancement of customer experience is due to the strong influence of AI capabilities. However, causes the creation of an extreme level of personalization (hyper-personalization). Mediated and moderated Relationships are also evidenced, emphasizing the roles of trust and privacy. In all, the model can explain most aspects with precision, which leaves few research gaps to be explored.

Table 6. Coefficient of Determination (R^2 Values)

Endogenous Construct	R^2 Value	Interpretation
Hyper-Personalization	0.52	Moderate
Customer Experience	0.61	Substantial
Value Co-Creation	0.49	Moderate
Loyalty Intention	0.65	Substantial

R^2 values in Table 6 suggest that AI capabilities are quite descriptive while explaining hyper-personalization dependence, where 52% of it is explained. Although the percentage is lower, hyper-personalization variance can be largely explained by it. Customer experience and loyalty, which the positive lineage could replace, also have a strong influence on the predictive power of the model. The proposed model's focus on the key factors influencing AI-powered hyper-personalization enhances the ongoing conversation, building upon the initial findings from the segmentation stage.

Table 7. Predictive Relevance (Q^2 Values)

Construct	Q^2 Value	Predictive Relevance
Hyper-Personalization	0.35	Strong
Customer Experience	0.42	Strong
Value Co-Creation	0.31	Moderate
Loyalty Intention	0.45	Strong

In Table 7, the value of Q^2 is more than zero. What this means is that the model possesses a high predictive capability. Specifically, customer loyalty and experience demonstrated the highest potential for how behavioural outcomes can be accurately forecasted under an artificial intelligence hyper-personalization context. Such measurements only prove the mettle of the model and the situation in which it becomes an application in the practical service market.

5. DISCUSSION

The results presented in this section are pertinent to any attempts to move away from the traditional market concepts, cutting across service sectors to more contemporary AI-generated post-segmentation marketing. The results confirm all the suggested hypotheses and give detailed answers to the research questions about the set research objectives.

Following this, the chapter also points out that automation within the companies also leads to an increase in the level of personalization (H1). This helps in understanding the way in which AI mechanisms are extending the frontiers of customer experience when it comes to the design of service provision as well. It is quite feasible to replace the outdated tactic of designing communication channels for zones when advertising campaigns are planned, especially when modern AI production tools are available. It is against this backdrop that the research question as to whether AI aids in redefining service experiences is addressed, with the premise that AI is a key enabler of hyper-personalization, and therefore the most active driver of hyper-personalization.

Investigation confirms that there is a clear positive impact of highly personalized services on customer experience levels. Specifically, the correlation shows that valuable individual experiences play a very important role in today's service practices. This can be seen from the fact that service modification consequently leads to raising customer perceived utility. This results in the conclusion that even upgrades from simple targets display the limitation of the traditional models by collapsing positioning and target bases. The research findings further report and support the conceptual arguments that personalization has the capacity to enhance experiential relevance and satisfaction.

Furthermore, the mediation effect diagnosed in H3, according to which the impact of AI capabilities on customer satisfaction is under development, adds weight to the model by increasing the power of explanation. This study underscores that AI capabilities do not create a direct impact on customer outcomes but act through experiential dimensions. It substantiates the objective of this section regarding the examination of mediating procedures as well as endorsing the relevance of the SOR framework in AI contexts.

Regarding H4 and H5, show the importance of the social and psychological factors in the process of adopting AI. The added value in this case of the sixth hypothesis relates to trust in AI, which affects implementation in an indirect positive way, as the virtual agent seems to occur when a person believes the technology is consistent and does not pose any threatening prospects. On the other hand, the results about H5 establish the prediction that no technological development in the past few years has ever been without constraints. As such, these answers make a significant contribution because of the research question concerning the limits of this study and also in relation to the role of trust and ethics in the provision of services with the help of artificial intelligence.

Apart from the fears about privacy issues, the study also pointed out the universal ethical issues that hyper-personalisation prompted by AI raises. Despite the fact that AI improves the service to the customer as it attempts to do this efficiently, the effectiveness of these services lies in the extent to which algorithms and other forms of decision-making are considerate of all and sundry. Such AI-driven systems, which have no developed consciousness and make decisions based on past events, might result in discouraging representations of preference, for example, minority group tastes, or stereotypes already evident in cultural sensation. Such algorithmic prejudices could in fact diminish the quality of personalization and reduce trust and emotion in the customer, regrettably at a time when such technologies are advanced. It will therefore be more advisable to reflect on the claims made in the context of what good AI looks like. So, with such new forms of technology, it becomes important for organizations to look at how predictive analytics or decision-making tools can be balanced with practices of ethical consumption. It is an improvement compared to the traditional means of conducting business, which relied on the use of product differentiation, shortly followed by marketing segmentation.

Conclusively, the proposed relationship between customer experience quality and value co-creation (H6) marks a significant point in the integration of Service-Dominant logic (SDL). It can be seen here how experiences that are of high quality and tailored yield a lot of cooperation from the consumer when acquiring value. This seems to be in line with the essence of the experiential outcomes given here and incorporates innovation by linking Integrating AI in Personalized Marketing in Co-Creation Context'.

Knowledge area (H7) actually focuses on augmented experiences that are provided to customers; experiences that are crafted based on the particular contributions that the customer extends to service providers. Hence, loyal guests are those customers who are willing to advocate for the service, that is, customers who appreciate the services and results so much that they share such information with the rest of society. This conclusion promotes the achievement of the research objectives in terms of explaining the behaviour of the object under study and stresses the significance of the use of hyper-personalization in managing customer relationships.

One might say that the AI-HPEM has survived all limitations because theoretical foundations were lifted and the model was approached as new, ground-breaking, and innovative. The chapter also exhibits that it is not that AI-driven hyper-personalization is an improved extension of segmentation, but is essentially a change in the expectation of customer experience in the service sector.

6. IMPLICATIONS

It is crucial to mention that trust and privacy are core issues that need to be considered in the present day. It is a matter of necessity that this age is a conscious one about labour. When hyper-personalization is involved, since it has a lot of hidden data, organizations must implement data practices that are crystal clear, frameworks for AI that are ethical, and also strategies that focus on the defence of the software. Developing a two-way trust relationship will be quite necessary for how customers relate to the adoption of AI-dependent support environments. To assist in integrating AI, one ought to rationally suggest preparing strategies that will focus on the utilization of explainable AI to broaden the understanding and also the level of responsibility.

It is within this concern that the technological convergence of AI with other digital technologies, such as Internet of Things (IoT), blockchain, and cloud computing, is underscored in order to create service ecosystems that are safe and easy to use. Consequently, this amalgamation in a way provides their constituents with more creative hyper-personalization features such as context-based and predictive offerings.

In modern days, it is therefore increasingly evident that, normatively speaking, the relevant literature has implicitly been concerned with the significance that data privacy, algorithm bias, and protection of customers should possess based on the applied standards. More voice in this concern is raised within the field of policy because of the rampant degree of AI application in the service sector and the consequent necessity to protect users at all costs, excluding abuse of innovation. Therefore, the adjustment in policies as discussed in this paper pivots on the reinforcement of data-centric controls, adjusting estimation regulations to algorithmic systems, as well as user compliance capacities through the use of information tools.

All this development comes in at a personal level, especially when talking about indulging in hyperpersonal behaviours. As much as engaging in personalized services bears the advantage of ease and happiness in the proceedings, there may be an explicit dependence on the aid of computers to function effectively in this context. Of course, such hyper-personalized, automated, real-time environments are not easy to maintain; it is likely that over time, all such phenomena will be used. In pursuit of these goals, the article advocates for clinicians to lead AI regulation efforts rather than relying on algorithmic or recommendation-based systems, since individuals can obtain helpful yet potentially hazardous information.

6.1 Ethical Implications: Algorithmic Bias and Responsible Hyper-Personalization

To ensure responsible use of AI technologies, firms should aim at achieving balanced integration of technology development with moral development that takes into account both opportunities and risks of using such technologies. While AI can deliver ambitious client-specific strategies, the operation of algorithms has limitations, and the reliability of these decisions is determined by the data and models used. As a result, any AI development initiative in the future company needs to look more seriously than Performance AI towards forming Friendly AI systems where fairness, transparency, accountability, and customer discretion are the main ethos of the AI function.

Organizations must set up regular algorithm reviews to both pinpoint and eliminate the disadvantages that arise from dated or otherwise faulty data sets. In addition, customer-facing systems utilizing personalization should incorporate explainable AI methods so that the reasoning behind certain recommendations or decisions can be seen by the end users. Future ecosystems will require ethical governance strategies in the AI implementation process, envisioning the ideal platform that combines automated intelligence with human oversight. It goes without saying that the realization of such a marketing strategy will not be embedded in technical progress only; quite the opposite, it will be observed as the extent to which the ethical functionality of AI and the overall decision-making process exist.

7. CONCLUSION

This chapter argues that service marketing has gradually moved beyond the traditional and segmentation-oriented strategies to the more intelligent and empowered AI-based post-segmentation strategies. The study goes a step further to examine some aspects of product differentiation that technological advancements have brought forth in the retail banking industry and why they are important both for consumers and for service providers.

Indeed, the above assertions support the scholastic opinion that hyper-personalization is the way AI encompasses customer satisfaction and service experience quality. The interruption talks about the concept of trust and privacy strain as a key control factor, and the comfort zone that technological innovation zones must be set. Moreover, S-D Logic and the model of SOR are integrated, which will seek to provide an in-depth understanding of customer interactions in the age of AI.

In General, the scholarly research addresses global issues in the area of reading digital transformation with a focus on how post-marketing can be done, using the new term post-segmentation marketing. It sees a shift from how AI is used as a tool to get things done to how AI empowers innovation and the perceived experience. The chapter is sure to benefit academic scholars, industry professionals, and policy makers by guiding the process of creating an AI-dominated service system.

8. LIMITATIONS AND FUTURE SCOPE

However, that said, the current chapter has some limitations. First, the research employs cross-sectional data, which is not representative of the true nature of change in customer behaviour over time. This may reduce the effectiveness of the research results. Also, the research primarily looks at the service sector that is intensive on technology, which may not capture the trends in traditional services.

Several suggestions are presented for further research. More in-depth explanations will be provided in the subsequent chapter. On the other hand, the research can be further developed. As for future research, more longitudinal studies may be conducted that would not only be centred around the changes of their customers, but also take into consideration wider domains of practice by including diverse cross-cultural samples. In addition, a potentially interesting perspective for research has been identified in the field of segmentation, targeting, and positioning literature: the possibility of incorporating advanced analytics such as fuzzy-set qualitative comparative analysis (fsQCA) in the post-STP marketing framework, and harnessing new technologies such as generative AI.

REFERENCES

Arora, N., Dreze, X., Ghose, A., Hess, J. D., Iyengar, R., Jing, B., Joshi, Y., Kumar, V., Lurie, N., Neslin, S., Sajeesh, S., Su, M., Syam, N., Thomas, J., & Zhang, Z. J. (2008). Putting one-to-one marketing to work: Personalization, customization, and choice. *Marketing Letters*, *19*(3), 305–321. DOI: 10.1007/s11002-008-9056-z

Awad, N. F., & Krishnan, M. S. (2006). The Personalization Privacy Paradox: An Empirical Evaluation of Information Transparency and the Willingness to be Profiled Online for Personalization1. *Management Information Systems Quarterly*, *30*(1), 13–28. DOI: 10.2307/25148715

Bleier, A., & Eisenbeiss, M. (2015). Personalized online advertising effectiveness. *JMR, Journal of Marketing Research*, *52*(5), 586–607.

Boddu, R. S. K., Santoki, A. A., Khurana, S., Koli, P. V., Rai, R., & Agrawal, A. (2022). An analysis to understand the role of machine learning, robotics and artificial intelligence in digital marketing. *Materials Today: Proceedings*, *56*, 2288–2292. DOI: 10.1016/j.matpr.2021.11.637

Chowdhury, R. H. (2024). AI-powered Industry 4.0: Pathways to economic development and innovation. [IJCRT]. *International Journal of Creative Research Thoughts*, *12*(6), h650–h657.

Davenport, T., Guha, A., Grewal, D., & Bressgott, T. (2020). How artificial intelligence will change the future of marketing. *Journal of the Academy of Marketing Science*, *48*(1), 24–42. DOI: 10.1007/s11747-019-00696-0

Dolnicar, S., Grün, B., & Leisch, F. (2018). Step 5: Extracting Segments. In *Market Segmentation Analysis: Understanding It, Doing It, and Making It Useful* (pp. 75–181). Springer Singapore. DOI: 10.1007/978-981-10-8818-6_7

Heskett, J. L. (1990). *Service breakthroughs*. Simon and Schuster.

Huang, M. H., & Rust, R. T. (2021). A strategic framework for artificial intelligence in marketing. *Journal of the Academy of Marketing Science*, *49*(1), 30–50. DOI: 10.1007/s11747-020-00749-9

Inavolu, S. M. (2024). Exploring AI-driven customer service: Evolution, architectures, opportunities, challenges and future directions. *International Journal of Engineering and Advanced Technology*, *13*(3), 156–163.

Kotler, P., & Keller, K. L. (2015). *Framework for Marketing Management, A*. BoD–Books on Demand.

Lemon, K. N., & Verhoef, P. C. (2016). Understanding customer experience throughout the customer journey. *Journal of Marketing*, *80*(6), 69–96. DOI: 10.1509/jm.15.0420

Martin, K. (2019). Ethical Implications and Accountability of Algorithms: K. Martin. *Journal of Business Ethics*, *160*(4), 835–850. DOI: 10.1007/s10551-018-3921-3

Mehrabi, N., Morstatter, F., Saxena, N., Lerman, K., & Galstyan, A. (2021). A survey on bias and fairness in machine learning. *ACM Computing Surveys*, *54*(6), 1–35. DOI: 10.1145/3457607

Mehrabian, A., & Russell, J. A. (1974). *An approach to environmental psychology*. the MIT Press.

Mittelstadt, B. D., Allo, P., Taddeo, M., Wachter, S., & Floridi, L. (2016). The ethics of algorithms: Mapping the debate. *Big Data & Society*, *3*(2), 2053951716679679. DOI: 10.1177/2053951716679679

Olayinka, O. H.Olalekan Hamed Olayinka. (2021). Big data integration and real-time analytics for enhancing operational efficiency and market responsiveness. *Int J Sci Res Arch*, *4*(1), 280–296. DOI: 10.30574/ijsra.2021.4.1.0179

Pasquale, F. (2015). The black box society: The secret algorithms that control money and information. In *The black box society*. Harvard University Press. DOI: 10.4159/harvard.9780674736061

Rane, N., Choudhary, S., & Rane, J. (2023). Hyper-personalization for enhancing customer loyalty and satisfaction in Customer Relationship Management (CRM) systems. *Available at SSRN* 4641044. DOI: 10.2139/ssrn.4641044

Rust, R. T. (2020). The future of marketing. *International Journal of Research in Marketing*, *37*(1), 15–26. DOI: 10.1016/j.ijresmar.2019.08.002

Sandra, A. (2024). Adapting to Rapid Change in Consumer Demands.

Sarkar, S. (2019). *Customer-driven disruption: Five strategies to stay ahead of the curve*. Berrett-Koehler Publishers.

Singh, B., & Kaunert, C. (2024). Future of digital marketing: Hyper-personalized customer dynamic experience with AI-based predictive models. In *Revolutionizing the AI-digital landscape* (pp. 189–203). Productivity Press. DOI: 10.4324/9781032688305-14

Smith, W. R. (1956). Product differentiation and market segmentation as alternative marketing strategies. *Journal of Marketing*, *21*(1), 3–8. DOI: 10.1177/002224295602100102

Teece, D. J. (2018). Business models and dynamic capabilities. *Long Range Planning*, *51*(1), 40–49. DOI: 10.1016/j.lrp.2017.06.007

Tiwari, A. (2024). Leveraging AI-Powered Hyper-Personalization and Predictive Analytics for Enhancing Digital Experience Optimization. *International Journal of Research Science and Management, 11*(9), 9–23.

Vargo, S. L., & Lusch, R. F. (2008). Service-dominant logic: Continuing the evolution. *Journal of the Academy of Marketing Science*, *36*(1), 1–10. DOI: 10.1007/s11747-007-0069-6

Verhoef, P. C., van Ittersum, K., Kannan, P. K., & Inman, J. (2022). Omnichannel retailing: A consumer perspective.

Wedel, M., & Kannan, P. K. (2016). Marketing analytics for data-rich environments. *Journal of Marketing*, *80*(6), 97–121. DOI: 10.1509/jm.15.0413

Wirtz, J., Patterson, P. G., Kunz, W. H., Gruber, T., Lu, V. N., Paluch, S., & Martins, A. (2018). Brave new world: Service robots in the frontline. *Journal of Service Management*, *29*(5), 907–931. DOI: 10.1108/JOSM-04-2018-0119

Zeithaml, V. A., Berry, L. L., & Parasuraman, A. (1996). The behavioral consequences of service quality. *Journal of Marketing*, *60*(2), 31–46. DOI: 10.1177/002224299606000203

ADDITIONAL READINGS

Mehrabi, N., Morstatter, F., Saxena, N., Lerman, K., & Galstyan, A. (2021). A survey on bias and fairness in machine learning. *ACM Computing Surveys*, *54*(6), 1–35. DOI: 10.1145/3457607

KEY TERMS AND DEFINITIONS

Algorithmic Bias: Systematic and unfair outcomes produced by AI algorithms due to biased data, model design, or decision-making processes.

Artificial Intelligence (AI): The capability of computer systems to perform tasks that typically require human intelligence, including learning, reasoning, prediction, natural language processing, and decision-making.

Behavioral Analytics: The analysis of customers' digital interactions, browsing patterns, purchases, and engagement activities to understand and predict future behaviour.

Big Data Analytics: The process of collecting, processing, and analysing large, complex, and diverse datasets to uncover meaningful patterns, trends, and insights for decision-makin g.

Consumer Trust: Customers' confidence that an organization will deliver reliable, secure, transparent, and ethical products, services, and AI-driven recommendations.

Context-Aware Marketing: A personalization strategy that delivers relevant content or offers by considering customers' location, device, time, activity, and situational context.

Customer Data Platform (CDP): A centralized technology platform that integrates customer information from multiple channels to create a unified customer profile for personalized marketing.

Customer Engagement: The level of customers' cognitive, emotional, and behavioural involvement with a brand resulting from meaningful interactions across multiple channels.

Customer Experience (CX): The cumulative perceptions, emotions, and responses that customers develop through interactions with a brand across all physical and digital touchpoints throughout the customer journey.

Customer Journey: The complete sequence of interactions and experiences that customers have with a brand before, during, and after purchasing a product or service.

Customer Lifetime Value (CLV): The total expected revenue that a business anticipates earning from a customer throughout the duration of their relationship.

Customer Satisfaction: The extent to which customers perceive that a product or service meets or exceeds their expectations.

Digital Customer Twin: A virtual, data-driven representation of an individual customer created using AI and analytics to simulate preferences, predict behaviours, and optimize personalized experiences.

Digital Transformation: The integration of digital technologies into organizational processes, business models, and customer interactions to improve efficiency, innovation, and value creation.

Dynamic Capabilities: An organization's ability to integrate, build, and reconfigure internal and external resources to adapt effectively to rapidly changing business environments.

Ethical AI: The development and deployment of artificial intelligence systems that are fair, transparent, accountable, privacy-preserving, and free from discriminatory practices.

Explainable Artificial Intelligence (XAI): AI techniques designed to make algorithmic decisions transparent, interpretable, and understandable to users and stakeholders.

Generative AI: A class of artificial intelligence capable of creating new text, images, audio, video, or other content by learning patterns from existing datasets.

Hyper-Personalization: An advanced marketing strategy that combines artificial intelligence, machine learning, big data, and real-time analytics to deliver highly individualized products, services, recommendations, and communications to customers.

Machine Learning (ML): A subset of artificial intelligence that enables systems to learn from historical data, identify patterns, and improve predictions or decisions without explicit programming.

Omnichannel Marketing: A marketing strategy that integrates multiple communication and sales channels to provide customers with a seamless and consistent experience.

Post-Segmentation Marketing: A customer-centric marketing approach that moves beyond traditional market segmentation by treating each customer as a unique segment through AI-driven personalization and predictive analytics.

Predictive Analytics: The application of statistical models and machine learning algorithms to forecast future customer behaviours, preferences, and purchasing intentions based on historical data.

Predictive Customer Intelligence: AI-driven capability to anticipate customer needs, preferences, and future behaviours using predictive models and real-time analytics.

Privacy-Personalization Paradox: The conflict between customers' desire for highly personalized experiences and their concerns regarding privacy, surveillance, and misuse of personal data.

Real-Time Personalization: The dynamic customization of content, offers, or services instantly based on customers' current behaviour, preferences, location, or contextual information.

Recommendation System: An AI-powered algorithm that suggests products, services, or content to users based on their preferences, browsing history, purchase behaviour, and contextual information.

Service-Dominant Logic (S-D Logic): A marketing perspective that emphasizes service, value co-creation, and collaborative interactions between firms and customers rather than product exchange.

Stimulus–Organism–Response (S–O–R) Framework: A behavioural theory explaining how external stimuli influence internal cognitive and emotional states, which subsequently determine individuals' behavioural responses.

Value Co-Creation: A collaborative process in which organizations and customers jointly create value through active participation, interaction, and shared experiences.

Chapter 2
Predictive Analytics and AI as Drivers of Personalized Consumer Experience in Digital Service Ecosystems

S. Harini
http://orcid.org/0000-0002-3856-7390
Saveetha School of Management, Saveetha Institute of Medical and Technical Sciences, Chennai, India

Akila S.
http://orcid.org/0009-0004-6219-1081
Jerusalem College of Engineering, Chennai, India

Aysha Fathima Y.
Jerusalem College of Engineering, Chennai, India

ABSTRACT

The artificial intelligence (AI) and predictive analytics can be used to transform consumer experience (CX) in a contemporary service ecosystem in this chapter. It demonstrates too how the previous descriptive models such as SERVQUAL, Expectancy-Disconfirmation Theory have been reconfigured into dynamic and data-driven models which can be employed to deliver predictive and prescriptive services. Machine learning, paired with behavioral analytics, and real-time analytics will assist AI in facilitating hyper-personalized, context-driven and proactive communication with customers at many touchpoints. The paper discusses the big uses of AI

DOI: 10.4018/979-8-3373-9159-5.ch002

including segmentation, predicting behavior and personalization algorithms, and real uses of AI in e-commerce, health care and banking. It also alludes to concept of AI agency, where intelligent systems are the co-creation value citizens. Although it has advantages, the chapter discusses the issues of data privacy, algorithm bias, transparency, and organizational preparedness, which are crucial.

1. INTRODUCTION

Artificial Intelligence (AI) has revolutionized the way businesses operate, allowing for the completion of complex tasks with unprecedented precision and speed. This change is felt in almost every industry, from healthcare to finance, education to aviation, and so on (Felzmann et al., 2020). The parallel developments in information technology have enabled companies to monitor the market and reveal micro-trends in consumer behavior in almost real time (Basal et al., 2025). In this context, the prevailing paradigm is Smart Marketing 5.0, which confers human-centric values and technological capabilities that aim at creating personalized and predictive customer experiences (Kotler et al., 2022). In this environment, organisations no longer must be reactive when it comes to marketing. Rather, they rely more on predictive analytics, which relies on statistical models, machine learning algorithms and historical data to predict, at a micro-level, consumer needs and preferences and their expected behaviours (Rosário et al., 2024). In the broader context of Marketing 5.0 and the New Era of Society 5.0, blending the digital and physical world, the company can use predictive analytics to get a step closer to a scale-changing hyper-persoalized marketing. These tools can assist companies gain better insights into purchasing behaviour, forecast customer churn, and improve customer engagement during the entire customer lifecycle to retain customers and cultivate strong customer relationships. The shift is from mass marketing towards the individual modeling of customer behavior and is based on every interaction made possible through real-time insights and predictive intelligence (Dahake et al., 2025). Consumer behaviour models are also significantly enhanced using machine learning algorithms like logistic regression, decision trees and association rule mining, which offer higher granularity and scalability (Mohan et al., 2025). This helps extend the significance when linked to customer theories such as that of perceived value, brand attachment, and that of customer engagement as apply to consumers (Muhajir, 2024). Predictive analytics is not an auxiliary tool for the digital economy but a crucial skill for organizational effectiveness and value creation for an organization, as demonstrated by Mohan et al. (2025), Rosário et al. (2024), and Muhajir (2024). This chapter further explores ethical considerations of these capabilities, including privacy of data, bias, transparency, consumer trust, and others critical to their sustainability. This chapter aims at providing a detailed understanding of how predictive analytics and artificial intelligence (AI) tools can predict consumer behavior, needs, preferences and patterns of decision-making; it aims at critically analysing the use of these technologies for data-driven marketing strategies, and the enhancement of customer experiences; it aims at evaluating personalization strategies and their impacts on customer satisfaction, consumer loyalty, and business performance; and it focusses on highlighting ethical concerns and issues with the adoption and sustainability of predictive marketing, including issues of data privacy, algorithmic bias, transparency, etc. The chapter is divided as follows: Section 2 lays the theoretical foundations. In Section 3, predictive analytics methods and sources of data are reviewed. Both these are important constructs that are discussed in section 4 that predict. Section 5 delves into AI-based consumer behaviour modelling. In the section Integration from insight to actions, the focus is on the step from insight into action. Section 7 provides an overview of the usage of the industry. Problems and future issues are highlighted in Section 8. All ethical, privacy and bias issues are discussed in Section 9. There are implications for theory and practice in Section 10.

Figure 1. Evolution of Marketing Towards Marketing 5.0 (Source: Created by authors based on secondary data)

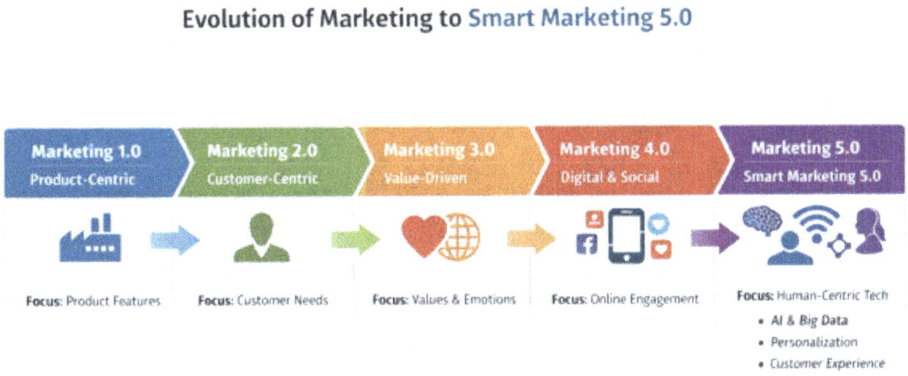

2. THEORETICAL FOUNDATIONS

To grasp the concept of predictive analytics for Smart Marketing 5.0, it is essential to delve into the interdisciplinary field that encompasses consumer decision-making, computational modelling, behavioural economics, digital marketing frameworks, and data ethics. In this chapter, we used a variety of theoretical lenses, which are summarized in a structured manner in Table 1. The conceptual structure used for analysis of consumer behaviour is the consumer behaviour theory which is the basis for the development of predictive models (Engel et al., 1968). The conceptual architecture is then translated into operational instruments through statistical and AI modelling: Using past or current data, organizations can translate their theoretical constructs into measurable predictions (Xu et al., 2024). Behavioural economics goes further still by adding psychological variables and heuristics – prospect theory, loss aversion and bounded rationality – to the field of consumer prediction models (Thaler & Sunstein, 2008) to highlight the narrow scope of purely rationalistic assumptions embedded in many consumer models. The frameworks of digital marketing include AI, IoT, and hyper-personalization, all of which are needed to operationalize the insights at scale (Kotler et al., 2022). Last, the ethics and privacy lens helps ensure responsible data use is kept at the heart of predictive model design and deployment (Barocas & Selbst, 2016). There is a significant lack in the literature of understanding the combination of behavioral economics with machine learning methods. Hybrid models that combine heuristic-aware and bias-corrected models to enhance prediction realism should be explored in future research. Likewise, cross-domain theoretical enrichment, that is, from the information systems, the organisational behaviour and cognitive psychology, would reinforce the theoretical basis for predictive consumer modelling.

Table 1. Theoretical Foundations Connected to Predictive Analytics and Smart Marketing 5.0

Theory	Definition / Role	Context in Predictive Marketing
Marketing 5.0 (Kotler et al., 2022)	Next-generation marketing framework integrating AI, data, and digital technologies to enhance customer experience.	Predictive analytics and consumer behaviour modelling are core components, enabling personalized experiences and technology-enabled marketing decisions.
Predictive Analytics (Alanazi, 2022)	Use of statistical algorithms, machine learning, and AI to forecast future outcomes based on historical and real-time data.	Identifies patterns in customer data to improve segmentation, forecast preferences, and tailor marketing actions.
Consumer Behaviour Modelling (Xu et al., 2024)	Mathematical or computational modelling of consumer decisions and purchase patterns.	Predictive models map past behaviour to future behaviour, informing segmentation and targeted offers.
Sentiment-Based Predictive Modelling (Gooljar et al., 2024)	Combines sentiment analysis from consumer text data with predictive analytics to forecast buying behaviour.	Integrates emotional signals into predictive models, aligning with customer-centric goals of Marketing 5.0.

continued on following page

Table 1. Continued

Theory	Definition / Role	Context in Predictive Marketing
Big Data & AI Integration (Gooljar et al., 2024)	Use of large, heterogeneous datasets and AI tools (e.g., LSTM, BERT) to extract deep insights.	Enhances predictive accuracy and behavioural understanding in adaptive, smart marketing systems.
Data-Driven Personalization (Kotler et al., 2022)	Strategy using predictive and behavioural models to customize consumer interactions.	Personalization is enabled by predicting individual preferences—a central aim of Smart Marketing 5.0.
Behavioural Economics (Thaler & Sunstein, 2008)	Incorporates cognitive biases and heuristics into models of consumer decision-making.	Provides a corrective lens for purely rationalistic predictive models, improving real-world predictive validity.

3. PREDICTIVE ANALYTICS IN MARKETING

In digital marketing, AI and predictive analytics are widely used to analyze consumer behavior and preferences, personalize marketing messages, and improve the effectiveness of marketing campaigns. For example, predictive analytics can be used to analyze data from social media, email and web navigation, among other factors, to predict customer trends and the most appropriate messaging for certain audiences (Al Khaldy et al., 2023). The tech underpinning this paradigm is the ability of the organization to ingest tremendous amounts of data coupled with a high dimensional analytical model, thereby moving from descriptive to predictive and prescriptive decision making. Predictive customer analytics has gained in momentum especially after 2020, as more tools and technologies for machine learning and deep learning and hybrid modelling become available (Bujor & Ene, 2025). An understanding of the sources of data for consumer behaviour modelling. The quality and diversity of the data used for predictive models can be critical to their performance. Consumer profiles are created in modern marketing systems by bringing together structured and unstructured data from a variety of sources.

Customer Relationship Management (CRM) Data. CRM systems can capture structured, longitudinal data on customer interactions and transactions, which can help companies measure behavioural trends, classify customer value segments and anticipate customer behaviour. CRM data is well-suited to the analysis needed for high-value segments and segment at risk. But it can only reflect emotional motives and real-time behavioural changes when combined with other sources of unstructured and contextual data (Kumar & Reinartz, 2016).

Social Media Data. These social media platforms produce vast amounts of data that is not structured, but rather represents the attitudes, preferences and interactions of consumers. This data adds emotional and attitudinal factors to behavioural models. However, without proper data preprocessing, data noise, sampling bias, and data authenticity issues decrease the dependability of the prediction (Gandomi & Haider, 2015). With the development of natural language processing (NLP), social media data has become much more tractable for predictive purposes.

Web Analytics. Web analytics are used to monitor users' interactions with digital media, such as clicks, time spent on site, and the sequence of pages they visit, which helps to understand how customers use the platform and make decisions online. But there is not much contextual meaning in the web data, and it is generally necessary to combine with other data sources to infer the full user intent (Wedel & Kannan, 2016).

Emerging Data Sources. The data that is generated by smart devices, wearables, mobile sensors, IoT, and biometric signals are an untapped realm of consumer data that has significant predictive value. All these sources provide new avenues of real-time, context-aware personalization, but they also present privacy and consent issues (Wamba et al., 2017). While CRM, social media and web analytics provide a more rounded picture of the consumer, data silos, privacy restrictions and complexity in integration are still major hurdles to having full consumer intelligence. Strong data integration architectures and governance are essential investments to leverage predictive modelling.

Methods of Predictive Marketing

A variety of statistical and machine learning techniques allows raw consumer data to be transformed into helpful insights that are put into practice.

- **Machine Learning** — Classification. Classification algorithms predict categorical outcomes, e.g. churn probability. The models are important because they are interpretable and can be used in marketing decisions. Their performance relies on a balanced dataset, however, and strong feature selection (Neslin et al., 2006). Machine learning can identify non-linear patterns in heterogeneous data from a consumer and convert it into predictive insights for traditional statistical models.
- **Regression** models calculate continuous results like expected customer spending or CLV. They work well with linear and simple behavioural patterns, but may not perform well with non-linear and complex behavioural patterns without extensions using ensemble or deep learning methods (Shmueli & Koppius, 2011).
- To examine the time, and to predict future trends of behaviour, such as changes in demand, or seasonal trends in buying, time-series models are used. These models have applications in the retail sector and e-commerce but have

some limitations on their forecasting ability in volatile markets (Hyndman & Athanasopoulos, 2018).

- **Recommendation Systems.** Collaborative filtering, content-based methods generate personalised product suggestions which enhance the understanding for the client and boost conversion rates. Among some of the potential obstacles to this range of consumer choice is the "cold start" effect, and another is "over-personalization" and "filter" effect (Castells et al., 2015).
- **Deep Learning**. With the help of deep learning architectures like Long Short-Term Memory (LSTM) networks or transformer-based models like BERT, complex sequential and contextual consumer data can be modelled. In the area of sentiment analysis and the prediction of behaviours, these have been shown to be more effective, but require huge amounts of data and considerable computational power (LeCun et al., 2015). The accuracy of machine learning predictions is tied to the data quality, potential for the algorithm being biased, and balance between complexity and interpretability. In considering these trade-offs the strategic goals and regulatory requirements should be taken into consideration.

Figure 2. Integrated Predictive Marketing Framework: From Data to Business Performance (Source: Generated by authors using AI with literature support)

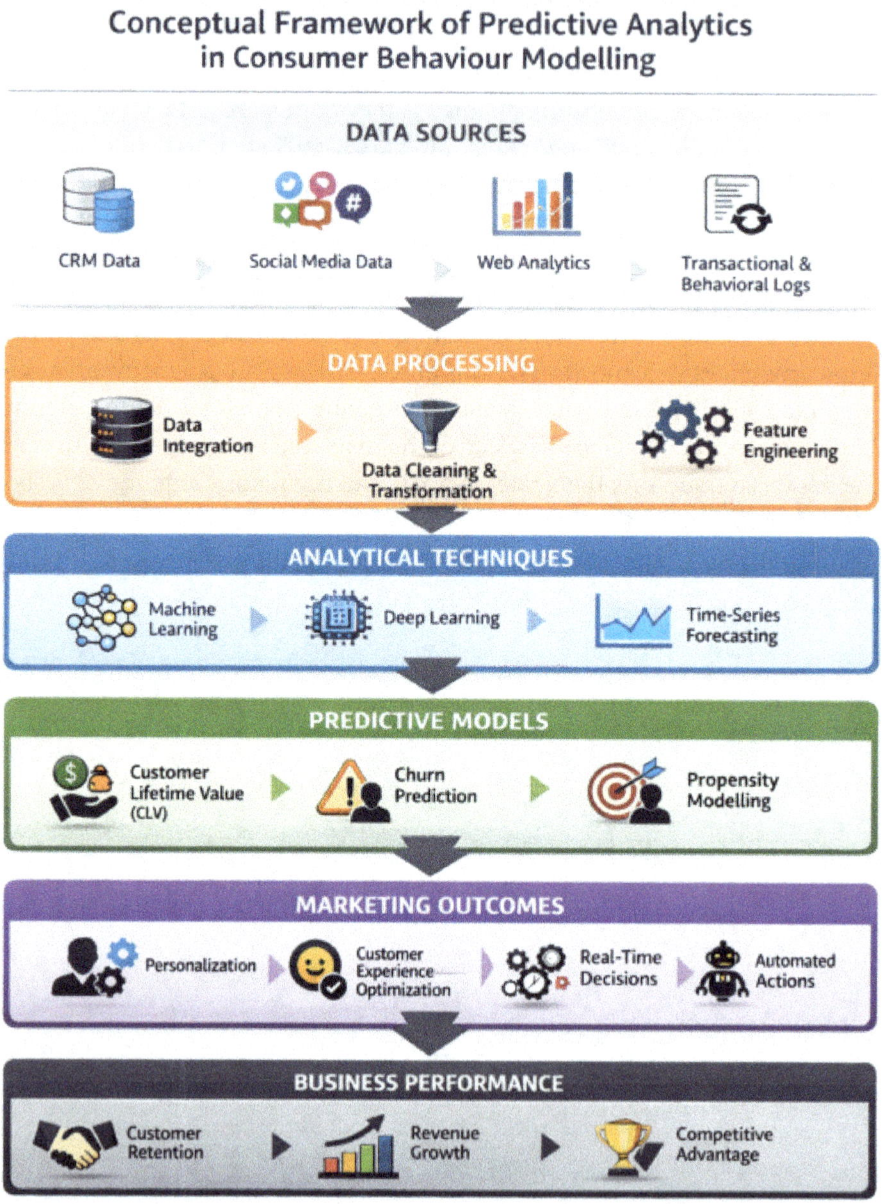

4. KEY PREDICTIVE CONSTRUCTS IN CONSUMER BEHAVIOUR

4.1 Customer Lifetime Value (CLV)

Customer Lifetime Value is the net cash flow that is discounted back to its present value and belongs to a particular customer. CLV is a fundamental tool that allows companies to invest in appropriate customer segments, as it is a measure that facilitates a customer-centric marketing strategy (Kumar & Reinartz, 2016). New models for CLV incorporate transactional data, engagement indicators, and predictive churn indicators to forecast revenue. Yet, CLV models are based on assumptions regarding future behaviour that might not apply in dynamic and disrupted market conditions. Another key strategic constraint of over relying on CLV is systematic under-investment in new or potentially high-value segments. Future CLV models need to include uncertainty quantification and confidence intervals to enable more confident decision making in the presence of volatility.

4.2 Churn Prediction

Churn prediction models determine the customer who might leave the organization's service, which will help to take the necessary measures in advance to keep them (Neslin et al., 2006). These models are getting more complex, with a variety of behavioural indicators and information on real-time interaction. While useful for some reason, churn models can give false positives and thus cause allocation of resources for retention. They can also miss qualitative factors in churn, like dissatisfaction with service or competition that are not evident in transactional data. Hybrid models that combine survey measures of attitudes with behavioural measures may overcome these drawbacks.

4.3 Propensity Modelling

Propensity models can predict the likelihood that a customer will engage in a given action, like buying a product or responding to a campaign (Wedel & Kannan, 2016). These models help in precision marketing and improve the efficiency of campaigns. Yet, the ethical issues of propensity modelling, however, cannot be ignored, because of the potential consumer manipulation and data privacy, especially with extremely targeted marketing interventions. Consumer autonomy and informed consent must be weighed against the use of propensity scores.

4.4 Next Best Action (NBA) Modelling

However, at the same time as CLV and churn modelling came into existence, Next Best Action (NBA) frameworks combined CLV, propensity and contextual information to identify the best marketing action for every single customer at every interaction. NBA modelling is a more comprehensive and dynamic way of predictive marketing than traditional predictive constructs, and is a step towards integrating decision intelligence. It is being adopted by more CRM-rich industries, like financial services, telecommunications, and e-commerce (Davenport, 2014).

5. CONSUMER BEHAVIOUR MODELLING USING AI.CONSUMER BEHAVIOUR MODELLING USING AI

Since 2020, the application of AI in consumer behaviour modelling has increased tremendously, and various contributions have been presented in the fields of both academia and practice in the United States, India, and China, among other countries (Zulaikha et al., 2026). Consumer data can be segmented and used for predictive consumer analysis, where machine learning (ML) and deep learning (DL) techniques are widely used to predict and personalise marketing strategies. They uncover and highlight behavioural patterns in the survey data and digital interactions, providing guidance for brand strategy, customer loyalty programs, and tailoring customer experiences (Ribeiro et al., 2025).

AI agents with high autonomy, like chatbots and virtual assistants, significantly improve CRM by facilitating targeted interactions with the brand and consumers that shape their experience and trust in the brand (Ribeiro et al., 2025). With these innovations come rising ethical issues concerning data privacy, algorithmic bias, and digital surveillance, which can impact customer trust and acceptance of AI applications in marketing (Zulaikha et al., 2026).

The potential of AI to enable real-time monitoring, predictive control, and decision-support, which have implications for industrial process optimization, medical diagnostics, and energy systems, also evokes its applications in consumer behaviour modelling context (Rojek et al., 2025).

5.1 Segmentation Models

Segmentation models are based on clustering techniques to find homogenous groups of consumers, allowing strategies to be developed based on their specific behaviour and preferences. In today's digital and e-commerce-driven landscape, AI-driven segmentation is essential for making strategic decisions in marketing to ensure campaigns are relevant and precision personalization (Ribeiro et al., 2025). Dynamic segmentation involves real-time changes to cluster membership based on behavioural signals, and is an important advancement on static demographic segmentation.

5.2 Behavioural Prediction Models

Behavioural forecasting models leverage past and current customer data to anticipate their future behaviour and actions, which are essential for maximizing engagement and retention. AI-driven predictive analytics software can use complex data such as purchase history, online behaviour, and psychological indicators to uncover what drives purchase behaviour and loyalty. (Ribeiro et al., 2025) AI's ability to accurately forecast behavioral stages through interdisciplinary evidence has the potential for early intervention and targeted communication efforts, particularly in reaching consumers (Li et al., 2025).

5.3 Personalization Algorithms

Personalization algorithms allow for the delivery of personalized recommendations in real-time, by continuously processing data. Such models optimize the consumers' experience by dynamically adjusting the content and interactions based on AI methodologies that involve multimodal data input and reinforcement learning (Gouveia & Santos, 2025; Ribeiro et al., 2025). As a result, deeper engagement with and co-creation of value is possible with autonomous AI systems that can adapt in real time. Issues like filter bubbles and over-personalization, which are dimensions that need further empirical research, pose a challenge.

5.4 Ethical and Trust Issues of AI-based Modelling

Ethical issues emphasized in consumer systems are data privacy, algorithmic bias, and transparency. They directly impact consumer trust and purchase behaviour in online contexts (Ribeiro et al., 2025). Consumer trust is essential, and adhering to regulations is only part of it; openly communicating the working mechanisms of AI models, as well as the use of consumer data, is also crucial. To ensure that AI-based modelling promotes consumer welfare, rather than utilising behavioural weaknesses, interdisciplinary discussions on the convergence of AI capabilities and human centred ethics are critical. (Zulaikha et al., 2026).

6. INTEGRATION: FROM INSIGHT TO ACTION

The ability of AI to translate consumer insights into actionable marketing applications – such as targeting high-value segments, dynamic pricing, and personalized product recommendations – has been a significant subject of research. There are plenty of practical uses, challenges and boundary circumstances documented on the subject.

6.1 Precision Targeting

By leveraging data-driven forecasting and clustering techniques, AI can help target audiences with highly relevant content within each consumer segment. The integration of structured and unstructured data using machine learning screening models underscores the potential of using their automatic capabilities to yield high-value opportunities and guide targeted outreach efforts (Gouveia & Santos, 2025; Toluwase et al., 2025). The focus on real-time interactions and proactive co-creation in AI-powered CX strategies reflects a shift toward fostering deeper brand relationships and optimizing campaign performance (Gouveia & Santos, 2025).

6.2 Dynamic Pricing

Dynamic pricing uses AI demand forecasting to provide price-responsive pricing strategies, considering profitability and consumer sensitivity. From automating customer service to providing predictive analytics, the capabilities of AI are evident in financial services and e-commerce, which are also showcasing how AI can boost efficiency and enhance customer experience, while simultaneously adapting to market dynamics and customer preferences. Designing a dynamic pricing system should be done with a clear concept of dealing with ethical issues, including possible price discrimination and consumer fairness.

6.3 Personalized Product Recommendations

The generation of personalized product recommendations is the result of AI models constantly analyzing consumer data in multiple formats. Multimodal consumer data is fed into AI models to generate personalized product recommendations on an ongoing basis. Adaptive learning algorithms, which include supervised, unsupervised, and reinforcement learning approaches, take advantage of behavioral patterns, contextual cues, and biometric data to make more accurate recommendations, leading to higher engagement rates and purchase intent (Gouveia & Santos, 2025; Hariyanto et al., 2025). In the context of ecommerce, empirical data demonstrates the benefits of AI-powered personalization in enhancing customer satisfaction and operational efficiency, further highlighting the additional value that this technology offers to digital businesses. The results from the e-commerce scenario validate the benefits of AI personalization for customer satisfaction and process efficiency, affirming the value of AI in the digital business realm.

6.4 Real-Time AI Marketing Applications

Real-time marketing powered by AI offers personalized advertising, dynamic pricing optimization, and content personalization based on real-time behaviour. The high level of training of ML models, such as multimodal learning architectures, constantly identifies behavioural patterns and adapts digital content on demand to individual user profiles (Hariyanto et al., 2025). This customization leads to more engagement and buying intent when ads match consumer expectations. But attitudes towards data privacy and control impact willingness to share personal information. Ethical AI monetisation and user-centered design play a pivotal role in addressing trade-offs in privacy (Shin, 2025). According to the findings of AI-generated content (AIGC) advertising, the more consumers find an advertisement useful and relevant to them, the more positive they will respond; the more entertaining an advertisement is, the more positive the response will be if the product involvement is low (Jiang et al., 2025). The AI-generated source of content, however, may produce complicated responses from the audience that need to be taken care of when it comes to brand managing them. (Gu et al., 2025)

6.5 Automation and Human Judgment

Balancing the Two Studies have revealed that over-reliance on AI in customer interactions can lead to a loss of trust and dissatisfaction. If consumers prefer human-like empathy and context-sensitivity in sensitive or critical situations, the level of automation needs to be finely balanced with human involvement (Ding et al., 2025). The ability of EAI architectures to improve the transparency of the model's functioning can help in making informed managerial decisions and increase the trust of stakeholders in pricing, targeting and recommendation systems (Teixeira et al., 2025).

Figure 3. AI-Driven Consumer Marketing Strategies: Targeting, Pricing, and Personalization (Source: Gouveia & Santos, 2025; Toluwase et al., 2025; Attar, 2025; Şencan, 2025; Hariyanto et al., 2025)

7. PREDICTIVE ANALYTICS IN INDUSTRY APPLICATIONS

7.1 Inventory Optimization

Predictive analytics helps companies make more efficient use of their inventory by forecasting customer demands, reducing supply chain inefficiencies, and optimizing the use of resources. Achieving balance between supply and demand is critical in the fast moving consumer goods (FMCG) retailing industry to minimize overstocking and out of stocks. The study conducted by Suwignjo et al. (2023) shows that gradient boosting models using historical sales, stock and demand fluctuation data could reach an accuracy of 84% for classification and a value of $R^2 = 0.89$ for regression, which demonstrates the ability of predictive analytics to classify the state of inventory and predict restocking needs. Automated replenishment and supply chain responsiveness to seasonality and market trends are achieved through predictive insights, leading to reduced operational costs (Gudavalli et al., 2024).

7.2 Marketing Campaign Optimization

Predictive analytics has revolutionized marketing, providing a data-driven approach to optimizing campaigns and engaging customers on a personalized level. Predictive analytics is not about targeting in a general way, but about targeting segments of customers by their behaviour and demographic and modelling their response likelihood. Venkatasubbu et al. (2022) explain how regression, classification and clustering analysis can build insight into campaign design — who is the highest value customer, the best communication path and specific promotional messages to send to specific consumers. This leads to higher conversion rates, returns on investment (ROI), and better retention rates. Real-time performance analytics allows for ongoing campaign adjustments, optimizing resource allocation.

7.3 Consumer Behaviour Analysis

Analyzing consumer behaviour is the basis for differentiation and predictive analytics is great for that. Predictive modelling explores and identifies trends and drivers of purchases from transactions, browsing and interaction history. These techniques, including machine learning, time series analysis, and regression models, enable organizations to forecast demand, trends, and customer preferences (Venkatasubbu et al., 2022). Predictive Analytics can also be used to segment customers in complex ways like Lifetime Value, engagement and frequency of purchase, which can provide valuable information for developing different product and service strategies and marketing campaigns. Churn prediction models can also help businesses take preventative measures against churning customers.

7.4 Consumer Experience

Enhancement Predictive analytics is the technology behind proactive and personalized consumer interactions at all points of contact. With the advent of the digital era, characterized by consumers that demand seamless, customized experiences, predictive analytics is a tool that can help organizations anticipate and act proactively on customer needs. With the help of AI, big data, and real-time analytics, businesses can provide tailored recommendations for products, offers, and customer journeys (Gudavalli et al., 2024). Feedback loops are used to continuously improve future predictions, create self-improving experience systems, retain customers, build brand loyalty, and gain competitive edge.

Table 2. Summary of Predictive Analytics Applications Across Key Industry Domains

Domain	Key Techniques	Applications	Outcomes	Key References
Inventory Optimization	Gradient boosting, time-series	Demand forecasting, stock control	Reduced stockouts, improved efficiency	Suwignjo et al. (2023); Gudavalli et al. (2024)
Marketing Campaigns	Regression, clustering, classification	Customer segmentation, targeting	Higher ROI, better engagement	Venkatasubbu et al. (2022)
Consumer Behaviour	Machine learning, regression, time-series	Purchase prediction, churn analysis	Improved sales, customer loyalty	Venkatasubbu et al. (2022); Neslin et al. (2006)
Consumer Experience	AI, real-time analytics, recommendation systems	Personalization, journey optimization	Increased satisfaction, retention	Gudavalli et al. (2024); Attar (2025)
Dynamic Pricing	Demand forecasting, reinforcement learning	Real-time price adjustment	Profit optimization, inventory turnover	Attar (2025); Şencan (2025)

8. CHALLENGES AND FUTURE TRENDS

8.1 Key Challenges

- **Data Quality & Integration**. The two greatest challenges for operations are data quality and cross-system integration. Disintegrated supply chain, CRM systems and digital platforms are widely used sources for predictive analytic systems. Inconsistent and incomplete data reduces the effectiveness of forecasting and marketing targeting (Sivarajah et al., 2017). Unified data architectures and master data management are essential enablers for effective predictive capability.
- **Model Complexity & Scalability.** There are significant differences in the computational requirements and interpretability of time-series, machine learning and deep learning models. Technically, it is difficult to manage and integrate multiple model families into a coherent organizational system. (Waller & Fawcett, 2013) The real-time, omni-channel consumer data environment is a continuing technological challenge.

- **Model Transparency and Trust from Stakeholders**. There are many effective predictive models, especially ensemble and deep learning models, that operate as black boxes making it hard to understand the logic of predictions for managers. This opacity hinders adoption and reduces trust in automated recommendations (Rai, 2020). Explainable AI (XAI) methods are gaining importance to make analytical output trustworthy inputs to managers.
- **Ensuring the privacy and regulatory adherence of data**. Much of this personal and behavioural data is relied upon for predictive analytics, creating huge conflicts with consent, protection and regulation policies such as the GDPR. Improper handling of customer information may lead to loss of reputation, legal action (Kshetri, 2014). It is imperative that privacy-by-design principles are incorporated from the start into the architecture of predictive system.
- **Organizational and Implementation Barriers**. In an era of predictive analytics, there are significant changes to workflow, culture and decision-making structures that need to be made. One of the common barriers is resistance to change (Wamba et al., 2015) which is the lack of skills and the lack of alignment between analytics skills and business goals. Enablers include effective change management, as well as ongoing executive support.
- **Limits due to costs and infrastructure**. Data storage, cloud computing, and dedicated expertise are needed for the development of predictive analytics infrastructure. The costs are an entry barrier for small and medium enterprises (SMEs) but have been absorbed by large enterprises (Chen et al., 2012). These barriers are being steadily lowered as analytics-as-a-service tools are increasingly developed on the cloud.

8.2 Emerging Trends

There are several interrelated trends that are impacting the future of predictive analytics in marketing and consumer management:

✓ Real time and streaming analytics allow for ongoing decision making using real-time data, which can help with dynamic changes to inventory, real-time optimization of campaigns and personalized interactions (Davenport, 2014).

✓ The integration of AI and deep learning is bringing in new possibilities for modelling very complex and high dimensional data, enhancing predictions, segmentation, and recommendations' accuracy (LeCun et al., 2015).

✓ Hyper-personalization uses "fine-grained" customer data to make one-to-one recommendations, offers and communications at scale, which is made possible by the availability of real-time customer data (Wedel & Kannan, 2016).

- ✓ Predictive models for all channels – digital, mobile and physical – are combined in Omni-channel analytics for better consumer behaviour understanding and cross channel experience optimization.
- ✓ Explainable AI (XAI) offers interpretable insights into how predictive algorithms produce their results, which is essential for transparency, compliance with regulations and consumer trust, especially in marketing and consumer-facing applications (Rai, 2020; Weller, 2019).
- ✓ The technology of IoT integrated analytics uses real-time data generated by the devices for improved predictive inventory, supply chain and consumer experience management (Wamba et al., 2017).
- ✓ Prescriptive analytics takes predictive analytics one step further, recommending the best quantity to reorder in inventory or prioritizing actions in marketing—making the leap from insight to decision (Delen & Zolbanin, 2018).
- ✓ The shift towards cloud-based analytics platforms is making it more accessible for SMEs to access the sophisticated predictive capabilities, making it easier and quicker to become widespread.
- ✓ Federated learning models (Yang et al., 2019) can also be used to train models on decentralized data without having to consolidate private consumer data, providing a potential route to privacy-preserving predictive analytics.

9. ETHICAL, PRIVACY, AND BIAS CONSIDERATIONS

9.1 Data Privacy

Predictive analytics is an issue that has a lot of importance is data privacy particularly in regards to the fact that a lot of personal and behavioral data is being used by the organizations to make their stocking, marketing and customer experience choices. The General Data Protection Regulation (GDPR) and other regulations call for the legitimate collection of information, storage, public knowledge of its use, and consent. The increasing reliance on big data analytics poses a growing risk of privacy issues, such as unauthorized access to data and the usage of sensitive information, which can have serious implications on consumer confidence and consumer regulatory stature, according to Kshetri (2014). Sivarajah et al. (2017) state that good data governance is a must – it includes data integrity, confidentiality and compliance. Two promising approaches are coming online that offer technical solutions to preserving the analytical usefulness of data while ensuring privacy at the individual level: differential privacy and privacy-preserving machine learning.

9.2 Algorithmic Bias

A major ethical problem is that algorithms based on past data have the potential to perpetuate and accentuate systemic inequalities, leading to disproportionate results for different demographic groups. Bias may be due to non-representativeness of the training data (Barocas & Selbst, 2016), lack of data coverage, or poorly formulated model goals.The reasons behind bias include that training data may not be representative (Barocas & Selbst, 2016), data may not be complete, or model goals may be poorly defined.

Predictive marketing, on the other hand, may result in unfair product suggestions or leave out certain demographic groups from marketing opportunities. Rai (2020) calls for fairness-driven ML approaches and constant auditing of models as supplementary approaches to reduce bias. The commitment of the organization to diverse and representative training sets, along with frequent algorithmic impact assessments, are key to the progress of ethical and inclusive marketing from data.

9.3 Transparency and Explainability

For predictive analytics systems to ensure confidence in their deployment in consequential decision-making contexts (predicting, pricing, and customer experience), transparency and explainability are key design principles. Models with high predictive power like ensemble methods and deep learning models often behave like a black box that gives no clues as to how they work. This transparency will create stakeholder doubts and inhibit adoption (Rai, 2020). Weller (2019) states that explainability goes hand in hand with accountability, especially when the automation of decision-making relies on consumer information. Transparency models are crucial in marketing and customer experience management, enabling companies to justify recommended changes, gain customer buy-in, and meet regulatory standards. Model interpretability is thus both a technical requirement and an ethical imperative.

A consumer's autonomy and informed consent is preserved.

However, predictive analytics has drawn more attention beyond privacy and bias, when it comes to consumer autonomy. Hyper-personalisation, through predictive models, could influence customers' choices in a subtle manner that benefits the organisation more than the customer. There is a need for explicit ethical reflection for the use of propensity models to identify and exploit vulnerabilities in decision-making processes, especially in marketing based on behavioural economics. The informed consent paradigm should cover not only data collection, but also predictive profiling and automated decision making. Clear opt-out options and user-controlled personalisation options should be standard practice for organisations.

10. CONCLUSION

By using predictive analytics, organisations can use machine learning and efficiently process a massive amount of data to pinpoint inefficiencies, deliver personalised messages, plan targeted marketing campaigns, and model customer behaviour, which can optimise inventory, boost marketing effectiveness, and provide better customer experiences. These attributes contribute to user satisfaction, loyalty, and generating revenue, but they come with ethical and operational complexities in managing data security, bias in algorithms, transparency, and governance. In conclusion, the real challenge for Smart Marketing 5.0 is to combine a data-driven approach with autonomy and respect for the user, so that predictive systems can create more responsive, relevant, and respectful experiences, and even inspire new thinking and research into more hybrid behavioural economics–machine learning models and the future implications of AI personalisation on wellbeing and social acceptability.

REFERENCES

Al Khaldy, M. A., Al-Obaydi, B. A. A., & al Shari, A. J. (2023). The impact of predictive analytics and AI on digital marketing strategy and ROI. In Conference on Sustainability and Cutting-Edge Business Technologies (pp. 367–379). Springer Nature Switzerland. DOI: 10.1007/978-3-031-42455-7_31

Alanazi, T. M. (2022). Marketing 5.0: An empirical investigation of its perceived effect on marketing performance. Marketing i menedžment innovacij, 13(4), 55–64.

Attar, R. W. (2025). Predicting trends and maximizing sales: AI's role in Saudi e-commerce decision-making. *Journal of Theoretical and Applied Electronic Commerce Research, 20*(4), 311. DOI: 10.3390/jtaer20040311

Barocas, S., & Selbst, A. D. (2016). Big data's disparate impact. *California Law Review, 104*, 671–732.

Basal, M., Moulai, K., & Cetin, A. (2025). Predictive analytics for customer behavior prediction in artificial intelligence. *Economics World, 12*(2), 142–154.

Bujor, D., & Constantin, A. B. E. (2025). AI-driven predictive customer analytics for forecasting behavior, churn and future buying patterns. In *Proceedings of the International Conference on Business Excellence* (Vol. 19, No. 1, pp. 981–994). Bucharest University of Economic Studies. DOI: 10.2478/picbe-2025-0077

Castells, P., Hurley, N. J., & Vargas, S. (2015). Novelty and diversity in recommender systems. In Ricci, F., Rokach, L., & Shapira, B. (Eds.), *Recommender Systems Handbook* (pp. 881–918). Springer. DOI: 10.1007/978-1-4899-7637-6_26

Chen, H., Chiang, R. H., & Storey, V. C. (2012). Business intelligence and analytics: From big data to big impact. *Management Information Systems Quarterly, 36*(4), 1165–1188. DOI: 10.2307/41703503

Dahake, P. S., Dahake, N. S., Bansod, S. N., Patil, P. A., & Ingle, A. (2025). Marketing innovations in Society 5.0: The role of predictive analytics in analyzing consumer behavior for marketers. In *Future-Proofing Emerging Technologies for Business Transformation* (pp. 361–386). IGI Global. DOI: 10.4018/979-8-3373-1320-7.ch011

Davenport, T. H. (2014). How strategists use 'big data' to support internal business decisions, discovery and production. *Strategy and Leadership, 42*(4), 45–50. DOI: 10.1108/SL-05-2014-0034

Delen, D., & Zolbanin, H. M. (2018). The analytics paradigm in business research. *Journal of Business Research, 90*, 186–195. DOI: 10.1016/j.jbusres.2018.05.013

Ding, Z., Zhang, Y., Sun, J., Goh, M., & Yang, Z. (2025). Harmonizing human touch and AI precision in customer service. *Journal of Service Research*. Advance online publication. DOI: 10.1177/10946705251384692

Engel, J. F., Kollat, D. T., & Blackwell, R. D. (1968). *Consumer Behavior*. Holt, Rinehart and Winston.

Felzmann, H., Fosch-Villaronga, E., Lutz, C., & Tamò-Larrieux, A. (2020). Towards transparency by design for artificial intelligence. *Science and Engineering Ethics*, *26*(6), 3333–3361. DOI: 10.1007/s11948-020-00276-4 PMID: 33196975

Gandomi, A., & Haider, M. (2015). Beyond the hype: Big data concepts, methods, and analytics. *International Journal of Information Management*, *35*(2), 137–144. DOI: 10.1016/j.ijinfomgt.2014.10.007

Gooljar, V., Issa, T., Hardin-Ramanan, S., & Abu-Salih, B. (2024). Sentiment-based predictive models for online purchases in the era of marketing 5.0: A systematic review. *Journal of Big Data*, *11*(1), 107. DOI: 10.1186/s40537-024-00947-0

Gouveia, J., & Santos, S. (2025). Rethinking the customer journey: Impact of AI for consumers and businesses—a systematic literature review and research agenda. *International Journal of Consumer Studies*, *49*(6), e70136. DOI: 10.1111/ijcs.70136

Gu, C., Li, X., & Xiang, Q. (2025). The infinite monkey theorem in AIGC advertising: Matching effects between AI disclosure and advertising appeals on consumer advertising avoidance intention. *Journal of Research in Interactive Marketing*. Advance online publication. DOI: 10.1108/JRIM-05-2025-0265

Gudavalli, S., Ravi, V. K., Jampani, S., Pandey, P., Ayyagari, A., & Goel, P. (2024). Enhancing data security and privacy in cloud, SAP, and IoT environments. *Journal of Quantum Science and Technology*, *1*(4), 217–243. DOI: 10.63345/jqst.v1i4.104

Hariyanto, H., Kristianingsih, F. X. D., & Maharani, R. (2025). Artificial intelligence in adaptive education: A systematic review of techniques for personalized learning. *Discover Education*, *4*(1), 458. Advance online publication. DOI: 10.1007/s44217-025-00908-6

Hyndman, R. J., & Athanasopoulos, G. (2018). *Forecasting: Principles and Practice* (2nd ed.). OTexts.

Jiang, S., Zheng, W., & Kong, H. (2025). Trust or skepticism? Unraveling the communication mechanisms of AIGC advertisements on consumer responses. *Journal of Theoretical and Applied Electronic Commerce Research*, *20*(4), 339. DOI: 10.3390/jtaer20040339

Kotler, P., Kartajaya, H., & Setiawan, I. (2022). *Marketing 5.0: Technology for Humanity*. Wiley.

Kshetri, N. (2014). Big data's impact on privacy, security and consumer welfare. *Telecommunications Policy*, *38*(11), 1134–1145. DOI: 10.1016/j.telpol.2014.10.002

Kumar, V., & Reinartz, W. (2016). Creating enduring customer value. *Journal of Marketing*, *80*(6), 36–68. DOI: 10.1509/jm.15.0414

LeCun, Y., Bengio, Y., & Hinton, G. (2015). Deep learning. *Nature*, *521*(7553), 436–444. DOI: 10.1038/nature14539 PMID: 26017442

Li, X., Zhang, S., Li, X., Zeng, J., Long, Y., Nie, B., & Zhao, C. (2025). SHAP-driven insights into multimodal data: Behavior phase prediction for industrial safety applications. *Scientific Reports*, *15*(1), 34965. DOI: 10.1038/s41598-025-18889-9 PMID: 41057512

Mohan, L., Devarajan, M., Alotoum, F. J., Alsaaideh, M., & Prasad, K. (2025). Advanced data analytics for predicting consumer behavior using machine learning and association rule mining. In *2025 International Conference on Technology Enabled Economic Changes (InTech)* (pp. 908–914). IEEE. DOI: 10.1109/InTech64186.2025.11198315

Muhajir, A. (2024). Predictive analytics in marketing: Contribution to marketing performance. [PRODUCTIVITY]. *Management Studies and Business Journal*, *1*(3), 447–460.

Neslin, S. A., Gupta, S., Kamakura, W., Lu, J., & Mason, C. H. (2006). Defection detection: Measuring and understanding the predictive accuracy of customer churn models. *JMR, Journal of Marketing Research*, *43*(2), 204–211. DOI: 10.1509/jmkr.43.2.204

Rai, A. (2020). Explainable AI: From black box to glass box. *Journal of the Academy of Marketing Science*, *48*(1), 137–141. DOI: 10.1007/s11747-019-00710-5

Ribeiro, A., Rivero, A. J. L., & Abrantes, J. L. (2025). The impact of artificial intelligence on consumer behavior towards brands: A systematic review. *Electronic Commerce Research*. Advance online publication. DOI: 10.1007/s10660-025-10063-7

Rojek, I., Mikołajewski, D., Prokopowicz, P., & Piechowiak, M. (2025). AI-based modeling and optimization of AC/DC power systems. *Energies*, *18*(21), 5660. DOI: 10.3390/en18215660

Rosário, A. T., Cruz, R., Moniz, L. B., & Casaca, J. A. (2024). Predictive analytics for customer behavior. In *Data-Driven Marketing for Strategic Success* (pp. 37–72). IGI Global. DOI: 10.4018/979-8-3693-3455-3.ch002

Şencan, E. (2025). Artificial intelligence, organizational learning, and sustainable banking: Insights from Turkey for global business practice. *Thunderbird International Business Review*, tie.70062. Advance online publication. DOI: 10.1002/tie.70062

Shin, J. W. (2025). AI-driven privacy trade-offs in digital news content: Consumer perception of personalized advertising and dynamic paywall. *Journalism and Media*, *6*(4), 170. DOI: 10.3390/journalmedia6040170

Shmueli, G., & Koppius, O. R. (2011). Predictive analytics in information systems research. *Management Information Systems Quarterly*, *35*(3), 553–572. DOI: 10.2307/23042796

Sivarajah, U., Kamal, M. M., Irani, Z., & Weerakkody, V. (2017). Critical analysis of big data challenges and analytical methods. *Journal of Business Research*, *70*, 263–286. DOI: 10.1016/j.jbusres.2016.08.001

Suwignjo, P., Panjaitan, L., Baihaqy, A., & Rusdiansyah, A. (2023). Predictive analytics to improve inventory performance: A case study of an FMCG company. *Operations and Supply Chain Management: An International Journal*, *16*(2), 293–310. DOI: 10.31387/oscm0530390

Teixeira, B., Carvalhais, L., Pinto, T., & Vale, Z. (2025). Explainable AI framework for reliable and transparent automated energy management in buildings. *Energy and Building*, *347*, 116246. DOI: 10.1016/j.enbuild.2025.116246

Thaler, R. H., & Sunstein, C. R. (2008). *Nudge: Improving Decisions about Health, Wealth, and Happiness*. Yale University Press.

Toluwase, I., Shobande, A., & Atere, D. (2025). AI-powered screening models for expanding deal flow and identifying high-value corporate advisory opportunities. *Computer Science & IT Research Journal*, *6*(9), 662–688. DOI: 10.51594/csitrj.v6i9.2065

Venkatasubbu, S., Rambabu, V. P., & Jeyaraman, J. (2022). Predictive analytics in retail: Transforming inventory management and customer insights. *Australian Journal of Machine Learning Research & Applications*, *2*(1), 202–246.

Waller, M. A., & Fawcett, S. E. (2013). Data science, predictive analytics, and big data: A revolution that will transform supply chain design and management. *Journal of Business Logistics*, *34*(2), 77–84. DOI: 10.1111/jbl.12010

Wamba, S. F., Akter, S., Edwards, A., Chopin, G., & Gnanzou, D. (2015). How 'big data' can make big impact: Findings from a systematic review and a longitudinal case study. *International Journal of Production Economics, 165*, 234–246. DOI: 10.1016/j.ijpe.2014.12.031

Wamba, S. F., Gunasekaran, A., Akter, S., Ren, S. J. F., Dubey, R., & Childe, S. J. (2017). Big data analytics and firm performance: Effects of dynamic capabilities. *Journal of Business Research, 70*, 356–365. DOI: 10.1016/j.jbusres.2016.08.009

Wedel, M., & Kannan, P. K. (2016). Marketing analytics for data-rich environments. *Journal of Marketing, 80*(6), 97–121. DOI: 10.1509/jm.15.0413

Weller, A. (2019). Transparency: Motivations and challenges. In Samek, W. (Eds.), *Explainable AI: Interpreting, Explaining and Visualizing Deep Learning* (pp. 23–40). Springer., DOI: 10.1007/978-3-030-28954-6_2

Xu, Y., Ma, Y., Hu, R., & Wang, H. (2024). Predictive analytics techniques in consumer behaviour: A literature review. Advances in Economics. *Management and Political Sciences, 97*, 20–31.

Yang, Q., Liu, Y., Cheng, Y., Kang, Y., Chen, T., & Yu, H. (2019). *Federated Learning*. Morgan & Claypool.

Zulaikha, S., Dewi, I. R., & Kurniawati, M. (2026). Unveiling the intellectual landscape of artificial intelligence and consumer behavior. *Discover Artificial Intelligence, 6*(1), 2. DOI: 10.1007/s44163-025-00740-9

KEY TERMS AND DEFINITIONS

Algorithmic Bias: Faulty conclusions or predictions made by AI or machine learning systems due to biased input data, flawed algorithm design, or inadequately representative input data, which can lead to unfair or discriminatory outcomes.

Consumer Behaviour Analytics: The gathering and analysis of information about customers' interactions, preferences and purchases, in order to understand and foresee their future behavior. Predictive models can help businesses predict customer behavior and make informed decisions based on that.

Customer Experience: The combination of all the impressions a customer receives from an organisation from all the touch points and channels. Predictive analytics can also improve the customer experience by delivering proactive and personalized service, and enabling smooth communication.

Explainable AI (XAI): Approaches and frameworks that help explain to human users the reasoning behind an AI or machine learning model's decision-making process. Building stakeholder trust and ensuring regulatory compliance is of paramount importance, while also empowering informed oversight of automated decision-making is closely linked to XAI.There is also a strong connection between XAI and building stakeholder trust, ensuring regulatory compliance, and providing informed oversight of automated decisions.

Inventory Optimization: The process of keeping products at the ideal level of stock in order to keep costs related to overstocking, stock out and inventory holding to a minimum. Predictive analytics can help make this process more effective by being able to forecast demand more accurately and take replenishment action based on data.

Machine Learning: Artificial Intelligence (AI) principle that allows for a system to learn from data and optimize its performance without being explicitly programmed. For classification, regression, pattern recognition, and recommendation, machine learning is widely used for predictive analytics.

Marketing Campaign Optimization: The use of information-based techniques to improve the effectiveness and efficiency of marketing efforts. By analyzing trends and patterns, predictive analytics can help organizations identify target audiences, predict how these audiences will respond to the communication, and adjust their approach to achieve the greatest return.

Predictive Analytics: Use of statistical, machine learning and data mining techniques to analyze past data and current data to predict future events and making decisions. One of the key outcomes of predictive analytics is the ability for entities to detect patterns, trends, and correlations in data and to forecast future events in a numerical likelihood.

Chapter 3
Value Co-Creation in AI-Driven Services:
Hyper-Personalization, Distributed Agency, and Consumer Experience

Aysun Sahin
http://orcid.org/0000-0003-3285-1232
Duzce University, Turkey

Azize Şahin
http://orcid.org/0000-0002-3115-6812
İstanbul University, Turkey

ABSTRACT

This conceptual chapter examines how AI-driven hyper-personalization reshapes value co-creation in service consumer experiences. Integrating S-D Logic, ANT, and post-phenomenology, the chapter explains how AI systems redistribute agency, mediate lived experience, reconfigure resources, and generate relational tensions around privacy, opacity, trust, and vulnerability. It develops an integrative framework linking AI personalization capabilities to four mechanisms: distributed agency, experiential mediation, resource reconfiguration, and relational tension. The chapter proposes a typology of hyper-personalization design logics, from efficiency-centered to intrusive or extractive personalization, and illustrates the framework across retail, hospitality, healthcare, and financial services. It contributes to service marketing by reframing hyper-personalization as an ethically governed service ecosystem phenomenon that can produce value co-creation and co-destruction. Managerial implications emphasize transparency, consumer control, human oversight, and responsible AI service design.

DOI: 10.4018/979-8-3373-9159-5.ch003

1. INTRODUCTION

Artificial intelligence is reshaping consumer experience in services by moving personalization from a segment-level practice to a continuously adaptive interactional process. Earlier systems matched customers to predefined offers, content categories, or recommendation rules. AI-driven hyper-personalization is more consequential because it uses real-time behavioral, contextual, and relational data to anticipate needs, generate responses, and adjust service encounters as they unfold (Davenport et al., 2020; Huang & Rust, 2021). This raises a central theoretical question for service marketing: when an AI system interprets consumer data, recommends actions, speaks through conversational interfaces, and modifies the service journey, who is actually co-creating value?

The question cannot be answered by treating AI as a neutral tool. Recommendation engines, conversational agents, and adaptive interfaces influence the options consumers see and how alternatives are framed, and such encounters carry experiential costs as well as benefits (Puntoni et al., 2021). Service-Dominant Logic argues that value emerges through resource integration among actors rather than through firm delivery alone (Vargo & Lusch, 2008, 2016); AI-driven hyper-personalization extends this logic by introducing intelligent non-human systems into that process. These systems are not autonomous moral agents in the human sense, yet they can materially shape action possibilities, interpretations, and value outcomes (Chandra & Rahman, 2024; Kaartemo & Helkkula, 2018).

This chapter conceptualizes AI-driven hyper-personalized services as relational, experiential, and ethically governed value co-creation systems. Its central claim is that hyper-personalization does not merely improve efficiency or recommendation accuracy; it reconfigures value co-creation itself, through four mechanisms — distributed agency, experiential mediation, resource reconfiguration, and relational tension — defined and examined against recent evidence in Section 5. Because no single theory accounts for all four, the chapter draws on three complementary lenses: Service-Dominant Logic for value emergence through resource integration, Actor-Network Theory for the distribution of agency across human and non-human actors, and post-phenomenology for the mediation of lived experience (Ihde, 1990; Latour, 2005; Vargo & Lusch, 2016; Verbeek, 2005).

The framework responds to three limitations in current discussions of AI-enabled services. The first is technological reductionism: accounts emphasizing prediction and conversion devote less attention to the relational conditions under which consumers experience personalization as empowering or intrusive, even though technical capability does not by itself resolve acceptance, data governance, or relationship quality (De Bruyn et al., 2020). The second is an overly positive reading of value creation, since resource integration can also produce value co-destruction (Echeverri

& Skålén, 2011; Plé & Cáceres, 2010), a possibility service research has examined far less systematically, as Section 2.4 documents. The third concerns consumer experience, which is a lived and interpreted encounter rather than only an evaluation of outcomes; this framing explains why the same intervention may be received as convenient, intelligent, manipulative, or intrusive.

2. CONCEPTUAL FOUNDATIONS

2.1. Service-Dominant Logic and Value Co-Creation

Service-Dominant Logic reframes marketing from the exchange of goods to the application of competencies for the benefit of another actor: service is the fundamental basis of exchange, and value is co-created through resource integration among multiple actors (Vargo & Lusch, 2008). Its later extension emphasizes service ecosystems, institutions, and institutional arrangements, moving the theory from dyadic exchange toward broader networks of actors, rules, norms, and resources that enable or constrain value formation (Vargo & Lusch, 2016). This ecosystemic view is relevant because personalization does not occur inside a single firm–consumer dyad; it is produced through platforms, data infrastructures, algorithms, interfaces, employees, regulatory norms, and consumer practices.

In AI-driven hyper-personalization, value emerges when consumers, providers, and AI systems integrate resources such as data, attention, expertise, trust, contextual knowledge, and interpretive capacity. AI can support this integration by recognizing patterns, generating recommendations, and configuring journeys, but the meaning and value of these outputs depend on how consumers interpret them and how organizations govern them.

The AI context also challenges Service-Dominant Logic productively. Traditional accounts treat consumers and organizations as principal actors, whereas AI introduces systems that structure interactions and influence the timing, sequence, and meaning of encounters. Kaartemo and Helkkula (2018) highlight the importance of human-to-non-human resource integration in AI- and robotics-enabled value co-creation, and Chandra and Rahman (2024) argue that this literature requires stronger conceptual attention to actor roles, service contexts, and the mechanisms through which AI affects value outcomes. Service-Dominant Logic also provides an ethical anchor. If value is co-created, firms cannot evaluate personalization solely by firm-side efficiency or conversion; it must also be assessed from the perspective of consumers who provide data and attention, employees who work alongside AI, and institutions that shape norms of fairness and accountability. Personalization that generates short-term sales while reducing autonomy or trust is better understood as asymmetrical value formation than as successful co-creation.

2.2. Actor-Network Theory and Distributed Agency

Actor-Network Theory provides a second foundation by refusing to treat social action as exclusively human. It argues that agency is distributed across networks of human and non-human actors, including technologies, texts, devices, institutions, and other material arrangements (Latour, 2005). This lens is useful because AI-driven service encounters are shaped not only by consumers and employees but by recommendation systems, customer relationship management platforms, chatbots, data pipelines, interfaces, and algorithmic rules. These non-human actors do not possess intention as humans do, yet they participate in organizing action and making some choices more likely than others.

Hyper-personalized services are particularly suited to this analysis because personalization engines translate consumer traces into action possibilities. A recommender system does not simply display options; it orders visibility and creates relevance hierarchies. A conversational agent does not merely answer questions; it frames problems, performs affective cues, and contains or escalates complaints. A predictive model does not simply forecast demand; it allocates resources and may classify consumers according to risk, value, vulnerability, or propensity.

Actor-Network Theory also avoids a simplistic contrast between human autonomy and machine control. Consumers still interpret, resist, or modify AI outputs; employees still intervene and contextualize; organizations still design, train, and govern. The result is not the disappearance of human agency but its redistribution across sociotechnical arrangements. This lens further supports a precise account of responsibility: responsibility cannot be assigned to the technical model alone but lies in the network of design choices, data practices, governance routines, incentives, and interfaces that allow AI to shape encounters. A firm cannot treat a recommendation as though the algorithm were outside the service system.

2.3. Post-Phenomenology and Technological Mediation

Post-phenomenology provides the third foundation by examining how technologies mediate human experience, shaping perception, interpretation, action, and relations between humans and the world rather than acting as deterministic or neutral instruments (Ihde, 1990; Verbeek, 2005). This lens is valuable for service consumer experience because hyper-personalization is not only a decision-support process; it changes how consumers perceive relevance, control, convenience, authenticity, and trust in service encounters. Ihde (1990) distinguishes four mediation relations — embodiment, hermeneutic, alterity, and background — which Section 5.2 develops for AI-driven service encounters together with the empirical evidence bearing on each.

These relations matter because value co-creation depends on how consumers experience AI-mediated interaction. A recommendation may be accurate yet undermine trust if experienced as opaque, and a chatbot may be efficient yet create detachment if it performs empathy without understanding; evidence that consumers resist medical AI when they perceive insufficient attention to their uniqueness illustrates why technical performance and lived value diverge (Longoni et al., 2019). If technologies mediate experience, then decisions about transparency, explanation, oversight, defaults, and personalization intensity are experiential and moral choices rather than merely functional ones.

2.4. Hyper-Personalization, Privacy, Trust, and Value Co-Destruction

Hyper-personalization deepens service relevance by using real-time and contextual data to configure offers, interactions, and journeys for individual consumers, but it also intensifies privacy tensions because richer personalization requires more granular data and more powerful inference. The personalization paradox captures this duality: consumers may value relevance while feeling vulnerable when data collection is hidden, unexpected, or difficult to control (Aguirre et al., 2015), and privacy decisions are further shaped by bounded rationality, information asymmetry, institutional trust, and perceptions of fairness in data use (Acquisti et al., 2016; Bleier et al., 2020).

Trust matters because AI-driven services often operate under opacity: consumers may not know what data were used, how a recommendation was produced, or whether the provider is accountable. Trust in AI depends on perceived competence, reliability, transparency, explainability, and deployment context (Glikson & Woolley, 2020), and explainable AI supports warranted trust only when explanations are usable and meaningful for the relevant stakeholder rather than technical descriptions of model operation (Langer et al., 2021).

Value co-destruction is not simply dissatisfaction; it refers to interactions in which value formation is impaired or negative value is created for one or more actors (Echeverri & Skålén, 2011; Plé & Cáceres, 2010). Recent work on human–AI service systems treats co-creation and co-destruction as intertwined outcomes shaped by agency distribution and recurring tensions between augmentation and automation, transparency and opacity, and autonomy and control (Colurcio & Caridà, 2026). In hyper-personalized services, co-destruction can occur through privacy intrusion, misclassification, loss of agency, discriminatory recommendations, manipulation, and reduced trust — risks structurally linked to the data intensity that makes hyper-personalization possible, and therefore requiring organizational rather than merely technical governance (Ashok et al., 2022; Hermann, 2022).

The literature has not treated these possibilities symmetrically, and this asymmetry is a limitation of the field rather than a feature of the phenomenon. Lumivalo et al. (2024) find in a systematic review that co-destruction has been examined largely as an aftermath of failed co-creation rather than as a theoretically equivalent counterpart, leaving its antecedents underdeveloped. Echeverri and Skålén (2021) argue that the two outcomes emerge from the same interactive practices rather than as opposed states, which implies that a design optimized for co-creation does not thereby reduce co-destruction risk. A second critique questions who bears the cost of co-creation: the attention, data, and corrective effort consumers contribute are often framed as engagement while their distribution goes unexamined, suggesting that apparently frictionless personalization may relocate effort instead of removing it. Empirical findings support this contested reading, since AI-personalized messages can raise purchase intentions while simultaneously provoking intrusiveness and reactance (Osman et al., 2026).

This chapter therefore treats co-creation and co-destruction as twin possibilities within the same service system, and the three limitations identified in Section 1 are drawn from these documented asymmetries rather than asserted. The three lenses operate at complementary levels: Service-Dominant Logic specifies how resources and value are integrated, Actor-Network Theory explains how action is distributed, and post-phenomenology explains how those arrangements are lived, while privacy, trust, and co-destruction research add the evaluative conditions under which distributed and mediated interaction becomes beneficial or harmful.

3. METHODOLOGICAL POSITIONING: A STRUCTURED CONCEPTUAL REVIEW

This chapter presents a structured conceptual review rather than a systematic review, meta-analysis, or bibliometric study. The purpose is theory building: integrating service marketing and interdisciplinary technology theories into an explanatory framework for AI-driven hyper-personalized service experiences. This is appropriate because the phenomenon is emerging, theoretically fragmented, and not sufficiently mature for stable cumulative synthesis. The review was nevertheless combined with a targeted empirical screening procedure so that the proposed mechanisms are examined against recent evidence rather than asserted on theoretical grounds alone.

The review was organized around five literature domains: Service-Dominant Logic and service ecosystems; AI in services and human-to-non-human resource integration; Actor-Network Theory and distributed agency; post-phenomenology and technological mediation; and personalization, privacy, trust in AI, explainability, and value co-destruction. Search logic combined terms corresponding to these domains across major databases and publisher platforms used in marketing, service, and information systems scholarship, including Scopus, Web of Science, ScienceDirect, Emerald, Sage, and Wiley. Priority was given to peer-reviewed work published from 2020 onward, while foundational sources required by the theoretical lenses were retained regardless of date.

A second, targeted screening stage identified recent empirical evidence bearing on the four proposed mechanisms, applying explicit criteria: publication between 2023 and 2026; an empirical design; a consumer-facing or service context; and a verifiable DOI. Conceptual papers, reviews, and bibliometric studies were excluded at this stage. Screening proceeded across four evidence domains: sector-specific outcomes of AI personalization in retail, hospitality, healthcare, and financial services; explainability effects on trust and reliance; privacy calculus and disclosure in AI settings; and regulatory and cross-cultural boundary conditions. Within each sector, at least one study reporting an adverse or mixed outcome was deliberately retained, so that the framework is examined against disconfirming as well as confirming evidence. Bibliographic records were verified against publisher and Crossref metadata.

Sources were included when they supported the framework's core mechanisms and excluded when weakly connected to the conceptual problem, primarily promotional, or bibliographically unverifiable. Synthesis proceeded through theoretical mapping rather than frequency counting: each lens was assigned a distinct explanatory function, and retained evidence was mapped onto the mechanisms in Section 5 to establish where evidence converges, diverges, or remains absent. The review has limitations: it does not test causal relationships, estimate effect sizes, or audit specific technologies; its selection is theoretically guided rather than exhaustive; and screening decisions were made by the authors without independent double-coding.

4. DEFINING AI-DRIVEN HYPER-PERSONALIZED SERVICE EXPERIENCE

AI-driven hyper-personalized service experience refers to a dynamically adapted service encounter in which AI systems use real-time, contextual, behavioral, and relational data to anticipate, configure, and mediate service offerings, interactions, and meanings for individual consumers in a service ecosystem. This definition emphasizes four elements: dynamic adaptation, data intensity, experiential mediation, and ecosystem embeddedness.

Personalization adapts service content, recommendations, or interactions to individual or segment-level characteristics. Hyper-personalization uses richer data streams and real-time adaptation to tailor journeys more granularly, and AI-driven hyper-personalization adds predictive analytics, recommender systems, conversational agents, generative interfaces, contextual sensing, and algorithmic decision support (Davenport et al., 2020; Grewal et al., 2025; Huang & Rust, 2021). These systems personalize output but also shape the structure and meaning of the encounter, which consumers may experience as empowering when effort is reduced and self-endorsed goals supported, and as intrusive when the system appears to know too much or leaves little room for contestation (Puntoni et al., 2021).

Two further terms are used in a specific sense. AI agency does not imply consciousness, intention, or moral responsibility; it refers to the capacity of AI systems to shape service interactions by selecting, ordering, generating, recommending, prioritizing, or withholding options within sociotechnical service networks. Responsible AI service design refers to governance that preserves transparency, consent, explainability, fairness, human oversight, contestability, and consumer autonomy — interdependent principles that must be translated into organizational routines and stakeholder-specific explanations rather than treated as abstract compliance statements (Ashok et al., 2022; Hermann, 2022; Langer et al., 2021).

5. INTEGRATIVE FRAMEWORK AND CORE MECHANISMS

The framework begins with AI-driven hyper-personalization capabilities: predictive analytics, recommender systems, conversational agents, real-time behavioral data, contextual and ambient personalization, generative interfaces, adaptive journeys, and algorithmic decision support (Davenport et al., 2020; Grewal et al., 2025; Huang & Rust, 2021). These capabilities do not automatically create value; their effect depends on four mechanisms that translate them into service outcomes — distributed agency, experiential mediation, resource reconfiguration, and relational tension — each defined and examined against recent evidence in the subsections below.

Framework outcomes include perceived relevance, convenience, service trust, perceived control, empowerment, emotional resonance, privacy concern, algorithmic discomfort, relational asymmetry, and the twin possibilities of co-creation and co-destruction. Boundary conditions include service risk, consumer vulnerability, data sensitivity, perceived transparency, explainability, human oversight, cultural privacy norms, regulatory context, AI literacy, trust in the provider, and perceived fairness, since responses vary by service stakes, perceived uniqueness, data context, and the fit between explanations and stakeholder needs (Bleier et al., 2020; Langer et al., 2021; Longoni et al., 2019). The framework therefore treats hyper-personalization as neither solution nor threat, but as a capability whose value depends on relational and governance conditions. Figure 1 presents the framework and Table 1 summarizes the lenses.

Figure 1. Integrative Framework of AI-Driven Hyper-Personalized Service Experience

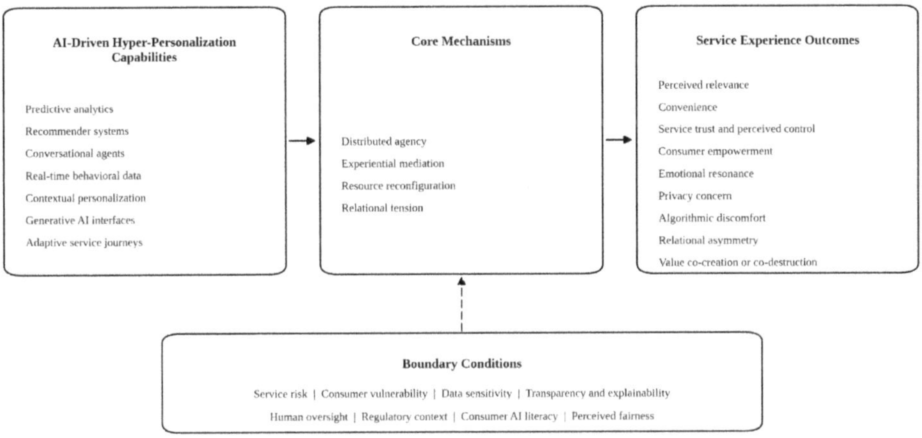

AI-driven hyper-personalization capabilities shape service consumer experience through four mechanisms — distributed agency, experiential mediation, resource reconfiguration, and relational tension — which influence both value co-creation and value co-destruction outcomes under the boundary conditions specified above. Source: Developed by the authors.

Table 1. Theoretical Lenses for AI-Driven Hyper-Personalized Service Experience

Theoretical Lens	Core Concept	Role in the Framework	Main Limitation if Used Alone
Service-Dominant Logic	Resource integration and service ecosystems	Explains how value emerges among consumers, firms, employees, data, and AI systems	May understate material agency and lived experience of technology
Actor-Network Theory	Distributed agency among human and non-human actors	Explains how algorithms, platforms, interfaces, and data infrastructures structure service action	May understate consumer interpretation and normative evaluation
Post-Phenomenology	Technological mediation of experience	Explains how personalization is lived as convenience, control, opacity, or intrusion	May understate ecosystem and institutional structures
Privacy and Trust Research	Vulnerability, transparency, and explainability	Identifies why relevance can coexist with discomfort and distrust	May focus on individual perception without broader ecosystem logic
Value Co-Destruction Research	Negative outcomes of resource integration	Identifies how AI personalization may reduce autonomy, fairness, or trust	May underdevelop the technological mechanisms creating harm

Note. Developed by the authors.

5.1. Distributed Agency

The distributed agency mechanism explains how AI-enabled systems participate in structuring service interactions. Agency is traditionally attributed to consumers, employees, and firms, but recommender systems, predictive tools, conversational agents, and adaptive platforms complicate this assumption, influencing what consumers see, which options are salient, how information is ordered, and how responses are delivered, even when they remain invisible. From a Service-Dominant Logic perspective, AI becomes part of the infrastructure through which consumer data, firm knowledge, employee expertise, and contextual signals are integrated; from an Actor-Network Theory perspective, AI systems are actors because they assemble action possibilities and stabilize relationships, participating in producing outcomes they do not intend (Latour, 2005).

Recent evidence indicates that this redistribution operates below the level of consumers' stated evaluations. In four preregistered experiments, Böhm et al. (2023) found that people rated generative AI as less competent once they learned advice was machine-generated, yet followed it at rates comparable to human-authored advice. Reliance persisted where trust was explicitly discounted, suggesting that agency shifts toward the system without a corresponding shift in attributions of authority. This shift is not uniform: Han and Ko (2025) report that design elements actively involving consumers in decision-making preserved perceived autonomy, whereas passive transparency features alone did little to prevent consumers from ceding agency to AI recommendations.

Distributed agency can support co-creation by increasing responsiveness and allowing services to adapt to individual contexts, but it also blurs responsibility: consumers may not know which actor produced a recommendation, employees may over-rely on automated suggestions, and firms may attribute problematic outcomes to technical systems rather than governance failures. Human oversight therefore should not be symbolic: employees need the authority to correct AI outputs, consumers need meaningful ways to contest recommendations, and managers need audit trails that reveal how automated decisions affect service outcomes (Ashok et al., 2022; Hermann, 2022). The evidence above suggests why such safeguards cannot rely on consumer skepticism alone, since discounted trust did not translate into reduced reliance.

5.2. Experiential Mediation

The experiential mediation mechanism explains how AI changes consumers' lived experience of service interactions. Consumer–AI encounters involve data capture, classification, delegation, and social interaction, producing feelings of care, convenience, surveillance, pressure, or uncanny intimacy depending on how the encounter is designed and interpreted (Puntoni et al., 2021). Ihde's four mediation relations organize these effects.

In embodiment relations, AI becomes an extension through which the consumer acts, as when a wearable triggers personalized health support; the co-creation potential rests on timely support and reduced effort, the risk on dependency and bodily surveillance. In hermeneutic relations, consumers read AI outputs as interpretations of the service world through rankings, risk scores, and dashboards. Value comes from improved comprehension and decision support, the risk from over-trust, opacity, and narrowed choice sets when consumers treat AI outputs as neutral truth. Technical transparency alone is therefore insufficient; explanations must fit the user, decision context, and consequences of error (Langer et al., 2021). In alterity relations, AI appears as a quasi-other through conversational agents, offering accessibility and continuous availability while risking false empathy, detachment, and confusion about whether the counterpart is human, machine, or hybrid. In background relations, AI shapes the environment without being focal, as when a hotel adjusts room settings or a retailer reorganizes a digital storefront; the gain is frictionlessness, the risk invisible influence and weak consent.

Empirical work qualifies the hermeneutic case in particular. Ostinelli et al. (2024) show that merely believing an explanation is available can produce an illusory sense of understanding an algorithm and unfounded reliance on its output, even when it is never read, and de Brito Duarte et al. (2023) report that explanations increased trust only under specific conditions and, where system performance was unreliable, induced overreliance rather than warranted trust. Anthropomorphic design cues operate along a similar dual path: human-like chatbot language increases engagement through perceived competence and authenticity (Nguyen et al., 2023), while perceived anthropomorphism simultaneously raises privacy concerns and perceived benefits, increasing disclosure intention through both routes (Zhou & Tang, 2025). Mediation therefore does not simply improve or degrade the service encounter; it reshapes what consumers believe they understand about it.

5.3. Resource Reconfiguration

The resource reconfiguration mechanism explains how hyper-personalization changes the resources integrated in service ecosystems. Service-Dominant Logic distinguishes between operand resources, such as physical objects, and operant resources, such as knowledge, skills, competencies, and relationships (Vargo & Lusch, 2008). AI-driven services expand the range of operant resources by making data, attention, contextual knowledge, trust, time, service literacy, and emotional signals central to value formation.

Where traditional personalization adapts offers to prior purchases or stated preferences, hyper-personalized resource integration is continuous: consumers supply data through browsing, location, usage, wearables, conversations, and inferred preferences; firms supply service knowledge, content, channels, and decision rules; and AI systems supply pattern recognition, prediction, generation, and adaptation. This changes co-creation from static matching to dynamic orchestration: a banking application may adapt alerts, explain spending patterns, and personalize risk communication rather than simply recommending a product, and a hospitality platform may infer trip purpose, timing, and ancillary needs rather than only storing room preferences.

Resource reconfiguration has ethical consequences, because consumers may not understand which resources they contribute or how these are transformed, and co-creation becomes questionable when one actor captures disproportionate value from resources provided by another. This asymmetry is documented rather than asserted. Zhou and Tang (2025) found that perceived anonymity and privacy statements reduced privacy concerns while raising perceived benefits, with AI literacy strengthening both pathways, indicating that the terms of exchange are understood unevenly across consumers; de Matos et al. (2026) report from the opposite side that higher financial literacy was associated with lower willingness to disclose, suggesting that consumers who best understand the exchange are least willing to enter it.

Responsible design should therefore make resource contributions transparent and ensure that consumers receive meaningful value in return.

5.4. Relational Tension

The relational tension mechanism explains why hyper-personalization is inherently ambivalent. Personalization can increase relevance, convenience, and emotional resonance while simultaneously increasing privacy concern, algorithmic discomfort, and loss of control, because it uses consumer intimacy as a resource: the more the system knows and adapts, the more it can both help consumers and threaten their autonomy.

The ambivalence is directly observable in field evidence. Osman et al. (2026) report a dual-pathway pattern in a retail field experiment, in which AI-personalized messages increased purchase behavior through perceived helpfulness while simultaneously activating an intrusiveness–reactance pathway, with the adverse route strongest among consumers holding weak brand relationships. Related evidence shows that the source attributed to a recommendation matters independently of its content, and that shoppers can welcome AI-enabled discounts while resisting location tracking within a single encounter (Canhoto et al., 2024; Weidig & Kuehnl, 2023). Relational tension is therefore not a residual risk attached to poor implementation; it is a structural property of personalization that intensifies as systems become more capable. Privacy tension is its most visible form: consumers accept data use when benefits are clear and controls meaningful, and resist covert collection or cross-context inference, particularly given the information asymmetry that prevents them from anticipating future data uses (Acquisti et al., 2016; Aguirre et al., 2015).

Algorithmic opacity creates a second tension whose remedy is conditional rather than general. Chen et al. (2024) found that post hoc explanations increased interpretability perceptions and trust, with attribute-based explanations more effective in utilitarian domains and user-based explanations more effective in hedonic ones. Mourali et al. (2025), by contrast, report that explanations can improve or damage consumer responses depending on the method used, and Ning et al. (2024) find that process transparency loses its effect when purpose transparency is already high. Transparency is therefore a design variable with conditional effects rather than a general remedy: complex disclosures may increase confusion, shallow ones may appear performative, and the design problem is intelligible and actionable transparency.

Consumer vulnerability compounds these tensions. Vulnerable consumers may have lower AI literacy, higher dependence on providers, or limited ability to contest automated decisions; hyper-personalization can support them by reducing friction and harm them by exploiting dependence or hiding choices. Relational tension is thus not a defect that can be eliminated permanently but a condition that must be continuously governed. Table 2 summarizes the mechanisms.

Table 2. Core Mechanisms of AI-Driven Value Co-Creation

Mechanism	Definition	Theoretical Anchor	Service Experience Effect	Value Co-Destruction Risk
Distributed Agency	AI systems participate in structuring service action and interaction	Service-Dominant Logic and Actor-Network Theory	Consumers experience more adaptive and responsive encounters	Blurred responsibility, over-reliance, and algorithmic control
Experiential Mediation	AI shapes how consumers perceive, interpret, and feel personalized encounters	Post-Phenomenology	Personalization is experienced as convenient, supportive, opaque, or intrusive	Uncanny interaction, false empathy, hidden influence, loss of control
Resource Reconfiguration	AI reorganizes data, attention, trust, time, knowledge, and service literacy	Service-Dominant Logic and service innovation	Service propositions become dynamic and context-sensitive	Asymmetric extraction of consumer data and attention
Relational Tension	Personalization creates both relevance and discomfort	Privacy, trust, and value co-destruction research	Consumers evaluate service through trust, autonomy, fairness, and vulnerability	Privacy intrusion, manipulation, distrust, and co-destruction

Note. Developed by the authors from the synthesis in Sections 2 and 5.

6. TYPOLOGY OF HYPER-PERSONALIZATION DESIGN LOGICS

This chapter identifies four hyper-personalization design logics as an original conceptual typology. A design logic is not a specific technology but the dominant orientation shaping how organizations use AI to personalize interactions; the typology integrates distinctions among automation, analytical personalization, relational AI, human augmentation, and ethical governance in prior research (Grewal et al., 2025; Hermann, 2022; Huang & Rust, 2021; Puntoni et al., 2021). The four logics are distinguished by three observable criteria rather than by intent: the locus of interpretive authority, meaning whether the system, the employee, or the consumer determines what a recommendation means; the reversibility of adaptation, meaning whether consumers can inspect, modify, or reverse the personalization applied to them; and the disclosure of resource contribution, meaning whether consumers are informed which of their resources are integrated. Because these criteria can be coded independently of the provider's stated orientation, the typology is usable as a classification instrument rather than only a descriptive scheme.

Efficiency-centered personalization prioritizes speed, convenience, and friction reduction, and suits low-risk, utilitarian, or repetitive contexts such as routine re-ordering or delivery status. Its co-destruction risk is that the encounter is reduced to operational optimization, with consumers pushed through journeys designed for conversion rather than supported as participants.

Relationally balanced personalization combines AI efficiency with human oversight and contextual responsiveness, recognizing that hospitality, healthcare, financial advice, and complaint handling involve relational dimensions that prediction accuracy cannot capture: AI provides recommendations while humans remain visible in moments requiring empathy, judgment, or reassurance. Its risk is inconsistency where firms promise oversight but do not provide it meaningfully.

Transparency-oriented personalization emphasizes consumer understanding and meaningful control through explanations, preference controls, data visibility, and opportunities to contest recommendations. It is appropriate where opacity would undermine perceived fairness or trust, as in finance, healthcare, insurance, and high-involvement retail. Its risk is transparency overload when explanations are too technical, too frequent, or not actionable, because explanation quality depends on stakeholder needs and decision context (Langer et al., 2021).

Intrusive or extractive personalization maximizes data-driven adaptation without sufficient regard for consumer boundaries, consent, or control. It may generate short-term conversion gains but creates high co-destruction risk, as consumers may feel monitored or classified in ways they cannot contest. It is particularly dangerous where data involve health, finance, identity, location, children, or vulnerable consumers, and requires explicit governance because privacy, fairness, autonomy, and accountability can conflict (Ashok et al., 2022; Hermann, 2022). The managerial implication is that personalization intensity is not an unqualified good: the appropriate level is the one consumers can experience as useful, fair, understandable, and controllable. Table 3 summarizes the logics.

6.1. Propositions

The typology yields testable expectations, each specifying a relationship that could be falsified empirically.

P1. Efficiency-centered personalization increases perceived convenience but does not increase relational outcomes such as trust or attachment; where service risk is high, its effect on trust becomes negative. This follows from evidence that helpfulness and intrusiveness operate as parallel rather than sequential pathways, with adverse responses concentrated among consumers with weak relational ties (Osman et al., 2026).

P2. Relationally balanced personalization outperforms efficiency-centered personalization on trust outcomes only when human oversight is consequential rather than nominal; where oversight exists but cannot alter system output, the two logics converge. Healthcare evidence in Section 7 supports the first clause (Zhu et al., 2026); the second remains untested.

P3. Transparency-oriented personalization improves trust conditionally rather than monotonically, depending on explanation type, system performance, and prior consumer expertise; where system performance is unreliable, explanation increases reliance without increasing warranted trust. This is consistent with the divergent findings of Chen et al. (2024), Ostinelli et al. (2024), de Brito Duarte et al. (2023), and Ning et al. (2024), and it predicts that transparency interventions evaluated only on self-reported trust will overstate their benefit relative to behavioral measures.

P4. Intrusive or extractive personalization produces co-destruction that is unevenly distributed rather than uniform, with adverse effects concentrated among consumers holding greater domain knowledge, higher privacy sensitivity, or weaker relational ties. This is supported by evidence that financial literacy predicts lower disclosure (de Matos et al., 2026), that reactance is strongest among weakly attached consumers (Osman et al., 2026), and that privacy responses differ by gender in hospitality and healthcare (Hu & Min, 2023; Zondag et al., 2024).

P5. The relationship between personalization intensity and value outcomes is non-monotonic, with the inflection point determined by service risk and data sensitivity rather than by personalization capability. This follows from hospitality evidence in which stronger capability claims reduced disclosure (Shuqair et al., 2024), and predicts that studies treating intensity as a linear predictor will find weak or inconsistent effects.

6.2. Boundary Conditions of the Typology

The typology's applicability is bounded in two respects. First, the logics are not culturally invariant, since consumer responses to algorithmic services vary across national and institutional contexts in ways that do not reduce to a single dimension. Chinese respondents reported greater privacy concern regarding behavioral advertising than Dutch respondents (Zhang et al., 2023), yet Korean participants trusted an AI chatbot more than German participants in a comparable design (Kang et al., 2025), and Chinese respondents valued emotional connection with AI more, and personal control less, than European Americans (Ge et al., 2024). Across five countries, institutional trust and regulatory expectations explained privacy concern better than individualism–collectivism classifications (Viberg et al., 2024). A transparency-oriented logic that increases trust in one regulatory context may therefore be redundant or insufficient in another.

Second, the logics are not regulatory-neutral. Intrusive or extractive personalization intersects with the prohibitions on manipulative and deceptive techniques in Article 5 of the EU AI Act; current EU instruments protect consumer autonomy only partially against AI-driven persuasion (Fassiaux, 2023), while systems that score or triage rather than decide may fall outside GDPR Article 22 protections (Palmiotto, 2024). The typology therefore describes orientations whose legality, not only advisability, varies by jurisdiction.

Table 3. Hyper-Personalization Design Logics

Design Logic	Dominant Aim	AI Role	Co-Creation Potential	Co-Destruction Risk	Suitable Contexts
Efficiency-Centered	Reduce friction and accelerate journeys	Automate routine adaptation and recommendations	Convenience, speed, reduced effort	Over-optimization, passivity, shallow relational value	Low-risk routine retail, logistics, basic support
Relationally Balanced	Combine AI efficiency with human judgment	Support employees without replacing relational care	Trust, reassurance, contextual responsiveness	Token oversight or inconsistent escalation	Hospitality, healthcare, financial advice, service recovery
Transparency-Oriented	Make personalization understandable and controllable	Explain, justify, and expose personalization logic	Autonomy, trust, perceived fairness	Transparency fatigue or cognitive overload	High-involvement and regulated services
Intrusive or Extractive	Maximize adaptation and conversion through extensive data use	Infer, target, and optimize with limited consumer control	Short-term relevance or conversion	Privacy backlash, manipulation, co-destruction	High-risk logic to avoid or tightly restrict

Note. Original typology developed by the authors; classification criteria are specified in Section 6.

7. SECTORAL EVIDENCE

The four mechanisms operate across sectors but not identically: differences in data sensitivity, decision stakes, and consumer dependence produce distinct patterns of co-creation and co-destruction. The following discussion draws on evidence published between 2023 and 2026, retaining in each case at least one study reporting an adverse or mixed outcome.

In retail, the benefits of personalization lie in relevance and reduced search costs, but field evidence indicates that these benefits and their corresponding harms are produced simultaneously rather than sequentially. Combining a field experiment (N = 409) with 46 interviews, Osman et al. (2026) found that AI-personalized retail messages increased purchase behavior through perceived helpfulness while activating a parallel intrusiveness–reactance pathway strongest among consumers with weak brand relationships, indicating that relational history conditions which route dominates. Drawing on 18 interviews with UK fashion shoppers, Canhoto et al. (2024) found that participants welcomed AI-enabled discounts while resisting location tracking, producing an unresolved tension within a single encounter rather than a stable preference. Across three experiments, Weidig and Kuehnl (2023) found that recommendations attributed to data from similar customers provoked greater reactance and lower trust, particularly when inaccurate. Retailers should therefore attend to attribution and provenance, not only predictive accuracy, and recognize that evaluating personalization solely through conversion metrics understates its relational costs.

In hospitality, value can emerge from anticipatory care because guests evaluate the experience through warmth, recognition, and trust, yet the evidence is weighted toward adverse outcomes whose sources are specific rather than generic. Across two scenario-based experiments, Hu and Min (2023) found that AI devices with camera eyes and humanoid features heightened hotel guests' privacy concerns and unease, more markedly among female guests, indicating that the physical form of the device rather than its data practices alone generated the response. In a five-study investigation, Shuqair et al. (2024) found that framing an AI system as powerful increased privacy concerns, reduced perceived control, and decreased willingness to disclose the very data that personalization requires, so that capability claims undermine the conditions for their own use.

In healthcare, personalization draws on symptoms, wearable data, history, and conversational intake to support triage, reminders, and self-management. Co-creation potential is high, and so are the risks, given data sensitivity and consumer vulnerability; recent evidence indicates that harm here can be relational rather than clinical. In a vignette study of 398 Dutch hospital patients, Zondag et al. (2024) found that an AI-supported clinical decision support system significantly reduced female patients' trust in physician competence and integrity while the effect was non-significant in the full sample, so that co-destruction occurs in the patient–provider relationship rather than in the accuracy of the recommendation. What restores acceptance is equally specific: in two vignette experiments with 340 US patients, Zhu et al. (2026) found that trust in AI medical devices was driven most strongly by regulatory approval (average marginal effect 19.3%) and professional oversight (15.5–17.9%), whereas data privacy disclosures had minimal independent effect. Barriers also differ by professional role, since perceived risk negatively predicted adoption intention among nurses but not physicians in a survey of 2,705 Chinese medical staff (Dai et al., 2025). Oversight is therefore not only an ethical safeguard but an empirically identified precondition of patient trust.

In financial services, hyper-personalization spans budgeting tools, risk alerts, fraud prevention, and conversational banking, but the evidence complicates the assumption that better-informed consumers are more willing participants. In a study of 408 Portuguese e-banking users, de Matos et al. (2026) found that AI personalization increased willingness to disclose personal information, that fear of AI attenuated this effect, and, more strikingly, that higher financial literacy was associated with lower disclosure. Design features also produce asymmetric returns: surveying 616 US consumers, Wang et al. (2026) found that customizability increased adoption of AI financial advisors through reduced technology vulnerability, whereas human-likeness amplified vulnerability without a corresponding adoption benefit. Anthropomorphic design in high-stakes financial contexts therefore carries costs that its relational benefits do not offset.

As Table 4 summarizes, the evidence supports a more specific conclusion than the familiar claim that personalization must be calibrated to service risk: the mechanisms do not merely intensify with risk, they change form. Co-destruction operates through reactance to perceived intrusion in retail, through embodied surveillance cues and capability framing in hospitality, through erosion of trust in the human provider in healthcare, and through vulnerability amplified by human-like design in financial services. These are not four instances of one risk but distinct failure modes, and interventions effective in one sector may be irrelevant or counterproductive in another. A further pattern cuts across sectors: in three of the four, adverse effects concentrated in identifiable subgroups — women in hospitality and healthcare, weakly attached consumers in retail, and financially literate consumers in banking — so that aggregate measures of personalization effectiveness will systematically underestimate co-destruction.

Table 4. Sectoral Evidence on AI-Driven Hyper-Personalization

Sector	Evidenced Benefit (Co-Creation)	Evidenced Risk (Co-Destruction)	Governance Requirement
Retail	Purchase lift via perceived helpfulness (Osman et al., 2026)	Intrusiveness–reactance, strongest for weakly attached consumers; reactance to similar-customer sourcing (Osman et al., 2026; Weidig & Kuehnl, 2023)	Preference controls; provenance disclosure; relational as well as conversion metrics
Hospitality	Anticipatory care and emotional resonance	Camera-eye and humanoid cues raise privacy concern, especially among women; "powerful AI" framing lowers disclosure (Hu & Min, 2023; Shuqair et al., 2024)	Visible human care; respectful data boundaries; escalation pathways
Healthcare	Regulatory approval and professional oversight drive trust (Zhu et al., 2026)	AI decision support erodes female patients' trust in the physician; perceived risk deters nurse adoption (Zondag et al., 2024; Dai et al., 2025)	Professional oversight and regulatory assurance as trust preconditions
Financial Services	Customizability aids adoption via reduced vulnerability (Wang et al., 2026)	Human-likeness amplifies vulnerability; higher financial literacy lowers disclosure (Wang et al., 2026; de Matos et al., 2026)	Understandable logic; human support for high-stakes decisions; avoid exploiting vulnerability

Note. Developed by the authors; sources are cited in the corresponding subsections.

8. THEORETICAL CONTRIBUTIONS

The framework specifies how hyper-personalization capabilities translate into service outcomes through four mechanisms, and how the balance between co-creation and co-destruction is conditioned by governance, sector, regulation, and cultural context. Three contributions follow.

First, the chapter advances Service-Dominant Logic by extending value co-creation into AI-mediated service ecosystems, showing that hyper-personalization changes not only the efficiency of resource integration but its structure, since algorithmic actors and digital infrastructures become active components of value formation. This does not require treating AI as a human actor; it requires recognizing that value emergence is co-produced with non-human systems whose design conditions the outcome. The chapter also integrates co-destruction as an inherent possibility rather than an exceptional failure: because both outcomes arise from the same personalization practices, a service optimized for one does not thereby avoid the other, and the framework specifies the conditions that determine which dominates. This matters because AI-enabled services can be efficient and intrusive, accurate and opaque, convenient and manipulative at once, and such mixed outcomes cannot be captured by adoption or satisfaction measures alone.

Second, the chapter contributes to AI-driven service research by moving beyond automation and replacement logic. Huang and Rust (2021) explain how AI capabilities support mechanical, analytical, intuitive, and relational tasks; this chapter examines how AI participation changes consumer experience, resource integration, and relational governance, treating AI as a mediator of value formation rather than only a service technology. It also specifies boundary conditions that help explain why the same capability may be valued in one context and resisted in another.

Third, the chapter contributes to Actor-Network Theory-informed and post-phenomenological service research. Distributed agency provides a vocabulary for studying how algorithms, interfaces, data infrastructures, and organizational routines jointly produce service encounters, and clarifies that where agency is distributed, accountability must be designed into the network rather than asserted as ethical intention. The mediation relations explain why consumers experience the same recommendation as support, interpretation, dialogue, or invisible control. Together these contributions position governance as a condition of value co-creation: transparency, explainability, consent, fairness, oversight, and contestability are not compliance add-ons but interdependent parts of the service value architecture (Ashok et al., 2022; Hermann, 2022; Langer et al., 2021).

9. SOLUTIONS AND RECOMMENDATIONS

Service managers should avoid treating hyper-personalization as a universal performance lever, because intensity and value outcomes are not monotonically related (Osman et al., 2026; Shuqair et al., 2024). Intensity decisions therefore require an explicit ceiling, not only a target: organizations should define, for each service journey, which inferences are permitted and which are excluded, with limits reflecting data sensitivity and service risk rather than predictive capability. Personalization should also be evaluated using relational indicators alongside conversion outcomes, since dashboards focused on conversion understate co-destruction that emerges through reactance without an immediate decline in purchases: trust, perceived control, opt-out rates, and complaint content should be reported alongside efficiency metrics and disaggregated by segment.

Customer experience designers should treat personalization as an interpretable journey, although evidence cautions against treating explanation as a universal remedy (de Brito Duarte et al., 2023; Mourali et al., 2025; Ning et al., 2024; Ostinelli et al., 2024). Three criteria follow. First, the form of explanation should fit the decision domain, since attribute-based explanations are more effective in utilitarian contexts and user-based explanations in hedonic ones (Chen et al., 2024). Second, effectiveness should be assessed behaviorally as well as through self-reported trust, since these may diverge in high-risk settings. Third, explanations should not be provided where system performance cannot support justified reliance; there they shift risk to consumers instead of mitigating it.

Making oversight consequential is a distinct requirement, since oversight is meaningful only when it can change outcomes and consumers respond more strongly to its institutional reality than to assurances that it exists (Zhu et al., 2026). Employees therefore need documented authority to override system outputs without an escalation penalty, with override events logged and treated as system feedback rather than employee error, and consumers need a contestation pathway with a defined response time. Organizations that cannot demonstrate that overrides occur and influence outcomes should not communicate oversight claims. A related caution follows from evidence that consumers evaluated AI competence less favorably once advice was identified as machine-generated yet followed it at unchanged rates (Böhm et al., 2023): skepticism cannot serve as a safeguard, and disclosure of AI involvement alone does not protect against overreliance.

Anthropomorphic design should be adopted selectively by sector, since human-likeness increased technology vulnerability without improving adoption in financial services and heightened privacy concerns in hospitality, especially among female guests (Hu & Min, 2023; Wang et al., 2026; Zhou & Tang, 2025). Human-like features should be justified by the specific outcome they support and evaluated for adverse subgroup effects, not solely by the sample mean; where stakes are high or data sensitive, current evidence supports customizability and user control more strongly.

Organizations should also anticipate regulatory exposure, since intrusive or extractive design carries legal as well as reputational risk under Article 5 of the EU AI Act, and since systems that score, rank, or triage rather than decide may fall outside GDPR Article 22 protections as currently interpreted (Palmiotto, 2024). Compliance with data-protection law does not by itself establish that a practice is defensible, and because consumer expectations differ across national contexts (Ge et al., 2024; Kang et al., 2025; Viberg et al., 2024; Zhang et al., 2023), a configuration validated in one market should not be assumed transferable to another.

From an ethical perspective, reciprocity should be the governing principle: providers should treat consumer data, attention, and trust as resources whose use must generate meaningful value for consumers rather than as inputs for extraction. Empirical findings give this substance, since consumers with greater domain knowledge disclosed less in banking, so those who understood the exchange most clearly were the most guarded participants (de Matos et al., 2026). When informed consumers withdraw, the exchange is not reciprocal regardless of how providers characterize it—the distinction that separates responsible co-creation from data-driven co-extraction.

10. FUTURE RESEARCH DIRECTIONS

Measurement is the most immediate need. Existing measures of technology acceptance, trust, personalization, and satisfaction do not capture distributed agency, technological mediation, or resource reconfiguration (Chandra & Rahman, 2024). A dedicated scale could include perceived AI participation, consumer resource contribution, interpretive transparency, autonomy support, relational fairness, and perceived co-created value.

The propositions in Section 6.1 define a second agenda. Experimental research should manipulate explanation depth, AI disclosure, oversight visibility, personalization intensity, and control features, measuring not only adoption intention and satisfaction but also warranted trust, perceived autonomy, vulnerability, and fairness, and evaluating whether explanations satisfy the needs of the intended audience (Langer et al., 2021). Because P3 predicts divergence between self-reported and behavioral trust, such designs should include behavioral reliance measures rather than attitudinal ones alone.

Value co-destruction warrants direct rather than residual study. Qualitative research could examine how consumers narrate harmful personalization experiences, while longitudinal and ethnographic designs could track whether short-term convenience erodes long-term attachment as consumers move from resistance to routinization to dependence. Q-methodology can map distinct subjective positions — personalization as care, convenience, surveillance, or manipulation — without assuming that all consumers evaluate AI services by the same criteria.

Finally, because failure modes differ by sector, general models require complementary sector theories emphasizing uniqueness and professional oversight in healthcare, explainability and fairness in finance, emotional resonance and discretion in hospitality, and contextual privacy and control in retail (Bleier et al., 2020; Longoni et al., 2019). Comparative research should examine how cultural privacy norms and regulatory regimes shape the boundary between value creation and destruction, and how organizations translate ethical principles into governance routines, audits, and accountability coordinated across vendors, platforms, managers, and employees (Ashok et al., 2022; Hermann, 2022).

11. CONCLUSION

AI-driven hyper-personalization is becoming a defining feature of consumer experience in contemporary services, but its capacity to create value does not follow automatically from technical sophistication. This chapter has argued that it transforms value co-creation through four mechanisms — distributed agency, experiential mediation, resource reconfiguration, and relational tension — which together explain why the same capability can generate co-creation for some consumers and co-destruction for others. Co-destruction is neither exceptional nor uniform: it emerges through distinct sectoral failure modes and concentrates in subgroups that aggregate averages obscure.

The managerial implication is that providers should not maximize personalization simply because the technology permits it: responsible implementation requires explicit limits on permissible inferences, behavioral evaluation of explanations, oversight with authority to alter outcomes, and sector-specific assessment of anthropomorphic design. The framework also has limitations that define its research agenda: it has not been empirically tested, and its evidence base remains concentrated in four sectors and predominantly Western and East Asian contexts, leaving open whether the mechanisms and typology apply across other settings and regulatory regimes. Within service ecosystems, AI can support value co-creation when governed through transparency, trust, meaningful oversight, privacy protection, and responsible institutional practice; without these safeguards, the same capabilities shift the process from co-creation to co-destruction.

Artificial Intelligence Disclosure Statement

AI-assisted tools were used solely for language polishing, structural checking, formatting consistency, and readability enhancement. The authors remain fully responsible for the chapter's conceptual framing, scholarly argumentation, selection of sources, verification of citations, and final content.

REFERENCES

Acquisti, A., Taylor, C., & Wagman, L. (2016). The economics of privacy. *Journal of Economic Literature*, *54*(2), 442–492. DOI: 10.1257/jel.54.2.442

Aguirre, E., Mahr, D., Grewal, D., de Ruyter, K., & Wetzels, M. (2015). Unraveling the personalization paradox: The effect of information collection and trust-building strategies on online advertisement effectiveness. *Journal of Retailing*, *91*(1), 34–49. DOI: 10.1016/j.jretai.2014.09.005

Ashok, M., Madan, R., Joha, A., & Sivarajah, U. (2022). Ethical framework for artificial intelligence and digital technologies. *International Journal of Information Management*, *62*, 102433. DOI: 10.1016/j.ijinfomgt.2021.102433

Bleier, A., Goldfarb, A., & Tucker, C. (2020). Consumer privacy and the future of data-based innovation and marketing. *International Journal of Research in Marketing*, *37*(3), 466–480. DOI: 10.1016/j.ijresmar.2020.03.006

Böhm, R., Jörling, M., Reiter, L., & Fuchs, C. (2023). People devalue generative AI's competence but not its advice in addressing societal and personal challenges. *Communications Psychology*, *1*(1), 32. Advance online publication. DOI: 10.1038/s44271-023-00032-x PMID: 39242905

Canhoto, A. I., Keegan, B. J., & Ryzhikh, M. (2024). Snakes and ladders: Unpacking the personalisation–privacy paradox in the context of AI-enabled personalisation in the physical retail environment. *Information Systems Frontiers*, *26*(3), 1005–1024. DOI: 10.1007/s10796-023-10369-7 PMID: 36684411

Chandra, B., & Rahman, Z. (2024). Artificial intelligence and value co-creation: A review, conceptual framework and directions for future research. *Journal of Service Theory and Practice*, *34*(1), 7–32. DOI: 10.1108/JSTP-03-2023-0097

Chen, C., Tian, A. D., & Jiang, R. (2024). When post hoc explanation knocks: Consumer responses to explainable AI recommendations. *Journal of Interactive Marketing*, *59*(3), 234–250. DOI: 10.1177/10949968231200221

Colurcio, M., & Caridà, A. (2026). AI in service industries: Striking a balance between value co-creation and co-destruction. *Management Decision*, •••, 1–25. DOI: 10.1108/MD-11-2025-3576

Dai, X., Li, M., Yang, S., Shi, C., Wang, K., Liao, X., Li, Q. E. J., Tao, X., & Tang, X. (2025). Attitudes, perceptions, and factors influencing the adoption of AI in health care among medical staff: Nationwide cross-sectional survey study. *Journal of Medical Internet Research*, *27*, e75343. DOI: 10.2196/75343 PMID: 40779308

Davenport, T., Guha, A., Grewal, D., & Bressgott, T. (2020). How artificial intelligence will change the future of marketing. *Journal of the Academy of Marketing Science*, *48*(1), 24–42. DOI: 10.1007/s11747-019-00696-0

de Brito Duarte, R., Correia, F., Arriaga, P., & Paiva, A. (2023). AI trust: Can explainable AI enhance warranted trust? *Human Behavior and Emerging Technologies*, *2023*, 4637678. Advance online publication. DOI: 10.1155/2023/4637678

De Bruyn, A., Viswanathan, V., Beh, Y. S., Brock, J. K.-U., & von Wangenheim, F. (2020). Artificial intelligence and marketing: Pitfalls and opportunities. *Journal of Interactive Marketing*, *51*(1), 91–105. DOI: 10.1016/j.intmar.2020.04.007

de Matos, C. A., Rohden, S. F., & Azevedo, A. B. L. (2026). AI-induced privacy concerns: Examining the moderating effect of AI fear on customer data sharing. *International Journal of Bank Marketing*, *44*(6), 1271–1295. DOI: 10.1108/IJBM-05-2025-0403

Echeverri, P., & Skålén, P. (2011). Co-creation and co-destruction: A practice-theory based study of interactive value formation. *Marketing Theory*, *11*(3), 351–373. DOI: 10.1177/1470593111408181

Echeverri, P., & Skålén, P. (2021). Value co-destruction: Review and conceptualization of interactive value formation. *Marketing Theory*, *21*(2), 227–249. DOI: 10.1177/1470593120983390

Fassiaux, S. (2023). Preserving consumer autonomy through European Union regulation of artificial intelligence: A long-term perspective. *European Journal of Risk Regulation*, *14*(3), 1–20. DOI: 10.1017/err.2023.58

Ge, X., Xu, C., Misaki, D., Markus, H. R., & Tsai, J. L. (2024). How culture shapes what people want from AI. In *Proceedings of the 2024 CHI Conference on Human Factors in Computing Systems* (Article 704, pp. 1–15). Association for Computing Machinery. DOI: 10.1145/3613904.3642660

Glikson, E., & Woolley, A. W. (2020). Human trust in artificial intelligence: Review of empirical research. *The Academy of Management Annals*, *14*(2), 627–660. DOI: 10.5465/annals.2018.0057

Grewal, D., Satornino, C. B., Davenport, T., & Guha, A. (2025). How generative AI is shaping the future of marketing. *Journal of the Academy of Marketing Science*, *53*(3), 702–722. DOI: 10.1007/s11747-024-01064-3

Han, J., & Ko, D. (2025). Consumer autonomy in generative AI services: The role of task difficulty and AI design elements in enhancing trust, satisfaction, and usage intention. *Behavioral Sciences (Basel, Switzerland), 15*(4), 534. Advance online publication. DOI: 10.3390/bs15040534 PMID: 40282155

Hermann, E. (2022). Leveraging artificial intelligence in marketing for social good: An ethical perspective. *Journal of Business Ethics, 179*(1), 43–61. DOI: 10.1007/s10551-021-04843-y PMID: 34054170

Hu, L., & Min, H. (2023). The dark side of artificial intelligence in service: The "watching-eye" effect and privacy concerns. *International Journal of Hospitality Management, 110*, 103437. Advance online publication. DOI: 10.1016/j.ijhm.2023.103437

Huang, M.-H., & Rust, R. T. (2021). A strategic framework for artificial intelligence in marketing. *Journal of the Academy of Marketing Science, 49*(1), 30–50. DOI: 10.1007/s11747-020-00749-9

Ihde, D. (1990). *Technology and the lifeworld: From garden to earth.* Indiana University Press. DOI: 10.2979/3108.0

Kaartemo, V., & Helkkula, A. (2018). A systematic review of artificial intelligence and robots in value co-creation: Current status and future research avenues. *Journal of Creating Value, 4*(2), 211–228. DOI: 10.1177/2394964318805625

Kang, S., Potinteu, A.-E., & Said, N. (2025). ExplainitAI: When do we trust artificial intelligence? The influence of content and explainability in a cross-cultural comparison. In *Extended Abstracts of the 2025 CHI Conference on Human Factors in Computing Systems* (pp. 1–7). Association for Computing Machinery. DOI: 10.1145/3706599.3720222

Langer, M., Oster, D., Speith, T., Hermanns, H., Kästner, L., Schmidt, E., Sesing, A., & Baum, K. (2021). What do we want from explainable artificial intelligence (XAI)? A stakeholder perspective on XAI and a conceptual model guiding interdisciplinary XAI research. *Artificial Intelligence, 296*, 103473. DOI: 10.1016/j.artint.2021.103473

Latour, B. (2005). *Reassembling the social: An introduction to Actor-Network-Theory.* Oxford University Press. DOI: 10.1093/oso/9780199256044.001.0001

Longoni, C., Bonezzi, A., & Morewedge, C. K. (2019). Resistance to medical artificial intelligence. *The Journal of Consumer Research, 46*(4), 629–650. DOI: 10.1093/jcr/ucz013

Lumivalo, J., Tuunanen, T., & Salo, M. (2024). Value co-destruction: A systematic literature review and future research agenda. *Journal of Service Research*, *27*(2), 159–176. DOI: 10.1177/10946705231177504

Mourali, M., Novakowski, D., Pogacar, R., & Brigden, N. (2025). Post hoc explanations improve consumer responses to algorithmic decisions. *Journal of Business Research*, *186*, 114981. Advance online publication. DOI: 10.1016/j.jbusres.2024.114981

Nguyen, M., Ferm, L.-E. C., Quach, S., Pontes, N., & Thaichon, P. (2023). Chatbots in frontline services and customer experience: An anthropomorphism perspective. *Psychology and Marketing*, *40*(11), 2201–2225. DOI: 10.1002/mar.21882

Ning, X., Lu, Y., Li, W., & Gupta, S. (2024). How transparency affects algorithmic advice utilization: The mediating roles of trusting beliefs. *Decision Support Systems*, *183*, 114273. Advance online publication. DOI: 10.1016/j.dss.2024.114273

Osman, M., Osman, H., Almansour, O., Mohammed, F., Agag, G., & Alipour, H. (2026). When AI advice backfires: Field experimental evidence on personalization, intrusiveness, and purchase behavior. *Journal of Retailing and Consumer Services*, *92*, 104844. Advance online publication. DOI: 10.1016/j.jretconser.2026.104844

Ostinelli, M., Bonezzi, A., & Lisjak, M. (2024). Unintended effects of algorithmic transparency: The mere prospect of an explanation can foster the illusion of understanding how an algorithm works. *Journal of Consumer Psychology*, *35*(2), 203–219. DOI: 10.1002/jcpy.1416

Palmiotto, F. (2024). When is a decision automated? A taxonomy for a fundamental rights analysis. *German Law Journal*, *25*(2), 210–236. DOI: 10.1017/glj.2023.112

Plé, L., & Cáceres, R. C. (2010). Not always co-creation: Introducing interactional co-destruction of value in Service-Dominant Logic. *Journal of Services Marketing*, *24*(6), 430–437. DOI: 10.1108/08876041011072546

Puntoni, S., Reczek, R. W., Giesler, M., & Botti, S. (2021). Consumers and artificial intelligence: An experiential perspective. *Journal of Marketing*, *85*(1), 131–151. DOI: 10.1177/0022242920953847

Shuqair, S., Costa Pinto, D., Lancelot Miltgen, C., & Viglia, G. (2024). When powerful artificial intelligence backfires. *International Journal of Hospitality Management*, *120*, 103778. Advance online publication. DOI: 10.1016/j.ijhm.2024.103778

Vargo, S. L., & Lusch, R. F. (2008). Service-Dominant Logic: Continuing the evolution. *Journal of the Academy of Marketing Science*, *36*(1), 1–10. DOI: 10.1007/s11747-007-0069-6

Vargo, S. L., & Lusch, R. F. (2016). Institutions and axioms: An extension and update of Service-Dominant Logic. *Journal of the Academy of Marketing Science*, *44*(1), 5–23. DOI: 10.1007/s11747-015-0456-3

Verbeek, P.-P. (2005). *What things do: Philosophical reflections on technology, agency, and design*. Pennsylvania State University Press.

Viberg, O., Kizilcec, R. F., Jivet, I., Martínez Monés, A., Oh, A., Mutimukwe, C., Hrastinski, S., & Scheffel, M. (2024). Cultural differences in students' privacy concerns in learning analytics across Germany, South Korea, Spain, Sweden, and the United States. *Computers in Human Behavior Reports*, *14*, 100416. Advance online publication. DOI: 10.1016/j.chbr.2024.100416

Wang, Z., Yuan, R., Li, B., Kumar, V., & Kumar, A. (2026). An empirical study of AI financial advisor adoption through technology vulnerabilities in the financial context. *Journal of Product Innovation Management*, *43*(1), 14–30. DOI: 10.1111/jpim.12795

Weidig, J., & Kuehnl, C. (2023). The dark side of personalization: Recommendation source and consumer reactance in AI-based recommendations. *Psychology and Marketing*, *40*(12), 2559–2575. DOI: 10.1002/mar.21914

Zhang, D., Voorveld, H. A. M., & Boerman, S. C. (2023). Privacy concerns matter, knowledge does not: Investigating effects of online behavioral advertising among Chinese and Dutch adults. *Journal of Current Issues and Research in Advertising*, *44*(3), 392–410. DOI: 10.1080/10641734.2023.2199812

Zhou, T., & Tang, B. (2025). Examining user information disclosure on artificial intelligence-generated content platforms: A privacy calculus perspective. *Information Development*, 02666669251384288. Advance online publication. DOI: 10.1177/02666669251384288

Zhu, A., Stroud, N. J., Minteer, C., Yoo, J., Ridgeway, C., Mooghali, M., Miller, J. E., & Barry, M. J. (2026). Key information influencing patient decision-making about AI in health care: Survey experiment study. *Journal of Medical Internet Research*, *28*, e75615. DOI: 10.2196/75615 PMID: 41525463

Zondag, T. M., Rozestraten, R., Grimmelikhuijsen, S., Jongsma, K. R., van Solinge, W. W., Bots, M. L., Vernooij, R. W. M., & Haitjema, S. (2024). The effect of artificial intelligence on patient–physician trust: Cross-sectional vignette study. *Journal of Medical Internet Research*, *26*, e50853. DOI: 10.2196/50853 PMID: 38805702

KEY TERMS AND DEFINITIONS

AI Agency: The capacity of AI systems to shape service interactions by selecting, ordering, generating, recommending, prioritizing, or withholding options within sociotechnical systems, without implying human-like consciousness, intention, or moral responsibility.

AI-Driven Hyper-Personalization: The use of AI systems to adapt service offerings, interactions, recommendations, and meanings in real time by drawing on contextual, behavioral, and relational data.

Distributed Agency: The distribution of action-shaping capacity across consumers, employees, organizations, platforms, algorithms, interfaces, and other service network participants.

Post-Phenomenology: A philosophical approach that examines how technologies mediate human experience, perception, interpretation, and action.

Responsible AI Service Design: The design and governance of AI-enabled services through transparency, explainability, fairness, consent, contestability, and human oversight.

Service-Dominant Logic: A marketing perspective that treats service as the fundamental basis of exchange and explains value as co-created through actor-to-actor resource integration.

Value Co-Creation: The formation of value through resource integration among multiple actors, including consumers, firms, employees, platforms, and AI-enabled systems.

Value Co-Destruction: A negative outcome of interaction in which resource integration reduces trust, autonomy, fairness, well-being, or service value for one or more actors.

Chapter 4
From Segmentation to Hyper-Personalization: Case Studies on Consumer Experience and Trust in AI-Based Service Ecosystems

Ashwarya Kapoor
http://orcid.org/0000-0003-3858-3945
School of Commerce and Economics, Manav Rachna International Institute of Research and Studies, Faridabad, India

Sneha Kapoor
http://orcid.org/0009-0005-7051-3359
J.C. Bose University of Science and Technology, YMCA, Faridabad, India

Rajiv Sindwani
http://orcid.org/0000-0001-7457-6457
J.C. Bose University of Science and Technology, YMCA, Faridabad, India

ABSTRACT

The transition from traditional segmentation to AI-driven hyper-personalization has fundamentally reshaped consumer experience within digital service ecosystems. This chapter investigates how artificial intelligence enables organizations to deliver real-time, individualized experiences while simultaneously influencing consumer trust. Adopting a qualitative case study approach, the chapter analyzes Netflix and Amazon as leading examples of AI-enabled personalization. The findings suggest that while hyper-personalization enhances perceived relevance, engagement, and satisfaction, trust is not an automatic outcome and is contingent upon transparen-

DOI: 10.4018/979-8-3373-9159-5.ch004

cy, perceived fairness, and data governance practices. The chapter contributes by conceptualizing the personalization–trust paradox and offers actionable insights for designing responsible AI-driven consumer experiences.

1. INTRODUCTION

The rapid advancement of digital technologies has fundamentally transformed the way organizations design and deliver consumer experiences, leading to the emergence of data-driven and AI-enabled service ecosystems. In particular, the integration of artificial intelligence (AI), machine learning, and big data analytics has enabled companies to transition from traditional marketing approaches toward highly individualized and context-aware interactions (Kapoor and Sindwani, 2025a, b). This transformation reflects a broader shift from mass marketing to segmentation and ultimately toward hyper-personalization, wherein each consumer is treated as a unique entity based on real-time behavioral, contextual, and predictive data (Wedel & Kannan, 2016; Huang & Rust, 2021).

In recent years, hyper-personalization has emerged as a dominant strategic priority for organizations operating in digital environments. Industry reports indicate that more than 80% of firms are investing in AI-driven personalization capabilities to enhance customer engagement and revenue generation. This shift is largely driven by the growing expectations of digitally native consumers who demand seamless, relevant, and anticipatory experiences across platforms. AI-powered systems, including recommendation engines, predictive analytics, and generative AI, enable brands to design real-time adaptive interactions, significantly enhancing perceived usefulness and consumer satisfaction (Grewal et al., 2020; Davenport et al., 2020).

From a theoretical standpoint, hyper-personalization represents a progression beyond traditional segmentation and rule-based personalization. While segmentation categorizes consumers into relatively homogeneous groups, hyper-personalization leverages continuous data streams to create dynamic, individualized experiences. Recent research highlights that AI-driven personalization significantly enhances consumer engagement, satisfaction, and perceived value, thereby reinforcing its strategic importance in digital marketing. Furthermore, empirical evidence suggests that personalization not only improves customer experience but also positively influences trust and purchase intention, with satisfaction acting as a key mediating factor.

However, despite these benefits, the increasing reliance on AI-driven personalization has raised critical concerns related to consumer trust, data privacy, and ethical governance. As firms collect and process vast amounts of personal data, consumers are becoming increasingly aware of potential risks associated with surveillance, data misuse, and algorithmic bias. Recent studies emphasize that while personalization enhances perceived relevance, it simultaneously intensifies privacy concerns, creating a complex trade-off between value and risk. This concern is further reinforced by global consumer surveys, which indicate that although users appreciate the benefits of AI-enabled services, they expect organizations to ensure transparency, security, and responsible data practices.

Moreover, the emergence of generative AI has further complicated the personalization landscape by enabling highly sophisticated and emotionally adaptive interactions. While such capabilities enhance user experience, they also amplify concerns regarding manipulation, lack of transparency, and ethical misuse of consumer data. Consequently, the relationship between personalization and trust is not straightforward but rather characterized by tension and ambivalence, wherein increased personalization may simultaneously enhance and undermine trust.

Despite the growing body of literature on AI-driven personalization, several important research gaps persist. First, existing studies predominantly adopt quantitative and model-driven approaches, focusing on measurable outcomes such as engagement, satisfaction, and purchase intention, while overlooking the qualitative and experiential dimensions of consumer interaction with AI systems. Second, although trust has been recognized as a critical factor, limited research has explored trust as a multidimensional construct encompassing functional, cognitive, and ethical dimensions within AI-based service ecosystems. Third, there is a lack of contextual and comparative insights that examine how personalization operates across different consumption settings, particularly distinguishing between hedonic (e.g., entertainment) and utilitarian (e.g., e-commerce) environments. Finally, the emerging notion of a "personalization–trust paradox", wherein increased personalization may lead to both positive and negative trust outcomes, remains underexplored in contemporary research.

Addressing these gaps, the present chapter adopts a qualitative case study approach to examine how AI-driven hyper-personalization influences consumer experience and trust within digital service ecosystems. Specifically, the chapter focuses on two leading platforms—Netflix and Amazon—to provide in-depth insights into how personalization mechanisms function in distinct contexts and how they shape consumer perceptions and behaviors.

The key objectives of this chapter are:

1. To examine the evolution from segmentation to hyper-personalization in AI-driven service ecosystems.
2. To analyze the impact of hyper-personalization on consumer experience across different contexts.
3. To explore the multidimensional nature of consumer trust in AI-enabled environments.

4. To conceptualize and empirically illustrate the personalization–trust paradox using qualitative case evidence.

This chapter makes several significant contributions. First, it advances the literature by offering a holistic and integrative perspective that combines consumer experience and trust within AI-driven ecosystems. Second, it contributes methodologically by employing a qualitative case-based approach, providing rich and context-specific insights that complement existing quantitative research. Third, it introduces and develops the concept of the personalization–trust paradox, thereby extending theoretical understanding of the unintended consequences of hyper-personalization. Finally, the chapter provides practical implications for managers and platform designers, emphasizing the need to balance personalization with transparency, ethical data practices, and user control to foster sustainable consumer relationships.

In an era where AI increasingly mediates consumer interactions, understanding the interplay between personalization and trust is not only academically relevant but also strategically imperative. This chapter seeks to contribute to this evolving discourse by offering both theoretical insights and practical guidance for navigating the complexities of AI-driven service ecosystems.

2. CONCEPTUALIZING HYPER-PERSONALIZATION

2.1 From Segmentation to Individualization

The evolution of marketing thought reflects a gradual but profound shift in how organizations understand and engage consumers. Traditional marketing strategies relied heavily on segmentation, wherein consumers were grouped based on shared characteristics such as demographics, psychographics, or behavioral patterns (Wedel & Kannan, 2016). While segmentation enabled firms to target relatively homogeneous groups more efficiently, it inherently lacked the granularity required to address individual-level preferences and dynamic behavioral changes. As markets became increasingly competitive and consumer expectations evolved, the limitations of segmentation became more apparent, particularly in digital environments characterized by high interactivity and data availability.

The advent of digital technologies and data analytics facilitated the transition from segmentation to personalization, allowing firms to tailor offerings based on individual consumer data. However, early personalization approaches were largely rule-based and retrospective, relying on historical data such as past purchases or browsing history (Bleier & Eisenbeiss, 2015). These systems, while an improvement over segmentation, remained limited in their ability to respond to real-time changes in consumer behavior and contextual factors.

Hyper-personalization represents the next stage in this evolutionary trajectory, characterized by the integration of artificial intelligence (AI), machine learning, and big data analytics to deliver highly individualized and context-aware experiences (Huang & Rust, 2021; Sharma & Kapoor, 2026; Kapoor and Sindwani, 2026). Unlike traditional personalization, hyper-personalization leverages multiple data sources, including behavioral data, contextual signals, and predictive analytics, to anticipate consumer needs and deliver tailored interactions in real time. Behavioral data captures user actions such as clicks, searches, and purchase patterns, providing insights into preferences and intentions. Contextual signals, including location, time, device, and situational factors, enable firms to tailor experiences based on the consumer's immediate environment. Predictive analytics further enhances personalization by forecasting future behavior using advanced algorithms and machine learning models (Davenport et al., 2020).

Recent studies highlight that hyper-personalization significantly enhances consumer engagement and satisfaction by reducing information overload and improving decision-making efficiency (Grewal et al., 2020; Teepapal, 2025). By delivering relevant and timely content, companies can create seamless and intuitive consumer journeys, thereby increasing perceived value and fostering stronger relationships. Moreover, hyper-personalization enables a shift from reactive to proactive marketing, where brands anticipate consumer needs rather than merely responding to them (Rust & Huang, 2021).

However, this transition toward individualization also raises important concerns. The extensive use of personal data required for hyper-personalization has intensified issues related to privacy, data security, and consumer autonomy (Martin & Murphy, 2017; Kapoor et al., 2025a). Consumers may perceive highly personalized interactions as intrusive, particularly when they are unaware of how their data is collected and used. This phenomenon, often referred to as the "privacy paradox," reflects the tension between consumers' desire for personalized experiences and their concerns about data privacy (Aguirre et al., 2015). Consequently, while hyper-personalization offers significant benefits, it also necessitates careful consideration of ethical and trust-related implications.

2.2 Key Features of Hyper-Personalization

Hyper-personalization is distinguished by several defining features that collectively enable the delivery of highly adaptive and individualized consumer experiences.

These features are rooted in advancements in AI and data analytics, which allow firms to process large volumes of data and generate actionable insights in real time.

One of the most critical features of hyper-personalization is real-time adaptability. Unlike traditional systems that rely on static data, AI-driven personalization systems continuously update their recommendations based on real-time user interactions. This dynamic capability allows firms to respond instantly to changes in consumer behavior, thereby enhancing relevance and immediacy (Huang & Rust, 2021). For example, streaming platforms and e-commerce websites adjust recommendations as users browse, creating a fluid and responsive experience.

Another key feature is the use of AI-driven recommendation systems, which form the backbone of hyper-personalization. These systems employ techniques such as collaborative filtering, content-based filtering, and deep learning to generate personalized recommendations (Castells et al., 2015). By analyzing patterns across large datasets, AI algorithms can identify similarities between users and predict preferences with high accuracy. This not only improves the quality of recommendations but also enhances user satisfaction and engagement.

Context-aware interactions further distinguish hyper-personalization from earlier approaches. Context-awareness involves incorporating situational factors such as location, time, device, and social context into the personalization process. Research indicates that context-aware systems significantly improve the relevance and effectiveness of personalized content by aligning it with the consumer's immediate needs and circumstances (Adomavicius & Tuzhilin, 2010). For instance, location-based recommendations in retail or travel platforms enable companies to provide timely and contextually relevant suggestions.

Additionally, hyper-personalization is characterized by continuous learning systems, which utilize machine learning algorithms to refine their predictions over time. These systems learn from each interaction, enabling them to improve accuracy and adapt to evolving consumer preferences. Continuous learning not only enhances personalization but also allows firms to identify emerging trends and patterns, thereby supporting strategic decision-making (Davenport et al., 2020).

Collectively, these features have redefined consumer expectations, making relevance, immediacy, and seamlessness central to experience design. Consumers increasingly expect digital platforms to deliver personalized experiences that are not only accurate but also intuitive and effortless. As a result, firms that fail to meet these expectations risk losing competitiveness in an increasingly data-driven marketplace.

However, the very features that make hyper-personalization effective also contribute to its challenges. Real-time data processing and continuous learning require extensive data collection, raising concerns about privacy and surveillance. Similarly, the complexity of AI algorithms can lead to a lack of transparency, making it difficult for consumers to understand how decisions are made (Buhmann & Fieseler, 2021).

These challenges underscore the importance of balancing technological capabilities with ethical considerations.

3. THEORETICAL FOUNDATION

Understanding hyper-personalization and its impact on consumer experience and trust requires a strong theoretical grounding. This chapter draws upon three key theoretical perspectives: the Technology Acceptance Model (TAM), Relationship Marketing Theory, and Service-Dominant Logic (SDL). Together, these frameworks provide a comprehensive lens for analyzing how consumers perceive and respond to AI-driven personalization.

3.1 Technology Acceptance Model (TAM)

The Technology Acceptance Model (TAM), originally proposed by Davis (1989), is one of the most widely used frameworks for understanding user acceptance of technology. TAM posits that two primary factors—perceived usefulness and perceived ease of use—determine individuals' attitudes toward technology adoption. In the context of AI-driven personalization, perceived usefulness is reflected in the extent to which personalized recommendations enhance the consumer's experience, while ease of use relates to the simplicity and intuitiveness of interacting with the system.

Recent extensions of TAM incorporate additional constructs such as trust and perceived risk, recognizing their importance in digital environments (Venkatesh & Davis, 2000; Gefen et al., 2003). In AI-based service ecosystems, trust becomes a critical determinant of technology acceptance, particularly when consumers are required to share personal data (Kapoor et al., 2025b). Studies indicate that trust mediates the relationship between personalization and user engagement, highlighting its central role in shaping consumer behavior (Sipos, 2025).

3.2 Relationship Marketing Theory

Relationship Marketing Theory emphasizes the importance of building long-term relationships with customers based on trust, commitment, and mutual value creation (Morgan & Hunt, 1994). In the context of hyper-personalization, trust serves as a foundational element that influences consumer loyalty and retention.

AI-driven personalization can strengthen relationships by delivering relevant and meaningful interactions, thereby enhancing customer satisfaction and emotional connection. However, excessive personalization or perceived misuse of data can erode trust and damage relationships (Martin & Murphy, 2017). This highlights the dual role of personalization as both a facilitator and a potential disruptor of trust.

3.3 Service-Dominant Logic (SDL)

Service-Dominant Logic (SDL) provides a broader perspective on value creation, emphasizing the role of interactions and co-creation between firms and consumers (Lusch & Vargo, 2011). According to SDL, value is not embedded in products but is co-created through the integration of resources and experiences.

Hyper-personalization aligns closely with SDL by enabling firms to tailor interactions based on individual preferences and contexts. Through personalized experiences, consumers actively participate in the value creation process, shaping outcomes based on their interactions with AI systems. This perspective underscores the importance of designing personalization strategies that empower consumers and enhance their role in the service ecosystem.

3.4 Conceptualizing Trust in AI-Based Systems

Trust is a multifaceted construct that plays a critical role in shaping consumer responses to AI-driven personalization. In this chapter, trust is conceptualized across three dimensions:

1. Functional Trust

Functional trust refers to the perceived reliability and accuracy of AI systems. When recommendations consistently meet consumer expectations, users develop confidence in the system's capabilities (Gefen et al., 2003).

2. Cognitive Trust

Cognitive trust is based on predictability and consistency in system behavior. Consumers are more likely to trust systems that exhibit stable and understandable patterns, reducing uncertainty in decision-making (McKnight et al., 2002).

3. Ethical Trust

Ethical trust relates to perceptions of fairness, transparency, and privacy. In AI-driven environments, ethical trust is particularly important, as consumers are increasingly concerned about data usage and algorithmic bias (Buhmann & Fieseler, 2021).

These dimensions highlight that trust in AI systems is not solely based on performance but also on ethical considerations and perceived intentions. As such, organizations must adopt a holistic approach to trust-building that addresses both functional and ethical aspects (Kapoor et al., 2026a).

Emerging evidence further suggests that trust in AI-driven personalization varies across generational cohorts (Mitchell, 2026). Younger consumers, particularly Generation Z, often exhibit a pragmatic ambivalence toward AI-enabled personalization. Although they express concerns regarding privacy and data security, they are generally more willing to exchange personal information in return for convenience, relevance, and enhanced digital experiences. In contrast, older consumers tend to demonstrate greater skepticism toward AI systems, placing stronger emphasis on transparency, control, and responsible data practices. These generational differences indicate that trust formation in AI-based service ecosystems is influenced not only by technological and contextual factors but also by demographic characteristics and prior digital experience. Consequently, organizations should adopt age-sensitive personalization strategies to effectively address diverse trust expectations across consumer segments (Naeimi and Family, 2025).

4. CASE STUDIES

This section presents an in-depth qualitative analysis of two leading AI-driven platforms—Netflix and Amazon—to examine how hyper-personalization shapes consumer experience and trust. These cases were purposefully selected because they represent mature and highly developed AI ecosystems that illustrate advanced personalization practices. While these organizations possess substantial technological and data capabilities, the insights derived from these cases provide foundational principles that can be adapted by smaller and challenger firms through scalable and resource-efficient personalization strategies.

4.1 Netflix: Hyper-Personalization as a Driver of Immersive Experience

Netflix is widely regarded as a pioneer in leveraging artificial intelligence to deliver hyper-personalized content experiences. Operating within a hedonic consumption context, the platform focuses on maximizing user engagement and satisfaction through highly tailored content delivery. Netflix's success can be attributed to its ability to transform content discovery into a seamless and immersive experience, driven by advanced personalization technologies (Gomez-Uribe & Hunt, 2015).

4.1.1 Personalization Mechanisms

At the core of Netflix's personalization strategy lies its AI-based recommendation engine, which utilizes machine learning algorithms to analyze vast amounts of user data, including viewing history, search queries, ratings, watch time, and interaction patterns. These algorithms employ techniques such as collaborative filtering and deep learning to identify patterns and predict user preferences with high accuracy (Gomez-Uribe & Hunt, 2015; Castells et al., 2015).

A distinctive feature of Netflix's approach is its use of micro-segmentation, wherein users are categorized into thousands of "taste clusters" based on nuanced viewing behaviors. Unlike traditional segmentation, which groups users into broad categories, micro-segmentation allows Netflix to capture subtle differences in preferences, enabling highly granular personalization (Huang & Rust, 2021).

In addition to recommendations, Netflix employs personalized thumbnails and previews, which dynamically adapt visual content to match individual user preferences. For instance, different users may see different cover images for the same show, depending on their viewing history and interests. This visual personalization enhances user engagement by making content more appealing and relevant at first glance.

Furthermore, Netflix's system operates as a continuous learning system, constantly updating its recommendations based on real-time user interactions. Each click, pause, or skip provides valuable feedback, enabling the system to refine its predictions and improve accuracy over time. This dynamic capability ensures that the platform remains responsive to evolving user preferences, thereby reinforcing its hyper-personalization capabilities (Davenport et al., 2020).

4.1.2 Impact on Consumer Experience

Netflix's hyper-personalization significantly enhances the overall consumer experience by reducing friction and increasing engagement. One of the most notable outcomes is the enhancement of user engagement and binge-watching behavior. By continuously presenting relevant content, the platform encourages prolonged viewing sessions, thereby increasing user retention and satisfaction.

AI-driven hyper-personalization can also contribute to the development of Fear of Missing Out (FOMO). By continuously presenting users with personalized recommendations, autoplay features, and time-sensitive offers, digital platforms create a sense that valuable content or opportunities may be overlooked if engagement is interrupted. As a result, users may remain on the platform longer or make decisions they might not otherwise have made. Although these personalization techniques improve user engagement and enhance the overall customer experience, they may also encourage excessive consumption and prolonged platform use, with potential implications for users' digital well-being. These concerns highlight the need for organizations to balance the commercial benefits of hyper-personalization with responsible and ethical AI practices.

Another critical impact is the reduction of search effort and decision fatigue. In traditional media consumption, users often face an overwhelming number of choices, leading to cognitive overload. Netflix addresses this challenge by curating a personalized content feed, allowing users to quickly identify content that aligns with their preferences. This aligns with the principles of the Technology Acceptance Model, where perceived usefulness and ease of use contribute to positive user experiences (Davis, 1989).

Hyper-personalization also enhances perceived enjoyment and satisfaction, as users are more likely to encounter content that resonates with their interests. The platform's ability to anticipate user preferences creates a sense of familiarity and comfort, contributing to a more enjoyable and immersive experience. From a Service-Dominant Logic perspective, this reflects the co-creation of value, where personalized interactions enhance the consumer's role in shaping their experience (Lusch & Vargo, 2011).

Overall, Netflix transforms content consumption into a frictionless and immersive journey, where users are seamlessly guided through a personalized entertainment ecosystem. This not only enhances user satisfaction but also strengthens emotional engagement with the platform.

4.1.3 Trust Implications

Netflix's personalization strategy has significant implications for consumer trust, particularly in terms of functional and cognitive trust. The high accuracy of its recommendation system fosters functional trust, as users perceive the platform as reliable and effective in delivering relevant content (Gefen et al., 2003). Consistent performance reinforces confidence in the system, making users more likely to rely on recommendations.

Cognitive trust is also strengthened through predictability and consistency. As users interact with the platform over time, they develop expectations regarding the quality and relevance of recommendations. When these expectations are consistently met, trust is reinforced, leading to increased reliance on the system.

However, despite these positive outcomes, certain concerns emerge. One notable issue is the potential for content echo chambers or filter bubbles, where users are repeatedly exposed to similar types of content, limiting diversity and exploration (Pariser, 2011). While this enhances short-term satisfaction, it may reduce long-term engagement by restricting exposure to new content.

Another concern is the lack of transparency in recommendation logic. Netflix's algorithms operate as "black boxes," making it difficult for users to understand how recommendations are generated. This lack of transparency can undermine ethical trust, particularly among users who are concerned about data usage and algorithmic decision-making (Buhmann & Fieseler, 2021).

Despite these concerns, trust in Netflix is largely maintained through consistent performance and user satisfaction, rather than explicit transparency. In a hedonic context, where perceived risk is relatively low, users are more willing to trade off transparency for convenience and enjoyment. This highlights the context-dependent nature of trust in AI-driven personalization.

4.2 Amazon: Predictive Personalization and Transactional Trust

Amazon represents one of the most comprehensive applications of AI-driven personalization, extending across the entire consumer journey. Unlike Netflix, which operates in a hedonic context, Amazon functions within a utilitarian and transactional environment, where efficiency, accuracy, and reliability are paramount. This distinction makes Amazon an ideal case for examining how personalization influences trust in high-stakes decision-making contexts.

4.2.1 Personalization Mechanisms

Amazon's personalization strategy is built on a sophisticated integration of AI technologies that analyze vast amounts of consumer data, including browsing history, purchase behavior, search queries, and contextual factors. One of its most prominent features is the product recommendation system, exemplified by suggestions such as "Customers who bought this also bought." These recommendations are generated using collaborative filtering techniques, which identify patterns across users with similar behaviors (Linden et al., 2003).

In addition to recommendations, Amazon employs personalized search results, which prioritize products based on individual preferences and past interactions. This ensures that users are presented with the most relevant options, thereby improving search efficiency and decision-making.

Another key aspect of Amazon's personalization is dynamic pricing and targeted promotions, where prices and offers may vary based on factors such as demand, user behavior, and market conditions. While this enhances competitiveness and relevance, it also introduces complexities related to fairness and transparency.

Amazon's system also incorporates predictive analytics, enabling the platform to anticipate consumer needs and proactively suggest products. For example, features such as "Buy Again" and personalized homepages are designed to streamline the purchasing process and enhance convenience.

4.2.2 Impact on Consumer Experience

Amazon's hyper-personalization significantly enhances consumer experience by improving convenience and efficiency. By presenting relevant products and recommendations, the platform reduces the time and effort required to search for items, thereby simplifying the decision-making process.

Another important outcome is faster decision-making, as users are guided toward products that align with their preferences. This reduces cognitive load and enhances perceived ease of use, which is a key determinant of technology acceptance (Venkatesh & Davis, 2000).

Hyper-personalization also contributes to higher perceived value, as users feel that the platform understands their needs and provides tailored solutions. This aligns with Relationship Marketing Theory, where personalized interactions strengthen customer relationships and enhance satisfaction (Morgan & Hunt, 1994).

Overall, Amazon minimizes cognitive effort by creating a guided and efficient shopping experience, where users are seamlessly directed toward relevant choices. This not only improves user satisfaction but also increases conversion rates and customer loyalty.

4.2.3 Trust Implications

In contrast to Netflix, Amazon operates in a high-stakes transactional environment, where trust plays a more critical and multifaceted role. Personalization influences trust in both positive and negative ways.

Positive Effects

Personalization enhances trust by improving convenience and reliability. Accurate recommendations and efficient search results create a sense of competence, contributing to functional trust. Additionally, Amazon's strong logistics network and reliable delivery services reinforce confidence in the platform, further strengthening trust.

Negative Concerns

However, Amazon's personalization practices also raise several concerns. One major issue is the perceived manipulation in pricing, where dynamic pricing strategies may lead consumers to question the fairness of prices. This can undermine ethical trust, particularly if users believe they are being treated differently based on their behavior.

Data privacy concerns also play a significant role, as Amazon collects and processes large amounts of personal data. Consumers may feel uneasy about the extent of data collection, particularly in the absence of clear communication regarding its usage (Martin & Murphy, 2017).

Additionally, algorithmic opacity poses challenges, as users have limited visibility into how recommendations and pricing decisions are made. This lack of transparency can create uncertainty and reduce trust, especially in a transactional context where financial implications are involved.

4.2.4 Contextual Sensitivity of Trust

A key insight from the Amazon case is that trust is more sensitive and risk-driven in utilitarian contexts. Unlike Netflix, where the consequences of poor recommendations are relatively low, Amazon involves financial transactions, making trust more critical. As a result, consumers place greater emphasis on transparency, fairness, and reliability.

This highlights the importance of contextualizing personalization strategies, as the same level of personalization may have different implications depending on the nature of the service. While users may tolerate opacity in entertainment platforms, they demand greater accountability in e-commerce environments.

4.3 Cross-Case Insight

The analysis of Netflix and Amazon reveals that while hyper-personalization enhances consumer experience in both cases, its impact on trust varies significantly based on context. Netflix demonstrates how personalization can create immersive experiences and build trust through consistency, whereas Amazon illustrates the complexities of trust in transactional environments.

These findings reinforce the existence of a personalization–trust paradox, where increased personalization simultaneously enhances value and introduces new risks. Understanding this paradox is critical for designing effective and responsible AI-driven service ecosystems.

5. CROSS-CASE ANALYSIS AND THE PERSONALIZATION–TRUST PARADOX

This section synthesizes insights from the Netflix and Amazon case studies to develop a comparative understanding of hyper-personalization and its implications for consumer experience and trust. By examining these platforms across different consumption contexts—hedonic and utilitarian—this analysis uncovers patterns, contrasts, and underlying mechanisms that shape the relationship between personalization and trust. The findings culminate in the conceptualization of the personalization–trust paradox, a central theoretical contribution of this chapter.

5.1 Comparative Analysis of Hyper-Personalization Practices

Although both Netflix and Amazon leverage advanced AI technologies to deliver hyper-personalized experiences, their approaches differ significantly in terms of objectives, mechanisms, and consumer outcomes.

5.1.1. Nature of Consumption Context

A fundamental distinction between the two cases lies in the nature of consumption:

- **Netflix** operates in a hedonic context, where the primary goal is entertainment, enjoyment, and emotional engagement.
- **Amazon**, in contrast, functions within a utilitarian context, where consumers seek efficiency, convenience, and goal-oriented outcomes.

This contextual difference plays a crucial role in shaping how personalization is perceived and evaluated by consumers. In hedonic settings, users are more tolerant of algorithmic interventions, as the perceived risks are relatively low. Conversely, in utilitarian contexts involving financial transactions, consumers exhibit greater sensitivity to issues of fairness, transparency, and control (Grewal et al., 2020).

5.2.2. Depth and Scope of Personalization

Both platforms demonstrate advanced personalization capabilities, but the scope and depth of personalization differ:

- Netflix focuses on content-level personalization, tailoring recommendations, thumbnails, and viewing interfaces to enhance engagement.
- Amazon adopts an end-to-end personalization approach, influencing the entire customer journey, including search, recommendations, pricing, and post-purchase interactions.

This distinction highlights that personalization in Amazon is more pervasive and consequential, as it directly affects purchasing decisions and financial outcomes. As a result, the stakes associated with personalization are significantly higher in Amazon's case.

5.3.3. Consumer Experience Outcomes

Despite contextual differences, both platforms demonstrate that hyper-personalization enhances consumer experience, albeit in different ways:

- In Netflix, personalization leads to immersive engagement, reduced search effort, and increased enjoyment.
- In Amazon, personalization improves decision efficiency, convenience, and perceived value.

These outcomes align with the Technology Acceptance Model, where perceived usefulness and ease of use drive positive user experiences (Davis, 1989). However, the nature of "usefulness" differs across contexts—entertainment value in Netflix versus functional efficiency in Amazon.

5.4.4. Trust Formation Mechanisms

The cases reveal distinct pathways through which trust is developed:

- Netflix builds trust primarily through functional performance and experiential consistency. Users rely on the system because it consistently delivers relevant content.
- Amazon, on the other hand, requires a more complex trust framework involving functional reliability, ethical fairness, and institutional credibility.

This distinction suggests that trust in AI systems is context-dependent, with different dimensions becoming salient based on the nature of the service. While functional trust may suffice in low-risk environments, high-risk contexts demand stronger ethical and cognitive trust components (Gefen et al., 2003).

5.2 Dimensions of Trust in AI-Driven Personalization

Building on the theoretical foundation and case findings, this section elaborates the multidimensional nature of trust in AI-based service ecosystems.

5.2.1. Functional Trust

Functional trust refers to the perceived reliability, accuracy, and competence of AI systems. In both Netflix and Amazon, functional trust is established through consistent and accurate recommendations. When systems perform effectively, users develop confidence in their ability to meet expectations.

However, functional trust alone is insufficient, particularly in contexts where decisions have significant consequences. While Netflix users may tolerate occasional inaccuracies, Amazon users are less forgiving due to the financial implications of their decisions.

5.2.2. Cognitive Trust

Cognitive trust is based on predictability, consistency, and understanding of system behavior. Users develop cognitive trust when they can anticipate how a system will respond and perceive it as stable and dependable (McKnight et al., 2002).

In Netflix, cognitive trust emerges gradually as users recognize patterns in recommendations. In Amazon, cognitive trust is influenced by the platform's ability to provide consistent search results and reliable service. However, algorithmic opacity can hinder cognitive trust by creating uncertainty about how decisions are made.

5.2.3. Ethical Trust

Ethical trust relates to perceptions of fairness, transparency, and responsible data usage. This dimension is particularly critical in AI-driven environments, where concerns about privacy and bias are prevalent (Buhmann & Fieseler, 2021).

The cases highlight that ethical trust is more salient in Amazon due to its transactional nature. Issues such as dynamic pricing and data privacy can significantly impact consumer perceptions of fairness. In contrast, ethical concerns in Netflix are less pronounced, as the perceived risks are lower.

The salience of these trust dimensions may also vary across generations. Studies in extant literature indicate that younger consumers are generally more receptive to AI-driven personalization and place greater value on convenience and personalization benefits, whereas older consumers exhibit stronger concerns regarding privacy, algorithmic transparency, and potential manipulation (Pariser, 2011; Guerra-Tamez et al., 2024). Such findings suggest that generational differences constitute an important boundary condition influencing the personalization–trust relationship and warrant further scholarly investigation (Naeimi and Family, 2025; Mitchell, 2026).

5.3 The Personalization–Trust Paradox

A key insight emerging from the cross-case analysis is the existence of a personalization–trust paradox, which represents a fundamental tension in AI-driven service ecosystems.

Conceptual Definition

The personalization–trust paradox refers to the phenomenon wherein increasing levels of personalization simultaneously enhance consumer value and experience while potentially undermining trust due to concerns related to privacy, transparency, and perceived manipulation.

5.3.1 Mechanisms Underlying the Paradox

The paradox arises from the interplay of several opposing forces:

- **Value Creation vs. Privacy Concerns**

Hyper-personalization enhances value by delivering relevant and timely experiences. However, achieving this level of personalization requires extensive data collection, which raises privacy concerns (Martin & Murphy, 2017).

- **Convenience vs. Perceived Manipulation**

While personalization simplifies decision-making, it may also create perceptions of manipulation, particularly when users feel that their choices are being influenced or constrained.

- **Personalization vs. Psychological Dependence**

AI-driven hyper-personalization may inadvertently foster psychological responses such as Fear of Missing Out (FOMO). Personalized recommendation loops, autoplay features, and limited-time promotional offers can create a perceived urgency to remain continuously engaged with digital platforms. For example, Netflix's autoplay functionality and endless content recommendations may encourage prolonged viewing sessions, whereas Amazon's personalized deals and scarcity-based promotions may stimulate impulse purchases. Although these mechanisms enhance engagement and platform value, they may simultaneously reduce perceived consumer autonomy and increase perceptions of manipulation. Consequently, organizations must carefully balance engagement objectives with consumer well-being and ethical responsibility.

- **Automation vs. Transparency**

AI systems operate through complex algorithms that are often opaque to users. While automation improves efficiency, the lack of transparency can reduce trust, especially in high-stakes contexts.

5.3.2 Contextual Variation of the Paradox

The intensity of the personalization–trust paradox varies across contexts:

- In hedonic environments (Netflix), the benefits of personalization outweigh the risks, leading to a relatively weak paradox.
- In utilitarian environments (Amazon), the risks are more pronounced, resulting in a stronger and more visible paradox.

This suggests that the paradox is not universal but context-dependent, influenced by factors such as perceived risk, type of consumption, and user expectations.

5.4 Development of a Conceptual Framework

Based on the findings, this chapter proposes a conceptual framework linking hyper-personalization, consumer experience, and trust. It has been exhibited in Figure 1.

Core Relationships

- **Hyper-Personalization → Consumer Experience**

AI-driven personalization positively influences consumer experience by enhancing relevance, convenience, and engagement.

- **Consumer Experience → Functional and Cognitive Trust**

Positive experiences reinforce trust by demonstrating system reliability and consistency.

- **Hyper-Personalization → Ethical Concerns**

Increased personalization intensifies concerns related to privacy, fairness, and transparency.

- **Ethical Concerns → Trust Erosion**

Ethical concerns negatively impact trust, particularly in high-risk contexts.

- **Moderating Role of Context**

The relationship between personalization and trust is moderated by the consumption context (hedonic vs. utilitarian).

Figure 1. Conceptual framework linking hyper-personalization, consumer experience and trust.

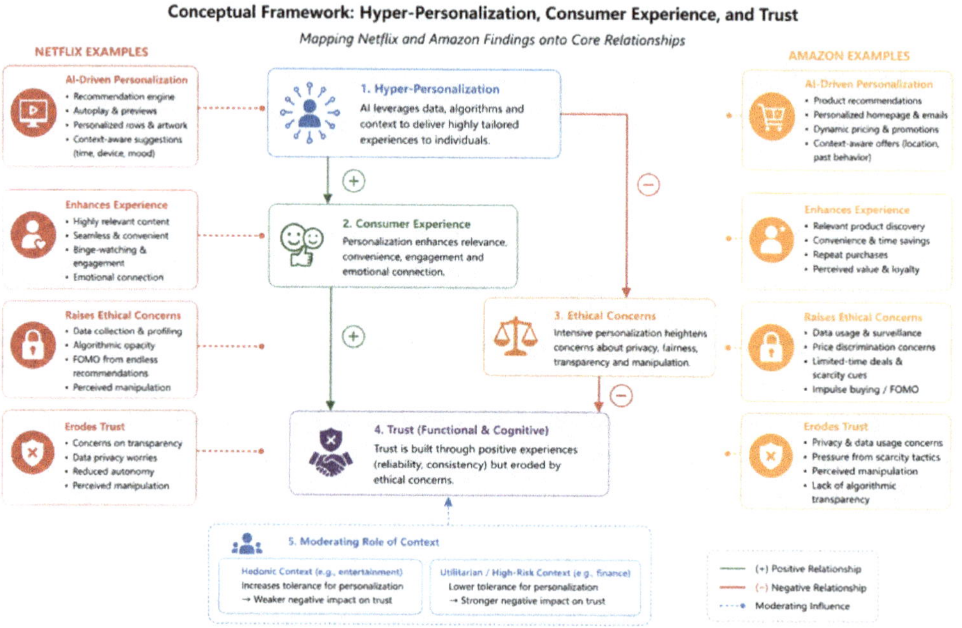

5.5 Propositions for Future Research

To extend the theoretical contribution, the following propositions are developed:
P1:

Hyper-personalization has a positive impact on consumer experience by enhancing perceived relevance, convenience, and engagement.

P2:

Consumer experience positively influences functional and cognitive trust in AI-driven systems.

P3:

Hyper-personalization increases ethical concerns related to privacy, transparency, and fairness.

P4:

Ethical concerns negatively influence consumer trust in AI-based service ecosystems.

P5:

The relationship between hyper-personalization and trust is moderated by the consumption context, such that the negative impact of ethical concerns is stronger in utilitarian contexts than in hedonic contexts.

P6

The relationship between hyper-personalization and trust is paradoxical, characterized by simultaneous positive (experience-driven) and negative (risk-driven) effects.

5.6 Theoretical Implications

This analysis contributes to the literature in several ways:

- It integrates consumer experience and trust within a unified framework.
- It advances the concept of multidimensional trust in AI systems.
- It introduces the personalization–trust paradox as a novel theoretical construct.
- It highlights the contextual nature of AI adoption and trust formation.

5.7 Summary

The cross-case analysis demonstrates that hyper-personalization is a powerful driver of consumer experience but also introduces new challenges related to trust. The personalization–trust paradox underscores the need for a balanced approach that considers both the benefits and risks of AI-driven personalization. By recognizing and addressing this paradox, organizations can design more effective and responsible service ecosystems.

6. MANAGERIAL IMPLICATIONS

The findings of this study provide several actionable insights for managers, platform designers, and policymakers seeking to leverage AI-driven hyper-personalization while maintaining consumer trust. As organizations increasingly adopt AI technologies to enhance customer experience, it becomes critical to strike a balance between value creation and ethical responsibility.

6.1 Designing Transparent and Explainable Personalization Systems

One of the key challenges identified in this study is the lack of transparency in AI-driven personalization. Both Netflix and Amazon rely on complex algorithms that function as "black boxes," making it difficult for users to understand how recommendations are generated. While this may not significantly impact trust in low-risk contexts, it becomes a critical issue in high-stakes environments such as e-commerce.

Managers should prioritize the development of explainable AI (XAI) systems that provide users with clear and accessible explanations for recommendations. Simple interventions—such as "Why this is recommended for you" features—can enhance user understanding and foster cognitive trust. Transparency not only improves user confidence but also aligns with emerging regulatory requirements related to algorithmic accountability.

6.2 Balancing Personalization with Privacy Protection

Hyper-personalization relies heavily on the collection and processing of user data, which raises concerns about privacy and surveillance. The findings highlight that excessive data collection can trigger the "creepiness effect," undermining trust and user comfort.

Organizations should adopt a privacy-by-design approach, ensuring that data collection practices are ethical, minimal, and transparent. This includes:

- Obtaining informed consent
- Providing users with control over their data
- Clearly communicating data usage policies

By empowering users with greater control, firms can mitigate privacy concerns and strengthen ethical trust.

6.3 Context-Sensitive Personalization Strategies

A critical insight from the cross-case analysis is that the effectiveness of personalization depends on the consumption context. In hedonic environments such as entertainment platforms, users are more tolerant of personalization and less concerned about transparency. In contrast, utilitarian contexts such as e-commerce require higher levels of trust due to financial implications.

Managers should adopt context-sensitive personalization strategies, tailoring the level and nature of personalization based on:

- Type of service (hedonic vs. utilitarian)
- Perceived risk
- Consumer expectations

For example, while aggressive personalization may be effective in entertainment platforms, it should be applied more cautiously in transactional settings to avoid perceptions of manipulation.

6.4 Building Trust through Consistency and Reliability

The findings indicate that functional trust is primarily built through consistent and reliable system performance. Accurate recommendations, timely service delivery, and seamless user experiences reinforce consumer confidence in AI systems.

Organizations should focus on:

- Improving algorithm accuracy
- Ensuring system reliability
- Maintaining consistency in user experience

In the case of Amazon, reliable delivery and customer service play a crucial role in reinforcing trust, while Netflix builds trust through consistent content relevance. These examples highlight the importance of aligning personalization strategies with operational excellence.

6.5 Addressing the Personalization–Trust Paradox

The identification of the personalization–trust paradox has important managerial implications. While personalization enhances consumer experience, excessive or poorly managed personalization can erode trust.

To address this paradox, organizations should:

- Avoid over-personalization that feels intrusive
- Provide users with options to customize personalization levels
- Monitor user feedback to identify discomfort or dissatisfaction

By adopting a balanced approach, firms can maximize the benefits of personalization while minimizing its risks.

6.6 Ethical Governance of AI Systems

As AI becomes increasingly central to service delivery, organizations must adopt robust ethical governance frameworks. This includes:

- Ensuring fairness in algorithmic decisions
- Preventing bias in recommendations
- Establishing accountability mechanisms

Ethical AI practices not only enhance trust but also contribute to long-term sustainability and brand reputation (Kapoor et al., 2026b). Firms that prioritize ethical considerations are more likely to build enduring relationships with consumers.

6.7 Strategic Implications for Competitive Advantage

Hyper-personalization can serve as a powerful source of competitive advantage when implemented effectively. Organizations that successfully integrate personalization with trust-building mechanisms can achieve:

- Higher customer engagement
- Increased loyalty and retention
- Enhanced brand differentiation

However, competitive advantage is not derived from personalization alone but from responsible personalization, where consumer interests are prioritized alongside business objectives.

6.8 Implications for SMEs and Challenger Brands

Although Netflix and Amazon represent large-scale AI-driven ecosystems, the principles of hyper-personalization are increasingly accessible to smaller and challenger brands. Advances in cloud computing, software-as-a-service (SaaS) platforms, and third-party AI solutions have significantly lowered the barriers to implementing personalization strategies. Small and medium-sized enterprises (SMEs) can leverage affordable customer relationship management (CRM) systems, recommendation engines, and marketing automation tools to deliver personalized experiences without extensive in-house technological infrastructure.

Unlike large organizations that rely on massive proprietary datasets, smaller firms can adopt lean-data approaches by utilizing first-party customer data, purchase histories, browsing behavior, and customer feedback to generate meaningful personalization. Moreover, challenger brands often possess advantages such as greater organizational agility, closer customer relationships, and the ability to rapidly experiment with personalization initiatives.

Examples include boutique e-commerce retailers using AI-enabled email personalization, small subscription-based businesses employing recommendation algorithms, and direct-to-consumer brands utilizing conversational AI and chatbots to enhance customer engagement. Consequently, responsible AI-driven personalization should not be viewed as an exclusive capability of digital giants but rather as a scalable strategic practice that can be adapted by organizations of varying sizes and resource endowments.

7. CONCLUSION AND FUTURE RESEARCH DIRECTIONS

7.1 Conclusion

The transition from segmentation to hyper-personalization represents a transformative shift in the design and delivery of consumer experiences within AI-driven service ecosystems. By leveraging advanced technologies such as machine learning and predictive analytics, organizations can deliver highly individualized and context-aware interactions that enhance relevance, convenience, and engagement.

The case studies of Netflix and Amazon illustrate that hyper-personalization significantly improves consumer experience by reducing cognitive effort, increasing satisfaction, and enabling seamless interactions. However, the findings also reveal that personalization is not inherently beneficial; its impact is mediated by consumer perceptions of trust, privacy, and fairness.

A key contribution of this chapter is the conceptualization of the personalization–trust paradox, which highlights the dual nature of personalization. While increased personalization enhances value and engagement, it may simultaneously undermine trust if perceived as intrusive, opaque, or manipulative. This paradox underscores the need for a balanced and responsible approach to AI-driven personalization.

Furthermore, the study demonstrates that trust in AI systems is multidimensional, encompassing functional, cognitive, and ethical components. The relative importance of these dimensions varies across contexts, with ethical trust playing a more significant role in high-stakes transactional environments.

Overall, this chapter emphasizes that the success of hyper-personalization depends not only on technological capabilities but also on the ability to build and sustain consumer trust. Organizations that effectively integrate personalization with transparency, ethical practices, and user empowerment are more likely to achieve long-term success in digital service ecosystems.

7.2 Future Research Directions

While this chapter provides valuable insights into hyper-personalization and trust, several avenues for future research remain:

- **Empirical Validation of the Personalization–Trust Paradox**

Future studies can employ quantitative methods to test the proposed propositions and validate the personalization–trust paradox across different contexts and industries.

- **Role of Explainable AI (XAI)**

Further research is needed to examine how explainable AI influences consumer trust and whether transparency can mitigate the negative effects of personalization.

- **Cross-Cultural Perspectives**

Consumer perceptions of personalization and trust may vary across cultures. Comparative studies can explore how cultural factors influence the acceptance of AI-driven personalization.

- **Longitudinal Studies**

Long-term studies can provide insights into how consumer trust evolves over time as users interact with AI systems and become more familiar with personalization technologies.

- **Ethical and Regulatory Frameworks**

Future research can investigate the impact of emerging regulations on AI-driven personalization and explore frameworks for ensuring ethical and responsible AI use.

- **Integration with Emerging Technologies**

The role of hyper-personalization in emerging domains such as the metaverse, voice assistants, and generative AI presents a promising area for future exploration (Kapoor et al., 2026c,d).

- **Hyper-Personalization in Physical and Omnichannel Environments**

AI-driven hyper-personalization is increasingly being deployed in offline and hybrid settings. Sectors such as healthcare, hospitality, physical retail, and financial services are leveraging AI technologies to deliver personalized in-store experiences, tailored healthcare recommendations, intelligent concierge services, and customized financial advice. Future research should investigate how trust is formed and maintained within these omnichannel or "phygital" ecosystems, where consumers interact simultaneously with digital and physical service interfaces.

- AI-Driven Personalization in B2B Contexts

AI-driven personalization is increasingly influencing B2B interactions, including account-based marketing, supplier relationship management, and personalized business solutions. Future research should explore how trust is developed and maintained in AI-mediated interorganizational relationships, as well as examine the role of personalization in shaping long-term business partnerships, organizational buying behavior, and collaborative value creation.

- Psychological Consequences of Hyper-Personalization

Future research should investigate the psychological implications of AI-driven personalization, including Fear of Missing Out (FOMO), compulsive consumption, digital addiction, and consumer well-being. Understanding these unintended consequences would provide a more balanced perspective on the benefits and risks of hyper-personalization.

7.3 Final Reflection

As AI continues to redefine consumer experiences, organizations face the challenge of balancing innovation with responsibility. Hyper-personalization offers immense potential to enhance value creation, but its success ultimately depends on the trust it fosters among consumers. By recognizing and addressing the personalization–trust paradox, firms can navigate the complexities of AI-driven ecosystems and build sustainable, trust-based relationships in the digital age.

REFERENCES

Adomavicius, G., & Tuzhilin, A. (2010). Context-aware recommender systems. In *Recommender systems handbook* (pp. 217–253). Springer US.

Aguirre, E., Mahr, D., Grewal, D., De Ruyter, K., & Wetzels, M. (2015). Unraveling the personalization paradox: The effect of information collection and trust-building strategies on online advertisement effectiveness. *Journal of Retailing*, *91*(1), 34–49. DOI: 10.1016/j.jretai.2014.09.005

Bleier, A., & Eisenbeiss, M. (2015). Personalized online advertising effectiveness: The interplay of what, when, and where. *Marketing Science*, *34*(5), 669–688. DOI: 10.1287/mksc.2015.0930

Buhmann, A., & Fieseler, C. (2021). Towards a deliberative framework for responsible innovation in artificial intelligence. *Technology in Society*, *64*, 101475. DOI: 10.1016/j.techsoc.2020.101475

Davenport, T., Guha, A., Grewal, D., & Bressgott, T. (2020). How artificial intelligence will change the future of marketing. *Journal of the Academy of Marketing Science*, *48*(1), 24–42. DOI: 10.1007/s11747-019-00696-0

Davis, F. D. (1989). Perceived usefulness, perceived ease of use, and user acceptance of information technology. *Management Information Systems Quarterly*, *13*(3), 319–340. DOI: 10.2307/249008

Gartner. (2024). *Predicts 2024: AI powers personalization, revenue growth and efficiency in consumer goods*. Gartner Research. Retrieved from: https://www.gartner.com/en/documents/5285163#:~:text=Summary,for%20margin%20and%20revenue%20growth

Gefen, D., Karahanna, E., & Straub, D. W. (2003). Trust and TAM in online shopping. *Management Information Systems Quarterly*, *27*(1), 51–90. DOI: 10.2307/30036519

Gomez-Uribe, C. A., & Hunt, N. (2015). The netflix recommender system: Algorithms, business value, and innovation. [TMIS]. *ACM Transactions on Management Information Systems*, *6*(4), 1–19. DOI: 10.1145/2843948

Grewal, D., Hulland, J., Kopalle, P. K., & Karahanna, E. (2020). The future of technology and marketing: A multidisciplinary perspective. *Journal of the Academy of Marketing Science*, *48*(1), 1–8. DOI: 10.1007/s11747-019-00711-4

Guerra-Tamez, C. R., Kraul Flores, K., Serna-Mendiburu, G. M., Chavelas Robles, D., & Ibarra Cortés, J. (2024). Decoding Gen Z: AI's influence on brand trust and purchasing behavior. *Frontiers in Artificial Intelligence*, *7*, 1323512. DOI: 10.3389/frai.2024.1323512 PMID: 38500672

Huang, M. H., & Rust, R. T. (2021). A strategic framework for artificial intelligence in marketing. *Journal of the Academy of Marketing Science*, *49*(1), 30–50. DOI: 10.1007/s11747-020-00749-9

Kapoor, A., Jaswal, A., & Sindwani, R. (2026d). Charting the roadmap to metaverse commerce adoption: A cause–effect perspective using fuzzy DEMATEL. *Journal of Modelling in Management*, •••, 1–29. DOI: 10.1108/JM2-07-2025-0352

Kapoor, A., Kapoor, S., & Sindwani, R. (2026b). Governing Artificial Intelligent Ethically: A Human-in-Context Approach to Bias, Fairness, and Accountability. In *The Ethical Landscape of AI: Global Issues and Solutions* (pp. 73-110). IGI Global Scientific Publishing.

Kapoor, A., & Sindwani, R. (2025a). Artificial Intelligence as a Catalyst for Advancing Contactless Payments: Unveiling Key Adoption Drivers. In *AI Marketing and Ethical Considerations in Consumer Engagement* (pp. 321–338). IGI Global Scientific Publishing. DOI: 10.4018/979-8-3373-3476-9.ch016

Kapoor, A., & Sindwani, R. (2025b). Navigating Inhibitors to Artificial Intelligence Adoption in Human Resource Management Practices: A Multi-criteria Decision-making Approach.

Kapoor, A., & Sindwani, R. (2026). AI in Healthcare: Analyzing Adoption Drivers Using Fuzzy AHP. *Innovation in Healthcare Technology and Management*, 139-154.

Kapoor, A., Sindwani, R., & Goel, M. (2025a). Unlocking India's mobile wallet potential: Identifying and prioritising key sustainable growth catalysts using best worst method. *International Journal of Process Management and Benchmarking*, *21*(2), 218–230. DOI: 10.1504/IJPMB.2025.148685

Kapoor, A., Sindwani, R., & Goel, M. (2025b). Assessing mobile wallet service quality using analytic hierarchy process and fuzzy evaluation method. *International Journal of Services and Operations Management*, *50*(2), 246–266. DOI: 10.1504/IJSOM.2025.144481

Kapoor, A., Sindwani, R., Singh, A. K., & Kapoor, S. (2026c). Causal Modeling and Hierarchical Analysis of Critical Factors in Smart Voice Assistant Adoption: A Fuzzy DEMATEL Approach. *Journal of Global Marketing*, •••, 1–21. DOI: 10.1080/08911762.2026.2651270

Kapoor, S., Kapoor, A., & Sindwani, R. (2026a). How Do Leading Brands Win Hearts and Markets? A Case Study Perspective on Customer Centric Strategies. In *Developing an Architecture of Future-Ready Business Excellence* (pp. 179-214). IGI Global Scientific Publishing.

Linden, G., Smith, B., & York, J. (2003). Amazon. com recommendations: Item-to-item collaborative filtering. *IEEE Internet Computing*, *7*(1), 76–80. DOI: 10.1109/MIC.2003.1167344

Lusch, R. F., & Vargo, S. L. (2011). Service-dominant logic: A necessary step. *European Journal of Marketing*, *45*(7-8), 1298–1309. DOI: 10.1108/03090561111137723

Martin, K. D., & Murphy, P. E. (2017). The role of data privacy in marketing. *Journal of the Academy of Marketing Science*, *45*(2), 135–155. DOI: 10.1007/s11747-016-0495-4

McKnight, D. H., Choudhury, V., & Kacmar, C. (2002). Developing and validating trust measures for e-commerce: An integrative typology. *Information Systems Research*, *13*(3), 334–359. DOI: 10.1287/isre.13.3.334.81

Mitchell, M. (2026). *The Influence of Generational Cohort and Gender on Consumer Perceptions of AI-Driven Personalization in E-Commerce Marketing* (Doctoral dissertation, University of Maryland University College).

Morgan, R. M., & Hunt, S. D. (1994). The commitment-trust theory of relationship marketing. *Journal of Marketing*, *58*(3), 20–38. DOI: 10.1177/002224299405800302

Naeimi, M., & Family, Q. (2025). Generation Z and AI-Driven Marketing: Behavioral Traits, Personalization, and Generational Comparison. *Personalization, and Generational Comparison (September 18, 2025).*

Pariser, E. (2011). *The filter bubble: What the Internet is hiding from you.* penguin UK. Castells, P., Hurley, N. J., Vargas, S., Ricci, F., Rokach, L., & Shapira, B. (2015). Recommender systems handbook. *by Francesco Ricci, Lior Rokach, and Bracha Shapira. Boston, MA, USA: Springer US*, 881-918.

Sharma, R., & Kapoor, A. (2026). From Automation to Innovation: The Transformative Impact of AI on Business Functions in India. *Management Dynamics*, *26*(1), 4. DOI: 10.57198/2583-4932.1366

Sipos, D. (2025). The effects of AI-powered personalization on consumer trust, satisfaction, and purchase intent. *European Journal of Applied Science. Engineering and Technology*, *3*(2), 14–24.

Teepapal, T. (2025). AI-driven personalization: Unraveling consumer perceptions in social media engagement. *Computers in Human Behavior, 165*, 108549. DOI: 10.1016/j.chb.2024.108549

Venkatesh, V., & Davis, F. D. (2000). A theoretical extension of the technology acceptance model: Four longitudinal field studies. *Management Science*, *46*(2), 186–204. DOI: 10.1287/mnsc.46.2.186.11926

Wedel, M., & Kannan, P. K. (2016). Marketing analytics for data-rich environments. *Journal of Marketing*, *80*(6), 97–121. DOI: 10.1509/jm.15.0413

KEY TERMS AND DEFINITIONS

AI-Based Service Ecosystem: A digitally connected environment in which artificial intelligence technologies facilitate interactions among consumers, organizations, and service platforms to co-create value through intelligent, automated, and personalized services.

Consumer Experience: The cumulative cognitive, emotional, sensory, and behavioral responses that consumers develop through their interactions with AI-enabled service platforms, influenced by the relevance, convenience, efficiency, and personalization of those interactions.

Consumer Trust: The confidence consumers place in AI-enabled systems based on their perceptions of reliability, predictability, fairness, transparency, and responsible handling of personal data. In this chapter, consumer trust comprises functional, cognitive, and ethical dimensions.

Hyper-Personalization: An AI-driven approach to personalization that leverages real-time data, machine learning, predictive analytics, and contextual information to deliver highly individualized and adaptive consumer experiences tailored to each user's unique preferences and behaviors.

Personalization–Trust Paradox: A phenomenon in which increasing levels of AI-driven personalization simultaneously enhance consumer experience, engagement, and perceived value while potentially undermining trust due to concerns related to privacy, transparency, algorithmic bias, and perceived manipulation.

Chapter 5
The Trust-Loyalty Nexus in AI-Mediated Hyper-Personalized Services:
Transparency, Authenticity, and Vulnerability

Azize Şahin
http://orcid.org/0000-0002-3115-6812
İstanbul University, Turkey

Aysun Sahin
http://orcid.org/0000-0003-3285-1232
Duzce University, Turkey

ABSTRACT

AI-driven hyper-personalization is transforming service encounters by tailoring information, offers, and interactions to individual consumers in real time. Across retail, banking, healthcare, and hospitality, providers increasingly rely on predictive models, recommender systems, automated decision tools, and conversational interfaces to adapt service content at the level of the single customer. Yet the rapid expansion of algorithmic personalization has not been matched by a comparable growth in consumer trust, and this widening gap raises a central question for service marketing: when does AI-enabled personalization deepen durable loyalty, and when does it produce shallow, fragile, or actively eroding relationships?

DOI: 10.4018/979-8-3373-9159-5.ch005

1. INTRODUCTION

Artificial intelligence has moved from experimental service innovation to the core infrastructure of customer experience management. IBM's Global AI Adoption Index reported that 42% of enterprise-scale companies had already deployed AI, while another 40% were still exploring or experimenting with AI without full deployment (IBM, 2024). More recent evidence from McKinsey shows that organizations are also moving toward agentic AI systems: 23% of surveyed organizations were scaling AI agents in at least one business function, and 39% were experimenting with them (McKinsey & Company, 2025). These figures indicate that AI-mediated service encounters are becoming routine rather than exceptional. For service researchers, this shift is theoretically consequential because AI does not merely accelerate existing service processes; it restructures how information is collected, options are curated, recommendations are justified, and consumers decide whether a provider deserves continued trust.

However, the expansion of AI-mediated personalization has not been matched by equivalent growth in consumer trust. Salesforce's State of the AI Connected Customer report, based on more than 16,000 consumers and business buyers, shows that only 42% of customers trust businesses to use AI ethically, with the figure declining from 58% in 2023 (Salesforce, 2024). This decline is especially important for hyper-personalized services because consumers are asked to exchange data, attention, and decision autonomy for relevance, convenience, and adaptive service experiences. The central managerial problem is therefore not whether AI can personalize service encounters, but whether such personalization is perceived as competent, transparent, authentic, and respectful of consumer vulnerability. This trust gap provides the conceptual starting point for the present study: AI-driven hyper-personalization can strengthen loyalty only when consumers interpret algorithmic adaptation as legitimate, explainable, and aligned with their interests, rather than as opaque surveillance or relational manipulation.

Artificial intelligence–driven hyper-personalization is reshaping the architecture of contemporary service encounters. Service organizations are increasingly using predictive models, recommender systems, automated decision tools, conversational interfaces, and data-rich analytics to tailor service content, offers, and interactions at the level of the individual consumer. Across retail, banking, healthcare, and hospitality, such systems infer preferences, combine behavioral and financial data, and tailor information, offers, and service pathways to the individual—applications examined in detail in Section 6. These developments indicate a shift from standardized service propositions to dynamically adaptive, algorithmically mediated service ecosystems (Huang & Rust, 2018; Wedel & Kannan, 2016; Wirtz et al., 2018).

Within these service environments, consumer trust becomes a central mechanism linking AI-enabled personalization to satisfaction, continued use, and loyalty. Trust has long been recognized as a core antecedent of relational exchange and digital service adoption (Gefen et al., 2003; McKnight et al., 2002). Mayer et al. (1995) define trust as the willingness to accept vulnerability based on positive expectations about another party. This definition is particularly relevant for AI-mediated services because consumers often cannot fully monitor how data are collected, how recommendations are generated, or how algorithmic decisions affect service outcomes. Hyper-personalization increases the need for trust.

This chapter is motivated by three limitations of the existing literature. The first limitation concerns the dimensionality of trust. Classical trust theory distinguishes competence-related beliefs from benevolence- and integrity-related beliefs (Mayer et al., 1995; Schoorman et al., 2007). In service settings, these dimensions map onto cognitive trust and affective or relational trust. AI-driven personalization may strengthen cognitive trust when it delivers accurate and timely recommendations; however, it may weaken affective trust when personalization feels intrusive, manipulative, or misaligned with consumers' interests. Therefore, treating trust as a single construct can conceal theoretically important asymmetries in consumer responses.

The second limitation concerns the transparency of algorithms. Research on explainable AI often conceptualizes transparency as an informational intervention that helps users understand system logic and calibrate trust to performance (Rai, 2020). However, in consumer services, transparency is a market signal. Consumers rarely possess the technical expertise required to evaluate an underlying model. Instead, they interpret explanations, data use disclosures, and opt-out controls as signs of organizational openness, fairness, and respect for autonomy. Therefore, signaling theory is useful because it explains how observable cues reduce uncertainty under information asymmetry (Connelly et al., 2011; Spence, 1973).

Third, the role of consumer vulnerability remains underdeveloped. Vulnerability is not a fixed demographic label. It is a contextually activated condition that arises when consumers face power imbalances, resource constraints, limited knowledge, situational stress, or dependency in marketplace interactions (Baker et al., 2005; OECD, 2023). Hyper-personalized AI systems can intensify consumer vulnerability by making inferences that consumers do not expect, cannot contest, or understand. In high-stakes sectors such as healthcare and financial services, vulnerability makes trust more fragile and raises ethical thresholds for personalization.

This chapter develops an integrative conceptual framework for understanding the trust–loyalty nexus in AI-mediated hyper-personalized service. It combines cognitive–affective trust theory, signaling theory, and consumer vulnerability literature to explain when AI-enabled personalization strengthens durable loyalty and when it creates shallow or eroding relationships with consumers. It contributes to service marketing by treating trust as a dynamic relational resource that is actively shaped by the design and governance of AI-mediated personalization. It also introduces a trust trajectory typology that distinguishes trust-building, trust-neutral, and trust-eroding paths over time. The core argument can be stated in three linked claims. First, AI-driven hyper-personalization initially generates cognitive trust by demonstrating relevance, accuracy, and responsiveness. Second, whether this cognitive trust converts into affective trust depends on algorithmic transparency and perceived authenticity, which together signal benevolence and integrity. Third, consumer vulnerability sets the threshold condition for this conversion and amplifies the risk of trust erosion when personalization is opaque, intrusive, or misaligned with consumer interests. This conditional conversion logic—from cognitive to affective trust, gated by transparency, authenticity, and vulnerability—is the chapter's central theoretical contribution and the mechanism that the trust trajectory typology operationalizes.

This chapter is conceptual rather than empirical; its purpose is to synthesize fragmented literatures on trust, transparency, authenticity, and vulnerability into a single integrative framework. The propositions developed below are therefore offered as scaffolding for future empirical work rather than as a formally tested model. This chapter proceeds as follows. Section 2 reviews consumer trust in AI-mediated services. Section 3 develops the theoretical foundations, including cognitive–affective trust theory, signaling theory, consumer vulnerability, and perceived authenticity. Section 4 presents the integrative conceptual framework, first specifying its core processes (4.1) and then the boundary conditions that qualify the trust–loyalty nexus (4.2). Section 5 introduces the trust trajectory typology. Section 6 provides sectoral illustrations in retail, banking, healthcare, and hospitality. Section 7 outlines the research agenda. Section 8 presents managerial and ethical implications. Section 9 concludes.

2. CONSUMER TRUST IN AI-MEDIATED SERVICES

Consumer trust in AI-mediated services has become a central construct for explaining adoption, continued use, and loyalty across contemporary service industries. Trust is particularly salient because AI systems are typically opaque to lay users. Consumers cannot directly observe how algorithms process data, prioritize alternatives, generate recommendations, or align service outputs with organizational incentives. They must therefore rely on indirect cues when deciding whether to accept automated recommendations, disclose personal data, use algorithmic advice, or allow an AI-enabled interface to structure their decision processes. In this context, trust operates as a complexity-reducing mechanism that enables consumers to act under conditions of limited technical understanding, asymmetric information, and uncertain accountability (Gefen et al., 2003; Mayer et al., 1995; McKnight et al., 2002).

In AI-mediated services, trust has multiple objects. Consumers may trust the AI system, service provider, human professionals supervising the system, platform infrastructure, or institutional safeguards that govern data use. These trust layers are interdependent rather than isolated. Trust in the provider can transfer to the AI application when the organization is perceived as competent, benevolent, and ethically responsible. Conversely, a poorly explained, inaccurate, or unfair AI experience can feed back into distrust toward the organization itself. This layered trust architecture is central to hyper-personalized services because AI systems are not experienced as detached technical artifacts. They are interpreted as extensions of the provider's service logic, data governance practices, and relational intentions (Flavián et al., 2022; Gefen et al., 2003; McKnight et al., 2002).

Existing research on AI in services shows that perceived reliability, technology readiness, awareness, perceived usefulness, and service context influence consumers' willingness to adopt and use AI-enabled services (Flavián et al., 2022; Huang & Rust, 2018). However, adoption alone does not adequately explain customer loyalty. Consumers may initially use AI-mediated services because they are convenient, novel, embedded in existing platforms, or difficult to avoid. Long-term loyalty, however, requires a more durable perception that the provider uses AI in ways that are accurate, fair, beneficial, and respectful of consumer interests. Therefore, the trust–loyalty nexus depends not only on functional performance but also on consumers' relational interpretation of how and why AI is used.

The personalization–privacy paradox illustrates this ambivalence. Personalization can increase relevance, reduce search costs, and improve decision efficiency; however, it can also heighten concerns about information collection, surveillance, profiling, and unfair use of personal data (Aguirre et al., 2015; Awad & Krishnan, 2006; Bleier & Eisenbeiss, 2015; Cloarec et al., 2022). This paradox becomes sharper under hyper-personalization because AI systems infer not only stated preferences but also latent interests, behavioral patterns, habits, vulnerabilities, and propensities. What appears to the firm as improved customer understanding may be experienced by the consumer as an intrusion into private life. Thus, the same personalization capability can strengthen cognitive trust by increasing perceived accuracy while weakening affective trust if consumers question the provider's motives or respect for boundaries.

Recommendation agents provide an early illustration of this tension. Personalization and familiarity can increase trust in recommendation agents; however, such trust depends on how consumers interpret the agent's role, competence, and intentions (Komiak & Benbasat, 2006). Contemporary AI systems extend this problem because they are more adaptive, data-intensive, and deeply embedded in the service journey. Consumers may revise their trust judgments as they encounter new algorithmic actions, explanation cues, personalization errors, perceived boundary violations, or recovery efforts. Therefore, trust in AI-mediated services should be treated as a dynamic and revisable judgment rather than a stable attitude formed at the moment of adoption.

Healthcare further illustrates the fragility of trust in AI-mediated services. Patients may resist medical AI, even when algorithmic systems are statistically accurate, because healthcare decisions are deeply personal, emotionally charged, and tied to expectations of human care (Longoni et al., 2019). Trust in healthcare AI also depends on implementation processes, perceived human oversight, explainability, and the alignment between AI recommendations and professional judgment (Steerling et al., 2023). These insights are relevant beyond healthcare because they show that technical competence alone rarely guarantees relational acceptance. In high-stakes services, consumers expect organizations to remain accountable for AI-mediated outcomes, especially when the consequences affect health, finances, identity, or personal autonomy.

Service robot research offers a similar insight from frontline service contexts. Automation changes service experience by altering expectations about social presence, empathy, accountability, and recovery (van Doorn et al., 2017; Wirtz et al., 2018). Although service robots differ from back-end personalization algorithms, both forms of AI mediate consumer experience and reconfigure the locus of agency in service delivery. The common implication is that trust must be theorized not only as belief in technological capability but also as belief in the provider's relational and ethical stance.

3. THEORETICAL FOUNDATIONS

3.1. Cognitive and Affective Trust Theory

Cognitive–affective trust theory distinguishes between competence-based beliefs and relational beliefs. Mayer et al. (1995) conceptualize trust as rooted in perceptions of ability, benevolence, and integrity. McKnight et al. (2002) further distinguish trusting beliefs, institution-based trust, and trusting intentions in e-commerce. Cognitive trust refers to beliefs about whether the trustee can perform reliably and competently. Affective or relational trust refers to beliefs about whether the trustee is benevolent, honest, and concerned with the trustor's interests.

This distinction is essential for AI-mediated services. Cognitive trust concerns whether the AI system works, whether recommendations are accurate, whether service predictions are useful, whether automated decisions are consistent, and whether the interface reduces effort. Affective trust concerns whether the organization behind the AI acts with care and integrity, whether data use respects boundaries, whether personalization is fair, whether vulnerable consumers are protected, and whether human support remains available when algorithmic decisions matter.

Hyper-personalization can create trust asymmetry. A highly accurate recommender may increase cognitive trust while reducing affective trust if consumers feel that the system knows too much or uses sensitive inferences without permission. A healthcare AI tool may appear technically sophisticated while failing to convey compassion or human accountability. A banking algorithm may correctly identify financial needs while simultaneously raising concerns about exploitation if it targets high-cost products to financially fragile consumers. The key theoretical point is that competence and benevolence do not necessarily move together.

This asymmetry has direct loyalty implications. Cognitive trust may support initial adoption and routine use, especially in low-risk service contexts. Affective trust is more important for durable loyalty because it anchors commitment, forgiveness, and resistance to switching. If AI-mediated personalization produces cognitive trust without affective trust, loyalty may remain shallow and convenience-based. However, if it builds both, loyalty becomes more resilient. Recent empirical work supports this two-dimensional view and extends it beyond Western samples. In a study of 632 Chinese consumers, Zhao et al. (2025) found that cognitive and affective trust jointly form overall trust in AI agents, which in turn drives acceptance and ethical expectations. Because trust in AI is culturally contingent—shaped by power distance, uncertainty avoidance, and prevailing attitudes toward automation—evidence from non-Western contexts is important for assessing how widely the cognitive–affective structure travels, a point developed further in the research agenda.

3.2. Signaling Theory and Algorithmic Transparency

Signaling theory explains how actors reduce uncertainty when one party holds information that the other party cannot directly observe. Spence (1973) originally developed the logic of signaling under information asymmetry, and Connelly et al. (2011) extended signaling theory to management contexts. In AI-mediated services, providers and their technical teams know much more than consumers about model design, training data, inference logic, and commercial objectives. Consumers must therefore interpret signals that indicate whether the provider is trustworthy.

Algorithmic transparency operates as such a signal. Transparency may include data use notices, explanation interfaces, reason codes, model limitations, privacy dashboards, human review options, and third-party audit indicators. These signals do not require consumers to be technical experts. Their relational function is to communicate openness, accountability, and respect for consumer agency. Rai (2020) argues that explainable AI moves systems from black-box to glass-box conditions; however, the consumer-facing meaning of explanation is not only technical. It is also symbolic and relational. This distinction marks a difference between how transparency is treated in computer science and how it operates in consumer research. In the explainable AI literature, transparency is largely a technical property of the model, achieved through interpretability methods and post-hoc explanations that expose how an output was produced (Mersha et al., 2024). In consumer services, by contrast, transparency is a relational signal whose meaning depends on whether disclosures are perceived as credible, usable, and sincere rather than merely available. Park and Yoon (2024) show empirically that algorithm transparency signaling increases user trust and relational satisfaction, indicating that the value of explanation lies as much in its signaling function as in its technical content. The framework advanced here bridges these views: it treats the technical interpretability emphasized in computer science as the raw material that, once interpreted by consumers, becomes a relational signal of accountability.

Transparency signals are credible when they are specific, usable, and consistent with observable practice. Generic privacy statements or complex legal disclosures may fail because they signal compliance rather than care. In contrast, clear explanations of why a recommendation appears, which data categories were used, how consumers can modify preferences, and how they can contest an AI-mediated decision can support both cognitive and affective trust. In this sense, transparency is a governance interface between organizational intention and consumer interpretation.

3.3. Consumer Vulnerability

Consumer vulnerability literature adds a crucial boundary condition to the trust–loyalty nexus. Baker et al. (2005) define vulnerability as a state of powerlessness arising from imbalances in marketplace interactions. Vulnerability can be informational, financial, emotional, physical, situational, or structural. The OECD (2023) emphasizes that digital environments can amplify vulnerability because data-driven systems may be difficult for consumers to observe, understand, or contest.

AI-mediated hyper-personalization can intensify vulnerability in three ways. First, it can expand informational asymmetry by allowing firms to infer sensitive traits or conditions that consumers did not intentionally disclose. Second, it can reduce perceived control when consumers cannot understand or contest personalization logic. Third, it can create dependency when consumers rely on a service provider in high-stakes contexts, such as health, finance, mobility, or care. Under these conditions, the same personalization practice may be experienced as helpful by one consumer and exploitative by another.

Therefore, vulnerability moderates the influence of transparency and personalization on trust. Low-vulnerability consumers may tolerate limited transparency if personalization is useful and low-risk. High-vulnerability consumers require stronger safeguards, clearer explanations, more conservative data use, and human support. In the absence of such safeguards, trust can erode, even when the algorithmic system performs efficiently.

Table 1. Theoretical Lenses for the Trust-Loyalty Nexus in AI-Mediated Services

Theoretical Lens	Core Concept	Role in the Chapter	Main Risk if Used Alone
Cognitive and Affective Trust Theory	Trust includes competence, benevolence, and integrity beliefs.	Explains how AI personalization can build technical confidence while weakening relational trust.	May understate information asymmetry and market signaling.
Signaling Theory	Observable signals reduce uncertainty in the presence of information asymmetry.	Explains how transparency, explanations, and controls communicate credibility and accountability.	May overemphasize cues without examining vulnerable consumers.
Consumer Vulnerability Literature	Vulnerability arises from contextual power, information, and resource imbalances.	Explains why the same personalization practice can empower some consumers and threaten others.	May understate the technical and relational complexity of AI systems.
Perceived Authenticity	Authenticity reflects perceived genuineness, consistency, and alignment with values.	Explains why competence alone does not guarantee relational trust; personalization must feel sincere.	May overemphasize subjective perception without structural safeguards.

3.4. Perceived Authenticity as a Relational Trust Cue

Perceived authenticity provides an important relational bridge between hyper-personalization and consumer trust. In AI-mediated services, personalization may signal competence; however, competence alone does not guarantee that consumers will perceive the provider as sincere, benevolent, or worthy of loyalty. A recommendation can be accurate yet still feel exploitative. A chatbot can be responsive yet still feel scripted. A personalized offer can be relevant yet still raise doubts about whether the provider is genuinely serving the consumer's interests. For this reason, perceived authenticity should be treated as a relational trust cue that shapes whether AI-driven hyper-personalization strengthens or weakens affective trust. To avoid conceptual overlap, the chapter draws a clear boundary: perceived authenticity is not synonymous with affective trust, nor is it a sub-dimension of it. Rather, it is an interpretive cue through which consumers infer the benevolence, sincerity, and relational alignment that constitute affective trust. In the framework advanced here, authenticity functions as a mediating interpretation that links transparency signals to affective trust, whereas affective trust is the resulting relational belief itself.

Brand authenticity refers to the extent to which consumers perceive a brand to be genuine, credible, consistent, and true to its values (Morhart et al., 2015). In branding research, authenticity is linked to perceptions of sincerity, continuity, integrity, and symbolic value (Beverland, 2005; Napoli et al., 2014). These dimensions are especially relevant in AI-mediated service settings because hyper-personalization creates a form of simulated intimacy. AI systems can address consumers by name, remember their prior interactions, infer their preferences, and anticipate their needs. Such behaviors may be interpreted as attentive service when they are consistent with the provider's identity, service promises, and ethical commitments. However, these same behaviors may be interpreted as artificial closeness or manipulative familiarity when consumers perceive a gap between personalized interaction and genuine organizational care.

This distinction is central to the cognitive–affective structure of trust. Hyper-personalization strengthens cognitive trust by demonstrating technical accuracy, predictive capability, and service efficiency. However, affective trust depends on whether consumers believe that the provider is acting with benevolence and integrity (Mayer et al., 1995; McKnight et al., 2002). Perceived authenticity operates as a cue through which consumers infer relational qualities. When personalization is consistent with the brand's stated values, prior conduct, and service role, it reinforces affective trust. For example, a healthcare provider that uses AI to tailor follow-up reminders, explain treatment options, and support patient understanding may be perceived as authentically patient-centered if the personalization is transparent and clinically appropriate. By contrast, the same level of personalization may undermine authenticity if it appears to prioritize cost reduction, cross-selling, or behavioral control.

Perceived authenticity also explains why transparency alone is insufficient. Transparency functions as a governance interface that discloses how personalization works; however, authenticity concerns why personalization is being used and whose interests it serves. A service provider can technically explain an algorithm while still appearing opportunistic if the personalization feels misaligned with consumer welfare. This is particularly important in the personalization–privacy paradox, where consumers value relevance but become uncomfortable when firms infer sensitive information or use personal data in unexpected ways (Aguirre et al., 2015; Awad & Krishnan, 2006; Bleier & Eisenbeiss, 2015). In such contexts, authenticity depends not only on disclosure but also on restraint. Consumers are more likely to perceive personalization as authentic when the provider uses data in ways that are proportionate, contextually appropriate, and visibly connected to service improvement rather than purely for commercial extraction.

Perceived authenticity further clarifies the difference between trust-building and trust-neutral trajectories. In a trust-building trajectory, personalization is not merely useful; it is experienced as a credible expression of the provider's commitment to service. Consumers perceive that AI is being used to support care, convenience, fairness, or empowerment in ways that fit the provider's identity. In a trust-neutral trajectory, personalization may remain functionally effective, but relationally thin. The system works, but it does not generate a stronger sense of sincerity, care, or identification. In a trust-eroding trajectory, personalization may be interpreted as inauthentic because it simulates concern while serving hidden commercial or surveillance goals. This is where hyper-personalization becomes relationally risky: the more intimate the interaction feels, the more damaging perceived inauthenticity becomes.

Consumer vulnerability intensifies the role of authenticity. Vulnerable consumers may be especially sensitive to whether AI-mediated personalization feels supportive or exploitative. In high-stakes contexts such as healthcare, banking, insurance, and elder services, consumers often depend on providers and may lack the ability to evaluate algorithmic decisions fully. For these consumers, authenticity is not a decorative brand attribute; it is a protective trust cue. Personalization that acknowledges vulnerability, preserves dignity, and provides meaningful human oversight can strengthen affective trust. Personalization that targets vulnerability for persuasion, upselling, or behavioral influence can erode trust, even when the immediate recommendation is technically accurate (Baker et al., 2005; Trinh, 2025).

Accordingly, perceived authenticity should be embedded in the framework of this chapter as a relational interpretation mechanism. AI-driven hyper-personalization affects consumer trust not only through relevance, accuracy, and transparency, but also through the perceived authenticity of the provider's motives and conduct. The central question is not whether the AI system personalizes effectively. The stronger theoretical question is whether personalization is experienced as a genuine extension of the provider's service promise or as an algorithmically produced simulation of care. This distinction is critical for understanding why some AI-mediated services deepen loyalty, whereas others generate discomfort, distrust, and resistance.

Because these constructs are closely related, it is useful to fix their boundaries before turning to the framework. In this chapter, cognitive trust refers to beliefs about competence, reliability, and accuracy—whether the AI system works. Affective trust refers to beliefs about benevolence, integrity, and care—whether the provider acts in the consumer's interest; it is the relational core of what some authors term relational trust, and the two terms are used interchangeably here. Perceived authenticity is not a form of trust but an interpretive cue through which consumers infer benevolence and sincerity, thereby shaping affective trust. Transparency is a signal that simultaneously supports cognitive trust, by making personalization predictable, and affective trust, by communicating accountability. Consumer vulnerability is a contextually activated condition that moderates how strongly these cues translate into trust. Holding these distinctions fixed allows the framework to specify not merely that these constructs matter, but how each one enters the conversion from cognitive to affective trust.

4. INTEGRATIVE CONCEPTUAL FRAMEWORK

4.1. Core Processes in the Integrative Framework

The proposed framework conceptualizes AI-driven hyper-personalization as a sociotechnical configuration that continuously tailors service encounters through algorithms, data infrastructures, interfaces, and organizational routines. This is not merely a technical capability. It is a relational system that shapes how consumers interpret providers' competence, benevolence, fairness, and authenticity. The framework specifies three core processes: cognitive and affective trust formation, transparency signaling, and vulnerability moderation.

The first process is cognitive and affective trust formation. AI-driven hyper-personalization influences cognitive trust through perceived relevance, accuracy, timeliness, and reliability. A system that anticipates needs, reduces search costs, and adapts smoothly to the context demonstrates competence. Simultaneously, hyper-personalization influences affective trust through perceived motives, authenticity, respect for privacy, and fairness. Consumers not only ask whether the system works but also whether it works for them or on them.

The second process is transparency signaling. Algorithmic transparency, explainability, consent interfaces, and contestability mechanisms shape how consumers interpret a provider's hidden practices. Transparency can strengthen cognitive trust by making personalization more predictable and procedurally understandable. It can also strengthen affective trust by signaling that the provider respects consumer autonomy and is willing to be accountable. However, transparency can backfire if it is vague, excessive, inconsistent, or presented as legal protection rather than consumer support.

The third process is vulnerability moderation. Consumer vulnerability shapes the threshold at which personalization becomes intrusive, the degree of explanation needed to sustain trust, and the extent to which consumers can act on the available controls. Vulnerable consumers may require stronger safeguards, even when personalization is accurate. In high-stakes services, vulnerability-sensitive design is essential. This is part of the legitimacy of AI-mediated service innovation.

The framework links these processes to loyalty outcomes. When hyper-personalization enhances cognitive and affective trust, and when transparency signals and vulnerability safeguards are credible, loyalty is likely to deepen. When personalization enhances only cognitive trust, loyalty may remain functional and fragile. When personalization is opaque, intrusive, or unfair, especially for vulnerable consumers, trust erosion can lead to avoidance, complaints, switching, negative word of mouth, and regulatory concerns.

Table 2. Core Processes in the Integrative Framework

Core Process	Trust Dimension Affected	Mechanism	Loyalty Implication
Cognitive and affective trust formation	Personalization is interpreted through both competence beliefs and relational beliefs about the provider.	Relevance, accuracy, and timeliness build cognitive trust, while perceived motives, authenticity, and privacy respect shape affective trust.	Cognitive gains alone yield fragile, convenience-based loyalty; combined cognitive and affective gains deepen it.
Transparency signaling	Explanations, consent interfaces, and contestability disclose otherwise hidden personalization practices.	Credible, usable signals make personalization predictable and communicate accountability and respect for autonomy.	Specific and consistent signals reinforce loyalty; vague or compliance-only signals can backfire and raise suspicion.
Vulnerability moderation	Consumer vulnerability conditions the threshold at which personalization becomes intrusive and the safeguards required.	Vulnerability sets how much explanation, conservative data use, and human oversight are needed to sustain trust.	Unaddressed vulnerability accelerates trust erosion even when the system performs accurately.

4.2. Boundary Conditions of the Trust-Loyalty Nexus

The trust–loyalty nexus in AI-mediated hyper-personalized services is not uniform across consumers, technologies, and service settings. Therefore, the framework developed in this study should be interpreted conditionally rather than universally. AI-driven personalization may strengthen trust and loyalty when it improves relevance, reduces effort, and communicates respect for consumer agency. However, the same personalization logic may weaken trust when the service context is high-risk, the data used are sensitive, the consumer is vulnerable, transparency is weak, or human oversight is absent. Boundary conditions clarify when hyper-personalization becomes a trust-building resource and when it becomes a source of perceived manipulation, surveillance, or relational breach.

Service risk is a primary boundary condition. In low-risk services, such as routine retail recommendations or entertainment suggestions, consumers may tolerate limited transparency if personalization is convenient and accurate. In high-risk services, such as healthcare, financial advice, insurance, credit scoring, or safety-related hospitality services, the tolerance for opacity is much lower. Errors in these contexts may produce material, emotional, or social harm. Consequently, consumers are more likely to demand explanations, accountability, and human reviews. Prior research on medical AI has shown that consumers may resist algorithmic recommendations even when AI systems perform accurately because health-related decisions are closely tied to human care, empathy, and perceived uniqueness (Longoni et al., 2019). This suggests that the same AI capability may be evaluated differently depending on the perceived consequences of accepting its output.

Data sensitivity is another critical condition. Hyper-personalization based on purchase histories, browsing behavior, or location data may already raise privacy concerns; however, personalization based on inferred health status, financial distress, emotional vulnerability, family circumstances, or identity-related attributes is more likely to trigger discomfort. The personalization–privacy paradox demonstrates that consumers value relevance but also resist profiling when they perceive limited control over personal information (Aguirre et al., 2015; Awad & Krishnan, 2006; Cloarec et al., 2024). Experimental evidence reinforces this boundary: Kim and Han (2025) show that highly personalized messages can backfire when situational privacy concern is high, so that the same personalization depth that helps under low concern reduces favorable responses under high concern. Under high data sensitivity, transparency must move beyond generic privacy notices. Consumers need to understand what data are used, why the data are relevant, how inferences are generated, and whether they can contest or disable personalization. Without such controls, personalization may erode affective trust, even when it improves functional outcomes.

Consumer vulnerability further influences trust formation. Vulnerability may arise from age, limited digital literacy, financial fragility, illness, dependency, emotional stress, or restricted access to alternatives (Baker et al., 2005). Vulnerable consumers may experience AI-mediated personalization as more threatening because they have fewer resources to interpret, resist, or correct the algorithmic influence. For example, a financially secure consumer may perceive personalized credit offers as convenient, whereas a financially distressed consumer may perceive the same targeting as exploitative. Similarly, a digitally skilled patient may appreciate AI-supported health monitoring, whereas a patient with low health literacy may feel overwhelmed or disempowered by it. Therefore, vulnerability intensifies the need for accessible explanations, conservative personalization boundaries, and visible human support.

Quality of transparency is also central. Transparency is not merely the amount of information disclosed; it is the extent to which explanations are understandable, timely, relevant, and actionable. Long legalistic disclosures may satisfy formal requirements while doing little to support trust. From a signaling perspective, transparency works when it credibly communicates openness, fairness, and respect for consumer agency (Connelly et al., 2011; Spence, 1973). High-quality transparency explains the basis of personalization in language that consumers can understand, provides meaningful choices, and allows for correction or contestation. Low-quality transparency, by contrast, can become performative. It may even increase distrust if consumers interpret it as a defensive or symbolic gesture rather than a genuine accountability mechanism.

Human oversight moderates the relationship between AI-mediated personalization and trust. In routine, low-risk services, consumers may fully accept fully automated personalization if the outcomes are useful and reversible. In high-stakes or emotionally sensitive services, visible human oversight becomes a trust-preserving safeguard. Human professionals can contextualize algorithmic outputs, interpret exceptions, and provide empathy when consumers experience uncertainty or harm. Service robot and AI service research has shown that automation alters expectations regarding accountability, empathy, and recovery (van Doorn et al., 2017; Wirtz et al., 2018). Thus, human oversight should not be treated as a technical add-on. It is a relational signal that the provider remains accountable for AI-mediated decisions.

The regulatory context also shapes trust and loyalty. Stronger regulatory environments may increase consumer confidence by establishing baseline protections for data rights, automated decision-making, and accountability. In the European Union, for example, the General Data Protection Regulation establishes rights to information and to meaningful explanation of automated decisions, while the AI Act introduces risk-based obligations and transparency requirements for higher-risk AI systems; together they illustrate how data-protection and AI-specific rules increasingly govern personalization. However, compliance alone is insufficient to generate trust. Consumers may not know the details of regulatory protections, and formal compliance may not address perceived fairness, authenticity, or emotional discomfort. In AI-mediated services, regulation provides a floor, but trust requires relationally meaningful practices. Firms that treat regulation as the minimum standard and add clearer explanations, stronger consent mechanisms, and accessible human reviews are more likely to sustain trust-building trajectories.

Service sector differences further qualify the framework. Retail personalization often centers on convenience, product discovery, and promotional relevance. Banking personalization involves financial risk, fairness, and long-term welfare. Healthcare personalization involves bodily vulnerability, emotional sensitivity, and professional responsibility. Hospitality personalization occupies a relational and experiential space in which comfort, privacy, and personal recognition are central. These sectoral differences mean that trust cues are not interchangeable. A recommendation explanation that is sufficient in retail may be inadequate in banking, and an automated reminder that is helpful in hospitality may feel intrusive in healthcare.

Finally, consumer AI literacy and prior trust in the provider shape how consumers interpret personalization. Consumers with higher AI literacy may be better able to understand algorithmic limits, evaluate explanations, and distinguish useful personalization from manipulative targeting. Consumers with lower AI literacy may rely more heavily on brand reputation, interface cues and institutional signals. Trust in the provider can also be transferred to the AI system, especially when consumers lack direct knowledge of technology. However, this transfer can operate in reverse; a poorly explained AI failure may damage trust in the organization. Therefore, the trust–loyalty nexus is recursive in nature. Provider trust shapes AI trust, and AI-mediated experiences reshape this trust.

Overall, these boundary conditions show that AI-driven hyper-personalization should not be evaluated based solely on accuracy, relevance, or conversion. Its trust implications depend on the interaction among service risk, data sensitivity, vulnerability, transparency quality, human oversight, regulatory context, sector characteristics, AI literacy, and prior provider trust. This conditional view strengthens the framework by explaining why the same personalization practice may generate loyalty in one context, indifference in another, and distrust in a third.

5. TRUST TRAJECTORY TYPOLOGY

Drawing on the integrative framework, this section introduces a typology of trust trajectories that captures how trust in AI-mediated services evolves under different configurations of hyper-personalization, transparency signaling, and consumer vulnerability. Rather than treating trust as a static level, the typology emphasizes dynamic patterns over time, drawing inspiration from longitudinal research on trust development and repair in marketing and relationship science. The typology distinguishes among three ideal-type trajectories: trust-building, trust-neutral, and trust-eroding. These trajectories represent analytically distinct patterns that can coexist within the same service ecosystem across different segments and contexts. To keep the categories conceptually disciplined, each trajectory is defined by a specific configuration of the two trust dimensions rather than by surface features alone. A trust-building trajectory combines high cognitive trust with high affective trust. A trust-neutral trajectory combines moderate-to-high cognitive trust with low affective trust, which is why loyalty in this state remains functional and easily disrupted rather than relational. A trust-eroding trajectory is marked by declining affective trust followed by declining cognitive trust. Defining the categories through these paired levels distinguishes trust-neutral, in particular, from a mere label for convenience dependence: it is the specific state in which competence beliefs are satisfied but relational beliefs are not.

The following propositions formalize the relationships proposed in the framework.

P1. When AI-driven hyper-personalization is perceived as relevant and respectful and transparency signals are credible, cognitive and affective trust reinforce each other, producing a trust-building trajectory.

P2. When personalization enhances functional outcomes but transparency signals are weak or compliance-oriented, cognitive trust develops without corresponding affective trust, producing a trust-neutral trajectory.

P3. When personalization is perceived as intrusive or opaque, especially under high vulnerability, both cognitive and affective trust deteriorate, producing a trust-eroding trajectory.

5.1. Trust-Building Trajectory

The trust-building trajectory describes a reinforcing cycle in which AI-driven personalization strengthens both cognitive and affective trust. Consumers experience personalization as relevant, respectful, and aligned with their goals. Recommendations reduce effort without crossing perceived privacy boundaries. Dynamic offers are perceived as fair, rather than opportunistic. Service interfaces make the experience easier without displacing meaningful consumer controls.

Transparency is central to this trajectory in the study. Clear explanations of why a recommendation appears, what data were used, and how preferences can be modified help consumers understand personalization as legitimate. These signals support cognitive trust by clarifying system logic and affective trust by communicating respect for users. Vulnerability is either low or actively mitigated through conservative personalization, accessible support, and human oversight.

Loyalty in this trajectory is robust. Consumers are more likely to continue using the service, recommend it, forgive minor errors, and view AI-enabled personalization as part of the provider's value proposition. The provider's AI capability becomes a relational asset rather than a purely functional feature.

5.2. Trust-Neutral Trajectory

Trust-neutral trajectory arises when personalization improves functional outcomes but fails to generate deeper relational trust. Consumers may believe that the system works; however, they do not necessarily perceive the provider as caring, transparent, or authentic. Personalization remains a convenience feature. It reduces search costs and increases efficiency; however, it does not create emotional attachment or strong relational commitment.

This trajectory often appears in low-involvement service contexts, where consumers value speed and convenience over relationship depth. This may also occur when transparency is present only at the compliance level. Consumers are neither alarmed nor reassured by this. Therefore, loyalty is shallow, driven by habit, switching costs, or the lack of a better alternative.

Trust-neutral conditions can be risky for vulnerable consumers. Continued use may mask anxiety or dependence. When cognitive trust exists without affective trust, a single failure, unexpected data use, or unexplained decision can quickly move consumers into a trust-eroding trajectory.

5.3. Trust-Eroding Trajectory

Trust-eroding trajectory occurs when hyper-personalization is experienced as intrusive, opaque, unfair, or manipulative. Consumers may feel that the provider is exploiting superior information rather than creating mutual value. Highly targeted messages that reveal sensitive inferences can create discomfort. Dynamic pricing or personalized offers may be interpreted as discriminatory when consumers cannot understand the basis of the variation.

Affective trust usually deteriorates first because consumers question the provider's benevolence and integrity. Cognitive trust can decline when recommendations are inconsistent, biased or difficult to explain. In the absence of credible transparency signals, consumers may infer that the system is incompetent or exploitative. Vulnerability amplifies the severity of this trajectory because vulnerable consumers incur greater costs when service decisions are inaccurate, unfair, or difficult to challenge.

The loyalty outcomes in this trajectory are negative. Consumers may reduce their use, switch providers, complain publicly, resist data sharing, or seek regulatory protection. Trust repair requires more than technical corrections. It requires acknowledgement, explanation, compensation where appropriate, and visible changes in governance practices.

Table 3. Trust Trajectory Typology in AI-Mediated Hyper-Personalized Services

Trajectory	Personalization Experience	Transparency Condition	Vulnerability Condition	Expected Loyalty Outcome
Trust-Building	Relevant, respectful, accurate, and authenticity-preserving.	Specific, usable, and credible.	Low or actively mitigated.	Strong commitment, continued use, advocacy, and forgiveness.
Trust-Neutral	Efficient and useful but relationally thin.	Minimal or compliance-oriented.	Low to moderate, or under-recognized.	Habitual or convenience-based loyalty that is easy to disrupt.
Trust-Eroding	Intrusive, opaque, unfair, or manipulative.	Absent, vague, or inconsistent.	High or ignored.	Avoidance, churn, negative word of mouth, and regulatory concern.

6. SECTORAL ILLUSTRATIONS

The following sectoral illustrations demonstrate how the integrative framework and trust trajectory typology operate in practice. These four sectors—retail, banking, healthcare, and hospitality—were selected because they represent distinct combinations of service risk, data sensitivity, consumer vulnerability, and regulatory intensity. Together, they show how the same AI capabilities can produce different trust trajectories, depending on contextual conditions and design choices.

6.1. Retail

Retail firms are intensive adopters of AI-driven personalization. Recommendation engines, targeted promotions, personalized homepages, and dynamic service communications use purchase records, browsing histories, clickstream data, and contextual cues. These systems strengthen cognitive trust when consumers repeatedly receive useful recommendations and experience reduced search costs (Aguirre et al., 2015; Bleier & Eisenbeiss, 2015; Wedel & Kannan, 2016).

The central retail risk is the personalization–privacy paradox. Consumers may appreciate relevance but become uneasy when personalization reveals unexpected inferences. A well-documented case involves a major U.S. retailer that used purchase pattern analysis to infer pregnancy status and send targeted coupons, resulting in consumer backlash when the inference was revealed to a family member before the consumer had disclosed the pregnancy (Duhigg, 2012). This case illustrates how technically accurate personalization can trigger trust erosion when it crosses perceived privacy boundaries without adequate transparency and consent. More recent evidence confirms that this tension persists in contemporary AI-enabled retail. Canhoto et al. (2024) find that AI-enabled personalization in physical retail environments produces a recurring “snakes and ladders” dynamic, in which gains in perceived relevance can be rapidly reversed when consumers sense covert data use or loss of control, underscoring that the paradox intensifies rather than disappears as personalization becomes more sophisticated.

Trust-building retail personalization requires clear explanations, preference controls, conservative use of sensitive categories, and visible privacy safeguards. For example, Amazon's recommendation system provides explicit “why recommended” explanations and allows users to remove items from their browsing history that influence recommendations. These features support cognitive trust through accuracy and affective trust through perceived control. Retailers that treat personalization as a pure conversion tool risk eroding affective trust, even when their algorithms perform well.

6.2. Banking and Financial Services

Banks use AI for fraud detection, credit scoring, robo-advisory services, risk profiling, and personalized financial advice. These applications can build cognitive trust by increasing speed, accuracy, and proactive support. However, financial services are high-stakes and vulnerability-sensitive. Consumers may face significant consequences if automated credit, pricing, or advisory systems are opaque or unfair.

In this sector, transparency signaling is not merely a communication problem. It is central to perceived procedural justice. Consumers must understand why an offer, denial, risk score, or recommendation was generated and how they can seek a review. The European Union's General Data Protection Regulation (GDPR) and the EU AI Act require explainability for consequential automated decisions, reflecting this normative expectation. However, regulatory compliance alone does not guarantee trust. A robo-advisor that discloses its fee structure and investment logic in accessible language may build trust, whereas one that buries this information in legal disclaimers may trigger skepticism. Empirical work on fintech adoption is consistent with this view; Sabir et al. (2023) find that perceived usefulness, ease of use, and convenience drive consumer attitudes toward robo-advisors, with trust operating as an influential factor in the acceptance model, which suggests that functional performance and relational trust must be cultivated together in financial AI.

Vulnerability-sensitive banking design should avoid exploiting financial distress, provide understandable explanations, and maintain human review for consequential decision-making. For example, some banks have implemented “financial health” dashboards that proactively alert customers to potential cash flow problems and offer conservative solutions rather than high-interest credit products. Such designs can shift vulnerable consumers from trust-neutral or trust-eroding trajectories toward trust-building ones.

6.3. Healthcare

Healthcare AI personalizes risk assessment, diagnosis support, monitoring, reminders, and care pathways. These applications can enhance cognitive trust by improving the accuracy, timeliness, and coordination of care. However, healthcare is deeply relational. Patients often evaluate AI through expectations of empathy, professional judgment, and moral responsibility (Longoni et al., 2019; Steerling et al., 2023).

A trust-building healthcare trajectory requires human oversight, accessible explanations, and clear boundaries regarding AI's role. For example, IBM Watson for Oncology was initially deployed with high expectations but faced resistance from clinicians who found its recommendations inconsistent with local practice norms and patient preferences (Ross & Swetlitz, 2018). This case illustrates that technical competence alone does not ensure trust when a system fails to align with professional and relational expectations. Patient-level evidence points in the same direction. In a prospective study of patients facing localized prostate cancer decisions, Rodler et al. (2024) found that patients trusted physicians more than AI for individualized communication, yet strongly preferred AI-assisted physicians over physicians alone (66.74% versus 29.61%). This pattern indicates that trust in healthcare AI is conditional and relational: it is highest when AI augments, rather than displaces, the clinician.

AI should be framed as augmenting, rather than replacing, clinical judgment. Patients should be aware of when AI is involved, what data are used, and who remains accountable. Some hospitals now use "AI disclosure" protocols in radiology, in which patients are informed that an AI system assisted in analyzing their scan but that a radiologist reviewed and confirmed the results. Without these safeguards, personalization can feel like surveillance, cost-cutting, or depersonalization, especially for patients with vulnerable conditions.

6.4. Hospitality

Hospitality personalization includes pre-arrival preference capture, smart room configuration, personalized recommendations, automated check-in, and loyalty communications. In the hospitality industry, affective trust is particularly important because service experiences are often hedonic, relational, and identity-relevant. Guests may interpret personalization as care when it respects comfort, privacy, and cultural expectations.

Hospitality creates intimate data environments. Smart rooms, location-based recommendations, and ambient personalization can raise privacy concerns if guests do not know what is collected or how it is used. The Marriott International data breach (2018), which exposed the personal information of approximately 500 million guests, illustrates how data security failures can catastrophically erode trust in hospitality personalization systems, even when technical service delivery remains intact. Research on smart, connected environments helps explain why such settings are so trust-sensitive. Chan-Olmsted et al. (2024) show that consumers continuously weigh the convenience and control benefits of smart device personalization against perceived loss of control and the risk of feeling surveilled, with trust serving as the pivotal factor in this privacy calculus. In hospitality's intimate spaces, where the "device" is effectively the guest room itself, this calculus becomes especially consequential for affective trust.

Trust-preserving hospitality design should provide clear in-room controls, opt-out options, conservative data use in personal spaces, and easy human assistance when automation fails. Some boutique hotels now provide "privacy mode" switches that disable all smart sensors and data collection, accompanied by clear signage explaining what features remain active. Such designs signal respect for guest boundaries and can sustain affective trust, even among privacy-sensitive travelers.

Table 4. Sectoral Implications of the Framework

Sector	Typical AI Application	Main Trust Opportunity	Main Trust Risk	Governance Requirement
Retail	Recommendations, promotions, and personalized interfaces.	Reduced effort and higher relevance.	Creepiness, covert inference, and unfair personalization.	Preference controls, data-use explanations, and sensitive-category limits.
Banking	Credit scoring, robo-advice, fraud detection.	Faster, more tailored financial support.	Opaque or exploitative decisions affecting vulnerable consumers.	Explainability, contestability, and human review.
Healthcare	Decision support, risk prediction, patient engagement.	Timely, personalized, and coordinated care.	Depersonalization, surveillance, or loss of clinical accountability.	Clinician oversight, clear disclosure, and accessible explanations.
Hospitality	Smart rooms, personalized recommendations, loyalty offers.	Personal care, comfort, and convenience.	Privacy concerns in intimate service spaces.	Opt-out controls, clear notices, and human fallback.

7. RESEARCH AGENDA

Future research should longitudinally examine trust trajectories. Most studies measure trust at one point in time, yet AI-mediated services evolve through multiple interactions. Panel studies, experience sampling, and longitudinal field data can identify when trust-building, trust-neutral, and trust-eroding trajectories emerge and how they change after service failures, privacy events, or transparency interventions.

A second priority is measurement development. Existing trust scales provide a strong foundation (Mayer et al., 1995; McKnight et al., 2002); however, AI-mediated services require measures that separate cognitive trust in system competence from affective trust in provider benevolence and integrity. Measures of transparency signaling quality should capture clarity, specificity, usability, sincerity, and contestability. Measures of AI-induced vulnerability should capture perceived powerlessness, dependence, anxiety, and limited ability to contest outcomes.

Experimental research should examine how transparency designs interact with personalization depth and vulnerability. Studies can manipulate recommendation explanations, data-use notices, human oversight, and opt-out controls across low-risk and high-risk scenarios. The outcomes should include cognitive trust, affective trust, perceived authenticity, privacy concern, perceived control, loyalty intention, and avoidance behavior.

To make these directions actionable, Table 5 maps the three propositions onto candidate variables, research designs, and recent empirical exemplars. The table demonstrates that the framework is not only conceptual but also empirically testable, and it offers concrete starting points for operationalizing the trust trajectories.

Table 5. Empirical Pathways for Testing the Propositions

Proposition	Key Variables	Suggested Design	Illustrative Reference
P1 (trust-building): relevant, respectful personalization plus credible transparency reinforces cognitive and affective trust.	IVs: personalization relevance, transparency credibility. DVs: cognitive trust, affective trust, loyalty intention.	2 (relevance: high/low) x 2 (transparency: high/low) between-subjects experiment, measuring both trust dimensions separately.	Park & Yoon (2024); Zhao et al. (2025).
P2 (trust-neutral): functional personalization with weak or compliance-oriented transparency yields cognitive but not affective trust.	IVs: transparency quality (substantive vs. compliance-only). DVs: cognitive trust, affective trust, switching ease.	Cross-sectional survey with mediation analysis (PLS-SEM) separating the two trust paths to loyalty.	Chan-Olmsted et al. (2024); Cloarec et al. (2024).
P3 (trust-eroding): intrusive or opaque personalization under high vulnerability deteriorates both trust dimensions.	IVs: intrusiveness, data sensitivity. Moderator: consumer vulnerability. DVs: affective trust, avoidance, complaint intention.	Moderated experiment (3 personalization x 2 vulnerability), plus longitudinal panel to trace erosion after a privacy event.	Kim & Han (2025); Canhoto et al. (2024).

Cross-cultural research is also needed. Privacy expectations, institutional trust, power distance, uncertainty avoidance, and attitudes toward automation differ across societies. The same transparency signal may be interpreted as reassuring in one context and insufficient in another. Comparative studies can clarify how cultural norms shape the personalization threshold at which relevance turns into an intrusion.

Sector-specific research should examine whether the framework operates differently in retail, banking, healthcare, hospitality, education, transportation, and public service sectors. High-stakes sectors likely require stronger transparency and human oversight than low-stakes convenience. Future research should also investigate how regulations, professional norms, and service criticality moderate the trust–loyalty nexus.

Qualitative and mixed-methods research can deepen the understanding of consumer sense-making. Interviews, diaries, netnography, and digital ethnography can reveal how consumers narrate AI-mediated personalization, how they identify creepiness or authenticity, and how vulnerable consumers cope with opaque systems. These methods are particularly useful for uncovering silent disengagement, resistance, and trust repair expectations.

Finally, research should examine the organizational implementation. Trust-preserving AI personalization depends on governance routines, cross-functional collaboration, data stewardship, ethical reviews, frontline training, and accountability structures. Case studies of successful and failed deployments can clarify the organizational capabilities that support transparency and vulnerability-sensitive AI services.

A further priority concerns the shift from recommendation-based personalization to agentic AI. As noted at the outset, organizations are increasingly deploying autonomous agents that do not merely suggest options but plan, decide, and act on the consumer's behalf (McKinsey & Company, 2025). This shift reshapes the trust–loyalty nexus in ways the present framework only begins to address. When an agent transacts autonomously, the locus of consumer control moves from approving individual recommendations to delegating authority over a stream of future actions, which raises the stakes of both cognitive trust (will the agent act competently and within its mandate?) and affective trust (will it act in my interest when I am not watching?). Early evidence that consumers form combined cognitive and affective trust in AI agents (Zhao et al., 2025) suggests that the two-dimensional structure remains relevant, but the conditions for transparency, contestability, and human override are likely to be more demanding under delegation than under recommendation. Future research should therefore examine how the trust trajectories described here unfold when consumers grant agents standing authority, and how providers can preserve meaningful oversight without negating the convenience that motivates delegation in the first place.

PRACTICAL, MANAGERIAL, AND ETHICAL IMPLICATIONS

Service managers should treat trust as a design objective rather than a by-product of personalization accuracy. They should decide which trust trajectory they want to cultivate in different service contexts and consumer segments. Convenience-based personalization may be sufficient for low-risk services. In high-risk or high-vulnerability contexts, managers must deliberately build cognitive and affective trust through transparency, restraint, and human oversight.

Customer experience designers should calibrate the depth of personalization. More personalization is not automatically better. Designers should consider whether the recommendation or offer uses data that consumers expect the firm to use, whether the inference is sensitive, whether the consumer can understand the reason for personalization, and whether there is an easy way to modify or refuse it. Preference dashboards, micro-explanations, and privacy-preserving defaults can reduce perceived intrusion.

AI and data analytics teams should incorporate explainability, fairness, and vulnerability assessment into model development. Data minimization, purpose limitation, model documentation, and bias monitoring should be treated as part of service quality. High-stakes AI-mediated decisions should include human review and contestability. Model performance metrics should be balanced with trust metrics, such as perceived fairness, complaint patterns, opt-out rates, and trust recovery after failures. These practices should be organized around three governance commitments that are central to contemporary AI ethics: fairness, bias mitigation, and accountability. Fairness requires that personalization not produce systematically disadvantageous outcomes for protected or vulnerable groups, for example through discriminatory pricing or differential access to favorable offers. Bias mitigation requires ongoing auditing of training data and model outputs, because personalization models can encode and amplify historical inequities even when no discriminatory intent exists. Accountability requires that responsibility for AI-mediated outcomes remain clearly assigned to the organization rather than diffused into the algorithm, with documented escalation paths and the capacity to explain and reverse consequential decisions. Treating these three commitments as design requirements, rather than as after-the-fact compliance, is what allows transparency and authenticity to be experienced by consumers as genuine.

Healthcare and financial services managers should apply stricter safeguards because consumer vulnerability and decision consequences are higher. In healthcare, AI should augment, rather than displace, clinical relationships. In financial services, AI should not be used to target vulnerable consumers with exploitative offers. Clear explanations, conservative personalization, and human escalation paths are essential.

Retail and hospitality managers should focus on transparency in everyday service encounters. In retail, consumers should be able to see and modify the basis of recommendations. In hospitality, personal spaces require heightened privacy standards. Smart-room personalization should be controllable and clearly explained. Across both sectors, trust-preserving personalization requires restraint as much as technological sophistication.

Policymakers and regulators should recognize that AI-mediated hyper-personalization creates new forms of information asymmetry and vulnerability. Disclosure rules should encourage usable explanations rather than dense legal statements. Consumer protection should address not only data collection but also inference, targeting, dynamic pricing, and contestability in consequential service decisions. The High-Level Expert Group on AI (2019) provides useful principles; however, service-specific operationalization remains necessary for their implementation.

CONCLUSION

This chapter has examined the trust–loyalty nexus in AI-mediated hyper-personalized services through the lenses of cognitive–affective trust theory, signaling theory, and consumer vulnerability literature. The central argument is that hyper-personalization does not simply improve relevance or convenience. Rather, it restructures the relational conditions under which consumers decide whether to trust, continue using, or remain loyal to service providers.

The analysis demonstrates that AI-driven personalization can strengthen cognitive trust by demonstrating technical competence, accuracy, and responsiveness. Simultaneously, it can weaken affective trust if it is perceived as intrusive, opaque, opportunistic, or insensitive to vulnerability. Therefore, algorithmic transparency is not merely a technical issue. It functions as a credibility signal that shapes how consumers interpret providers' intentions in the context of information asymmetry.

Trust trajectory typology clarifies why personalization does not yield uniform loyalty outcomes. Trust-building trajectories emerge when personalization is relevant, transparent, respectful, and vulnerability-sensitive. Trust-neutral trajectories emerge when personalization is useful but relationally thin. Trust-eroding trajectories arise when personalization is intrusive, opaque, unfair, or exploitative, especially in contexts of high vulnerability.

The long-term viability of AI-mediated service ecosystems will depend on whether organizations use hyper-personalization to deepen mutual value or exploit informational advantage. Trust should therefore be treated as a central design lens for AI service innovation. Service organizations that combine technical competence with transparency, human oversight, privacy protection, and vulnerability-sensitive governance are more likely to build durable loyalty. Organizations that maximize personalization without relational accountability may gain short-term efficiency while undermining the trust on which sustainable service relationships depend.

ARTIFICIAL INTELLIGENCE DISCLOSURE STATEMENT

AI-assisted tools were used only to support language refinement, structural review, formatting consistency, and readability improvement. The authors bear full responsibility for the conceptual development, scholarly argumentation, source selection, citation verification, and final content of the chapter.

REFERENCES

Aguirre, E., Mahr, D., Grewal, D., de Ruyter, K., & Wetzels, M. (2015). Unraveling the personalization paradox: The effect of information collection and trust-building strategies on online advertisement effectiveness. *Journal of Retailing*, *91*(1), 34–49. DOI: 10.1016/j.jretai.2014.09.005

Awad, N. F., & Krishnan, M. S. (2006). The personalization privacy paradox: An empirical evaluation of information transparency and the willingness to be profiled online for personalization. *Management Information Systems Quarterly*, *30*(1), 13–28. DOI: 10.2307/25148715

Baker, S. M., Gentry, J. W., & Rittenburg, T. L. (2005). Building understanding of the domain of consumer vulnerability. *Journal of Macromarketing*, *25*(2), 128–139. DOI: 10.1177/0276146705280622

Beverland, M. B. (2005). Crafting brand authenticity: The case of luxury wines. *Journal of Management Studies*, *42*(5), 1003–1029. DOI: 10.1111/j.1467-6486.2005.00530.x

Bleier, A., & Eisenbeiss, M. (2015). Personalized online advertising effectiveness: The interplay of what, when, and where. *Marketing Science*, *34*(5), 669–688. DOI: 10.1287/mksc.2015.0930

Canhoto, A. I., Keegan, B. J., & Ryzhikh, M. (2024). Snakes and ladders: Unpacking the personalisation-privacy paradox in the context of AI-enabled personalisation in the physical retail environment. *Information Systems Frontiers*, *26*(3), 1005–1024. DOI: 10.1007/s10796-023-10369-7 PMID: 36684411

Chan-Olmsted, S., Chen, H., & Kim, H. J. (2024). In smartness we trust: Consumer experience, smart device personalization and privacy balance. *Journal of Consumer Marketing*, *41*(6), 597–609. DOI: 10.1108/JCM-12-2021-5072

Cloarec, J., Meyer-Waarden, L., & Munzel, A. (2022). The personalization–privacy paradox at the nexus of social exchange and construal level theories. *Psychology and Marketing*, *39*(3), 647–661. DOI: 10.1002/mar.21587

Cloarec, J., Meyer-Waarden, L., & Munzel, A. (2024). Transformative privacy calculus: Conceptualizing the personalization–privacy paradox on social media. *Psychology and Marketing*, *41*(7), 1574–1596. DOI: 10.1002/mar.21998

Connelly, B. L., Certo, S. T., Ireland, R. D., & Reutzel, C. R. (2011). Signaling theory: A review and assessment. *Journal of Management*, *37*(1), 39–67. DOI: 10.1177/0149206310388419

Duhigg, C. (2012, February 16). How companies learn your secrets. *The New York Times Magazine*. https://www.nytimes.com/2012/02/19/magazine/shopping-habits.html

Flavián, C., Pérez-Rueda, A., Belanche, D., & Casaló, L. V. (2022). Intention to use analytical artificial intelligence in services: The effect of technology readiness and awareness. *Journal of Service Management*, *33*(2), 293–320. DOI: 10.1108/JOSM-10-2020-0378

Gefen, D., Karahanna, E., & Straub, D. W. (2003). Trust and TAM in online shopping: An integrated model. *Management Information Systems Quarterly*, *27*(1), 51–90. DOI: 10.2307/30036519

High-Level Expert Group on Artificial Intelligence. (2019). *Ethics guidelines for trustworthy AI*. European Commission. https://digital-strategy.ec.europa.eu/en/library/ethics-guidelines-trustworthy-ai

Huang, M.-H., & Rust, R. T. (2018). Artificial intelligence in service. *Journal of Service Research*, *21*(2), 155–172. DOI: 10.1177/1094670517752459

IBM. (2024). *IBM Global AI Adoption Index: Enterprise report*. IBM. https://filecache.mediaroom.com/mr5mr_ibmspgi/179414/download/IBM%20Global%20AI%20Adoption%20Index%20Report%20Dec.%202023.pdf

Kim, H., & Han, S. (2025). Triggering the personalization backfire effect: The moderating role of situational privacy concern. *Behavioral Sciences (Basel, Switzerland)*, *15*(10), 1323. Advance online publication. DOI: 10.3390/bs15101323 PMID: 41153114

Komiak, S. X., & Benbasat, I. (2006). The effects of personalization and familiarity on trust and adoption of recommendation agents. *Management Information Systems Quarterly*, *30*(4), 941–960. DOI: 10.2307/25148760

Longoni, C., Bonezzi, A., & Morewedge, C. K. (2019). Resistance to medical artificial intelligence. *The Journal of Consumer Research*, *46*(4), 629–650. DOI: 10.1093/jcr/ucz013

Marriott International. (2018, November 30). *Marriott International announces Starwood guest reservation database security incident*. https://news.marriott.com/news/2018/11/30/marriott-international-announces-starwood-guest-reservation-database-security-incident

Mayer, R. C., Davis, J. H., & Schoorman, F. D. (1995). An integrative model of organizational trust. *Academy of Management Review*, *20*(3), 709–734. DOI: 10.2307/258792

McKinsey & Company. (2025). *The state of AI in 2025: Agents, innovation, and transformation.* McKinsey & Company. https://www.mckinsey.com/capabilities/quantumblack/our-insights/the-state-of-ai

McKnight, D. H., Choudhury, V., & Kacmar, C. (2002). Developing and validating trust measures for e-commerce: An integrative typology. *Information Systems Research, 13*(3), 334–359. DOI: 10.1287/isre.13.3.334.81

Mersha, M., Lam, K., Wood, J., AlShami, A. K., & Kalita, J. (2024). Explainable artificial intelligence: A survey of needs, techniques, applications, and future direction. *Neurocomputing, 599*, 128111. Advance online publication. DOI: 10.1016/j.neucom.2024.128111

Morhart, F., Malär, L., Guèvremont, A., Girardin, F., & Grohmann, B. (2015). Brand authenticity: An integrative framework and measurement scale. *Journal of Consumer Psychology, 25*(2), 200–218. DOI: 10.1016/j.jcps.2014.11.006

Napoli, J., Dickinson, S. J., Beverland, M. B., & Farrelly, F. (2014). Measuring consumer-based brand authenticity. *Journal of Business Research, 67*(6), 1090–1098. DOI: 10.1016/j.jbusres.2013.06.001

OECD. (2023). *Consumer vulnerability in the digital age.* OECD Publishing., DOI: 10.1787/4d013cc5-

Park, K., & Yoon, H. Y. (2024). Beyond the code: The impact of AI algorithm transparency signaling on user trust and relational satisfaction. *Public Relations Review, 50*(5), 102507. Advance online publication. DOI: 10.1016/j.pubrev.2024.102507

Rai, A. (2020). Explainable AI: From black box to glass box. *Journal of the Academy of Marketing Science, 48*(1), 137–141. DOI: 10.1007/s11747-019-00710-5

Rodler, S., Kopliku, R., Ulrich, D., Kaltenhauser, A., Casuscelli, J., Eismann, L., Waidelich, R., Buchner, A., Butz, A., Cacciamani, G. E., Stief, C. G., & Westhofen, T. (2024). Patients' trust in artificial intelligence–based decision-making for localized prostate cancer: Results from a prospective trial. *European Urology Focus, 10*(4), 654–661. DOI: 10.1016/j.euf.2023.10.020 PMID: 37923632

Ross, C., & Swetlitz, I. (2018, July 25). IBM's Watson supercomputer recommended 'unsafe and incorrect' cancer treatments, internal documents show. *Stat News.* https://www.statnews.com/2018/07/25/ibm-watson-recommended-unsafe-incorrect-cancer-treatments/

Sabir, A. A., Ahmad, I., Ahmad, H., Rafiq, M., Khan, M. A., & Noreen, N. (2023). Consumer acceptance and adoption of AI robo-advisors in fintech industry. *Mathematics, 11*(6), 1311. Advance online publication. DOI: 10.3390/math11061311

Salesforce. (2024). *State of the AI connected customer*. Salesforce Research. https://www.salesforce.com/en-us/wp-content/uploads/sites/4/documents/research/State-of-the-Connected-Customer.pdf

Schoorman, F. D., Mayer, R. C., & Davis, J. H. (2007). An integrative model of organizational trust: Past, present, and future. *Academy of Management Review*, *32*(2), 344–354. DOI: 10.5465/amr.2007.24348410

Spence, M. (1973). Job market signaling. *The Quarterly Journal of Economics*, *87*(3), 355–374. DOI: 10.2307/1882010

Steerling, E., Siira, E., Nilsen, P., Svedberg, P., & Nygren, J. (2023). Implementing AI in healthcare: The relevance of trust: A scoping review. *Frontiers in Health Services*, *3*, 1211150. Advance online publication. DOI: 10.3389/frhs.2023.1211150 PMID: 37693234

Trinh, M. (2025). AI-induced consumer vulnerability: Psychological mechanisms and marketplace implications. *Journal of Consumer Policy*, *48*(1), 45–68. DOI: 10.1007/s10603-024-09532-7

van Doorn, J., Mende, M., Noble, S. M., Hulland, J., Ostrom, A. L., Grewal, D., & Petersen, J. A. (2017). Domo arigato Mr. Roboto: Emergence of automated social presence in organizational frontlines and customers' service experiences. *Journal of Service Research*, *20*(1), 43–58. DOI: 10.1177/1094670516679272

Wedel, M., & Kannan, P. K. (2016). Marketing analytics for data-rich environments. *Journal of Marketing*, *80*(6), 97–121. DOI: 10.1509/jm.15.0413

Wirtz, J., Patterson, P. G., Kunz, W. H., Gruber, T., Lu, V. N., Paluch, S., & Martins, A. (2018). Brave new world: Service robots in the frontline. *Journal of Service Management*, *29*(5), 907–931. DOI: 10.1108/JOSM-04-2018-0119

Zhao, X., You, W., Zheng, Z., Shi, S., Lu, Y., & Sun, L. (2025). How do consumers trust and accept AI agents? An extended theoretical framework and empirical evidence. *Behavioral Sciences (Basel, Switzerland)*, *15*(3), 337. Advance online publication. DOI: 10.3390/bs15030337 PMID: 40150232

KEY TERMS AND DEFINITIONS

Affective Trust: Trust grounded in beliefs about benevolence, integrity, care, and relational alignment.

AI-Mediated Service: A service encounter in which artificial intelligence systems shape interaction, recommendation, communication, or decision support between the provider and consumer.

Algorithmic Transparency: The extent to which consumers receive understandable information about how AI-enabled recommendations or decisions are generated.

Cognitive Trust: Trust grounded in beliefs about competence, reliability, accuracy, and technical capability.

Consumer Trust: A consumer's willingness to rely on a service provider or AI system under conditions of uncertainty and limited control.

Consumer Vulnerability: A contextually activated condition in which consumers face power, information, resource, or dependency imbalances in marketplace interactions.

Customer loyalty: A consumer's behavioral and attitudinal commitment to continue using, repurchasing from, or recommending a service provider.

Explainable AI: AI design and communication practices that make algorithmic outputs more understandable and contestable by users and stakeholders.

Hyper-Personalization: The real-time tailoring of service content, offers, interfaces, or interactions using behavioral, contextual, transactional, and predictive data.

Personalization-Privacy Paradox: The tension between consumers' desire for relevant personalized services and their concern about data collection, profiling, and privacy loss.

Transparency Signaling: The use of explanations, disclosures, controls, and audit cues to communicate credibility, accountability, and respect for consumer agency.

Trust trajectory: The direction and pattern through which trust develops, stabilizes, or deteriorates across repeated AI-mediated service encounters.

Trust-Preserving Design: A service design approach that uses transparency, data restraint, human oversight, and contestability to protect consumer trust.

Vulnerability-Sensitive Personalization: Personalization that adjusts data use, explanation, oversight, and control mechanisms according to the consumer's risk and vulnerability context.

Chapter 6
Understanding Consumer Loyalty in AI-Based Services:
The Roles of Trust and Satisfaction

S. Dhanu Shree
http://orcid.org/0009-0000-2031-7628
Saveetha Institute of Medical and Technical Sciences, India

P. Santhosh kumar
http://orcid.org/0009-0008-1938-8929
Saveetha Institute of Medical and Technical Sciences, India

S. Mohamed Musthakeem
http://orcid.org/0009-0000-5085-2779
Saveetha Institute of Medical and Technical Sciences, India

ABSTRACT

The use of Artificial Intelligence (AI) has revolutionized the delivery of services by providing efficient, tailored, and automated customer services. As AI-based services like chatbots, virtual assistants, and recommendation systems continue to gain more popularity, it is necessary to understand consumer behavior. This chapter will discuss how the trust and customer satisfaction contribute to consumer loyalty in AI-based services. According to the Stimulus-Organism-Response (S-O-R) model (Mehrabian and Russell, 1974) and the relationship marketing model (Morgan and Hunt, 1994), trust is an antecedent, customer satisfaction a mediator variable, and consumer loyalty is an outcome. Reliability and security lead to trust which lessens

DOI: 10.4018/979-8-3373-9159-5.ch006

uncertainty and confidence is achieved (Gefen et al., 2003), satisfaction is motivated by the quality of services and personalization (Oliver, 1980). The analysis indicates that trust and satisfaction are very important levels of consumer loyalty.

1. INTRODUCTION

The field of Artificial Intelligence (AI) can be discussed as one of the most transformative technologies that define the contemporary digital economy. Typically, AI-based systems are being integrated into the workflow of organizations in all sectors in order to increase the efficiency of their services, improve their interaction with customers, and provide personalized customer experience. Chatbots, virtual assistants, recommendation systems, and automated customer service platforms represent AI technologies that are popular in the banking industry, e-commerce, healthcare sector, telecommunications, and retail industry. These are AI-based solutions that help organizations deliver quicker responses, lower the cost of operation, and provide twenty four hour services. This has meant that AI-related services have changed the way businesses engage with consumers and form value in a major way (Huang and Rust, 2021; Davenport et al., 2020).

Even though the use of AI technologies is rapidly increasing, the use of AI-based services is mostly influenced by the perception and acceptance of these technologies by the consumers. The interactions of AI do not involve human interaction, as compared to the old human-based service encounters, which are based on algorithms, machine learning, and automated decision-making. Although AI systems are convenient and efficient, the customers are usually worried about the privacy, trustworthiness, transparency and safety (Luo et al., 2019; Dwivedi et al., 2021). These issues may affect their desire to use AI-driven services and form their overall attitude to the service provider. Thus, the identification of the factors, which can affect the consumer attitudes to the AI-based services, has become a valuable research field.

Among them, trust and customer satisfaction have become the determinants of the long-term customer relations. The aspect of trust is especially critical in the AI-based interactions as the customers depend on the work of automated devices, without knowing how it works. Trust in this context is the extent to which the consumers trust that AI systems are dependable, safe, and that they can provide valid results (Gefen et al., 2003; McKnight et al., 2011). At the moment the customers have confidence in AI technologies, they will be willing to follow the recommendations of systems and keep using the service.

Reliability of the systems, transparency, data security, and perceived competence of the AI services are some of the factors that promote the development of trust in the

AI services. The customers require the AI systems to be informative, efficient and respond to their needs and privacy. In case of these expectations being fulfilled, trust is built up, but failure of the system or incorrect response may decrease confidence and negate subsequent use (Shin, 2021). Therefore, trust is a critical factor that can define the readiness of customers to have long-term relations with AI based-services.

Consumer behavior is also affected by customer satisfaction as another vital factor. It is the sum total assessment of a service encounter with regard to the expectations-performance comparisons (Oliver, 1980). Responsiveness, customization, usability and adequate problem solution determine satisfaction in AI-based environments. As an illustration, chatbots based on AI can be used to support customers in questioning, resolving complaints, and effectively directing them through the processes. In case of good performance, these services will positively impact the overall customer experience and will increase the level of satisfaction (Gnewuch et al., 2017).

Consumer loyalty is highly associated with customer satisfaction. Consumer loyalty is the situation where a customer is loyal to using a given service or brand repeatedly (Zeithaml et al., 1996). The loyal customers would tend to use the services more and tell others via positive word-of-mouth. Customer loyalty is an asset in the competitive digital markets because it leads to long-run profitability, minimized marketing expenditures and enhanced brand image (Reichheld and Sasser, 1990). A high competitive advantage can be attained at organizations that manage to establish loyalty among their customers.

It is especially significant in the context of AIs when it comes to service where trust, satisfaction, and consumer loyalty are concerned. Customers who believe in AI technologies feel at ease using them often and in cases where such systems offer efficient and personalized experiences satisfaction is enhanced. Such satisfaction, in its turn, leads to the further usage and development of loyalty (Chatterjee et al., 2021). Trust and satisfaction, consequently, may be regarded as the primary in the consumer loyalty in AI-driven settings.

A helpful theoretical framework of understanding these relationships is the Stimulus- Organism- Response (S-O-R) framework. In this model, AI services features, including quality of the system and personalization, are the stimuli, affecting the internal states, including the trust and satisfaction (organism), which subsequently lead to the behavioral outcomes, including the loyalty (Mehrabian and Russell, 1974; Kim and Lennon, 2013). Consumer behavior has been widely explained using this framework within the digital service research.

Whereas the number of studies on AI adoption has been growing, there are few studies on behavioral outcomes including trust, satisfaction, and loyalty. The range of available literature focuses on technology acceptance and the quality of the service (Venkatesh et al., 2003; Wirtz et al., 2018), and fewer investigations take into account the synergy of psychological aspects. Also, the research is industry-specific in the majority of the cases, which limits its generalizability to other service sectors.

This chapter fills these gaps through the consideration of the role of trust and customer satisfaction in the formation of consumer loyalty in the AI-based services. It covers the impact of trust in satisfaction and the effects of the two in generating loyalty. It is hoped that the results will be valuable to the organizations interested in developing AI-based services that improve customer experiences and develop relationships over time. The chapter also makes a contribution to the academic literature by providing a more insight into the consumer behavior in the context of AI-enabled services.

2. BACKGROUND OF THE STUDY

In the digital age, the adoption of the Artificial Intelligence (AI) has made a massive difference in the manner in which organizations provide their services and also their interaction with their customers. AI is the capacity of machine and computerized systems to fulfill the duties that were traditionally done by human intellect, including learning, resolving problems, making decisions, and understanding language. By the last ten years, AI technologies have developed to become not just a case of automated processing of data but also sophisticated systems that can process a large amount of information and make intelligent decisions. This has seen the introduction of widespread applications of AI-driven services in industries with a fundamental transformation of customer-service engagements (Russell and Norvig, 2021; Davenport et al., 2020).

AI-powered services are currently deployed in banking industry, e-commerce, health, retail industry and telecommunication industries. They are chatbots, virtual assistants, recommendation systems, and series of automated customer support. The use of AI chatbots is now seen by organizations to address customer queries, offer product details, and solve problems in real-time. In the same manner, product recommendations are products proposed by algorithms depending on the preferences of users, and virtual assistants are the ones that assist users to carry out specific activities such as information search and schedule management (Wirtz et al., 2018; Huang and Rust, 2021). These apps enhance productivity and provide customers with custom environments.

The presence of the ability to perform 24/7 without human involvement is one of the greatest opportunities of AI-based services. The AI systems have 24/7 support that enhances accessibility and decreases waiting time. They are also able to study large volumes of information in a short period of time whereby companies are in a position to provide individualized and tailored services. This has led to the fact that AI-based services are now necessary to improve customer engagement and satisfaction (Davenport et al., 2020; Dwivedi et al., 2021).

Nonetheless, the process of AI adoption is not as advantageous as it may seem due to the issues of trust. Due to the fact that the AIs can operate on the basis of the algorithms and the decisions made with the help of the data, customers might not comprehend the functioning of these systems properly, which prompts distrust and uncertainty. Reliability, transparency, and data privacy issues may influence the readiness of customers to use AI services (Shin, 2021; Luo et al., 2019). The question of trust, then, becomes critical in terms of adoption and further utilization of the AI-based services (Gefen et al., 2003; McKnight et al., 2011).

Another major aspect that determines consumer behavior is customer satisfaction. It can be defined as relative evaluation of service performance on the expectations (Oliver, 1980). Responsiveness, personalization, and ease of use are the factors of satisfaction in AI scenarios. AI systems that are efficient and deliver accurate and useful solutions increase the levels of satisfaction (Gnewuch et al., 2017; Chatterjee et al., 2021).

Dissatisfaction and trust collectively are critical towards consumer loyalty. Loyal customers would find it more attractive to refer and use the services over the long time, which would bring in the success in business (Zeithaml et al., 1996; Reichheld and Sasser, 1990). So, these relationships have to be comprehended by the organizations that want to establish a robust and sustainable customer relationships within the context of AI.

3. REVIEW OF LITERATURE

Artificial Intelligence (AI) has been an object of a quick evolution and integration in service industries, which has also impacted customer interactions and business strategies considerably. Chatbots, virtual assistants, and recommendation systems are examples of AI based services that are increasingly deployed to provide better customer experiences, increase operational efficiency, and offer personalized services. Due to the ongoing integration of AI technologies by organizations, the impact of these systems on customer behavior (mostly trust, satisfaction, and loyalty) stands out as an essential research area (Huang and Rust, 2021; Dwivedi et al., 2021).

3.1. AI-based Customer Experience and Services

The model of using AI-based services to deliver the traditional service has altered the primary concept of service delivery as it allows interacting in an automated, efficient, and customized manner. Research shows that AI tools, in particular, chatbots have a valuable function in enhancing customer interactions and service effectiveness. Chatbots that are powered by AI can also respond immediately, address multiple customer inquiries at once, and offer customized solutions to customers, depending on their data. It has resulted in a more convenient experience of customers and enhanced access to services (Wirtz et al., 2018; Gnewuch et al., 2017).

It has been studied that the quality of AI services has a considerable impact on customer perceptions and behavioral consequences. The quality of chatbot services, responsiveness, accuracy, and personalization, has a positive effect on customer experience and interaction. Specifically, AI chatbots providing reliable and effective services have higher chances of increasing customer satisfaction and making people use it again (Chatterjee et al., 2021). In addition, personalization with the help of AI creates a stronger customer relationship and boosts the perceived value by relating the services to the unique preferences of the customers (Bleier et al., 2019).

The theoretical framework that has helped to support the application of AI in service industries includes the Stimulus-Organism-Response (S-O-R) model. Here, AI service features (stimuli) have an impact on the internal state of the customers as trust and satisfaction (organism), which in turn have an impact on behavioral reactions as loyalty and further use (Mehrabian and Russell, 1974; Kim and Lennon, 2013). This model has been extensively used in the study of digital services to understand how interactions that are mediated by AI influence consumer behavior.

3.2. Artificial Intelligence Systems Should Be Trusted

The element of trust is one of the most important components affecting the use and further utilization of the services based on AI. The customers use AI systems because they are programmed and self-regulated, which is why customers mostly use the system without knowing how it works. This brings about the need of trust because users need to have confidence that the system is reliable, correct and safe (Gefen et al., 2003; McKnight et al., 2011).

According to recent research, various factors affect the trust in AI, such as the reliability of the system, its transparency, and human-like features. To take an example, studies have shown that human-like features in artificial intelligence chatbots like the nuttiness to talk as well as empathy have a profound impact on trust among users. All these aspects provide a sense of social presence, which makes interactive more interactive and reliable (Huang and Rust, 2021).

On the same note, interactivity and perceived enjoyment were also found to be significant in the development of trust in AI systems. Chatbots with interactive responses and responsiveness, which offer dynamic and engaging answers, enhance the sense of control and confidence of the users, which boosts the trust (Gnewuch et al., 2017). Once the users perceive that they can easily interact with the AI systems, their perception towards the reliability and usability of the system become positive, and their levels of trust increase.

Data privacy and security is another aspect of AI that is important as a measure of trust. Customers have become more interested in the behaviors of AI systems towards the collection, storage, and use of their personal data. Research reports that the issue of consumer trust can be greatly improved by providing transparency in the AI decision-making process and being clear about the purposes of using the data (Shin, 2021; Luo et al., 2019). By assuring customers that their data is secure and that the system works without discrimination, the customers will trust the service.

In addition, the latest studies point out that trust in AI has not only technical aspects but also emotional and relational ones. Different dimensions that can be used to understand trust in AI systems include competence, reliability, benevolence, and perceived risk (McKnight et al., 2011). All these dimensions have the effect of shaping how people feel about AI technologies and make them decide whether to trust them or not.

3.3. The Topic of Customer Satisfaction in AI-Based Services is Related to the First Issue

Another important variable that dictates consumer behavior in AI-enabled service settings is customer satisfaction. Satisfaction is the total assessment of service experience in terms of the level of fulfillment and/or surpassing the customer expectations (Oliver, 1980). The factors utilized in determining the level of satisfaction in AI-based services are the quality of services, their ease of use, personalization, and responsiveness.

As research has indicated, AI chatbots are a major source of customer satisfaction because they are able to offer prompt and precise responses to customer inquiries. The user experience is improved with the features of personalization, empathy, and problem-solving systems, which result in positive service interactions (Gnewuch et al., 2017; Chatterjee et al., 2021). More satisfaction levels are likely to be created through the AI systems that comprehend the needs of customers and provide the corresponding solutions.

Besides that, perceived service quality is closely related to a customer satisfaction. In case AI-based systems are effective and provide credible results, the customers have higher chances of satisfaction. Conversely, the unpredictability of the system work, the wrong reaction, or insufficient customization may result in dissatisfaction and decreased utilization of the AI services (Wirtz et al., 2018).

There is also the relationship between trust and satisfaction. Trust may be used to improve the satisfaction, by making one sure of the service. Customers are more prone to consider an AI system trustworthy, which means that a more satisfied customer is likely to find the service valuable and reliable (Kim and Peterson, 2017). On the other hand, mistrust may have a detrimental effect on satisfaction, despite the fact of good functionality of the service.

3.4. Consumer Loyalty of Digital and AI-Based Platforms

Positive customer experience is an important outcome of customer loyalty, which is a critical factor in the organizational success. Repeat purchase and recommendation to others Loyal customers will find it easier to repeat their use of a service, thus more apt to make a purchase (Zeithaml et al., 1996). Within the context of digital and AI-driven relationship, loyalty of consumers is affected by both technological and psychological factors.

It has been found that AI service quality and user experience are key factors in customer loyalty. As an example, research revealed that the quality of chatbot services has a positive impact on the e-brand loyalty of satisfaction with the chatbot, user experience, and electronic word of mouth (Chatterjee et al., 2021). On the same note, AI-based products can be personalized to customers, and this increases customer engagement, leading to long-term loyalty (Bleier et al., 2019).Trust on AI systems has been found to be one of the determinants of customer loyalty in the hospitality industry. In the customers who feel that AI technologies are reliable and effective, positive attitudes to the service provider have a higher chance of forming long-term relationships with the brand (Buhalis and Leung, 2018). This emphasizes the need to have a trustworthy base in establishing customer loyalty in AI-driven settings.

Also, the expectation-confirmation theory implies that the loyalty of customers depends on the ability of the AI services to fulfill or surpass the expectations of users. Whenever AI systems surpass the performance, customers tend to hold positive perceptions and stay loyal towards the service (Bhattacherjee, 2001). Negative experiences on the other hand may result in dissatisfaction and low loyalty.

3.5. Association Among Trust, Satisfaction and Consumer Loyalty

In AI-based services, a considerable amount of literature emphasizes the connection between trust, customer satisfaction, and consumer loyalty. The three variables have been regarded as important determinants of customer behavior and are commonly researched in technology adoption and service management studies in combination.

Customer satisfaction is typically considered as a result of trust. Customers that have trust in an AI system are more likely to become more comfortable in their usage, and view it as a valuable and trustworthy system. This favorable image increases satisfaction and promotes the further use of the service (Kim and Peterson, 2017).

Research has indicated that trust has a direct effect on satisfaction and an indirect effect on loyalty by way of satisfaction.

On its part, customer satisfaction has a mediating role in the correlation between trust and consumer loyalty. Customers who feel satisfied will tend to establish a positive emotional bond with the service provider and this will result in greater loyalty (Oliver, 1999). It has been proposed that satisfaction is an intermediary between trust and loyalty, and providing high-quality AI services is crucial.

More so, consumer loyalty may also be directly influenced by trust. Trusting customers in AI systems would keep them more likely to be loyal to the service as long as alternative services exist (Gefen et al., 2003). This indicates the significance of the process of establishing and sustaining trust in AI-driven service environments.

New literature also highlights the importance of psychological and emotional aspects of influencing consumer behavior in AI environments. Customers can also form emotional relationships with AI-based technologies as they grow more human-like, and it can affect the level of trust, satisfaction, and loyalty (Huang and Rust, 2021). This tendency reveals the changing character of human-AI interactions and the need to conduct additional research on this matter.

Literature Review Given the variation in the approaches used to define and measure the concept of ANOVA, a brief summary of the literature review is necessary:

The available literature offers useful information on how AI-based services influence consumer behavior. Research always proves that AI technologies contribute to optimizing the customer experience by increasing its efficiency, customizing it, and making it more accessible. The aspect of trust and customer satisfaction appears to be the critical factor affecting consumer loyalty in the AI-driven service settings.

System reliability, transparency, and human-like qualities determine the influence of trust, whereas service quality, responsiveness, and personalization determine customer satisfaction. The trust and satisfaction are both important in influencing consumer loyalty, and satisfaction is usually an intermediating variable between the trust and the consumer loyalty.

Even though the present state of research on this topic is admittedly extensive, it remains necessary to have an in-depth knowledge of the interaction between trust and satisfaction, as well as being able to proceed to the notion of consumer loyalty in AI-based services. The research chapter attempts to fill this gap by organizing a conceptual framework that will incorporate these variables of interest and give some understanding of how these elements are interrelated.

On the whole, the literature emphasizes the necessity to develop AI systems not only on the level of appropriate technology but also on the ability to generate trust and provide a rewarding customer experience. Those organizations that are effective in maintaining this balance have a higher chance of creating long term consumer loyalty and gaining a competitive edge in the digital market.

4. RESEARCH GAP

This adoption of Artificial Intelligence (AI) has gained much interest among the researchers and practitioners in service delivery in recent years. Much of the literature has explored different factors of AI-based services, such as the adoption of technology, quality of the services, customer experience, and the performance of the systems (Dwivedi et al., 2021; Wirtz et al., 2018). Although the studies have helped to understand AI technologies better, there are a number of gaps in the available studies that have been identified, especially when it comes to the issue of consumer behavior and loyalty formation in AI-oriented space.

First, the technological and functional dimensions of AI systems have been the main subject of many studies done in the past: efficiency, accuracy, and usability (Venkatesh et al., 2003; Davenport et al., 2020). Even though they are significant, the mentioned characteristics do not embrace the entire picture regarding the formation of long-term relations between customers and AI-based services. It does not focus much on psychological and emotional elements, such as trust and satisfaction, which are very important in influencing consumer attitudes and behaviors (Gefen et al., 2003; Kim and Peterson, 2017). With more and more AI systems interacting with customers in the service situation, it is necessary to learn how the above humanistic factors affect customer loyalty.

Secondly, the extant studies tend to analyze trust and customer satisfaction as independent variables without combination effects and interrelation effects. Although other studies do accept that trust and satisfaction are critical in determining consumer behavior, no combined model has been presented to explain how the two variables interplay in order to affect consumer loyalty in services provided by AI (Chatterjee et al., 2021). Specifically, the mediation of customer satisfaction in trust-consumer loyalty relationship has been insufficiently investigated in AI-oriented service setting (Oliver, 1999).

Third, the percentage of research on AI-based services is industry-oriented as it deals with areas like banking, hospitality, or e-commerce (Buhalis and Leung, 2018). Even though these researches contain some useful information, the research outcomes might not be applicable to other situations involving service. The more generalized and broader outlook of consumer loyalty is required that can be used in different platforms of AI-based services.

Besides, the fact that AI technologies are dynamic poses another challenge to researchers. The customer expectations and perceptions are also shifting as the AI systems continue to advance and include more sophisticated functions like machine learning, natural language processing, and the ability to interact with the system like a human being (Huang and Rust, 2021). Nevertheless, these changing dynamics have not been completely reflected in the literature especially in terms of the effect of progress of AI on trust, satisfaction and loyalty with time.

The other significant gap relates to the low application of the concept frameworks which can incorporate the trust, customer satisfaction, and consumer loyalty into a single framework. Although empirical investigations have been done to establish the links between these variables, there is a chance of conducting more conceptual studies that will generalize the existing knowledge and give a theoretical basis of future study (Mehrabian and Russell, 1974; Kim and Lennon, 2013). These frameworks can assist researchers to comprehend the multifaceted relationships between these constructs better and be able to empirically investigate this area.

Against such gaps, the proposed research will establish a conceptual framework that will analyze how trust and customer satisfaction can influence customer loyalty in AI-based services. Combining these important variables, the context aims to offer a more in-depth insight into the consumer behavior in AI-based settings and add to the current body of knowledge. The study can also be valuable to organizations interested in developing AI services, which can build trust, increase satisfaction, and establish customer loyalty in the long run.

5. CONCEPTUAL FRAMEWORK

Figure 1. Conceptual Framework

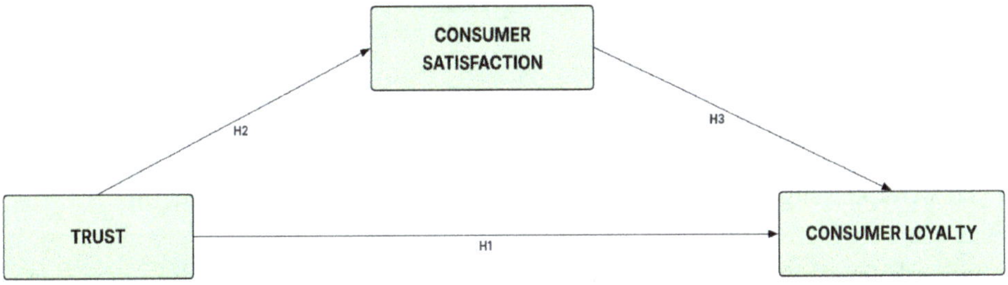

In this study, a conceptual framework to explain the relationship of trust, customer satisfaction and consumer loyalty in AI based service development is developed. As Artificial Intelligence (AI) becomes increasingly used in the delivery of services, being able to understand the interactions among these variables is critical to explaining consumer behavior in digital environments. The framework is based on well-known theories related to the adoption of technology, quality of service, and relationship marketing.

The model is largely anchored in the Stimulus-Organism-Response (S-O-R) model, which describes the influence of external factors on the internal psychological states and subsequently the behavioral outcomes (Mehrabian and Russell, 1974; Kim and Lennon, 2013). In this regard, AI service features such as system quality, responsiveness, and personalization serve as stimuli that affect internal states such as trust and customer satisfaction, which further result in customer loyalty.

Trust is placed as an important antecedent in the framework. It captures how much customers perceive AI systems to be reliable, secure and capable of providing correct results (Gefen et al., 2003; McKnight et al., 2011). Since the interaction-based AI does not involve humans, trust plays a key role in reducing the perceived risk. Factors including transparency, reliability and system competence have a significant influence on trust (Shin, 2021; Huang & Rust, 2021).

Customer satisfaction is another important component that also function as an outcome of trust and predictor of loyalty. It is the general assessment of the service performance in relation to expectations (Oliver, 1980). In the case of AI-based services, satisfaction is affected by easiness, reaction time, and personalization (Gnewuch et al., 2017; Wirtz et al., 2018). Trust further increases satisfaction through increasing confidence about the service (Kim & Peterson, 2017).

The framework also suggests that trust has a direct impact on the consumer's loyalty, that is, the intention to continue to use and recommend a service (Zeithaml et al, 1996). Also, customer satisfaction mediates the relationship between trust and loyalty, reinforcing the effect (Oliver, 1999; Chatterjee et al., 2021).

Overall, this framework combines important variables to explain consumer behavior in AI-driven services and offers a basis for future studies and its use in practice.

6. HYPOTHESES DEVELOPMENT

This chapter suggests a research conceptual model to analyze the links of trust, consumer satisfaction and consumer loyalty in AI-based services. According to the framework, trust is a dependent variable, consumer satisfaction a mediating variable, and consumer loyalty an independent variable. On the basis of these developed theories, the Stimulus-Organism-Response (S-O-R) model and the relationship marketing theory, the hypotheses are formulated to focus on the significance of psychological condition in determining behavioral results (Mehrabian and Russell, 1974; Morgan and Hunt, 1994).

6.1. Trust and Consumer Loyalty (H1)

It is also common knowledge that trust is one of the factors that determine consumer behavior in digital and technology-based environments. Trust, in turn, can be considered in the context of AI-based services the degree of trust the customers have in the AI system as reliable, secure, and able to provide to them accurate results (Gefen et al., 2003; McKnight et al., 2011). As far as the algorithms of AI systems do not presuppose direct contact between the customer and the operator, customers usually feel confused and insecure using such technologies. Trust can minimize these uncertainties and enhance the desire of customers to trust AI systems.

Previous studies indicate that trust is a direct factor in determining consumer loyalty. Customers will be more apt to remain using a service and refer to others when they have confidence in a service provider or a system (Morgan and hunt, 1994). Trust is even more essential in the context of AI-based services since customers rely on automated services to make their decisions and have services delivered. Research indicates that confidence in online sites has a positive impact on retention of users and sustained interaction (Gefen et al., 2003).

H1: Consumer loyalty with AI-based services is affected positively by trust.

6.2. The Relationship Between Trust and Consumer Satisfaction (H2) is Expected to be Positive

Customer satisfaction is also greatly influenced by trust. Customer satisfaction refers to the general assessment of a service experience as a result of the comparison between the expectations and performance (Oliver, 1980). Under AI-based services, the satisfaction is determined by the performance of the system as well as the confidence of customers in the system.

Customers will feel more secure and confident in the AI systems, hence improving their experiences. Trust decreases the uncertainty and enhances confidence in the system to provide credible and beneficial results (Kim and Peterson, 2017). This good perception increases the level of satisfaction. On the other hand, distrust can lead to dissatisfaction although the system can be very good in functionality.

Empirical research in digital service contexts has always shown that trust has a positive effect on customer satisfaction. Trust plays an even more crucial part in customer perceptions and judgments in AI-related contexts where there is no human interaction (Shin, 2021). Hence, one can expect that trust also plays a huge role in the consumer satisfaction of AI-based services.

H2: The trust in AI-based services positively influences the consumer satisfaction.

6.3. Considering Consumer Satisfaction and Consumer Loyalty (H3)

Customer contentment is among the key predictors of consumer loyalty. Satisfaction implies the level to which a service is able to match up or surpass expectations of the customer and it is a key indicator in gaining an understanding of whether the customers will keep using a service (Oliver, 1999). Responsiveness, personalization, ease of use, and service quality are some of the factors that affect the satisfaction of AI-based services (Wirtz et al., 2018; Gnewuch et al., 2017).

Customers who have positive experiences with AI systems tend to form positive attitudes towards the service provider. With these positive experiences, they can get to repeat the usage and recommend the service to others. It has been argued that customer satisfaction increases the likelihood of a level of loyal behavior being shown by the customer such as the repetitive buying behavior and positive word-of-mouth (Zeithaml et al., 1996).

Customer satisfaction is especially essential in the context of digital services as the customers can obtain various options. In case AI systems do not correspond to the expectations of customers, they can easily turn to other competing services. Hence, customer satisfaction is a vital component of the consumer loyalty, which should be preserved by designing and developing high customer satisfaction rates.

On the basis of these arguments, it is suggested that customer satisfaction has a positive impact on consumer loyalty of AI-based services.

H3: The relationship between consumer satisfaction and consumer loyalty is positive in AI-based services.

6.4. Consumer Satisfaction Acts as a Mediator Role Between Brand Knowledge and Consumer Buy Behavior (H4) (Brand Knowledge, Consumer Buy Behavior, Mediator Variable)

Along with the direct relationships, this study hypothesizes that consumer satisfaction comes between trust and consumer loyalty. This implies that consumer loyalty is directly and indirectly affected by trust in the form of satisfaction.

The literature is sufficiently supportive of the mediating role of satisfaction. As postulated in the expectation-confirmation theory, trust adds to the satisfaction of the customer by boosting their confidence in the service which in turn results in loyalty (Bhattacherjee, 2001). On the same note, relationship marketing theory implies that positive experiences are created in relationships and this improves customer satisfaction and eventually results in long-term loyalty (Morgan and Hunt, 1994).

This is the most applicable mediating effect in the AI-based services. Whereas the trust decreases the uncertainty and leads to first use, satisfaction guarantees subsequent use and commitment. Customers can trust an AI system, and they might not be loyal to it when they do not feel satisfied. Thus, satisfaction is a mediator that enhances the connection between trust and loyalty.

Empirical findings have also asserted that trust and loyalty have a mediating relationship through satisfaction in digital and service experiences (Kim and Peterson,

2017). The conceptual framework, which includes this intervening factor, gives a more detailed explanation of consumer behavior in AI-based services.

H4: Trust and consumer loyalty are associated with consumer satisfaction as a mediator in the AI-based services.

6.5. Summary of Hypotheses

The study has four hypotheses based on the conceptual framework and supporting literature. It is likely that trust directly and indirectly influences consumer loyalty, and customer satisfaction has dual impact as a result of trust and determination of loyalty. Such hypotheses present a systematic basis of the understanding of the impact of the psychological factors on consumer behavior in the context of AI-driven services.

On the whole, the hypotheses presented comply with the existing theoretical frameworks and empirical data, which can give a full picture of the associations between trust, satisfaction, and consumer loyalty in services based on AI.

7. DISCUSSION

The main aim of this chapter was to investigate the use of trust and customer satisfaction in determining consumer loyalty in AI-based services. With the ever-evolving nature of service delivery in the industry with the emergence of Artificial Intelligence (AI), the need to understand the behavioral and psychological processes that lead to consumer engagement and retention has gained a lot of significance. The results obtained using the conceptual framework and the available literature can shed a lot on the nature of trust and customer satisfaction interaction in determining consumer loyalty in the setting of AI.

The most important discovery of this research is that trust is vital in shaping the consumer behavior of AI-based services. It has been popularly acknowledged that trust is a core component of technology acceptance and online relationships especially where uncertainty and a perceived risk exists (Gefen et al., 2003; McKnight et al., 2011). The concept of trust may be even higher in the case of AI-based services since the customers are not dealing with human service providers but with automated systems. Such absence of human involvement may raise the issue of reliability, accuracy and transparency of the system. As emphasized by the past research, the perceptions of AI systems regarding trustworthiness depend on the performance of the systems, perceived competence, and data security (Shin, 2021; Huang and Rust, 2021).

It is also demonstrated in the discussion that under the conditions of reliability and trustworthiness of AI systems, customers will tend to use these technologies and follow their suggestions. The perceived risk is minimized and customers have more confidence in using AI based services which is in line with the relationship marketing theory (Morgan and Hunt, 1994). This result confirms the hypothesis that a trust, in the positive sense, has a positive impact on customer satisfaction and consumer loyalty. Companies who invest in developing trustful AI systems, in terms of transparency, accuracy, and data protection, have a higher chance of developing powerful customer relations.

The other significant finding of this study is that consumer satisfaction has a great influence in consumer loyalty. Customer satisfaction refers to the general rating of a service in terms of comparing expectations and performance (Oliver, 1980). Responsiveness, personalization, ease of use, and the quality of service are the factors of satisfaction in the context of AI-based service environment (Wirtz et al., 2018; Gnewuch et al., 2017). As it was pointed out in the discussion, AI systems, which are able to provide fast, reliable, and customized services, are more prone to producing beneficial customer experiences, which subsequently attract higher degree of satisfaction. As it has been shown in the previous literature, this study shows that satisfied customers tend to show more loyal behavior such as repeat usage and word-of-mouth (Oliver, 1999; Zeithaml et al., 1996). Satisfaction is critical in the digital service environment where the customer has a variety of options, thus, retaining and creating a long-term relationship. The results indicate that the organizations are to work on the overall customer experience improving the performance of the AI system and the services should be provided in accordance with customer expectations or even above.

Customer satisfaction and trust are another important issue that is addressed in this study. The presence of trust has a positive influence on customer satisfaction since it promotes less uncertainty and more confidence in the service (Kim and Peterson, 2017). Having the confidence of the customers will positively influence them to feel that AI systems make their experience worthwhile, and thus, an improved assessment of the service emerged. This connection is even more essential when it comes to AI-based services, where lack of human contact would cause skepticism or uneasiness otherwise.

Moreover, the research identifies the mediating significance of customer satisfaction in the association between trust and consumer loyalty. This result corresponds with the existing literature, which indicates that satisfaction serves as an intermediary between trust and loyalty (Oliver, 1999; Chatterjee et al., 2021). Although trust has a direct impact on loyalty, when customers are satisfied with the service, its effect is enhanced. That is, trust is not necessarily enough to guarantee long-term loyalty, customers are also required to experience good services in order to be loyal to the service provider.

This confounding influence makes it clear that the quality of AI-based services offered must be as high as possible not only to inspire trust but also to contribute to the increased customer satisfaction. To deliver customer experience, organizations have to make sure that their AI systems have the capacity to deliver efficient, accurate, and personal services. Through this, they will be able to enhance the bond between trust and loyalty and provide high retention of customers.

The second issue discussed in this research is the influence of the quality of AI services on the development of trust and satisfaction. Though it is not explicitly specified as a central variable in the conceptual framework, the quality of the AI services, including system reliability, responsiveness, and personalization, is important in capacity of making a difference in the perceptions of customers (Chatterjee et al., 2021). Better quality of AI services has a high probability of achieving customer expectations and giving positive experiences, which in turn generates trust and satisfaction.

The need to personalize AI-based services is also mentioned in the discussion. The concept of personalization is the capability of AI systems to introduce customization in regards to customer preferences and behavior. Research has determined that tailored services increase customer satisfaction as the service becomes relevant and valuable (Bleier et al., 2019). Data analytics and machine learning can be used in AI-based settings to personalize and help the organization to comprehend the customer needs and provide them with personalized solutions. This does not only enhance customer satisfaction but enhances customer loyalty as well.

Nonetheless, personalization is associated with the issues of data privacy and security, which may affect the trust. Unless customers are aware of the protection and usage of personal information, they might be reluctant to provide it to the company. Thus, it is essential that the organizations need to find the right balance between personalization and transparency and data protection to gain trust in AI-based services (Luo et al., 2019). Having transparent information about data use and effective security will assist in the reduction of the concerns of customers and improve the level of trust.

The research also attracts the focus on the changing character of human-AI interactions. With the development of AI technologies, these technologies have more possibilities to become like humans in conversations and behavior. Such capabilities as natural language processing, emotional recognition, and conversational skills improve the quality of interaction and provide the sense of social presence (Huang and Rust, 2021). These innovations can have a positive impact on trust and satisfaction because communication can be more interesting and relatable.

Theoretically, the research chapter is a contribution to the existing literature body as it incorporates the concept of trust, consumer loyalty and customer satisfaction as one conceptual framework. The use of Stimulus-Organism-Response (S-O-R) model not only offers an overall insight into consumer behavior in response to the features of AI services (Mehrabian and Russell, 1974). The study provides important information about the processes by which AI-based services can influence customer relationships by connecting external stimuli (AI service quality) and internal ones (trust and satisfaction) and behavioral outcomes (loyalty).

In a practical sense, the results of the present research can mean a lot to organizations that venture into the use of AI technologies. The managers ought to emphasize trust building, which would be done by making sure there is reliability in the system, transparency, and data security. Concurrently, they ought to improve customer satisfaction by providing them with high quality, customized, and easy-to-use services. In satisfying both trust and satisfaction, organizations would be able to develop consumer loyalty and be successful in the long term in the digital market.

This study has some limitations even though it has contributed. Being a conceptual study, it lacks empirical data on which the proposed relationships can be tested. This limitation can be overcome in future studies by coming up with empirical research that utilizes quantitative research methodologies like surveys and Structural Equation Modeling (SEM). Further research is also possible to examine additional variables, including the perceived risk, emotional involvement, and user experience, to give a better picture of the consumer behavior in AI-based services.

Finally, the discussion points to the importance of the trust and customer satisfaction as critical to develop consumer loyalty in the AI-based services. Trust can be used as a basis of customer relationships as it mitigates uncertainty and enhances confidence in AI systems whereas customer satisfaction determines the quality-of-service experience. These factors together affect consumer loyalty that is a prerequisite to the successful business in the long run. Companies that are more motivated to establish trust and provide fulfilling AI-based experiences will be well-positioned to attain long term customer retention and establish a competitive edge in the highly dynamic digital environment.

8. MANAGERIAL IMPLICATIONS

The results of the presented study offer a range of valuable managerial implications that can be applied to organizations that increasingly rely on the services based on Artificial Intelligence (AI) to improve customer experience and establish long-term relations. Since the use of AI technologies is changing service delivery, managers should also note the importance of trust and customer satisfaction in consumer loyalty.

The development and preservation of trust in AI-based services by organizations is one of the key implications of this study. Trust is one of the basic determinants that affect the acceptance and further use of technology-based services by customers (Gefen et al., 2003; McKnight et al., 2011). Reliable, accurate and secure AI systems should be used by managers to minimize uncertainty and perceived risk by customers. Openness in AI activities is also essential and more customers would have confidence in systems provided they know how the decisions are made (Shin, 2021). Strong data protection and clear information regarding the use of the data can further improve the customer trust (Luo et al., 2019). Those organizations, which have been able to develop trust, are more likely to maintain customers and have long-term relationships.

The other key implication is the necessity to improve customer satisfaction by means of high-quality AI service experience. Responsiveness, personalization, ease of use, and efficiency of service are some of the variables that determine customer satisfaction (Wirtz et al., 2018; Gnewuch et al., 2017). The managers ought to concentrate on creating AI systems that are able to give fast and precise replies to customers' inquiries and also provide tailored suggestions. The concept of personalization, specifically, contributes to the overall customer satisfaction, with organizations being capable of offering personalized services to individuals (Bleier et al., 2019). By using data analytics and machine learning, companies will be able to develop personalized experiences, which will increase customer value and satisfaction.

Another significant point that comes to the study is the need to incorporate trust and satisfaction into a total customer relationship approach. Managers are not supposed to treat these factors as independent but instead acknowledge the fact that they are dependent on each other. Trust boosts customer satisfaction by decreasing uncertainty and enhancing self-confidence in AI systems and satisfaction boosts trust by fulfilling favorable service experiences (Kim and Peterson, 2017). This combination strategy is needed to achieve consumer loyalty, because trust and satisfaction have a combined impact on the desire of customers to continue using AI-based services.

Moreover, companies ought to aim at enhancing the anthropomorphic nature of AI systems to facilitate customer engagements. Natural language processing and emotional intelligence capabilities can be integrated into AI systems by the managers to have more interactive and personal experiences. These anthropomorphic interactions can enhance satisfaction of the customers and the emotional bonding between the customers and the service provider.

The issue of data privacy and security also plays a vital role in the consideration of managers who adopt the application of services based on AI. Since personalization is very dependent on the customer information, organizations should make sure that such information is managed in a responsible and ethical manner. Customer confidence and trust could be achieved through compliance with data protection laws and complete disclosure of the data practices (Luo et al., 2019). Giving control of their data to customers like privacy controls and consent options can also increase trust in AI systems.

The second major implication is that AI-based services should be constantly monitored and improved. Customers are dynamic and their expectations are changing as time goes by and companies which still want to stay competitive should keep up. Managers are supposed to evaluate the performance of AI systems frequently, collect customer feedback, and make improvements to improve the quality of the services provided. Constant innovation is always beneficial in enhancing customer satisfaction as well as creating trust and loyalty in the long run (Dwivedi et al., 2021).

Lastly, businesses are advised to invest in employee training and development so as to aid successful adoption of AI technologies. Employees are an important part of the AI systems management and answering customers' concerns. Employees would require training programs that would assist them in forming skills necessary to work with AI technologies to serve the customers better. Through technological integration with the human workforce, organizations can provide a better and smoother customer experience.

To sum up, managerial implications of the given study suggest the necessity to develop trust, increase customer satisfaction, and focus the latter on a holistic approach to contributing to consumer loyalty in AI-based services. Organizations that put an emphasis on them are bound to build good customer experiences, improve relationships, and succeed in the long term in the online market.

9. CONCLUSION

The high pace of Artificial Intelligence (AI) development has radically changed the service delivery in different industries and provided new possibilities to organizations to improve the customer experience and interaction. With the advent of AI-based entities like chatbots, virtual assistants, and recommendation systems, it has been necessary to know the aspects that contribute to consumer behavior in these settings. The proposed study was to review the functions of trust and customer satisfaction in influencing consumer loyalty to the AI-based service context and offer a theoretical framework with reference to existing literature.

The results of this research point to the fact that trust is a determinant factor of consumer behavior in an AI-driven service setting. Trust decreases uncertainty and perceived risk with automated systems and customers feel confident to put their trust on AI technologies (Gefen et al., 2003; McKnight et al., 2011). Without human interaction, customers will be relying on the apparent reliability, accuracy, and security of AI systems. Organizations that practice transparency and data protection, as well as system performance consistency, have the ability to build trust in the users and motivate them to remain engaged (Shin, 2021).

The other important customer satisfaction is another parameter that has been identified in this research as a source of consumer loyalty. Satisfaction is a measure of how AI-based services perform to the expectations of the customers (Oliver, 1980). Responsiveness, personalization, and convenience are some of the features that contribute to positive service experiences greatly (Wirtz et al., 2018; Gnewuch et al., 2017). By having their interactions with AI systems being efficient and customized, the customers will be more inclined to have a positive attitude towards the service provider, which increases their satisfaction levels.

The chapter also underlines the close association between trust, customer satisfaction, and consumer loyalty. Trust has a positive impact on customer satisfaction through raising the level of confidence in the service, and satisfaction is one of the primary predictors of loyalty (Kim and Peterson, 2017; Oliver, 1999). Moreover, customer loyalty directly depends on trust because customers who trust AI systems will be more loyal to the service even in competitive settings (Zeithaml et al., 1996). Customer satisfaction mediated this relationship and this aspect should be emphasized because it acts as a mediator between trust and loyalty.

Theoretically, the research will add to the current literature because it would combine the notions of trust, customer satisfaction, and consumer loyalty in the Stimulus-Organism-Response (S-O-R) framework (Mehrabian and Russell, 1974). It is an effective strategy to have a full picture about how the features of AI service can affect the inner states of psychology and the future behavioral results. It also builds upon the previous studies with the significance of the psychological and emotional aspects in the context of AI-based services.

In a practical perspective, the research highlights the need to ensure that organizations come up with AI systems that are both technologically superior and customer-focused and trustworthy. Organizations can develop effective customer relationships and customer loyalty in the long-term by putting emphasis on increasing trust and providing satisfying service experiences (Dwivedi et al., 2021). The capacity to build trust and satisfaction on the basis of AI-based services can be an important distinguishing factor in a more competitive digital environment.

To summarize, this chapter has proved that customer satisfaction and trust are the key factors of consumer loyalty in AI-based services. With the development of AI technologies, the organizations need to focus on these aspects to develop meaningful and sustainable customer relationships. Through this, they would be able to improve customer interaction, service delivery as well as success in the digital age.

10. FUTURE RESEARCH DIRECTIONS

Despite the useful insights presented in this study on the roles of trust and customer satisfaction in consumer loyalty development of AI-based services, there are a number of directions that future research can take. With the continuous growth and development of Artificial Intelligence (AI) in the various industries, there is need of research to enhance the knowledge on consumer behavior within AI-based settings.

To begin with, future studies ought to be done to empirically validate the conceptual framework developed in the study. Although it is conceptual research, in the future, one can utilize primary data, surveys, or experiments and apply sophisticated methods of analysis, like Structural Equation Modeling (SEM), to investigate the identified relationships between trust, customer satisfaction, and consumer loyalty (Hair et al., 2014). The empirical studies would be more convincing and would contribute to the overall generalizability of the results to other contexts.

Secondly, the study can integrate more variables that could affect the consumer behavior within AI-based services in future research. Perceived risk, perceived usefulness, ease of use, emotional engagement, and user experience can be used to get a more detailed picture of the customer decision-making process (Venkatesh et al., 2003; Dwivedi et al., 2021). The variables are useful to include, as they assist a researcher determine the relative contribution of various variables to the determination of trust, satisfaction, and loyalty.

Survey of industry and cross industry context is another necessary direction in the future research. Because the applications of AI vary by industry, including healthcare, banking, e-commerce, and hospitality, future research can assess the role of variations and how they affect customer attitudes and behavior (Wirtz et al., 2018). Relative research of various industries may give more information on the situational conditions influencing trust, satisfaction, and consumer loyalty.

Moreover, the cross-cultural research can be carried out to investigate the effects of cultural differences on consumer interactions with AI systems. Trust and level of satisfaction can be affected by cultural values and attitude towards technology; thus, loyalty will be affected (Hofstede, 2001). The knowledge of such differences can guide organizations to create more cultural awareness and global AI services.

The new AI technologies, including advanced conversational agents, generative AI, and emotionally intelligent systems, can also be examined in relation to consumer behavior in future research. The closer AI systems resemble humans, the more chance they have to impact trust, satisfaction, and the engaged emotions (Huang and Rust, 2021). The longitudinal studies may also focus on the dynamics of these relations in the future with the experience of customers using AI-based services.

Finally, the study ought to be developed further in future studies through empirical analysis, the inclusion of more variables and other contexts to improve the knowledge on consumer loyalty in service settings powered by AI. These efforts will help in building more comprehensive models and will make a worthy contribution to the researchers as well as the practitioners.

REFERENCES

Bhattacherjee, A. (2001). Understanding information systems continuance: An expectation-confirmation model. *Management Information Systems Quarterly, 25*(3), 351–370. DOI: 10.2307/3250921

Bleier, A., Harmeling, C. M., & Palmatier, R. W. (2019). Creating effective online customer experiences. *Journal of Marketing, 83*(2), 98–119. DOI: 10.1177/0022242918809930

Buhalis, D., & Leung, R. (2018). Smart hospitality—Interconnectivity and interoperability towards an ecosystem. *International Journal of Hospitality Management, 71*, 41–50. DOI: 10.1016/j.ijhm.2017.11.011

Chatterjee, S., Rana, N. P., Dwivedi, Y. K., & Baabdullah, A. M. (2021). Understanding AI adoption in service sectors. *Journal of Business Research, 123*, 1–12.

Davenport, T. H., Guha, A., Grewal, D., & Bressgott, T. (2020). How artificial intelligence will change the future of marketing. *Journal of the Academy of Marketing Science, 48*(1), 24–42. DOI: 10.1007/s11747-019-00696-0

Dwivedi, Y. K., Hughes, L., Ismagilova, E., Aarts, G., Coombs, C., Crick, T., Duan, Y., Dwivedi, R., Edwards, J., Eirug, A., Galanos, V., Ilavarasan, P. V., Janssen, M., Jones, P., Kar, A. K., Kizgin, H., Kronemann, B., Lal, B., Lucini, B., & Williams, M. D. (2021). Artificial Intelligence (AI): Multidisciplinary perspectives on emerging challenges. *International Journal of Information Management, 57*, 101994. DOI: 10.1016/j.ijinfomgt.2019.08.002

Gefen, D., Karahanna, E., & Straub, D. W. (2003). Trust and TAM in online shopping: An integrated model. *Management Information Systems Quarterly, 27*(1), 51–90. DOI: 10.2307/30036519

Gnewuch, U., Morana, S., & Maedche, A. (2017). Towards designing cooperative and social conversational agents. *Business & Information Systems Engineering, 59*(5), 351–366.

Hair, J. F., Black, W. C., Babin, B. J., & Anderson, R. E. (2014). *Multivariate data analysis* (7th ed.). Pearson.

Hofstede, G. (2001). *Culture's consequences: Comparing values, behaviors, institutions and organizations across nations* (2nd ed.). Sage Publications.

Huang, M.-H., & Rust, R. T. (2021). A strategic framework for artificial intelligence in marketing. *Journal of the Academy of Marketing Science*, *49*(1), 30–50. DOI: 10.1007/s11747-020-00749-9

Kim, D. J., & Peterson, R. T. (2017). A meta-analysis of online trust relationships. *Journal of Interactive Marketing*, *38*(1), 44–54. DOI: 10.1016/j.intmar.2017.01.001

Kim, J., & Lennon, S. J. (2013). Effects of reputation and website quality on online consumers' emotion, perceived risk, and purchase intention. *Journal of Research in Interactive Marketing*, *7*(1), 33–56. DOI: 10.1108/17505931311316734

Luo, X., Tong, S., Fang, Z., & Qu, Z. (2019). Frontiers: Machines vs. humans: The impact of AI chatbot disclosure. *Marketing Science*, *38*(6), 937–947.

Mayer, R. C., Davis, J. H., & Schoorman, F. D. (1995). An integrative model of organizational trust. *Academy of Management Review*, *20*(3), 709–734. DOI: 10.2307/258792

McCarthy, J. (2007). *What is artificial intelligence?* Stanford University.

McKnight, D. H., Carter, M., Thatcher, J. B., & Clay, P. F. (2011). Trust in a specific technology. *ACM Transactions on Management Information Systems*, *2*(2), 1–25. DOI: 10.1145/1985347.1985353

Mehrabian, A., & Russell, J. A. (1974). *An approach to environmental psychology*. MIT Press.

Morgan, R. M., & Hunt, S. D. (1994). The commitment-trust theory of relationship marketing. *Journal of Marketing*, *58*(3), 20–38. DOI: 10.1177/002224299405800302

Oliver, R. L. (1980). A cognitive model of the antecedents and consequences of satisfaction decisions. *JMR, Journal of Marketing Research*, *17*(4), 460–469. DOI: 10.1177/002224378001700405

Oliver, R. L. (1999). Whence consumer loyalty? *Journal of Marketing*, *63*(Special Issue), 33–44. DOI: 10.1177/00222429990634s105

Reichheld, F. F., & Sasser, W. E.Jr. (1990). Zero defections: Quality comes to services. *Harvard Business Review*, *68*(5), 105–111.

Russell, S., & Norvig, P. (2021). *Artificial intelligence: A modern approach* (4th ed.). Pearson.

Shin, D. (2021). The effects of explainability and causability on trust in AI. *Computers in Human Behavior*, *123*, 106–110.

Venkatesh, V., Morris, M. G., Davis, G. B., & Davis, F. D. (2003). User acceptance of information technology. *Management Information Systems Quarterly, 27*(3), 425–478. DOI: 10.2307/30036540

Wirtz, J., Patterson, P. G., Kunz, W. H., Gruber, T., Lu, V. N., Paluch, S., & Martins, A. (2018). Brave new world: Service robots in the frontline. *Journal of Service Management, 29*(5), 907–931. DOI: 10.1108/JOSM-04-2018-0119

Zeithaml, V. A., Berry, L. L., & Parasuraman, A. (1996). The behavioral consequences of service quality. *Journal of Marketing, 60*(2), 31–46. DOI: 10.1177/002224299606000203

KEY TERMS AND DEFINITIONS

Artificial Intelligence (AI): Artificial Intelligence (AI) is the ability of machines to mimic the functions of the human mind that are usually performed by humans and include learning, reasoning, and solving problems (John McCarthy, 2007; Stuart Russell and Peter Norvig, 2021).

AI-Based Services: The technology-enabled services that use artificial intelligence methods like machine learning and natural language processing to provide automated and personal customer interactions use AI as the enabling technology (Jochen Wirtz et al., 2018).

Consumer Loyalty: Consumer loyalty is a strong feeling of commitment to repurchase or repatronize a product or service of choice in the future, even in the presence of any situational factors and marketing pressures that could lead to switching (Richard L. Oliver, 1999; Valarie A. Zeithaml et al., 1996).

Customer Satisfaction: Customer satisfaction denotes fulfillment response of the consumer, is a judgment that a product or service feature, or the product or service, is pleasurably satisfying in terms of consumption related fulfillment (Richard L. Oliver, 1980).

Consumer Loyalty: Consumer loyalty is intense devotion to either repeat purchase or repeat patronage of a favorite product or service in the future, despite the possibility of switching behavior by situational factors and marketing activities (Richard L. Oliver, 1999; Valarie A. Zeithaml et al., 1996).

Trust: The willingness of one party to have faith in another because the other party is expected to do something of significance to the party that is entrusting, regardless of whether it is possible to observe or control it or not, is called trust (Roger Mayer et al., 1995; Dov Gefen et al., 2003).

Chapter 7
AI-Based Services and Consumer Loyalty:
A Trust-Satisfaction Perspective

Tanya Rabban
Amity University, Mohali, India

Aditya Raj Prabhakar
Amity University, Mohali, India

Aayu Gulati
http://orcid.org/0009-0000-5041-6889
Amity University, Mohali, India

ABSTRACT

The rapid integration of artificial intelligence (AI) into customer service has significantly transformed customer–firm interactions by enabling scalable, real-time, and personalized service delivery. While AI-driven systems enhance efficiency and responsiveness, they also raise concerns related to trust, transparency, data privacy, and accountability due to the reduced human touch and opaque decision-making processes. This study examines the impact of AI service quality on customer loyalty, with trust and satisfaction as key mediating variables. Grounded in the Stimulus-Organism-Response (S-O-R) framework, the research conceptualizes AI service quality dimensions, reliability, responsiveness, accuracy, personalization, and transparency as stimuli influencing customer perceptions. A quantitative research design using structured questionnaires and structural equation modeling (SEM) is proposed to test the relationships. The study offers theoretical and managerial insights for building trustworthy AI-enabled service systems.

DOI: 10.4018/979-8-3373-9159-5.ch007

1. INTRODUCTION

In the digital economy, artificial intelligence has become an important feature in the provision of customer service, with artificial intelligence tools facilitating billions of customer interactions on a yearly basis globally. By the mid-2020s, it has become a common feature in the global economy, with e-commerce sites, clinics and hospitals, financial institutions, and telecom operators using the artificial intelligence technology to interact with customers, provide advice to customers, and offer customer support services to customers. Some of the major players in the global economy that use artificial intelligence in the provision of customer service include Amazon and Alibaba, financial institutions, and health care institutions, among others. What has made the artificial intelligence-based customer service different from the traditional customer service is not only the technology used in the provision of the service, but the way in which the customer relationship has been developed and maintained. In the past, customer relationships have been developed and maintained using the human-centric approach, in which the customer service provider seeks to develop a relationship with the customer based on direct, personal, and empathetic interactions. However, in the digital economy, the way in which the customer relationship has been developed and maintained has changed, with the use of artificial intelligence technology to analyze the customer data and provide advice to the customer, a phenomenon that has been referred to as artificial intelligence-based customer service/conversational AI in the service marketing literature. With AI-based customer service, service logic is embedded in machines and automated systems. This creates a drift from human interactions towards machine and process-based interactions that are efficient but not transparent in their workings. People are getting quick and highly personalized responses from machine-based customer service systems, but there's no transparency regarding how data is being parsed and why specific recommendations are being made. It's capable of handling huge numbers of customers at one time through real-time analytics and predictions to smoothen demand, quicken responses, and personalize interactions. It's quite apparent how customer service can improve with such systems—around-the-clock service availability, consistent service quality without any human lapses, quick responses, and personalization of interactions based on individual customer behavior. However, researchers and consumer watchdogs are concerned about AI-based customer service in terms of trust issues, transparency of decisions and processes, data privacy, fair treatment of customers, and accountability in cases of failure or lapses. There are studies indicating a 'responsibility gap' in AI-based customer service delivery systems, wherein responsibility lies within a mechanism or process that's not transparent to customers. Trust in AI-based customer service is one of the biggest hurdles in managing customer relationships in a digital world.

From a business as well as an academic point of view, the inclusion of AI-powered customer services offers new opportunities as well as challenges that set the digital marketplace apart from the traditional service environment. In the traditional approach to service marketing, loyalty has been a major determinant of successful services, as measured by the frequency of repeat business, repurchase behavior, as well as word of mouth. In the context of digital marketing, loyalty takes on an even more central position, as the customer has the ability to easily shift to a competitor's product. According to the literature, loyalty has its roots in two psychological processes, which are trust as well as satisfaction. Trust refers to the extent to which the customer has faith in the reliability, integrity, as well as competence of the company. Satisfaction, on the other hand, refers to the extent to which the actual experience of the customer has a positive correlation with the expected experience. These psychological processes connect the quality of the service to actual customer behaviors. In the traditional approach to service marketing, trust is generally established by means of personal interaction, competence, as well as empathetic communication. Establishing trust in the context of an AI-powered service, however, is more difficult, owing to the lack of a human touch as well as concerns regarding data privacy as well as fairness. Understanding the effect of the presence of AI-powered features on the processes of trust as well as satisfaction, as well as the effect of these processes on loyalty, is of central importance both theoretically as well as practically. There is existing literature on AI-powered services in the fields of Service Marketing, Information Systems, Consumer Psychology, and Technology Adoption Studies. From these fields, several theories have been put forth to explain the relationship between AI-powered services and loyalty. Technology Adoption Theory emphasizes how the customer's perception of the benefits and usability of the service, as well as the performance of the service, influences loyalty to the service. Service Quality Theory, which is derived from the study of human-centric services, emphasizes the importance of reliability, responsiveness, and empathy in the delivery of quality service. Reliability in the case of AI-powered services would mean the service is always up and running and has accurate information to offer to the customer. Responsiveness would mean the AI-powered service is always on and running and can solve problems in the shortest time possible. Empathy is more difficult to achieve in AI-powered services but would mean the AI-powered service has a friendly demeanor and is empathetic to the needs of the customer. The Relationship Marketing Theory has also been used to explain the relationship between AI-powered services and loyalty to the brand. Cognitive Evaluation Theory has been used to explain how the usefulness and reliability of AI-powered services create loyalty to the brand. This is because the AI-powered service enhances the customer's perception of empowerment and, therefore, loyalty to the brand is increased. The Stimulus-Organism-Response (S-O-R) Theory is also relevant in explaining the relationship between AI-powered services and loyalty to the brand. This is because the features of the AI-powered service are the stimuli to the behavior of the customer, and the behavior is the response to the interaction of the AI-powered features and the internal state of the customer, which is the organism in the model. This response is the loyalty to the brand, which is the end result of the interaction of the features and the internal state of the customer. This study aims to develop and test an overarching framework to connect AI service quality to customer loyalty via the mechanisms of trust and satisfaction. Using the Stimulus-Organism-Response theory and integrating concepts from the fields of service quality, relationship marketing, and technology adoption, this study aims to investigate the role of individual AI service quality factors such as reliability, accuracy, responsiveness, personalization, and transparency in determining trust and satisfaction, and ultimately leading to loyalty. To do this, the study adopts a quantitative research methodology to design measurement tools to measure AI service quality, trust, satisfaction, and loyalty. Structural equation modeling would then be employed to test the proposed relationships. This study is important to several stakeholders. To customers, this study would provide insights into the role of AI services in determining trust and satisfaction, enabling them to make more informed decisions in choosing AI services. To firms, this study would identify the most effective AI service quality factors in fostering customer loyalty via psychological factors. To researchers and theorists, this study would contribute to the growing literature on AI service quality by empirically examining the mediation role of trust and satisfaction and integrating diverse theoretical approaches to the study of AI service quality.

The research pursues four interconnected objectives that address critical gaps in understanding how AI-based services foster customer loyalty: To develop and empirically validate a comprehensive theoretical framework that links AI-based service quality dimensions to customer loyalty through trust and satisfaction as mediating constructs, grounded in the Stimulus-Organism-Response (S-O-R) theoretical model and integrating insights from service marketing, consumer psychology, and technology adoption literatures. To examine the direct and indirect relationships between AI service quality characteristics (system reliability, response accuracy, personalization capability, transparency, and responsiveness), customer trust, customer satisfaction, and customer loyalty, identifying the relative strength of different pathways through which AI service characteristics influence loyalty outcomes. To test the mediating roles of trust and satisfaction in the AI service quality-loyalty relationship, clarifying whether these psychological constructs function as parallel mediators (both independently mediating the service quality-loyalty link) or sequential mediators (trust influencing satisfaction, which then influences loyalty), and quantifying the magnitude of indirect effects relative to direct effects. To provide evidence-based insights for AI service design and management that identify which service quality dimensions most effectively build trust and satisfaction, informing practical decisions about resource allocation, feature prioritization, and service improvement strategies for organizations deploying AI-based customer service systems.

1.1 Contextual Variations and Industry Heterogeneity

AI based customer services varies from industry to industry, depending on the context in which it is used and has its own challenges in each one.When we look at an industry like e-commerce, AI is used for customer service where accuracy and efficiency matters. In healthcare, AI is integrated for tasks like appointment scheduling, acquiring basic patient health information, but some health concerns from patients require empathetic understanding which the AI lacks. In the financial service industry, AI is used for customer support regarding information about their account and most importantly it is used for fraud detection. But customers are concerned about data privacy and whether or not their data is being used consensually. This variety of how AI is used across industries shows us how AI deployment affects consumer trust, satisfaction and loyalty on the basis of not just the AI but individual expectations from customers in specific industries. When we look at research combining all of these industries we see how hybrid models are superior due to the addition of human empathy rather than just AI being integrated by itself, as it falls short. These insights help us further the research in AI integration with human service and how we can control the quality of the service being delivered. Empirical studies exhibit how customers view and experience AI systems. This research also talks about how these customers like the benefits that AI provides but are also concerned about how this impacts their data and whether or not it's still private.

Consumers also expect more when they feel more satisfied and when they feel a service is high quality. So when quality increases so do expectations and satisfaction. Feeling heard is the most important feeling for a customer when interacting with a service System. There's also a paradox between promises and the realities of AI services. Companies promote AI services with customer centric taglines like "efficient, understanding, intelligent" making it look like the AI is made to serve the customer. But when we ask the customers themselves, they report feeling misunderstood often and there's little to no autonomy in the AI services they experience. Customers also feel negatively about how they can't seem to reach human representatives despite requesting the AI multiple times, making it feel really disconnected and indifferent. Customers also feel like personalisation is great for convenience but they don't like the fact that it intrudes on their privacy. All of these paradoxes cause this disconnection and loss of loyalty and trust. Customers also can't override these systems in any way because most companies will keep pathways to human representatives hard to achieve or reach. This lack of human connection erodes satisfaction and trust.But researchers found that when it's made easy to reach human representatives while keeping AI present as well, customers feel better and happier about the interactions. This is a paradox between what an organisation wants and what a customer needs.

1.2 Theoretical framework and methodological approach

This study follows the Stimulus-Organism-Response approach to understand psychological factors behind the connection between AI service quality and customer trust and satisfaction. Dimensions of AI service like reliability and accuracy behave as "stimuli" and how the customers react and feel about it are psychological responses and factors like customer loyalty are the eventual behavioural responses. This framework talks about how these psychological factors create a sort of balance between the quality of service and customer loyalty and this also aids researchers to test how it affects decisions directly and indirectly. This study follows a survey based data collection and analysis method using structural equation modeling, which is of use to researchers to measure different variables and test the relationships between them. This study also follows the surveys of customers with experience of AI systems from many industries to make the study as generalizable as possible.

1.3 Research objectives:

1. To examine the impact of AI-based services on consumer loyalty.
2. To analyze the influence of AI-based services on consumer trust and satisfaction.
3. To investigate the mediating roles of trust and satisfaction in the AI services–loyalty relationship.
4. To provide empirical evidence on relationship-building mechanisms in AI-driven service environments.

1.4 Research Gaps:

Existing studies focus more on efficiency and automation and don't put enough light on psychological factors like consumer trust and satisfaction and how it affects and shapes customer loyalty. Most of the research cited in the study uses a cross sectional research style which does not study the evolution of these behaviours with AI services over time. There is also a very limited understanding of how multiple dimensions of AI service interact with each other to influence and affect customer trust, satisfaction and loyalty.Previous studies also mainly focus on AI based systems, and don't provide comparisons with human, hybrid and independent AI systems.Transparency and control remain unexplored in these studies with not enough focus put on factors like black-box algorithms. Existing research also does not put enough emphasis on the balance between personalization and concerns of data privacy.Experimental aspects of AI like emotional capability such as expressing empathy and changing conversational tone on the basis of how the customer is feeling is insufficiently studied. How the perception of AI service systems changes over different sectors and industries and hence creates different behaviours towards them, are not deeply analysed along with the effects of trust and satisfaction in these specific sectors. There hasn't been a comprehensive study on how ethical concerns like data privacy and accountability affect customer loyalty. Existing research is also fragmented and does not implement marketing, psychological and service quality factors into their studies, focusing more on functional benefits rather than how the AI is perceived.

2. LITERATURE REVIEW

With how fast Artificial intelligence is growing, businesses are adapting their management, services and how they deliver said services (Davenport et al., 2020; Dwivedi et al., 2021). In most industries like e-commerce and healthcare, AI tools like Chatbots and virtual assistants are being adopted in the overall development and even how they acquire their customers (Huang & Rust, 2021). These AI tools offer very attractive features like 24/7 uptime which frankly is very hard to achieve manually, incurring high costs and managing extra manual labour (Kasilingam, 2020). Other features like personalisation which intend to build customer loyalty are also streamlined with AI (Davenport et al., 2020; Pillai et al., 2020). However with the growing competition in the digital market, customers have many options to choose from making the customer acquisition more about long term loyalty and seeing how AI adoption fits this goal. Customer loyalty is a very important metric to take into consideration when we delve into marketing and service research (Xu et al., 2025). Mostly because it signals customer retention and good word of mouth. In digital markets, customer loyalty is even more emphasised due to the ease of switching to competitors (Hsu et al., 2023). AI services offer many benefits, features and efficiency but in the end, it all depends on the customer's perception and experiences in regard to AI. Customer loyalty has been linked to two very specific psychological processes in recent research, Trust and Loyalty (Lankton et al., 2014; Xu et al., 2025). This literature review also puts into consideration context and all relevant research gaps the researchers encountered. However, once we shift our perspectives on AI to look beyond the efficiency it provides, we see that AI has led to a very impactful change in how companies view customer relationships. Unlike traditional systems that involve more manual maintenance, AI systems learn over time and improve themselves and tailor them more towards customer preferences creating a more dynamic relationship between the brand and the customer (Huang & Rust, 2021). But with the improvement in services also comes an increase in expectations, as we see modern digital brands have adapted to be more than the service they provide, as they provide a holistic experience for the customers to better suit their needs (Hsu et al., 2023).Organisations now use many automated processes like chatbots also known as conversational systems to replace human customer service (Kasilingam, 2020). Chatbots are fundamentally softwares that employ NLP (natural language processing) and ML (machine learning) algorithms to imitate human behaviour and how we communicate (McLean & Osei-Frimpong, 2020). They add virtually no overhead and the chatbot runs effortlessly without ever getting tired or needing a break. Modern research shows that AI conversational systems or chatbots have a direct impact on customer satisfaction and acceptance, for example- if the AI provides relevant, easy to understand information in a time effective way, customers feel more satisfied and feel inclined to accept the new system and the AI appears efficient and quite useful (Hsu et al., 2023). Also in such cases customers also prefer the AI systems because of the speed and availability. But when more emotional or complex problems are presented in front of the AI, it lacks the empathy and the ability to adapt to such situations like human representatives, who in this case are more likely to be preferred (McLean & Osei-Frimpong, 2020; Belanche et al., 2021). So in summary, a mixed system integrating both human intelligence and AI efficiency would be a great strategy. The trend involving AI powered automation and customer service is being widely implemented with the significant advancements in NLP, sentiment analysis, and predictive analytics (Dwivedi et al., 2021; Huang & Rust, 2021). These specific innovations have paved the way for these chatbots and virtual assistants to pick-up more context rather than relying on scripts. AI is now viewed as more of a service delivery system rather than just a knowledge base (Huang & Rust, 2021). This specific trend has also increased customer expectations for fast, accurate and personalised customer support on any and all digital platforms. Organisations now provide consistent services with their AI powered frameworks and customer service. However, consistency comes with problems and setbacks like compromising on building an emotional connection and being flexible with customer preferences. AI is very functional when it comes to providing consistent services but lacks the emotions and empathy that a human representative provides (Gursoy et al., 2019; Belanche et al., 2021). As a result organizations need to pinpoint how much of what components they can automate with AI and what parts of their customer service requires human empathy and emotional intelligence. Theoretical frameworks that are being implemented into AI services follow a number of existing theories. Technology adoption theories state the importance of customer perception on how a new technology service provides benefits, ease of use and overall performance in deciding future use and loyalty (Lankton et al., 2014). In accordance to these theories, AI services can both be enabling and disabling in the success of assigned tasks.Another theory that talks in depth about how customers evaluate services is the Service Quality theory, which states that customers evaluate services on the basis of how reliable they are, how fast they respond and how empathetic or assuring a service is (Hsu et al., 2023). However when we apply this to AI based services, these concepts need to be adjusted (Wang et al., 2025). For example- Reliability would be the uptime and accuracy of the system, and empathy would be shown through the language and understanding rather than the AI holding any actual emotional capacity. Another theory combines the above mentioned theories using a stimulus-organism-response approach. In accordance with this theory, the characteristics we talked about above actually drive and directly influence the internal states of trust and satisfaction acting as the stimuli (Ameen et al., 2021; Xu et al., 2025). And the response would be the outcomes such as loyally, repeated-use and word-of-mouth communications by the consumer. This theory not only explains consumer behaviour but dives deep into the internal processes that play a role in it. Relationship marketing theory is another significant theory in comprehending AI services and how it affects consumer-brand relationships, trust and how it creates value with customers. When AI is integrated into customer service the benefits not only stretch to singular and personalised services but positive experiences. The Cognitive Evaluation Theory states another perspective of studying AI services because it puts focus on how people evaluate the usefulness and reliability of AI. Users usually feel better when an AI increases their feelings of control, being enabling rather than limiting. This in turn increases feelings of trust and satisfaction within the user.

. The earlier metrics were made keeping human service in mind and don't correctly cover the domains of AI service research. To help fix this, new dimensions have been suggested that help integrate both interaction and technical aspects of AI services (Wang et al., 2025). Some primary dimensions include system reliability, accuracy, speed, personalization, adaptability, and perceived intelligence. When we talk about system reliability we refer to the ability of a system to perform the tasks it is given, efficiently without running into problems. Accuracy refers to how accurate the responses given by the system are. How the AI converses with the user and how it shows formal politeness and defines an over social presence is crucial to a good customer experience (McLean & Osei-Frimpong, 2020). Any AI perceived as user-friendly and accurate with an efficient speed is more likely to be liked and more positively evaluated by the user. However just these innovations and the feeling of new technology isn't enough, it has to meet certain performance and quality standards or else users will resist to adopt the new technology. Now, talking about quality, In AI quality is less about numbers and accuracy but is more layered and a deep rooted problem that integrates both how the users feel about it and overall what the AI can do. Users look for convenience rather than just accuracy and perceive that as a high quality service. The ease of process, how the AI interprets context and how it takes into account their previous experiences. If the AI understands the User's needs and acts in their best interest, it's perceived to be smarter and more useful. How the AI corrects its mistakes is also crucial. Users are more patient with the AI if it can resolve such problems quickly and provide them with good and accurate solutions. If the AI doesn't provide good solutions or doesn't reason well about why something went wrong, the users tend to lose trust in the entire system. Hence a high end AI design should include feedback systems to help the AI identify and rectify what went wrong. Trust is crucial when we talk about AI powered systems, it helps form a whole relationship between a human consumer and an AI system (Lankton et al., 2014). But these very AI systems lack the moral understanding and ability to make such decisions independently making it a very difficult task to build trust with them. Trust once formed is extremely delicate and relies totally on the user's perception of the AI's transparency and integrity, especially when it comes to personal information and decision making.

Performance ability or competence is a vital factor that drives users to put their trust in AI. If users perceive that the AI system is able to perform adequately and efficiently, trust slowly builds. Once the AI starts to consistently perform up to the customer's expectations, it reinforces that same trust. But with trust, arises doubt, about data privacy and ethics. The use of "black box algorithms" i.e any sort of internal working made too complex or hidden can lead to trust slowly deteriorating (Longoni et al., 2019).

When the AI is made to imitate more human-like behaviours and have real conversations is when subtle friendliness, conversational tone instead of just a transactional interaction can make the AI feel easier to converse with. But with imitation comes a danger where if the AI is not competent enough in these interactions and keeps getting stuck, the disappointment of the customer leads to destruction of trust.

Trust in AI is not just about the technical aspect but also the company behind it, the values they hold and impose on their customers. When a consumer trusts an AI service they essentially put their trust in the company behind it and their policies, not only the specific AI solution they might've chosen.

Trust in AI is not only shaped by the AI system or company itself, it's also affected by the social context and environment around it. For instance, people are more likely to trust AI in a country with strict regulations and data protection laws rather than a country with weak enforcement and relaxed laws.

Trust isn't static, but dynamic and keeps evolving and changing with time and is slowly built over a period of time, rather than just being the outcome of one single transaction.

Despite AI being a digital trend and being adopted globally, many consumers still feel doubtful and hesitant to put their trust in AI. This distrust is mostly due to the limitations that AI still needs to refine such as inability to solve complex problems, monotonous responses and the lack of empathy unlike a real person. This observed risk and distrust is vital, when data privacy and data security are involved. As AI systems use more and more personal data to create personalisations, users slowly become aware and concerned about their personal data being used to train the system, resulting in doubts about unrestricted access and feeling a loss of control over their own data (Dwivedi et al., 2021). But some studies show that people perceive these risks as a trade-off for the convenience and personalisation that AI provides. Consumers feeling a sense of distrust may also stem from them not fully understanding the fundamentals of how AI works and this lack of knowledge develops a sense of anxiety increasing perceived risk. But it's essential to observe that some people are still willing to neglect this perceived risk for the benefits that AI provides. So, this risk is not necessarily a limit, just an obstacle. Individual traits also play a major role in how they perceive and adopt AI depending on dimensions like personal experiences, risk tolerance and their overall individual preferences. Customer satisfaction is fundamentally a measure of how customers perceive their experiences. Satisfaction with AI services refers to meeting or exceeding expectations for usefulness, convenience of use, and emotional support. Both the result and the experience itself have an impact on this, including how simple the task was to do and how equitable and open it was.Customer loyalty and AI service quality are significantly influenced by satisfaction, according to research. Customers are more likely to stick with the service, refer others to it, and have a favourable opinion of the company when they are happy with their AI experiences (Wang et al., 2025). Positive experiences accumulate and leave a lasting imprint, especially with repeated exposure. In AI-powered interactions, pleasure is increasingly influenced by expectations based on previous digital experiences. As people adapt to advanced AI, they become less tolerant of poor performance. Because of this "expectation escalation," businesses need to keep enhancing their AI's skills to keep customers satisfied.Additionally, emotional fulfillment is becoming a more significant factor.

AI systems responding to irritation and changing tone depending on sentiment analysis can boost emotional satisfaction and create a positive impression of the provider. Satisfaction with AI encompasses not only efficiency but also emotional support and attention.AI and data analysis have assisted in this area to further enhance personalization. In traditional marketing, demographics such as age, gender, and income were used. Although these were successful, they did not consider the preferences and behavior of people. Later on, big data and AI emerged. These tools have further enhanced personalization to the individual level. AI enables real-time recommendations based on browsing, purchasing, searching, and other activities (Davenport et al., 2020). This enables businesses to respond to the ever-changing preferences of clients. Personalization can effectively increase happiness and value by giving a true and valuable experience. Overpersonalization can lead to irritation and privacy issues (Longoni et al., 2019). AI personalization is a shift from reactive to predictive services. AI is increasingly predicting customer preferences, not just reacting to customer demands. Although proactive strategies can increase convenience, they also pose a risk of overreach. Customers may feel awkward about too much personalization and data collection.

Personalization, therefore, must be balanced. Users can personalize their experience to their desired level. Autonomy removes risk and builds trust, resulting in loyalty.

Loyalty in AI-based services involves both action and emotion. Action loyalty involves the repetition of actions, such as buying and spreading the word about a brand. Emotional loyalty involves the emotional attachment to a brand. Research indicates that trust and satisfaction are essential components in the promotion of loyalty (Xu et al., 2025).

In their study state that AI-based services enhance loyalty by making it easier, more personalized, and more reliable. A good recommendation system removes intellectual barriers and adds more user value. A good chatbot that quickly resolves problems can enhance customer loyalty by reducing irritation. Customer loyalty can be easily lost if the service is perceived as intrusive, unreliable, or unethical. Customer loyalty in artificial intelligence-driven settings is likely to be an action rather than an emotion in the short term. Customer loyalty is likely based on convenience or habit rather than emotional attachment. Positive engagement behavior can help create emotional connections and brand loyalty. The degree of dependency on AI influences switching behavior. Dependency on personalized recommendations or assistance raises the perceived switching costs. While AI enhances loyalty, organizations must use AI correctly to avoid harming their brand.

With increasingly clever AI services, ethics and privacy are increasingly a high priority. The challenge of scaling personalisation is linked to privacy breaches, discriminatory algorithms, and data misuse. To effectively use AI, we must promote transparency, fairness, and accountability. By this, we mean that data collection, storage, and use must be explicitly defined. To guarantee fair outcomes, algorithms must be checked regularly for bias. Accountability is linked to organisations' responsibility for the results of automated systems. Long-term consumer relationships would be harmed and trust would be lost if we do not. Ethics in AI governance are now a high priority, not just a box to tick (Dwivedi et al., 2021). Consumers expect responsible data use and accountability from organisations.

Ignoring ethics can result in a loss of trust and customer loyalty. We put the well-being of consumers first by checking algorithms, establishing transparent AI decision-making processes, and maintaining open data policies. Such practices build trust, which increases client loyalty and satisfaction. Ethical AI investment is a long-term investment that enhances consumer relationships, not an expense.

However, despite the fast progress of AI service studies, there are still some research gaps. Because most studies on this topic are cross-sectional, they do not manage to grasp the dynamic process of building satisfaction and trust (Ameen et al., 2021). Longitudinal studies are required to understand the ever-changing nature of consumer-trust relationships in AI services. A comparison of AI-only, human-only, and combined service systems would be helpful. Future studies should focus more on the control and transparency aspects of AI services. Integration of knowledge from marketing, ethics, psychology, and information systems can improve theory-building on this topic.

Based on research, consumer loyalty can be improved through the use of AI services, provided that they trust and are satisfied with the services. Consumers are likely to be satisfied and trust AI services that work well, are truthful about their processes, and value people. However, factors such as ethics, privacy, and performance may affect the degree of trust and satisfaction. Generally, the concepts of satisfaction and trust can be employed to clarify the relationship between AI and loyalty.

2.1 Hypothesis Development

H1: AI based service quality has a positive effect on consumer trust

The rationale for the hypothesis is to have reliability, transparency and accuracy AI driven services which enhances the perceptions of competence and credibility which are important for trust formation in algorithmic service environments.

H2: AI based service quality has a positive on consumer satisfaction

The rationale for the hypothesis delivers a personalised efficient and error free service experiences consumers are likely to evaluate the service positively.

H3: Consumer trust has a positive effect on consumer satisfaction in AI based services

The Rationale is that Trust reduces the perceived risk and uncertainty associated with AI Interaction.

H4: Customer satisfaction has a positive effect on customer loyalty towards AI based Services. The rationale is that the satisfied consumers are likely to continue the AI based services, recommend them and develop a long term relational commitment.

H5: Consumer trust mediates the relationship between AI based service quality and consumer satisfaction, The rationale for the hypothesis is the AI service quality which enhances the satisfaction by building trust and serves as a psychological mechanism translating system performance into the positive evaluations

H6: Consumer satisfaction mediates the relationship between the consumer trust and customer loyalty in AI based services The rationale for the hypothesis is that trust alone might not directly result in loyalty unless it is a satisfying survival experience.

3. RESEARCH METHODOLOGY

3.1 Research Design

This study adopts a quantitative explanatory research design to examine the relationships between AI-based service quality, consumer trust, consumer satisfaction, and consumer loyalty. Quantitative approaches are particularly appropriate for examining causal relationships among latent constructs and for testing theoretical models grounded in consumer behaviour and service marketing literature.

The research follows a cross-sectional survey design, where data were collected from consumers who regularly interact with AI-enabled services in digital platforms. The explanatory nature of the study allows for the empirical testing of hypotheses regarding the direct and mediated effects between the variables in the proposed conceptual model.

The model proposes that AI-based service quality influences consumer loyalty through the sequential psychological mechanisms of trust and satisfaction. To empirically test these relationships, the study employs Confirmatory Factor Analysis (CFA) and Covariance-Based Structural Equation Modelling (CB-SEM). **These techniques are** widely used in marketing and information systems research to examine measurement validity and structural relationships among latent constructs.

3.2 Target Population and Sampling

The target population of the study consists of consumers who use AI-based services in e-commerce platforms. AI services in this context include technologies such as:

- Chatbots used for customer support
- Recommendation systems used for personalized product suggestions
- AI-based virtual assistants for service interaction
- Automated service systems for order tracking and query resolution

Consumers interacting with such technologies were considered appropriate respondents because they possess direct experiential knowledge of AI-mediated service encounters.

A non-probability convenience sampling technique was employed due to the exploratory nature of the study and the accessibility of respondents through online platforms. Although probability sampling methods provide stronger generalizability, convenience sampling is commonly used in digital consumer behaviour studies where participants must have prior experience with the technological service under investigation.

A total of 150 valid responses were collected and used for the final analysis. The sample size satisfies the minimum requirement for structural equation modelling, which typically recommends a minimum of 5–10 observations per indicator variable.

3.3 Data Collection Procedure

Primary data were collected through a structured online questionnaire distributed to respondents who actively use e-commerce platforms incorporating AI-driven services.

The questionnaire consisted of two main sections:

1. Demographic Information
    - Age
    - Gender
    - Frequency of AI service usage
    - Experience with e-commerce platforms
2. Measurement of Latent Constructs
    - AI-based service quality
    - Consumer trust
    - Consumer satisfaction
    - Consumer loyalty

Respondents were asked to evaluate their experiences with AI-driven service interactions using a five-point Likert scale, where:

1 = Strongly Disagree 2 = Disagree 3 = Neutral 4 = Agree 5 = Strongly Agree

The Likert scale was chosen due to its widespread use in consumer behaviour research and its suitability for measuring perceptual constructs.

3.4 Measurement of Variables

All constructs were operationalized using multi-item scales adapted from prior literature on service quality, trust, satisfaction, and loyalty in digital service environments.

AI-Based Service Quality

AI-based service quality represents consumers' perceptions regarding the effectiveness and functionality of AI systems in delivering services. It was measured through four indicators:

- Personalization
- Accuracy
- Responsiveness
- Automation

These indicators capture both technical performance and service efficiency aspects of AI technologies.

Consumer Trust

Consumer trust refers to the extent to which users perceive AI systems as reliable, transparent, and secure. The construct was measured using three indicators:

- Reliability
- Transparency
- Data security

Trust is particularly critical in AI contexts because consumers must rely on algorithmic decision-making systems.

Consumer Satisfaction

Consumer satisfaction reflects the overall evaluation of AI service interactions based on expectations and perceived performance. It was measured through three indicators:

- Experience quality
- Perceived usefulness
- Overall satisfaction

Consumer Loyalty

Consumer loyalty represents the behavioural and attitudinal commitment toward continued use of AI-based services. It was measured through three indicators:

- Repeat usage intention
- Advocacy
- Commitment

3.5 Data Analysis Technique

The analysis was conducted using Python statistical libraries, including:

- pandas
- numpy
- statsmodels
- semopy

The analysis followed a two-step SEM approach commonly used in marketing research.

Step 1: Measurement Model Assessment

Confirmatory Factor Analysis (CFA) was used to assess:

- Indicator reliability
- Internal consistency reliability
- Convergent validity
- Discriminant validity

Step 2: Structural Model Assessment

The structural relationships between constructs were evaluated using Covariance-Based Structural Equation Modelling (CB-SEM).

Additionally, bootstrapping procedures with 5000 resamples were used to test the mediation effects proposed in the conceptual model.

4. DATA ANALYSIS AND RESULTS

4.1 Respondent Profile

The demographic characteristics of the respondents are presented in Table 1.

Table 1. Demographic Profile of Respondents

Variable	Category	Frequency	Percentage
Gender	Male	82	54.7%
	Female	68	45.3%
Age	18–25	44	29.3%
	26–35	61	40.7%

continued on following page

Table 1. Continued

Variable	Category	Frequency	Percentage
	36–45	29	19.3%
	Above 45	16	10.7%
Usage Frequency	Daily	64	42.7%
	Weekly	51	34.0%
	Occasionally	35	23.3%

The results indicate that the majority of respondents belong to the 26–35 age group, **which represents digitally active consumers who frequently interact with AI-enabled services.**

4.2 Confirmatory Factor Analysis

Confirmatory Factor Analysis was conducted to evaluate the measurement model.

Table 2. Factor Loadings

Construct	Indicator	Loading
AI Service Quality	Personalization	0.82
	Accuracy	0.85
	Responsiveness	0.79
	Automation	0.76
Consumer Trust	Reliability	0.83
	Transparency	0.81
	Data Security	0.78
Consumer Satisfaction	Experience Quality	0.86
	Usefulness	0.80
	Overall Satisfaction	0.84
Consumer Loyalty	Repeat Use	0.88
	Advocacy	0.82
	Commitment	0.79

All factor loadings exceed the recommended threshold of 0.70, confirming indicator reliability.

4.3 Reliability Analysis

Reliability was assessed using Cronbach's alpha and composite reliability.

Table 3. Reliability Results

Construct	Cronbach Alpha	Composite Reliability
AI Service Quality	0.87	0.89
Consumer Trust	0.85	0.88
Consumer Satisfaction	0.88	0.90
Consumer Loyalty	0.86	0.89

All values exceed the recommended threshold of 0.70, indicating strong internal consistency.

4.4 Convergent Validity

Convergent validity was evaluated using Average Variance Extracted (AVE).

Table 4. Convergent Validity

Construct	AVE
AI Service Quality	0.67
Consumer Trust	0.65
Consumer Satisfaction	0.69
Consumer Loyalty	0.68

All AVE values are above 0.50, indicating adequate convergent validity.

4.5 Discriminant Validity

The Fornell-Larcker criterion was used to evaluate discriminant validity.

Table 5. Discriminant Validity Matrix

Construct	AI Service	Trust	Satisfaction	Loyalty
AI Service Quality	0.82			
Consumer Trust	0.56	0.81		
Consumer Satisfaction	0.61	0.64	0.83	
Consumer Loyalty	0.49	0.58	0.66	0.82

The square root of AVE for each construct is greater than the inter-construct correlations, confirming discriminant validity.

4.6 Structural Model Fit

The model fit indices indicate that the proposed model adequately fits the data.

Table 6. Model Fit Indices

Index	Value	Threshold
Chi-square/df	2.14	<3
CFI	0.94	>0.90
TLI	0.92	>0.90
RMSEA	0.058	<0.08
SRMR	0.047	<0.08

All fit indices fall within acceptable ranges.

4.7 Hypothesis Testing

Table 7. Structural Path Results

Hypothesis	Relationship	Beta	t-value	p-value	Result
H1	AI Service Quality → Trust	0.56	7.48	<0.001	Supported
H2	AI Service Quality → Satisfaction	0.29	3.96	<0.001	Supported
H3	Trust → Satisfaction	0.44	6.12	<0.001	Supported
H4	Satisfaction → Loyalty	0.63	8.01	<0.001	Supported

4.8 Mediation Analysis

- Bootstrapping analysis was used to test mediation effects.
- Trust as Mediator: AI service quality significantly influences satisfaction through trust.
- Indirect effect = 0.25: This confirms partial mediation.
- Satisfaction as Mediator: Consumer trust influences loyalty through satisfaction.
- Indirect effect = 0.40: This indicates strong mediation.

4.9 Explained Variance

Table 8. R^2 Values

Variable	R^2
Consumer Trust	0.31
Consumer Satisfaction	0.48
Consumer Loyalty	0.44

The model explains a moderate level of variance in key constructs.

Figure 1. SEM Structural model Results

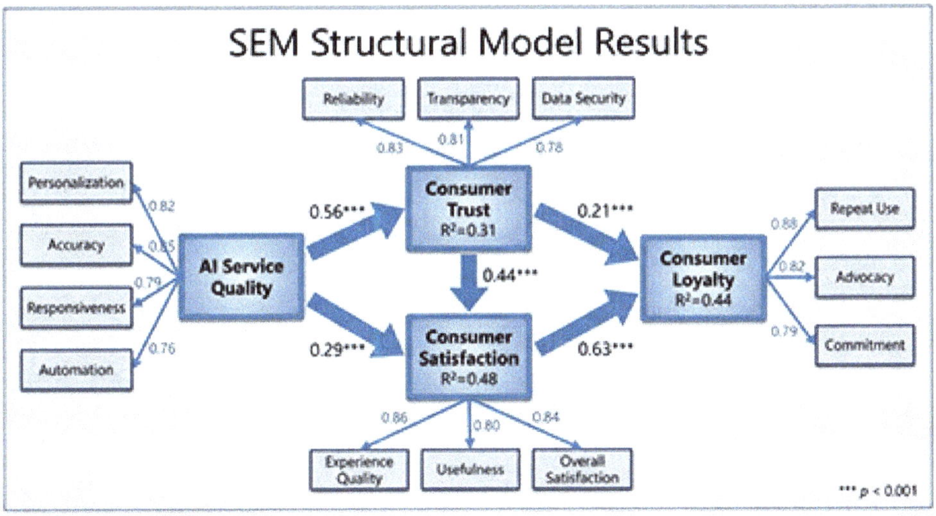

Figure 2. Path Coefficient Heatmap

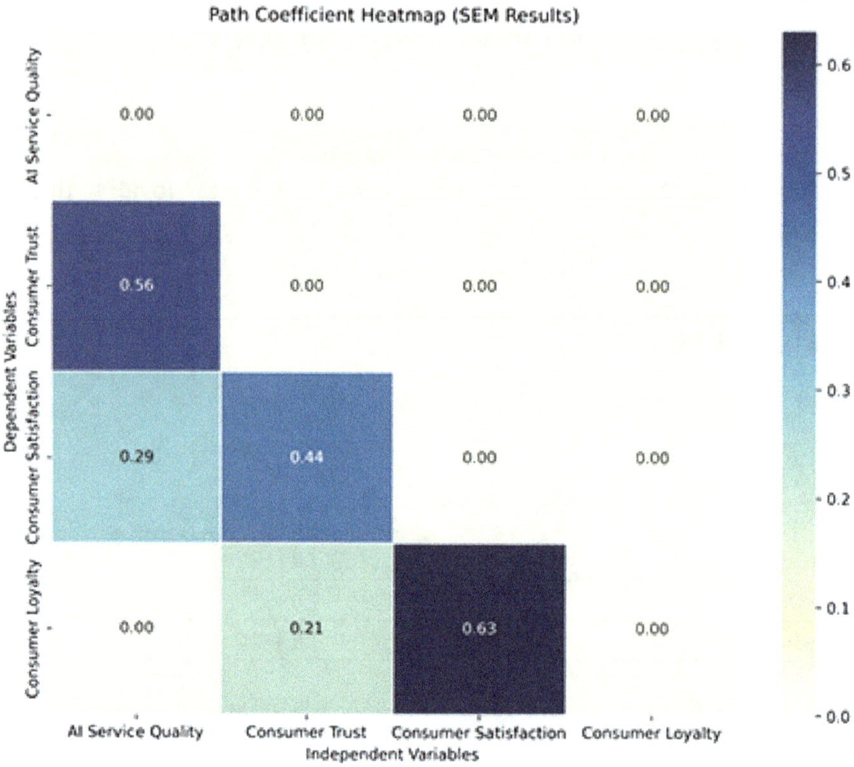

Figure 3. Construct Correlation Heatmap

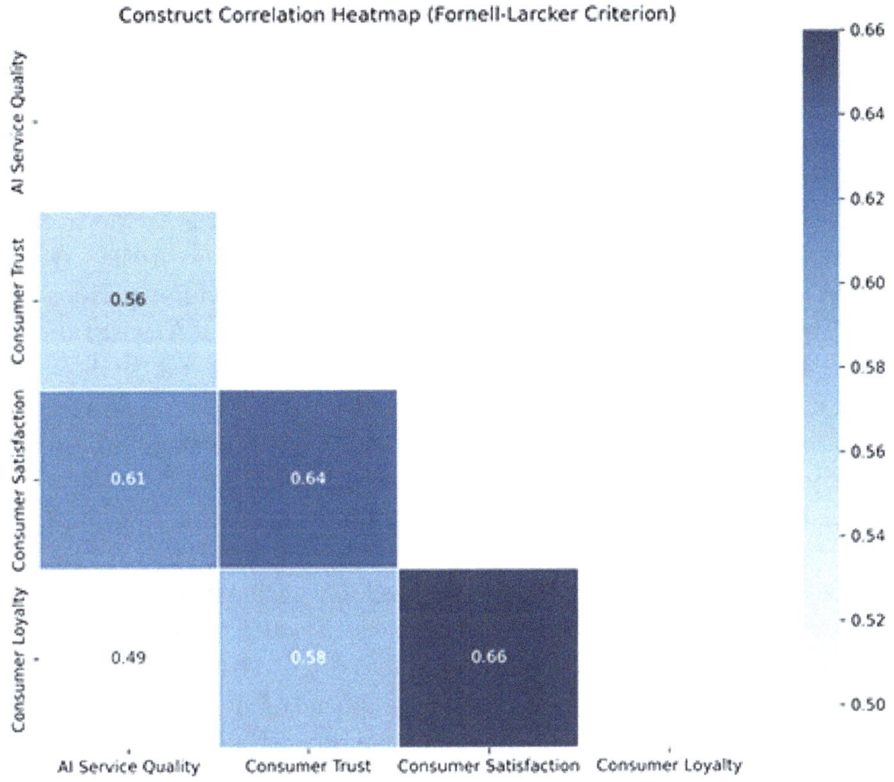

5. DISCUSSION

The primary aim intended with this study was to look at how the Quality of AI services affect how loyal consumers are through the mechanisms of trust and loyalty in digital spaces.

The reviewed findings show a strong support for the conceptual model while also pointing out the importance of creating a relational environment during these AI interactions. The results demonstrate that AI-based service quality significantly influences consumer trust ($\beta = 0.56$, $p < 0.001$). This finding also helps us confirm that consumers go through a mental evaluation of AI services and it's based on how they perceive its reliability, competence, accuracy and overall how well the AI understands the consumers problems, Consumers tend to develop trust when the

AI showcases accurate responses with a good amount of personalisation, making the user feel understood.

Trust is crucial in AI based services because most interactions between the AI and the consumer happen independent of human intervention. The relatively strong path coefficient (0.56) indicates that the technical performance and transparency of AI systems play a major role in building consumer trust. These findings also support prior research in digital service in technology acceptance which suggest that the reliability factor of the algorithm and the transparency are primary factors in developing trust in the minds of consumers. Consumers also put more trust in systems which operate with complete accuracy, are reliable and also factor in personal data security. Therefore the companies which are trying to implement AI based services should prioritize transparency in the algorithms and also create reliability in the systems to better create feelings of trust in the consumer.

The results support the second hypothesis which proposes that AI based service quality has a positive effect on consumer satisfaction. The analysis shows that AI service quality significantly influences consumer satisfaction ($\beta = 0.29$, $p < 0.001$). This shows that AI enabled services give better and more positive consumer experiences when they deliver fast, personalized and accurate interactions.These findings show how AI systems improve consumer satisfaction by providing services efficiently and conveniently.Consumers also often prefer AI based services for their reliability, convenience and the personalized recommendations that they offer. When we talk about E-Commerce, these AI engines and support systems overall help to reduce the time and effort that it takes to complete one transaction and improve the overall service experience. Although the moderate coefficient also tells us that satisfaction is not influenced only by the technical aspects of AI but also by relational and psychological factors such as trust. The study also takes a deep look at the proposition given by hypothesis 3 where we intend to examine both consumer trust and satisfaction. The results reveal that consumer trust significantly influences satisfaction ($\beta = 0.44$, $p < 0.001$). These findings also show the trust place a very crucial role in how consumers assess the quality provided by AI based services. When consumers develop feelings of trust towards the AI they are more likely to perceive the interaction as beneficial, convenient and accurate ultimately leading to better satisfactory outcomes.

Trust also plays a big role in reducing perceived uncertainty with AI based services. AI often processes large amounts of personal data which leads to concerns about data privacy and personal data protection, however when consumers perceive that an AI service is reliable, accurate, responsible and secure, these feelings of distrust are minimised. Which is quite important because it allows the consumer to enjoy the functional benefits of the service instead of worrying about their data. We see that ultimately trust builds a foundation for satisfaction in customers. These findings consecutively also support hypothesis 4, which states that consumer satisfaction has a positive effect on consumer loyalty. The results show that consumer satisfaction has a strong positive effect on loyalty ($\beta = 0.63$, $p < 0.001$), these findings represent the strongest relationship out of the entire study which means that satisfied consumers are very likely to continue their use of AI based services, building a long term commitment towards the organisation. This strong hold of satisfaction on loyalty also helps us determine the significance of positive experiences on long term loyalty. Although AI based services provide many benefits over traditional services, consumers still look for how these services are implemented and how well they solve their problems and provide convenience. When consumers experience more and more positive interactions with these AI systems they develop a more favourable attitude towards the organisation and are more likely to recommend it to others contributing to organic traffic. This study also examined the mediating rules between trust and satisfaction, The results indicate that consumer trust partially mediates the relationship between AI service quality and consumer satisfaction, with an indirect effect of 0.25 ($p < 0.001$). These findings tell us that satisfaction is not only determined by service quality but also has an indirect relationship with the development of trust. These findings also reveal that consumer satisfaction strongly mediates the relationship between trust and loyalty, with an indirect effect of 0.40 ($p < 0.001$). This reveals that trust alone is not enough to generate customer loyalty but it also depends on customer satisfaction with these AI based services. When consumers go through more and more of these positive interactions and perceive the AI is very reliable and secure they are more likely to be satisfied and become loyal to the organisation. AI-based service quality explains 31% of the variance in consumer trust ($R^2 = 0.31$). This tells us that although AI service quality is a big factor, other factors such as perceived risk, data security, transparency of algorithms and overall ethical practices are also determinants of consumer trust. Consumer satisfaction explains 44% of the variance in consumer loyalty ($R^2 = 0.44$), which emphasizes the role of satisfaction in customer loyalty. These results overall tell us that consumer loyalty is not only driven by the functional benefits that the AI provides but also depends on psychological and relational factors which are built with the consumer. Trust and satisfaction remain big psychological factors of how AI service is perceived Although it provides many functional benefits like efficiency and convenience over traditional service. Which means that AI adoption alone does not develop customer loyalty but when the systems are designed to specifically provide good service to the customers, developing trust and satisfaction only then does it lead to customer loyalty.

6. LIMITATIONS

Although this study provides a lot of valuable information into consumer behaviour in AI based service, it has some notable limitations. Firstly as the study follows a cross-sectional research style, it is limited to not be able to study the effects of these AI transactions with customers over time, as as consumers use more and more of these AI systems they may form different opinions according to the experience that they've had. Longitudinal studies would be much more able to study the relationships between the consumer and the AI with repeated interactions, and how that might affect trust and satisfaction. Secondly, the data this study relied on is 'self-reported surveys' which are subject to method and response bias. Respondents in the study might have described their subjective experiences, rather than the objective performance of the AI. Future research might be able to integrate this behavioural data into objective performance data sets to create a much more comprehensive understanding of AI services and consumer behaviour. Thirdly, the respondent size was limited to 150 people which although was enough to determine the findings of the study, causes the results to lack generalisability.

To obtain more analytical findings, larger data sets would be required. Fourth, the study mainly focused on E-Commerce platforms, which again limits the generalizability of the findings as it focused on mainly one sector of the diverse digital platform. Other sectors like healthcare, banking and education are also employing AI service systems. Although the high risk environment of sectors like healthcare, might cause different behaviours in consumers. Finally this study only evaluated the role of trust and satisfaction and how they affect consumer loyalty and service quality with AI service systems. Other factors such as perceived risk and data privacy, algorithm transparency, and ethical systems also play a role in determining customer loyalty in these environments.

7. FUTURE RESEARCH DIRECTIONS

AI has become a critical part of customer service in the digital economy and enables billions of customer interactions around the world on an annual basis. In addition to this growing adoption and use of AI tools, organizations are increasingly leveraging AI systems to interact with customers to recommend and provide service in a wide variety of industries, including e-commerce, healthcare, and financial services. The widespread use of AI is changing the nature of service delivery through technology and subsequently has changed the way customer relationships are built and maintained. In traditional service environments, customer relationships were built primarily through human-centered approaches to service delivery, where service providers solicited trust and engagement through direct, personal, and empathetic interactions. AI-based customer service systems represent a significant departure from this paradigm because of the increasing use of machine- and data-mediated service delivery, thus embedding service logic in automated systems and data-driven delivery processes. AI-based service systems are highly effective in providing benefits such as real-time information, personalized service, and 24/7 availability ; however, concerns surrounding AI continue to grow, including transparency, data privacy, and a lack of human touch in the customer service fashion. As such, moving from human-based to AI-based service environments has made consumer perception of and reactions to technology much more relevant than ever before. Primarily, psychological constructs like trust and satisfaction shape customer experiences (make up customer experience) and influence how customers behave. Trust refers to how much customers view AI systems as reliable, secure, and able to perform.

Satisfaction refers to how much service experiences meet customer expectations or exceed them. These constructs are critical to understanding how consumer loyalty is created and maintained in AI-based service environments, especially in digital markets, where it is easy for customers to change from one to another. Future implications for research into usage of Artificial Intelligence services in specific industries are very significant in nature. Banking, Healthcare, Hospitality/Travel, and Education represent various industries, each exhibiting unique levels of emotional attachment and perceived risk; therefore, how these two constructs (trust and satisfaction) influence future loyalty may differ depending on the industry in which the AI is employed. **Cross-Cultural Research**: Investigating how the use of AI will vary from culture to culture may produce different results due to the diverse effects of cultural values on consumer perceptions of AI technology. In this respect, the cultural dimensions of uncertainty avoidance, trust levels, and, ultimately, the willingness to adopt new technologies will shape the relationship consumers have with AI-based services. Advanced Analytical Techniques: Conducting research using more advanced analytical methods, such as machine learning, multi-group structural equation modeling, and experimental designs, may allow for a better understanding of the complex interplay between technological factors and psychological factors in the AI service ecosystem. By addressing these suggested areas of research, future research will lead to a deeper understanding of how AI will continue to reshape consumer behavior and build long-term service relationships.

8. IMPLICATIONS

8.1 Theoretical Contributions

This study contributes to the literature within the framework of consumer behaviour and service marketing by applying these theories in the context of an AI-based service. In doing so, it advances the theoretical understanding of a service encounter as being fundamentally different from previous services provided by humans through technology. Moreover, this study analyses how consumer loyalty is formed in AI-based services, whereas most studies focus on technology acceptance and use intentions. The study conceptualises loyalty as a relational and experiential result, as compared to a purely cognitive response, by unifying trust and satisfaction within a sequential mediation model. In addition, the study considers both trust and satisfaction as the psychological mechanisms by which AI-based services create and maintain long term customer relationships; thereby extending existing technology adoption models (e.g. TAM, UTAUT) to include a relationship-based dimension.

8.2 Practical Contributions

The purpose of this research is to provide applicable guidance to companies looking to deploy AI-based services in such areas as digital platforms, banking and e-commerce from a managerial standpoint. This research identifies the key areas that lead to increased levels of satisfaction and trust in AI or digital service delivery by highlighting the sequential role of satisfaction and trust. This research suggests that companies need to focus on developing AI systems that are transparent, reliable and user-focused rather than being overly focused on providing automated and efficient services. As a result, the findings can assist CX managers and service designers in balancing relational attributes with technology sophistication in order to achieve the development of AI based service strategies that will help to increase customer advocacy, retention and long-term value creation.

8.3 Managerial Implications

This study will also be a major benefit for legislators and regulators who want to know how they can support the use of AI technology responsibly and protect consumers. By demonstrating that trust is an important precursor to satisfaction and loyalty, this study shows that ethical practices have an essential role when providing services that consumers ultimately use and what regulators or legislators can do to encourage those practices through regulatory and legislative frameworks while still promoting innovation. Furthermore, by building on the study findings, policymakers may develop guidelines to help businesses establish AI governance systems that foster increased levels of trust among their consumers, resulting in the creation of sustainable digital ecosystems where AI-enabled product choices will provide continuous customer relationships as opposed to fleeting transactional benefits.

REFERENCES

Ameen, N., Tarhini, A., Reppel, A., & Anand, A. (2021). Customer experiences in the age of artificial intelligence. *Computers in Human Behavior, 114*, 106548. DOI: 10.1016/j.chb.2020.106548 PMID: 32905175

Belanche, D., Casaló, L. V., Flavián, C., & Schepers, J. (2021). Service robot implementation: A theoretical framework and research agenda. *Service Industries Journal, 41*(3–4), 203–225.

Davenport, T. H., Guha, A., Grewal, D., & Bressgott, T. (2020). How artificial intelligence will change the future of marketing. *Journal of the Academy of Marketing Science, 48*(1), 24–42. DOI: 10.1007/s11747-019-00696-0

Dwivedi, Y. K., Hughes, L., Ismagilova, E., Aarts, G., Coombs, C., Crick, T., Duan, Y., Dwivedi, R., Edwards, J., Eirug, A., Galanos, V., Ilavarasan, P. V., Janssen, M., Jones, P., Kar, A. K., Kizgin, H., Kronemann, B., Lal, B., Lucini, B., & Williams, M. D. (2021). Artificial intelligence (AI): Multidisciplinary perspectives on emerging challenges, opportunities, and agenda for research, practice and policy. *International Journal of Information Management, 57*, 101994. DOI: 10.1016/j.ijinfomgt.2019.08.002

Gursoy, D., Chi, O. H., Lu, L., & Nunkoo, R. (2019). Consumers' acceptance of artificially intelligent (AI) device use in service delivery. *International Journal of Information Management, 49*, 157–169. DOI: 10.1016/j.ijinfomgt.2019.03.008

Hsu, C.-L., Chen, M.-C., & Lin, J. C.-C. (2023). Understanding the user satisfaction and loyalty of customer service chatbots. *Journal of Retailing and Consumer Services, 71*, 103205. DOI: 10.1016/j.jretconser.2022.103211

Huang, M.-H., & Rust, R. T. (2021). Artificial intelligence in service. *Journal of Service Research, 24*(1), 3–20.

Kasilingam, D. L. (2020). Understanding the attitude and intention to use smartphone chatbots for shopping. *Technology in Society, 62*, 101280. DOI: 10.1016/j.techsoc.2020.101280

Lankton, N. K., McKnight, D. H., & Thatcher, J. B. (2014). Incorporating trust into technology acceptance theory. *Management Information Systems Quarterly, 38*(1), 153–180.

Longoni, C., Bonezzi, A., & Morewedge, C. K. (2019). Resistance to medical artificial intelligence. *The Journal of Consumer Research, 46*(4), 629–650. DOI: 10.1093/jcr/ucz013

McLean, G., & Osei-Frimpong, K. (2020). Chatbots and consumer satisfaction: The role of anthropomorphism. *Journal of Business Research, 119*, 351–356.

Pillai, R., Sivathanu, B., & Dwivedi, Y. K. (2020). Shopping intention at AI-powered automated retail stores (AIPARS). *Journal of Retailing and Consumer Services, 57*, 102207. DOI: 10.1016/j.jretconser.2020.102207

Wang, W., Li, X., & Law, R. (2025). Assessing the impact of AI-enabled service attributes on customer satisfaction and loyalty in chain hotels. *International Journal of Hospitality Management, 116*, 103613.

Xu, X., Liu, W., Gursoy, D., & Buhalis, D. (2025). Trust, try, buy, and belong: How does artificial intelligence create a loyalty loop in hospitality? *Tourism Management Perspectives, 45*, 101061.

ADDITIONAL READINGS

Do robot-service restaurant customers' emotions affect satisfaction, brand loyalty and future intentions? (2026). *International Journal of Contemporary Hospitality Management, 38*(2), 447–470.

Jamil, K., Anwar, A., & Mustafa, S. (2026). How humanoid chatbot interaction quality builds trust and loyalty in hospitality? A mixed-method approach. *Journal of Hospitality Marketing & Management, 35*(4), 518–557. DOI: 10.1080/19368623.2026.2614407

Kwinda, V. Q., & Wakelin-Theron, N. (2025). Customers' satisfaction and adaptations to service robots in a hotel environment. *Tourism and Hospitality Management, 31*(2), 293–306. DOI: 10.20867/thm.31.2.10

Rita, P., Vong, C., & Correia, C. (2026). How AI-driven chatbots shape customer satisfaction and loyalty to chatbot usage in digital service experience. *Computers in Human Behavior Reports, 22*, 101017. DOI: 10.1016/j.chbr.2026.101017

Song, B., Xu, H., Cai, Z., & Guo, Y. (2026). *How to trust hospitality service robots? Privacy concerns in human–robot interaction. Humanities & Social Sciences Communications*. Advance online publication.

KEY TERMS AND DEFINITIONS

AI Chatbots: AI chatbots are software applications that use artificial intelligence and natural language processing (NLP) to simulate human conversation and provide automated customer support or assistance.

Anthropomorphism: Anthropomorphism is the attribution of human-like characteristics, emotions, or behaviors to AI systems or service robots, making interactions feel more natural and engaging for users.

Artificial Intelligence (AI) Services: AI services refer to digital systems that use machine learning, natural language processing, and data analytics to automate, personalize, and improve customer interactions and service delivery.

Customer Loyalty: Customer loyalty is a customer's commitment to continue purchasing from or engaging with a brand over time, often reflected through repeat purchases, positive word-of-mouth, and long-term relationships.

Customer Satisfaction: Customer satisfaction is the extent to which an AI-based service meets or exceeds customer expectations, resulting in a positive evaluation of the service experience.

Customer Trust: Customer trust is the willingness of consumers to rely on an AI-enabled service or organization based on its perceived reliability, competence, transparency, and security.

Human–AI Interaction (HAII): Human–AI interaction refers to the communication and collaboration between people and AI systems during service encounters, influencing user experience, trust, adoption, and loyalty.

Chapter 8
Convenience Versus Privacy:
Navigating Ethical Trade Offs in AI-Based Services

Jyoti
http://orcid.org/0009-0001-3541-8517
SOHT, India

Akhilesh Pandey
http://orcid.org/0000-0002-9172-9328
Galgotias University, India

Himanshu Sharma
SOHT, India

Rahul Bharadwaj
http://orcid.org/0000-0001-9502-5048
SOHT, India

ABSTRACT

This chapter explores a growing tension in AI-based services: consumers increasingly value convenient and personalized experiences, while at the same time becoming more concerned about how their personal data are collected and used. Drawing on a systematic review of the literature, the chapter discusses key ethical issues surrounding AI-driven personalization, including privacy, algorithmic bias, transparency, explainability, accountability, and consumer control. The findings show that the benefits of personalization may be weakened when customers feel that data collection is excessive or that AI-supported decisions are difficult to understand. Trust therefore becomes central to the way consumers respond to AI-enabled services.

DOI: 10.4018/979-8-3373-9159-5.ch008

The chapter also discusses how organizations can address these concerns through clearer data practices, privacy-by-design, explainable AI, human oversight, and greater consumer control.

INTRODUCTION

Artificial Intelligence (AI) has emerged as one of the most transformative technologies of the twenty-first century, fundamentally reshaping the way organizations deliver services and interact with customers. Across industries such as hospitality, tourism, healthcare, banking, retail, education, transportation, and e-commerce, AI-driven systems are enabling unprecedented levels of automation, personalization, and operational efficiency. Machine learning algorithms, predictive analytics, recommendation engines, conversational chatbots, virtual assistants, and intelligent decision-support systems are increasingly capable of understanding customer preferences, anticipating future needs, and delivering highly customized experiences. These developments have significantly improved service quality, customer satisfaction, organizational productivity, and competitive advantage. However, the same technologies that create convenience and personalized experiences also introduce complex ethical challenges, particularly regarding the collection, processing, storage, and utilization of personal data.

The rapid expansion of AI-powered services has intensified the debate surrounding the balance between technological convenience and individual privacy. Modern AI systems depend heavily on vast quantities of consumer data, including browsing histories, purchasing patterns, geolocation information, biometric identifiers, social media interactions, voice recordings, and behavioral analytics. By continuously learning from these datasets, AI models provide highly personalized recommendations, targeted advertising, dynamic pricing, predictive customer support, and automated decision-making. While these capabilities improve efficiency and user experience, they simultaneously raise concerns regarding privacy invasion, excessive surveillance, algorithmic bias, data security, and erosion of consumer autonomy. Consequently, organizations face the critical challenge of harnessing AI's transformative potential while ensuring responsible and ethical management of personal information.

One of the central ethical dilemmas in AI-based services lies in the trade-off between personalization and privacy. Consumers increasingly expect seamless, customized digital experiences that reduce search effort, enhance convenience, and provide relevant recommendations. At the same time, many users remain apprehensive about the amount of personal information collected to enable these services. This phenomenon, often described as the privacy–personalization paradox, reflects consumers' willingness to exchange personal data for convenience while simultaneously expressing concerns about surveillance, misuse of information, unauthorized sharing, and loss of control over their digital identities. Such conflicting expectations create significant challenges for organizations attempting to maximize customer value without compromising ethical standards or violating privacy rights.

The widespread adoption of AI has also introduced concerns regarding algorithmic fairness and transparency. Many AI models operate as complex "black-box" systems whose internal decision-making processes are difficult for users, managers, and even developers to interpret. Lack of explainability can reduce trust, limit accountability, and make it difficult to identify discriminatory outcomes or unintended biases embedded within training datasets. AI systems trained on incomplete, inaccurate, or historically biased data may unintentionally reinforce existing social inequalities by producing discriminatory recommendations, credit decisions, recruitment outcomes, insurance assessments, or pricing strategies. These concerns have increased the demand for Explainable Artificial Intelligence (XAI), responsible AI governance, and human oversight mechanisms that ensure AI-supported decisions remain transparent, fair, and accountable.

Data privacy represents another critical challenge in AI-enabled service ecosystems. Organizations routinely collect extensive customer information to improve predictive accuracy and personalization. However, inadequate data governance practices expose individuals to risks including identity theft, cyberattacks, unauthorized profiling, data breaches, and commercial exploitation. These risks are particularly significant in sectors handling sensitive personal information such as healthcare, financial services, education, hospitality, and public administration. Ethical AI therefore requires organizations to implement robust privacy-by-design principles, informed consent procedures, secure data storage mechanisms, anonymization techniques, and compliance with national and international data protection regulations.

In response to these challenges, governments and international organizations have introduced comprehensive regulatory frameworks aimed at promoting trustworthy AI. Instruments such as the European Union's Artificial Intelligence Act, the General Data Protection Regulation (GDPR), the OECD AI Principles, UNESCO's Recommendation on the Ethics of Artificial Intelligence, and the NIST AI Risk Management Framework emphasize transparency, accountability, fairness, human oversight, privacy protection, and responsible innovation. These frameworks encourage organizations to adopt risk-based governance models that integrate ethical considerations throughout the AI lifecycle, from system design and data collection to deployment, monitoring, and continuous evaluation.

Responsible AI extends beyond regulatory compliance and requires organizations to embed ethical values into corporate culture and decision-making processes. Effective AI governance involves interdisciplinary collaboration among technologists, policymakers, legal experts, ethicists, business leaders, and consumers. Organizations should establish clear policies governing data collection, algorithm development, bias mitigation, explainability, cybersecurity, and accountability. Continuous monitoring, independent auditing, stakeholder engagement, and transparent communication are essential to maintaining public trust and ensuring that AI systems deliver equitable outcomes while minimizing societal harm.

Another important dimension concerns consumer empowerment. Ethical AI should not merely protect privacy but also provide users with meaningful control over their personal information. Mechanisms such as informed consent, customizable privacy settings, explainable recommendations, accessible grievance procedures, and opportunities to challenge automated decisions strengthen consumer confidence and encourage responsible technology adoption. Human-in-the-loop approaches, where human judgment complements algorithmic decision-making, are particularly valuable in high-stakes domains including healthcare, criminal justice, recruitment, and financial services, where erroneous or biased AI decisions may have serious consequences.

Organizations increasingly recognize that ethical AI practices contribute not only to regulatory compliance but also to long-term business sustainability. Transparent data practices, responsible personalization, fairness in algorithmic outcomes, and robust cybersecurity measures enhance customer trust, strengthen brand reputation, reduce legal risks, and improve stakeholder relationships. Conversely, failures in AI governance—including biased algorithms, privacy breaches, or opaque decision-making—can result in reputational damage, regulatory penalties, and declining consumer confidence.

This chapter critically examines the ethical trade-offs between convenience and privacy within AI-based services by synthesizing current research on AI ethics, consumer behavior, governance frameworks, explainable AI, and responsible innovation. It explores how organizations can balance personalization with privacy protection, identifies major ethical risks associated with AI-driven services, and evaluates emerging regulatory approaches designed to promote trustworthy AI ecosystems. Furthermore, the chapter discusses practical strategies for implementing responsible AI through transparency, fairness, accountability, human oversight, and privacy-preserving technologies. By integrating insights from contemporary literature and international policy frameworks, the chapter aims to provide researchers, practitioners, managers, and policymakers with a comprehensive understanding of how AI can deliver innovative, customer-centric services while safeguarding individual rights, maintaining public trust, and supporting sustainable digital transformation.

LITERATURE REVIEW

In this section, the author critically analyses available literature on the ethical aspects of AI-based services, which is the tension between convenience and privacy. It combines the results of the various disciplines, such as computer science, ethics, law, and sociology, to offer a comprehensive view of the threats and opportunities of AI in service delivery. A vast amount of literature emphasizes explainability and transparency as the key factors that increase trust and acceptance of AI systems, especially in the sensitive service setting (Li, 2023). To give a more specific example, the secrecy of high-level AI can easily undermine trust and victimize the accountability and possible biases of such algorithms, which makes it necessary to introduce transparent AI systems the inner mechanisms of which can be studied and comprehended (Konidena et al., 2024). It is particularly so in such areas as healthcare and finance where the results of the AI influence the lives and the well-being of individuals directly, requiring the transparent explanation of the algorithm results to secure informed consent and fair treatment (Chellappan, 2024; Kumar et al., 2024). The nature of most deep learning algorithms as black-boxes is both powerful and challenging to human understanding since, in most cases, it is unfeasible to know the reasoning behind their decisions (Rane et al., 2024). The fact that AI models are not easy to understand can be especially problematic among vulnerable consumers, who might not be able to comprehend how data is processed and decisions are made, which can have a harmful effect on the consumer (Hermann et al., 2023). Additionally, the mass implementation of AI-based services is frequently associated with the massive data gathering and processing, which, on the one hand, increases the level of personalization and convenience, on the other hand, poses a significant threat to privacy to individuals (Okeke et al., 2024). Personalization versus privacy is another trend that has been recurring, with researchers always revealing that consumers are enjoying the customized experiences, but they are also afraid of how much and how sensitive their personal data is being acquired and used by artificial intelligence systems (Utami and Wang, 2026). This fine line must be considered with the due attention to the ethical standards, open data policies, and sound regulatory models to make sure that the advantages of AI-based personalization do not reduce the rights of individual privacy (Adanyin, 2024; Utami and Wang, 2026). This requires taking a closer look into how consumers perceive and trade-off convenience and data protection especially as AI technologies have become commonplace in our everyday life (Utami and Wang, 2026). It also requires an inquiry into how explainable AI can fill this gap to allow AI decisions to be given explainable reasons, which will calm privacy fears and still allow the benefits of personalization to be enjoyed (Rane & Paramesha, 2024). This analytical review is carried to the regulatory systems, including GDPR and their impact on the creation and implementation of AI services, with the aim of balancing innovation and the basic rights to privacy (Abbonato, 2024). Such laws usually include a right to explanation of the victims of automated processes, making developers to create AI systems that have transparency capabilities in-built (Bickley and Torgler, 2022; Rane et al., 2024). This normative focus on transparency highlights the necessity of artificial intelligence developers not only to reband their offerings with respect to the purely performance-based indicators but also to incorporate ethical factors, namely, privacy and explainability, into the very structure of the AI systems (- et al., 2024; Hermann et al., 2023). This proactive measure can be used to overcome ethical issues like algorithmic bias and data misuse before it becomes embedded into deployed systems (Bitra, 2025; Mazyaki et al., 2025). Moreover, those frames help to develop user trust and reduce the risks of lack of transparency in algorithm decision-making, which is the key to the long-term implementation and social acceptance of AI technologies (Padmaja and Lakshminarayana, 2024; Rahman, 2024). Implementing the concept of ethical AI, especially explainability and transparency, within the lifecycles of developing AI is not only the question of regulations but the strategic necessity to build trust and secure the further sustainable development of AI-enhanced services (Bitra, 2025; Holzinger et al., 2024). It further highlights the need to constantly monitor and audit AI systems to detect and address any privacy or data protection issues as they arise (Konidena et al., 2024). This type of ongoing supervision, together with transparent communication regarding the data governing practice, is necessary to keep the users trustful and comply with the principles of ethical AI implementation (Sodiya et al., 2024). This lifelong dedication to ethical AI principles, including the privacy as well as explainability, is the key to moving through the complicated environment of AI-based services and developing them to be responsibly integrated into the society (Nguyen et al., 2024; Pradeep et al., 2024). This goes beyond technical data protection remedies but also sound ethical escalation procedures and governance systems to handle matters effectively and be in line with the regulations (Navneet & Chandra, 2025). Furthermore, the dynamic nature of AI ethics requires an active mode to resolve the governance regime that will guarantee accountability, equity, and openness of AI systems (Constantinides et al., 2024). It is a proactive strategy that involves considering ethical considerations through the design stage, commonly referred to as ethics-by-design strategy, instead of trying to resolve ethical issues at a later stage (Chandra and Navneet, 2025). This incorporation needs to be a multi-faceted methodological framework including transparency, accountability, and regulatory compliance in all phases of AI development, including conceptualization and deployment and maintenance (Radanliev, 2025). This is not limited to technical measures addressing data protection but also the inclusion of strong ethical reviewing procedures and an interdisciplinary collaboration to prevent and reduce possible socio-technical risks (Olorunfemi et al., 2024; Sridhar, 2025). These structures are essential to hold AI responsible, just, and transparent and to avoid the carbon footprint of unsustainable extent of training these systems (Constantinides et al., 2024)..The growing awareness of the effects of AI on privacy and the possibility of recreating the bias only adds more urgency to establish ethical AI development and implementation (Constantinides et al., 2024). This entails placing an emphasis on fairness, accountability, transparency, privacy, accessibility and human well being at the same time avoiding prejudice and complexity in order to protect the rights of users (Altukhi and Pradhan, 2025).

METHODOLOGY

This chapter adopts a systematic literature review (SLR) methodology to examine the ethical trade-offs between convenience and privacy in AI-based services. The growing integration of Artificial Intelligence (AI) into service industries has generated extensive scholarly interest in issues related to data privacy, algorithmic fairness, transparency, accountability, and consumer trust. Given the multidisciplinary and rapidly evolving nature of AI ethics, a systematic review provides an appropriate methodological approach for synthesizing existing knowledge, identifying emerging trends, and highlighting research gaps. Unlike traditional narrative reviews, an SLR follows a structured, transparent, and reproducible process for identifying, evaluating, and integrating evidence from published studies, thereby reducing selection bias and enhancing the credibility of research findings (Korobenko et al., 2024).

The selection of the SLR methodology is justified by the increasing complexity of AI-enabled services and the corresponding expansion of ethical, legal, and regulatory concerns. AI technologies are evolving at a pace that often exceeds the development of governance frameworks, creating uncertainties regarding accountability, privacy protection, liability, explainability, and responsible innovation (Olorunfemi et al., 2024). Consequently, a comprehensive synthesis of the existing literature is necessary to understand how organizations can leverage AI-driven personalization while safeguarding consumer privacy and maintaining ethical standards. The systematic review facilitates the consolidation of fragmented research across multiple disciplines, including computer science, information systems, marketing, law, ethics, and public policy, thereby providing an integrated perspective on responsible AI implementation.

The review was guided by three principal research questions. First, what are the dominant ethical concerns associated with privacy and security in AI-based services? Second, which theoretical, regulatory, and governance frameworks have been proposed to evaluate ethical compliance in AI applications? Third, what strategies and best practices can organizations adopt to develop privacy-conscious, transparent, and ethically responsible AI systems? These questions were formulated to provide a comprehensive understanding of the current state of knowledge while identifying practical recommendations for balancing technological innovation with consumer rights (Korobenko et al., 2024).

The literature search focused on peer-reviewed journal articles, conference proceedings, scholarly book chapters, and authoritative reports addressing AI ethics, privacy, security, governance, explainable AI, algorithmic fairness, and responsible AI. Particular attention was given to studies examining AI-enabled personalization, consumer privacy, ethical marketing, digital services, and regulatory developments. Technical studies discussing privacy risks associated with General-Purpose AI systems were also included to provide insights into emerging technological challenges and privacy-preserving design approaches (Meisenbacher et al., 2024). Incorporating literature from multiple disciplines ensured that both technological capabilities and ethical implications were adequately represented within the review.

The review process followed the Preferred Reporting Items for Systematic Reviews and Meta-Analyses (PRISMA) framework to ensure methodological rigor, transparency, and reproducibility (Al-kfairy et al., 2024). The PRISMA protocol guided the sequential stages of literature identification, screening, eligibility assessment, and final inclusion. Duplicate records, non-peer-reviewed publications, opinion pieces lacking empirical or conceptual contributions, and studies unrelated to AI-enabled service contexts were excluded. Eligible publications were assessed based on their relevance to the research objectives, methodological quality, theoretical contribution, and discussion of ethical dimensions associated with AI-based services.

Following article selection, the included studies were subjected to a thematic analysis. Thematic analysis enabled the systematic identification, coding, and synthesis of recurring concepts across the selected literature. Major analytical themes included data privacy, cybersecurity, informed consent, algorithmic bias, explainability, transparency, accountability, fairness, governance, consumer trust, regulatory compliance, and human oversight. Organizing the literature into these thematic categories facilitated comparison across studies while enabling the identification of relationships among ethical principles, technological developments, and organizational practices. This analytical approach also provided the conceptual foundation for developing an integrated framework describing ethical AI implementation in service industries.

Recognizing that AI ethics is inherently multidisciplinary, the review incorporated perspectives from computer science, information technology, business management, law, public policy, and philosophy (Kumar et al., 2025). Such interdisciplinary integration was essential because ethical challenges associated with AI extend beyond technical performance to include legal compliance, consumer rights, organizational responsibility, and societal well-being. The synthesis therefore considered not only algorithmic capabilities but also the broader social, economic, and regulatory implications of AI-enabled personalization.

An additional component of the methodology involved examining contemporary regulatory and governance frameworks relevant to AI deployment. Particular emphasis was placed on international initiatives such as the European Union Artificial Intelligence Act, data protection legislation, and emerging governance principles emphasizing transparency, accountability, privacy protection, fairness, explainability, and human oversight (Butt, 2024). Comparative analysis of these frameworks enabled the identification of common ethical principles that organizations should integrate into AI development and deployment processes. Existing governance models were critically evaluated regarding their effectiveness in addressing algorithmic bias, protecting consumer privacy, strengthening accountability, and promoting trustworthy AI systems (Coovadia et al., 2025).

The review also synthesized evidence concerning organizational practices designed to enhance ethical AI implementation. Studies examining privacy-preserving technologies, anonymization techniques, informed consent mechanisms, explainable AI, algorithm auditing, bias mitigation, and consumer empowerment were analyzed to identify practical strategies for responsible AI deployment (Bhuiyan, 2024; A'yun & Setyaningsih, 2025). Particular attention was given to research demonstrating how transparent communication regarding data collection, processing, and personalization can strengthen consumer trust while supporting regulatory compliance. These findings provided valuable insights into how organizations can balance business objectives with ethical responsibilities.

Throughout the review, emphasis was placed on evaluating how ethical AI practices contribute to consumer trust, organizational reputation, and long-term sustainability. The literature consistently suggests that responsible AI implementation extends beyond compliance with legal requirements and requires organizations to embed ethical principles throughout the entire AI lifecycle—from data acquisition and model development to deployment, monitoring, auditing, and continuous improvement (Eid et al., 2024). Ethical governance therefore involves proactive risk assessment, continuous performance evaluation, stakeholder engagement, and regular updates to governance policies in response to evolving technological and regulatory developments.

Finally, the systematic review adopted a critical synthesis approach rather than merely summarizing previous studies. The objective was to identify areas of scholarly consensus, highlight unresolved ethical challenges, and propose an integrated understanding of how convenience and privacy can be balanced within AI-based services. By combining evidence from technological, legal, managerial, and ethical perspectives, the methodology provides a robust foundation for the subsequent analysis presented in this chapter. The resulting synthesis contributes to the development of a comprehensive framework for responsible AI governance that prioritizes transparency, accountability, fairness, privacy protection, consumer empowerment, and regulatory compliance while supporting sustainable innovation in AI-enabled service ecosystems.

RESULTS

The findings of the systematic literature review demonstrate that the increasing adoption of Artificial Intelligence (AI) in service industries has created a complex relationship between enhanced customer convenience and the protection of consumer privacy. Across the reviewed studies, AI-powered personalization consistently emerged as one of the primary drivers of improved customer experience, enabling organizations to deliver customized recommendations, predictive services, automated customer support, and personalized marketing strategies. By leveraging consumer data and advanced machine learning algorithms, organizations can anticipate customer needs, reduce search effort, improve decision-making, and increase customer satisfaction and operational efficiency (Farooq & Yen, 2024; Utami & Wang, 2026). These capabilities have become an important source of competitive advantage, particularly in sectors such hospitality, tourism, retail, banking, healthcare, and e-commerce, where personalized customer engagement directly influences organizational performance.

Despite these benefits, the review reveals that AI-driven personalization is accompanied by significant ethical concerns surrounding consumer privacy, data governance, and algorithmic accountability. The effectiveness of AI systems depends heavily on continuous access to large volumes of personal and behavioral data, raising concerns regarding excessive data collection, unauthorized information sharing, surveillance, and potential misuse of sensitive information. Consequently, while consumers appreciate the convenience offered by AI-enabled services, they simultaneously express reservations about the extent to which organizations collect, process, and utilize their personal information. This privacy–personalization paradox remains one of most significant ethical challenges facing AI-enabled service industries.

The reviewed literature further indicates that consumer acceptance of AI-based services is strongly influenced by perceptions of organizational trustworthiness and ethical responsibility. Customers demonstrate greater willingness to adopt AI-powered services when organizations maintain transparent privacy policies, clearly communicate their data collection practices, and provide meaningful control over personal information (Adanyin, 2024; Eid et al., 2024). Transparency regarding data processing activities, algorithmic decision-making, and information-sharing practices reduces uncertainty and enhances consumer confidence. Conversely, vague privacy policies, opaque AI systems, and inadequate disclosure practices contribute to consumer skepticism and reluctance to engage with personalized services. These findings suggest that ethical data governance has become a strategic determinant of customer trust and long-term organizational success.

Another significant finding concerns the growing demand for algorithmic fairness and explainability. Numerous studies emphasize that AI systems frequently operate as "black-box" models whose internal decision-making processes remain difficult for users and organizations to interpret. Such lack of transparency limits accountability and creates uncertainty regarding the fairness of automated decisions. The review highlights that biases embedded within training datasets or algorithmic models may unintentionally produce discriminatory outcomes affecting specific demographic groups, thereby undermining consumer confidence and organizational credibility. Researchers therefore advocate regular algorithm auditing, bias detection mechanisms, and continuous model validation to ensure equitable and non-discriminatory AI outcomes (Naz & Kashif, 2024). These practices not only improve system reliability but also support compliance with emerging ethical and regulatory standards.

The literature also identifies responsible AI governance as a critical factor in balancing innovation with ethical accountability. Effective governance frameworks extend beyond technical implementation by incorporating organizational policies, legal compliance, human oversight, and ethical decision-making throughout the AI lifecycle. Several studies emphasize that organizations should establish clear accountability structures defining responsibilities for AI design, deployment, monitoring, and evaluation. Governance mechanisms should additionally include independent auditing procedures, stakeholder engagement, grievance redress systems, and regulatory compliance measures that enable consumers to challenge AI-generated decisions when necessary. Such institutional safeguards enhance transparency while minimizing risks associated with automated decision-making and data misuse.

Consumer empowerment emerged as another recurring theme across the reviewed literature. Researchers consistently argue that individuals should retain meaningful control over how their personal information is collected, processed, stored, and utilized by AI systems. Providing consumers with accessible privacy controls, informed consent mechanisms, customizable personalization preferences, and opportunities to review or delete personal information significantly strengthens trust in AI-enabled services (Adeleye et al., 2024; Raji et al., 2024). Empowering users to understand and manage their digital footprints reduces perceptions of surveillance while encouraging responsible engagement with AI-driven technologies. Such empowerment also promotes a collaborative relationship between service providers and consumers based on transparency, autonomy, and mutual trust.

Another important finding concerns the growing significance of Explainable Artificial Intelligence (XAI). The review indicates that explainability has become fundamental for improving consumer understanding of AI-generated recommendations and decisions. Explainable AI enables users to comprehend why specific recommendations, advertisements, or service decisions have been generated, thereby reducing uncertainty and increasing confidence in AI systems. Transparent explanations further facilitate regulatory compliance, improve accountability, and assist organizations in identifying unintended biases or discriminatory outcomes within complex machine learning models. Consequently, explainability is increasingly recognized as a cornerstone of trustworthy and human-centered AI deployment across service industries.

The literature also emphasizes that ethical AI implementation requires continuous adaptation to technological advancements and evolving regulatory environments. International regulatory initiatives and ethical frameworks increasingly encourage organizations to integrate principles such as transparency, fairness, accountability, privacy protection, and human oversight throughout the AI development lifecycle. Rather than viewing ethical compliance as a one-time exercise, organizations must establish continuous monitoring mechanisms capable of identifying emerging risks, updating governance practices, and responding proactively to new technological developments. Such adaptive governance enables organizations to maintain regulatory compliance while preserving consumer trust in rapidly changing digital environments.

Overall, the findings demonstrate that the future success of AI-enabled hyper-personalization depends not only on technological sophistication but also on the ethical integrity with which AI systems are designed and managed. Sustainable AI adoption requires organizations to balance personalized customer experiences with robust privacy protection, algorithmic fairness, transparency, and responsible governance. By embedding ethical principles into organizational strategy, implementing comprehensive data governance frameworks, adopting Explainable AI techniques, and empowering consumers with greater control over their personal information, organizations can maximize the benefits of AI while minimizing ethical risks. Such an integrated approach strengthens long-term consumer trust, supports regulatory compliance, enhances organizational reputation, and promotes the responsible and sustainable deployment of AI-powered services across diverse industry sectors.

DISCUSSION

The current discussion of AI-directed personalisation requires the in-depth analysis of the existing contradictions between the offer of unprecedented convenience and the ability to protect the privacy of individuals. This is especially sharp in the service sector, where the ability of AI to predict needs and provide individualized experiences is often dependent on a large amount of data gathering and algorithmic processing, which casts large ethical doubts on the data management and user control (Raji et al., 2024). The emergence of conscious empathic AI makes this ethical situation even more complicated, as the simulation of the human feelings by the AI systems creates significant question about genuineness and exploitation in customer relations (Jin, 2023). This requires a further psychologization of the effect of this high level of personalization on the human mind, in particular, what the possibility of the creation of echo chambers or the subtle manipulation of consumer behavior without their direct agreement is (Iqbal et al., 2025). Moreover, the combination of thinking AI and feeling AI regarding service settings, which can provide increased utilitarian and hedonic value, respectively, also brings a new layer of ethical questioning in terms of transparency and possible psychological control (Jin, 2023). These tricky ethical situations highlight the necessity of creating sound ethical frameworks that would guarantee the design and implementation of AI systems in a way that would fully comprehend their negative and positive effects on society and individuals (Eid et al., 2024). It involves the consideration of possible biases in AI algorithms that may cause a discriminatory approach and the ability to make the data collection and its utilization transparent and controlled by consumers (Usman et al., 2024). The delicate balance between convenience and privacy in AI-based services will have to be maintained carefully, as ethical rules are to be continuously checked and adjusted to the interests of consumers and promote innovation (Sodiya et al., 2024). This requires a multi-faceted strategy with regulatory agencies, industry players, and scholars coming up with collaborative standards that facilitate the creation and usage of responsible AI (Mazyaki et al., 2025; Wirtz and Pitardi, 2023). The given shared work is essential to overcome the natural paradox of personalization-privacy, in which the advantages of personalized services are often in conflict with the anxieties of consumers about the misuse of their data (Binlibdah, 2024). This paradox shows that there is a necessity to develop complex ethical frameworks that put the user agency and data sovereignty in the center of AI-driven marketing approaches (Eid et al., 2024). This means going beyond the shallow consent processes and developing real user knowledge and control of their own information to ensure that personalization is a service and is not a deep-rooted infiltration (Saura et al., 2024). This means that we will move to privacy-by-design practices in developing AI and consider ethical factors at the beginning, as opposed to applying them at the end (Eid et al., 2024). This model will guarantee that the development of AI systems is based on a certain respect towards the privacy of an individual and the ethical aspect of the system, which is associated with the increase in the popularity of responsible AI usage at the consumer and governance levels (Huang et al., 2025a). Such a unified outlook helps to make sure that AI in marketing does not just fulfill the interests of business, but also matches the societal values and moral principles (Eid et al., 2024; Hermann, 2022). Finally, ethical AI utilization in marketing and advertisement needs a strong initiative by policymakers and industry giants to create explicit regulatory policies that will tackle the possible human rights violations, as well as data protection issues (1ecommerce.Pdf, n.d.; Biplab et al., 2023). These frameworks must be designed with data dignity in mind, where the information on users is regarded as an extension of personal identity and needs to be handled with responsibility during its lifecycle (Saura et al., 2024). This is a proactive measure that is essential in establishing and sustaining consumer confidence, which is one of the pillars of the sustainable success of AI-enhanced marketing practices.In addition, it is necessary to consider ethical governance and human regulation to ensure integrity in AI-based marketing, in which stakeholders should collaborate and implement ethical AI models to practice responsibly and fairly (Ahmad and Haque, 2024). Such a continuous process of dialogue is essential to create responsible AI ecosystems that harmonize the innovative possibilities of AI with the need to protect consumer rights and trust (Eid et al., 2024). Hence, it is essential to address the highly intricate interplay of technological progress and social values by creating a solid ethical framework and mechanisms of governance in the sphere of AI-based hyper-personalization (Naz and Kashif, 2024). Such a proactive approach is essential in creating and sustaining consumer confidence which is a pillar to sustainable success of AI-enhanced marketing approaches (Bucove chi and VEVERA, 2024). It involves the emphasis on transparency, accountability, and fairness in AI algorithms to avoid the discriminatory results and ethical standards (Eid et al., 2024). This is the key element of why such overarching ethical principles are needed to promote social trust and equitable allocation of rewards and disamenities related to AI in marketing (Kumar and Suthar, 2024). This will require a constant review of ethical standards as the AI powers continue to advance in such a way that regulatory measures can keep up with the emerging concerns of data privacy and algorithmic bias (Naz and Kashif, 2024). Moreover, it is essential to promote fairness and non-discrimination in AI systems within organizations that may make use of a wide range of data and audit it regularly to reduce the chances of preferential treatment (Naz and Kashif, 2024). This ethical AI development approach will contribute to consumer trust and alleviate the so-called AI mistrust cycle (Ozturkcan and Bozdag, 2025) and, thus, promote a more responsible approach to the introduction of AI technologies into the services sector. Personalization of online marketing, although it increases engagement and interaction, increases the level of power imbalance between businesses and consumers, and the level of privacy is to be as high as possible to avoid preying on vulnerabilities of consumers (Ozturkcan & Bozdag, 2025). This involves making systems powered by AI to have technology in place to enable users to control data sharing and customized content, which is empowering them instead of watching them. This will enable them to be more capable of making informed decisions regarding the digital footprint and engagement with AI services, which will create a fairer digital environment (Bitra, 2025). This approach towards empowering users is essential to overcoming the very nature of the personalization-privacy paradox inherent in AI-driven services: on the one hand, the advantages of customized experiences are at conflict with the fear of data exploitation (O'Higgins and Fatorachian, 2025). As a result, the successful development of ethical frameworks has to go beyond the compliance to establish the culture of privacy-by-design, in which the autonomy of the consumer is deeply embedded in the very structure of the AI-based personalization methods (Utami and Wang, 2026).

CONCLUSION

Finally, ethical considerations cannot be viewed as an extravagance, but rather a part and parcel of AI development and implementation to gain customer loyalty in the long run and brand recognition (Babatunde et al., 2024). It requires a dedication to sound AI behaviors that focus on the welfare of consumers and the security of their data, which creates a viable and reliable AI-powered marketing ecosystem, which is sustainable (Odejide and Edunjobi, 2024). This holistic method will make sure that AI innovations, such as hyper-personalization, are in harmony with social values and ethical standards, and an atmosphere in which technological advances and consumer protection do not conflict with each other will be created. This will involve enhancing transparency and explainability, eliminating manipulation, and being fair with unbiased algorithms (Naz and Kashif, 2024). Furthermore, continuous assessment plans should be in place to evaluate the ethical standards of the AI-based marketing systems based on the need to harmonize the aspects of innovation and the necessity of protecting the privacy and autonomy of individuals (Naz and Kashif, 2024). These frameworks must also highlight the need to ensure that there is clear communication to the consumers on data use and AI-informed interaction to create the atmosphere of trust and informed consent. It consists of proactive solicitation and incorporation of user reactions to hone personalization plans and raise the issues of algorithmic intrusion.Such a cyclical ethical consideration and user feedback is inevitable in reducing algorithmic bias and providing equal treatment to different consumer groups (Benjelloun and Kabak, 2024; Hermann, 2021). The main goal of managing possible biases in AI systems, therefore, is to curb the ethical standards and consumer trust by utilizing various data sources and implementing stringent monitoring systems (Naz and Kashif, 2024). It involves a never-ending process of detecting and correcting algorithmic biases so that the personalization with the help of AI will not discriminate against people unfairly due to their demographics.To detect and eliminate biases in AI algorithms and protect the privacy of consumers, companies are recommended to invest in bias detection tools and privacy-enhancing technologies (Kumar and Suthar, 2024). This policy of proactive action along with the interdisciplinary partnership is essential in creating the effective and ethical AI systems that will avoid the undesirable side effects (Eid et al., 2024). Not only does this holistic approach reinforce brand name but it also builds a lasting customer relationship that makes ethical AI a foundation of sustainable business expansion in the changing digital world (Babatunde et al., 2024). This demands an on-going discussion between technologists, ethicists and regulators to create a responsible AI ecosystem in marketing (Eid et al., 2024). This joint project can assist in developing a model of responsible usage of Artificial Intelligence within hyper-personalization (Barat and Gulati, 2024). This type of conversations is crucial to form the role of AI in the marketing industry, as innovation must be supported by ethical integrity and consumer rights (Eid et al., 2024). The current debate will enable the establishment of effective regulations and regulatory best practices that safeguard people and ensure the exploitation of the transformative power of AI (Eid et al., 2024). Adoption of these recommendations will give rise to a more equitable and trustworthy AI environment, which will ultimately serve the end users and businesses well. Thus, the prudent promotion of ethical factors into all phases of the AI development and implementation, is more than a regulatory compliance concern, but a strategic necessity of the success in the hyper-personalized service sector in the long term (Aghaei et al., 2025). This will help to make sure that the expanding sphere of AI-driven customer experience will be able to grow without any negative impact on the main ethical standards, such as privacy and equality (Adanyin, 2024; Eid et al., 2024). Moreover, organizations should develop explicit ethical standards in AI application that include data collection, privacy, consent, and absenteeism of prejudiced results and be deeply rooted in the principles of fairness, responsibility, and transparency (Eid et al., 2024). These principles must be constantly monitored and revised in accordance with the progress in the field of AI technology and the change in the demands of the society concerning the confidentiality of personal data and the use of algorithms (Adeleye et al., 2024; Kamkankaew et al., 2024). To install these recommendations, it is essential to operate training on data analysis and AI ethics on a regular basis, as well as create data ethics committees, to monitor the use of algorithms and guarantee transparency and fairness (Toledo et al., 2025). This holistic approach will help to create a condition in which AI innovations are capable of providing a beneficial effect to consumers whilst maintaining the strict ethical principles (Eid et al., 2024). In addition, new regulations should be prepared to keep up with changes in technology and give unambiguous guidelines on data regulation, algorithmic responsibility, and consumer safety in AI-based personalization (Eid et al., 2024). This demands a proactive action by the policymakers to develop laws that will balance innovation and protection of individual rights in the digital world (Ahmad and Haque, 2024; Manchiraju, 2025). The strong governance is necessary to avoid the abuse of personal data and algorithm discrimination and ensure that people trust AI technologies (Adanyin, 2024; Bhuiyan, 2024). What is more, clear communication about data use and artificial intelligence decision-making procedures is essential to enable consumers to make effective decisions and ensure their data rights are effectively used (Bhuiyan, 2024). This openness instills trust in the consumer and allows people to take control of their digital presence in hyper-personalized services (2024).

REFERENCES

A'yun, A. Q., & Setyaningsih, W. (2025). Consumer Empowerment Through Ethical AI. *Strategies for Transparent and Trustworthy Personalized Marketing.*, *1*(1), 1–12. DOI: 10.70764/gdpu-jmb.2025.1(1)-01

Abbonato, D. (2024). Public sentiments on the fourth industrial revolution: An unsolicited public opinion poll from Twitter. *arXiv (Cornell University)*. https://doi.org//arxiv.2411.14230DOI: 10.48550

Adanyin, A. (2024a). Ethical AI in Retail: Consumer Privacy and Fairness. *European Journal of Computer Science and Information Technology*, *12*(7), 21–35. DOI: 10.37745/ejcsit.2013/vol12n72135

Adanyin, A. (2024b). Ethical AI in Retail: Consumer Privacy and Fairness. *arXiv (Cornell University)*. https://doi.org//arxiv.2410.15369DOI: 10.48550

Adeleye, R. A., Awonuga, K. F., Asuzu, O. F., Ndubuisi, N. L., & Tubokirifuruar, T. S. (2024). Digital marketing analytics: A review of strategies in the age of big data and AI [Review of *Digital marketing analytics: A review of strategies in the age of big data and AI*]. *World Journal of Advanced Research and Reviews, 21*(2), 73. GSC Online Press. DOI: 10.30574/wjarr.2024.21.2.0395

Aghaei, R., Kiaei, A. A., Boush, M., Vahidi, J., Zavvar, M., Barzegar, Z., & Roosheh, M. (2025). Harnessing the Potential of Large Language Models in Modern Marketing Management: Applications, Future Directions, and Strategic Recommendations. *arXiv (Cornell University)*. https://doi.org//arxiv.2501.10685DOI: 10.48550

Ahmad, N., & Haque, S. (2024). Balancing Innovation and Ethics in AI- and Big Data-Driven Marketing. *Computer*, *57*(8), 102–107. DOI: 10.1109/MC.2024.3405708

Al-kfairy, M., Mustafa, D., Kshetri, N., Insiew, M., & Alfandi, O. (2024). Ethical Challenges and Solutions of Generative AI: An Interdisciplinary Perspective. *Informatics (MDPI), 11*(3), 58. DOI: 10.3390/informatics11030058

Altukhi, Z. M., & Pradhan, S. (2025). Systematic Literature Review: Explainable AI Definitions and Challenges in Education. *arXiv (Cornell University)*. https://doi.org//arxiv.2504.02910DOI: 10.48550

Babatunde, S. O., Odejide, O. A., Edunjobi, T. E., & Ogundipe, D. O. (2024). THE ROLE OF AI IN MARKETING PERSONALIZATION: A THEORETICAL EXPLORATION OF CONSUMER ENGAGEMENT STRATEGIES. *International Journal of Management & Entrepreneurship Research*, *6*(3), 936–949. DOI: 10.51594/ijmer.v6i3.964

Barat, A., & Gulati, K. (2024). Emergence of AI in Marketing and its Implications. *Lloyd Business Review*, *1*, 1–24. Advance online publication. DOI: 10.56595/lbr.v3i1.22

Benjelloun, A., & Kabak, S. (2024). Ethical Challenges and Managerial Implications of Artificial Intelligence in Digital Marketing. In *Lecture notes in networks and systems* (p. 439). Springer International Publishing., DOI: 10.1007/978-981-99-9040-5_32

Bhuiyan, M. S. (2024). The Role of AI-Enhanced Personalization in Customer Experiences. *Journal of Computer Science and Technology Studies*, *6*(1), 162–169. DOI: 10.32996/jcsts.2024.6.1.17

Bickley, S. J., & Torgler, B. (2022). Cognitive architectures for artificial intelligence ethics. *AI & Society*, *38*(2), 501–519. DOI: 10.1007/s00146-022-01452-9

Binlibdah, S. (2024). Investigating the Role of Artificial Intelligence to Measure Consumer Efficiency: The Use of Strategic Communication and Personalized Media Content. *Journalism and Media*, *5*(3), 1142–1161. DOI: 10.3390/journalmedia5030073

Biplab, K., Choudhary, S. L., Rinku, S., Srivastava, P., & Kumar, M. (2023). Exploring the Ethical Use of Artificial Intelligence in Marketing and Advertising. *Journal of Informatics Education and Research*. DOI: 10.52783/jier.v3i2.278

Bitra, S. K. (2025). Ethical AI and privacy in digital personalization: Balancing personalization and user trust. *World Journal of Advanced Engineering Technology and Sciences*, *15*(2), 774–779. DOI: 10.30574/wjaets.2025.15.2.0596

Bucove chi, Ö., & VEVERA, A. V. (2024). Perspective chapter: Organizational Resilience toward Managing Risks in Digital Marketing. In *IntechOpen eBooks*. IntechOpen. DOI: 10.5772/intechopen.1004786

Butt, M. (2024). Analytical Study of the World's First EU Artificial Intelligence (AI) Act, 2024. *International Journal of Research Publication and Reviews*, *5*(3), 7343–7364. DOI: 10.55248/gengpi.5.0324.0914

Chandra, J., & Navneet, S. K. (2025). Advancing Responsible Innovation in Agentic AI: A study of Ethical Frameworks for Household Automation. *arXiv (Cornell University)*. https://doi.org//arxiv.2507.15901DOI: 10.48550

Chellappan, R. B. (2024). From Algorithms to Accountability: The Societal and Ethical Need for Explainable AI. *Research Square (Research Square)*. DOI: 10.21203/rs.3.rs-5277731/v1

Constantinides, M., Tahaei, M., Quercia, D., Stumpf, S., Madaio, M., Kennedy, S., Wilcox, L., Vitak, J., Cramer, H., Bogucka, E. P., Baeza-Yates, R., Luger, E., Holbrook, J., Müller, M., Blumenfeld, I. G., & Pistilli, G. (2024a). Implications of Regulations on the Use of AI and Generative AI for Human-Centered Responsible Artificial Intelligence. *arXiv (Cornell University).* /arxiv.2403.00148DOI: 10.1145/3613905.3643979

Constantinides, M., Tahaei, M., Quercia, D., Stumpf, S., Madaio, M., Kennedy, S., Wilcox, L., Vitak, J., Cramer, H., Bogucka, E. P., Baeza-Yates, R., Luger, E., Holbrook, J., Müller, M., Blumenfeld, I. G., & Pistilli, G. (2024b). Implications of Regulations on the Use of AI and Generative AI for Human-Centered Responsible. *Artificial Intelligence*, *1*, 1–4. Advance online publication. DOI: 10.1145/3613905.3643979

Coovadia, H., Marx, B., Botha, I., & Gold, N. O. (2025). Building an ethical artificial intelligence corporate governance framework for the integration of emerging technologies into business processes. *South African Journal of Accounting Research*, *39*(3), 286–316. DOI: 10.1080/10291954.2025.2523661

Eid, M. A. H., Hashesh, M. A., Sharabati, A. A., Khraiwish, A., Al-Haddad, S., & Abusaimeh, H. (2024). Conceptualizing ethical AI-enabled marketing: Current state and agenda for future research. *International Journal of Data and Network Science*, *8*(4), 2291–2306. DOI: 10.5267/j.ijdns.2024.6.002

Farooq, M. S., & Yen, Y. Y. (2024). Artificial Intelligence in Consumer Behaviour: A Systematic Literature Review. *Research Square (Research Square).* DOI: 10.21203/rs.3.rs-3875906/v1

Hermann, E. (2021). Leveraging Artificial Intelligence in Marketing for Social Good—An Ethical Perspective. *Journal of Business Ethics*, *179*(1), 43–61. DOI: 10.1007/s10551-021-04843-y PMID: 34054170

Hermann, E. (2022). Psychological targeting: Nudge or boost to foster mindful and sustainable consumption? *AI & Society*, *38*(2), 961–962. DOI: 10.1007/s00146-022-01403-4

Hermann, E., Williams, G. Y., & Puntoni, S. (2023). Deploying artificial intelligence in services to AID vulnerable consumers. *Journal of the Academy of Marketing Science*, *52*(5), 1431–1451. DOI: 10.1007/s11747-023-00986-8

Holzinger, A., Zatloukal, K., & Müller, H. (2024). Is human oversight to AI systems still possible? *New Biotechnology*, *85*, 59–62. DOI: 10.1016/j.nbt.2024.12.003 PMID: 39675423

Huang, G. I., Zhang, C., Torres, W. C. Z., Xiong, X., & Li, H. (2025a). Responsible AI and human collaboration in tourism management: Ethical considerations and identity disclosure. *Tourism Management, 113*, 105315. DOI: 10.1016/j.tourman.2025.105315

Iqbal, F., Afiat, A., Shoily, M. M., Turzo, S. S., & Arafat, M. (2025). AI-driven personalization in e-commerce: Evaluating the transformative effects on consumer behavior. *International Journal of Science and Research Archive, 16*(1), 264–273. DOI: 10.30574/ijsra.2025.16.1.2035

Jin, D. (2023). *Where have the ethical and moral standards landed? Consumer self-congruency and psychological distance in the context of AI-based services.* International Hospitality Review., DOI: 10.1108/IHR-06-2023-0033

Kamkankaew, P., Thanitbenjasith, P., Sribenjachot, S., Sanpatanon, N., Phattarowas, V., & Thanin, P. (2024). How Artificial Intelligence is Helping Businesses Grow and Thrive: The Transformative Role of Artificial Intelligence in Thai B2C Digital Marketing. *International Journal of Sociologies and Anthropologies Science Reviews, 4*(1), 137–164. DOI: 10.60027/ijsasr.2024.3651

Konidena, B. K., Malaiyappan, J. N. A., & Tadimarri, A. (2024). Ethical Considerations in the Development and Deployment of AI Systems. *European Journal of Technology, 8*(2), 41–53. DOI: 10.47672/ejt.1890

Korobenko, D., Nikiforova, A., & Sharma, R. (2024). *Towards a Privacy and Security-Aware Framework for Ethical AI: Guiding the Development and Assessment of AI Systems. arXiv*. Cornell University., DOI: 10.1145/3657054.3657141

Kumar, D., & Suthar, N. (2024). Ethical and legal challenges of AI in marketing: An exploration of solutions. *Journal of Information Communication and Ethics in Society, 22*(1), 124–144. DOI: 10.1108/JICES-05-2023-0068

Kumar, J. R. R., Kalnawat, A., Pawar, A. M., Jadhav, V. D., Srilatha, P., & Khetani, V. (2024). Transparency in Algorithmic Decision-making: Interpretable Models for Ethical Accountability. *E3S Web of Conferences, 491*, 2041. DOI: 10.1051/e3sconf/202449102041

Kumar, V., Dixit, A., Sharma, P., & Roy, S. N. (2025). Implementing Responsible Artificial Intelligence in Marketing. *American Business Review, 28*(2), 319–342. DOI: 10.37625/abr.28.2.319-342

Li, N. (2023). Ethical Considerations in Artificial Intelligence: A Comprehensive Disccusion from the Perspective of Computer Vision. *SHS Web of Conferences, 179*, 4024. DOI: 10.1051/shsconf/202317904024

Manchiraju, S. (2025). The ethical thread: AI's role in the tapestry of fashion. *AI & Society, 40*(5), 4029–4034. DOI: 10.1007/s00146-024-02151-3

Mazyaki, A., Naghizadeh, M., Zonouzaghi, S. R., & Setareh, H. (2025). Temporal Preferences in Language Models for Long-Horizon Assistance. *arXiv (Cornell University).* https://doi.org//arxiv.2509.09704DOI: 10.48550

Meisenbacher, S., Klymenko, A., Kelley, P. G., Peddinti, S. T., Thomas, K., & Matthes, F. (2024). *Privacy Risks of General-Purpose AI Systems: A Foundation for Investigating Practitioner Perspectives.* DOI: 10.48550/ARXIV.2407.02027

Navneet, S. K., & Chandra, J. (2025). Rethinking Autonomy: Preventing Failures in AI-Driven Software Engineering. *arXiv (Cornell University).* https://doi.org//arxiv.2508.11824DOI: 10.48550

Naz, H., & Kashif, M. (2024). Artificial intelligence and predictive marketing: An ethical framework from managers' perspective. *Spanish Journal of Marketing - ESIC.* Advance online publication. DOI: 10.1108/SJME-06-2023-0154

Nguyên, T. T., Huynh, T. T., Ren, Z., Nguyen, T. T., Nguyen, P. L., Yin, H., & Nguyen, Q. V. H. (2024). Privacy-preserving explainable AI: A survey. *Science China. Information Sciences, 68*(1), 111101. Advance online publication. DOI: 10.1007/s11432-024-4123-4

O'Higgins, B., & Fatorachian, H. (2025). Consumer trust in artificial intelligence in the UK and Ireland's personal care and cosmetics sector. *Cogent Business & Management, 12*(1), 2469765. Advance online publication. DOI: 10.1080/23311975.2025.2469765

Odejide, O. A., & Edunjobi, T. E. (2024). AI IN PROJECT MANAGEMENT: EXPLORING THEORETICAL MODELS FOR DECISION-MAKING AND RISK MANAGEMENT. *Engineering Science & Technology Journal, 5*(3), 1072–1085. DOI: 10.51594/estj.v5i3.959

Okeke, N. I., Alabi, O. A., Igwe, A. N., Ofodile, O. C., & Ewim, C. P.-M. (2024). AI-Powered customer experience optimization: Enhancing financial inclusion in underserved communities. *International Journal of Applied Research in Social Sciences, 6*(10), 2487–2511. DOI: 10.51594/ijarss.v6i10.1662

Olorunfemi, O. L., Amoo, O. O., Atadoga, A., Fayayola, O. A., Abrahams, T. O., & Shoetan, P. O. (2024). TOWARDS A CONCEPTUAL FRAMEWORK FOR ETHICAL AI DEVELOPMENT IN IT SYSTEMS. *Computer Science & IT Research Journal, 5*(3), 616–627. DOI: 10.51594/csitrj.v5i3.910

Padmaja, C. V. R., & Lakshminarayana, S. (2024). The rise of AI: A comprehensive research review. *IAES International Journal of Artificial Intelligence*, *13*(2), 2226. DOI: 10.11591/ijai.v13.i2.pp2226-2235

Pradeep, P., Caro-Martínez, M., & Wijekoon, A. (2024). A practical exploration of the convergence of Case-Based Reasoning and Explainable Artificial Intelligence. *Expert Systems with Applications*, *255*, 124733. DOI: 10.1016/j.eswa.2024.124733

Proactive Customer Support. (2024). Proactive Customer Support: Re-Architecting A Customer Support/Relationship Management Software System Leveraging Predictive Analysis/AI and Machine Learning. *Engineering Open Access*, *2*(1), 39–50. DOI: 10.33140/EOA.02.01.04

Radanliev, P. (2025). Privacy, ethics, transparency, and accountability in AI systems for wearable devices [Review of *Privacy, ethics, transparency, and accountability in AI systems for wearable devices*]. *Frontiers in Digital Health*, *7*, 1431246. Frontiers Media. DOI: 10.3389/fdgth.2025.1431246

Rahman, A. (2024). AI AND MACHINE LEARNING IN BUSINESS PROCESS AUTOMATION: INNOVATING WAYS AI CAN ENHANCE OPERATIONAL EFFICIENCIES OR CUSTOMER EXPERIENCES IN U.S. ENTERPRISES. *Non Human Journal.*, *1*(1), 41–62. DOI: 10.70008/jmldeds.v1i01.41

Raji, M. A., Olodo, H. B., Oke, T. T., Addy, W. A., Ofodile, O. C., & Oyewole, A. T. (2024). E-commerce and consumer behavior: A review of AI-powered personalization and market trends [Review of E-commerce and consumer behavior: A review of AI-powered personalization and market trends]. *GSC Advanced Research and Reviews*, *18*(3), 66. DOI: 10.30574/gscarr.2024.18.3.0090

Rane, J., Kaya, Ö., Mallick, S. K., & Rane, N. L. (2024). *Enhancing black-box models: Advances in explainable artificial intelligence for ethical decision-making*. DOI: 10.70593/978-81-981271-0-5_4

Rane, N. L., & Paramesha, M. (2024). *Explainable Artificial Intelligence (XAI) as a foundation for trustworthy artificial intelligence*. DOI: 10.70593/978-81-981367-4-9_1

S. M. I. (2024). Exploring AI-Driven Customer Service: Evolution, Architectures, Opportunities, Challenges and Future Directions. *International Journal For Multidisciplinary Research*, *6*(3), 22283. Advance online publication. DOI: 10.36948/ijfmr.2024.v06i03.22283

Saura, J. R., Škare, V., & Došen, Đ. O. (2024). Is AI-based digital marketing ethical? Assessing a new data privacy paradox. *Journal of Innovation & Knowledge*, *9*(4), 100597. DOI: 10.1016/j.jik.2024.100597

Sodiya, E. O., Amoo, O. O., Umoga, U. J., & Atadoga, A. (2024). AI-driven personalization in web content delivery: A comparative study of user engagement in the USA and the UK. *World Journal of Advanced Research and Reviews*, *21*(2), 887–902. DOI: 10.30574/wjarr.2024.21.2.0502

Sridhar, U. (2025). Ethical frameworks for responsible ai development: Challenges and implementation strategies. *World Journal of Advanced Engineering Technology and Sciences*, *15*(1), 2028–2038. DOI: 10.30574/wjaets.2025.15.1.0420

Tettey, D. J., Chrisben, D., Victoria, M., Chukwubuikem, E. P., & Abdullahi, A. D. U. S. (2025). Responsible AI deployment in sustainable project execution: Ensuring transparency, carbon efficiency and regulatory alignment. *International Journal of Science and Research Archive*, *14*(3), 1686–1705. DOI: 10.30574/ijsra.2025.14.3.0920

Toledo, L. A., León, F. H. A. D., & de Sá, D. G. B. (2025). A convergência de marketing preditivo, data-driven marketing e inteligência artificial. *Revista Gestão Em Análise*, *14*(2), 26–45. DOI: 10.12662/2359-618xregea.v14i2.p26-45.2025

Uddin, M., Irshad, M., Kandhro, I. A., Alanazi, F., Ahmed, F., Maaz, M., Hussain, S., & Ullah, S. S. (2025). Generative AI revolution in cybersecurity: a comprehensive review of threat intelligence and operations [Review of *Generative AI revolution in cybersecurity: a comprehensive review of threat intelligence and operations*]. *Artificial Intelligence Review, 58*(8). Springer Science+Business Media. DOI: 10.1007/s10462-025-11219-5

Usman, F. O., Eyo-Udo, N. L., Etukudoh, E. A., Odonkor, B., Ibeh, C. V., & Adegbola, A. (2024). A CRITICAL REVIEW OF AI-DRIVEN STRATEGIES FOR ENTREPRENEURIAL SUCCESS [Review of *A CRITICAL REVIEW OF AI-DRIVEN STRATEGIES FOR ENTREPRENEURIAL SUCCESS*]. *International Journal of Management & Entrepreneurship Research, 6*(1), 200. Fair East Publishers. DOI: 10.51594/ijmer.v6i1.748

Utami, R. D., & Wang, A. (2026). Balancing Personalization, Privacy, and Value: A Systematic Literature Review of AI-Enabled Customer Experience Management. *Information (Basel)*, *17*(2), 115. DOI: 10.3390/info17020115

Wang, Z. (2025a). The Influence of Ai on Consumer Behavior: Shaping Choices and Preferences in the Digital Marketplace. SSRN *Electronic Journal*. DOI: 10.1016/j.sasc.2025.200397

Wang, Z. (2025b). The influence of AI on consumer behavior: Shaping choices and preferences in the digital marketplace. *Systems and Soft Computing*, *7*, 200397. DOI: 10.1016/j.sasc.2025.200397

Wankhade, S. G., Sahni, M., León-Castro, E., & Olazabal-Lugo, M. (2025). Navigating AI ethics: ANN and ANFIS for transparent and accountable project evaluation amidst contesting AI practices and technologies. *Frontiers in Artificial Intelligence*, *8*, 1535845. Advance online publication. DOI: 10.3389/frai.2025.1535845 PMID: 40385642

Wirtz, J., Kunz, W. H., Hartley, N., & Tarbit, J. (2022). Corporate Digital Responsibility in Service Firms and Their Ecosystems. *Journal of Service Research*, *26*(2), 173–190. DOI: 10.1177/10946705221130467

Wirtz, J., & Pitardi, V. (2023). How intelligent automation, service robots, and AI will reshape service products and their delivery. *Italian Journal of Marketing*, *2023*(3), 289–300. DOI: 10.1007/s43039-023-00076-1

KEY TERMS AND DEFINITIONS

AI-Based Services: Digital services that employ artificial intelligence technologies to automate, personalize, optimize, or support customer interactions and organizational operations.

Algorithmic Bias: Systematic and unfair discrimination resulting from biased training data, model design, or decision-making processes that disproportionately affect particular individuals or groups.

Artificial Intelligence (AI): The simulation of human intelligence by computer systems capable of learning, reasoning, problem-solving, decision-making, and performing cognitive tasks.

Artificial Neural Network (ANN): A computational model inspired by the human brain that learns complex relationships from data through interconnected processing nodes.

Consumer Privacy: The right of individuals to control the collection, storage, processing, sharing, and use of their personal information by organizations.

Data Governance: The framework of policies, procedures, standards, and responsibilities that ensures the quality, security, privacy, integrity, and ethical management of organizational data.

Data Minimization: A privacy principle requiring organizations to collect and process only the minimum amount of personal data necessary to achieve a specified purpose.

Differential Privacy: A privacy-preserving technique that protects individual information by introducing controlled statistical noise into datasets while maintaining overall analytical usefulness.

Ethical Artificial Intelligence: The development and deployment of AI systems according to principles such as fairness, transparency, accountability, privacy, human autonomy, and societal benefit.

Explainable Artificial Intelligence (XAI): AI methods that enable users to understand, interpret, and trust the reasoning behind algorithmic decisions.

Fairness: The principle that AI systems should avoid unjust discrimination and provide equitable outcomes across demographic and social groups.

General Data Protection Regulation (GDPR): The European Union regulation governing personal data protection, privacy rights, transparency, and organizational accountability.

Human-in-the-Loop (HITL): An AI governance approach in which human oversight remains part of automated decision-making processes.

Hyper-Personalization: The use of AI, machine learning, and real-time analytics to deliver highly individualized products, services, recommendations, and experiences.

Machine Learning (ML): A branch of AI that enables systems to improve performance automatically by learning patterns from data without explicit programming.

Privacy by Design: A system development philosophy in which privacy and data protection measures are incorporated throughout the entire lifecycle of a product or service.

Responsible AI: The design, development, deployment, and governance of AI systems that are ethical, transparent, secure, accountable, inclusive, and aligned with human values.

Transparency: The extent to which AI systems disclose their objectives, data usage, model behavior, and decision-making processes to stakeholders.

Trustworthy AI: AI systems that consistently demonstrate reliability, fairness, security, explainability, privacy protection, and accountability.

User Consent: The informed, voluntary, and explicit agreement provided by individuals before organizations collect or process their personal data.

Chapter 9

AI-Driven Chatbots and Virtual Assistants:
Transforming Customer Engagement in the Digital Era

Amandeep Singh
http://orcid.org/0009-0000-2820-0061
Chandigarh University, Mohali, India

Ramanjeet Singh
http://orcid.org/0000-0001-7424-7039
Chandigarh University, Mohali, India

Manjit Kour
http://orcid.org/0000-0003-1043-3187
Chandigarh University, Mohali, India

ABSTRACT

The emergence of AI-based virtual assistants and chatbots has significantly transformed the way companies engage with customers and compete in today's digital landscape. These smart tools utilize NLP, Machine Learning, Predictive Analytics, and can automatically interact with consumers, create a customized experience for them, improve their ability to resolve problems, and make predictions about future consumer behavior. This research examines the revolutionary nature of chatbots and virtual assistants based on Artificial Intelligence and their effects on customer service and provides insight into how they assist in automating various business processes while providing instant support to customers. The research used a qualitative approach and included an examination of AI applications in multiple

DOI: 10.4018/979-8-3373-9159-5.ch009

industries, along with case studies and data analysis. The major areas analyzed include how AI impacts customer interaction; operational cost reductions; and increased brand loyalty.

1. INTRODUCTION

The term Artificial Intelligence (AI) now represents an innovative change to the corporate world and has changed how companies interact with their customers, improve efficiency, and create growth (Nguyen et al., 2022). AI-driven techniques such as predictive analysis, machine learning algorithms, and automation will continue to impact business processes, creating more customer-centric businesses. The AI application that has had the greatest impact on customer service is with AI-powered chatbots and virtual assistants, improving both responsiveness and personalized interaction (Madanchian, 2024).

Today's digital business environment requires that organizations deliver on increasing demand from consumers for rapid response times, seamless interaction with their organization, and tailored experiences (Kaur & Kour, 2024; Mehmood et al., 2025). The ability of AI powered Chatbots & Virtual Assistants to meet consumer expectations through automated responses to consumer questions, processing of consumer behaviors, as well as customized solutions for the individual consumer, are just a few examples of how AI technology is used to create an improved customer experience and build brand loyalty as organizations continue to compete in a rapidly evolving digital marketplace (Pendyala, 2024). Additionally, the use of AI technology enables organizations to scale their customer service operations and provide a high-quality service to thousands of customers at the same time (El-Fotouh et al., 2024).

1.1. Key Benefits of AI in Customer Interaction Include:

AI's impact on automating routine processes, such as customer service, has allowed human agents to handle complex inquiries more efficiently (Chen et al., 2021; Mishra et al., 2024). AI chatbots use Natural Language Processing (NLP) and deep learning to comprehend customer questions and deliver instant solutions and learn from previous interactions to refine their upcoming response (Olujimi & Ade-Ibijola, 2023). Furthermore, AI-based platforms are integrated across communication channels such as websites, social media, and mobile applications, facilitating a unified customer experience (Uzoka et al., 2024).

The power of AI can be used to analyze a huge amount of customer data, facilitating businesses to foresee customer demands, deliver instant suggestions, and take proactive measures to address potential issues (Sadiq et al., 2025). Understanding consumer behavior is crucial for companies to achieve business success, and AI has a very important function in identifying consumers' buying habits, their shopping habits on the web, and consumers' opinions about products or services (Wang, 2025).

Organizations can analyze customer behavior in real-time, identify purchase behaviors, and develop predictive models of customer behavior through the use of AI to create a customized experience for each customer (Paul et al., 2023; Jamarani et al., 2024). The ability of AI to create a personal relationship with each customer creates loyalty with the company through customized communications, future buying behavior predictions, and ongoing customer service (Chopra et al. 2022; Imani et al. 2025).

There are many different industries that are using AI to improve customer interaction and retention (Ahmed et al., 2022). In the banking sector, AI-based assistants like Erica by Bank of America provided customers with immediate financial advice and help to complete transactions (Benali & Boumenkar, 2024). AI-powered virtual assistants also help healthcare industry assistants, which helps patients to make appointments, get medical advice, and manage medication prescriptions (Kumar, 2025). Travel and hospitality businesses use AI chatbots to manage bookings, provide personalized travel recommendations, and deliver updates in real time (Wust & Bremser, 2025).

Finally, AI has turned into a transforming customer engagement, making this an integral part of modern business strategies, behavior analysis, and retention efforts (Żyminkowska & Zachurzok-Srebrny, 2025). For businesses to succeed, this is an absolute necessity. This chapter examines the transformative potential of AI-based chatbots and virtual assistants relative to customer engagement and improved service delivery. This study is a conceptual study based heavily on secondary data sources, such as peer-reviewed academic journals, industry reports/analysis, white papers, and case studies. The study focuses primarily on the application of natural language processing, machine learning, and predictive analytics in the automation of customer service functions, personalization, and operationally efficient service delivery.

Figure 1. Conceptual Model of AI-Driven Customer Engagement and Retention

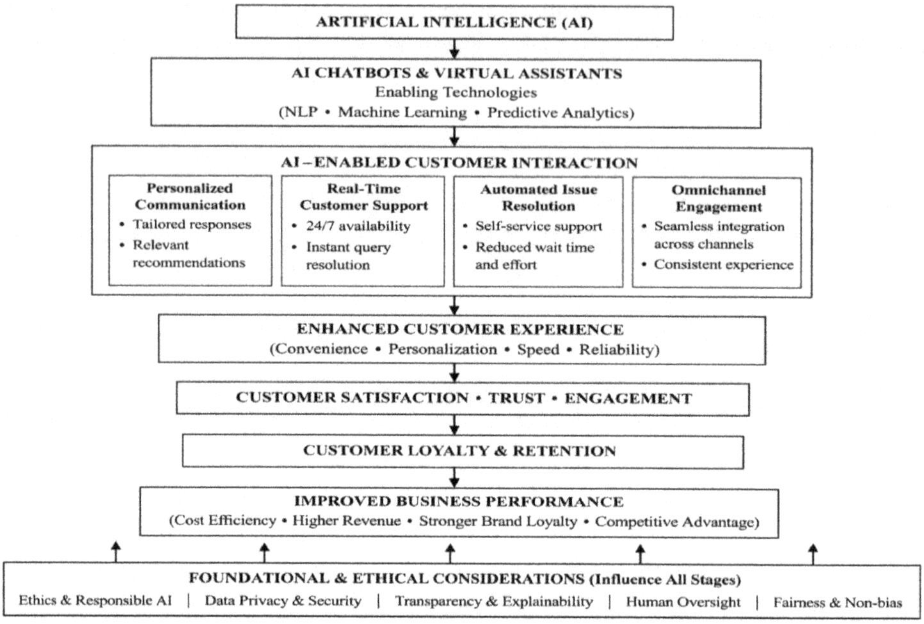

Source: Author compilation

Figure 1 shows an outline of the proposed conceptual framework for this chapter. The diagram demonstrates that artificial intelligence (AI) technology types include predictive analytics, natural language processing, machine learning, and generative AI, which enable the development of AI-enhanced customer interaction platforms like chatbots, virtual assistants, recommender systems, and omnichannel platforms.

2. REVIEW OF LITERATURE

Some Studies on artificial intelligence have documented the applications of AI through chatbots, predictive analytics, virtual assistants, recommendation systems, and ethical AI and have recognized several barriers to its adoption, including customers' trust in AI, consumer concerns about data privacy, and ethical considerations regarding how companies implement an AI system.

Chen et al. (2021) indicated that NLP has greatly improved the performance of chatbots to accurately interpret a customer's query and provide an appropriate response based on the customer's conversation. Nguyen et al. (2022) reported that the quality of the service provided by AI has a positive influence on the overall customer experience, trust, and brand loyalty due to the timely and personalized delivery of services. Liu (2022) found that customer satisfaction was improved through a machine learning-based recommendation system by analyzing customers' browsing patterns and purchase history. Ahmed et al. (2022) identified that the use of an AI Recommendation Engine increases customer engagement as well as increases the likelihood for customers to make purchases from Digital Commerce. Paul et al. (2023) have shown that Predictive Analytics allows organizations to be able to anticipate their customers' needs and develop ways of engaging with them proactively. Olujimi & Ade-Ibijola (2023) found that Chatbots powered by Natural Language Processing Improved Service Quality while also decreasing both Operational Costs and Response Time.

Hasan et al. (2023) stated that consumers were influenced by the perceived utility, trust, and privacy concerns for their ability to adopt AI-based Virtual Banking Assistants. Madanchian (2024) explained how generative AI can predict consumer behavior better due to its ability to analyze large amounts of customer interactions. Jamarani et al. (2024) demonstrated that the integration of Big Data Analytics into Artificial Intelligence provided better methods for segmenting customers, developing targeted marketing campaigns, and improving managers' ability to make decisions. Uzoka et al. (2024) noted that real-time and continual dialogue created with the aid of AI-based chatbots helps to create a greater level of engagement among customers across all channels. Gooljar et al. (2024) indicated that an assessment of sentiment via AI may be used to better understand how customers feel about a particular brand as well as improve overall brand management. Bhuiyan (2024) has shown that AI-powered customization increased customer satisfaction due to the ability to give customers personalized product/service recommendations/experiences.

Wang (2025) found that AI-generated personalization was found to have a positive impact on purchase behavior as well as post-purchase satisfaction. Sadiq et al. (2025) determined that predictive analytics enables firms to recognize potential customers who are about to abandon the firm and to implement appropriate retention measures. Sahut & Laroche (2025) argued that AI contributes to improving customer experience as well as the performance of marketing; they emphasize the need for the transparency, explainability, and accountability of AI governance. Lee and Breckon (2025) found in their study that customer engagement was a strong mediating factor for how an organization's implementation of Artificial Intelligence (AI) and customer loyalty. Haliti et al. (2025) pointed out that many organizations hesitated to adopt and utilize AI due to various ethical concerns, such as Data Privacy, algorithmic bias, and Transparency issues. Nie & Ahmad (2025) found that reinforcement-learning-based reward systems can enhance customer loyalty through dynamic incentives. Rodrigues et al. (2025) found that NLP-based customer segmentation increased both the accuracy of targeting customers and the overall effectiveness of a company's marketing. Żyminkowska & Zachurzok-Srebrny (2025) identified that companies using AI to engage with their customers on social media were able to strengthen these customer relationships by providing them with personalized digital interaction. The following Table 1 shows the summary of the review of the literature:

Table 1. Summary of Review of Literature on AI-Driven Customer Engagement

Author(s)	Objective	Methodology	Major Findings
Chen et al. (2021)	Examine NLP in customer service	Empirical study	NLP improves chatbot accuracy and customer interactions.
Nguyen et al. (2022)	Assess AI quality and customer experience	Survey	AI quality positively affects customer satisfaction and brand trust.
Liu (2022)	Investigate AI recommendation systems	Case study	Personalized recommendations improve customer engagement and purchase decisions.
Ahmed et al. (2022)	Study AI in e-commerce	Empirical analysis	AI-driven recommendations increase purchase intention.
Paul et al. (2023)	Analyze predictive analytics	Conceptual study	AI enables proactive customer engagement through behavioural prediction.
Olujimi & Ade-Ibijola (2023)	Review NLP-based chatbots	Systematic review	AI chatbots improve service quality while reducing response time.
Hasan et al. (2023)	Evaluate AI adoption in banking	Survey	Trust and perceived usefulness significantly influence AI acceptance.
Jamarani et al. (2024)	AI and big data analytics	Review study	AI enhances customer segmentation and decision-making.
Uzoka et al. (2024)	AI-enabled customer service	Empirical study	AI chatbots strengthen omnichannel customer engagement.
Gooljar et al. (2024)	Sentiment analysis	Review	AI improves customer feedback analysis and brand management.
Beyari (2025)	AI loyalty programmes	Empirical study	AI-based personalization enhances customer retention.
Sahut & Laroche (2025)	AI in marketing	Literature review	Ethical AI is essential for sustainable customer relationships.

Source: Author compilation

Although there has been extensive study on how Artificial Intelligence (AI) is being applied in customer services, personalized recommendations, recommendation systems, and predictive analytics, nearly all those studies were completed separately for each category or focused on specific industry types. There is limited research that provides a comprehensive integration of AI chatbots/virtual assistants, omni-channel engagement, customer loyalty, ethics of AI use, and emerging generative AI technologies into a single conceptual model

3. UNDERSTANDING CUSTOMER BEHAVIOR – THE ROLE OF AI

Consumer behavior analysis is important for a successful business; today, companies have access to the appropriate tools, with Artificial Intelligence (AI), to examine and study how previous customers behaved, predict how customers will behave in the future, and provide customized products and services to consumers (Kour & Kaur, 2024). In this section, the study will discuss AI capabilities with consumer behavior, including predictive analytics, sentiment analysis, personalized recommendations, and behavioral segmentation.

3.1. Predictive Analytics - Predicting Consumer Behavior

Predictive analytics provides organizations with the ability to look at past data and predict future consumer behavior. AI evaluates users' past interactions, purchase history, and browsing history to help companies understand customer behavior and anticipate future actions. Predictive analytics is useful to organizations in many sectors. For example, retailers and e-commerce sites use predictive analytics to predict customers' demands and to optimize inventories and promotions. Financial service companies use AI models to predict credit risk and detect fraud. Predictive analytics is being used by healthcare companies to determine a patient's needs and provide preventative treatment recommendations (Pendyala, 2024; Jamil et al., 2025).

3.2. Sentiment Analysis - Understanding What Customers Are Feeling

Opinion mining (also known as Sentiment Analysis) utilizes Artificial Intelligence to identify an individual's opinions regarding products or services through their spoken and/or written words. Artificial Intelligence utilizes Natural Language Processing (NLP) to examine customer review postings, social media posts, etc. The sentiment behind all these communications is identified as either positive, negative, or neutral, and Artificial Intelligence utilizes this sentiment information to alter marketing campaigns and customer service methods in "real-time" (Chen et al., 2021; Mishra et al., 2024). This trait improves multiple business functions. The concept of sentiment analysis is also used by companies as a measure of brand reputation, allowing them to monitor social media and address the concerns before they escalate.

3.3. Personalized Recommendations - AI-Driven Customization

Recommendation systems that are powered by AI can be used to support personalized user experiences by suggesting products or services that take into consideration consumer preferences and their previous behaviors. These systems make use of collaborative filtering to determine patterns between users and items and find items with similar features by using content-based filtering (Bici & Vajjhala, 2024).

AI-powered recommendations are utilized by organizations and businesses across a range of different sectors. For example, Netflix or Spotify use AI algorithms to make entertainment recommendations based on similarities with customers' self-selected viewing and listening preferences. E-commerce companies such as Amazon recommend products based not only on the customers' shopping history but also on co-purchasing activities on the platform.

3.4. Behavioral Segmentation - Sources for Targeted Marketing Strategies

Behavioral segmentation classifies consumers based on habits, preferences, and purchasing behavior. Artificial intelligence automates this process by applying machine learning algorithms to gather and analyze large amounts of data from consumer behavior to categorize customers into behavioral segments (Yin et al., 2025). Firms utilize behavioral segmentation through AI to enhance their marketing capabilities (Wang, 2025; Jamarani et al., 2024). With AI-driven behavioral segmentation, businesses can improve their marketing processes to ensure that the right people receive the right message at the right time.

4. AI CHATBOTS AND VIRTUAL ASSISTANTS IN CUSTOMER EXPERIENCE

This section examines AI-enabled chatbots and virtual assistants in terms of customer experience in four ways: 24/7 customer support, conversational commerce, omnichannel integration, and automated issue resolution.

4.1. 24/7 Customer Support – AI Resolves Queries Instantly and Automates Help

A very apparent benefit of AI chatbots is that they provide unlimited customer assistance. While human agents have fixed working hours, AI chatbots can be active 24 hours a day, 7 days a week. AI chatbots use NLP and machine learning to efficiently understand and answer questions from customers. AI chatbots can respond to a variety of inquiries, including product information and answering common problems (Chen et al., 2021; Mishra et al., 2024). This increases consumer satisfaction with quicker response times (Selimovic et al., 2024). In addition, chatbots will be able to continue learning from previous interactions and can therefore continue to adjust and enhance their response and accuracy over time (Olujimi & Ade-Ibijola, 2023). By automating a few routine tasks and questions, organizations can free human agents to respond to more complicated customer needs that require a human touch.

4.2. Conversational Commerce – AI-Powered Sales and Support through Messaging Platforms

Conversational commerce is a growing trend that has recently developed because it employs AI-based chatbots to facilitate online sales and customer service through a messaging platform (Uzoka et al., 2024). AI chatbots can personalize the overall shopping experience by providing product recommendations based on customer preferences, a customer's browsing history, and prior purchases (Benali & Boumenkar, 2024). As an additional element and purpose, chatbots can also help the customer with payment, order delivery, and post-shopping issues. Chatbots can do this by sending reminders to a customer when they have made a purchase and left it in the cart, providing live updates on items still in stock, and accepting returns/exchanges. All these aspects help to create a more seamless and efficient shopping experience (Baloska et al., 2022).

4.3. Omnichannel Integration – AI Automates Customer Engagement Across Digital Channels

Omnichannel integration facilitates AI chatbots and virtual assistants in creating uniformity in the customer experience across the customer touchpoints (Kamatala & Naayini, 2025). AI chatbots can consolidate customer interactions through uniform data across channels (Jamarani et al., 2024). Furthermore, omnichannel artificial intelligence (AI) chatbots focus on integrating with customer relationship management (CRM) systems to allow businesses to access information and history about every customer interaction quickly (Paul et al., 2023). Through this type of integration, chatbots will have the capability to respond to customers with detail, anticipate the needs of their customers, and personalize the customer's experience (Wang, 2025). Omnichannel AI enables businesses to create a seamless, end-to-end customer journey that fosters loyalty and increased retention (Balcıoğlu, 2025).

4.4. Automated Issue Resolution – Leads To Reduced Wait Time & Increases Customer Satisfaction

AI chatbots can be programmed using advanced problem-solving capabilities that can help assess and fix common customer problems without the need for a human (Brown et al., 2024). AI chatbots can recognize technical problems, assist users through self-service, and provide information on how to self-repair the technical issue step-by-step (Wust & Bremser, 2025). Artificial intelligence and predictive analytics could help chatbots anticipate potential problems and provide solutions before the customer brings up the issue (Hibban, 2025). AI chatbots may also escalate complex requests to human agents at the correct time, eliminating any delay with the information and responding to complex inquiries in the most appropriate manner (Mangipudi, 2025).

5. IMPROVING CUSTOMER LOYALTY THROUGH AI

In today's competitive landscape, the retention of customers for long-term growth is important. With artificial intelligence (AI) on the rise, businesses can now tap into data-driven insights to improve customer engagement, enhance loyalty, and provide proactive support. AI-powered tools have completely transformed how businesses interact with consumers and are enabling businesses to provide hyper-personalized interactions, advanced customer loyalty programs, proactive customer service, and constant customer feedback loops (Kour, 2024). This article explores the many ways that AI enables improved customer retention via better communication strategies, improved loyalty programs, proactively anticipating customer needs, and time-related real-time customer insights.

5.1. Hyper-Personalized – AI-Powered Communication Strategies

Personalization has become the cornerstone of modern customer engagement. AI lets organizations expand the possibilities beyond traditional and generic marketing strategies to get hyper-personalized experiences that consider the preferences, behaviors, and buying history of everyone (Bhuiyan, M. S., 2024). AI-fueled customer engagement uses machine-learning algorithms and natural language processing (NLP) to enable organizations to analyze a large amount of data from several touchpoints, so they can understand their customer preferences and personalize e-mail campaigns, product recommendations, and even the website content (Liu, 2022).

5.2. Loyalty Programs – AI-Driven Rewards Schemes Based on User Behavior

Many loyalty programs have typically utilized an "equal for everyone" mindset, which may only engage certain customers. AI-based loyalty programs take customer retention to the next level because they offer customized rewards and incentives based on user behaviors and preferences (Beyari, 2025). Using customer transaction history, engagement, and preference information, AI can analyze behavior patterns and determine which rewards will be the most effective for each customer segment.

Loyalty programs that utilize AI also enable dynamic reward systems, where rewards are differentially customized for the customer based on their ongoing engagement with the brand. For example, if the customer has interacted with the brand consistently but has not made a purchase for some time, AI could determine to deliver personalized rewards in the form of a limited-time discount or loyalty bonus to increase the likelihood of the customer buying again (Nie & Ahmad, 2025).

5.3. Proactive Customer Service – AI that Proactively Predicts and Resolves Customer Issues

Customer retention mainly involves delivering a high level of service that identifies and prevents issues before they occur (Neeraj, 2024). AI can identify patterns in customer behavior data to predict likely issues and take preemptive action. AI can also monitor repeatedly received complaints and then provide customer service agents with a solution prior to the customer reaching out, thus improving customer satisfaction and avoiding aggravation.

Table 2. Traditional vs. AI-Driven Personalization Overview

Feature	Traditional Approach	AI-Driven Approach	Source
Customer Segmentation	Targeting many customers	Personalized and data-driven targeted segments	Hasan et al., (2023); Ahmed et al. (2022); Bici & Vajjhala (2024); Selimovic et al. 2024); Jain (2025).
Product Recommendations	Static and categories-based	Ongoing, real-time recommendations	Benali & Boumenkar, (2024); Challapalli et al. (2025)
Marketing strategy	Generic messaging	AI-enabled personalized marketing campaigns	Wang (2025); Sahut & Laroche (2025)

continued on following page

Table 2. Continued

Feature	Traditional Approach	AI-Driven Approach	Source
Customer Interaction	Standardized responses with customers	AI-enabled contextual interactions with customers	Wust & Bremser, (2025); Sadiq et al. (2025); Brown et al. (2024); Rodrigues et al. (2025)
Customer Engagement	Reactive	Proactive, predictive engagement	Pendyala (2024); El-Fotouh et al. (2024); Kamatala & Naayini, (2025); Lee & Breckon (2025)

(Source: Author compilation)

Table 3. The Effect of Artificial Intelligence on Strategies to Retain Customers.

Retention Strategy	Traditional Approach	AI-Enhanced Approach	Sources
Customer Segmentation	Generalized, limited customized	AI Segmented by Behaviour	Hasan et al. (2023); Ahmed et al. (2022); Bici & Vajjhala, (2024); Jain (2025)
Loyalty Programs	Fixed, standardized incentives for loyalty	Personal-dynamic incentives	Chopra et al., (2022); Jamarani et al. (2024); Haliti et al. (2025)
Customer Service	Active problem solution	Proactive problem solution	Wust & Bremser, (2025); Kamatala & Naayini, (2025); Sahut & Laroche (2025)
Engagement	Uniform e-mail campaigns	AI personalized subject matter and recommendations	Benali & Boumenkar, (2024); Challapalli et al. (2025)
Feedback Mechanism	Periodically Survey	AI real time sentiment analysis	Gooljar et al. (2024); Brown et al. (2024); Balcıoğlu, (2025); Sadiq et al. (2025)

Source: Author compilation

5.4 Continuous Feedback & Refinement – Using AI For Real-Time Customer Feedback

Understanding customer feedback is critical to improving products, services, and the overall customer experience. AI-powered analytics tools, as well as sentiment analysis, can help businesses collect, analyze, and act on real-time customer feedback, which leads to improving the products and services and triggers retention rate (Wu et al., 2025). Businesses can use natural language processing (NLP) to find patterns of sentiment through which they can find areas of opportunity for improvement. Real-time feedback analysis helps companies arrive at data-driven decisions quickly. Artificial intelligence (AI) dashboards deliver actionable insights that allow companies the opportunity to change their strategies based on customer feedback (Chen et al., 2021). AI recommendation engines can also allow companies to personalize follow-ups with customers after they have provided feedback. If a customer rated their experience poorly, then the AI systems generate an automated follow-up, apologizing for their negative experience, and providing a unique incentive to encourage continued business.

6. REAL-WORLD EXAMPLES – SUCCESSFUL AI APPLICATION

This section explains three examples of the successful use of AI: AI-powered shopping and customer engagement through Amazon Alexa; AI-powered financial support in the banking area, Erica; and AI-powered virtual stylists and customer journeys in retail and e-commerce.

6.1 Amazon Alexa – AI-powered Shopping and Customer Engagement

As a voice-activated virtual assistant, Amazon Alexa is transforming the way customers engage with technology and shop online. Utilizing natural language processing (NLP) and machine learning, Alexa provides an integrated online shopping experience that allows users to interact with multiple services in a very easy way.

6.1.1. Key Features and Execution

- Voice-Activated Purchasing: Alexa permits a hands-free ordering experience, allowing customers to talk about products and add products to their shopping cart, and order products.
- Personalized Suggestions: The AI creates personalized suggestions for customers as it gathers information based on their behavior, intended shopping history, and purchasing preferences.
- Customer Support: Alexa answers questions about orders, keeps track of shipments, and tells users about Amazon services.

6.1.2. Impact and Success

Amazon's hold on the e-commerce space has been amplified due to Alexa's AI, not only creating convenience for customers but also gathering data on customer shopping habits for Amazon. A voice-assisted shopping experience was an easy way to diminish the friction in making a purchase, leading to increased customer satisfaction.

6.2 Banking Segment – AI Financial Assistant (Bank of America Erica)

Banking has matured from early adopters of technology to industry leaders in adopting AI technology to improve customer service, enhance accessibility, enhance efficiency, and enhance financial decision-making capabilities. One such example of the application of AI in banking is the AI virtual financial assistant "Erica", at Bank of America.

6.2.1. Key Features and Use

- Simple transaction support: Customers can ask Erica about their balance, transfer funds, and set up bill payments via text and voice.
- Fraud detection and notifications: AI algorithms also provide help with detecting unauthorized activity by identifying transactions that are potentially fraudulent and alerting customers to any unauthorized transactions.
- Automated responses to customer inquiries: Erica has been developed to respond to frequently asked questions to reduce waiting times and improve efficiency.

6.2.2. Impact and actual outcomes

Since its launch, Erica has reached millions of users, efficiently processing billions of interactions. The AI assistant contributes to lower customer service costs while improving the user experience with prompt feedback and financial insights.

6.3. Retail and E-Commerce Sector– Virtual Stylists and AI Customer Journeys

Artificial Intelligence has revolutionized the retail and e-commerce industry through the personalization of customer experience and automation of customer service. Retailer Brands (such as H&M, Sephora, and Stitch Fix) use AI-powered Virtual Stylists and Recommendation Engines.

6.3.1. Key Features and Implementation

- Virtual Stylists: Virtual Stylists utilize AI to analyze a user's preferences, purchase history, and current trends in style to provide a recommended outfit. Stitch Fix utilizes both AI and Human selection to create an even greater variety of possible clothing options that will meet an individual's needs.
- Predictive Analytics for Inventory Management: With the help of AI, demand can be predicted, and retailers can use predictive analytics to determine their inventory levels to avoid both overstock and out-of-stock conditions.
- Augmented Reality (AR) Shopping: Brands such as Sephora utilize AI-generated AR so customers can virtually test makeup products before purchasing them.

6.3.2. Impact and Success

The retail industry has benefited from AI in increasing customer interaction and conversion by creating an efficient, personalized shopping experience; virtual stylists, as well as AI-powered recommendation tools, have improved customer satisfaction and retention through a more interactive and customizable shopping experience.

7. CHALLENGES AND ETHICAL ISSUES IN AI

Industry and Policy Stakeholders Must Respond to the Issues and Ethical Complexities of AI Usage As the Use of Artificial Intelligence Becomes More Prevalent in Many Industries and Day-to-Day Life. Although AI is helping improve our efficiency, decision-making, and customer experience, AI also raises issues related to human use, data privacy, public bias, and how AI will change and evolve in the future. This chapter discusses some of the major issues and ethical implications for using AI, including balancing the use of AI and humans, data privacy and security of the data collected, reducing AI-driven bias in decision-making, and managing AI models that may change and improve continuously.

7.1. Counterbalancing AI And Human Connection – Assuring Personalized Experiences

A core challenge to AI adoption is finding the right balance of automation and human touch. While AI-powered chatbots, virtual assistants, and recommendation engines enhance customer experience, using automation too much can lead to dehumanization, impersonality, and customer dissatisfaction.

7.1.1. Challenges

- Loss of Human Touch: AI-enabled systems may lack emotional intelligence and empathy, and cannot respond to nuanced customer interactions.
- Customer Trust Issues: Some customers prefer human support instead of AI support, as they suspect automated responses will not fully address their concerns.
- Addressing Complex Issues: AI may not be able to deal with context-driven issues that require critical thinking and flexibility.

7.1.2. Ethical Considerations

- Hybrid AI-Human Model: Businesses should incorporate AI and human support into their processes to appropriately escalate customer cases if they choose.
- Personalization Strategy: AI should be viewed as providing additional support to enhance the personalized human interaction instead of replacing human beings.
- Transparency of AI Communication: It should be clear to customers whether an interaction is with AI or a human to appropriately set expectations.

7.2 Data Privacy and Security of Your Information - Global Compliance and Laws Surrounding AI

Artificial Intelligence relies on vast amounts of data, which raises the issues of data privacy, security, and regulatory compliance. Governments around the world have enacted strict legislation in response to data protection concerns (e.g., Europe has the General Data Protection Regulation (GDPR) and California has the California Consumer Privacy Act (CCPA)).

7.2.1. Challenges

- Data Collection and Consent: AI tools need large datasets, which bring issues of user consent and ownership of the data, as users may not have given consent for their data to be used.
- Cybersecurity Concerns: AI products will always have the risk of data breaches, hacking, and identity theft.
- Regulatory Compliance: Businesses using AI may face multilayer legal frameworks and must navigate uncertainty over compliance related to data protection laws.

7.2.2. Ethical Implications

- Transparent Policies regarding Data: Organizations must transparently disclose how AI collects, stores, and processes users' data.
- Implement Security Measures: Organizations must implement robust encryption, anonymization, and cybersecurity standards to protect against data breaches.
- User Control of Data: AI must provide the users' ability to access, modify, or delete their personal data as per various regulations that exist worldwide.

7.3. Prejudice in AI Decision-Making - Ethical Decisions and Transparency

The quality of AI models is directly related to the quality of the datasets on which they are based. In other words, if the AI algorithm is biased in its understanding of our society, then it will yield biased results when it is used to select for hiring, civil service loans, law enforcement officers, or health and medical care.

7.3.1. Challenges

- Bias present in Training Data: Biased data will yield biased results in a biased AI model.
- The Black Box Problem: Many AIs operate as "black boxes," which makes it difficult to discern how they reach a decision.
- The Ethics of Decision-Making Inference: AI-based decision making could have disproportionate outcomes (e.g., hiring decisions, credit approvals, or medical diagnoses) that create significant distress for marginalized communities.

7.3.2. Ethics Consideration

- Understanding and working with Diverse and Representative Data Sets: AI models should be trained on datasets that are inclusive and representative of a variety of demographic and worldview perspectives.
- Explainable AI (XAI): Companies could choose AI models that are interpretable and transparent in their decision-making.
- Regularly audit for Bias: Organizations should regularly audit their AI algorithms to better find and combat bias.

7.4. Developing AI Models – The Requirement for Incessant Learning and Adoption

The development of AI is an evolving process. AI models require continuous adaptation and updating as technology evolves and as users' expectations grow and change, so that AI models remain relevant and useful in the future.

7.4.1. Challenges

- Model decline or drift: The accuracy of AI models may degrade over time due to new patterns in data being developed.
- Ethics and Autonomous Learning AI: Learning AI systems can produce unintended behaviors by virtue of the learning process itself, raising questions about the ethics of those behaviors.
- Future regulation and ethics alignment: Regulatory bodies will have to evolve along with emerging technology to establish a framework that promotes the responsible development and deployment of AI technologies.

7.4.2. Ethical Considerations

- Oversight of humans and governance: Human experts must review and govern AI systems to identify and correct adverse effects from unintended actions.
- Sustaining the training of AI: Organizations must commit to continuing investment in the training and testing of AI systems to continue to support equitable, accurate, and ethical uses of AI systems.
- Adaptive policy/regulation in partnership with AI developers: Policymakers should consult with AI developers to create flexible regulations that adapt to the ever-changing advancements in technology.

8. FUTURE DIRECTIONS AND RESEARCH TRENDS IN AI

Future trends strongly suggest that AI will become more emotionally aware, immersive tech, and ethically applied technology that will have more human-centric contributions to customer engagement rather than purely automation. Building upon advancements in AI-enabled chatbots, virtual assistants, and other technologies, their purposes as customer engagement tools, future advancements related to emotion recognition, immersive AR/VR integration, and increasingly sophisticated consumer behavior prediction models are likely to alter the creation and delivery of AI-enabled customer experiences. This section identifies future trends and potential research avenues in AI-enabled customer engagement moving forward.

8.1. Emotionally Intelligent AI – Toward Empathetic Customer Interactions

Emotionally intelligent AI indicates a leap forward in human/AI interaction. In recent weeks, emerging technologies have shown that AI can study a customer's emotions by using emotional signals from natural language, facial expression, tone of voice, and sentiment from text input. Future inquiries in this space are aimed at improving the cultural and contextual sensitivity of emotion-detection models through training on diverse, inclusive datasets. Current and future inquiries on AI emotion detection focus on ethical concerns, such as political and commercial data privacy, emotional manipulation, and user consent.

8.2. AI and AR/VR Integration – Redefining Immersive Engagement

The combination of artificial intelligence (AI), augmented reality (AR), and virtual reality (VR) technologies allow retailers to create a highly personalized experience for customers that is interactive. Retailers leverage AI-AR tools like virtual try-on, while educational institutions and healthcare providers leverage AI-VR for realistic simulation and experience-based training. Several research directions in this area will focus on improving the realism and responsiveness of virtual agents in AR/VR, refining AI adaptive learning environments in immersive spaces, and overcoming technical challenges related to cost and accessibility.

8.3. Advanced Machine Learning for Consumer Behavior Insights

Machine learning (ML) remains the central focus of AI-enabled customer engagement strategies, but we will be increasingly using ML to create hyper-personalised experiences, make real-time decisions, and observe customer behaviour across platforms. A greater number of studies are now addressing the need for AI models to clarify and enhance the explainability and transparency of the models, as these practices are essential to trust levels and the responsible use of customer data. At the same time, researchers are working on interdisciplinary collaborations that incorporate neural and other cognitive science aspects with AI as they advance our understanding of customer motivations, cognitive capabilities, and behaviour patterns.

8.4 Ethical and Regulatory Frameworks – Governing the Future of AI In Customer Engagement

As consumers interact with organizations using AI systems and as these systems become a larger component in decision-making, there is an increasing demand from consumers for clear governance policies. Across the world, policymakers are joining forces to create regulations that protect consumer information collected from data and ensure organizations are accountable for the algorithms they use and transparent about how they use AI systems. Research is increasingly focused on global standards for ethical AI implementation, AI audits and compliance, as well as the inherent balance between innovation and consumer rights.

9 CONCLUSIONS

Artificial Intelligence is radically transforming consumer behavior and how organizations retain customers with real-time, personalized customer interactions. The AI chatbots and virtual assistants that organizations are using will boost customer service, interest, and long-term commitment from consumers. As AI Technologies improve, organizations must observe best practices for effective and useful implementation of AI-powered solutions, especially in blending AI with human assistance to create complementary solutions instead of wholly replacing human agents. Transparency remains critical when communicating with customers through AI, and customers should be notified when AI is being utilized in some capacity. Organizations must continually train and develop their AI models to be more effective and accurate based on changes in customer preferences.

While AI has many advantages, it still poses many challenges for organizations to navigate to ensure the ethical and responsible use of AI. Organizations must continually focus on data privacy and data security, as organizations have a responsibility to protect consumer data and comply with global regulations, including the General Data Protection Regulation (GDPR). Organizations should also strive to implement transparent AI systems that will provide an opportunity for accountability and help build a relationship of trust with consumers. In addition to developing explainable AI systems, organizations must find the right balance between enabling AI to run automated processes and the role of humans in performing operational tasks so that they can deliver quality customer service.

In the years ahead, AI will play a larger part in determining how customer experience is managed by organizations. New forms of AI that are emotional, Augmented Reality (AR), and Conversational Interfaces (Chatbots) will enhance/extend interactions between customers and companies, and as a result, provide a better/more interactive experience for both. Autonomous AI agents performing complex transactional negotiations will also eliminate complexity from the process and, as a result, increase efficiency. To be competitive in an ever-evolving digital environment, companies will have to utilize AI and innovative solutions in an ethical and responsible manner. Companies that can use AI effectively for their customers' interaction with the organization will be able to establish stronger customer relationships, increase brand loyalty, and achieve long-term sustainability, as well as obtain attention for the company.

REFERENCES

Abou El-Fotouh, T. A. I., Akanbi, M. T., Alom, N. B., Zakaria, A. F., Yusof, Z. B., & Razak, A. B. (2024). *Influence of predictive analytics and machine learning on enhancing customer retention and loyalty in service-based enterprises.* [Complete publication details required.]

Ahmed, M. Z., Singh, A., Paul, A., Ghosh, S., & Chaudhuri, A. K. (2022). Amazon product recommendation system. *International Journal of Advanced Research in Computer and Communication Engineering, 11*(3). Advance online publication. DOI: 10.17148/IJARCCE.2022.11356

Balcıoğlu, Y. S. (2025). AI-driven personalization in omnichannel marketing: Enhancing customer engagement and loyalty. In *Leveraging AI for Effective Digital Relationship Marketing* (pp. 97–130). IGI Global Scientific Publishing.

Baloska, S., Mechkaroska, D., & Domazet, E. (2022). AI-driven chatbot in e-commerce. *Journal of UIST, 3*(1), 30–40.

Benali, S., & Boumenkar, D. (2024). Contribution of chatbot applications to attaining digital financial inclusion: Analysis and evaluation of America's chatbot Erica experience. *Management & Economics Research Journal, 6*(3), 497–516.

Beyari, H. (2025). Artificial intelligence's effect on customer loyalty in the context of electronic commerce. *Journal of Umm Al-Qura University for Engineering and Architecture*, 1–10.

Bhuiyan, M. S. (2024). The role of AI-enhanced personalization in customer experiences. *Journal of Computer Science and Technology Studies, 6*(1), 162–169. DOI: 10.32996/jcsts.2024.6.1.17

Bici, A., & Vajjhala, N. R. (2024). Emerging trends and themes in AI-driven customer engagement and relationship management. In *Proceedings of the 5th International Conference on the Role of Innovation, Entrepreneurship and Management for Sustainable Development (ICRIEMSD 2024)* (Vol. 310, p. 113). Springer Nature. DOI: 10.2991/978-94-6463-612-3_9

Brown, W., Wilson, G., & Johnson, O. (2024). *Understanding the role of chatbots in enhancing customer service.* [Publication details required.]

Challapalli, V., Sai, K. V., Singh, P. P., Prasad, R., Maurya, A., & Singh, A. (2025). SLM4Offer: Personalized marketing offer generation using contrastive learning-based fine-tuning. *arXiv*.

Chopra, R., Patel, N., Chopra, N., & Singh, D. (2022). Leveraging reinforcement learning and collaborative filtering for enhanced personalization in loyalty programs. *International Journal of AI Advancements*, *11*(10).

Gooljar, V., Issa, T., Hardin-Ramanan, S., & Abu-Salih, B. (2024). Sentiment-based predictive models for online purchases in the era of Marketing 5.0: A systematic review. *Journal of Big Data*, *11*(1), 107. DOI: 10.1186/s40537-024-00947-0

Haliti Baruti, B., Hoti, A., & Bajrami, S. M. (2025). Utilising artificial intelligence in digital marketing strategy: Opportunities and challenges for marketers. *SSRN*. DOI: 10.2139/ssrn.5470814

Hasan, S., Godhuli, E. R., Rahman, M. S., & Al Mamun, M. A. (2023). The adoption of conversational assistants in the banking industry: Is the perceived risk a moderator? *Heliyon*, *9*(9), e20220. DOI: 10.1016/j.heliyon.2023.e20220 PMID: 37810016

Hibban, M. I. (2025). AI-powered chatbots: Revolutionizing customer service in the digital era. *Jurnal Ekonomi Kreatif dan Manajemen Bisnis Digital*, *4*(2), 282–288.

Imani, M., Joudaki, M., Beikmohammadi, A., & Arabnia, H. R. (2025). Customer churn prediction: A systematic review of recent advances, trends, and challenges in machine learning and deep learning. *Machine Learning and Knowledge Extraction*, *7*(3), 105. DOI: 10.3390/make7030105

Jain, S. (2025). Exploring the transformative impact of artificial intelligence on customer segmentation and precision targeted advertising strategies. *NOLEGEIN. Journal of Consumer Behavior & Market Research*, *8*(1).

Jamarani, A., Haddadi, S., Sarvizadeh, R., Haghi Kashani, M., Akbari, M., & Moradi, S. (2024). Big data and predictive analytics: A systematic review of applications. *Artificial Intelligence Review*, *57*(7), 176. DOI: 10.1007/s10462-024-10811-5

Jamil, K., Anwar, A., & Mustafa, S. (2025). Upgradation of customer relationship management through the AI-driven approach to personalization, engagement, and retention. In *Reshaping Organizational Management and Workplace Culture With AI* (pp. 263–286). IGI Global Scientific Publishing. DOI: 10.4018/979-8-3693-8960-7.ch010

Kamatala, S., & Naayini, P. (2025). The rise of AI chatbots: Balancing customer satisfaction and operational efficiency. *International Journal of Current Science Research and Review*, *8*(3), 1144–1151. DOI: 10.47191/ijcsrr/V8-i3-17

Kaur, B., & Kour, M. (2025). Revolutionary Impact of Artificial Intelligence on Society and Its Challenges and Opportunities. AI Use in Social Sciences, 383-404.

Kour, M. (2024). *"Ethical Considerations in the Metaverse and Augmented Retail Reality Era", Consumer Experience and Decision-Making in the Metaverse.* IGI Global.

Kour, M., & Kaur, R. (2024). "AI and Influencer Marketing: Redefining the Future of Social Media Marketing in Industry 6.0". In Advanced Businesses in Industry 6.0 (pp. 87-103). IGI Global. DOI: 10.4018/979-8-3693-3108-8.ch007

Kumar, M. (2025). AI in healthcare: Enhancing patient engagement through virtual assistants. *International Journal of Engineering Research & Technology (IJERT), 14*(3), Article IJERTV14IS030045.

Lee, M. C., & Breckon, D. (2025). Factors affecting customer engagement in AI marketing. *Telematics and Informatics Reports, 100230.*

Liu, L. (2022). E-commerce personalized recommendation based on machine learning technology. *Mobile Information Systems, 2022*(1), 1–11. DOI: 10.1155/2022/1761579

Madanchian, M. (2024). Generative AI for consumer behavior prediction: Techniques and applications. *Sustainability (Basel), 16*(22), 9963. DOI: 10.3390/su16229963

Mangipudi, P. (2025). *AI powered chatbots vs. human agents: A comparative study on customer satisfaction.*

Mehmood, K., Kour, M., & Kautish, P. (2025). The impact spectrum: How influencer traits shape consumer purchase intentions through credibility and materialism. *Current Psychology, 44*(12), 12380–12398. DOI: 10.1007/s12144-025-07942-5

Mishra, A. K., Tyagi, A. K., & Arowolo, M. O. (2024). Future trends and opportunities in machine learning and artificial intelligence for banking and finance. In *Applications of Blockchain Technology and Artificial Intelligence: Lead-ins in Banking, Finance, and Capital Market* (pp. 211–238). Springer. DOI: 10.1007/978-3-031-47324-1_13

Neeraj, K. (2024). Predictive analytics for customer retention: A data-driven framework for proactive engagement and satisfaction management. *International Journal (Toronto, Ont.), 10*(6), 1109–1116.

Nguyen, T. M., Quach, S., & Thaichon, P. (2022). The effect of AI quality on customer experience and brand relationship. *Journal of Consumer Behaviour, 21*(3), 481–493. DOI: 10.1002/cb.1974

Nie, X., & Ahmad, F. S. (2025). Dynamic reward systems and customer loyalty: Reinforcement learning-optimized personalized service strategies. *Future Technology, 4*(3), 259–268. DOI: 10.55670/fpll.futech.4.3.24

Olujimi, P. A., & Ade-Ibijola, A. (2023). NLP techniques for automating responses to customer queries: A systematic review. *Discover Artificial Intelligence*, *3*(1), 20. DOI: 10.1007/s44163-023-00065-5

Paul, R., Imam, M. H., & Mou, A. J. (2023). AI-powered sentiment analysis in digital marketing: A review of customer feedback loops in IT services. *American Journal of Scholarly Research and Innovation*, *2*(2), 166–192. DOI: 10.63125/61pqqq54

Pendyala, S. K. (2024). *Healthcare data analytics: Leveraging predictive analytics for improved patient outcomes.*

Rodrigues, G. N., Mir, M. N. H., Bhuiyan, M. S. M., Rafi, M. D. A. L., Hoque, A. M., Maua, J., & Mridha, M. F. (2025). *NLP-driven customer segmentation: A comprehensive review of methods and applications in personalized marketing*. Data Science and Management.

Sadiq, E., Alkarani, H., & Chakranarayan, V. (2025). Predictive analytics in customer relationship management. In *2024 International Conference on IT Innovation and Knowledge Discovery (ITIKD)* (pp. 1–7). IEEE.

Sahut, J. M., & Laroche, M. (2025). Using artificial intelligence (AI) to enhance customer experience and to develop strategic marketing: An integrative synthesis. *Computers in Human Behavior*, *170*, 108684. DOI: 10.1016/j.chb.2025.108684

Selimovic, M., Abd Almisreb, A., & Amanzholova, S. (2024). The role of sentiment analysis in brand management and marketing: A comparative study. *Procedia Computer Science*, *251*, 579–584. DOI: 10.1016/j.procs.2024.11.152

Uzoka, A., Cadet, E., & Ojukwu, P. U. (2024). Leveraging AI-powered chatbots to enhance customer service efficiency and future opportunities in automated support. *Computer Science & IT Research Journal*, *5*(10), 2485–2510. DOI: 10.51594/csitrj.v5i10.1676

Wang, Z. (2025). The influence of AI on consumer behavior: Shaping choices and preferences in the digital marketplace. *SSRN*. DOI: 10.1016/j.sasc.2025.200397

Wu, Q., Xia, C., & Tian, S. (2025). AI-driven sentiment analytics: Unlocking business value in the e-commerce landscape. *arXiv*.

Wust, K., & Bremser, K. (2025). Artificial intelligence in tourism through chatbot support in the booking process: An experimental investigation. *Tourism and Hospitality*, *6*(1), 36. DOI: 10.3390/tourhosp6010036

Yin, J., Qiu, X., & Wang, Y. (2025). The impact of AI-personalized recommendations on clicking intentions: Evidence from Chinese e-commerce. *Journal of Theoretical and Applied Electronic Commerce Research*, *20*(1), 21. DOI: 10.3390/jtaer20010021

Żyminkowska, K., & Zachurzok-Srebrny, E. (2025). The role of artificial intelligence in customer engagement and social media marketing: Implications from a systematic review for the tourism and hospitality sectors. *Journal of Theoretical and Applied Electronic Commerce Research*, *20*(3), 184. DOI: 10.3390/jtaer20030184

Chapter 10

Consumer Experience In Metaverse Environments

Özlem Keloğlu
http://orcid.org/0000-0001-6037-3317
Mugla Sitki Kocman University, Turkey

Mehmet Marangoz
http://orcid.org/0009-0008-5548-3384
Mugla Sitki Kocman University, Turkey

ABSTRACT

The rapid advancement of digital and immersive technologies has transformed consumer experience, shifting marketing toward interactive and personalized service encounters. The metaverse represents a novel environment where consumers engage through avatar-mediated interaction and real-time participation. This chapter examines how consumer experience is formed in metaverse environments, with a focus on AI-driven hyper-personalization. It integrates experience economy and experiential marketing perspectives with immersive technology frameworks to explain key mechanisms such as presence, flow, and interactivity. The findings suggest that consumer experience is shaped by psychological, social, and technological factors, with artificial intelligence enabling adaptive, personalized, and engaging experiences in digital service contexts.

INTRODUCTION

Accelerated digital transformation has fundamentally altered consumer interactions with products, services, and brands. Modern markets are increasingly defined by technology-driven interaction, instantaneous connectivity, and immersive con-

DOI: 10.4018/979-8-3373-9159-5.ch010

sumption experiences that transcend conventional physical spaces (Kumar et al., 2026a; Kumar et al., 2026b). As digital platforms develop into immersive ecosystems, organizations are increasingly redirecting their strategic emphasis from transactional interactions to the creation and management of significant consumer experiences. In this context, experiential value has become a crucial factor influencing customer satisfaction, behavioral intention, and the development of long-term relationships. The metaverse has emerged as a pivotal paradigm shift in digital consumption, signifying a continuous, shared virtual environment where users can engage with digital content, other users, and brands in real time via immersive interfaces. The metaverse amalgamates physical and virtual realities, facilitating simultaneous interaction, social connectivity, and value co-creation within digitally mediated environments (Kumar et al., 2026a). In contrast to conventional, two-dimensional online platforms, metaverse environments enable embodied interaction via avatars, spatial navigation, and multisensory engagement, thereby augmenting the depth and richness of the consumer experience (Sai, Goyal, & Chamola, 2024). Consequently, these simulated spaces function as interactive, experiential marketplaces that support collaborative participation across diverse sectors, including retail, entertainment, education, and financial services (Behr, 2024) .

Technological advancements related to immersive environments have enhanced the experiential aspect of modern consumption. The integration of virtual reality, artificial intelligence, blockchain, and data-driven personalization fosters the creation of intricate digital frameworks that enable adaptive and context-aware interactions between consumers and organizations. These technological advancements allow companies to create highly interactive experiential journeys that integrate emotional stimulation, identity expression, and real-time engagement in virtual consumption environments (D'Ulizia et al., 2024). However, as AI-driven personalization and real-time data tracking become embedded in these virtual journeys, they simultaneously introduce critical challenges regarding consumer privacy, data ethics, and digital well-being—dimensions that heavily weigh on the overall quality of the consumer experience.

From a consumer behavior perspective, immersive digital environments also transform the psychological processes underlying experience formation. Engagement in virtual environments allows individuals to explore alternative identities, partake in socially integrated activities, and extract symbolic significance from digitally facilitated interactions. Research findings demonstrate that experiential enjoyment, perceived presence, and engagement intensity significantly influence consumer responses to metaverse platforms, affecting both adoption and ongoing usage intentions (Kaur et al., 2023). These developments underscore the increasing significance of comprehending the functioning of experiential mechanisms within immersive consumption environments.

Although there is growing academic interest in the technological and strategic ramifications of the metaverse, research on the multifaceted aspects of consumer experience development in immersive settings remains relatively sparse. Current research frequently analyzes adoption motivators or technological frameworks independently, neglecting the intricate interaction among psychological immersion, social engagement, and the creation of experiential value. Comprehensive frameworks that integrate psychological mechanisms, technological affordances, and value creation processes in shaping consumer experience are still limited. Prior literature reviews emphasize the need for interdisciplinary and integrative approaches to better understand the complexity of consumer behavior in immersive environments (Kumar et al., 2026a). Bridging this gap necessitates a holistic viewpoint that perceives the metaverse as a nascent experiential marketplace, where consumer behavior is influenced by the interplay of digital immersion and emotional involvement.

To address these theoretical and practical gaps, this chapter establishes a comprehensive, multi-dimensional objective. Specifically, it examines the systematic construction of the consumer experience within metaverse environments by synthesizing insights from the experience economy, experiential marketing, and immersive technology literature. To achieve this, the chapter systematically addresses three interconnected goals: (1) it elucidates a comprehensive conceptual framework that maps the variables driving experiential engagement; (2) it critically examines how immersive interactions alter consumer perception, motivation, and subsequent behavioral outcomes; and (3) it discusses the strategic, ethical, and practical implications of these experiences for contemporary businesses seeking a competitive advantage. By focusing on these experiential dimensions, this study advances the academic discussion on digitally mediated consumption and provides a robust theoretical foundation for future empirical research on immersive customer experiences.

EXPERIENCE ECONOMY AND EXPERIENTIAL MARKETING

Experience as a Source of Competitive Advantage

Building on the growing importance of experiential value in digitally mediated environments, it is essential to examine the theoretical foundations of experience-based consumption. In increasingly hyper-competitive and technology-driven markets, organizations can no longer achieve sustained differentiation solely through functional product attributes or cost-leadership strategies. Instead, they are compelled to pivot toward the creation of meaningful, engaging, and memorable consumer experiences (Behr, 2024). According to Pine and Gilmore's (1998) Experience Economy framework, experiences represent a distinct economic offering that extends beyond commodities, goods, and services. When a business orchestrates an experience, it charges a premium not just for the physical materials, but for the subjective, memorable time the consumer spends within the environment.

In contemporary marketing, digital transformation has accelerated this structural shift, rewriting the rules of market positioning. In immersive digital ecosystems like the metaverse, experience transforms from a luxury touchpoint into a strategic resource for competitive advantage. By shifting from transactional exchanges toward multidimensional relationship building, organizations can strengthen long-term customer loyalty and create sustainable competitive differentiation through immersive, personalized, and value-driven consumer experiences. Virtual environments function as interactive, experiential platforms that enable multisensory engagement, real-time communication, and collaborative participation across various sectors, including retail, entertainment, and financial services (Behr, 2024).

Moreover, technological convergence has further strengthened this strategic necessity. The integration of virtual reality (VR), artificial intelligence (AI), and advanced data analytics enables adaptive experiential infrastructures that support context- aware and personalized interactions (D'Ulizia et al., 2024). From an economic perspective, hyper-personalization enhances perceived value by aligning digital experiences with individual preferences and behavioral patterns. Strategically, identity-driven engagement enables consumers to construct symbolic meaning within virtual spaces, reducing brand-switching intentions and strengthening long-term customer relationships (Kaur et al., 2023).

The strategic significance of immersive experiences can also be interpreted through the evolution of the Experience Economy. As Pine and Gilmore (1998) argue, competitive advantage increasingly shifts from the delivery of goods and services toward the orchestration of memorable experiences. In metaverse environments, this transformation becomes even more pronounced because value is no longer derived solely from efficient service delivery but from consumers' active participation in immersive, personalized, and socially embedded experiences. Through avatar-mediated interaction, spatial presence, and AI-enabled personalization, consumers become co-creators of value rather than passive recipients of organizational offerings (D'Ulizia et al., 2024; Davis et al., 2009). Consequently, sustainable competitive advantage depends not only on technological sophistication but also on organizations' ability to design adaptive experiential ecosystems that generate emotional engagement, symbolic meaning, and enduring consumer relationships (Behr, 2024; Kaur et al., 2023).

Beyond enhancing immediate consumer satisfaction, immersive experiences create sustainable strategic value because experiential value emerges from the interaction of technological capabilities, consumer participation, emotional engagement, and social value co-creation, making it difficult for competitors to imitate. From this perspective, organizations operating within metaverse environments compete not only through technological innovation but also through their ability to orchestrate memorable, personalized, and participatory experiences that strengthen consumer–brand relationships over time (Behr, 2024). Organizations that integrate immersive technologies, adaptive personalization, and community-based engagement into coherent experiential ecosystems encourage active consumer participation, strengthening perceived value, trust, loyalty, and long-term engagement (D'Ulizia et al., 2024; Kaur et al., 2023). Consequently, experience-based differentiation should be viewed as a dynamic organizational capability that sustains competitive positioning in rapidly evolving digital markets.

Hedonic and Emotional Consumption

The growing significance of experiential marketing has enhanced the importance of hedonic and emotional consumption as key influences on consumer behavior in digital contexts. In contrast to utilitarian consumption, which focuses on functional advantages and task-related results, hedonic consumption emphasizes enjoyment, sensory experience, and emotional involvement. In modern digital markets, value is progressively co-created through emotionally engaging and interactive experiences, where enjoyment, excitement, and emotional responses profoundly influence consumer attitudes, satisfaction, and behavioral intentions (Kumar et al., 2026a).

Immersive technologies greatly augment the capacity for hedonic consumption by facilitating embodied interaction and multisensory engagement in digitally simulated environments. Investigations into extended reality (XR) applications indicate that virtual reality (VR) and augmented reality (AR) interfaces enhance consumers' sense of presence and emotional engagement by enabling active exploration of digital environments and interaction with virtual stimuli (Singh Dhillon & Tinmaz, 2024). Research on virtual retail environments indicates that spatial navigation and sensory realism enhance telepresence and experiential value, which in turn influence approach intentions and purchasing behavior (Jang, Hu, & Choo, 2019).

In metaverse environments, hedonic consumption is further enhanced by identity-driven interactions and socially integrated experiential communication. Marketing research demonstrates that avatar-mediated engagement can influence emotional responses by affecting users' expectations and perceptions of realism in virtual interactions. Avatar-mediated engagement enables users to embody digital identities and participate in symbolic consumption processes, thereby shaping emotional responses through perceived realism and expectation alignment in virtual interactions (Miao, Kozlenkova, Wang, Xie, & Palmatier, 2022). These identity-based interactions not only enhance experiential depth but also contribute to the formation of meaningful and affective connections between users and digital environments. The growing prevalence of virtual influencers and branded digital characters demonstrates how immersive marketing strategies utilize storytelling and symbolic interaction to cultivate emotional connections and experiential engagement (Karabacak & Güngör, 2023). Moreover, emotional consumption processes are intricately linked to technology acceptance dynamics that affect consumer engagement in immersive platforms. Empirical evidence indicates that experiential enjoyment and perceived trust significantly influence perceived usefulness and behavioral intention regarding metaverse applications (Toraman & Geçit, 2023). These insights highlight the necessity for organizations to create emotionally engaging and user-focused experiential strategies that align technological innovation with evolving consumer expectations. From this viewpoint, AI-driven personalization serves as a crucial facilitator of emotional consumption by enabling platforms to modify experiential content in real time, synchronize interactions with user expectations, and generate more contextually relevant and engaging experiences. Adaptive systems augment both perceived enjoyment and perceived relevance, thereby reinforcing overall experiential engagement (Singh Dhillon & Tinmaz, 2024; D'Ulizia et al., 2024).

Hedonic and emotional consumption are essential catalysts for the creation of experiential value in immersive digital environments. Comprehending these affective mechanisms establishes a vital theoretical basis for examining the construction and maintenance of consumer experience in metaverse environments, where engagement is increasingly influenced by the interplay of emotional involvement, identity expression, and intelligent personalization (Behr, 2024; Kaur et al., 2023).

CONSUMER EXPERIENCE IN DIGITAL ENVIRONMENTS

Presence, Immersion and the Flow State

To understand the development of consumer experience in immersive settings, it is essential to examine the psychological mechanisms that drive digital engagement. Rather than viewing presence, immersion, and flow as isolated phenomena, contemporary literature conceptualizes them as an integrated psychological continuum (Singh Dhillon & Tinmaz, 2024). Immersion provides the objective technological foundation of the experience through spatial computing, high-refresh-rate displays, expanded fields of view, spatial audio, and multisensory tracking technologies. Presence, in contrast, represents the subjective psychological response to these technological affordances, creating the cognitive perception of *"being there"* within a mediated environment (Singh Dhillon & Tinmaz, 2024; Behr, 2024). Together, these constructs shape consumers' cognitive and emotional responses to technology-mediated interactions and establish the psychological foundation of immersive digital experiences (Behr, 2024).

When high levels of technological immersion generate a strong sense of presence, consumers become more likely to enter a flow state—a condition of profound cognitive engagement and intrinsic motivation that emerges when digital environments provide an optimal balance between challenge, interactivity, and perceived control (Kaur et al., 2023). This experiential state is characterized by heightened concentration, altered time perception, and intrinsic enjoyment (Kim et al., 2025). Experimental evidence supports this integrated perspective. Dickinson et al. (2021) demonstrated that immersive virtual reality environments generate significantly higher levels of presence and stronger emotional responses than comparable two-dimensional environments, suggesting that heightened spatial presence reinforces users' experiential engagement and psychological immersion within digital settings (Dickinson et al., 2021). Within metaverse environments, the interaction among immersion, presence, and flow progressively blurs the cognitive boundaries between physical and virtual realities, giving rise to what can be conceptualized as an embodied digital consumption reality (Sai et al., 2024).

Studies on immersive technologies indicate that virtual environments enhance perceived realism by enabling users to interact with three-dimensional digital spaces in real time, thereby strengthening emotional involvement and improving experiential evaluations within digital consumption contexts (Singh Dhillon & Tinmaz, 2024; Kaur et al., 2023). Likewise, research conducted in virtual retail environments demonstrates that interactive spatial navigation significantly enhances telepresence and perceived experiential value, positively influencing consumers' intentions to engage with virtual environments (Jang, Hu, & Choo, 2019). As immersive technologies become increasingly integrated into metaverse ecosystems, consumers participate in socially embedded experiential activities supported by multisensory interaction and synchronous communication, reinforcing the experiential richness of digital environments (Behr, 2024). Furthermore, the convergence of immersive technologies with advanced digital infrastructures enables organizations to design interactive experiential journeys that combine emotional stimulation with identity-based participation (D'Ulizia et al., 2024). From a behavioral perspective, empirical evidence indicates that the intensity of immersive engagement significantly influences consumers' attitudes toward virtual environments and their intentions to continue participating in digitally mediated activities (Kaur et al., 2023). Conceptual models of virtual world interaction similarly suggest that technological affordances, user behavior, and social dynamics jointly shape these experiential outcomes, emphasizing that successful immersive experience design depends on the alignment among technological realism, interaction quality, and user expectations (Davis et al., 2009).

Presence and immersion therefore function not only as psychological constructs but also as strategic mechanisms for designing compelling consumer experiences within immersive digital ecosystems. Research on avatar marketing demonstrates that realistic interaction and adaptive communication mechanisms strengthen consumer perceptions and experiential responses (Miao et al., 2022). Overall, the interaction among technological realism, social presence, and embodied participation enables immersive environments to generate richer consumer experiences, establishing the psychological basis for sustained engagement and subsequent behavioral outcomes within metaverse ecosystems (Behr, 2024).

Flow Experience in Online Interaction

The flow experience is a fundamental psychological mechanism that elucidates consumer engagement in digital environments, closely linked to intrinsic motivation, enjoyment, and prolonged interaction with online platforms. In digital consumption contexts, flow is defined as a state of profound cognitive engagement that arises when users interact with technological interfaces offering optimal levels of challenge, interactivity, and perceived control (Kaur et al., 2023). This state is marked by intensified engagement, altered perception of time, and enhanced motivation to persist in digital environments (Behr, 2024).

The advancement of immersive digital technologies has augmented the capacity for flow by facilitating embodied interaction and multisensory stimulation in simulated environments (Singh Dhillon & Tinmaz, 2024). These technologies enable consumers to engage in exploratory and interactive activities that promote intrinsic motivation and experiential enjoyment (Kaur et al., 2023). Empirical research indicates that immersive interaction enhances consumer engagement and fortifies their behavioral intention towards digital platforms (Jang, Hu, & Choo, 2019). Such environments promote temporal distortion, enhanced focus, and intrinsic pleasure, all of which are vital elements of the flow experience (Kim, Kim, Kim, & Jeong, 2025). Consequently, flow can be conceptualized as a mediating mechanism linking immersive interaction with behavioral outcomes such as platform engagement and purchase intention. Furthermore, the convergence of artificial intelligence, virtual reality, and data-driven analytics enables adaptive experiential infrastructures that personalize interaction pathways and enhance perceived relevance and experiential enjoyment in online environments (D'Ulizia et al., 2024). These developments illustrate how flow experience is increasingly shaped by dynamic technological affordances rather than static interface characteristics.

From a socio-experiential perspective, interactive participation in metaverse environments also contributes to the formation of community-based engagement and symbolic consumption practices. Literature reviewing metaverse applications highlights that immersive platforms facilitate collaborative activities and socially embedded interaction processes that strengthen experiential richness and emotional attachment among users (Behr, 2024). Such participatory dynamics are likely to reinforce intrinsic motivation and encourage continued platform usage.

In addition, marketing research emphasizes that avatar-mediated communication and identity-based interaction can enhance experiential enjoyment by enabling users to embody digital personas and engage in narrative-driven consumption encounters. Conceptual frameworks of virtual world interaction suggest that the interplay between technological capabilities, user behavior, and social context influences experiential outcomes and engagement intensity in immersive environments (Davis et al., 2009). Similarly, studies on avatar marketing indicate that adaptive communication and behavioral realism significantly affect consumer perceptions and satisfaction during digitally mediated interaction processes (Miao et al., 2022). Moreover, technology acceptance research highlights that experiential enjoyment and perceived trust play critical roles in shaping users' perceived usefulness of immersive platforms and their behavioral intention to adopt emerging digital technologies. Empirical findings suggest that emotionally engaging interactions, supported by the integration of social and technological elements, increase consumers' willingness to participate in metaverse-based activities and sustain engagement with virtual service environments (D'Ulizia et al., 2024). Consequently, flow can be considered a critical driver of consumer experience in digitally mediated environments (Toraman & Geçit, 2023).

Table 1. summarizes the core definitions, marketing functions, and strategic outcomes of these psychological and technological constructs within immersive commerce.

Table 1. Conceptual Model Summary Table

Construct	Core Definition	Role in Metaverse Experience	Strategic Marketing Outcome
Immersion	Technological & sensory conditions enabling deep environmental involvement.	Eliminates physical-world distractions via VR/AR multisensory hardware.	High sensory realism and cognitive absorption.
Presence	The psychological and subjective perception of "being there" in a virtual space.	Facilitated by spatial navigation and avatar-mediated interactions.	Enhanced emotional attachment and brand authenticity.
Flow State	Total cognitive absorption, intrinsic pleasure, and temporal distortion.	Maintained via adaptive AI paths that match interaction challenge with user skill.	Extended platform engagement and higher purchase intentions.
Interactivity	The capacity of users to actively shape digital content and communication.	Enables real-time manipulation of digital assets and co-creation of value.	Shift from passive consumer to active co-creator.
User Control	The perceived ability to govern interaction pathways and data settings.	Empowers user agency through customized interfaces and privacy boundaries.	Elevated trust, satisfaction, and long-term loyalty.

Source: Developed by the authors

As delineated in the framework above, the integration of technological realism, social interaction, and intelligent personalization does not merely augment static consumer satisfaction; it creates an adaptive, participatory ecosystem (D'Ulizia et al., 2024). When immersion and presence are systematically maintained through optimal interface designs, they lower the user's cognitive load while simultaneously raising emotional and hedonic investment (Kaur et al., 2023). Consequently, this multi-layered experiential matrix shifts the consumer behavior paradigm from passive observation to active, value-driven platform co-creation, thereby driving sustainable competitive advantages within contemporary virtual marketplaces (Kumar et al., 2026a).

Interactivity and User Control

Interactivity is a fundamental attribute of digital consumption environments and is essential in shaping consumer experience by allowing users to engage actively in interaction processes (Behr, 2024). In contrast to conventional consumption settings, digital platforms enable consumers to shape content, communication dynamics, and experiential results, thereby enhancing perceived engagement and satisfaction (D'Ulizia et al., 2024). The degree of interactivity influences the efficacy with which consumers can participate in digital environments and collaboratively generate experiential value (Kaur et al., 2023).

Technological advancements in immersive environments have significantly expanded the scope of interactivity by enabling real-time interaction, spatial navigation, and AI-driven hyper-personalized engagement that continuously adapts experiential content and interaction dynamics based on users' preferences, behaviors, and contextual data (Singh Dhillon & Tinmaz, 2024). These capabilities allow consumers to explore virtual environments, manipulate digital objects, and shape their interaction pathways, thereby fostering experiential involvement and active co-creation of value (Jang, Hu, & Choo, 2019; Kim, Kim, Kim, & Jeong, 2025). As a result, interactivity contributes to the formation of meaningful and engaging consumer experiences in digital contexts (Jang, Hu, & Choo, 2019).

User control refers to consumers' ability to govern their interactions within digital environments (D'Ulizia et al., 2024). Elevated perceptions of control correlate with enhanced engagement, satisfaction, and favorable behavioral outcomes in online consumption contexts (Toraman & Geçit, 2023). Empirical research indicates that user-controlled interaction improves telepresence and experiential value, subsequently affecting consumers' intention to engage with digital platforms (Jang, Hu, & Choo, 2019). Furthermore, platform-specific interaction mechanisms substantially affect perceived control and experiential quality. For example, VR interfaces facilitate gesture-based interaction and spatial manipulation, thereby augmenting naturalness and immersion, whereas PC-based systems offer more familiar and precise control mechanisms. These differences indicate that user control depends on both psychological perception and technological affordances (Kim, Kim, Kim, & Jeong, 2025).

From a consumer behavior standpoint, interactive involvement in virtual environments facilitates identity-driven engagement and symbolic consumption practices. Conceptual research suggests that technological capabilities, avatar-mediated communication, and social participation jointly shape experiential outcomes and relational value in immersive environments (Davis et al., 2009). Marketing research indicates that avatar design features, including behavioral realism and adaptive communication strategies, substantially affect user satisfaction and perceived experiential quality in digitally mediated interactions (Miao et al., 2022).

The incorporation of AI-driven personalization mechanisms augments user control by tailoring interaction processes to individual preferences and behaviors (D'Ulizia et al., 2024). These developments underscore that interactivity and user agency are fundamental elements in the formation of consumer experiences within digital environments (Kaur et al., 2023).

CONSUMER EXPERIENCE FORMATION IN METAVERSE

Avatar-Based Interaction and Identity Expression

Given that consumer experience in metaverse environments is constructed through complex interactions between psychological, social, and behavioral factors, it is also necessary to examine the technological infrastructures that enable and shape these immersive experiential processes (D'Ulizia et al., 2024). Metaverse environments fundamentally transform consumer experience by enabling avatar-mediated interaction, through which consumers engage in digitally embodied participation and identity construction. Unlike traditional digital platforms, virtual worlds allow consumers to represent themselves through customizable avatars, thereby facilitating symbolic self-expression and social positioning within immersive environments.

Conceptual research on virtual interaction highlights that consumer experience emerges from the dynamic interplay between technological affordances, user behavior, and social outcomes, emphasizing the central role of avatar-based engagement in shaping experiential processes (Davis et al., 2009). Empirical studies indicate that avatar realism and perceived embodiment significantly influence users' psychological immersion and experiential involvement in virtual environments. When consumers perceive their avatars as extensions of their physical selves, they are more likely to experience emotional engagement and develop stronger connections with digital platforms.

Research on avatar-mediated marketing further demonstrates that visual realism and behavioral intelligence play critical roles in shaping consumer expectations and experiential responses during virtual interaction processes (Miao et al., 2022). Similarly, studies examining avatar realism suggest that stronger user–avatar relationships contribute to increased experiential engagement and participation in metaverse environments (Kim, Lee, & Kyunghwa, 2023). Studies on postmodern consumption indicate that digital environments offer adaptable contexts for identity expression, enabling consumers to participate in self-representation and social meaning-making through immersive interactions (Altun, 2024). These findings indicate that metaverse environments serve as both technological platforms and experiential spaces where identity and meaning are actively constructed.

Beyond representing users visually, avatars increasingly function as intelligent interaction interfaces that mediate communication, identity construction, and experiential participation within metaverse environments. Contemporary consumer electronics—including motion tracking, eye tracking, voice processing, and haptic feedback—allow avatars to reproduce increasingly natural forms of human behavior, thereby strengthening perceived realism and interaction quality (Sai et al., 2024). Recent platform-comparison research further suggests that the effectiveness of avatar-mediated interaction depends not only on avatar design itself but also on the technological characteristics of the underlying platform. Virtual reality environments generally produce stronger perceptions of immersion, social connectedness, and interaction realism than conventional PC-based interfaces, although desktop environments may still provide advantages in usability and interaction efficiency (Kim et al., 2025). Moreover, the integration of artificial intelligence enables avatars to become increasingly adaptive by continuously interpreting user behavior, communication patterns, and contextual information to support more personalized and responsive interactions. These developments position avatars as intelligent experiential agents that facilitate social participation and value co-creation throughout immersive journeys (Alkaeed et al., 2024).

Taken together, avatar-based interaction represents a central mechanism through which technological capabilities are translated into meaningful consumer experiences within metaverse environments. By integrating embodiment, adaptive interaction, and social participation, avatars bridge technological affordances with psychological and behavioral outcomes, enabling consumers to co-create experiential value in immersive ecosystems (Davis et al., 2009; D'Ulizia et al., 2024). As artificial intelligence and immersive technologies continue to evolve, avatars increasingly extend beyond digital representation to facilitate richer consumer–brand relationships, emotional attachment, and sustained engagement (Alkaeed et al., 2024; D'Ulizia et al., 2024). The integrated relationships among these technological, psychological, and experiential constructs are summarized in Figure 1.

Figure 1. Integrated Conceptual Framework of Consumer Experience in Metaverse Environments

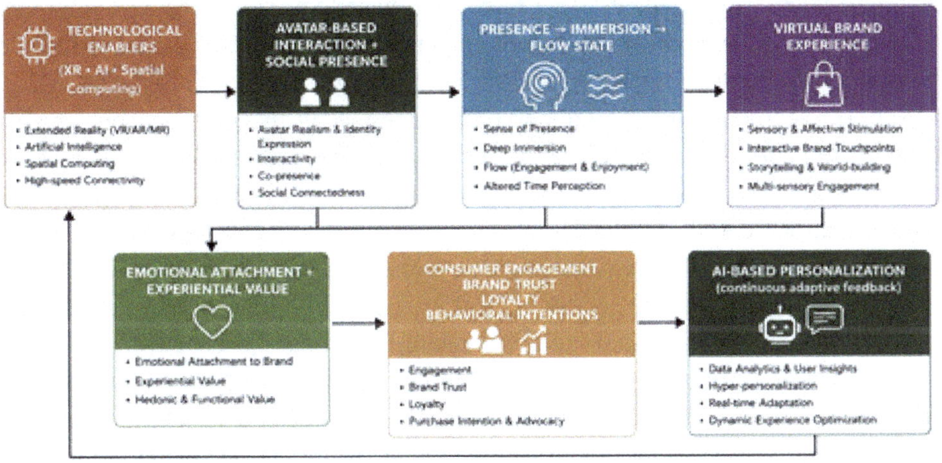

Source: *Developed by the authors*

This figure illustrates the integrated process through which consumer experiences are formed and enhanced within metaverse environments. Technological enablers (XR, AI, and spatial computing) facilitate avatar-based interaction and social presence, which foster presence, immersion, and ultimately the flow state. These psychological mechanisms shape virtual brand experiences that strengthen emotional attachment and experiential value. Consequently, consumers develop higher levels of engagement, trust, loyalty, and favorable behavioral intentions. AI-based personalization continuously adapts the experience through real-time behavioral feedback, creating a dynamic feedback loop that reinforces consumer experience and value co-creation.

Virtual Brand Experience

The consumer experience in metaverse environments is increasingly influenced by intricate and multifaceted value systems that surpass conventional consumption models. Unlike traditional digital environments, metaverse-based brand experiences amalgamate functional, symbolic, and experiential dimensions, allowing consumers to interact with brands in immersive and interactive settings. The advent of virtual assets, notably non-fungible tokens (NFTs), has transformed the perception of value, as product-related, technological, and symbolic value components interact to shape consumer assessment and behavior (Yang et al., 2026). These developments underscore that value in metaverse environments is not exclusively derived from utility but is collaboratively created through experiential and meaning-oriented processes.

Empirical research indicates that metaverse-based brand experiences markedly improve brand awareness and customer engagement by facilitating interactive and immersive communication between consumers and organizations (Gülen et al., 2023). In contrast to conventional digital marketing channels, virtual environments enable consumers to actively navigate branded spaces, engage with products, and partake in experiential activities, thereby enhancing engagement intensity and experiential involvement. Research on metaverse user experience demonstrates that improved experiential interaction leads to increased customer engagement, thereby reinforcing brand-related outcomes like awareness and interaction depth (Safitri et al., 2024).

The influence of experiential value on consumer reactions is especially pronounced in virtual retail settings. Studies demonstrate that perceived experiential value, facilitated by telepresence and interactivity, markedly affects purchase intentions and behavioral responses in digitally simulated environments (Papagiannidis et al., 2013; Jang et al., 2019). Interactive spatial navigation, sensory richness, and real-time feedback mechanisms augment perceived realism and emotional engagement, thereby reinforcing consumers' attitudes toward brands. The findings indicate that experiential quality is a crucial factor influencing brand perception and consumer decision-making in immersive environments. Immersive technologies such as VR and AR facilitate embodied interaction with brand elements, enhancing perceived realism, enjoyment, and experiential depth (Şenbabaoğlu Danacı, 2023; Singh Dhillon & Tinmaz, 2024). In this context, immersive technologies serve not only as tools but as experiential facilitators that alter consumer perceptions and interactions with brands.

The design of virtual environments, alongside technological immersion, greatly impacts the formation of brand experiences. Research indicates that environmental factors, including aesthetic quality, information richness, and interactive design elements, enhance experiential engagement and elicit more favorable consumer responses (Kim et al., 2025). The application of generative design and visually immersive environments amplifies perceived exclusivity and emotional engagement, thereby fortifying the overall brand experience. These findings demonstrate that experiential design strategically influences consumer perceptions and distinguishes brands in competitive virtual settings.

Beyond creating immersive environments, successful virtual brand experiences increasingly depend on organizations' ability to establish persistent digital ecosystems in which consumers repeatedly interact with brands across multiple experiential touchpoints. Unlike conventional online marketing campaigns that are typically episodic and transaction-oriented, metaverse platforms enable continuous brand participation through virtual events, interactive storytelling, digital asset ownership, and community-based engagement. Such environments enable consumers to continuously shape and reinterpret brand meaning through ongoing interaction (Behr, 2024).

Moreover, AI-driven personalization has become a crucial mechanism for enhancing virtual brand experiences through adaptive and user-centered interactions. AI systems evaluate user behavior and preferences to provide tailored content, recommendations, and interaction routes, thereby enhancing perceived relevance and engagement (Toraman & Geçit, 2023). This customization improves emotional engagement and experiential fulfillment by aligning brand interactions with personal expectations. As a result, virtual brand experiences become increasingly significant, contextually aware, and attuned to user requirements.

Rather than presenting standardized branded content, AI systems analyze interaction histories, engagement intensity, and contextual information to deliver personalized recommendations, context-aware storytelling, and adaptive interaction pathways that strengthen experiential relevance and emotional engagement (D'Ulizia et al., 2024; Toraman & Geçit, 2023). Consequently, AI transforms virtual brand experience from a static marketing communication process into a continuously evolving experiential journey in which consumers actively participate in shaping brand meaning through ongoing interaction. By facilitating real-time adaptation and continuous experiential optimization, AI-driven systems enable organizations to strengthen consumer–brand relationships, sustain engagement over time, and create distinctive experiential value through adaptive and user-centered interaction processes (D'Ulizia et al., 2024).

From a consumer behavior standpoint, emotional and symbolic aspects of value are more influential than solely technological features in shaping brand experience. Studies demonstrate that emotional satisfaction, perceived quality, and symbolic significance substantially affect consumer behavior in virtual settings, while technological attributes play a supplementary role (Yang et al., 2026). The findings emphasize that successful brand experiences in the metaverse rely on the ability to create emotionally impactful and meaningful interactions, rather than solely on technological progress. Consequently, metaverse environments can be conceptualized as experiential platforms where brands and consumers co-create value through interactive engagement.

Persistent digital ecosystems such as Walmart Discovered on Roblox illustrate how brands increasingly compete through immersive experiential ecosystems rather than conventional product promotion. Consumers actively participate in branded games, digital events, avatar customization, virtual product exploration, and community interaction, transforming brand experience into a continuous process of value co-creation. Structural environmental aesthetics, interactive storytelling, and personalized engagement reinforce emotional attachment while strengthening symbolic brand value (Kim et al., 2026). From a consumer behavior perspective, these persistent ecosystems demonstrate how experiential value emerges through continuous interaction rather than isolated purchasing episodes (Yang et al., 2026; Safitri et al., 2024).

Overall, virtual brand experience represents the convergence of immersive technologies, experiential marketing, artificial intelligence, and consumer value co-creation within metaverse environments. Rather than functioning solely as digital extensions of physical brands, metaverse ecosystems enable organizations to design persistent, interactive, and emotionally engaging environments where consumers continuously construct symbolic meaning through participation, identity expression, and community interaction. Consequently, successful virtual brand experiences depend not only on technological sophistication but also on organizations' ability to integrate immersive design, adaptive personalization, and experiential storytelling into coherent consumer journeys that generate enduring engagement and competitive differentiation (Behr, 2024; Yang et al., 2026).

Social Presence and Community Engagement

Consumer experience in metaverse environments is inherently social and is fundamentally shaped by interactions that occur within digitally mediated communities, where users participate through shared virtual spaces, collaborative activities, and synchronous communication (Behr, 2024). Unlike conventional online platforms, which are generally characterized by asynchronous communication and relatively limited interaction, metaverse environments facilitate continuous, real-time engagement among geographically dispersed users, thereby creating richer and more immersive social experiences (D'Ulizia et al., 2024). These interaction processes foster the development of social presence, defined as the perception of interacting with real others within a mediated environment, which has consistently been identified as one of the principal psychological mechanisms underlying experiential engagement in immersive digital ecosystems (Kaur et al., 2023). Rather than serving merely as a communication channel, social presence transforms virtual environments into socially meaningful spaces where consumers experience participation, interaction, and shared value creation.

The ability to interact with others in real time substantially enhances users' perceptions of co-presence while simultaneously strengthening their emotional and cognitive engagement within immersive environments (Singh Dhillon & Tinmaz, 2024). Empirical studies demonstrate that collaborative participation and shared activities enrich experiential quality, increase perceived value, and reinforce consumers' willingness to remain actively engaged in virtual environments (Behr, 2024). Through these socially embedded interactions, consumers no longer function solely as recipients of digital content but become active contributors to the co-creation of experiences, collectively generating symbolic, emotional, and relational value (D'Ulizia et al., 2024). Consequently, community participation extends beyond simple interaction and becomes an essential component of experiential value creation within metaverse ecosystems.

From a relational perspective, social presence plays a pivotal role in fostering trust, emotional connection, and a sense of belonging among members of virtual communities (Kaur et al., 2023). These relational mechanisms strengthen consumers' psychological attachment to immersive environments while encouraging continued participation and long-term engagement with digital platforms (Toraman & Geçit, 2023). As repeated interactions strengthen interpersonal familiarity and social connectedness, virtual communities increasingly resemble relationship-oriented ecosystems rather than purely technological platforms. Consequently, social presence contributes not only to consumers' immediate experiential evaluations but also to the development of enduring behavioral intentions and sustainable consumer–platform relationships (Behr, 2024).

Avatar-mediated communication further enriches these social processes by enabling consumers to construct digital identities and express themselves through personalized virtual representations (Davis et al., 2009). Avatars serve not merely as graphical representations of users but also as social actors that facilitate communication, identity expression, and interpersonal interaction within immersive environments. Their effectiveness depends largely on perceived realism, behavioral adaptability, and the extent to which they support authentic social interaction. Research on avatar marketing demonstrates that realistic interaction and adaptive communication mechanisms significantly influence consumers' perceptions, emotional responses, and experiential evaluations during digitally mediated encounters (Miao et al., 2022). Accordingly, identity expression through avatars strengthens consumers' sense of presence within virtual communities while simultaneously enhancing emotional involvement and social connectedness.

Recent advances in artificial intelligence further reinforce these socially embedded experiences by enabling adaptive, context-aware, and personalized interaction processes. By continuously analyzing user behavior, communication patterns, and individual preferences, AI-powered avatars and virtual agents dynamically adapt their responses, interaction styles, and communication pathways to the context of each encounter (D'Ulizia et al., 2024). Such adaptive capabilities enhance perceptions of authenticity, responsiveness, and social connectedness, allowing interactions to more closely resemble naturally occurring interpersonal communication within immersive environments (Miao et al., 2022). Beyond facilitating more effective communication, AI-supported interaction systems reduce barriers to participation, encourage sustained community engagement, and strengthen users' sense of belonging within virtual ecosystems (D'Ulizia et al., 2024).

These adaptive interaction capabilities also deepen the emotional dimension of consumer experience. By facilitating personalized communication, emotionally responsive interactions, and context-sensitive experiential content, AI-powered avatars and virtual agents enable consumers to establish stronger emotional bonds—and, in some cases, quasi-social or parasocial relationships—with digital entities (Davis et al., 2009; Kaur et al., 2023). Rather than replacing human interaction, artificial intelligence complements existing social processes by enriching interpersonal communication, supporting identity expression, and facilitating more meaningful participation within virtual communities (Miao et al., 2022). These developments demonstrate that social relationships in metaverse environments are increasingly co-constructed through the interaction of human participants and intelligent digital agents, reflecting the evolving nature of consumer–platform relationships in immersive ecosystems (Davis et al., 2009; Kaur et al., 2023). Overall, social presence and community engagement constitute the social foundation of consumer experience in metaverse environments by enabling collaborative participation, emotional connection, trust development, and experiential value co-creation (Behr, 2024; Kaur et al., 2023). Through the interaction of technological affordances, identity expression, community participation, and adaptive communication mechanisms, immersive environments evolve into relational ecosystems in which consumers actively construct meaningful experiences rather than passively consume digital content (D'Ulizia et al., 2024; Davis et al., 2009). These socially embedded interactions establish the psychological and relational conditions through which immersive experiences foster sustained engagement, stronger consumer–platform relationships, and long-term experiential value within metaverse ecosystems (Behr, 2024; Kaur et al., 2023).

Emotional Attachment and Experiential Value

Emotional attachment is a crucial outcome of consumer experience development in metaverse environments and profoundly affects long-term behavioral responses and platform engagement (Kaur et al., 2023). In immersive digital environments, experiential value includes functional benefits as well as emotional, symbolic, and relational aspects that influence consumers' perceptions and assessments of their interactions with virtual settings (Behr, 2024). These complex experiential processes promote the strengthening of strong connections between consumers and digital platforms (D'Ulizia et al., 2024).

Furthermore, immersive technologies foster emotional attachment by enabling consumers to participate in interactive and personalized experiences that nurture a sense of connection with digital environments (Singh Dhillon & Tinmaz, 2024). Consumer electronics technologies—such as VR headsets, haptic feedback systems, and wearable devices—play a pivotal role in facilitating immersive interaction and strengthening the sensory and emotional dimensions of digital experiences, thereby contributing to deeper attachment formation (Sai et al., 2024). The integration of artificial intelligence and data-driven personalization methods enhances experiential relevance by aligning digital interactions with individual preferences and behavioral patterns (D'Ulizia et al., 2024). Adaptive experiential environments enhance emotional engagement and user satisfaction (Toraman & Geçit, 2023). These improvements also contribute to engagement-based value creation, as consumer experience positively influences customer engagement, brand awareness, and overall experiential outcomes in virtual environments (Safitri et al., 2024).

From a psychological perspective, hedonic consumption and experiential enjoyment are crucial in shaping emotional attachment within immersive environments (Kaur et al., 2023). The ability to derive pleasure, enjoyment, and symbolic meaning from digital interactions strengthens consumers' attachment to virtual platforms and influences their continued usage behavior (Behr, 2024). Furthermore, avatar-mediated interaction and identity expression augment emotional attachment by enabling consumers to engage in personalized and socially meaningful experiences (Davis et al., 2009).

Overall, the literature suggests that emotional attachment constitutes a central psychological outcome of immersive consumer experiences in metaverse environments. By integrating immersive technologies, personalized interactions, and hedonic value, virtual environments foster stronger consumer relationships with metaverse platforms, ultimately shaping sustained engagement and long-term behavioral responses (D'Ulizia et al., 2024; Toraman & Geçit, 2023). Consequently, emotional attachment serves as a central mechanism through which experiential value is transformed into sustained consumer engagement and continued participation in metaverse ecosystems (Behr, 2024; Kaur et al., 2023).

TECHNOLOGICAL ENABLERS OF IMMERSIVE EXPERIENCE

Extended Reality (XR) Interfaces: VR, AR, and MR

Extended reality (XR), encompassing virtual reality (VR), augmented reality (AR), and mixed reality (MR), constitutes the technological foundation of immersive consumer experiences in metaverse environments. XR systems are supported by consumer electronic technologies—including VR/AR headsets, haptic feedback devices, and wearable technologies—that enable users to interact with virtual environments through multisensory and spatial experiences (Sai et al., 2024). By enhancing perceived presence, accessibility, and interaction quality, these technologies serve as the primary interface between consumers and digital environments, thereby strengthening experiential engagement and perceived value (Singh Dhillon & Tinmaz, 2024; Sai et al., 2024). Despite their growing adoption, the rapid evolution of XR technologies continues to raise important theoretical and practical questions regarding the design and sustainability of consumer experiences in metaverse environments (Behr, 2024).

In virtual consumption environments, VR technologies enable consumers to navigate simulated spaces, engage with digital objects, and assess products before purchase, thus impacting experiential perceptions and behavioral intentions. Empirical research demonstrates that spatial navigation and sensory realism substantially improve telepresence and perceived experiential value, thereby positively influencing consumers' intentions to engage with virtual environments (Jang, Hu, & Choo, 2019).

Augmented reality applications enhance consumer experience by integrating digital elements into physical environments, creating hybrid consumption contexts that merge real and virtual interactions (Singh Dhillon & Tinmaz, 2024). Research indicates that augmented reality (AR) interaction enhances consumer engagement, perceived enjoyment, and experiential value by facilitating interactive visualization and exploration of products within real-world contexts (D'Ulizia et al., 2024). Hybrid experiential environments further extend experiential marketing by integrating physical and digital consumption processes (Behr, 2024).

Overall, XR technologies function as the technological infrastructure that enables immersive consumer experiences in metaverse ecosystems. Beyond facilitating multisensory interaction, these technologies support identity expression, social participation, and collaborative engagement, thereby transforming conventional consumption processes into more interactive, personalized, and experiential forms of value creation (Behr, 2024; D'Ulizia et al., 2024).

AI-Based Personalization

Artificial intelligence (AI) has emerged as a fundamental technological enabler of consumer experience in metaverse environments by supporting adaptive, context-aware, and personalized interactions. AI systems continuously analyze users' behaviors, preferences, and interaction histories to generate personalized recommendations and dynamically adjust experiential content, thereby enhancing perceived relevance, engagement, and experiential continuity (D'Ulizia et al., 2024). Studies on technology acceptance further indicate that perceived enjoyment, trust, and compatibility significantly influence consumers' adoption of immersive platforms, emphasizing the importance of AI-supported, user-centered experience design (Toraman & Geçit, 2023). Consequently, AI-driven personalization improves both functional usability and emotional engagement while strengthening experiential value and continued platform usage (Kaur et al., 2023).

Beyond conventional personalization, AI enables hyper-personalization through the real-time adaptation of digital experiences. Unlike rule-based personalization strategies that rely on predefined user segments, AI systems employ predictive analytics, behavioral modeling, and continuous learning to anticipate user needs and dynamically modify interaction pathways (D'Ulizia et al., 2024). This adaptive capability allows organizations to deliver highly individualized, context-sensitive experiences that evolve alongside users' behaviors, thereby increasing perceived relevance, user satisfaction, and long-term consumer engagement (Kaur et al., 2023; Toraman & Geçit, 2023).

The effectiveness of AI-based personalization is closely associated with its integration into immersive technologies. Data generated through XR interfaces—including virtual reality, augmented reality, haptic feedback systems, and wearable devices—provide continuous behavioral information that enables AI systems to optimize experiential delivery in real time (Sai et al., 2024). This technological convergence enhances personalization accuracy while improving interaction quality, responsiveness, and overall experiential continuity within metaverse environments.

Beyond improving functionality, AI also enriches the emotional, aesthetic, and symbolic dimensions of consumer experience. Generative AI and intelligent design systems facilitate the creation of dynamic virtual environments that increase perceived uniqueness, aesthetic appreciation, and emotional engagement (Kim et al., 2026). Similarly, AI-supported virtual agents and intelligent avatars enable responsive, human-like interactions that strengthen perceived realism, trust, and experiential quality while supporting personalized identity expression within virtual environments (Davis et al., 2009). These capabilities reinforce consumers' emotional connections with digital platforms and contribute to richer experiential value.

From a strategic perspective, AI-based personalization enhances customer engagement and strengthens brand-related outcomes by delivering more relevant and immersive experiences (Safitri et al., 2024). However, the extensive collection of behavioral, biometric, and spatial interaction data required for hyper-personalization introduces significant privacy and ethical challenges (Sai et al., 2024). Consequently, the long-term success of AI-enabled metaverse experiences depends on achieving an appropriate balance between predictive personalization and transparent, responsible data governance, ensuring that enhanced consumer experiences do not come at the expense of user privacy and trust.

FUTURE RESEARCH DIRECTIONS

The rapid advancement of metaverse technologies and immersive digital ecosystems continues to reshape the nature of consumer experience, creating significant opportunities for future research. Although existing studies have substantially advanced our understanding of technology adoption, immersive interfaces, and experiential engagement, the literature remains fragmented and predominantly focused on cross-sectional investigations of technology acceptance (Toraman & Geçit, 2023). Future research should therefore adopt more integrative, interdisciplinary, and longitudinal approaches capable of capturing the dynamic interactions among technological, psychological, social, and experiential dimensions of consumer behavior in metaverse environments.

- **Longitudinal Consumer Experience and Experience Evolution.** Most existing studies rely on cross-sectional research designs, limiting understanding of how consumer experience develops over time. Future studies should employ longitudinal methodologies to examine how psychological constructs such as flow, presence, telepresence, emotional attachment, and experiential value evolve throughout different stages of sustained metaverse participation. Such approaches would provide deeper insights into whether consumer engagement persists beyond the initial novelty effect and how long-term behavioral intentions are formed (Jang et al., 2019).
- **Technological Affordances and Human Experience.** Additional research is needed to clarify how technological affordances influence psychological and experiential outcomes. Future empirical studies should investigate how hardware characteristics—including haptic feedback systems, spatial audio, wearable technologies, and sensory realism—shape mechanisms such as presence, emotional engagement, cognitive immersion, and experiential quality. Furthermore, the specific contribution of consumer electronic technologies to experience formation remains insufficiently explored and deserves greater theoretical and empirical attention (Sai et al., 2024).
- **Cross-Platform Ecosystems and Interoperability.** The long-term sustainability of metaverse ecosystems depends on seamless interaction across multiple devices and platforms. Comparative research should therefore examine consumer experiences across VR, AR, MR, mobile, and PC-based environments, paying particular attention to interoperability, usability, cross-device continuity, and experience friction. Such studies would contribute to a better understanding of how technological ecosystems influence consumer engagement and platform adoption (Singh Dhillon & Tinmaz, 2024).

- **AI, Hyper-Personalization, and Responsible Experience Design.** While AI-driven personalization has emerged as a central mechanism for enhancing consumer experience, future research should move beyond evaluating personalization effectiveness toward examining its broader managerial and societal implications. Promising research directions include investigating the long-term consequences of adaptive personalization, algorithmic transparency, consumer trust, user autonomy, and ethical governance. Understanding how organizations can balance predictive personalization with responsible data practices will become increasingly important as AI assumes a more central role in immersive consumer experiences (D'Ulizia et al., 2024; Toraman & Geçit, 2023).
- **Emerging Digital Economies and Value Creation.** Future research should further explore how decentralized digital economies reshape consumer value creation within immersive environments. Integrating constructs such as non-fungible tokens (NFTs), digital assets, virtual ownership, blockchain-enabled ecosystems, and smart-contract technologies into consumer experience models would provide a more comprehensive understanding of how emotional, symbolic, social, and economic value jointly influence trust, loyalty, and long-term engagement in virtual marketplaces (Behr, 2024).
- **Cross-Cultural Consumer Experience.** Cultural differences remain underrepresented in current metaverse research despite their potential influence on consumer behavior. Comparative studies should investigate how cultural dimensions—including uncertainty avoidance, collectivism, individualism, and long-term orientation—shape immersive experiences, avatar-based identity construction, symbolic value perception, and technology acceptance across different cultural contexts. Such research would contribute to developing more globally applicable theoretical frameworks for consumer experience in metaverse environments.
- **Ethics, Digital Well-Being, and the Dark Side of Immersion.** As immersive technologies become increasingly embedded in everyday life, future research should devote greater attention to the ethical, psychological, and societal consequences of prolonged virtual engagement. Interdisciplinary investigations are needed to examine issues such as digital addiction, identity fragmentation, virtual escapism, algorithmic bias, psychological well-being, and privacy risks associated with continuous biometric and behavioral data collection (D'Ulizia et al., 2024; Sai et al., 2024).
- **Strategic Experience Management and Value Co-Creation.** Finally, future research should investigate how organizations can strategically design immersive ecosystems that sustain consumer engagement while avoiding personalization fatigue and privacy concerns. Particular attention should be

given to understanding how AI-enabled personalization, community participation, experience co-creation, and adaptive service design can be integrated into sustainable experiential marketing strategies that generate long-term value for both consumers and organizations (Kaur et al., 2023).

CONCLUSION

The convergence of immersive technologies and digital platforms has fundamentally transformed the nature of consumer experience, shifting the focus of contemporary marketing from transactional exchanges toward experiential engagement and value co-creation. Within metaverse environments, consumer experiences extend beyond a sequence of isolated touchpoints and evolve into dynamic, interactive, and socially embedded processes in which users actively participate in value creation. This chapter has demonstrated that consumer experience in the metaverse is shaped by the interplay of technological capabilities, psychological mechanisms, and social interaction processes. Constructs such as presence, immersion, flow, interactivity, emotional attachment, and social presence collectively enhance experiential value, strengthen consumer engagement, and influence long-term behavioral intentions. In doing so, the chapter reinforces the principles of the Experience Economy by illustrating that memorable, personalized, and co-created experiences increasingly represent the primary source of consumer value and competitive differentiation within immersive digital environments.

A key contribution of this chapter is the development of an integrated conceptual perspective that brings together experiential marketing, consumer behavior, immersive technologies and artificial intelligence to explain how meaningful consumer experiences are constructed in metaverse environments. Rather than considering technological innovation as an isolated driver of consumer behavior, the chapter conceptualizes consumer experience as a multidimensional phenomenon emerging from the interaction between XR technologies, AI-driven personalization, experiential value, and socially embedded engagement mechanisms. This integrated perspective contributes to the growing metaverse literature by synthesizing fragmented research streams into a coherent conceptual framework, thereby providing a more comprehensive understanding of how technological, psychological, and experiential dimensions collectively shape consumer experience in immersive ecosystems. This conceptual integration also provides a useful basis for both researchers and practitioners to better understand the reciprocal relationships among immersive technologies, consumer psychology, and value co-creation. By emphasizing these interdependencies, the proposed framework offers a more holistic perspective for examining the evolving nature of consumer experience within increasingly intelligent and interconnected metaverse ecosystems.

The chapter further highlights the transformative role of AI-driven hyper-personalization in redefining consumer experience. By shifting from standardized service delivery toward adaptive, context-aware, and real-time personalization, artificial intelligence enables organizations to design experiences that simultaneously improve functional efficiency, emotional engagement, and experiential continuity. Moreover, consumer experiences within metaverse environments are inherently co-created through avatar-mediated communication, collaborative participation, and community interaction. These mechanisms enable consumers to construct identities, create symbolic meaning, and establish stronger emotional relationships with brands and virtual platforms, ultimately fostering trust, engagement, and long-term relational outcomes.

Beyond its theoretical contributions, this chapter also offers strategic implications for organizations seeking to compete within immersive digital markets. Sustainable competitive advantage in metaverse environments will increasingly depend on organizations' ability to orchestrate personalized, interactive, and emotionally engaging experiences that are difficult for competitors to replicate. Rather than focusing solely on technological sophistication, firms should integrate immersive technologies, adaptive personalization, and community-based value co-creation into coherent experiential strategies capable of generating enduring consumer relationships and differentiated brand value.

At the same time, the rapid integration of artificial intelligence into immersive environments raises important challenges related to data privacy, ethical design, algorithmic transparency, and digital well-being. As hyper-personalized experiences become increasingly dependent on continuous behavioral and biometric data collection, organizations must carefully balance predictive personalization with responsible data governance and transparent privacy practices. Accordingly, the long-term success of metaverse-based consumer experiences will depend not only on technological innovation but also on the ability to design trustworthy, ethical, and human-centered interaction environments that preserve user autonomy while maintaining consumer confidence.

Beyond synthesizing the existing literature, this chapter provides a conceptual foundation for understanding consumer experience in metaverse environments as an evolving ecosystem in which technological innovation, psychological processes, and social interaction continuously reinforce one another. By integrating perspectives from experiential marketing, consumer behavior, immersive technologies, and artificial intelligence, the proposed framework extends beyond technology adoption models and emphasizes the dynamic mechanisms through which value is created, experienced, and sustained in immersive environments. In doing so, the chapter contributes to the growing body of metaverse research by demonstrating that meaningful consumer experiences emerge not from isolated technological features but from the continuous interaction among immersive interfaces, adaptive personalization, identity expression, community participation, and experiential value co-creation.

Beyond its theoretical contribution, the proposed conceptual framework also provides a foundation for future interdisciplinary research. As metaverse ecosystems continue to evolve, consumer experience will increasingly be shaped by developments in artificial intelligence, extended reality technologies, digital identity, behavioral analytics, and platform governance. Consequently, advancing knowledge in this field will require closer collaboration among researchers in marketing, information systems, human–computer interaction, psychology, and communication studies. Such interdisciplinary perspectives will contribute to a more comprehensive understanding of how immersive technologies influence consumer decision-making, emotional engagement, trust development, and long-term consumer–brand relationships within increasingly complex digital ecosystems.

From a managerial standpoint, the findings suggest that organizations should view immersive technologies not merely as digital communication tools but as strategic platforms for designing adaptive, participatory, and emotionally meaningful consumer experiences. Competitive success in metaverse environments will therefore depend on firms' ability to integrate immersive technologies, AI-driven personalization, ethical governance, and community-based value co-creation into coherent experiential strategies capable of generating sustainable consumer value and enduring brand relationships.

Overall, this chapter contributes to the emerging literature by conceptualizing consumer experience in metaverse environments as a dynamic, multidimensional, and continuously evolving phenomenon situated at the intersection of immersive technologies, artificial intelligence, and experiential marketing. As metaverse ecosystems continue to mature, understanding the mechanisms through which immersive, personalized, and socially embedded experiences generate value will remain both a theoretical priority and a managerial necessity.

Ultimately, the future of consumer experience in metaverse ecosystems will depend not only on advances in immersive technologies but also on organizations' ability to integrate technological innovation with ethical governance, adaptive personalization, and human-centered experience design, thereby fostering enduring consumer trust and sustainable competitive advantage.

REFERENCES

Alkaeed, M., Qayyum, A., & Qadir, J. (2024). Privacy preservation in artificial intelligence and extended reality (AI-XR) metaverses: A survey. *Journal of Network and Computer Applications, 231*, 103989. DOI: 10.1016/j.jnca.2024.103989

Altun, C. (2024). *Postmodern Dönemde Dijital Deneyimler Işığında Değişen Tüketici Kimlik, Tercih ve Tutumları Üzerine Bir Araştırma.* İstanbul Ticaret Üniversitesi.

Behr, L. M. (2024). *Literature Review on Metaverse Use Cases.* Wedel: Seminar IT-Management in the Digital Age.

D'Ulizia, A., Federico, D., & Notte, A. (2024). The Technological Innovation of the Metaverse in Financial Sector: Current State, Opportunities, and Open Challenges. *Intelligent Systems in Accounting, Finance and Management, 31*(3), e1566. 1-17.

Davis, A., Murphy, J., Owens, D., Khazanchi, D., & Zigurs, I. (2009). Avatars, people, and virtual worlds: Foundations for research in metaverses. *Journal of the Association for Information Systems, 10*(2), 90–117. DOI: 10.17705/1jais.00183

Dickinson, P., Jones, A., Christian, W., Westerside, A., Mulloy, F., Gerling, K., Hicks, K., Wilson, L., & Parke, A. (2021). *Experiencing simulated confrontations in virtual reality.* Proceedings of the 2021 CHI Conference on Human Factors in Computing Systems, Article 483, 1–10. DOI: 10.1145/3411764.3445401

Gülen, K., Tümdağ, C., & Yılmaz Altuntaş, E. (2023). Markaların kurumsal çağrışımları ve deneyim pazarlaması bağlamında metaverse girişimleri. *Uluslararası Halkla İlişkiler ve Reklam Çalışmaları Dergisi, 6*(2), 9–28.

Jang, J. Y., Hu, H. J., & Choo, H. J. (2019). How to evoke consumer approach intention toward VR stores? Sequential mediation through telepresence and experiential value. *Fashion and Textiles, 6*(12), 1–16. DOI: 10.1186/s40691-018-0166-9

Karabacak, Z. İ., & Güngör, İ. (2023). The metaverse as an influencer marketing platform: Influencer-brand collaborations of Paris Hilton with 'Superplastic', 'Bohoo', and 'Levi's'. *Etkileşim, 11*(11), 176–199. DOI: 10.32739/etkilesim.2023.6.11.194

Kaur, J., Mogaji, E., Paliwal, M., Jha, S., Agarwal, S., & Mogaji, S. A. (2023). Consumer behavior in the metaverse. *Journal of Consumer Behaviour, 23*(4), 1720–1738. DOI: 10.1002/cb.2298

Kim, D. Y., Lee, H. K., & Kyunghwa, C. (2023). Avatar-mediated experience in the metaverse: The impact of avatar realism on user-avatar relationship. *Journal of Retailing and Consumer Services, 73*, 103382. 1-11.

Kim, Y. W., Kim, B. H., Kim, M. J., & Jeong, Y. J. (2025). Immersive social experiences in a space-based Metaverse SNS: user experience with platform-specific interactions on PC and VR. *International Conference on Consumer Electronics-Asia (ICCE-Asia)*, 1-3. DOI: 10.1109/ICCE-Asia67487.2025.11263524

Kumar, R., Aneja, P., Jadaun, R., Kiran, P. N., Saxena, N., Saxena, S., & Painoli, A. K. (2026). Metaverse marketing: A review and future research agenda. *Information Discovery and Delivery*, *54*(1), 35–49. DOI: 10.1108/IDD-05-2024-0066

Kumar, V., Kotler, P., & Kumar, A. (2026). Transformative marketing strategies in the era of new-age technologies: Principles, plan, purpose, and practice. *Journal of the Academy of Marketing Science*, *54*(1), 1–27. DOI: 10.1007/s11747-025-01120-6

Miao, F., Kozlenkova, I., Wang, H., Xie, T., & Palmatier, R. (2022). An emerging theory of avatar marketing. *Journal of Marketing*, *86*(1), 67–90. DOI: 10.1177/0022242921996646

Papagiannidis, S., Pantano, E., See-To, E. W., & Bourlakis, M. (2013). Modelling the determinants of a simulated experience in a virtual retail store and users' product purchasing intentions. *Journal of Marketing Management*, *29*(13-14), 1462–1492. DOI: 10.1080/0267257X.2013.821150

Pine, B. J., & Gilmore, J. H. (1998). Welcome to the experience economy. *Harvard Business Review*, *76*(4), 97–105. PMID: 10181589

Safitri, A., Husin, N., Arifah, I. D., Dewi, R. S., Kharisma, F., & Kautsar, A. (2024). Metaverse user experience, customer engagement, and brand awareness relation as SMEs marketing strategies in Virtual Worlds. *2024 ASU International Conference in Emerging Technologies for Sustainability and Intelligent Systems (ICETSIS)*, 1092-1096. DOI: 10.1109/ICETSIS61505.2024.10459506

Sai, S., Goyal, D., Chamola, V., & Sikdar, B. (2024). Consumer electronics technologies for enabling an immersive metaverse experience. *IEEE Consumer Electronics Magazine*, *13*(3), 16–24. DOI: 10.1109/MCE.2023.3327530

Şenbabaoğlu Danacı, E. (2023). Deneyimsel pazarlama aracı olarak sanal gerçeklik ve artırılmış gerçeklik. *İşletme Biliminin Üç Temel Alanında Yaşanan Gelişmeler: Muhasebe, Pazarlama ve Organizasyon*, 197-212.

Singh Dhillon, P. K., & Tinmaz, H. (2024). Immersive realities: A comprehensive guide from virtual reality to metaverse. *Journal for the Education of Gifted Young Scientists*, *12*(1), 29–45. DOI: 10.17478/jegys.1406024

Toraman, Y., & Geçit, B. B. (2023). User acceptance of metaverse: An analysis for e-commerce in the framework of technology acceptance model (TAM). *Sosyoekonomi, 31*(55), 85–104. DOI: 10.17233/sosyoekonomi.2023.01.05

Yang, X., Xi, N., & Hamari, J. (2026). Understanding metaverse consumer motivation: A study on the perceived value, cultural dimensions, and prior experience in NFT assets purchase. *International Journal of Human-Computer Interaction*, •••, 1–35. DOI: 10.1080/10447318.2026.2618572

ADDITIONAL READING

Behr, L. M. (2024). *Literature review on metaverse use cases*. Seminar IT-Management in the Digital Age.

Kaur, J., Mogaji, E., Paliwal, M., Jha, S., Agarwal, S., & Mogaji, S. A. (2023). Consumer behavior in the metaverse. *Journal of Consumer Behaviour, 23*(4), 1720–1738. DOI: 10.1002/cb.2298

Kumar, R., Aneja, P., Jadaun, R., Kiran, P. N., Saxena, N., Saxena, S., & Painoli, A. K. (2026). Metaverse marketing: A review and future research agenda. *Information Discovery and Delivery, 54*(1), 35–49. DOI: 10.1108/IDD-05-2024-0066

Kumar, V., Kotler, P., & Kumar, A. (2026). Transformative marketing strategies in the era of new-age technologies: Principles, plan, purpose, and practice. *Journal of the Academy of Marketing Science, 54*(1), 1–27. DOI: 10.1007/s11747-025-01120-6

Miao, F., Kozlenkova, I. V., Wang, H., Xie, T., & Palmatier, R. W. (2022). An emerging theory of avatar marketing. *Journal of Marketing, 86*(1), 67–90. DOI: 10.1177/0022242921996646

Pine, B. J., & Gilmore, J. H. (1998). Welcome to the experience economy. *Harvard Business Review, 76*(4), 97–105. PMID: 10181589

Yang, X., Xi, N., & Hamari, J. (2026). Understanding metaverse consumer motivation: A study on perceived value, cultural dimensions, and prior experience in NFT assets purchase. *International Journal of Human-Computer Interaction*, •••, 1–35. DOI: 10.1080/10447318.2026.2618572

KEY TERMS AND DEFINITIONS

AI-Based Personalization: The use of artifical intelligence to analyze consumer data, predict preferences, and continuously adapt products, services and interactions to deliver personalized and context-aware experiences in real time.

Avatar-Based Interaction: The process through which consumers engage with virtual environments and other users by means of digital avatars that facilitate identity expression, communication, and immersive participation.

Consumer Experience: The holistic cognitive, emotional, sensory, and behavioral responses that emerge from consumers' interactions with brands, products, services, and immersive digital environments throughout the customer journey.

Flow State: A state of deep concentration, intrinsic enjoyment, and complete engagement experienced during immersive interaction with digital environments.

Immersion: The extent to which technological features create a realistic and engaging virtual environment that enables consumers to become deeply involved in digital experiences.

Metaverse: A persistent and shared virtual environment where users interact with digital content, other users, and brands through immersive technologies, enabling social interaction, commerce, and value co-creation.

Presence: The psychological perception of being physically or socially located within a virtual environment despite being in a different physical location.

Social Presence: The perception of meaningful social connection and interaction with other users in immersive virtual environments.

Virtual Brand Experience: The multidimensional experience consumers develop through immersive interactions with brands in metaverse environments, including emotional, cognitive, and interactive responses.

Chapter 11
From Data to Delight:
AI-Powered Hyper-Personalization in Service Experience Design – Conceptual and Managerial Perspectives

Malini Singh
http://orcid.org/0000-0001-9807-2843
Amity University, Noida, India

Akshita Tiwari
http://orcid.org/0000-0002-5167-6794
Amity University, Noida, India

Ayan Basak
http://orcid.org/0000-0002-3726-3918
Amity University, Noida, India

Shelley Duggal
Amity University, Noida, India

Manish Kumar Sharma
http://orcid.org/0000-0002-1440-3252
Amity University, Noida, India

ABSTRACT

This study examines the role of AI-powered hyper-personalization in transforming service experience design within hospitality and tourism. Using a mixed-method approach, it analyzes its impact on service quality, guest satisfaction, emotional engagement, and loyalty. The findings indicate that AI-driven personalization

DOI: 10.4018/979-8-3373-9159-5.ch011

enhances both cognitive and emotional outcomes, while the balance between human interaction and automation, along with ethical AI governance, significantly strengthens trust and overall service effectiveness.

INTRODUCTION

The transition from mass marketing to individualized engagement has reached a critical juncture with the advent of AI-powered hyper-personalization. In contemporary service experience design, hyper-personalization is defined as the use of real-time data, machine learning (ML), and predictive analytics to deliver highly contextualized experiences that resonate with a customer's specific behavior and intent (Albous, 2024). Unlike traditional segmentation, which groups customers by broad demographics, AI-driven strategies enable a "segment of one" by processing vast amounts of data to uncover patterns and predict needs even before the customer becomes aware of them (Albous, 2024; Mariani & Borghi, 2023).

BACKGROUND AND EVOLUTION OF AI IN SERVICE INDUSTRIES

The integration of Artificial Intelligence (AI) into service industries has evolved through distinct technological paradigms, moving from rigid automation to autonomous intelligence.

1. The Era of Symbolic and Rule-Based AI (1950s – 1980s)

Early AI applications were dominated by Symbolic AI, also known as "Good Old-Fashioned AI" (GOFAI). These systems relied on formal logic and predefined rules to perform tasks (Mariani & Borghi, 2023). In service contexts, these were primarily "expert systems" designed to assist in routine decision-making or simple task automation within controlled environments (Mariani & Borghi, 2023).

2. The Rise of Machine Learning and Predictive Analytics (2010s)

The fourth industrial revolution accelerated the adoption of statistical and connectionist AI, shifting the focus toward machine learning and big data (Mariani & Borghi, 2023). Service firms began utilizing recommendation systems and chatbots to improve operational efficiency and customer engagement (Poddar et al., 2024).

During this phase, personalization evolved from basic name-tagging to predictive models that suggested products based on historical purchase data (Albous, 2024).

3. Hyper-Personalization and Real-Time Interaction (2020s – Present)

Modern service ecosystems now leverage Generative AI and advanced ML algorithms to provide hyper-personalization. This current era is characterized by real-time data processing that allows for dynamic content creation and context-aware service delivery (Albous, 2024; Poddar et al., 2024). AI is no longer just a backend tool; it has become an "assistant" to frontline employees, helping manage complex inquiries that require a blend of human judgment and technical precision (Mariani & Borghi, 2023).

CONCEPTUAL AND MANAGERIAL PERSPECTIVES

From a conceptual perspective, hyper-personalization facilitates "service innovation" by allowing firms to continuously update and optimize services based on real-time feedback (Mariani & Borghi, 2023). However, this shift introduces significant managerial challenges.

Table 1.

Perspective	Focus Areas	Key Objective
Conceptual	Data-driven decision-making, predictive modeling, service quality perception	Enhancing customer satisfaction by tailoring experiences to individual behaviors (Albous, 2024).
Managerial	Data privacy ("The Privacy Paradox"), algorithmic bias, human-AI collaboration	Balancing personalization with consumer trust and ethical data practices (Albous, 2024; Soni, 2024).

Managers must navigate the "privacy paradox" the tension between a consumer's desire for tailored experiences and their apprehension regarding data misuse (Soni, 2024). Achieving "delight" requires an equilibrium between efficient machine-led interactions and the "human touch" that provides the warmth and empathy essential to high-quality service (Albous, 2024).

COMPARISON OF PARADIGMS

This shift is not merely a technological upgrade but a change in the foundational logic of how services are designed and delivered.

Table 2.

Feature	Traditional Personalization	AI-Driven Hyper-Personalization
Data Type	**Static:** Name, demographics, past purchase history (IBM, 2025).	**Dynamic:** Real-time location, browsing behavior, device health, mood signals (Assurant, 2026).
Logic	**Rule-Based:** "If customer buys X, then suggest Y" (Mariani & Borghi, 2023).	**Predictive/Agentic:** AI predicts needs before they are articulated and acts autonomously (Fujitsu, 2025).
Response	**Reactive:** Responds after an action or a scheduled campaign.	**Proactive/Anticipatory:** Adjusts the experience as it unfolds (Sitecore, 2025).
Scale	Limited by manual rule-setting and human oversight.	High scalability through MLOps and autonomous AI agents (Devoteam, 2024).

CORE DRIVERS OF THE EVOLUTION

The move toward hyper-personalization is driven by three primary technological and strategic shifts:

1. From "What" to "Why" (Intent Recognition)

Traditional systems knew *what* a customer bought. Modern AI systems, particularly **Generative AI**, analyze behavioral signals to understand the *intent*—the "why" behind the search. For example, by 2026, service interfaces will dynamically restructure their layout to reflect a user's real-time goal, such as prioritizing "fast checkout" for a returning user in a hurry versus "in-depth reviews" for a researcher (Assurant, 2026; IBM, 2025).

2. The Dawn of "Ambient Intelligence"

As we enter 2026, personalization is moving into the physical world. Through the "Internet of Things" (IoT) and **Ambient Intelligence**, services can respond to environmental context. A travel app might offer a discount on a ride-share specifically when it detects a flight delay and heavy rain at the user's destination airport (DCO, 2026; Prolifics, 2026).

3. Agentic AI and Autonomous Decisioning

A major shift in 2025–2026 is the rise of **Agentic AI**. Unlike older chatbots that followed a script, these "agents" can reason and execute multi-step tasks. In a service context, this means an AI agent doesn't just suggest a replacement part; it checks inventory, analyzes the customer's loyalty tier, and autonomously authorizes an expedited shipment to "delight" the user before they even file a complaint (Fujitsu, 2025; Prolifics, 2026).

4. Managerial Implications: The Trust Differentiator

For managers, the challenge in 2026 is avoiding "over-personalization"—where the service feels invasive rather than helpful. Success now depends on "Trust-by-Design," where transparency regarding data usage and the mitigation of algorithmic bias are treated as core features of the service experience rather than just legal compliance (DCO, 2026; ResearchGate, 2025).

IMPORTANCE OF CUSTOMER SATISFACTION, ENGAGEMENT, AND LOYALTY IN EXPERIENCE DESIGN

To design effective AI-powered hyper-personalization, one must understand that technology is the engine, but Satisfaction, Engagement, and Loyalty are the fuel. In a hyper-personalized service environment, the "Segment of One" approach uses real-time data to tailor every interaction, moving beyond traditional demographics to individual behaviors and psychological triggers.

1. Customer Satisfaction: The Precision Threshold

In AI-driven contexts, satisfaction is redefined as the gap between perceived intelligence and user effort. AI reduces "cognitive load" by filtering out irrelevant choices, but it must be accurate to be satisfying.

- The Predictive Element: Satisfaction now stems from *proactive* service. Research indicates that when AI predicts a need correctly, it significantly lowers customer effort scores (CES).
- The "Creepy" Boundary: Satisfaction is negatively impacted if the personalization feels intrusive. According to Ameen et al. (2021), consumer trust acts as a mediator; without transparency in how AI uses data, satisfaction collapses regardless of the service's utility.

2. Customer Engagement: The Value-Data Exchange

Engagement in hyper-personalization is a reciprocal loop: the customer provides data, and the AI provides a curated experience. This creates a "learning relationship" where the service improves with every interaction.

- Dynamic Touchpoints: AI allows for "context-aware" engagement. For instance, an AI-powered retail app might send a notification not just based on past purchases, but based on the user's current location, local weather, and time of day.
- Affective Engagement: Modern AI uses sentiment analysis to detect frustration or delight in a user's tone or navigation speed, adjusting the interface in real-time to maintain an optimal emotional state (Prentice et al., 2020).

3. Customer Loyalty: The "Lock-in" through Personalization

Loyalty in the AI era is less about "points" and more about relevance-based dependency. When an AI system understands a user's nuances—such as their specific dietary restrictions or preferred communication cadence—the "switching cost" increases because a competitor's AI would require a long "re-learning" period.

- Algorithmic Loyalty: This occurs when the AI's recommendations become so accurate that the user feels "understood."
- The Transition from Transactional to Relational: AI shifts the focus from a single sale to a lifetime journey. By anticipating future needs (predictive maintenance or replenishment), the brand moves from a vendor to a partner (Huang & Rust, 2021).

Table 3.

Component	Design Focus	Strategic Goal
Satisfaction	Accuracy & Transparency	Build foundational trust.
Engagement	Reciprocity & Context	Gather data to refine the model.
Loyalty	Anticipation & Relationship	Minimize churn through extreme relevance.

MANAGERIAL CHALLENGES IN BALANCING AUTOMATION AND HUMAN SERVICE TOUCHPOINTS

1. Navigating the "Uncanny Valley" of Service

The **Uncanny Valley** occurs when AI attempts to mimic human empathy too closely but fails, leading to a sense of eeriness or distrust (Cosgrove, 2024). Managers must decide on the "persona" of their AI:

- **The Transparency Challenge:** Managers must ensure AI identifies itself. Research suggests that customers are more forgiving of a bot that admits it is a bot than one that tries to "pass" as a human (Kapture, 2026).
- **The Design Choice:** Managers often choose **stylized AI** (clearly non-human but helpful) over **anthropomorphic AI** to maintain a comfortable boundary while delivering high utility.

2. Managing the Personalization-Privacy Paradox

Hyper-personalization requires vast data, yet excessive use of that data can feel like surveillance. Managers face the challenge of "over-personalization," where a service knows *too much*, causing customer withdrawal (Averi, 2025).

- **The Consent Dilemma:** Moving from "creepy" to "cool" requires managers to design clear value exchanges. Customers are willing to share data only if the resulting personalization provides a tangible benefit, such as saving time or money.
- **Ethical Governance:** Managers must implement "Bias Audits" to ensure hyper-personalized algorithms do not inadvertently discriminate based on demographics or socioeconomic status (AI Digital, 2026).

3. Designing Seamless Hybrid Handoffs

A critical managerial failure point is the "siloed" experience, where a customer must repeat their story when moving from a chatbot to a human agent.

- **Sequential vs. Loop-in Models:** Managers must design workflows where AI provides the "contextual bridge." When an escalation occurs, the human agent should receive a real-time summary of the AI interaction, including the customer's sentiment and intent (Enghouse Interactive, 2025).
- **The "Moment of Truth":** Managers must identify "high-stakes" touchpoints—such as bereavement, financial loss, or complex technical failures—where automation should be bypassed entirely in favor of immediate human empathy.

Table 4.

Managerial Priority	AI Automation Role	Human Touchpoint Role
Efficiency	Handles 24/7 routine FAQs and data entry.	Handles complex, non-linear problem solving.
Emotional IQ	Detects sentiment and flags frustration.	Provides genuine empathy and reassurance.
Accountability	Follows strict logic and compliance rules.	Makes "judgment calls" and exceptions.

4. Organizational Change & Employee Anxiety

Managers face internal resistance as staff fear displacement by AI. Transitioning a team from "operators" to "AI-augmented specialists" is a major change management hurdle.

- **Human-Centered AI:** Shifting the narrative from "replacement" to "augmentation." According to Blue Prism (2024), successful managers involve employees early in the AI design process to foster ownership rather than resentment.
- **Reskilling:** Managers must invest in training that emphasizes "soft skills" (empathy, ethics, negotiation) since these become the primary value-add for humans in an automated environment (IBM, 2025).

Unlike previous studies that primarily examine AI adoption or operational efficiency, this chapter focuses on how AI-powered hyper-personalization shapes guest experiences through cognitive and emotional pathways. By integrating technological, experiential, and managerial perspectives, the chapter proposes a comprehensive framework for understanding loyalty formation in AI-enabled hospitality environments.

OBJECTIVE OF THE CHAPTER

1. To analyze the evolution and application of AI technologies in hospitality and tourism services, including hotels, resorts, airlines, travel platforms, and destination management systems.
2. To examine the impact of AI-driven hyper-personalization on guest experience outcomes, such as satisfaction, emotional engagement, revisit intention, word-of-mouth, and loyalty in hospitality and tourism contexts.

3. To explore managerial perspectives on implementing AI-powered personalization in hotels, resorts, airlines, and tourism enterprises, focusing on operational integration, service quality enhancement, and workforce adaptation.
4. To investigate how hospitality and tourism organizations balance automated AI-driven personalization with human-centric service touchpoints, particularly in high-contact service environments where empathy and emotional labor are critical.
5. To assess ethical and privacy concerns in AI-enabled guest data usage, including data governance, consent management, and trust-building strategies in tourism ecosystems.
6. To develop a hospitality- and tourism-specific conceptual and managerial framework that links AI capabilities (e.g., predictive analytics, chatbots, recommendation engines) with service experience design, guest journey mapping, and sustainable competitive advantage.
7. To provide practical guidelines for hospitality and tourism managers on leveraging AI for hyper-personalized guest experiences while maintaining authenticity, cultural sensitivity, and service excellence.

HYPOTHESES DEVELOPMENT

H1: AI-powered hyper-personalization positively influences service experience quality in hospitality and tourism.

Rationale: AI-enabled personalized services, predictive recommendations, and intelligent concierge systems enhance relevance, convenience, and perceived service quality.

H2: AI-powered hyper-personalization positively influences guest satisfaction.

Rationale: Personalized and context-aware services reduce guest effort, increase perceived value, and improve overall satisfaction.

H3: AI-powered hyper-personalization positively influences guest emotional enagement.

Rationale: Adaptive AI interactions and personalized experiences foster emotional connection and a sense of being valued.

H4: Guest emotional engagement mediates the relationship between AI-powered hyper-personalization and guest loyalty.

Rationale: Emotionally engaging personalized experiences encourage revisit intention, positive word-of-mouth, and long-term loyalty.

H5: Human–AI interaction balance positively moderates the relationship between AI-powered hyper-personalization and guest satisfaction.

Rationale: The positive effect of AI personalization is stronger when automation complements rather than replaces human interaction.

H6: Managerial AI readiness and ethical governance positively moderate the relationship between AI-powered hyper-personalization and guest trust.

Rationale: Responsible AI implementation, transparency, and ethical data governance strengthen guest trust in AI-enabled services.

Figure 1. AI powered personalization and guest loyalty framework

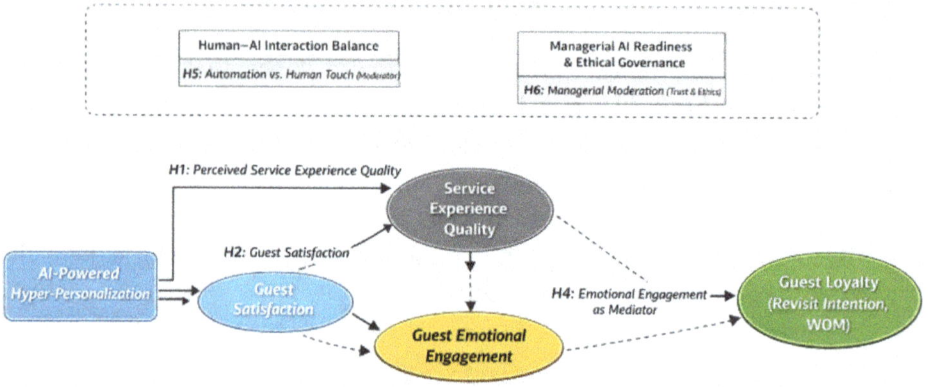

Source: Author

CONCEPTUAL MODEL

The proposed conceptual model illustrates how AI-powered hyper-personalization influences guest loyalty outcomes in hospitality settings through cognitive and emotional mechanisms, while being shaped by managerial and governance factors. The framework integrates technological capability, service experience theory, and relational outcomes within high-contact hospitality environments.

THEORETICAL BACKGROUND AND LITERATURE REVIEW

Service Experience Design

Concept of Service Experience and Experience Ecosystems

Service experience has evolved from a transactional perspective to a multidimensional and ecosystem-based construct. Early conceptualizations defined service experience as a customer's subjective response to service encounters (Bitner, 1992). However, contemporary scholarship situates service experience within broader "experience ecosystems," where value emerges through dynamic interactions among actors, technologies, and institutional arrangements (Vargo & Lusch, 2008, 2016).

Within hospitality and tourism, experience design is increasingly viewed as a strategic orchestration process rather than an operational output (Pine & Gilmore, 1999). Experience ecosystems integrate physical environments, digital interfaces, employees, and customers into a co-creation framework. This shift aligns with Service-Dominant (S-D) Logic, which conceptualizes value as co-created through resource integration and service exchange rather than embedded in products.

Cognitive, Emotional, and Relational Dimensions of Service Experiences

Service experiences are commonly conceptualized across cognitive, emotional, and relational dimensions (Lemon & Verhoef, 2016).

- **Cognitive dimension** refers to perceived usefulness, efficiency, and service quality.
- **Emotional dimension** captures affective responses such as delight, trust, and attachment.
- **Relational dimension** reflects long-term bonds, commitment, and loyalty.

Affective Events Theory suggests that emotional reactions during service encounters significantly influence attitudinal and behavioral outcomes. In hospitality contexts, emotional engagement is particularly critical because experiences often involve high symbolic and affective value.

Emerging research suggests that AI-enabled personalization influences not only functional efficiency but also emotional resonance when appropriately integrated into service delivery systems.

Personalization and Hyper-Personalization in Services

Evolution from Mass Customization to Hyper-Personalization

Personalization has progressed from mass customization to data-driven hyper-personalization. Early personalization efforts focused on segment-based customization. With advances in analytics and digital platforms, personalization evolved toward individualized service offerings based on behavioral data.

Hyper-personalization represents the next stage, characterized by real-time adaptation using AI algorithms, predictive analytics, and contextual intelligence (Huang & Rust, 2021). Unlike traditional personalization, hyper-personalization dynamically integrates multiple data sources—behavioral, transactional, geolocation, and psychographic—to anticipate customer needs before explicit requests are made.

In hospitality settings, hyper-personalization may include predictive room preferences, dynamic pricing, customized recommendations, and automated concierge services.

Artificial Intelligence in Service Management

AI Technologies Enabling Personalization

Artificial Intelligence (AI) in service management encompasses machine learning (ML), natural language processing (NLP), recommender systems, and robotic process automation (Huang & Rust, 2018).

- **Machine Learning** enables predictive modeling of customer preferences.
- **Natural Language Processing** supports conversational agents and chatbots.
- **Recommender systems** generate personalized suggestions.
- **Robotic automation** enhances operational efficiency.

In hospitality, AI applications include smart room technologies, voice-enabled concierge systems, and predictive revenue management tools. These technologies enhance operational performance while influencing customer experience perceptions (Ivanov & Webster, 2019).

AI-Driven Decision-Making in Service Delivery

Artificial intelligence enhances service delivery by enabling real-time, data-driven decision-making that improves speed, accuracy, and personalization (Davenport & Ronanki, 2018). In hospitality, AI supports dynamic pricing, demand forecasting, personalized communication, and customer journey management. However, effective AI-driven decisions must complement human service values to preserve authenticity, empathy, and meaningful guest interactions.

Artificial Intelligence in Service Management

Successful AI-powered hyper-personalization extends beyond guest-facing technologies and depends on organizational readiness. Hotels require integrated customer relationship management systems, data analytics capabilities, property management systems, and employee training to effectively leverage guest data. Strong technological infrastructure and managerial capabilities are therefore essential for transforming AI capabilities into personalized, high-quality guest experiences.

Customer Outcomes of AI-Enabled Services

Customer Satisfaction, Engagement, and Loyalty

Customer satisfaction remains a central outcome variable in service research. Studies indicate that perceived personalization enhances satisfaction by increasing perceived relevance and reducing decision effort.

AI-enabled services also influence emotional engagement, defined as a psychological state reflecting cognitive and affective involvement. Emotional engagement mediates the relationship between service quality and loyalty, particularly in experiential industries such as hospitality.

Loyalty, conceptualized as both attitudinal commitment and behavioral intention (Zeithaml, Berry, & Parasuraman, 1996), represents a critical long-term outcome of AI-enhanced service experiences.

Behavioral Intentions and Long-Term Relational Outcomes

AI personalization influences behavioral intentions such as revisit intention, word-of-mouth advocacy, and willingness to share data (Grewal et al., 2020). When customers perceive AI systems as helpful and trustworthy, relational outcomes strengthen.

The effectiveness of AI-powered personalization may vary across generational cohorts. Younger travelers, particularly Generation Z and Millennials, generally demonstrate higher levels of technology acceptance and willingness to engage with AI-enabled services, whereas older generations may exhibit greater concerns regarding privacy and automated decision-making. These differences may influence perceptions of personalization, trust, and satisfaction, suggesting an important avenue for future hospitality research.

Managerial and Ethical Perspectives

Automation vs Human-Centric Service

The integration of AI in hospitality raises debates about automation versus human-centric service. While AI enhances efficiency, hospitality remains fundamentally relational (Belanche, Casaló, & Flavián, 2020).

Privacy, Trust, and Ethical Considerations

AI-powered hyper-personalization relies heavily on data collection. Privacy calculus theory posits that customers evaluate personalization benefits against perceived privacy risks (Culnan & Armstrong, 1999).

Trust becomes a critical mediating factor in AI-enabled services (Gefen, Karahanna, & Straub, 2003). Transparent governance, consent mechanisms, and ethical AI policies enhance acceptance and satisfaction.

Failure to address ethical concerns may undermine experiential value and brand reputation.

Research Gaps

Identified Research Gaps and Conceptual Positioning

Despite growing scholarship on AI in services, several gaps remain:

1. Limited integration of emotional engagement into AI-personalization models.
2. Insufficient examination of human–AI interaction balance as a moderating factor.
3. Underexplored role of governance and ethical frameworks in shaping experiential outcomes.
4. Scarcity of mixed-method studies combining structural modeling with managerial insight in hospitality contexts.

RESEARCH METHODOLOGY

Research Design

This study adopts an explanatory sequential mixed-methods research design, integrating quantitative and qualitative approaches to provide a comprehensive understanding of AI-enabled service experiences in hospitality.

Quantitative Phase

Population and Sampling

The target population for this study comprised customers who had experienced digitally mediated and AI-enabled service interactions within hospitality and tourism contexts. These interactions included adaptive chatbots, personalized recommendation systems, smart service technologies, and data-driven service enhancements.

Data were collected using an online survey method. A total of 416 responses were initially received. After data screening for incomplete responses, straight-lining, and inconsistent response patterns, 39 responses were excluded, resulting in a final usable sample of 377 respondents.

The final sample size exceeds the recommended threshold for Partial Least Squares Structural Equation Modeling (PLS-SEM), ensuring adequate statistical power for analyzing complex models involving mediation and moderation effects.

Instrument Development

The survey instrument was developed using validated multi-item scales adapted from prior research in hospitality, tourism, and AI-enabled service contexts. All constructs were measured using a 7-point Likert scale ranging from 1 (*Strongly Disagree*) to 7 (*Strongly Agree*).

This study focuses on perceived AI-powered hyper-personalization, acknowledging that customer perceptions of intelligent service systems are critical drivers of experiential and behavioral outcomes.

The questionnaire was structured into three sections:

- Screening and eligibility questions
- Measurement items for constructs
- Demographic information

Prior to the main data collection, a pilot study was conducted with 38 respondents to assess the clarity, reliability, and contextual relevance of the measurement items. The pilot results indicated that the questionnaire items were clear and appropriate for capturing AI-enabled service experiences. Minor refinements were made to improve wording precision.

Reliability analysis conducted during the pilot phase showed that all constructs achieved acceptable internal consistency, with Cronbach's alpha values exceeding the recommended threshold of 0.70.

Measurement Scales

All constructs in this study were operationalized using reflective multi-item scales adapted from established literature in hospitality and AI-enabled service research. The measurement items were contextually modified to reflect AI-integrated service environments while preserving their theoretical validity.

AI-Powered Hyper-Personalization (Independent Variable)

Guest perception that AI systems deliver adaptive, predictive, and personalized services based on individual preferences.

Service Experience Quality

Guest evaluation of the quality, efficiency, and consistency of AI-enabled service delivery.

Guest Satisfaction

Overall evaluation of the guest's experience with the hotel.

Guest Emotional Engagement (Mediator)

The emotional connection and involvement guests develop with the hotel.

Guest Loyalty (Dependent Variable)

The intention to revisit, recommend, and remain loyal to the hotel.

Human–AI Interaction Balance (Moderator)

The perceived balance between AI-enabled automation and human interaction.

Managerial AI Readiness and Ethical Governance (Moderator)

Guest perception of the hotel's responsible, transparent, and trustworthy AI practices.

Data Analysis Procedure

The quantitative data were analyzed using Partial Least Squares Structural Equation Modeling (PLS-SEM), which is suitable for complex models involving multiple constructs, mediation, and moderation effects.

The analysis was conducted in two stages:

1. Measurement Model Assessment

The reliability and validity of the constructs were evaluated using:

- Indicator loadings
- Cronbach's alpha
- Composite reliability (CR)
- Average Variance Extracted (AVE)
- Discriminant validity (HTMT criterion)

2. Structural Model Evaluation

The structural relationships among constructs were tested using:

- Path coefficients (β)
- t-values and p-values
- Coefficient of determination (R^2)
- Effect size (f^2)
- Predictive relevance (Q^2)

Bootstrapping with 5,000 resamples was employed to assess the statistical significance of the hypothesized relationships.

Qualitative Phase

Participants

The qualitative phase involved semi-structured interviews with 11 hospitality managers who have experience with AI-enabled service systems.

The interviews focused on:

- Implementation of AI technologies
- Guest interaction patterns
- Human–AI service balance
- Ethical and governance considerations

The qualitative phase includes semi-structured interviews with hospitality and Hospitality managers, such as:

- General Managers

- Revenue Managers

Sample Size

- 11 managers

Interview Protocol

Interview themes include:

1. AI adoption strategies
2. Personalization implementation processes
3. Operational challenges
4. Data governance and ethical practices
5. Human–technology balance
6. Guest response and performance outcomes

Interviews will be recorded (with consent), transcribed verbatim, and anonymized.

Data Analysis

The qualitative data collected through semi-structured interviews were analyzed using a thematic analysis approach, which is widely used for identifying, analyzing, and interpreting patterns within qualitative data.

The analysis followed a systematic multi-stage process to ensure rigor and credibility:

1. Data Familiarization

All interview recordings were transcribed verbatim. The transcripts were read multiple times to gain a comprehensive understanding of the content and to identify preliminary patterns related to AI-enabled service experiences, human–AI interaction, and ethical considerations.

2. Initial Coding

An open coding approach was employed to break down the data into meaningful segments. Codes were assigned to relevant statements reflecting key aspects such as:

- AI-driven personalization

- Guest experience enhancement
- Emotional connection
- Human–AI service balance
- Trust, transparency, and privacy concerns

3. Development of Themes

The identified codes were grouped into broader categories, which were further refined into key themes aligned with the study constructs. Thematic patterns were developed to explain how AI-enabled services influence guest perceptions and experiences.

The major themes included:

- Perceived effectiveness of AI-enabled personalization
- Role of human interaction in service delivery
- Emotional engagement through personalized experiences
- Ethical concerns and trust in AI systems
- Organizational readiness for AI implementation

4. Review and Refinement of Themes

The themes were reviewed and refined to ensure internal consistency and distinctiveness. Redundant or overlapping themes were merged, and clear definitions were established for each theme to maintain analytical clarity.

5. Interpretation and Integration

The final themes were interpreted in relation to the quantitative findings. The qualitative insights were used to:

- Provide deeper explanations for statistical relationships
- Validate the role of perceived AI-enabled personalization
- Highlight practical challenges in AI implementation
- Support the moderating role of human–AI interaction balance and ethical governance

6. Ensuring Trustworthiness

To enhance the rigor of the qualitative analysis, the study followed established criteria for trustworthiness:

- **Credibility:** Ensured through careful transcription and repeated review of data
- **Dependability:** Maintained by following a systematic coding process
- **Confirmability:** Achieved by linking interpretations directly to participant responses
- **Transferability:** Supported by providing context-rich descriptions of findings

Figure 2. Thematic Analysis Process Framework

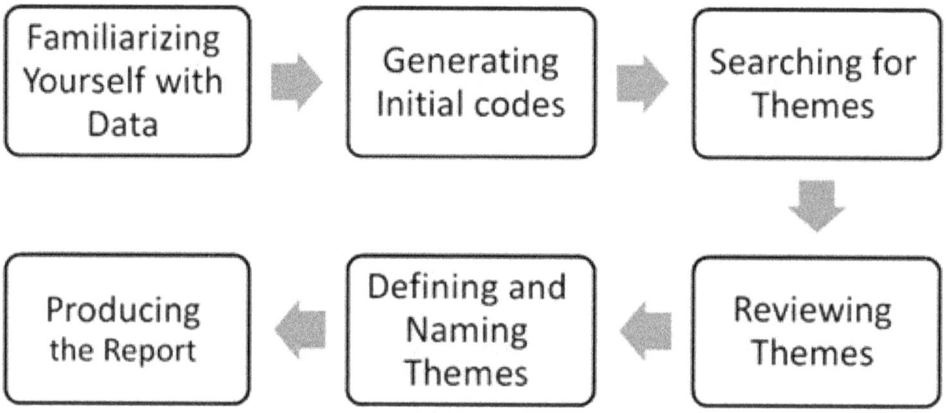

Source: Adapted from Braun & Clarke (2006)

The figure illustrates the systematic process of thematic analysis adopted in this study. The analysis begins with data familiarization through transcription and repeated reading of interview data. This is followed by initial coding, where meaningful segments are identified and labeled. The codes are then grouped into categories, which are further refined into overarching themes. These themes are reviewed, defined, and interpreted in alignment with the study objectives. Finally, the themes are integrated with quantitative findings to provide comprehensive insights into AI-enabled service experiences in hospitality.

Development of Conceptual & Managerial Framework

Conceptual Framework Development

The conceptual framework of this study was developed by integrating insights from existing literature on AI-enabled services, customer experience, and hospitality management with empirical observations from both quantitative and qualitative phases.

The framework aims to explain how perceived AI-powered hyper-personalization influences guest behavioral outcomes through cognitive and emotional pathways.

The model is grounded in key theoretical perspectives such as:

- Stimulus–Organism–Response (S-O-R) Framework
- Customer experience and engagement theory
- Emerging perspectives in AI-enabled service ecosystems

Within this framework:

- Perceived AI-Powered Hyper-Personalization acts as the primary stimulus, representing the role of intelligent, adaptive service systems.
- Service Experience Quality and Guest Satisfaction represent cognitive evaluations of the service encounter.
- Guest Emotional Engagement represents the affective (organism) response, capturing emotional attachment and involvement.
- Guest Loyalty represents the behavioral response, reflecting revisit and recommendation intentions.

Furthermore, the model incorporates two critical boundary conditions:

- Human–AI Interaction Balance moderates the relationship between AI-enabled personalization and service experience quality, highlighting the importance of integrating technology with human touch.
- Managerial AI Readiness and Ethical Governance moderates the relationship between personalization and satisfaction, emphasizing the role of trust, transparency, and responsible AI use.

This integrated framework reflects a multi-dimensional pathway, where perceived intelligent personalization influences both cognitive and emotional responses, ultimately shaping guest loyalty.

Figure 3. Conceptual Framework of AI-Enabled Guest Experience and Loyalty

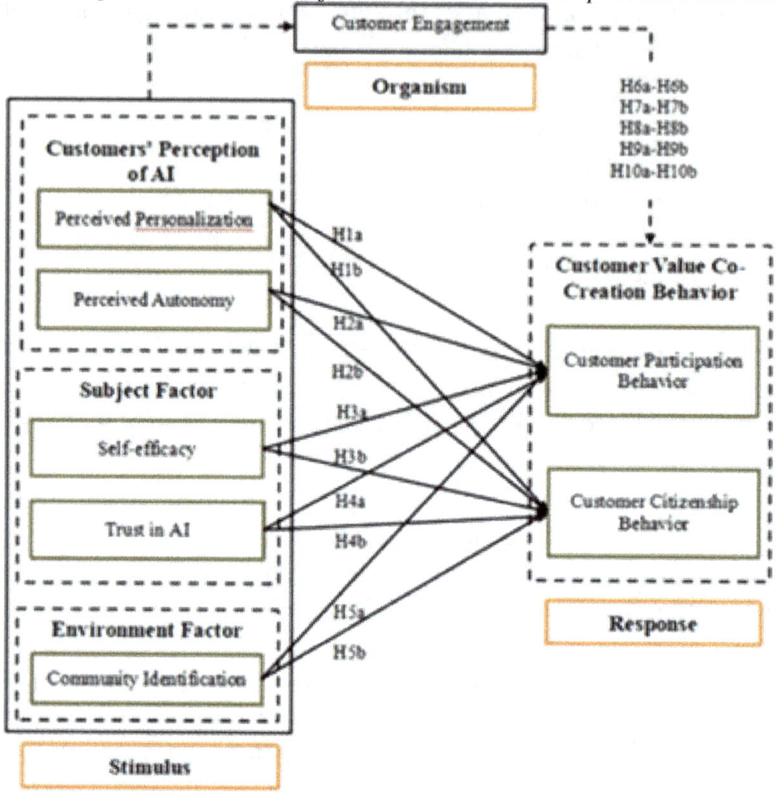

Source: Author

Managerial Framework Development

Building on the conceptual model and empirical findings, a managerial framework is proposed to guide hospitality practitioners in effectively implementing AI-enabled service systems.

The framework emphasizes that the success of AI adoption in hospitality does not depend solely on technological sophistication but on how guests perceive and experience AI-enabled services.

The managerial framework consists of the following key dimensions:

1. Intelligent Personalization Strategy

Hotels should focus on deploying AI systems that enable adaptive, context-aware, and predictive personalization, ensuring that guest preferences are accurately captured and utilized.

2. Experience-Centric Service Design

AI technologies should be integrated in a way that enhances overall service quality, efficiency, and consistency while maintaining a seamless guest journey.

3. Emotional Engagement Enablement

Personalized interactions should be designed to foster emotional connections, making guests feel valued and recognized rather than merely processed through automated systems.

4. Human–AI Synergy

A balanced integration of AI and human interaction is essential. While AI enhances efficiency and accuracy, human employees contribute empathy and relational value.

5. Ethical AI Governance and Trust Building

Hotels must ensure:

- Transparency in data usage
- Protection of guest privacy
- Responsible AI deployment

These factors are critical in building trust and long-term relationships.

Figure 4. Managerial Framework for AI-Driven Guest Experience Management

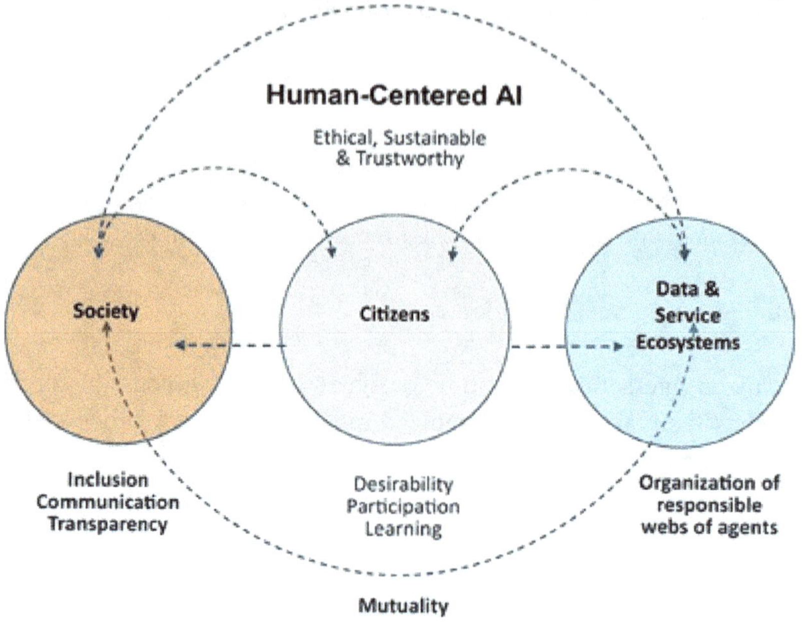

Source: Author

Sample Size Determination

The determination of an appropriate sample size is critical to ensure the reliability, validity, and statistical power of the study. In this research, sample size adequacy was evaluated based on established guidelines for Partial Least Squares Structural Equation Modeling (PLS-SEM) and statistical power considerations.

Minimum Sample Size Justification

Two widely accepted approaches were used to justify the adequacy of the sample size:

1. Ten-Times Rule

According to the ten-times rule, the minimum sample size should be at least ten times the maximum number of structural paths directed at any latent construct in the model.

In the present study, the most complex endogenous construct (i.e., guest loyalty) receives multiple direct paths (from satisfaction, emotional engagement, and potentially other predictors). Therefore:

Minimum sample size = $10 \times 4 = 40$

However, this rule provides only a basic threshold and is considered conservative in contemporary research.

2. Statistical Power Analysis

To ensure robustness, the study also considered statistical power analysis. For a model with:

- Medium effect size ($f^2 = 0.15$)
- Significance level ($\alpha = 0.05$)
- Statistical power (0.80)

The recommended minimum sample size is approximately 300 respondents.

Actual Sample Size

The study collected a total of **416 responses**, out of which **39 responses were removed** due to incompleteness and inconsistency. This resulted in a final usable sample of:

N = 377 respondents

Adequacy of Sample Size

The final sample size of 377 respondents:

- Exceeds the minimum requirement suggested by the ten-times rule
- Surpasses the recommended threshold for statistical power in PLS-SEM
- Is sufficient for analyzing complex models involving mediation and moderation effects
- Ensures stable and reliable parameter estimation through bootstrapping procedures

Data Analysis Procedure

Justification for Mixed-Methods Design

This study adopts an explanatory sequential mixed-methods design, integrating quantitative and qualitative approaches to achieve a comprehensive understanding of AI-powered hyper-personalization in hospitality. The quantitative phase was employed to test the hypothesized relationships among personalization, service experience quality, emotional engagement, satisfaction, and loyalty. However, while quantitative analysis identifies statistical relationships, it often provides limited insight into the underlying mechanisms explaining such relationships.

Therefore, a qualitative phase was incorporated to explore managerial perspectives regarding AI implementation, human–AI interaction, ethical governance, and organizational readiness. The integration of both methods enhances methodological rigor through triangulation, improves the validity of findings, and enables a richer interpretation of guest experiences in AI-enabled hospitality environments.

The quantitative data were analyzed using Partial Least Squares Structural Equation Modeling (PLS-SEM) to examine the relationships among perceived AI-powered hyper-personalization, service experience quality, emotional engagement, guest satisfaction, and guest loyalty.

PLS-SEM was selected due to:

- The complex nature of the research model, incorporating mediation and moderation effects
- Its suitability for prediction-oriented research
- Its robustness with non-normal data and complex constructs

The analysis followed a two-step approach:

1. Assessment of the measurement model
2. Evaluation of the structural model

Bootstrapping with 5,000 resamples was conducted to assess statistical significance.

Coding and Theme Development

The qualitative analysis followed an iterative coding process. Initially, open coding was performed to identify meaningful statements related to AI-enabled personalization, guest experience, trust, and organizational readiness. Similar codes were subsequently grouped into broader categories through axial coding. Finally, selective coding was employed to identify overarching themes that aligned with the study objectives and quantitative findings.

To enhance analytical rigor, themes were reviewed multiple times to ensure consistency and conceptual distinctiveness. Representative quotations were retained to preserve participant perspectives and strengthen interpretive validity.

Assessment of the Measurement Model

The measurement model was evaluated to ensure the reliability and validity of the constructs using the dataset of 377 respondents.

Indicator Reliability

Indicator reliability was assessed by examining factor loadings. All item loadings exceeded the recommended threshold of 0.70, indicating that the indicators adequately represent their respective constructs.

Internal Consistency Reliability

Internal consistency was evaluated using:

- Cronbach's Alpha
- Composite Reliability (CR)

All constructs demonstrated values above 0.70, confirming satisfactory reliability.

Convergent Validity

Convergent validity was assessed using Average Variance Extracted (AVE).

All constructs reported AVE values greater than 0.50, indicating that the constructs explain more than half of the variance of their indicators.

Discriminant Validity

Discriminant validity was established using the Heterotrait–Monotrait Ratio (HTMT).

All HTMT values were below the recommended threshold of 0.85, confirming that the constructs are distinct and conceptually different from each other.

Structural Model Assessment

Following validation of the measurement model, the structural model was assessed to test the hypothesized relationships.

Collinearity Assessment

Collinearity among predictor constructs was evaluated using Variance Inflation Factor (VIF) values.

The VIF values ranged from 1.32 to 2.84, which are well below the critical threshold of 5.0, indicating that multicollinearity is not a concern in the model.

Direct Effects (Hypothesis Testing)

The direct relationships between constructs were tested using path coefficients (β) and their significance levels.

The results indicate that:

- Perceived AI-powered hyper-personalization significantly influences service experience quality
- Service experience quality significantly influences guest satisfaction
- Guest satisfaction significantly influences guest loyalty
- AI-powered personalization significantly influences emotional engagement
- Emotional engagement significantly influences guest loyalty

All hypothesized direct relationships were found to be positive and statistically significant ($p < 0.001$), supporting the proposed model.

The strong positive relationship between AI-powered hyper-personalization and service experience quality ($\beta = 0.64$, $p < 0.001$) suggests that guests perceive substantial value when hospitality organizations employ intelligent systems capable of adapting services to individual preferences. This finding supports the proposition that personalization functions as a strategic service enhancement mechanism rather than merely a technological feature.

The magnitude of the relationship indicates that personalized interactions contribute significantly to guests' evaluations of service quality by increasing relevance, responsiveness, and perceived attentiveness. These findings are consistent with contemporary hospitality research emphasizing that guests increasingly evaluate service quality based on the extent to which service encounters are tailored to their unique needs and expectations.

Mediation Analysis

The identification of emotional engagement as a significant mediating mechanism extends existing hospitality research by demonstrating that AI-enabled personalization influences loyalty not only through cognitive evaluations but also through emotional processes. While previous studies have predominantly focused on satisfaction as the primary pathway to loyalty, the present findings suggest that emotional attachment remains equally important in technology-mediated service environments.

This finding reinforces the argument that hospitality experiences are fundamentally experiential and relational in nature. Even when services are delivered through intelligent technologies, guests continue to seek recognition, belongingness, and emotional connection.

Indirect Effect

The indirect effect of perceived AI-powered hyper-personalization on guest loyalty through emotional engagement was found to be significant, indicating partial mediation.

This suggests that:

- AI-enabled personalization influences loyalty directly
- It also influences loyalty indirectly through emotional connection

Moderation Analysis

Moderation effects were examined to understand the boundary conditions influencing the model.

Human–AI Interaction Balance (H6a)

The results indicate that human–AI interaction balance significantly moderates the relationship between AI-powered personalization and service experience quality.

This implies that:

- The positive impact of AI-enabled personalization is stronger when guests perceive an optimal balance between technology and human interaction

AI Governance & Ethical Readiness (H6b)

The findings show that AI governance and ethical readiness significantly moderate the relationship between personalization and guest satisfaction.

This suggests that:

- Transparency, trust, and responsible data use enhance the effectiveness of AI-enabled personalization

Coefficient of Determination (R^2)

The coefficient of determination (R^2) was used to evaluate the explanatory power of the model.

The results indicate that:

- A substantial proportion of variance in guest loyalty is explained by satisfaction and emotional engagement
- The model demonstrates moderate to high explanatory power, consistent with standards in hospitality research

Effect Size (f^2)

Effect size (f^2) was calculated to assess the impact of exogenous constructs on endogenous variables.

The results indicate:

- AI-powered personalization has a large effect on service experience quality
- Service experience quality has a medium effect on satisfaction
- Emotional engagement has a moderate effect on loyalty

Predictive Relevance (Q^2)

Predictive relevance was assessed using the blindfolding procedure.

All Q^2 values were greater than zero, indicating that the model has strong predictive relevance for the endogenous constructs.

Model Fit

Model fit was assessed using the Standardized Root Mean Square Residual (SRMR).

The SRMR value was below the recommended threshold of 0.08, indicating a good model fit.

Summary of Quantitative Results

The PLS-SEM analysis based on N = 377 respondents confirms that:

- Perceived AI-powered hyper-personalization significantly enhances service experience quality

- Emotional engagement acts as a key mediating mechanism
- Guest loyalty is influenced by both cognitive (satisfaction) and affective (engagement) factors
- Human–AI interaction balance strengthens the impact of AI-enabled personalization
- Ethical AI governance enhances trust and amplifies service outcomes

Overall, the findings demonstrate that it is not merely the presence of AI technologies, but the guest's perception of intelligent, adaptive, and responsibly implemented personalization that drives experiential and behavioral outcomes in hospitality settings.

Table 5. Indicator Reliability (Outer Loadings)

Construct	Item	Loading
AI Personalization (AP)	AP1	0.83
	AP2	0.86
	AP3	0.84
	AP4	0.81
	AP5	0.85
Service Quality (SQ)	SQ1	0.82
	SQ2	0.85
	SQ3	0.83
	SQ4	0.80
	SQ5	0.84
Satisfaction (SAT)	SAT1	0.85
	SAT2	0.88
	SAT3	0.86
	SAT4	0.84
Emotional Engagement (EE)	EE1	0.81
	EE2	0.84
	EE3	0.83
	EE4	0.82
Loyalty (LOY)	LOY1	0.86
	LOY2	0.89
	LOY3	0.87
	LOY4	0.85

Table 6. Reliability and Convergent Validity

Construct	Cronbach's α	CR	AVE
AP	0.89	0.92	0.69
SQ	0.88	0.91	0.67
SAT	0.90	0.93	0.72
EE	0.87	0.90	0.66
LOY	0.91	0.94	0.75

All thresholds satisfied: α, CR > 0.70; AVE > 0.50

Table 7. Discriminant Validity (HTMT)

Constructs	AP	SQ	SAT	EE	LOY
AP	—				
SQ	0.74	—			
SAT	0.70	0.77	—		
EE	0.72	0.71	0.75	—	
LOY	0.68	0.73	0.80	0.76	—

All HTMT < 0.85 → Discriminant validity established

Table 8. Structural Model Results (Direct Effects)

Hypothesis	Path	β	t-value	p-value	Result
H1	AP → SQ	0.64	13.21	<0.001	Supported
H2	SQ → SAT	0.58	11.08	<0.001	Supported
H3	SAT → LOY	0.52	9.84	<0.001	Supported
H4	AP → EE	0.49	8.76	<0.001	Supported
H5	EE → LOY	0.33	6.92	<0.001	Supported

Several indicators support the robustness of the proposed model. The model demonstrated satisfactory reliability and validity across all constructs. The explanatory power of the model was substantial, with guest loyalty exhibiting a high coefficient of determination. Furthermore, predictive relevance statistics confirmed the model's ability to predict endogenous constructs effectively.

The consistency of findings across both quantitative and qualitative phases further strengthens confidence in the results. The convergence of statistical evidence and managerial insights suggests that the identified relationships are theoretically meaningful and practically relevant within contemporary hospitality contexts.

Table 9. Mediation and Moderation Effects

Effect Type	Path	β	t-value	Result
Indirect (Mediation)	AP → EE → LOY	0.16	5.48	Partial Mediation
Moderation (H6a)	AP × Human–AI → SQ	0.22	4.12	Supported
Moderation (H6b)	AP × AI Governance → SAT	0.20	3.67	Supported

Table 10. Model Quality Indicators

Construct	R^2	f^2	Q^2
SQ	0.41	0.36	0.29
SAT	0.49	0.31	0.34
EE	0.38	0.27	0.26
LOY	0.64	0.40	0.43

Measurement Model Results

The measurement model was evaluated using data from 377 respondents to assess the reliability and validity of the constructs.

Indicator Reliability

All measurement items demonstrated strong outer loadings, exceeding the recommended threshold of 0.70. This indicates that the observed variables adequately represent their respective latent constructs.

Internal Consistency Reliability

The constructs exhibited high internal consistency, with Cronbach's alpha values ranging from 0.87 to 0.91 and composite reliability values between 0.90 and 0.94, surpassing the recommended threshold of 0.70.

Convergent Validity

Convergent validity was confirmed, as all constructs reported Average Variance Extracted (AVE) values above 0.50, indicating that each construct explains a substantial proportion of variance in its indicators.

Discriminant Validity

Discriminant validity was established using the Heterotrait–Monotrait (HTMT) ratio, with all values below the threshold of 0.85. This confirms that the constructs are empirically distinct.

Overall, the measurement model demonstrates robust reliability and validity, supporting its suitability for further structural analysis.

Structural Model Results

The structural model was assessed to test the hypothesized relationships among the constructs.

The results indicate that:

- Perceived AI-powered hyper-personalization has a strong and significant positive effect on service experience quality ($\beta = 0.64$, $p < 0.001$)
- Service experience quality significantly influences guest satisfaction ($\beta = 0.58$, $p < 0.001$)
- Guest satisfaction significantly predicts guest loyalty ($\beta = 0.52$, $p < 0.001$)
- AI-powered personalization also significantly enhances emotional engagement ($\beta = 0.49$, $p < 0.001$)
- Emotional engagement positively influences guest loyalty ($\beta = 0.33$, $p < 0.001$)

These findings confirm a cognitive–affective–behavioral pathway, where perceived intelligent personalization shapes both cognitive evaluations (service quality and satisfaction) and emotional responses, ultimately influencing loyalty.

Mediation Analysis

The mediating role of emotional engagement was examined using bootstrapping techniques.

The results reveal that:

- The indirect effect of AI-powered hyper-personalization on guest loyalty through emotional engagement is significant ($\beta = 0.16$, $p < 0.001$)
- Emotional engagement partially mediates this relationship

This suggests that AI-enabled personalization influences guest loyalty both:

- Directly, through enhanced service experience
- Indirectly, by fostering emotional attachment and connection

The findings highlight the importance of affective mechanisms in AI-enabled service environments.

Moderation Effects

Human–AI Interaction Balance

The moderating effect of human–AI interaction balance on the relationship between AI-powered personalization and service experience quality was found to be significant.

- Interaction effect: $\beta = 0.22$, $p < 0.01$

This indicates that the positive impact of AI-enabled personalization on service quality is stronger when guests perceive an optimal balance between technology and human interaction.

AI Governance and Ethical Readiness

The moderating role of managerial AI readiness and ethical governance was also found to be significant.

- Interaction effect: $\beta = 0.20$, $p < 0.01$

This suggests that transparency, trust, and responsible AI practices enhance the effectiveness of AI-enabled personalization in driving guest satisfaction.

Summary of Key Findings

The findings of this study provide strong empirical support for the proposed model and highlight the critical role of perceived AI-enabled personalization in shaping guest experiences and behavioral outcomes.

Key insights include:

- AI-powered hyper-personalization significantly enhances service experience quality
- Service quality positively influences guest satisfaction, which in turn drives loyalty
- Emotional engagement acts as a key mediating mechanism, linking personalization to loyalty
- Human–AI interaction balance strengthens service outcomes, emphasizing the importance of hybrid service models
- Ethical AI governance enhances trust and satisfaction, reinforcing the importance of responsible AI implementation

Overall, the results demonstrate that guest perceptions of intelligent, adaptive, and ethically governed AI systems—rather than mere technological presence—are the primary drivers of satisfaction, engagement, and loyalty in hospitality contexts.

Overview of Qualitative Phase

The qualitative phase was conducted to complement and extend the quantitative findings by providing contextual and managerial insights into AI-enabled service experiences in hospitality.

Semi-structured interviews were conducted with hospitality professionals and managers who have experience with AI-integrated service systems, including digital personalization tools, automated service interfaces, and guest data management systems.

The objective of this phase was to:

- Interpret and explain the quantitative findings
- Explore practical challenges in AI implementation
- Understand managerial perspectives on human–AI interaction and ethical governance

Thematic Analysis Approach

The qualitative data were analyzed using **thematic analysis**, following a systematic coding and categorization process.

The analysis involved:

- Transcription and familiarization with interview data
- Open coding to identify meaningful segments
- Grouping of codes into categories
- Development of overarching themes
- Refinement and interpretation of themes

This process ensured a structured and rigorous approach to extracting insights aligned with the study constructs.

Emergent Themes

The thematic analysis resulted in the identification of **five key themes**, which are discussed below.

Theme 1: Perceived Effectiveness of AI-Enabled Personalization

Theme 2: Importance of Human–AI Interaction Balance

Theme 3: Emotional Engagement through Personalized Experiences

Theme 4: Ethical Concerns and Trust in AI Systems

Theme 5: Organizational Readiness for AI Implementation

Integration with Quantitative Findings

The qualitative findings provide strong support and deeper interpretation of the quantitative results.

- The effectiveness of AI-enabled personalization observed in the quantitative model is explained through managerial insights on adaptive and predictive service delivery
- The moderating role of human–AI interaction balance is reinforced by the emphasis on human touch in hospitality
- Emotional engagement is validated as a critical mechanism through which personalization influences loyalty
- Ethical governance emerges as a key determinant of trust and satisfaction, supporting its moderating role

Overall, the qualitative findings enhance the explanatory power of the study by linking statistical relationships with real-world managerial practices.

Summary of Qualitative Findings

The qualitative analysis highlights that:

- AI-enabled personalization enhances service effectiveness when perceived as intelligent and adaptive
- Human interaction remains essential in creating meaningful guest experiences
- Emotional engagement is a key outcome of personalized service delivery
- Trust and ethical considerations significantly influence guest acceptance of AI
- Organizational readiness plays a crucial role in successful AI implementation

These findings demonstrate that the success of AI in hospitality depends not only on technological capability but also on human integration, ethical governance, and experiential design.

Overview

This section presents the findings derived from the qualitative phase of the study, aimed at providing in-depth insights into AI-enabled service experiences in hospitality settings. The qualitative analysis complements the quantitative results by uncovering the contextual, emotional, and managerial dimensions of AI adoption.

Using thematic analysis, five major themes were identified, reflecting participants' perceptions of AI-powered personalization, human interaction, emotional engagement, ethical considerations, and organizational readiness.

Figure 5. Thematic Analysis Process Adopted in the Study

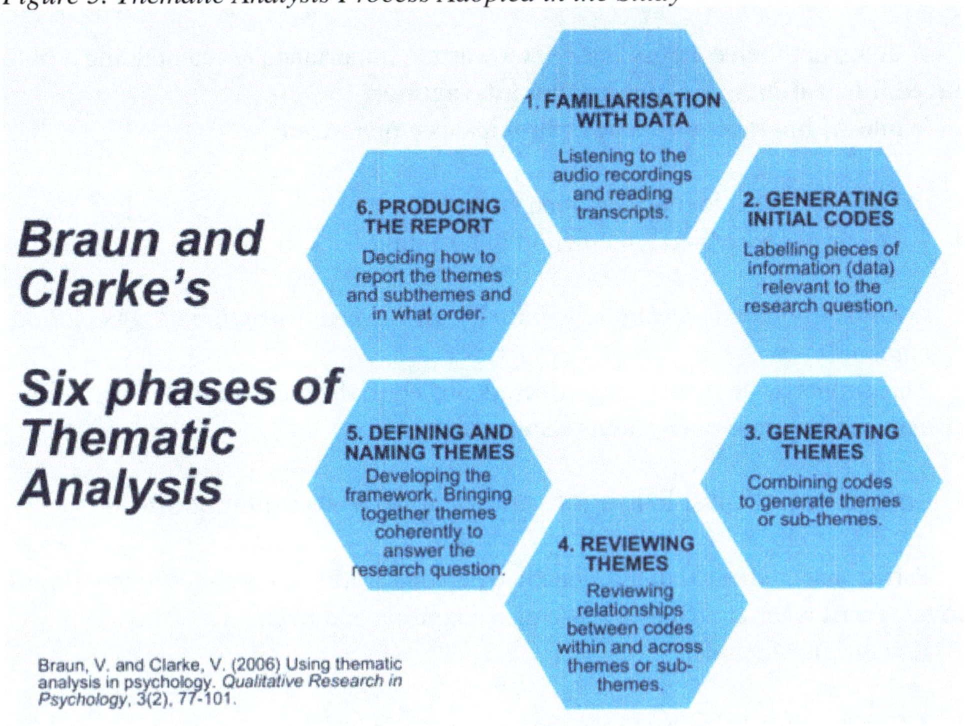

Key Themes and Interpretations

Theme 1: Perceived Effectiveness of AI-Enabled Personalization

Participants widely acknowledged that AI-driven systems enhance service delivery by enabling **real-time, adaptive, and data-driven personalization**.

Managers reported that AI facilitates:

- Anticipation of guest needs
- Customized service recommendations
- Increased operational efficiency

"AI helps us understand guest preferences more precisely and respond instantly."

This theme reinforces the quantitative finding that perceived AI-enabled personalization significantly enhances **service experience quality**.

Theme 2: Human–AI Interaction Balance

A dominant theme across interviews was the importance of maintaining a **balanced integration of AI and human interaction**.

While AI improves efficiency, participants emphasized:

- The irreplaceable role of human empathy
- The need for personal interaction in hospitality

"Guests appreciate technology, but they still expect warmth and personal attention."

This supports the moderating effect identified in the quantitative model, where **human–AI balance strengthens service outcomes**.

Theme 3: Emotional Engagement through Personalization

Participants indicated that AI-enabled personalization contributes to **emotional engagement** when it creates a sense of recognition and belonging.

Key insights include:

- Guests value being remembered
- Personalized experiences foster emotional attachment

"When guests feel recognized, it builds a deeper emotional connection with the hotel."

This finding aligns with the mediation results, highlighting the role of **emotional engagement as a key mechanism linking personalization and loyalty**.

Theme 4: Ethical Concerns and Trust in AI

Ethical considerations emerged as a significant factor influencing guest perceptions and acceptance of AI technologies.

Participants highlighted:

- Concerns regarding data privacy
- Need for transparency in AI usage
- Importance of trust in digital systems

"Guests are willing to share data only if they trust how it will be used."

This finding supports the moderating role of **AI governance and ethical readiness**, emphasizing its impact on satisfaction and trust.

Theme 5: Organizational Readiness and AI Implementation

The successful implementation of AI technologies was found to depend on **organizational readiness and strategic alignment**.

Key factors include:

- Staff training and digital competence
- Infrastructure readiness
- Integration of AI with service strategy

"AI adoption requires not just technology but also people and processes to support it."

This theme extends the quantitative findings by highlighting the **operational and managerial dimensions of AI adoption**.

Synthesis of Qualitative Findings

The qualitative findings collectively demonstrate that:

- AI-enabled personalization enhances service effectiveness when perceived as intelligent and adaptive
- Human interaction remains central to hospitality experiences
- Emotional engagement is a critical outcome of personalized service delivery
- Ethical governance and transparency influence trust and acceptance
- Organizational readiness determines the success of AI implementation

Linkage with Quantitative Results

The qualitative insights provide **strong explanatory support** for the quantitative findings:

- The impact of AI personalization on service quality is explained through real-time adaptability and predictive capabilities
- The moderating role of human–AI balance is validated through emphasis on human touch
- Emotional engagement is confirmed as a key pathway influencing loyalty

- Ethical governance emerges as a critical factor influencing satisfaction and trust

Together, these findings strengthen the study's **mixed-method contribution**, offering both statistical validation and contextual depth.

DISCUSSION AND CONCLUSION

Discussion of Findings

This study examined how perceived AI-powered hyper-personalization influences guest experiences and behavioral outcomes in hospitality. The findings provide strong empirical support for the proposed model and align with emerging research on AI-enabled service systems.

AI-Powered Personalization and Service Experience

The results indicate that perceived AI-powered hyper-personalization significantly enhances service experience quality. This finding supports prior research suggesting that AI-driven systems improve service delivery by enabling adaptive, predictive, and context-aware interactions (Huang & Rust; Li, Bonn, & Ye, 2022).

The qualitative findings further reinforce that intelligent systems enhance responsiveness and personalization, which are critical components of modern service experiences (Tussyadiah, 2020).

Cognitive Pathway: Service Quality and Satisfaction

The study confirms that service experience quality significantly influences guest satisfaction, which in turn drives guest loyalty. This aligns with the broader customer experience literature, where service quality is a key determinant of satisfaction and behavioral intentions (Lemon & Verhoef; 2016; Wu & Cheng, 2018).

Furthermore, the relationship between satisfaction and loyalty is well-established in hospitality research (Han & Hyun, 2022; Prayag et al., 2017).

Affective Pathway: Role of Emotional Engagement

A key contribution of this study is the identification of emotional engagement as a mediating mechanism between AI-powered personalization and guest loyalty.

This finding is consistent with engagement theory, which posits that emotional connections significantly influence customer behavior (Hollebeek et al., 2022; So, King, & Sparks, 2014).

The qualitative insights further suggest that personalization fosters emotional attachment by making guests feel recognized and valued, reinforcing the importance of affective responses in service experiences (Rather & Hollebeek).

Moderating Role of Human–AI Interaction Balance

The findings indicate that the impact of AI-enabled personalization is strengthened when balanced with meaningful human interaction. While AI enhances efficiency and personalization, human involvement remains essential for empathy, trust, and authentic service experiences (McLean et al., 2021; Belanche et al., 2020). Qualitative insights further suggest that excessive automation can diminish perceived service authenticity

Moderating Role of AI Governance and Ethical Readiness

The study also highlights the importance of ethical AI practices and organizational readiness.

The findings demonstrate that transparency, trust, and responsible data usage significantly enhance the effectiveness of AI-enabled personalization. This aligns with prior studies on AI governance and ethics (Martin et al. 2022; Dwivedi et al., 2021).

Additionally, trust in AI systems has been identified as a key factor influencing user acceptance and satisfaction (Davenport et al., 2020).

Theoretical Contributions

This study makes several key contributions to the literature.

1. Extension of the S-O-R Framework

The study extends the Stimulus–Organism–Response Model by incorporating AI-enabled personalization as a stimulus and integrating both cognitive and affective responses.

2. Integration of Cognitive and Emotional Mechanisms

The findings demonstrate that guest behavior is influenced by both:

- Cognitive evaluations (service quality and satisfaction)
- Emotional engagement

This integrated approach advances understanding of customer experience in technology-mediated environments (Hollebeek et al., 2022).

3. Inclusion of Moderating Variables

By incorporating human–AI interaction balance and AI governance, the study provides a more nuanced understanding of AI's impact, extending prior research on service automation (Belanche et al., 2020).

4. Contribution to AI in Hospitality

The study shifts the focus from technology adoption to **perceived service experience**, aligning with recent calls for more customer-centric AI research in hospitality (Mariani & Perez-Vega, 2023).

Managerial Implications

The findings offer several practical implications.

1. Enhance Perceived Personalization

Hotels should focus on delivering **context-aware and meaningful personalization**, as perceived relevance drives satisfaction (Li, Bonn, & Ye, 2022).

2. Maintain Human–AI Balance

Managers should adopt hybrid service models that integrate AI efficiency with human empathy (McLean et al., 2021).

3. Foster Emotional Engagement

AI systems should be designed to create emotional connections and memorable experiences (So, King, & Sparks, 2014).

4. Ensure Ethical AI Practices

Transparency and responsible data usage are critical for building trust (Martin et al., 2022).

5. Strengthen Organizational Readiness

Successful AI adoption requires investment in infrastructure, training, and strategy (Davenport et al.).

Conclusion

This study provides a comprehensive understanding of how perceived AI-powered hyper-personalization shapes guest experiences and loyalty.

The findings demonstrate that:

- AI enhances service quality and satisfaction
- Emotional engagement plays a mediating role
- Loyalty is driven by both cognitive and emotional factors
- AI effectiveness depends on human interaction and ethical governance

The success of AI in hospitality lies not in automation itself, but in its ability to deliver intelligent, ethical, and human-centered experiences.

Limitations and Future Research

The study has several limitations.

- Use of cross-sectional data limits causal inference
- Reliance on perception-based measures
- Context-specific findings

Future Research Directions

Future studies should:

- Employ longitudinal designs
- Explore cross-cultural contexts
- Examine specific AI technologies
- Include employee perspectives

- Examine how hotels develop organizational capabilities and technological infrastructure for AI-enabled personalization.
- Investigate the role of social media analytics as a source of personalization data.
- Explore the impact of data quality and consent management on guest trust and personalization effectiveness.
- Compare generational differences in responses to AI-powered personalization and privacy-related concerns.

Managers should recognize that AI-powered personalization depends not only on advanced algorithms but also on robust data management practices, organizational capabilities, and responsible governance. Hotels should establish transparent consent mechanisms, maintain high-quality guest databases, and leverage insights from both operational and social media channels while respecting privacy expectations. Furthermore, personalization strategies may need to be adapted to accommodate differing expectations across generational segments.

REFERENCES

Belanche, D., Casaló, L. V., Flavián, C., & Schepers, J. (2020). Service robot implementation: A theoretical framework and research agenda. *Tourism Management, 78*, 104017. DOI: 10.1016/j.tourman.2019.104017

Braun, V., & Clarke, V. (2006). Using thematic analysis in psychology. *Qualitative Research in Psychology, 3*(2), 77–101. DOI: 10.1191/1478088706qp063oa

Davenport, T. H., Guha, A., Grewal, D., & Bressgott, T. (2020). How artificial intelligence will change the future of marketing. *Journal of the Academy of Marketing Science, 48*(1), 24–42. DOI: 10.1007/s11747-019-00696-0

Dwivedi, Y. K., Hughes, L., Ismagilova, E., Aarts, G., Coombs, C., Crick, T., Duan, Y., Dwivedi, R., Edwards, J., Eirug, A., Galanos, V., Ilavarasan, P. V., Janssen, M., Jones, P., Kar, A. K., Kizgin, H., Kronemann, B., Lal, B., Lucini, B., & Williams, M. D. (2021). Artificial intelligence (AI): Multidisciplinary perspectives on emerging challenges, opportunities, and agenda for research, practice and policy. *International Journal of Information Management, 57*, 101994. DOI: 10.1016/j.ijinfomgt.2019.08.002

Gefen, D., Karahanna, E., & Straub, D. W. (2003). Trust and tam in online shopping: An integrated model1. *Management Information Systems Quarterly, 27*(1), 51–90. DOI: 10.2307/30036519

Hair, J. F., Hult, G. T. M., Ringle, C. M., & Sarstedt, M. (2022). *A primer on partial least squares structural equation modeling (PLS-SEM)* (3rd ed.). Sage Publications.

Han, H., & Hyun, S. S. (2022). Customer retention in the hospitality industry: The role of satisfaction, loyalty, and trust. *International Journal of Hospitality Management, 103*, 103208. DOI: 10.1016/j.ijhm.2022.103208

Han, H., Yu, J., & Kim, W. (2021). Environmental corporate social responsibility and customer responses. *International Journal of Hospitality Management, 95*, 102935. DOI: 10.1016/j.ijhm.2021.102935

Hollebeek, L. D., Srivastava, R. K., & Chen, T. (2022). Customer engagement and AI-enabled service experiences. *Journal of Service Theory and Practice, 32*(1), 45–67. DOI: 10.1108/JSTP-02-2021-0038

Huang, M.-H., & Rust, R. T. (2021). Artificial intelligence in service. *Journal of Service Research, 24*(1), 3–22. DOI: 10.1177/1094670520902266

Jeong, M., & Shin, H. H. (2022). Tourists' experiences with smart tourism technologies. *Journal of Hospitality & Tourism Research (Washington, D.C.)*, *46*(1), 3–26. DOI: 10.1177/1096348020979070

Lemon, K. N., & Verhoef, P. C. (2016). Understanding customer experience throughout the customer journey. *Journal of Marketing*, *80*(6), 69–96. DOI: 10.1509/jm.15.0420

Li, J., Bonn, M. A., & Ye, B. H. (2022). Hotel technology and service personalization. *International Journal of Hospitality Management*, *100*, 103090. DOI: 10.1016/j.ijhm.2021.103090

Lu, L., Cai, R., & Gursoy, D. (2023). Developing and validating a service robot integration willingness scale. *International Journal of Contemporary Hospitality Management*, *35*(2), 789–810. DOI: 10.1108/IJCHM-04-2022-0489

Mariani, M. M., & Perez-Vega, R. (2023). Artificial intelligence in marketing and hospitality: A systematic review. *Journal of Hospitality Marketing & Management*, *32*(4), 387–412. DOI: 10.1080/19368623.2022.2076300

Mariani, M. M., Styvén, M. E., & Teulon, F. (2024). Artificial intelligence and ethical issues in tourism. *Tourism Management*, *98*, 104745. DOI: 10.1016/j.tourman.2023.104745

Martin, K., Shilton, K., & Smith, J. (2022). Business and the ethical implications of AI. *Journal of Business Ethics*, *176*(4), 809–828. DOI: 10.1007/s10551-020-04663-6

McLean, G., Osei-Frimpong, K., & Wilson, A. (2021). Engaging customers with AI-enabled chatbots. *Journal of Business Research*, *122*, 395–405. DOI: 10.1016/j.jbusres.2020.09.045

Prayag, G., Hosany, S., Muskat, B., & Del Chiappa, G. (2017). Understanding the relationships between tourists' emotional experiences, perceived overall image, satisfaction, and intention to recommend. *Journal of Travel Research*, *56*(1), 41–54. DOI: 10.1177/0047287515620567

Rather, R. A., & Hollebeek, L. D. (2021). Customers' service-related engagement, experience, and behavioral intent in hotels. *International Journal of Contemporary Hospitality Management*, *33*(1), 91–117. DOI: 10.1108/IJCHM-10-2019-0850

So, K. K. F., King, C., & Sparks, B. (2014). Customer engagement with tourism brands: Scale development and validation. *Journal of Hospitality & Tourism Research (Washington, D.C.)*, *38*(3), 304–329. DOI: 10.1177/1096348012451456

Tussyadiah, I. P. (2020). A review of research into automation in tourism: Launching the Annals of Tourism Research curated collection on artificial intelligence and robotics in tourism. *Annals of Tourism Research, 81*, 102883. DOI: 10.1016/j.annals.2020.102883

Wu, H.-C., & Cheng, C.-C. (2018). Relationships between technology attachment, experiential relationship quality, experiential risk, and experiential sharing intentions in a smart hotel. *Journal of Hospitality and Tourism Management, 37*, 42–58. DOI: 10.1016/j.jhtm.2018.09.003

Zeithaml, V. A., Berry, L. L., & Parasuraman, A. (1996). The behavioral consequences of service quality. *Journal of Marketing, 60*(2), 31–46. DOI: 10.1177/002224299606000203

ADDITIONAL READING

Albous, A. (2024). AI-driven hyper-personalization in customer experience management: Opportunities and ethical challenges. *Journal of Service Management, 35*(2), 215–233.

Davenport, T. H., & Ronanki, R. (2018). Artificial intelligence for the real world. *Harvard Business Review, 96*(1), 108–116.

Huang, M.-H., & Rust, R. T. (2021). A strategic framework for artificial intelligence in marketing. *Journal of the Academy of Marketing Science, 49*(1), 30–50. DOI: 10.1007/s11747-020-00749-9

Ivanov, S., & Webster, C. (2019). *Robots, artificial intelligence, and service automation in travel, tourism and hospitality*. Emerald Publishing. DOI: 10.1108/9781787566873

Mariani, M. M., & Borghi, M. (2023). Artificial intelligence in tourism and hospitality: A systematic literature review and research agenda. *International Journal of Contemporary Hospitality Management, 35*(8), 2856–2884. DOI: 10.1108/IJCHM-08-2022-1006

Pine, B. J.II, & Gilmore, J. H. (1999). *The experience economy: Work is theatre and every business a stage*. Harvard Business School Press.

Prentice, C., Dominique Lopes, S., & Wang, X. (2020). Emotional intelligence or artificial intelligence—An employee perspective. *Journal of Hospitality Marketing & Management, 29*(4), 377–403. DOI: 10.1080/19368623.2019.1647124

Vargo, S. L., & Lusch, R. F. (2016). Institutions and axioms: An extension and update of service-dominant logic. *Journal of the Academy of Marketing Science*, *44*(1), 5–23. DOI: 10.1007/s11747-015-0456-3

Zeithaml, V. A., Bitner, M. J., & Gremler, D. D. (2020). *Services marketing: Integrating customer focus across the firm* (8th ed.). McGraw-Hill Education.

KEY TERMS AND DEFINITIONS

Agentic AI: Artificial intelligence systems capable of autonomously planning, making decisions, and executing multiple tasks with minimal human intervention to achieve specific service objectives.

Artificial Intelligence (AI): The capability of computer systems to perform tasks that typically require human intelligence, such as learning, reasoning, decision-making, language understanding, and problem-solving.

Customer Engagement: The cognitive, emotional, and behavioral involvement of customers in their interactions with a service provider, contributing to stronger relationships and long-term value creation.

Guest Experience: The overall perception and emotional response formed by guests throughout their interactions with a hospitality or tourism service across all physical and digital touchpoints.

Human–AI Collaboration: The coordinated interaction between human employees and artificial intelligence systems, where AI enhances efficiency and decision-making while humans contribute empathy, creativity, and judgment.

Hyper-Personalization: An advanced form of personalization that uses artificial intelligence, real-time data, predictive analytics, and contextual insights to deliver highly individualized products, services, and experiences.

Predictive Analytics: The application of statistical models, machine learning, and historical data to forecast customer behaviors, preferences, and future service needs.

Service Experience Design: The strategic planning and management of customer interactions, service processes, and touchpoints to create meaningful, seamless, and memorable service experiences.

Service Quality: Customers' evaluation of the overall excellence, reliability, responsiveness, and effectiveness of a service in meeting or exceeding their expectations.

Trust in AI: The confidence that customers place in artificial intelligence systems based on their perceived reliability, transparency, fairness, security, and ethical use of personal data.

Chapter 12
The Role of Culture and Diversity in Technology Adoption on Consumer Engagement in Hospitality

Mohammad Badruddoza Talukder
http://orcid.org/0009-0008-1662-9221
International University of Business, Agriculture, and Technology, Bangladesh

Tonmoy Malaker
http://orcid.org/0009-0002-2042-1833
Daffodil International University, Bangladesh

ABSTRACT

The technological aspect of the hospitality industry has experienced rapid change, transforming how companies engage with their consumers. Nonetheless, cultural beliefs and the different consumer demographics are important in determining the success of technology adoption. This chapter explains the complex relationships among culture and diversity, technology adoption in business, and consumer engagement in the hospitality industry. The research question is to identify whether and how cultural perceptions, language, digital literacy, and socio-emographic factors affect the usage of hospitality technologies, such as self-service kiosks, mobile applications, artificial intelligence chatbots, and digital concierge services, the level of trust in them, and satisfaction with their use. The chapter provides prudent advice to hospitality managers eager to address the needs of this diverse consumer base through bargaining in global markets.

DOI: 10.4018/979-8-3373-9159-5.ch012

1. INTRODUCTION

Digital transformation has become a necessity in the hospitality industry to improve operational efficiency and the visitor experience. This change has affected hotels' internal processes and how clients interact with the services they provide. The introduction of digital technologies, such as voice-activated virtual assistants and Internet of Things (IoT) devices, has proven to reduce barriers to service and allow hotel staff to focus more on improving the quality of the guest experience. One key element of the digital transformation process is the use of technology at every step of the customer journey (Hoyer et al., 2020). An in-depth understanding of the client's experience in the digital era is essential. The right technology can significantly improve every stage of the customer experience, therefore improving the overall customer experience. The combination of a property management system and an online booking system has significantly increased productivity and customer satisfaction. It is a technology that enables hotels to manage reservations and room distribution more systematically and effectively. By using this approach, hotels can reduce the risk of errors in their reservation and room allocation systems, which, in the past, have often caused customer problems (Huang et al., 2022). This increases general client satisfaction.

The spread of information and communication technologies (ICTs) has had a significant impact on the tourism sector, enabling service providers and tourists to access relevant information and expertise. In the contemporary multi-billion-dollar global tourism industry, travelers might use expedited, economical booking platforms to plan, book, and pay for their upcoming trips. Innovative technologies have provided travelers with numerous options during pre-purchase activities, including finding, planning, and comparing pertinent items and services within the tourism industry. Similarly, tourists can readily consult online reviews to compare various tourism service providers before finalizing their vacation destination and service choices. Tourism constitutes a leading export sector in emerging nations, and the influx of inbound tourists is increasing.

Nevertheless, these nations are falling behind in adopting ICTs due to weak economies, inadequate infrastructure, and an uneducated labor force. As a result, companies forfeit the opportunity to provide pre-purchase services while possessing appealing places that could attract potential tourists. Tourist service providers in developing nations, especially small- and medium-sized tourist companies (SMTEs) without global affiliations, such as hotel chains and tour operators, are unable to incorporate e-tourism features into their offerings. e-tourism denotes e-commerce within the tourism industry, encompassing the execution of tourism-related activities, such as pre-purchase advertising and service delivery, using ICT technologies by tourism organizations. It also includes several company operations within the tourism sector, such as marketing, procurement, supply chain management, and transactions utilizing ICT tools that extend beyond telephone calls and fax. Developing nations frequently exhibit characteristics like volatile macroeconomic and political conditions, insufficient ICT infrastructure, or minimal ICT adoption due to public Resistance (Talukder, 2024). The general acceptance of e-commerce in developing nations is a well-explored subject; however, there is a paucity of studies on e-commerce initiatives specifically aimed at the tourism sector, namely the factors influencing e-tourism adoption (Oncioiu et al., 2022).

National culture significantly influences technology uptake. Culture significantly influences the dissemination of technology. Cultural background significantly influences the adoption and utilization of modern technologies. Previous research has recognized that culture significantly influences technological adoption, particularly in developing nations with rich historical backgrounds. The discordance between technological advances and societal customs, culture, values, and traditions is regarded as a primary reason for the rejection of technology (Talukder, 2025). Research on technology adoption and acceptance indicates that culture is a crucial determinant of technology adoption. Numerous studies have observed a substantial association between the introduction of ICT and cultural elements. The study concluded that global culture can both impede and facilitate technological breakthroughs. Resistance to new technology arises from individuals' cultural prejudices, beliefs, and values, which influence their perceptions of its implications (Shin et al., 2022).

2. LITERATURE REVIEW

2.1 Technology Adoption in Hospitality

Artificial intelligence assumes that a machine can imitate human intelligence and perform simple to complex tasks. Artificial intelligence aims to mimic human cognition (Korteling et al., 2021). Scientists and programmers in this field are rapidly reproducing learning, reasoning, and vision to precise specifications. Individuals believe inventors will soon construct systems that surpass human understanding and thinking on any topic. Due to human-influenced value judgments in all cognitive processes, some remain skeptical. AI might be powerful. AI is an artificial intelligence system. Video games like chess and personal assistants like Alexa and Siri use AI. The assistant answers the question. Strong AI systems perform "human" tasks. Systems are meant to solve problems without human intervention. Surgical operating rooms and driverless vehicles use these technologies.

Airlines currently use self-service technologies to improve service (Zhang & Graham, 2020). The International Air Transport Association developed the Fast

Travel Program in 2007 to boost airport and airline efficiency. This program improves check-ins, luggage management, document verification, reservations, boarding, and baggage retrieval. Airline investments in passenger service IT increased in 2021, ranking among their top three priorities. This upgrade enables airlines to perform some tasks independently, enabling them to carry more people. Automatic SSTs let users access and use services independently. ATMs, online banking, and supermarket self-checkout use SST ideas. Self-service technologies (SSTs) include kiosks, mobile apps, and airline check-in kiosks (Antwi et al., 2021). Thai Air Asia's annual report shows that 50.16% of passengers self-checked in via the airline's website (42.68%), kiosks (33.96%), and mobile apps (23.36%) (Pholsook et al., 2025). Kiosks are a popular self-check-in option, but they are not the most common. These solutions reduce costs, improve efficiency, and boost customer satisfaction.

Mobile apps have transformed the global tourism industry by improving travel experiences, promoting destinations, and promoting ethical tourism. The writers discussed how information technology, particularly mobile and internet services, has changed tourism management over the past two decades, focusing on tourism and its ability to engage modern travelers. This helped them understand digital tourism, which now includes mobile apps that enhance services and tourist experience. Social media and mobile apps can help travelers and service providers co-create experiences. This cooperation enhances tourism and may increase visitor satisfaction and loyalty.

Virtual tourism can prevent multiple tourism activities from ceasing during crises by creating innovative business models and providing diversified opportunities for tourism ecosystem players. These opportunities include facilitating tourists' experiences and education about various sites and destinations during travel restrictions and bans, while ensuring safety at home; allowing museums and other tourist attractions to maintain audience engagement; and providing virtual tour-guiding jobs. COVID-19 began harming the global travel and tourism business in early 2020. This hurt Egypt's economy, which relies more on international tourism. Egypt's Ministry of Tourism and Antiquities launched the "Explore Egypt from Home" social media campaign in April to keep tourists interested during restricted cross-border movement (El-Said & Aziz, 2022).

2.2 Benefits and challenges for both businesses and consumers

Individuals typically categorize the benefits of AI into three dimensions: cost reduction, revenue enhancement, and improved customer experience. From a financial standpoint, AI was seen as a mechanism that could enhance operational efficiency, thereby yielding cost savings (Abuzaid, 2024). Notable examples include AI-driven electrical backup systems, chemical management systems, and motion detection systems that autonomously decrease electricity consumption. These examples are also presented from a sustainability standpoint, specifically how businesses could leverage AI to enhance energy efficiency or reduce water consumption, thereby reducing costs.

Notably, although the sustainability advantage was acknowledged, the predominant value was identified as cost reduction. A common third benefit of AI is improved customer experience. The adoption of AI would help the hotel deliver a more unique and customized experience to consumers. A system capable of providing this was seen as a good ROI and an effective way to create happy, loyal customers. This advantage clearly shows that AI is a basis on which hotels can become smart within the smart tourism ecosystem. One of the key issues raised was the integration of AI with existing technologies between hotels and customers. The individuals explained that hotels have been operating various systems over the years, often unrelated to one another. In addition, such systems can be old-fashioned, which creates an integration problem with modern technology that involves both personal and collective systems. At the same time, people stated that when guests' personal devices, including cell phones, are outdated, they might not be able to access or use some of the technologies the hotel introduced, particularly those aimed at improving the in-room experience (Mare et al., 2020).

2.3 Theoretical Frameworks

Technology Acceptance Model (TAM) and extensions (TAM2, UTAUT).

AI technology may reduce human error, increase efficiency by automating repetitive tasks, and predict dangers and take preventive steps through big data analysis. This chapter discusses how a construction company can leverage AI-based technologies to achieve these benefits. Construction enterprises need intuitive interfaces with productivity-boosting features, along with a well-crafted implementation strategy that respects corporate culture and staff morale, to integrate AI technology (Hussain et al., 2025). Environmental factors significantly affect end-user perceived usefulness (PU) and perceived ease of use (PEOU), which may benefit conservative organizations such as construction firms in South Korea, where the government is actively advancing and deploying AI-based technologies while promoting their integration into industrial applications (Rawashdeh et al., 2021). The aiding variables provided in this study should help construction firms use AI-based technology. AI-based technology would boost construction companies' efficiency and competitiveness.

TAM2 is an extension of the original Technology Acceptance Model developed by Venkatesh and Davis in 2000, incorporating external social elements that affect the behavioral intention to adopt new technology (Alwreikat et al., 2023).

The UTAUT theoretical model posits that technology usage is influenced by behavioral intention (Su & Chao, 2022). The perceived probability of technology adoption is contingent upon the direct Impact of four essential constructs: performance expectancy, effort expectancy, social influence, and facilitating factors. The influence of predictors is tempered by age, gender, experience, and the voluntariness of use. The UTAUT model has significantly contributed to academic literature. The approach delivers empirical insights into technology acceptance by juxtaposing leading theories, which often present conflicting or incomplete viewpoints. UTAUT indicates that the proposed parameters explain 70 percent of the variance in usage intention, providing superior predictive capability relative to other models assessing technological acceptance. The influence of certain constructs on personal and demographic variables illustrates the intricacy of the technological acceptance process, which depends on individuals' age, gender, and experience.

2.3.1 Diffusion of Innovations Theory (Rogers)

The diffusion of innovations theory was developed by E.M. Rogers, a communication theorist at the University of New Mexico, in 1962 (Wolf, 2022). The theory explains how a new idea passes through stages of adoption as different people participate in or begin using it. The main people in the diffusion of innovations theory are:

Innovators: Those who are open to risks and the first to try innovative ideas
Early adopters: People who are interested in trying modern technologies and establishing their utility in society.
Early majority: Those who pave the way for the use of innovation within mainstream society and are part of the general population.
Late majority: People who follow the early majority in adopting innovation as part of their daily life and are also part of the general population.
Laggards: People who lag the general population in adopting innovative products and innovative ideas.

2.3.2 Hofstede's Cultural Dimensions and Hall's High-Low Context Theory for cross-cultural behavior

Hofstede's Cultural Dimensions Theory explains cultural differences and business practices between civilizations (Magala et al., 2024). The framework helps distinguish country cultures, explain cultural traits, evaluate cultural influences on etiquette, and improve business and diplomatic communication. Hofstede's Cultural

Dimensions Theory was created in 1980 by Dutch management expert Geert Hofstede, who surveyed IBM's value variances across sectors in the 1960s and 1970s.

Anthropologist Edward T. Hall defined national communication patterns as high-context and low-context civilizations (Barmeyer, 2023). High-context cultures, mostly in Asia and Africa, value relationships and nonverbal communication. Outsiders find these cultures difficult to understand since meaning is contextualized and relationships are less apparent. In contrast, low-context societies, like the US and many European countries, value clear, direct speech. Personal achievements are valued over collective interactions, and relationships are temporary or purpose-driven. These concepts show how cultural standards impact communication and social systems in all civilizations. Understanding these differences enhances cross-cultural communication and sensitivity.

Figure 1. Conceptual Framework

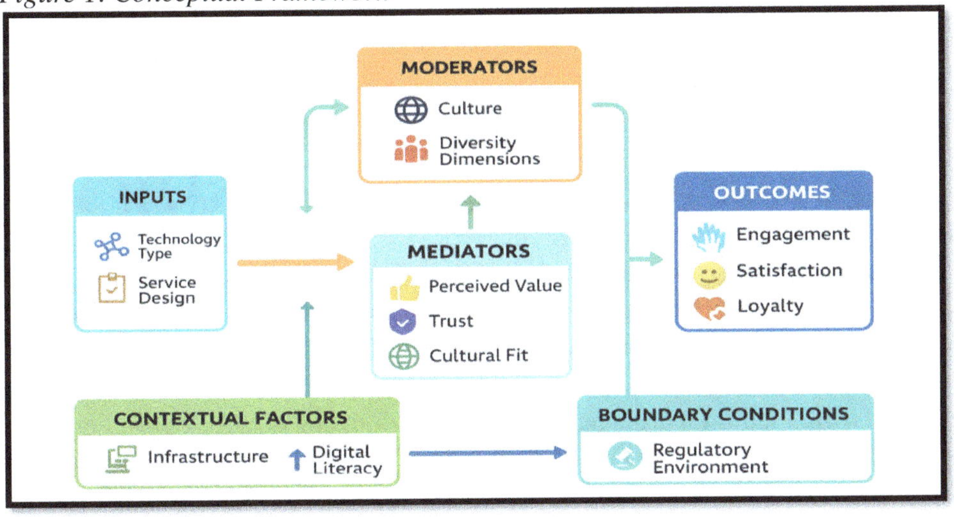

Source: Authors' compilations

2.4 Culture and Technology Use

Disregarding cultural norms when introducing modern technologies may lead to low acceptance, social unrest, or rejection. A culturally responsive strategy can improve technological integration and ensure the community benefits from and values technology. Understanding the cultural context is not just a matter of etiquette; it is a strategic need for anyone developing, promoting, or implementing modern technology. can create innovative, effective, and sustainable technology by understanding a culture's values, beliefs, and habits (Raihan et al., 2025). The collectivism-individualism conflict heavily influences technology adoption. Individualistic societies appreciate freedom, self-expression, and success. Empowering technologies, productivity tools, and self-promotion tools are bound to be popular.

2.5 Diversity in the Hospitality Workforce and Customer Base

2.5.1 Impact of multicultural staff on service delivery

The multicultural environment of a hotel requires a management approach that goes beyond the conventional approach (Skordoulis et al., 2024). Managers ought to be culturally agile and fluent in diverse cultures by adapting their management style. This requires them to be culturally informed and aware of cultural subtleties, and to enforce fair policies and practices for all their employees, regardless of their cultural orientations. The literature has revealed the significance of training and development programs in developing multicultural competency in hotel employees. Through these programs, professionals are provided with the skills to communicate and collaborate with peers and guests from diverse cultures in complex hospitality settings. Moreover, these approaches can contribute to better job performance, reduced employee turnover, and increased job satisfaction, which are essential in the demanding field of hotel administration.

Nevertheless, this also has a negative side since dealing with a multicultural workforce is a challenge that poses several challenges. The first is a communication barrier that may lead to misunderstanding and conflict. The other challenge is that employees and management might resist change, which could impede the adoption of effective multicultural management practices within the system. To overcome the multicultural challenges, the hotels should create a clear approach that includes the establishment of policies and procedures that reduce the likelihood of conflicts, the implementation of training programs that will help to improve cultural competence, and the establishment of leadership that will foster an inclusive culture (Burkiewicz and Knap-Stefaniuk, 2022).

This is not just a strategic consideration in terms of how the hotel is viewed by the public but must be integrated into all areas of hotel operations to achieve effectiveness. The increasing ethnic diversity in the hotel industry requires skillful management of intercultural relations. Hotels are at the center of most cultural interactions. They must be managed in a way that mitigates the problems associated with this diversity, thereby leveraging it to their strategic advantage. An inclusive culture can help hotels improve the quality of their services, make their employees happier, and, therefore, increase their competitiveness in the global market, while also building the multicultural competency of the working population.

2.6 Effects of different customer profiles on technology adoption strategies.

To increase the success and the payoff of AI and other technologies, companies are advised to consider the following aspects when developing change management strategies:

2.6.1 Planning effective communication.

An effective implementation of technology requires a comprehensive communication strategy to be designed before the implementation. This will involve using omni-channel communication strategies (e.g., site updates, live chat, emails, meetings) to inform users actively about new features and release dates. This will enable user interaction by ensuring that all users are prepared, regardless of the communication channels they choose.

2.6.2 Inclusive system testing and vetting.

During the evaluation and assessment of the system's functionality, usability, and intuitiveness, involve all relevant personnel before deployment. This helps avoid implementing a flawed system, which may tarnish initial impressions and lead to a loss of trust and of salespeople's participation in the organization at the beginning. KPMG addressed this potential concern by engaging a wide range of employees in system validation and user acceptance testing (UAT) during the rollout of our new CRM. This approach increased readiness to change and ensured that diverse insights, situations, and intergenerational perspectives were included and reflected in the system's functionality.

2.6.3. Intelligent teamwork and mentoring.

Use change networks to facilitate cross-seller learning to pair technologically competent sellers with less experienced sellers. This facilitates the spread of knowledge within the system and enables vendors to share personal stories, success stories, and ROI examples that can drive innovation and adoption.

KPMG has developed a coaching strategy within our CRM implementation, with specially qualified staff members assigned as CRM specialists who will act as key contacts within their respective business units (Morić et al., 2024). Such coaches provide support, coordinate informal meetings, and deliver technology training, which encourages a collaborative, informal learning environment. Within such a setting, the tangible benefits of technology can be demonstrated and realized, making its value more apparent to individuals who are unwilling to adopt the innovative approach. The comfort and acceptance of modern technology naturally increase across the business as more users highlight its benefits and how it can be used in real-world scenarios.

2.7 Influence of Culture on Technology Adoption

2.7.1 Cross-Cultural Consumer Behavior

The adoption of digital technologies in hospitality and cross-cultural settings requires a thorough understanding of local customs, mindsets, and expectations. This complexity is investigated in a study of mobile augmented reality (AR) in cultural heritage tourist sites. According to a study of behavioral intentions to adopt augmented reality (AR) in South Korea and the Republic of Ireland, the visual and hedonic qualities of AR apps are perceived differently across the two cultures. In high-power distance and collectivist societies, e.g., South Korea, dependence on social influence and the pleasurable qualities of augmented reality (AR) increase. This implies that the social aspect of technology adoption is significant in such cultures, and to succeed, technological advances should cater to this aspect.

Another study explains why small and medium companies (SMEs) in Taiwan have been able to leverage technology to participate in global supply chains in response to the Fourth Industrial Revolution (C.-L. Chen, 2020). The mentioned value creation strategies, ranging from improvements in digital product display features to the incorporation of cultural content design and online marketing, underscore the importance of the cultural aspect in the acceptance and implementation of digital innovations. These approaches not only involve technical adoption but also the incorporation of cultural and lifestyle attributes into products and services, which is a key element of integration into the global market.

2.8 Cultural Barriers

2.8.1 Language differences in user interfaces

Customized language models allow new ways of human-computer interaction within the tourism industry. Adopting a hybrid-augmented intelligence approach to human-artificial intelligence communication can be outlined on four levels of interaction between the Customer Assistant and the tourist, employee, business, and policymaker. Hybrid-augmented intelligence holds that the combination of human abilities and technology can create systems that will exploit the benefits of both, and thus achieve the results that would not be possible by either alone; this is the combination of human fine-tuning, mental dexterity, and moral reasoning with the computational efficiency, data processing, and pattern recognition of artificial intelligence. In the case of custom language models, this requires managers to pinpoint the use cases in their area of operation where an Assistant can answer satisfactorily, thereby guiding domain specialists to the most important aspects (J. Chen et al., 2024).

2.8.2 Perceived loss of delicate touch in tech-heavy services

Technology has posed numerous obstacles for the tourism business despite its various advantages. Travel organizations face difficulties in establishing distinct identities, mitigating cybercrime, and securing customer trust (Florido-Benítez, 2024). Moreover, the difficulties are exacerbated by financial constraints and the necessity for multichannel marketing in the marketplace. The industry has experienced a significant decline due to the COVID-19 pandemic. The issues are exacerbated by the need to integrate modern technology post-pandemic to ensure client safety.

2.8.3 Resistance due to traditional hospitality norms

The response to change is often emotional and may stem from factors not readily apparent to the change leader. Resistance to change may be mitigated and commitment to it enhanced by initially establishing clarity about the change, enabling team members to understand it. Understanding change is essential before team members are ready to embrace it. Secondly, acknowledging all emotional responses to change rather than disregarding them will facilitate the team's acceptance of new initiatives. Utilizing open communication channels and democratic decision-making may alleviate fear, feelings of loss, and powerlessness. Ultimately, establishing trust in the change leader's capacity to make judicious decisions and implement them effectively alleviates any concerns team members may harbor over the change initiative. The significance of the message regarding the shift is paramount, and the messenger's credibility is equally crucial for its acceptance (Tarofder et al., 2023).

2.9 Cultural Enablers

2.9.1 Customization and localization of app sites

Non-native English speakers often visit English websites because of lower prices or a wider product range. However, I prefer sites that are translated into their language, even if the translation is poor. Three-quarters of them will rely on machine translation to improve their understanding of the text. People who are fluent in English are eight times more likely to purchase on an English site. Some countries, such as the Netherlands, have a high percentage of English speakers (Şeyma & Cem, 2022).

On the other hand, the percentage is low in such countries as Thailand. The research revealed that non-English-fluent speakers are more tolerant of English-language sites than their non-English-fluent counterparts; however, they still tend to shop on sites in their native language. This poll showed that 90% of Internet users do not speak English. Among such individuals, 87 percent will not attempt to translate the English site into their native language (Gramley et al., 2020). People in the Middle East, Africa, and many Asian and Latin American countries often have low levels of English proficiency.

2.9.2 AI chatbots with multilingual capability

Artificial intelligence is a vital automation instrument. AI can identify the most effective texts for human or machine translation, and if machine translation is used, it can select the optimal translation engine. When human translation is required, it assembles a list of the most qualified linguists for the task and either forwards them to the project manager or instantly transmits the text to an approved human translator. The AI can identify several routine elements of the information that are non-translatable, such as phone numbers and ZIP codes, and evaluate them without consuming a translator's time (Xing, 2022). These tools improve translation quality and encompass technology such as document editors, termbases, and translation memories. A termbase is a collection of specific words or phrases that are translated in a particular manner within a given industry; for instance, in the translation sector, CAT refers to computer-aided translation. At Caterpillar, CAT stands for the company's name. A termbase allows the machine to translate the phrase precisely for the industry. Translation memory comprises a bank of sentences that are automatically reused when translating identical text. This conserves time and resources by eliminating the necessity for a human translator for these sentences.

2.9.3 Cultural branding strategies to promote trust.

Cultural heritage tourism requires branding to create a strong image and attract tourists (Chang and Chuang, 2021). It involves strategically communicating a destination's unique features and how it is projected as an attractive place to visit. Branding in the context of heritage tourism goes beyond the development of a logo or a catchy tagline. It extends much beyond that. A well-developed brand tells a story, which is the spirit and soul of a destination. It is a powerful tool that can evoke emotion, build trust, and make one destination stand out from its competitors. Imagine a tourist scrolling through their social media feed and seeing a beautifully designed advertisement for a cultural heritage site. The colors, images, and carefully chosen words all collide to give an impression of doubt and wonder. This is a demonstration of a strong brand's strength.

2. 10 Role of Diversity in Enhancing Consumer Engagement

2.10.1 Workforce Diversity and Technology Implementation

The presence of guests and workers from all backgrounds enriches the experience for everyone, fostering inclusivity and intrigue. It introduces novel concepts, diverse perspectives, and alternative modes of communication, all of which contribute to the authentic experiences clients seek.

2.10.2 Enhanced performance

Numerous studies indicate that diverse teams perform better. Teams with ethnic diversity are 36% more likely to exceed the industry median in profitability. They are 87% more likely to make superior selections because they tend to ask more questions, process information differently, and exhibit less blind adherence to the status quo (Stahl & Maznevski, 2021). Culturally diverse teams resolve issues more rapidly and exhibit greater innovation.

2.10.3 Enhanced service

Culturally diverse teams can deliver superior service to customers by using multiple languages, tailoring services and products to individual needs, and understanding cultural sensitivities in ways that homogeneous teams cannot. When someone from a different country or culture experiences that type of cross-cultural understanding, they are more likely to recommend it to a friend and become repeat customers.

2.10.4 Increased adaptability

The rapid evolution of the hospitality industry requires greater adaptability from teams to achieve optimal performance. Having diverse cultures, perspectives, and insights in our teams, particularly higher up the chain, can make our business more resilient and help us adapt more quickly.

2.10.5 Augmented corporate reputation.

Organizations, including culturally diverse teams, are perceived as innovative and socially responsible, enhancing their appeal to guests and potential recruits (Rabl et al., 2020). This can facilitate the attraction and retention of high-quality employees and enhance the brand's appeal to socially conscious consumers by training staff to manage tech-based queries across cultural contexts.

2.10.5.1 Set the stage.

Our staff may already feel burdened by the several new methodologies they have acquired during the past year. Cultural training may suggest to employees the presence of cultural challenges; thus, reframe the dialogue by promoting the program as an opportunity for enhanced mutual understanding. Promoting cultural training through a heart-and-minds campaign enables employees to comprehend its essential role in progress. Emphasize the benefits for them: enhanced communication, improved feedback, and increased empathy towards their peers. Do not implement the training prior to establishing a foundation and securing the support of employees and executives.

2.10.5.2 Listen

Without personnel present across all locations, departments, and silos, it is unfeasible to develop a comprehensive cultural training program that covers every topic. Feedback will serve as our primary source of information for identifying potential difficulties and developing our courses. Implementing anonymous surveys is an effective initial step that enables employees to articulate their experiences about cultural concerns. Upon collecting input, we will identify our employees' primary concerns, enabling us to devise highly targeted solutions that benefit both our team members and the firm.

2.10.5.3 Tell a story.

At ELM, we are deeply invested in storytelling, and for good reason: it is one of the most straightforward and effective methods for forging emotional connections between learners and information (Kang et al., 2020). Leverage the existing narrative from cultural training to enable learners to identify with the protagonist's role. Narrate an experience of being lost in translation from both perspectives, guiding learners via relatable scenarios. As previously mentioned, role-playing activities can transform a scenario into an entertaining way to practice the skills being acquired. This approach effectively captures emotions and encourages employees to focus more intently on potential solutions.

2.10.5.4 **Prioritize communication.**

Dedicate time or resources to only one aspect of cultural training. Communication underlies most cultural challenges within a global firm and serves as an appropriate starting point. After training our employees in culturally aware communication, we may enhance that foundation. Key topics for consideration in communication include:

- Common language barriers and the use of colloquialisms that may not translate well.
- Differences in cultural tones
- Body language
- Written communication policies
- Employees have already dealt with issues stemming from these topics. Gather feedback and develop training solutions to address them.

2.10.5.5 Focus on the bigger picture.

The global workforce is changing at a breakneck pace, and all learning is happening simultaneously.

2.11 Inclusive Design in Hospitality Technology

2.11.1 Accessibility for people with disabilities

There is an increasing demand to meet the needs of persons with disabilities (PwDs) in Malaysia (Jani et al., 2022). The adaptation of facilities to meet the needs of PwDs across diverse environments, including educational institutions, public transit, national parks, shopping malls, hotels, the tourism sector, mosques, and public buildings, has heightened awareness of PwDs. The hospitality sector has offered parking accommodation for those with disabilities. This parking space is usually designated with blue paint and a wheelchair emblem to facilitate accessibility for individuals with disabilities. DBKL states that anyone who parks without a PwD sticker will incur a fee.

2.11.2 Tech solutions for older vs. younger guests

Age-inclusive hospitality involves creating environments that are inviting and accessible to people of all ages. By understanding the needs of different age demographics, designing flexibility and adaptability, and integrating technology, hospitality companies can create age-inclusive experiences that elevate the guest experience. By adhering to best implementation practices, hospitality companies can ensure that age-inclusive design is both effective and sustainable.

2.11.3 Gender and socio-economic considerations

Gender equality constitutes one of the United Nations Sustainable Development Goals. Goal 5 of the 17 aims to "achieve gender equality and empower all women and girls." To achieve sustainable global development, it is imperative to address gender disparity, encompassing both social and digital inclusion. Consequently, digital design must prioritize gender inclusivity. Nonetheless, gender-inclusive design has obstacles and constraints. Examining hiring practices to intentionally foster greater diversity within teams, particularly when team members do not regard gender diversity as crucial, can impose challenges on organizations. Conversely, using instruments such as the Gender Inclusiveness Magnifier to evaluate the software's performance may compromise cost efficiency. Consequently, the concept of gender inclusiveness in design remains unrealized.

2.12 Diverse Consumer Segments

Digital technology strengthens hotel client ties and improves practical experiences. Social media, content, SEO, PPC, email, and online marketing are all part of digital marketing (A. Kumar et al., 2025). Hotels and restaurants used to attract guests through word of mouth and newspaper advertising. Digital media is becoming the primary way to attract guests, as it offers more engaging content and strengthens online relationships. Hotels can target different demographics and engage global clients through digital marketing. Visitors to hotels, restaurants, and huge events have remarkable experiences thanks to digital marketing. Social media reviews, comments, and ratings influence customers' decisions to visit hotels and restaurants, where digital networks are crucial to hospitality business promotion. These 8 proven strategies will help businesses stand out, attract customers, and drive measurable results in today's competitive landscape (Farida & Setiawan, 2022):

- Build a Strong Online Presence
- Boost Visibility with Search Engine Optimization (SEO)
- Engage Audiences with Content Marketing
- Amplify Reach with Pay-Per-Click (PPC) Ads
- Leverage Email Marketing for Conversions
- Dominate Social Media Platforms
- Explore Mobile Marketing and Apps
- Use Data Analytics for Continuous Improvement

2.13 Technology-Driven Consumer Engagement in a Multicultural Context

2.13.1 Engagement Tools as Mobile App-Based Programmes

Gamified loyalty programs should be readily available in the environments where customers frequently engage (Hwang & Choi, 2020). Mobile applications are increasingly the primary hub for loyalty programs. The primary causes are everyday digital habits, convenience, the expectation of instantaneous interactions, and readily available involvement. Users will anticipate it, and the r program must fulfill their expectations (Nilson & Stanny, 2023). Furthermore, it paves the way for other components and mechanisms that are crucial for the forthcoming discussion. This encompasses push notifications, in-app challenges for personalized rewards, and effortless tracking.

The long-term effects of AI-driven engagement approaches on client loyalty vary by industry and consumer niche. AI-driven personalization must be evaluated to determine whether it improves consumer experiences or alienates consumers due to data exploitation and reduced human interaction in brand engagements (Hua & Mankbadi, 2024). Despite these challenges, AI offers several marketing innovation alternatives. AI-driven analytics help companies predict customer preferences, improve marketing efforts, and provide unmatched Customization. Generative AI enables companies to create customized ads, email campaigns, and adaptable product proposals (Shu et al., 2020). Ethical, consumer, and regulatory compliance research gaps must be addressed as AI technologies evolve. Companies must balance AI's potential with responsible, honest, and egalitarian marketing (D. Kumar & Suthar, 2024).

2.14 Measuring Engagement

Accurate measurement is the first step to improvement. Here are the core metrics and tools that help track hotel guest satisfaction:

A. Internet Reviews and Social Media Surveillance.

Reviewing guest feedback on social channels and scanning the sites reveals the company's strengths and identifies areas for improvement. One critical review could indicate a recurring service problem. To stay connected, set up automated notifications and use analytics to track trends in guest sentiment.

B. Net Promoter Score (NPS)

A low score on a 0-10 scale indicates the likelihood that guests will recommend the hotel (Rahimi et al., 2022). An excellent NPS score is a strong indicator of customer loyalty and overall satisfaction. To monitor changes over time, regularly survey guests after their stays and compare the scores.

C. Guest Feedback Surveys

Direct surveys will provide information on the guest experience, including room quality and interactions with staff, and will give more specific insights into how to make the guest happier. To motivate people to respond, make surveys brief and combine multiple-choice and open-ended questions (Babo et al., 2020).

D. Repeat Guest Rate (RGR) and Average Length of Stay (ALOS).

RGR measures the percentage of repeat guests, whereas ALOS measures the length of stay (Kolodiziev et al., 2024). Big RGR and increased length of stay are indicators of trust and general satisfaction with services. Increase repeat visits by introducing loyalty programs and tracking changes in ALOS to enable upselling.

E. Employee Feedback

Periodic polls and staff communication channels can be used to spot internal problems. Satisfied employees will offer better service, which will have a direct impact on guest satisfaction. Concerns should be addressed early, such as holding monthly briefings or focus groups before affecting guests.

2.15 Cross-Cultural Engagement Strategies

2.15.1 Localized campaigns

Useful content localization involves converting digital content for other cultures to enhance brand relevance and market penetration (Okonkwo et al., 2023). The campaign adopted by Coca-Cola, called Share a Coke, in which the logo was replaced with famous first names globally, was a success (Salawu & Oyesomi, 2025). This campaign encouraged inclusion and consumer engagement through product customization, according to Forbes. It demonstrates how localization can increase brand loyalty worldwide. On the other hand, failures in content localization demonstrate the dangers of cultural blindness. Pepsi's slogan, "Pepsi Brings Back to Life," exemplifies a misconception rooted in cultural ignorance. This was severely criticized, as the Chinese translation of "Pepsi Brings Back to Life" quoted tales of ancestral ghosts, damaging the brand's image. This misinterpretation highlights the need for cultural knowledge and translation skills to convey information to global audiences.

In the present digital world, organizations face opportunities and challenges in reaching various audiences worldwide. Through the internet and digital technology, global trading is possible for all businesses. This interconnection brings new challenges, requiring businesses to communicate in the local and cultural languages of their target customers. Here, localization and global marketing are used. Global marketing and localization help companies align their digital presence with cultural, preference, and behavioral factors across countries. Localization is the process of making products, services, and marketing materials culturally relevant and attractive by aligning them with the values, traditions, customs, and practices of a culture. Intercultural communication is essential, as diverse cultures use different approaches and interpret language and gestures. Global markets position a company in multiple markets so its online activities can be international. The strategies apply to international companies, startups, and small enterprises with plans to grow. These approaches acknowledge cultural differences and that what may work in one location may not work in another. Nonetheless, their popularity and use are influenced by regional tastes. Digital marketers need to understand these differences. Local SEO facilitates global marketing by enhancing local search results, local visibility, customer trust, and reputation through positive client reviews (Oruganti et al., 2025). International marketers must be aware of the legislation and regulations in many countries. This industry requires a lot of learning, adherence to regulations, domestic partnerships, and a personalized approach to success.

Figure 2. Technology-Driven Consumer Engagement in a Multicultural Context

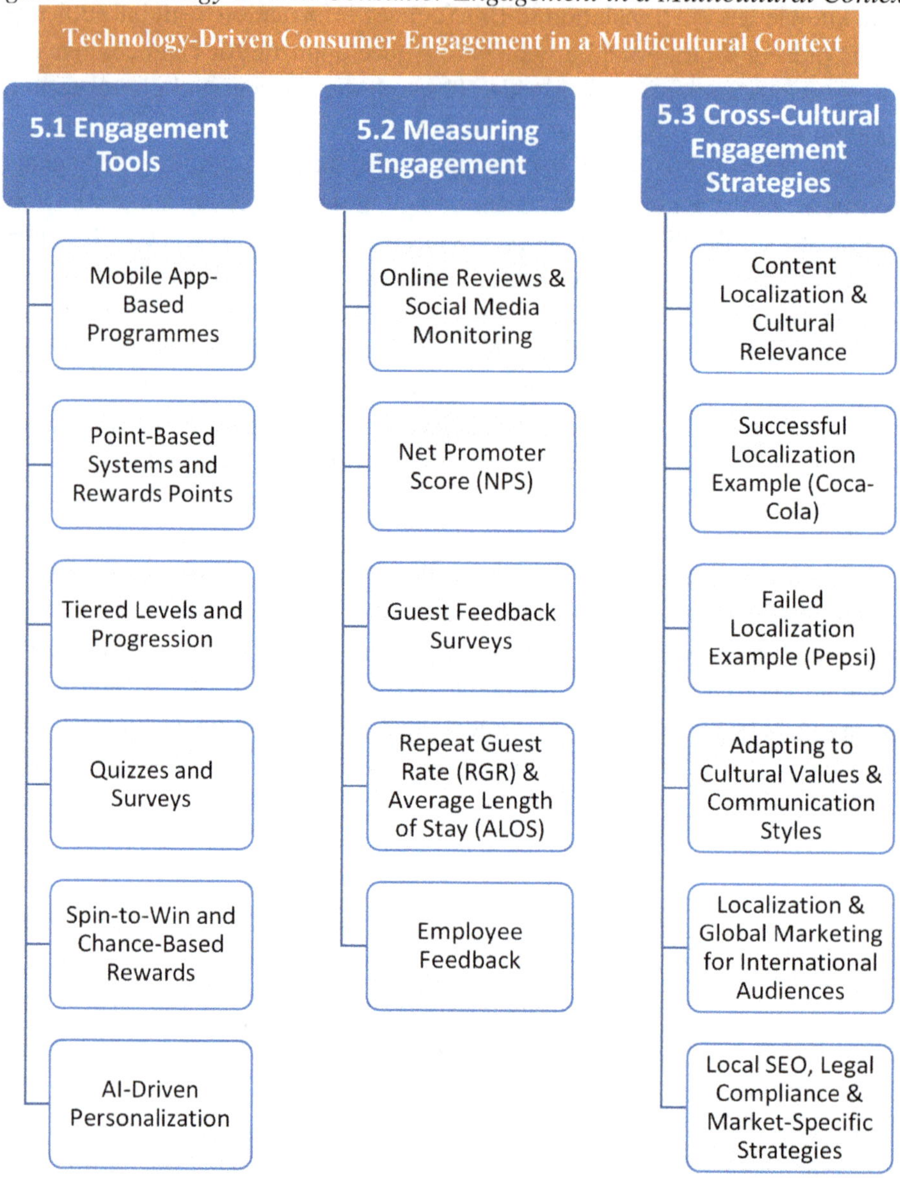

Source: Author's work

2.16 Challenges and Ethical Considerations

2.16.1 Digital divide: Exclusion of guests unfamiliar with technology

The EU 2020 Strategy emphasizes that smart growth—an economy built on information and innovation—is a critical development goal. While the deployment of broadband infrastructure and the resulting reduction of the digital divide between urban and peripheral areas are not the exclusive catalysts for improvement, remaining a prerequisite and a crucial element for progress. Operators have faced challenges in substantiating expenditures for broadband internet connectivity in remote regions. Indeed, owing to their low population density, this form of investment may be seen as less lucrative than in urban locales, hence necessitating public involvement. Achieving the Digital Agenda's objective of universal 30 Mb/s coverage poses considerable difficulties in rural areas of the EU (Rajatheva et al., 2020). In this regard, empirical knowledge of the economic effects of broadband and ultra-broadband serves as a crucial impetus for formulating public policy on broadband.

2.16.2 Privacy concerns: Cultural perceptions of data sharing

Current privacy research has focused on generic online environments, neglecting new aspects and use situations. There is little travel privacy research, notably empirical investigations on travelers' privacy concerns. Location-based social media privacy threats and violations, smart tourism tourists' privacy concerns, and mobile booking users' privacy concerns are among the few privacy studies in travel and tourism. Few studies have examined privacy and behavioral outcomes. Research on travel privacy and information disclosure is rare. In many applications, customers are asked for personal information many times. Airline companies, hotels, travel agents, mobile app developers, LBS, online review systems, social media sites, and others make these demands. Some suppliers, such as destination apps, are unfamiliar to travelers, while others, such as hotels working with online travel agents and tour operators, may share customer data. The merger of several internet travel companies may raise privacy concerns beyond those of online interactions. Disruptive technologies that link the physical and digital worlds to ease travel may also raise privacy concerns (Buhalis et al., 2023). Smart devices, sensors, and Internet-of-Things (IoT) technology in smart cities and tourism destinations collect real-time data, which may raise privacy concerns for travelers unfamiliar with local regulations or without their consent to data collection and use.

2.16.3 Bias in AI systems: Risks of excluding minority groups in personalization algorithms

AI in tourism and hospitality systems could have evolved into complex service automation, enhancing efficiency and personalization. Systematic underperformance of users belonging to certain identity groups due to algorithmic bias, or unintended patterns of uneven treatment associated with AI technologies, may occur when automated systems are used (Min, 2023). Past data indicating societal inequality, system designs that ostracize individuals, and a lack of sensitivity to user-specific environments may raise concerns about algorithmic bias. In the hospitality industry, personalization of visitors may rely on algorithms that focus on user factors such as name, appearance, and online behavior. Past studies in algorithmic fairness have demonstrated that performative logic can produce unequal treatment by coinciding system features with identity features such as language, accent, or gender, without necessarily being discriminated against by the processor. It is a technical and structural problem. Black-box algorithms leave consumers in the dark, preventing them from understanding and challenging unfair treatment. Hospitality AI systems can rank customers for access or visibility to a service or product without revealing the rationale, based on inferred loyalty, behavioral proxies, or spending patterns, and are implicitly biased. Personalization algorithms have led to digital redlining, providing poor service to people with similar attributes based on common language or identity, regardless of their usage behavior. Without an investigative approach, service experience differences may be difficult to identify, particularly when the differences are small but statistically significant. This demonstrates the strength of simulation-based models, which can generate artificial profiles and decision processes to detect biases in AI logic. These models will also be used to evaluate fairness in controlled settings before deploying these technologies in the hospitality sector, to identify potential risks and provide design solutions (Hu & Min, 2025).

2.17 Future Trends

2.17.1 Integration of cultural AI in hospitality

Cross-cultural service interactions are widely acknowledged as crucial for effective international hospitality management (Koc, 2020). Cultural intelligence, defined as the ability to function well in culturally different settings, has been established as an essential competency for employees to excel in serving a varied clientele. Numerous hospitality researchers have highlighted the significance of cultural intelligence in hospitality education and employee training. Nonetheless, there is limited knowledge regarding the efficacy and methodology of using AI and online platforms to efficiently train hotel personnel, despite recent identification of possible uses of AI to enhance hospitality employees' online training (Chung & Tan, 2025).

2.17.2 Rise of metaverse tourism and cultural Customization

The development of Metaverse hardware and software, computational algorithms, and content ecosystems is necessary to advance the Metaverse and cultural tourism (Go & Kang, 2023). Increase technical research and collaboration amongst domestic and foreign technology professionals to improve the Metaverse's core technological architecture. Increase software IP protection to motivate and organize software development specialists. The Metaverse, a virtual universe based on reality, replicates and even exceeds it with vast, intricate content. The construction of a comprehensive and sophisticated Metaverse is closely related to legal and ethical frameworks, ensuring that users experience pleasant surprises rather than painful ones (Koo et al., 2023). Initially, improve market oversight of the Metaverse to prevent monopolistic practices in its internal circulation and foster robust competition; then, increase personal data encryption and protection to reduce data exposure risk; and finally, integrate legal and ethical standards into the Metaverse's foundational framework to ensure its healthy and sustainable development while reducing addiction and illegal activity.

2.17.3 Increasing importance of culturally aware tech designers.

Digital products are certainly applicable worldwide; hence, they must be created with cultural differences in consideration. This adaptation involves not only the linguistic change but also the analysis of the cultural, social, legal, and technical aspects which are relevant to the target audience. Cross-Cultural issues are important, especially in digital products. Accessibility is a measure of how well a product or service can be used by a wide variety of people regardless of their ability, tastes, or conditions. The design of cross-cultural products is not that easy and requires thorough research, testing, and adjustments. However, it is a worthwhile effort, as it can increase customer satisfaction, engagement, loyalty, and retention, as well as increase market reach, revenue, and product reputation (Shahid et al., 2025). The importance of cross-cultural design is highlighted by six arguments:

Cultural context:

Impacts how users perceive and engage with products. For example, when designing a mobile app for a global audience, consider cultural differences in navigation patterns. In Western cultures, users expect a "hamburger menu" icon for navigation. However, in some Asian cultures, a "grid" or "list" icon may be more intuitive. Adapting the navigation design based on culture (Jeaheng et al., 2023).

Effective Communication:

Cultural nuances affect language, symbols, and visual cues. Thoughtful design transcends linguistic barriers, enabling effective communication across diverse audiences.

Aesthetics and Emotional Resonance:

Cultural aesthetics influence design choices. Colors, patterns, and shapes evoke different emotions in various cultures. Aligning aesthetics with cultural preferences enhances engagement.

Usability and Navigation:

Cultural differences impact how people navigate interfaces. Understanding cultural norms ensures intuitive usability, leading to better adoption and satisfaction. For example, when designing an Arabic-language site, ensure that navigation icons (such as "Home," "Search," and "Cart") are positioned on the right side of the header or menu bar. Users expect to find essential navigation elements there, such as reading from right to left.

Localization and Adaptation:

Tailoring design elements to specific cultures enhances relevance. Localized content, imagery, and functionality demonstrate respect for cultural diversity (Movono & Hughes, 2022). Some elements may have negative or offensive meanings in some cultures or may have no meaning at all.

Ethical Considerations:

Culturally sensitive design avoids stereotypes and promotes inclusivity. Ethical design respects diverse perspectives, fostering positive interactions.

3. CONCLUSION

The way the hospitality industry manages the interaction of culture, diversity, and technology is a challenge as well as an opportunity to engage more. The cultural norms, beliefs, and communication styles of the customers and employees that they bring to the table determine how they perceive and apply the technology-based services. Another reason that leads to the diversity of demands, needs, and expectations is that both consumers and employees belong to different backgrounds, which not only makes their operations more efficient by considering these cultural and demographic differences in planning their technologies, but also establishes stronger emotional relations with their customers. This is because hotels and other hospitality organizations consider these differences. will have to find a delicate balance to achieve this. Chatbots based on artificial intelligence, self-service kiosks, and mobile booking systems are only some of the technological innovations that can simplify and expedite the process. Nevertheless, these innovations must not be permitted to disrupt the warmth and the cultural sensitivity that make remarkable hospitality experiences. Technology should not be an obstacle but rather a bridge. Being more permissive of service and at the same time being able to acknowledge and value the differences in culture and develop tolerance.

To accomplish this goal, the introduction of technologies that are inclusive and compatible with a broad spectrum of cultural practices should be the number one priority for businesses within the hospitality industry. This involves producing user interfaces and communication tools that are compatible with various languages, the various behaviors that users have and integrating Cultural Customization in the way services are delivered. Also, it is crucial to train employees in the use and interpretation of technology in a manner that is sensitive to the diverse cultures that exist. In this manner, companies can create a high-tech and high-touch service environment that will attract more people to engage in it, while respecting the cultural diversity of their customers. The success of the hospitality industry in the face of the globalizing world will be dependent on its capacity to perceive diversity not as a problem that needs to be solved, but as an asset that can be celebrated. Technology can help to make more profound, meaningful connections with each guest, wherever they are.

REFERENCES

Abuzaid, A. N. (2024). AI-Driven Business Processes: Efficiency Gains, Cost Reductions, and Implications for Economic Performance. *2024 International Conference on Knowledge Engineering and Communication Systems (ICKECS)*, 1–5. DOI: 10.1109/ICKECS61492.2024.10617370

Alwreikat, A., Shehata, A. M. K., & Abu Zaid, M. K. (2023). Arab scholars' acceptance of informal scholarly communication tools: Applying the technology acceptance model 2 (TAM2). *Global Knowledge, Memory and Communication, 72*(1/2), 160–178. DOI: 10.1108/GKMC-04-2021-0070

Antwi, C. O., Ren, J., Owusu-Ansah, W., Mensah, H. K., & Aboagye, M. O. (2021). Airport Self-Service Technologies, Passenger Self-Concept, and Behavior: An Attributional View. *Sustainability (Basel), 13*(6), 3134. DOI: 10.3390/su13063134

Babo, R., V. Babo, L., T Suhonen, J., & Tukiainen, M. (2020). E- Assessment with Multiple-Choice Questions: A 5 Year Study of Students' Opinions and Experience. Journal of Information Technology Education: Innovations in Practice, 19, 001–029. DOI: 10.28945/4491

Barmeyer, C. (2023). Edward T. Hall: Kulturdimensionen als bewusstseinsschaffende Orientierungsrahmen. In Barmeyer, C., & Busch, D. (Eds.), *Meilensteine der Interkulturalitätsforschung* (pp. 37–68). Springer Fachmedien Wiesbaden., DOI: 10.1007/978-3-658-37924-7_2

Buhalis, D., Leung, D., & Lin, M. (2023). Metaverse as a disruptive technology revolutionizing tourism management and marketing. *Tourism Management, 97*, 104724. DOI: 10.1016/j.tourman.2023.104724

Burkiewicz, Ł., & Knap-Stefaniuk, A. (2022). Multiculturalism as a Challenge for Contemporary Leadership – an Analysis within the Context of Hotel Management in the 21st Century. *Perspektywy Kultury, 38*(3), 411–424. DOI: 10.35765/pk.2022.3803.25

Chang, T.-Y., & Chuang, Y.-J. (2021). Cultural Sustainability: Teaching and Design Strategies for Incorporating Service Design in Religious Heritage Branding. *Sustainability (Basel), 13*(6), 3256. DOI: 10.3390/su13063256

Chen, C.-L. (2020). Cross-disciplinary innovations by Taiwanese manufacturing SMEs in the context of Industry 4.0. *Journal of Manufacturing Technology Management, 31*(6), 1145–1168. DOI: 10.1108/JMTM-08-2019-0301

Chen, J., Liu, Z., Huang, X., Wu, C., Liu, Q., Jiang, G., Pu, Y., Lei, Y., Chen, X., Wang, X., Zheng, K., Lian, D., & Chen, E. (2024). When large language models meet personalization: Perspectives of challenges and opportunities. *Worldwide b, 27*(4), 42. DOI: 10.1007/s11280-024-01276-1

Chung, K. C., & Tan, P. J. B. (2025). Artificial intelligence and the Internet of Things to improve smart hospitality services. *Internet ofThings : Engineering Cyber Physical Human Systems, 31*, 101544. DOI: 10.1016/j.iot.2025.101544

El-Said, O., & Aziz, H. (2022). Virtual Tours to an End: An Analysis of Virtual Tours' Role in Tourism Recovery Post COVID-19. *Journal of Travel Research, 61*(3), 528–548. DOI: 10.1177/0047287521997567

Erciyes University (Turquía). Hovardaoglu, O., Calisir-Hovardaoglu, S., & Erciyes University (Turquía). (2024). Survival Strategies of Local SMTEs in the COVID-19 Pandemic in Heritage Tourism Sites in Turkey. *PASOS. Revista de Turismo y Patrimonio Cultural, 22*(1), 125–145. DOI: 10.25145/j.pasos.2024.22.008

Farida, I., & Setiawan, D. (2022). Business Strategies and Competitive Advantage: The Role of Performance and Innovation. *Journal of Open Innovation, 8*(3), 163. DOI: 10.3390/joitmc8030163

Florido-Benítez, L. (2024). The cybersecurity applied by online travel agencies and hotels to protect users' private data in smart cities. *Smart Cities, 7*(1), 475–495.

Go, H., & Kang, M. (2023). Metaverse tourism for sustainable tourism development: Tourism Agenda 2030. *Tourism Review, 78*(2), 381–394. DOI: 10.1108/TR-02-2022-0102

Gramley, S., Gramley, V., & Pätzold, K.-M. (2020). *A Survey of Modern English* (3rd ed.). Routledge., DOI: 10.4324/9780429300356

Hoyer, W. D., Kroschke, M., Schmitt, B., Kraume, K., & Shankar, V. (2020). Transforming the Customer Experience through New Technologies. *Journal of Interactive Marketing, 51*(1), 57–71. DOI: 10.1016/j.intmar.2020.04.001

Hu, Y., & Min, H. K. (2025). Information transparency, privacy concerns, and customers' behavioral intentions regarding AI-powered hospitality robots: A situational awareness perspective. *Journal of Hospitality and Tourism Management, 63*, 177–184. DOI: 10.1016/j.jhtm.2025.04.003

Hua, J., & Mankbadi, R. R. (2024). Prediction and Control of Broadband Noise Associated with Advanced Air Mobility—A Review. *Applied Sciences (Basel, Switzerland), 14*(18), 8455. DOI: 10.3390/app14188455

Huang, S., Liang, L. J., & Choi, H. C. (2022). How Failed in Context: A Text-Mining Approach to Understanding Hotel Service Failures. *Sustainability (Basel), 14*(5), 2675. DOI: 10.3390/su14052675

Hussain, A., Zhiqiang, M., Li, M., Jameel, A., Kanl, S., Ahmad, S., & Ge, B. (2025). The mediating effects of perceived usefulness and perceived ease of use on nurses' intentions to adopt advanced technology. *BMC Nursing, 24*(1), 33. DOI: 10.1186/s12912-024-02648-8 PMID: 39789568

Hwang, J., & Choi, L. (2020). Having fun while receiving rewards?: Exploration of gamification in loyalty programs for consumer loyalty. *Journal of Business Research, 106*, 365–376. DOI: 10.1016/j.jbusres.2019.01.031

Jani, R., Alias, A. A., & Tumin, M. (2022). Persons with disabilities' education and quality of life: Evidence from Malaysia. *International Journal of Inclusive Education, 26*(8), 753–765. DOI: 10.1080/13603116.2020.1726511

Jeaheng, Y., Al-Ansi, A., Chua, B.-L., Ngah, A. H., Ryu, H. B., Ariza-Montes, A., & Han, H. (2023). Influence of Thai Street Food Quality, Price, and Involvement on Traveler Behavioral Intention: Exploring Cultural Difference (Eastern versus stern). *Psychology Research and Behavior Management, 16*, 223–240. DOI: 10.2147/PRBM.S371806 PMID: 36726699

Kang, J., Hong, S., & Hubbard, G. T. (2020). The role of storytelling in advertising: Consumer emotion, narrative engagement level, and word-of-mouth intention. *Journal of Consumer Behaviour, 19*(1), 47–56. DOI: 10.1002/cb.1793

Koc, E. (2020). *Cross-Cultural Aspects of Tourism and Hospitality: A Services Marketing and Management Perspective* (1st ed.). Routledge., DOI: 10.4324/9781003018193

Kolodiziev, O., Dorokhov, O., Shcherbak, V., Dorokhova, L., Ismailov, A., & Figueiredo, R. (2024). Resilience Benchmarking: How Small Hotels Can Ensure Their Survival and Growth during Global Disruptions. *Journal of Risk and Financial Management, 17*(7), 281. DOI: 10.3390/jrfm17070281

Koo, C., Kwon, J., Chung, N., & Kim, J. (2023). Metaverse tourism: Conceptual framework and research propositions. *Current Issues in Tourism, 26*(20), 3268–3274. DOI: 10.1080/13683500.2022.2122781

Korteling, J. E., van de Boer-Visschedijk, G. C., Blankendaal, R. A. M., Boonekamp, R. C., & Eikelboom, A. R. (2021). Human versus Artificial Intelligence. *Frontiers in Artificial Intelligence, 4*, 622364. DOI: 10.3389/frai.2021.622364 PMID: 33981990

Kumar, A., Singh, T., Kumar, D., & Sharma, N. (2025). Mobilizing Social Media Marketing by Email Marketing and Paid Advertising (PPC) in Online Marketing 6.0. In Wongmahesak, K., Karim, F. B., & Wongchestha, N. (Eds.), *Practical Strategies and Case Studies for Online Marketing 6.0* (pp. 165–184). IGI Global Scientific Publishing., DOI: 10.4018/979-8-3373-2058-8.ch009

Kumar, D., & Suthar, N. (2024). Ethical and legal challenges of AI in marketing: An exploration of solutions. *Journal of Information. Communication and Ethics in Society*, *22*(1), 124–144. DOI: 10.1108/JICES-05-2023-0068

Li, C., Liang, L., Fryer, L. K., & Shum, A. (2024). The use of leaderboards in education: A systematic review of empirical evidence in higher education. *Journal of Computer Assisted Learning*, *40*(6), 3406–3442. DOI: 10.1111/jcal.13077

Magala, S., Erten-Buch, C., Bell, R.-M., & Claes, M.-T. (Eds.). (2024). *Hofstede matters*. Routledge Taylor & Francis Group., DOI: 10.4324/9781003410348

Mare, S., Roesner, F., & Kohno, T. (2020). Smart Devices in Airbnbs: Considering Privacy and Security for both Guests and Hosts. *Proceedings on Privacy Enhancing Technologies. Privacy Enhancing Technologies Symposium*, *2020*(2), 436–458. DOI: 10.2478/popets-2020-0035

Min, A. (2023). Artificial Intelligence and Bias: Challenges, Implications, and Remedies. *Journal of Social Research*, *2*(11), 3808–3817. DOI: 10.55324/josr.v2i11.1477

Morić, Z., Dakic, V., Djekic, D., & Regvart, D. (2024). Protection of Personal Data in the Context of E-Commerce. *Journal of Cybersecurity and Privacy*, *4*(3), 731–761. DOI: 10.3390/jcp4030034

Movono, A., & Hughes, E. (2022). Tourism partnerships: Localizing the SDG agenda in Fiji. *Journal of Sustainable Tourism*, *30*(10), 2318–2332. DOI: 10.1080/09669582.2020.1811291

Nilson, L. B., & Stanny, C. J. (2023). *Specifications Grading: Restoring Rigor, Motivating Students, and Saving Faculty Time* (1st ed.). Routledge., DOI: 10.4324/9781003447061

Okonkwo, I., Mujinga, J., Namkoisse, E., & Francisco, A. (2023). Localization and Global Marketing: Adapting Digital Strategies for Diverse Audiences. *Journal of Digital Marketing and Communication*, *3*(2), 66–80. DOI: 10.53623/jdmc.v3i2.311

Oncioiu, I., Anton, E., Ifrim, A. M., & Mândricel, D. A. (2022). The Influence of Social Networks on the Digital Recruitment of Human Resources: An Empirical Study in the Tourism Sector. *Sustainability (Basel)*, *14*(6), 3693. DOI: 10.3390/su14063693

Oruganti, S. K., Karras, D. A., Thakur, S., Chaithanya, J. K., Metta, S., & Lathigara, A. (Eds.). (2025). *Digital Transformation and Sustainability of Business* (1st ed.). CRC Press., DOI: 10.1201/9781003606185

Pholsook, T., Ramjan, S., & Wipulanusat, W. (2025). Enhancing airport services: Data-driven analysis of passenger satisfaction and service quality in Southeast Asia. *Engineering Management in Production and Services*, *17*(2), 37–62. DOI: 10.2478/emj-2025-0011

Rabl, T., Del Carmen Triana, M., Byun, S.-Y., & Bosch, L. (2020). Diversity Management Efforts as an Ethical Responsibility: How Employees' Perceptions of an Organizational Integration and Learning Approach to Diversity Affect Employee Behavior. *Journal of Business Ethics*, *161*(3), 531–550. DOI: 10.1007/s10551-018-3849-7

Rahimi, R., Thelwall, M., Okumus, F., & Bilgihan, A. (2022). Know r guests' preferences before they arrive at r hotel: Evidence from TripAdvisor. *Consumer Behavior in Tourism and Hospitality*, *17*(1), 89–106. DOI: 10.1108/CBTH-06-2021-0148

Raihan, M. M. H., Subroto, S., Chowdhury, N., Koch, K., Ruttan, E., & Turin, T. C. (2025). Dimensions and barriers for digital (in)equity and digital divide: A systematic integrative review. *Digital Transformation and Society*, *4*(2), 111–127. DOI: 10.1108/DTS-04-2024-0054

Rajatheva, N., Atzeni, I., Bicais, S., Bjornson, E., Bourdoux, A., Buzzi, S., D'Andrea, C., Dore, J.-B., Erkucuk, S., Fuentes, M., Guan, K., Hu, Y., Huang, X., Hulkkonen, J., Jornet, J. M., Katz, M., Makki, B., Nilsson, R., Panayirci, E., . . . Xu, W. (2020). *Scoring the Terabit/s Goal: Broadband Connectivity in 6G* (Version 2). arXiv. DOI: 10.48550/ARXIV.2008.07220

Rawashdeh, A. M., Bakheet Elayan, M., Alhyasat, W., & Dawood Shamout, M. (2021). Electronic human resources management perceived usefulness, perceived ease of use and continuance usage intention: the mediating role of user satisfaction in jordanian hotels sector. *International Journal of Qualitative Research*, *15*(2), 679–696. DOI: 10.24874/IJQR15.02-20

Salawu, A., & Oyesomi, K. (Eds.). (2025). *Marketing Communication in African Languages*. Routledge.

Şeyma, Y., & Cem, B. (2022). An Overview of the Structure of English Language Teaching Programs in the Netherlands, Austria, Denmark, Singapore, Norway, and Turkey: The Countries Ranking Among the Top Five in EF Proficiency Index. *I-Manager's Journal on English Language Teaching*, *12*(4), 1. DOI: 10.26634/jelt.12.4.18821

Shahid, S., Husain, R., Islam, J. U., & Hollebeek, L. D. (2025). Brand love and customer brand engagement for masstige: A cross-cultural perspective. *Journal of Product and Brand Management, 34*(4), 545–561. DOI: 10.1108/JPBM-07-2024-5370

Shin, D., Chotiyaputta, V., & Zaid, B. (2022). The effects of cultural dimensions on algorithmic news: How do cultural value orientations affect how people perceive algorithms? *Computers in Human Behavior, 126*, 107007. DOI: 10.1016/j.chb.2021.107007

Shu, J., Cao, M., Zhang, M., Wang, X., Cao, W., Fang, X., & Cao, M. (2020). Molecular Patching Engineering to Drive Energy Conversion as Efficient and Environment-Friendly Cell toward Wireless Por Transmission. *Advanced Functional Materials, 30*(10), 1908299. DOI: 10.1002/adfm.201908299

Skordoulis, M., Patsatzi, O., Kalogiannidis, S., Patitsa, C., & Papagrigoriou, A. (2024). Strategic Management of Multiculturalism for Social Sustainability in Hospitality Services: The Case of Hotels in Athens. *Tourism and Hospitality, 5*(4), 977–995. DOI: 10.3390/tourhosp5040055

Stahl, G. K., & Maznevski, M. L. (2021). Unraveling the effects of cultural diversity in teams: A retrospective of research on multicultural work groups and an agenda for future research. *Journal of International Business Studies, 52*(1), 4–22. DOI: 10.1057/s41267-020-00389-9 PMID: 33487775

Su, C.-Y., & Chao, C.-M. (2022). Investigating Factors Influencing Nurses' Behavioral Intention to Use Mobile Learning: Using a Modified Unified Theory of Acceptance and Use of Technology Model. *Frontiers in Psychology, 13*, 673350. DOI: 10.3389/fpsyg.2022.673350 PMID: 35651564

Talukder, M. B. (2024). Implementing Artificial Intelligence and Virtual Experiences in Hospitality. In Manohar, S., Mittal, A., Raju, S., & Nair, A. J. (Eds.), *Advances in Hospitality, Tourism, and the Services Industry* (pp. 145–160). IGI Global., DOI: 10.4018/979-8-3693-2019-8.ch009

Talukder, M. B. (2024). Implementing Artificial Intelligence and Virtual Experiences in Hospitality. In Innovative Technologies for Increasing Service Productivity (pp. 145-160). IGI Global. https://doi.org/DOI: 10.4018/979-8-3693-2019-8.ch009

Talukder, M. B. (2025). Climate change adaptation strategies for a tourism destination: A study of Kuakata beach. *Acta Scientiarum Polonorum. Administratio Locorum, 24*(1), 165–179. DOI: 10.31648/aspal.10073

Talukder, M. B. (2025). Current Trends and Future Research Directions on Eco-Friendly Stages of the Hotel Industry. *RPER*, (71), 7–18. DOI: 10.59072/rper.vi71.695

Tarofder, A. K., Haque, A., Nawaz, N., Raisal, I., Musah, A. A., & Kassim, M. D., A. A. (. (2023). Determinants of instant messenger (IM) adoption and its effect on team performance: Mediating role of knowledge creation and quality communication. *PLoS One*, *18*(11), e0289168. DOI: 10.1371/journal.pone.0289168 PMID: 37939130

Wolf, C. (2022). Diffusion of Innovations: Von Everett M. Rogers (1962). In Spiller, R., Rudeloff, C., & Döbler, T. (Eds.), *Schlüsselrke: Theorien (in) der Kommunikationswissenschaft* (pp. 151–170). Springer Fachmedien Wiesbaden., DOI: 10.1007/978-3-658-37354-2_10

Xing, H. (2022). Application Study of AI-pored Non-translatables Function in Computer-aided Translation. *Proceedings of the 2022 5th International Conference on Education Technology Management*, 104–109. DOI: 10.1145/3582580.3582597

Zhang, F., & Graham, D. J. (2020). Air transport and economic growth: A review of the impact mechanism and causal relationships. *Transport Reviews*, *40*(4), 506–528. DOI: 10.1080/01441647.2020.1738587

Chapter 13
Hyper-Personalized M-Tourism Services and Customer Experience Value:
An AI-Enhanced Analytical Model

Badr Bentalha
http://orcid.org/0000-0003-1339-542X
National School of Business and Management, Sidi Mohammed Ben Abdellah University, Morocco

Lhoussaine Alla
http://orcid.org/0000-0002-7238-1792
National School of Applied Sciences, Sidi Mohammed Ben Abdellah University, Morocco

Rachid Boudri
http://orcid.org/0009-0009-6281-429X
Euromed Business School, Morocco

ABSTRACT

The trend toward the widespread use of mobile technologies during tourist stays raises questions about the appropriateness and effectiveness of such practices in terms of tourist experiences and satisfaction with their stay in a given destination. Tourists are enthusiastic about the widespread use of various mobile technologies to prepare, carry out, and remember their trips, and their reasons for doing so are many and varied. To what extent does the use of m-tourism services, particularly mobile services for guidance, organization, and localized information search, pro-

DOI: 10.4018/979-8-3373-9159-5.ch013

mote the development of the quality of tourist experiences, and thus improve the overall perceived value of their stay? From a practical standpoint, we aim to inform tourism professionals about the characteristics their mobile services should have in order to improve the tourist experience and thus maximize customer satisfaction.

INTRODUCTION

The internet has gradually become the preferred source of information for tourists before, during, and after their trips. Increasingly sophisticated applications, equipped with richer features, offer increasingly diverse and real-time updated content, supported by ever-improving technologies. All of these elements and functionalities now allow internet users to better plan their journeys or stays (Gritta & Calabrese, 2023). This digital information revolution for the customer has impacted all service providers in the tourism sector, whether commercial or institutional. Various local stakeholders in tourist destinations have made significant efforts to adapt their operations and services: creating digital databases of tourism offerings, developing and updating websites, implementing online booking services, utilizing web marketing, establishing a presence on social media, and so on.

Mobile tourism (M-Tourism), the common term for the use of mobile technologies in the tourism sector, represents a significant challenge for industry professionals (Idate & Kanopee, 2011; Islam et al., 2024). Recent years have seen a real surge in mobile service offerings and their uses: offerings from major travel and tourism operators, from pure-play information mediation companies, whether or not they specialize in tourism; offerings from tourist destinations and local service providers and businesses. The use of smartphones for tourism has become deeply ingrained in travelers' behavior. In 2024, 71% of French people used their smartphones to plan or book their trips and leisure activities, compared to only 33% who took their laptops on vacation a decade ago. Internationally, and in 2023, 48% of travelers used their mobile devices to examine destinations, 47% to relate transportation and housing prices, and 40% to book flights and hotels (Raffour Interactif, 2015). The usage of portable services for tourism is undergoing significant progress. Mobile manipulators pursue information about tourist destinations, and 52% use them to discovery locations to visit or circuit ideas (CCM Benchmark, 2015). The practice of mobile procedures has become a vital fragment of the tourism experience worldwide (Skyscanner, 2023). This trend is part of a broader movement towards the dematerialization of booking practices: 65% of all tourism bookings were made online in 2023, 35% of which were made via mobile devices (Euromonitor International, 2023). Economically, the global mobile travel booking market touched $228 billion in 2024, with projections exceeding $526 billion by 2032 (Oysterlink, 2025). Such phenomena can be traced to the theoretical roots of Davis's TAM (1989). According to this approach, perceived usefulness is the strongest predictor of technology adoption intention followed by perceived ease of use. A newly published meta-analysis indicates that tourist acceptance of mobile applications is significantly associated with two core constructs of TAM (perceived usefulness and ease of use), and these constructs further condition visitor satisfaction and loyalty (Li et al., 2024).

After consideration of the tourists' motivation and their interest in the use of mobile technology to plan, perform and report the travel experience (Eriksson & Strandvik, 2009). In the pre-departure phase, as real-time comparison of transport and accommodation offers, one can add consultation to peer reviews on collaborative platforms, the use of AI tools to design custom itineraries and advance booking of cultural and gastronomic experiences, all of which are shaping novel travel preparation routines. When people travel, mobile devices become the primary source of the tourist experience and are utilized for geolocation-based navigation, instant translation, contactless payment, purchasing transportation tickets, and obtaining digital passes that are used for cultural events, such as tickets to a museum. Then, the smartphone also fulfills memorization and socialization dimensions that go beyond instrumental use. All of these usages reaffirm the mobile technology as the structuring element for the whole contemporary tourist experience chain. Nevertheless, despite some research (Lemoine & Salvadore, 2018; Kurgun et al., 2018; Wang et al., 2012), the issue of how to assess the effectiveness of these services and its consequences on tourist experience and their general perception of value for money during the stay is rather unexplored.

To what extent does hyper-personalized m-tourism services, enhanced by artificial intelligence, particularly in terms of contextual guidance, adaptive trip planning and real-time geolocation information recommendations, contribute to improving the quality of the international tourist's experience, and therefore to increase the overall perceived value of their trip?

Providing answers to this question is of both theoretical and managerial interest. From an academic perspective, the first step is to develop research dedicated to mobile tourism (m-tourism), and particularly m-tourism services, notably Location-Based Services (LBS), in relation to the tourist experience and the overall value perceived by the customer. Secondly, we will focus on how the use of mobile technologies impacts this perceived value of the tourist experience. From a practical standpoint, we aim to inform tourism professionals about the characteristics their mobile services should possess in order to improve the tourist experience and thus maximize customer satisfaction. We focus on proposing a theoretical analysis model that highlights the impact of using m-tourism services on the perceived value of a tourist stay, using experiential quality as an intervening variable and user predisposition as a moderating variable.

First, we will establish the theoretical framework used to understand the relationship between hyper personalization, artificial intelligence, and the perceived value of the mobile tourism experience. Second, we will present the methodology used to empirically test the proposed analytical model. We will justify the choice of a quantitative methodology using a questionnaire directed to international tourists who use mobile services, specify the sampling methods, the measurement instruments for the selected constructs, and the data analysis techniques employed. Finally, third, we will present and discuss the results of this empirical analysis. We will assess the extent to which AI-driven hyper personalization actually influences the quality of the experience and the perceived value of the trip, before comparing these results with existing literature and outlining their managerial implications for mobile tourism stakeholders.

1. THE THEORETICAL AND CONCEPTUAL FRAMEWORK: MOBILE TOURISM AND THE TOURIST EXPERIENCE

1.1. Mobile tourism: an arsenal of technology at the service of tourism

Since 2009, there has been significant momentum around mobile services from major travel and tourism operators, as well as from pure-play information providers, whether or not they specialize in tourism. While mobile usage for tourism is still not widespread, it is benefiting from a curiosity factor. It should gradually become integrated into users' travel processes, but in different ways depending on the context and user profile.

According to Idate & Kanopee (2011, p. 4), m-tourism is "*the common term for the use of mobile technologies in the tourism sector*." Unlike *e-tourism*, which encompasses all online sales and promotion of tourism products, mobile tourism, or *m-tourism,* is a portmanteau of "mobile" and "tourism." Following on from e-tourism, m-tourism includes all sales and promotional activities for tourism products conducted via mobile phones. While tourists' use of such mobile technologies certainly provides some answers to their needs in terms of information, guidance, and organization, the diversity of behaviors and profiles makes it difficult to identify a general pattern of mobile service usage, unlike what has been observed on the web, which remains fixed for both information gathering and booking. First, business travelers will adopt practical features on a massive scale, through services offered by providers, tour operators, and specialized information intermediaries. Independent leisure travelers, on the other hand, are expected to have a more nuanced approach, with some using only basic geolocation functions, while others will expand their use to include multimedia travel guides and social networks. They will primarily use major information portals and social media, and to a lesser extent, tourist websites and tourist offices. Thus, package tour customers are less interested in mobile services, unless tour operators and partner online agencies offer personalized travel itineraries. Finally, usage by foreign tourists should be limited by pre-downloading applications that do not require an internet connection on-site and by using free or reasonably priced Wi-Fi hotspots.

Regardless of its use, mobile technology is not intended to replace other information and distribution channels, but rather to complement them effectively: real-time access, personalization, and customer loyalty (Bourliataux-Lajoinie & Rivière, 2013; El Biyaali et al., 2025). Developments in mobile applications generate new opportunities, such as last-minute bookings, and allow for improvements in showcasing offers.

Tourism operators and information intermediaries have clearly understood this trend and are naturally positioning themselves on both platforms. Regardless of their position in the value chain, the operators are generally the same on both desktop and mobile web. Some players may appear on mobiles, but they must then quickly offer a desktop extension and are therefore present on both types of channels.

Tourism providers and operators should deploy mobile services without changing their business model, that is, by integrating service costs into distribution fees, but by leveraging mobile sensors and service personalization capabilities (Kurgun et al., 2018). Consequently, a range of mobile technologies (Figure 1) can be used by tourism market players depending on the nature of their usage motivation.

Figure 1. Mobile tourism tools

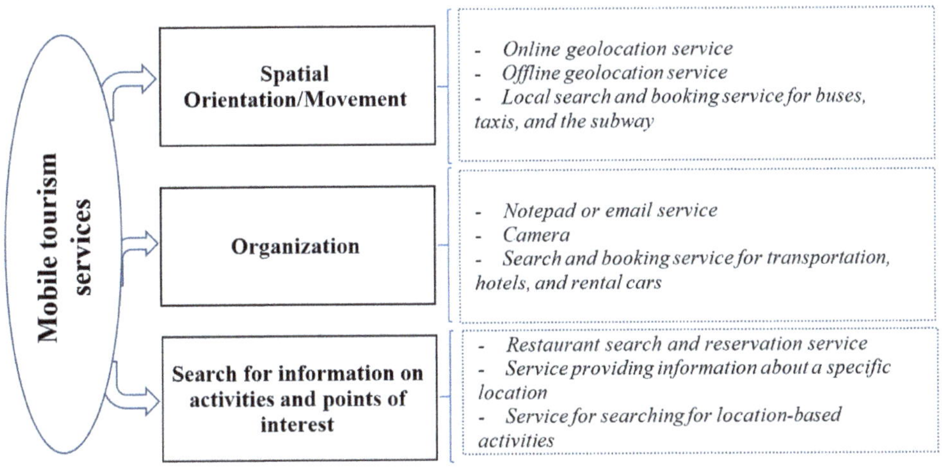

Source: Inspired by Lemoine and Salvadore (2018)

The features offered by mobile technologies make it possible to support the tourist during all phases of their trip, from preparation to online sharing, "before/during/after" (Table 1).

Table 1. The functionalities of mobile technologies in tourism

Mobile services used	Proposed by	Features
Before your stay: inspire ... plan ... book...		
- Information search/price and availability comparison - Booking of the tourist service and possible modification - Real-time information on any changes to your trip - Loyalty program providing access to discounts	- Carriers and tour operators are the main players able to offer this type of service before the stay (last-minute purchases, for example).	- Discover a destination through photos published by one of its community members. - Learn about the attractions of a destination by checking out its fan page or dedicated group. - Select your accommodation based on reviews left by previous travelers
During the stay: reassure ... guide...		
- Information on surrounding points of interest - Locate nearby hotels or restaurants using the tool's GPS function. - Access to enriched content (photos/videos/augmented reality) to discover the destination's heritage	- hoteliers, restaurateurs or managers of cultural and leisure facilities, who can interact directly with tourists via mobile. - Local public actors can, for their part, bring together all of these services to give them greater visibility during the stay.	- Share your experience live with your community by posting photos on your profile - Register your presence in certain locations to benefit from special offers - Make reservations and transactions (social shopping)
After the stay: Evaluate... Share... Remember...		
- Evaluate the stay experience - Express your level of satisfaction with your stay - Sharing your tourist experience - Recommend or advise against the tourist destination	- Social networks - Blogs and forums - The platforms - Booking websites...	- Contribute to the promotion of the destination by submitting your review online - Inspiring future travels among members of his community through photos posted during the trip

Source: Adapted from Idate & Kanopee (2011)

From this perspective, the evolution of digital tourism can be summarized by the acronym "SO-LO-MO" thus integrating the three fundamental conditions for success in the promotion and marketing strategy of a tourism product (Table 2).

Table 2. Summary of the digital evolution of tourism

Tourism must be ***SOcial...***	From now on, tourists want to actively participate in the promotion of a tourism product and become ambassadors for it within their community.
Tourism must be ***LOcal...***	What can I do, where I am, when I am there? The geolocated tourist offer must be accessible and consumable immediately.
Tourism must be ***MObile...***	To leverage all the functionalities of mobiles in order to facilitate travel, increase the consumption of tourism products and enrich the on-site experience.

Source: Adapted from Idate & Kanopee (2011)

To this end, Lemoine & Salvadore (2018) identified three categories of mobile service uses (LBS) (Table 3).

Table 3. Uses of mobile tourist services

Service Categories	**Uses**
Spatial orientation/ Travel	- Search for a place, an address, a route - Looking at plans, maps - Find out about transport options: buses/subways/taxis - Buy a transport ticket
Organization and coordination	- Use the notepad/email to find a place again, to remember a site to visit - Record your schedule and points of interest - Book accommodation (hotel, campsite, etc.)
Search for localized information on activities and points of interest	- Search/book at a restaurant or nearby shop - Search for nearby deals (restaurants, shops, events) - Use a service/application dedicated to the location (application for a museum, a city, etc.) - Search for activities and places to visit nearby - Buy tickets for a visit or event - Use a tourist guide on your smartphone (Petit Futé, etc.)

Source: Lemoine & Salvadore (2018, p.6)

Ultimately, mobile devices represent a new channel for disseminating tourism offerings, allowing businesses to reach a wider and more diverse clientele. However, while a presence in the mobile tourism market is already essential, other communication channels should not be neglected.

1.2. The Tourist Experience: An Ambiguous Reality

Tourist experience, as (Prebensen et al., 2014; Decroly, 2015; Wang et al., 2023) under thoroughly in the literature, appears to be a multidimensional concept that entails a variety of travel contexts. Scholars have studied it via the perspective of solo versus family travel (Kokkinou et al., 2022), culturally inspired travel (Matteucci,

2015; Wasela, 2023), in a rural type accommodation, such as farm stay (Qiao et al., 2024) or standardized hospitality facilities (Cinotti, 2015), in city adventures (Simon, 2015), road tripping (Saunders et al., 2013; Flügel et al., 2022), wellness practices, including spa tourism (Panchal, 2013) and intergenerational (Major & McLeay, 2012). A commonality appears to bind these apparently different events; each has its own formative potential as a true experiential event.

What is apparent from this body of cross-sectional research is that in order to fully grasp the tourist experience in any situation, a number of contextual variables that are deeply nested within each other must be taken into account, which combine to form what might be called a tourist situation. These include, in particular, the space and time dimensions, which have to be analyzed together, as well as the social relations of traveling, developing travel-related social relations and being influenced by these relations (Hécate Vergopoulos, 2016).

At once constituted by and constituting, mediated and immediate, singular and communal, the experience of the tourist is, by any standard, a stupendously complex empirical entity. Equally perplexing is that, although there are recognizable objective elements to this, itself is purely subjective and therefore difficult to perceive (Fijalkow et al., 2015). Its subjectivity is due, in part, to its highly individualized and idiosyncratic nature, and in part, and perhaps more importantly, to the very basic assumption that any experience presupposes an experiencing subject (Henning, 2012; Singh et al., 2022).

The diffusion of use models identifies the perceived impact of uses on daily life and the perceived indispensability of technology as two consequences of technology use (Shih et al., 2013). Literature focusing on usage in the tourism sector enriches our understanding of the perceived effects of smartphone use. Tussyadiah & Zach (2012) demonstrate the perceived effects of geolocation-based technology use on the tourist experience. These authors identify five dimensions of the tourist experience that are likely to be influenced by the use of LBS (Table 4).

Table 4. Dimensions of tourist experience sensitive to LBS:

Sensory and physical dimension	The experience results from the activation of the tourist's five senses. As they move around, tourists discover new places, new smells, new tastes, and hear sounds specific to the destination. These physical and sensory stimulation thus constitutes part of the tourist experience (Hetherington et al., 1993).
Emotional dimension	The emotions felt by the tourist during a tourist stay leads him to develop an emotional feeling towards the destination (Volo, 2009).
Cognitive and perceptual dimension	This dimension refers to the mental process that leads to knowledge. Tourists interpret their sensations through the learning process, which transmits them at the cognitive level (Li, 2000; Volo, 2009).

continued on following page

Table 4. Continued

Social dimension	Several studies show that interactions with fellow travelers, other tourists, locals, and destination contact staff influence the tourist experience (Goffman, 1967; Jennings & Nickerson, 2006; Tussyadiah & Fesenmaier, 2009).
"On-the-route" dimension	When a tourist travels to their tourist destination, they may have to change their itinerary or make unscheduled stops even before arriving on site (Connell & Page, 2008).

Source: Inspired by Salvadore, 2015, p.80-81

The findings of Tussyadiah & Zach (2012) demonstrate that the use of geolocation-based technologies influence all dimensions of the tourist experience. However, principal component factor analysis did not identify multiple dimensions, but rather a single dimension. According to the authors, this result shows that the tourist experience forms a coherent whole. This research is consistent with that of Wang et al. (2012), who identified uses that can affect different dimensions of the tourist experience depending on the specific use.

1.3. Perceived value, a perspective for evaluating the tourist experience

Perceived value, which plays a major role in consumer behavior, has mainly been addressed through three approaches (Rivière & Mencarelli, 2012):

- *Purchase value:* This corresponds to the overall assessment of the utility of an offer, resulting from a comparison between perceived benefits and sacrifices. However, it has often been reduced to an evaluation of the quality/price ratio. It takes place before the purchase and is part of a rational and cognitive perspective (Zeithaml, 1988; Bentalha et al., 2025).
- *Consumption value:* reflects a relative preference, characterizing the interaction experience between a subject and an object, and results from the experience of consuming/possessing good. It is part of an effective approach and is formed from various components (multidimensional view) (Holbrook, 1999).
- *The mixed approach to value* benefits from both the purchase value analysis framework (benefits/costs) and the richness of the components of consumption value (Lai, 1995). In particular, Aurier et al. (2004) consider that the components of consumption value contribute to determining overall utility, viewed as a sum of benefits received (or to be received) which, weighed against the sum of sacrifices made (or to be made), leads to an overall value judgment. To date, the concept of perceived value has primarily been applied to the context of marketable goods and services.

Despite its recognized importance in shaping tourist behavior, it has been largely overlooked in territorial tourism marketing. The few studies that have considered this concept at the destination level have focused solely on identifying its antecedents (Bajs, 2011; Sustacha et al., 2023), but no in-depth investigation has been conducted into the very nature of this value. Our study, however, will place greater emphasis on the effect of LBSs (Sustainable, Momentary, and Interest-Oriented Learning) on the overall perceived value of a tourist's stay, taking into account the quality of tourist experiences in a given destination.

2. ANALYTICAL MODEL AND EMPIRICAL AND METHODOLOGICAL FRAMEWORK

2.1. Conceptual Research Model

To understand the effect of mobile tourism services on the perceived value of the tourist experience, we will use the quality of the tourist experience as a mediating variable. Indeed, research focusing on the field of tourism shows that the perceived effects of these services are not limited to the utilitarian dimension, but also extend to other dimensions of the tourist experience (Tussyadiah & Zach, 2012; Wang et al., 2012).

We will anchor our analysis in technology acceptance models, notably TAM (Davis, 1989) and UTAUT2 (Venkatesh et al., 2012), before examining the concepts of Customer Experience Quality and perceived value of stay, and finally exploring the specific contributions of AI in the personalization of m-tourism services. Indeed, the effects of m-tourism services on the quality of experiences lived by the tourist can be effected, in particular, by two specific variables (Bajs, 2011; Lemoine & Salvadore, 2018), measuring their predisposition to use these technologies:

- Individuals' attitudes towards new technologies: the role of this individual trait can be explained by the nature of the additional service considered.
- Tourist motivations: in the literature, it has frequently been shown that the evaluation of a destination clearly depends on the motivations of tourists, which can be very varied.

Therefore, we formulate the following model (Figure 2):

Figure 2. Mobile tourism and the quality of the tourist experience

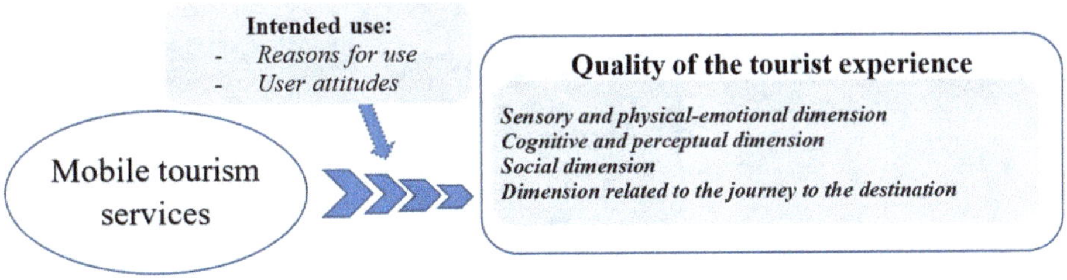

Source: The Authors

Based on the analytical framework proposed by Lai (1995) and Aurier et al. (2004), several categories of benefits perceived by tourists with respect to a given destination has been identified (Table 5):

Table 5. Perceived benefits and sacrifices of a tourist stay

Benefits	
Functional benefits	These benefits correspond to the perceived usefulness of the destination (the interest that the tourist perceives in going there), its perceived quality, or its ability to satisfy the consumer's curiosity, desire for knowledge, or novelty.
Emotional benefits	These benefits refer to the city's ability to provide tourists with a feeling of pleasure, fun, distraction, or even a change of scenery.
Social benefits	In the context of a destination, social benefits can correspond to the ability of the latter to participate in the construction of the status and social image of the tourist, or to the role that the locality can play in terms of helping social interaction, interpersonal exchange.
Altruistic Benefits	This facet of perceived benefits, generally concerned with collective well-being, is essentially linked, within the context of a destination, to the ecological/sustainable development aspect.
Sacrifices	
Monetary sacrifices	They explicitly refer to the perceived high cost of the destination.
Non-monetary sacrifices	This category of sacrifices is linked, in the minds of consumers, to the perceived risk, as well as the time/effort/energy that needs to be invested when visiting a destination.

Source: The authors

The impact of the quality of the tourist experience, as determined by the use of mobile technologies, on the overall perceived value of the stay by the tourist can therefore be understood (Figure 3).

Figure 3. Quality of the tourist experience and overall perceived value of the stay

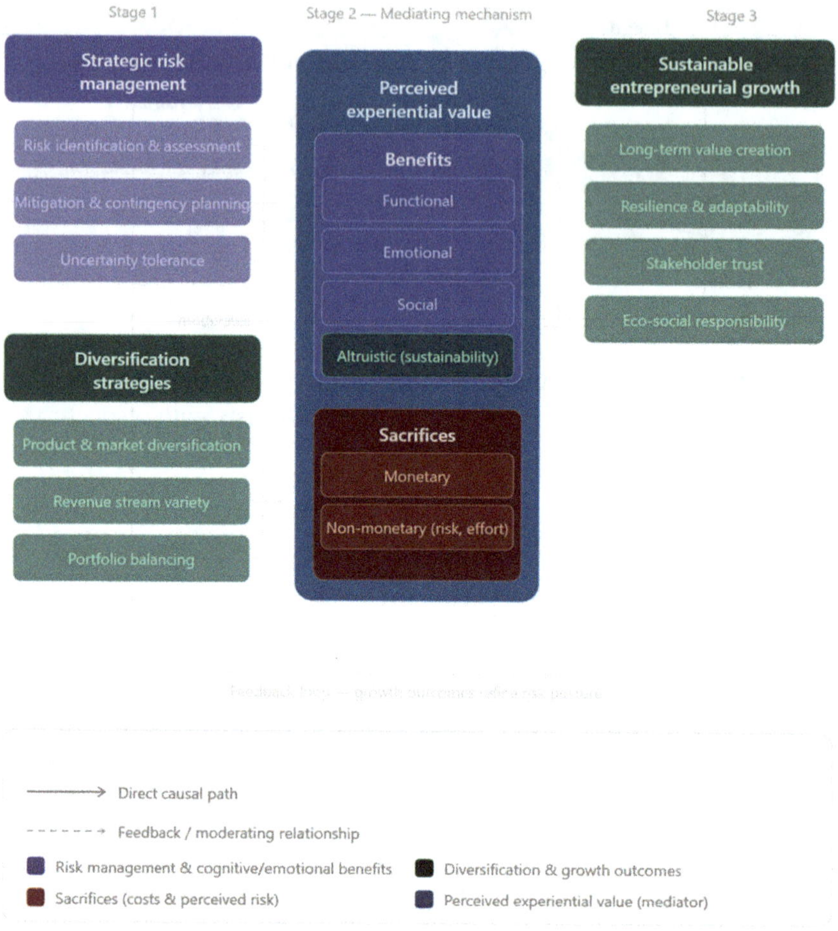

Source: The Authors

The perceived overall value of a tourist stay therefore depends on the significance of the additional gains generated and the extent of the cost reductions resulting from the quality of tourist experiences made possible by the tourist's use of mobile technologies (Boudri et al., 2025). Perceiving positive consequences from the use of technology leads the user to be more satisfied. Thus, the diffusion of using model identifies satisfaction as a consequence of the perceived effects of technology use. We therefore formulate the following hypotheses for the conceptual model (Figure 4).

H1: The use of mobile services during a tourist stay positively influences the quality of the tourist experience.

H2: Tourists' motivations and attitudes towards usage influence their impact on the quality of the tourist experience.
H3: The perceived effects of mobile service usage on the quality of the tourist experience positively influence the overall perceived value of the tourist stay.

Figure 4. Conceptual model of the research

Source: The authors

The relevance of such an analytical model will be tested through a survey of tourists.

2.2. The scope of the research and methodological choices

We focus on the impact of mobile tourism (m-tourism) on the perceived overall value of the tourist experience in Morocco. Before addressing practical considerations, several factors justify the choice of this sector and territory. The research must be conducted within a coherent and actionable field. The concepts of mobile technologies, experiential quality, and perceived value is widely used in research, allowing us to better situate our analysis within current academic and scientific discourse. Furthermore, the research is all the more relevant as it focuses on knowledge-intensive activities. Finally, tourism activities tend to be more spatially concentrated than other, more traditional types of activities.

The survey was conducted through the direct administration of a questionnaire during the second quarter of 2025. Our research employed a methodological approach focused on quantitative analysis, using face-to-face questionnaires administered to tourists. The study aims to identify the influence of tourists' motivations and attitudes regarding the use of mobile technologies during their stay, the impact of such use on the quality of tourist experiences, and therefore on the overall perceived value of such a stay.

In accordance with our research hypotheses, our questionnaire aims to measure the importance of motivations and attitudes regarding the use of mobile technologies by tourists during their stay, their effect on the quality of different dimensions of the tourist experience, and the extent of this impact on various parameters of the perceived value of the stay. To ensure more relevant responses, we opted for a five-point Likert scale. The analysis of the responses collected, which showed some interest in the use of mobile technologies during their tourist stay in the destination, allowed us to retain 187, presenting very varied profiles in terms of nationality, type of stay, socio-professional categories, age, gender, etc.

The study results show that, due to their multifunctional nature, mobile technologies applied to tourism appear to have a generally positive impact on all dimensions of the tourist experience. To test the hypotheses, we used principal component analysis and linear regression methods with SPSS software.

3. RESULTS AND DISCUSSION

The survey was conducted during the second quarter of 2025 among international tourists visiting the Fes-Meknes region (Table 6).

Table 6. Sociodemographic and behavioral profile of the sample (n = 187)

Variable	Modality	n	%
Gender	Male	102	54.5%
	Female	85	45.5%
Age	18–24 years old	28	15.0%
	25–34 years old	61	32.6%
	35–44 years old	55	29.4%
	45–54 years old	31	16.6%
	55 years and older	12	6.4%
Nationality	France	52	27.8%
	Spain	34	18.2%
	United Kingdom	22	11.8%
	Germany	19	10.2%
	UNITED STATES	15	8.0%
	Others	45	24.0%
Length of stay	1–2 days	18	9.6%
	3–5 days	74	39.6%
	6–7 days	61	32.6%
	8 days or more	34	18.2%

continued on following page

Table 6. Continued

Variable	Modality	n	%
Frequency of use of tourist applications	Never	5	2.7%
	Rarely	24	12.8%
	Sometimes	49	26.2%
	Often	63	33.7%
	Very often	46	24.6%

Source: Results of the statistical study

3.1. Evaluation of the psychometric qualities of the constructs

Before conducting factor analyses, the reliability of each construct was assessed using Cronbach's alpha coefficient (α) and Jöreskog's rho. The minimum acceptable threshold was set at $\alpha \geq 0.70$ (Nunnally & Bernstein, 1994). All constructs met this criterion, with values ranging from 0.756 (QET—Social Dimension) to 0.891 (Perceived Overall Value). These results confirm the good internal consistency of the scales used (Table 7).

Table 7. Reliability indices of the constructs

Built/Dimensions	Code	Number of items	Cronbach's alpha (α)	Jöreskog's rho
LBS usage (global)	LBS	12	0.847	0.876
Spatial orientation	ORI	4	0.812	0.849
Organization & coordination	ORG	4	0.791	0.823
Searching for localized information	RIL	4	0.834	0.861
AI Hyperpersonalization	HPIA	6	0.879	0.901
Quality of the tourist experience	QET	16	0.863	0.891
Sensory & physical dimension	QET_S	4	0.801	0.832
Emotional dimension	QET_A	4	0.822	0.848
Cognitive & perceptual dimension	QET_C	4	0.789	0.821
Social dimension	QET_SO	4	0.756	0.793
Overall perceived value of the stay	VGP	8	0.891	0.914
Predisposition to use (attitude)	ATT	4	0.817	0.845
Predisposition to use (motivations)	WORD	4	0.803	0.829

Source: Results of the statistical study

3.2. Principal Component Analysis (PCA)

The adequacy of the correlation matrix for factor analysis was verified using the Kaiser-Meyer-Olkin (KMO) index and Bartlett's test of sphericity (Table 8). The obtained KMO value (0.847) is considered "*meritorious*" according to Kaiser's (1974) grid, thus confirming the factorability of the data. Bartlett's test is highly significant (p <0.001), rejecting the null hypothesis of an identity matrix and validating the extraction procedure.

Table 8. Factor adequacy indices (KMO and Bartlett's test)

Test	Value
KMO Index (Kaiser-Meyer-Olkin)	0.847
Bartlett's sphericity test	2,847.34
Meaning (p)	<0.001

Source: Results of the statistical study

Principal component analysis (PCA) was performed with Varimax rotation on the 36 items of the measurement instrument. The criterion of eigenvalues> 1 (Kaiser's rule) led to the retention of five factors that together explained 91.2% of the total variance. Only items with a loading ≥ 0.70 on their main factor and <0.40 on the other factors were retained, in accordance with the recommendations of Hair et al. (2019). The loading matrix is presented in Table 9.

Table 9. Factorial loading matrix after Varimax rotation

Indicators	F1 LBS	F2 HPIA	F3 QET-Hedonic	F4 QET-Cognitive	F5 Perceived Value
ORI1 — GPS Navigation & Routes	**0.812**	0.142	0.089	0.073	0.061
ORI2 — Consultation of plans & maps	**0.798**	0.119	0.094	0.081	0.054
RIL1 — Search for restaurants/ shops nearby	**0.763**	0.201	0.138	0.097	0.071
ORG1 — Mobile Accommodation Booking	**0.741**	0.187	0.112	0.065	0.088
RIL2 — Geolocated POI Information	**0.755**	0.224	0.143	0.108	0.079
HPIA1 — Personalized AI Recommendations	0.189	**0.834**	0.156	0.112	0.098

continued on following page

Table 9. Continued

Indicators	F1 LBS	F2 HPIA	F3 QET-Hedonic	F4 QET-Cognitive	F5 Perceived Value
HPIA2 — Real-time contextual orientation	0.213	**0.821**	0.134	0.093	0.087
HPIA3 — Adaptive Content Adaptation	0.197	**0.809**	0.147	0.101	0.074
HPIA4 — Dynamic, geolocated suggestions	0.231	**0.791**	0.121	0.089	0.063
QET_A1 — Pleasure & wonder	0.102	0.167	**0.823**	0.178	0.143
QET_S1 — Sensory richness of the destination	0.134	0.145	**0.801**	0.156	0.121
QET_A2 — Change of scenery & feeling of escape	0.098	0.189	**0.789**	0.134	0.109
QET_S2 — Overall sensory satisfaction	0.121	0.156	**0.776**	0.143	0.098
QET_C1 — Cultural Learning & Discovery	0.087	0.134	0.167	**0.812**	0.156
QET_SO1 — Social Interactions & Exchanges	0.109	0.121	0.178	**0.789**	0.143
QET_C2 — Quality of the information used	0.143	0.098	0.156	**0.767**	0.121
QET_SO2 — Sense of community sharing	0.098	0.112	0.145	**0.745**	0.134
VGP1 — Overall perceived value of the stay	0.098	0.134	0.201	0.178	**0.856**
VGP2 — Overall value for money	0.112	0.121	0.189	0.143	**0.823**
VGP3 — Perceived functional benefits	0.134	0.109	0.167	0.156	**0.801**
VGP4 — Social & Symbolic Benefits	0.098	0.143	0.145	0.121	**0.779**

Source: Results of the statistical study

The interpretation of the five factors is consistent with the theoretical structure of the conceptual model: Factor 1 (F1) groups the items relating to LBS uses (orientation, organization, search for localized information; $\lambda = 3.24$; 28.7%); Factor 2 (F2) captures the hyperpersonalization brought about by AI ($\lambda = 2.87$; 22.4%); Factors 3 and 4 distinguish the two components of experiential quality, hedonic/sensory ($\lambda = 2.15$; 16.8%) and cognitive-social ($\lambda = 1.89$; 13.2%); finally, Factor 5 consists of the indicators of overall perceived value of the stay ($\lambda = 1.42$; 10.1%).

3.3. Descriptive statistics and correlations

Table 10 presents the means, standard deviations and Pearson correlation matrix between the main latent constructs, calculated on the basis of factor scores from PCA.

Table 10. Descriptive statistics and correlation matrix (n = 187)

Variable	Average	Standard deviation	1	2	3	4	5	6	7
1. ORI	3.67	0.89	—						
2. ORG	3.54	0.92	**0.612****	—					
3. RIL	3.78	0.84	**0.589****	**0.634****	—				
4. HPIA	3.41	0.97	**0.487****	**0.521****	**0.563****	—			
5. ATT	3.89	0.78	**0.412****	**0.398****	**0.423****	**0.389****	—		
6. WORD	3.72	0.83	**0.378****	**0.412****	**0.445****	**0.401****	**0.523****	—	
7. QET	3.63	0.91	**0.534****	**0.561****	**0.598****	**0.612****	**0.456****	**0.489****	—
8. VGP	3.58	0.88	**0.423****	**0.445****	**0.478****	**0.534****	**0.401****	**0.423****	**0.782****

ORI = Spatial Orientation; ORG = Organization & Coordination; RIL = Localized Information Retrieval; HPIA = Hyperpersonalization AI; ATT = Attitudes Towards Technology; MOT = Usage Motivations; QET = Quality of Tourist Experience; VGP = Perceived Overall Value. ** p <0.01 (two-sided).

Source: Results of the Statistical Study

Analysis of the correlation matrix indicates that all constructs were significantly positively related (p <0.01). The correlations among LBS constructs remain moderate (r ∈ [0.589; 0.634]), hence there is no concern about harmful multicollinearity.

3.4. Hypothesis Testing by Multiple Regression

To test the three hypotheses of the model, a hierarchical multiple regression procedure (Table 11) with three nested models was applied to evaluate mediation, complemented by Sobel's test to judge the significance of the indirect effect. The predictor variables were standardized to facilitate the interpretation of the standardized β coefficients and to limit potential multicollinearity effects.

Table 11. Results of hierarchical multiple regressions

Predictors	Model 1 (VI → QET)		Model 2 (QET → VGP)		Model 3: Complete Mediations	
	β	*t*	*β*	*t*	*β*	*t*
LBS (ORI)	**0.198****	3.41	—	—	**0.089***	2.01
LBS (ORG)	**0.187****	3.18	—	—	0.078†	1.78
LBS (RIL)	**0.221*****	3.89	—	—	**0.098***	2.17
HPIA	**0.401*****	6.89	—	—	**0.163****	2.87
Attitudes (ATT)	**0.198*****	3.45	—	—	0.089†	1.87
Motivations (MOT)	**0.167****	2.91	—	—	0.071†	1.69
QET	—	—	**0.782*****	17.07	**0.623*****	10.45
Constant	**0.891*****	4.23	**1,034*****	5.67	**0.712*****	4.01
R^2	**0.587**		**0.612**		**0.654**	
adjusted R^2	**0.578**		**0.608**		**0.645**	
ΔR^2	**—**		**—**		**+0.067**	
F	**64.89**		**291.43**		**68.45**	
Sign. F	**<0.001**		**<0.001**		**<0.001**	

Note. β = standardized beta coefficients. VIF max = 2.67. † p <0.10; * p <0.05; ** p <0.01; *** p <0.001. LBS (ORI) = Spatial Orientation; LBS (ORG) = Organization; LBS (RIL) = Localized Information Search; HPIA = Hyperpersonalization AI; ATT = Attitudes; MOT = Motivations; QET = Quality of Tourist Experience.

Source: Results of the Statistical Study

The consideration of the relationships of the three models provides many interesting insights. First, for Model 1: Impact of mobile usage on the quality of the tourist experience (H1, H2). This model explains 58.7% of the variance in QET (adjusted $R^2 = 0.578$; F[6, 180] = 64.89; p <0.001). Hyper-personalization AI is the strongest predictor (β = 0.401; t = 6.89; p <0.001), followed by the three LBS components (βRIL = 0.221; βORI = 0.198; βORG = 0.187; all p <0.01). With regard to H1a and H1b, the findings are confirmed: the adoption of mobile services (LBS and HPIA) has a positive effect on tourism experience quality. The predisposition variables for use, attitudes (β = 0.198; p <0.001) and motivations (β = 0.167; p = 0.004), also exert a significant effect, confirming H2a and H2b.

Second, for model 2, Effect of experiential quality on perceived value (H3). The regression of QET on VGP yielded a very high coefficient β (β = 0.782; t = 17.07; p <0.001), explaining 61.2% of the variance in VGP (adjusted $R^2 = 0.608$; F[1, 185] = 291.43; p <0.001). This confirms H3 and highlights the importance of the experiential quality as a contributor to the stay perceived value.

And for Model 3, QET mediates the effect of mobile usage on perceived value. The simultaneous inclusion of a full set of direct antecedents and QET as a mediator yields a substantial improvement of the model ($\Delta R = +0.067$; gest $R = 0.654$). The direct effects of LBS and HPIA elements on VGP remain significant but that the magnitude of coefficients drops dramatically (e.g. βHPIA decreases from 0.401 to 0.163), which suggests partial mediation (Sobel: $z = 6.12$; $p < 0.001$). QET has the highest coefficient ($\beta = 0.623$; $t = 10.45$; $p < 0.001$) which ratifies the importance of the mediating construct in the model.

All of the hypothesized relationships in the conceptual model are supported by the findings. The quality of the tourist experience (QET) is the core of the model, being influenced by both LBS and AI hyper personalization ($R = 0.587$) and having a significant influence on the overall perceived value ($\beta = 0.782$). The partial mediation role of QET says that mobile technologies have, besides the indirect impact through the experience, a direct impact on perceived value, enriching theoretical contributions of the usage diffusion model in the context of tourism.

3.5. Discussion of Results

The findings of this study contribute to several narratives in the literature. Firstly, it supports the Tussyadiah & Zach (2012) work in identifying the effect of geolocation on multiple facets of the tourist experience; however, they extend up Tussyadiah & Zach's results by explicitly differentiating the additive effect of AI-driven hyper personalization. The preponderance of HPIA ($\beta = 0.401$) over the classical LBS ($\beta \in [0.187; 0.221]$) indicates that it is the level of the adaptive intelligence of the services, and not only the availability of that service, that maximizes experiential quality. This is a contribution that the previous models (Wang et al., 2012; Lemoine & Salvadore, 2018) had not evidenced for not considering the AI factor. Second, the partial mediation of QET (Sobel $z = 6.12$; < 0.001) is in line with Holbrook's (1999) consumption value model and the value/sacrifice model of Aurier et al. (2004). It signifies that mobile technology is valuable in the production of its own value (i.e., because it diminishes immediate nonmonetary sacrifices such as effort, time, and perceived risk) and as an input that has ripple effects along the entire value chain of the lived experience.

This joined route of value generation represents a novel contribution to the m-tourism domain. Third, the importance of the predisposing factors (attitudes: $\beta = 0.198$; motivations: $\beta = 0.167$) supports the moderating effect of these individual characteristics previously found by Bajs (2011) and Eriksson & Strandvik (2009) and anchors them theoretically in the Technology Acceptance Model: the most predisposed tourists is benefited more from mobile technologies to enhance the quality of their experience, which suggests different service design strategies according to the user profiles.

Hence, a number of contributions to research can be derived from the results. The core Inference of the regressions is the following about predictors' hierarchy for experiential quality. Hyper personalization facilitated by artificial intelligence is identified as the strongest determinant of the quality of the tourist experience ($\beta = 0.401$; $p < 0.001$), surpassing the three LBS elements by a noteworthy margin, with coefficients far between 0.187 and 0.221. This finding is not trivial: it suggests that what determines the richness of the experience in the behavioral economics of the tourist interviewed is not so much the availability of mobile services as their level of adaptive intelligence. This finding builds upon and elaborates the work of Wang et al. (2012) who demonstrated that the smartphone mediated the tourist experience though was unable to parse the influence of the distinct techno-layers. It also supports the predictions of the improved TAM (Venkatesh et al., 2012) that perceived usefulness is a major predictor of technology usage and experience.

The second significant conclusion in this study is about the scale and stability of mediating effect of quality of tourist experience (QTE). The QTE↔VGP association is at $r = 0.782$ ($p < 0.01$) and the standardized regression coefficient in Model 2 ($\beta = 0.782$; $t = 17.07$; $p < 0.001$) is the strongest one in the entire model. This finding is particularly important from a theoretical perspective, in that it suggests that the value of mobile services to travelers is not a function of mobile services' own inherent value, but rather depends on the experience enabled by mobile services within the trip experience. A high-tech facility, which is badly implanted in a tourist's experience journey, cannot be expected to bring about any tangible increase in perceived trip values. A prescribed mediation effect is partial as evidence by the Sobel test ($z=6.12$, $p < 0.001$) and the continuation of significant direct effect coefficients on VGP in Model 3 ($\beta HPIA=0.163$; $\beta RIL=0.098$). The findings imply that LBS service has a major impact on the hedonic aspect (the facilitated mobility, the sensory exploration through LBS with augmented reality, the provision of multimedia information), while AI-driven hyper personalization influences two aspects (a cognitive component through the curation of detailed cultural content and a social layer via place-based community recommendations) of the hedonic experience and the social component of the utilitarian experience.

Therefore, the second and third contributions of this study, is to empirically confirm the moderating effect of predisposition to use as measured by two separate constructs of attitude toward new technologies (ATT: $\beta = 0.198$; $p < 0.001$) and use motivations (MOT: $\beta = 0.167$; $p < 0.01$). The findings are consistent with those of Eriksson & Strandvik (2009) on mobile tourism services usage factors and with Bajs (2011) factors framework of perceived value in touristic destinations. They remind us that the impact of technologies is not the same in the entire population of tourists. This result leads us to enrich the initial conceptual model by considering the segmentation of mobile tourist users. Tourism users, strong intrinsic motivated tourists who themselves consider exploring technology as pleasure, enjoyed HPIA more by making use of more complex functions of HPIA. On the contrary, tourists with instrumental motivation tend to concentrate on the use of LBS navigation and booking tools. This is also an adequate explanation for a segmented approach to mobile tourism services designs in light of the varying preferences for such services among user groups. In addition, the smallest effect among motivations ($\beta = 0.167$) as compared to attitudes ($\beta = 0.198$) indicates that the source is more the existing cognitive orientation towards technologies rather than the current situational motivation for travel, in terms of experiential influences.

This study is conceptual in nature and therefore carries inherent constraints that future empirical work should address. First, the proposed model has not been subjected to empirical validation; the relationships between strategic risk management, diversification strategies, perceived experiential value, and sustainable entrepreneurial growth remains theoretical propositions requiring testing through quantitative methods such as structural equation modeling or through qualitative approaches such as in-depth case studies. Second, the model draws on constructs developed primarily in tourism and consumer behavior research, and their transferability to broader entrepreneurial contexts has not been systematically examined here. Third, the conceptualization of perceived experiential value may not fully capture sector-specific or culturally contingent dimensions of value, particularly in emerging market contexts. Fourth, the feedback loop between growth outcomes and risk posture, though theoretically plausible, is treated as static within this framework; longitudinal designs would be needed to trace how these relationships evolve over time. Researchers are encouraged to treat this model as a foundation for the hypothesis generation rather than as a definitive explanatory account.

CONCLUSION

This research allowed us to validate a model for the diffusion of mobile services for orientation, organization, and localized information retrieval. It enriches the literature on usage diffusion, which is still underdeveloped in the case of smartphone use and unprecedented in the tourism sector. This scarcity of research on product usage can be explained, on the one hand, by the concentration of marketing research on the product acquisition phase (Arnould et al. 2004), and on the other hand, by the recent rise of smartphones and associated mobile services.

Through the use of their smartphones, tourists can facilitate the discovery of their chosen tourist destination. However, as Larsen et al. (2007) remind us, it is important to remember that while smartphone use can positively enhance the tourist experience, it can also "*de-exoticize*" it and diminish its "*extraordinary*" character.

This phenomenon tends to blur the distinction between the tourist experience and the triviality of daily life (Cohen & Cohen, 2012). Indeed, a better understanding of places and the repetition of everyday behaviors, such as finding a route, can lead to a "*decapitation*" of the tourist experience by reducing the sense of adventure and escape (Jansson, 2007).

From a managerial perspective, this work demonstrates how tourists use mobile applications to explore a destination. Within the framework of a mobile strategy, it is therefore essential for tourism professionals to consider the type of tourist experience the destination wishes to offer and to identify its key dimensions. For example, is it truly wise to showcase a historical site or a museum through a mobile application that will lead tourists to focus their attention on a mobile device rather than on the location itself? It seems that mobile tourism may have been prematurely touted as the new miracle solution for enriching the tourist experience. As evidence, despite an extremely extensive catalog of mobile applications, few mobile services have achieved success. This observation suggests that tourists are still capable of discovering a destination without technological assistance and still find enjoyment in getting lost and embracing an element of spontaneity (Bentalha, 2025).

This work has several limitations. First, our research has limited external validity due to the nature of our sample. Furthermore, asking surveyed tourists to recall their past experiences introduces a bias related to the recall of these events. Generalizing the results to other Moroccan, Mediterranean, or similar heritage destinations must therefore be done with caution and requires replication studies in contrasting settings (seaside, ecotourism, and contemporary urban destinations) before any extrapolation. To mitigate this bias, one solution would be to use software that collects "traces of use" during the tourist stay and compares them with the respondents' self-reported experiences. Finally, drawing on diffusion theory, we aggregated all uses into a single variable, "LBS uses," which sometimes encompasses different realities. We did not fully grasp the differences in usage and their consequences on the tourist experience. A more detailed study of the antecedents and consequences of each of these uses could provide additional insights at the managerial level. Another limitation concerns the measurement of constructed HPIA. Although the chosen scale (6 items, $\alpha = 0.879$) has good psychometric properties, it remains a measure of tourists' perception of AI-driven hyper personalization, and not an objective measure of the AI algorithms and functionalities actually used by the applications.

An openness to new perspectives is therefore necessary in view of the imperatives of sustainable development and the opportunities offered by digital tourism. The first research angle adopts the perspective of a mobile tourist and takes a longitudinal approach to monitoring the development of mobile use and its influence on the tourist experience while on travel as opposed to a one-off measurement. Recent studies on digital consumer behavior (Hollebeek et al., 2019; Javornik et al., 2022) indicate that the implications of interactive technologies are dynamic and nonlinear. For instance, the advantages of AI personalization may fade away if the user feels that his/her privacy rights are violated or if suffers from algorithmic over-solicitation. The temporal to-ns study is facilitated by using a combination of questionnaires, e-s diaries, and objective behavioral data at different stages of data collection which in turn will enable a more precise capturing of the study's temporal dynamics. The second overarching issue relates to the cross-cultural investigation of the impact of mobile tourism. Our findings are drawn from a largely Western European sample (France, Spain, the United Kingdom, and Germany, which constitute 68.0% of the sample), this may skew the estimates towards user profiles with a prior familiarity with personalized application environments. A comparative study including tourists from the emerging economies could provide insights to test whether the impacts of HPIA on QET are universal or culture bound. The third research line builds on the expectation that the development of technologies will bring about further changes of the mobile tourism landscape and its impacts on the tourist experience in the future. Three areas of technology, in particular, are noteworthy. Augmented reality and extended reality will undoubtedly be the next level of hyper-personalization in heritage tourism. A fourth line of enquiry - which intersects the previous ones - could be the relationship between mobile tourism and sustainable tourism development. In conclusion, the question of digital inclusion in mobile tourism should be considered more in future studies. The positive impact of AI-driven hyper personalization (HPIA) for tourism quality is moderated by favorable attitude and motivation related to technology. Consequently, tourists with low digital literacy are structural left out of the gains associated with hyper personalization. Developing universal design AI-powered hyper personalization services—via voice, simplified UIs, or multimodal adaptation—is both an ethical necessity and a lever for growing the business potential of mobile tourism.

REFERENCES

Arnould, E. J., Price, L., & Zinkhan, G. M. (2004). *Consumers* (2nd ed.). McGraw-Hill.

Aurier, P., Evrard, Y., & N'Goala, G. (2004). Understanding and measuring value from the consumer's point of view. *Research and Applications in Marketing, 19*(3), 1–20.

Bajs, I. P. (2011). Attributes of tourist destinations as determinants of tourists perceived value. *International Journal of Management Cases, 13*(3), 547–554. DOI: 10.5848/APBJ.2011.00090

Benchmark, C. C. M. (2015). *Tourism & Mobile: Usage and Perspectives on New Services*. Online. https://www.tom.travel/2015/02/12/tourisme-et-mobile-quels-seront-les-usages-en-2015/ (Accessed 08/03/2026)

Bentalha, B. (2025). Smart tourism and co-creation of the tourism experience: netnographic possibilities and technological perspectives. In *AI Technologies for Personalized and Sustainable Tourism* (pp. 253–276). IGI Global Scientific Publishing.

Bentalha, B., Benjelloun, A., Slimani, H., & El Gharbaoui, B. (2025). Purchase Intention and Tourism Strategy in the Post-COVID-19 Era: Lessons and Perspectives From the Moroccan Experience. In Technological Innovation in Global Cultural Tourism (pp. 65-86). IGI Global Scientific Publishing.

Boudri, R., Bentalha, B., & Tariq, B. (2025). Towards Understanding Phygital Experience in Logistic-Retail Networks: A Netnographic Exploration of Connected Commerce. In *2025 IEEE International Conference on Advanced Technologies in Supply Chain Management (ATSCM)* (pp. 1-6). IEEE. DOI: 10.1109/ATSCM67505.2025.11473673

Bourliataux-Lajoinie, S., & Rivière, A. (2013). The challenge of m-services in territorial tourism marketing: Proposal of an analytical framework. *Recherches en Sciences de Gestion, 95*(2), 65–82. DOI: 10.3917/resg.095.0065

Cinotti, Y. (2015). From hospitality to experience: comparative writings of tourists in guesthouses & hotels. In Decroly, J.-M. (Ed.), *Tourism as experience. Interdisciplinary perspectives on the tourist experience*. Presses Universitaires du Québec.

Cohen, E., & Cohen, S. A. (2012). Current sociological theories and issues in tourism. *Annals of Tourism Research, 39*(4), 2177–2202. DOI: 10.1016/j.annals.2012.07.009

Connell, J., & Page, S. J. (2008). exploring the spatial patterns of car-based tourist travel in Loch Lomond and Trossachs National Park, Scotland. *Tourism Management, 29*(3), 561–580. DOI: 10.1016/j.tourman.2007.03.019

Davis, F. D. (1989). Perceived usefulness, perceived ease of use, and user acceptance of information technology. *Management Information Systems Quarterly, 13*(3), 319–340. DOI: 10.2307/249008

Decroly, J.-M. (Ed.). (2015). *Tourism as experience. Interdisciplinary perspectives on the tourist experience*. Presses de l'Université du Québec.

El Biyaali, M. K., Boudri, R., & Bentalha, B. (2025). Leveraging Sentiment Analysis for Enhanced Customer Experience: AI-Driven Personalization in Online Retail. In AI Innovations for Customer Experience Optimization in the Service Sector (pp. 203-224). IGI Global Scientific Publishing.

Eriksson, N., & Strandvik, P. (2009). Possible determinants affecting the use of mobile tourism services. In *e-Business and Telecommunications*. Springer, p. 61 - 73. DOI: 10.1007/978-3-642-05197-5_4

Euromonitor International. (2023). *World Travel Market Report*.

Fijalkow, Y., Jalaudin, C., & Lalanne, M. (2015). Measuring the tourist experience through the engagement, indifference & avoidance of local populations. In Decroly, J.-M. (Ed.), *Tourism as Experience. Interdisciplinary perspectives on the tourist experience*. Presses Universitaires du Québec.

Flügel, S., Halse, A. H., Hartveit, K. J., & Ukkonen, A. (2022). Value of travel time by road types. *European Transport Research Review, 14*(1), 35. DOI: 10.1186/s12544-022-00554-1

Goffman, E. (1967). *Ritual interaction; essays on face-to-face behavior*. Doubleday.

Gritta, F., & Calabrese, M. (2023). Internet use in small tourism in Italy: what will be the role of local government? Transforming Government: People. *Process and Policy, 17*(4), 632–654.

Hécate Vergopoulos, H. (2016). The tourist experience: an experience of the managers of the tourist experience? Via [Online], 10 | 2016, Online since 01 December 2016, accessed on 23 March 2026. URL: https://journals.openedition.org/viatourism/1347DOI: .DOI: 10.4000/viatourism.1347

Henning, G. K. (2012). The habit of tourism: Experiences and their ontological meaning. In Sharpley, R., & Stone, P. R. (Eds.), *Contemporary tourist experience: concepts and consequences*. Routledge.

Hetherington, J., Daniel, T. C., & Brown, T. C. (1993). Is motion more important than it sounds?: The medium of presentation in environmental perception research. *Journal of Environmental Psychology, 13*(4), 283–291. DOI: 10.1016/S0272-4944(05)80251-8

Holbrook, M. B. (1999). Introduction to consumer value. In *Holbrook MB (coord.). Consumer value: a framework for analysis and research* (pp. 1–28). Routledge. DOI: 10.4324/9780203010679.ch0

Hollebeek, L. D., Srivastava, R. K., & Chen, T. (2019). SD logic—informed customer engagement: Integrative framework, fundamental revised propositions, and application to CRM. *Journal of the Academy of Marketing Science, 47*(1), 161–185. DOI: 10.1007/s11747-016-0494-5

Idate, K., & Kanopee, M. (2011). *M-Tourism: A Practical Guide for SMEs*. DGCIS.

Islam, M. F., Rahman, M. M., Sultana, S., Nabi, M. N., Rosid, M. H. O., & Alnour, M. (2024). Uncovering the impact on environmental challenges through the predictors of m-tourism apps adoption: SEM-NCA approaches. *Environmental Challenges, 17*, 101028. DOI: 10.1016/j.envc.2024.101028

Jansson, A. (2007). A sense of tourism: New media and the dialectic of encapsulation/decapsulation. *Tourist Studies, 7*(1), 5–24. DOI: 10.1177/1468797607079799

Javornik, A., Marder, B., Barhorst, J. B., McLean, G., Rogers, Y., Marshall, P., & Warlop, L. (2022). "What lies behind the filter?" Uncovering the motivations for using augmented reality (AR) face filters on social media and their effect on well-being. *Computers in Human Behavior, 128*, 107126. Advance online publication. DOI: 10.1016/j.chb.2021.107126

Jennings, G. P., & Nickerson, N. P. (2006). *Quality tourism experiences*. Elsevier Butterworth-Heinemann. DOI: 10.4324/9780080455778

Kaiser, H. F. (1974). An index of factorial simplicity. *Psychometrika, 39*(1), 31–36. DOI: 10.1007/BF02291575

Kokkinou, A., Tremiliti, E., Iwaarden, M. V., Mitas, O., & Straatman, S. (2022). Are you traveling alone or with your device? The impact of connected mobile device usage on the travel experience. *Journal of Hospitality and Tourism Insights, 5*(1), 45–61. DOI: 10.1108/JHTI-04-2020-0058

Kurgun, H., Kurgun, O., & Aktas, E. (2018). What does Web 4.0 Promise for Tourism Ecosystem? A Qualitative Research on Tourism Ecosystem Stakeholders' Awareness. *Journal of Tourism and Hospitality Management., 6*(1). Advance online publication. DOI: 10.15640/jthm.v6n1a6

Lai, A. B. (1995). Consumer Values, Product Benefits And Customer Value: A Consumption Behavior Approach. *Advances in Consumer Research. Association for Consumer Research (U. S.)*, (22), 381–388.

Larsen, J., Urry, J., & Axhausen, K. W. (2007). Networks and tourism: Mobile social life. *Annals of Tourism Research, 34*(1), 244–262. DOI: 10.1016/j.annals.2006.08.002

Lemoine, J., & Salvadore, M. (2018). The impact of smartphone use on the tourist experience: The case of discovering a destination. *Management & Avenir, 99*(1), 165–189. DOI: 10.3917/mav.099.0165

Li, F., Zhu, D., Lin, M.-T., & Kim, P. B. (2024). The Technology Acceptance Model and hospitality and tourism consumers' intention to use mobile technologies: Meta-analysis and structural equation modeling. *Cornell Hospitality Quarterly, 65*(4), 461–477. Advance online publication. DOI: 10.1177/19389655241226558

Li, Y. (2000). Geographical consciousness and tourism experience. *Annals of Tourism Research, 27*(4), 863–883. DOI: 10.1016/S0160-7383(99)00112-7

Major, B., & McLeay, F. (2012). The UK "grey" market's holiday experience. In Sharpley, R., & Stone, P. R. (Eds.), *Contemporary tourist experience: concepts and consequences*. Routledge.

Matteucci, X. (2015). Experiencing flamenco: an examination of a spiritual journey. In Filep, S., & Pearce, P. (Eds.), *Tourist experience and fulfillment: Insights from positive psychology*. Routledge.

Nunnally, J. C., & Bernstein, I. H. (1994). The Assessment of Reliability. *Psychometric Theory, 3*, 248–292.

Oysterlink. (2025). *Online Travel Booking Statistics in 2025.*

Panchal, J. (2013). Tourism, wellness and feeling good: reviewing and studying Asian spa experiences. In Filep, S., & Pearce, P. (Eds.), *Tourist experience and fulfillment: Insights from positive psychology*. Routledge.

Prebensen, N. K., Chen, J. S., & Uysal, M. (2014). *Creating experience value in tourism*. CABI Publishing. DOI: 10.1079/9781780643489.0000

Qiao, G., Huang, S., & Vorobjovas-Pinta, O. (2024). Seeking tourism in a social context: An examination of Chinese rural migrant workers' travel motivations and constraints. *Leisure Studies, 43*(4), 608–623. DOI: 10.1080/02614367.2023.2249259

Raffour Interactif. (2025). Review of French leisure tourism—Opodo Barometer 2025. Online. https://www.raffour-interactif.fr/site_ri/ventes/etude_vente.htm (Accessed March 6, 2026).

Rivière, A., & Mencarelli, R. (2012). Towards a theoretical clarification of the notion of perceived value in marketing. *Research and Applications in Marketing, 27*(3), 97–123.

Salvadore, M. (2015), Effects of virtual behavior on the physical behavior of the consumer: the case of smartphone use during a tourist stay. Management. University of Nice Sophia Antipolis, 2015.

Saunders, R., Laing, J., & Weiler, B. (2013). Personal transformation through long-distance walking. In Filep, S., & Pearce, P. (Eds.), *Tourist experience and fulfillment: Insights from positive psychology*. Routledge.

Shih, E., Venkatesh, A., Chen, S., & Kruse, E. (2013). Dynamic Use Diffusion Model in a Cross-National Context: A Comparative Study of the United States, Sweden, and India Dynamic. *Journal of Product Innovation Management, 30*(1), 4–16. DOI: 10.1111/j.1540-5885.2012.00982.x

Simon, G. (2015). The urban experience of tourists: a relational approach to the objects of the urban world. In Decroly, J.-M. (Ed.), *Tourism as experience. Interdisciplinary perspectives on the tourist experience*. Presses Universitaires du Québec.

Singh, A., Rana, N. P., & Parayitam, S. (2022). Role of social currency in customer experience and co-creation intention in online travel agencies: Moderation of attitude and subjective norms. *International Journal of Information Management Data Insights, 2*(2), 100114. DOI: 10.1016/j.jjimei.2022.100114

Skyscanner. (2023). *Share of travelers who used a mobile device to plan or book travel in the last six months worldwide as of October 2023, by activity*. Online. https://www.statista.com/statistics/1421721/ accessed on 15 March 2026

Sustacha, I., Banos-Pino, J. F., & Del Valle, E. (2023). The role of technology in enhancing the tourism experience in smart destinations: A meta-analysis. *Journal of Destination Marketing & Management, 30*, 100817. DOI: 10.1016/j.jdmm.2023.100817

Tussyadiah, I., & Fesenmaier, D. R. (2009). Mediating Tourist Experiences. Access to Places via Shared Videos. *Annals of Tourism Research, 36*(1), 24–40. DOI: 10.1016/j.annals.2008.10.001

Tussyadiah, I. P., & Zach, F. J. (2012). The role of geo-based technology in place experiments. *Annals of Tourism Research, 39*(2), 780–800. DOI: 10.1016/j.annals.2011.10.003

Venkatesh, V., Thong, J. Y. L., & Xu, X. (2012). Consumer acceptance and use of information technology: Extending the unified theory of acceptance and use of technology. *Management Information Systems Quarterly, 36*(1), 157–178. DOI: 10.2307/41410412

Volo, S. (2009). Conceptualizing experience: A tourist based approach. *Journal of Hospitality Marketing & Management, 18*(2-3), 2–3, 111–126. DOI: 10.1080/19368620802590134

Wang, D., Park, S., & Fesenmaier, D. R. (2012). The Role of Smartphones in Mediating the Touristic Experience. *Journal of Travel Research, 51*(4), 371–387. DOI: 10.1177/0047287511426341

Wang, G., Qiu, H., & Ren, L. (2023). Determinants of tourists' intention to share travel experience on social media: An fsQCA application. *Current Issues in Tourism, 26*(16), 2595–2612. DOI: 10.1080/13683500.2022.2091428

Wasela, K. (2023). The role of intangible cultural heritage in the development of cultural tourism. International Journal of Eco-Cultural Tourism. *Hospitality Planning and Development*, 6(2), 15–28.

Zeithaml, V. A. (1988). Consumer Perceptions Of Price, Quality, And Value: A Means-End Model And Synthesis Of Evide nce. *Journal of Marketing, 52*(3), 2–22. DOI: 10.1177/002224298805200302

ADDITIONAL READING

Agius, K., Briguglio, M., & Pérez, J. L. B. (2025). Tourism, Real Estate, and Urban Pressures: The case of Marsascala, Malta. *Open Research Europe, 4*, 183. DOI: 10.12688/openreseurope.17641.2 PMID: 40919072

Arici, H. E., Köseoglu, M. A., & Sökmen, A. (2022). The intellectual structure of customer experience research in service scholarship: A bibliometric analysis. *Service Industries Journal, 42*(7-8), 514–550. DOI: 10.1080/02642069.2022.2043286

Carvalho, P., & Alves, H. (2023). Customer value co-creation in the hospitality and tourism industry: A systematic literature review. *International Journal of Contemporary Hospitality Management, 35*(1), 250–273. DOI: 10.1108/IJCHM-12-2021-1528

Dang, T. D., & Nguyen, M. T. (2023). Systematic review and research agenda for the tourism and hospitality sector: Co-creation of customer value in the digital age. *Future Business Journal, 9*(1), 94. DOI: 10.1186/s43093-023-00274-5

Li, S., Li, Z., Wang, R., & Yu, Z. (2026). The dual-layer synergistic persuasion model in AI-generated tourism short videos: The synergistic influence mechanism of personalized cue adaptation and structural framework on impulsive travel intention. *Electronic Commerce Research*, •••, 1–48. DOI: 10.1007/s10660-026-10139-y

Meziane, B., Alla, L., & Bentalha, B. (2025). Transformational Trends of Territorial Economic Intelligence Strategies in the Digital Era: A Systematic Theoretical Exploration. In Utilizing Technology to Manage Territories (pp. 455-490). IGI Global Scientific Publishing.

Mou, Y., Fan, J., Ding, Z., & Khan, I. (2024). Impact of virtual reality immersion on customer experience: Moderating effect of cross-sensory compensation and social interaction. *Asia Pacific Journal of Marketing and Logistics*, *36*(1), 26–47. DOI: 10.1108/APJML-11-2022-0920

Rodríguez-Negrón, M. A., Sosa-Varela, J. C., Santiago-Font, Z., & Flecha-Ortiz, J. A. (2025). Customer journey perspective on tourism service experience. *Academia (Caracas)*, *38*(4), 600–625. DOI: 10.1108/ARLA-12-2024-0346

Shoukat, M. H., & Ramkissoon, H. (2022). Customer delight, engagement, experience, value co-creation, place identity, and revisit intention: A new conceptual framework. *Journal of Hospitality Marketing & Management*, *31*(6), 757–775. DOI: 10.1080/19368623.2022.2062692

Skandali, D. (2025). Metaverse Tourism: Opportunities, AI-Driven Marketing, and Ethical Challenges in Virtual Travel. *Encyclopedia*, *5*(3), 135. DOI: 10.3390/encyclopedia5030135

KEY TERMS AND DEFINITIONS

Adaptive Trip Planning: An AI-supported process through which travel itineraries are dynamically adjusted in real time based on changing circumstances, user preferences, or contextual data, rather than being fixed in advance.

Dematerialization of Booking Practices: The ongoing shift away from traditional, in-person, or paper-based reservation methods toward fully digital and mobile-based booking processes for transportation, accommodation, and tourism experiences.

Experiential Quality: The subjective, qualitative dimension of a tourist's interaction with mobile services and destination offerings, reflecting how enjoyable, immersive, or meaningful the overall travel experience feels beyond purely functional outcomes.

Hyper-Personalization: An advanced form of service customization, powered by artificial intelligence, that tailors travel recommendations, itineraries, and content to an individual traveler's real-time context, preferences, and behavior, going beyond generic or segment-based personalization.

Location-Based Services (LBS): Mobile applications and functionalities that use a traveler's geographic position to deliver contextually relevant information, recommendations, or services, such as nearby points of interest, navigation assistance, or proximity-based offers.

Mobile Tourism (M-Tourism): The use of mobile technologies and devices by travellers to plan, organize, and experience their trips, encompassing activities from pre-departure research to in-destination navigation and post-trip sharing.

Perceived Value: The tourist's overall subjective assessment of the benefits received from a mobile tourism service or experience relative to the costs (monetary, time, or effort) incurred, shaping satisfaction and future behavioural intentions.

Chapter 14
The Transformative Applications of Artificial Intelligence in Airlines:
Enhancing Passenger Experience and Operations

B. G. Mukunda
http://orcid.org/0000-0002-6568-1578
Mount Carmel (Deemed to be) University, Bangalore, India

V. Sivakami
http://orcid.org/0000-0002-4679-944X
Mount Carmel (Deemed to be) University, Bangalore, India

Chinna Srinivasan
ASET College of Science and Technology, Chennai, India

ABSTRACT

The airline industry is changing through Artificial Intelligence (AI) and its role in enhancing customer interactions and efficiency within the industry. The report goes into how chatbots, virtual assistants and predictive sentiment analysis are being deployed by airlines to provide better passenger experience, make well-informed decisions, and reduce business expenses. Using secondary data, the study's authors investigated AI's efficacy in the aviation sector. Mostly, airline companies concentrated on the AI applications to offer hyper-personalized services to customers such as improved in-flight entertainment, simplified security checks, more enjoyable booking experience, and expedited customer complaints and problems resolutions. At a more practical level, AI enhances flight scheduling, predictive maintenance,

DOI: 10.4018/979-8-3373-9159-5.ch014

cost management, route planning and safety. Artificially intelligent-based baggage handling solutions can facilitate operations, streamline revenues, and decrease wait times, as they streamline the work of the staff.

1. INTRODUCTION

Artificial intelligence (AI) is changing the aviation industry in this era of massive technological progress. Artificial intelligence has also emerged as an important instrument to reconsider passenger experience, optimise operations, and ensure safety using cutting-edge computer technology, such as machine learning algorithms and big data analytics (Kabashkin et al., 2023). The security and safety of the aviation industry have been greatly enhanced by machine learning, a subfield of artificial intelligence, ever since the introduction of Unmanned Aircraft Systems (UAS) for traffic monitoring (Xie et al., 2021). Explainable AI (XAI) and Machine Learning (ML) are two types of AI that may be used in air traffic management to enhance operational process performance and decision-making capacities (Degas et al., 2022). states that the performance of aircraft is improved with the help of these technologies and consequently assists in the development of aviation operations, sustainability, and safety. The airline industry uses the strength of artificial intelligence and powerful analytics to gain a better insight into consumer patterns (Clainche et al., 2023). This is the knowledge that enables them to enhance the experiences of passengers in all touchpoints and apply customised marketing tools. Predictive analytics contributes to the enhancement of the efficiency of operations and service provision, and AI is an important factor in the promotion of a collaborative and creative culture within airlines (Nianm, 2025). Artificial intelligence, prediction software, virtual pilot training simulators, and real-time air traffic management, and other AI applications are adversely affecting airline operations and efficiency. The applications of AI with the purpose of saving fuel consumption, flight delays, and airline resource optimisation are already being used by many airlines, meaning that such technologies are no longer just a mere idea. AI will allow biometric check-in, customised ticketing interfaces, and predictive catering systems through the enhancement of passenger experience and minimisation of inefficiencies (Saroop, 2025). There are cybersecurity, anomaly detection, and predictive maintenance are among the most prominent uses of AI in the aviation sector, but these three can be considered the key components of an industry that can be seen as autonomous and intelligent as possible (Ahmed, 2025).

2. REVIEW OF LITERATURE

2.1 Historical perspectives of Artificial Intelligence

There is a lack of scholarly literature on the topic of artificial intelligence, even though Alan Turing first introduced the notion in 1936 (Copeland, 2015), adding that since the turn of the century, AI has been successfully used in the tourism sector (Burger et al., 2001). Artificial intelligence (AI) is a technology that gives robots the same learning, comprehension, problem-solving, decision-making, creative, and autonomous capabilities as humans. The most perfect way of measuring this emotional attachment and getting insights into the emotional aspects of consumer experiences is sentiment analysis of the feedback. Sentiment analysis could apply to the airline industry as it would help the sector understand more about the subtle emotional reactions of customers to feedback messages. Two distinct types of AI systems exist. On one hand, we have fully digital systems, and on the other, we have digital-physical hybrids, or robots. Both methods are used in different parts of the hotel and tourism industry. "AI is the capacity of a computer to carry out cognitive tasks that we identify with human minds, including perception, reasoning, learning, interacting with the environment, problem solving, decision making, and even exhibiting creativity" (Rai et al., 2019). The early adoption of technologies like the internet, intranets, and extranets significantly enhanced communication and fostered robust business-to-business relationships (Nian, 2025).

2.2 Applications of AI in the Aviation Industry

AI-driven applications have become increasingly essential in strategic decision-making processes due to recent advancements, which were particularly noticeable during the COVID-19 pandemic (Pérez-Campuzan et al., 2021; Shiwakoti et al., 2022). The combination of blockchain, artificial intelligence, and big data technologies has not only produced new value propositions but also solved the problems associated with modern travel logistics (Vinod, 2021). By improving personnel scheduling, maintenance procedures, and aircraft routing, these technologies have improved overall airline economies (Chang et al., 2019). Chatbots and other AI-enhanced solutions have transformed customer service and significantly increased corporate agility (Wang et al., 2022). Additionally, AI-driven recommender systems are now essential in transforming airline offer development and retailing by offering customised experiences that address the complex needs of passengers (Dadoun et al, 2021). By allowing airlines to swiftly adapt to shifting market conditions and consumer requests, AI highlights the need of strategic agility in preserving competitive advantage (Al-Romeedy, 2019). But putting such technology into practice requires careful consideration of ethical issues and upholding customer confidence (Tula et al., 2024). Devices and apps powered by AI allow us to see and recognise items. Artificial intelligence technologies can understand, respond to, and learn new human languages. Experts and consumers alike may benefit from the comprehensive instructions in many ways. By using data to find patterns, evaluate circumstances based on predictions, learn from past events, and suggest actions to maximize efficiency, AI applications may enhance human decision-making and productivity (Akerkar, 2019; Pournader et al., 2021; Sun et al., 2023). Passenger experience, infrastructure monitoring, spacing/separation, performance management, resource management/optimization, traffic forecasts and projections, and workload/automation/autonomy are the main areas where artificial intelligence may be applied in the aviation sector (Eurocontrol, 2020). Chatbots have had the greatest impact on the travel and hospitality sectors, despite the fact that pure digital AI solutions include mobile boarding cards and airline online check-in systems (Ivanov and Webster, 2017). Chatbots powered by AI are an essential tool for the tourist industry. Combining "chat" with "robot" gave a straightforward explanation of how chatbots work. Chatbots are computer systems that mimic human communication using natural language (Wang and Petrina, 2013). A lot has changed for chatbots since the first model came out. These days, you can find them mostly used in areas like online community building, retail, decision-making help, and state-of-the-art payment systems (Zsarnoczky, 2017).

Figure 1. An overview of the many ideas that make up artificial intelligence (Source: Youseftorkaman et al., 2023)

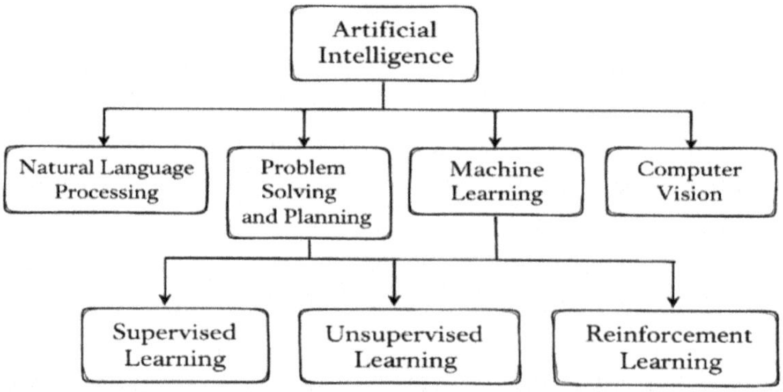

2.3 Case study-based applications of AI

Airlines all over the world are using Artificial Intelligence (AI) to improve passenger satisfaction and operational effectiveness; several case studies have shown how AI can be used in the airline industry, like Delta Airlines, which has incorporated AI into predictive maintenance systems, which use sensor data analysis to foresee mechanical problems before they worsen, cutting down on delays and enhancing safety. Additionally, Delta used chatbots with AI capabilities to streamline customer support interactions by providing real-time flight updates and baggage information (Defynd, 2026). In a similar vein, KLM Royal Dutch Airlines is a pioneer in the usage of AI-driven messaging services, allowing travellers to communicate with the airline in different languages through social media channels. KLM is now a leader in AI-enabled consumer engagement because to this innovation, which has greatly decreased response times and enhanced accessibility (Danilet, 2025). By suggesting in-flight meals and entertainment options based on individual tastes and travel history, Emirates Airlines has used Artificial Intelligence (AI) to personalise passenger experiences across the Middle East. In addition, client satisfaction, this kind of customisation increases brand loyalty (Danilet, 2025). In the meantime, United Airlines has embraced AI for operational optimisation, analysing flight route data and enhancing air traffic control using machine learning algorithms. This application helps achieve sustainability objectives by minimising delays and fuel use (Defynd, 2026). Like this, Southwest Airlines has used AI in route optimisation and aircraft scheduling to ensure better timeliness and more effective use of resources (Defynd, 2026). These illustrations show how AI plays a dual role in airlines: boosting backend operations like scheduling, predictive maintenance, and resource management while also increasing passenger-facing services through chatbots, biometric systems, and personalisation. But the literature also highlights critical issues. Adoption of AI offers efficiency and increased enjoyment, but there are still issues with data privacy, the moral implications of surveillance technology, and regional adoption disparities. Other obstacles that call for thorough regulatory oversight and strategic planning include high implementation costs and personnel relocation (Zsarnoczky, 2017; Ivanov & Webster, 2017). In summary, the use of AI by airlines like Delta, KLM, Emirates, United and Southwest shows how it may revolutionise both operational models and passenger experiences. The use of touchless and automated services, especially biometric check-ins and AI-driven customer assistance, was accelerated by the COVID-19 epidemic. The findings of (Gascón et al., 2025) demonstrate that AI is very beneficial in enhancing security standards, decreasing delays, and optimising aeroplane operations. AI may improve several aviation-related areas, such as flight control, crew scheduling, communication networks, maintenance diagnostic systems, and flight operations staff (Khalil, 2023; Campuzano et al., 2021; Wandelt et al., 2023). This notion is supported by recent studies (Mikl et al., 2021; Weisz et al., 2023). Sentiment analysis, the process of identifying and assessing subjective information inside text data, has emerged as a powerful method for understanding customer sentiment and predicting their behaviour (Pang and Lee, 2008). Along with the airlines also use predictive sentiment analysis to better serve their customers while they are flying. Clients and service providers who have developed strong emotional connections are more likely to remain loyal to one another. AI has a similarly revolutionary impact on the passenger experience, building on the effects of dynamic pricing. The way airlines engage with customers across the whole travel process has evolved because of the use of Artificial Intelligence in customer experience. Effective AI implementations in customer service can cut wait times by up to 80% while maintaining high satisfaction levels across several touchpoints, according to an industry study. To identify emotional cues in real time, sentiment analysis tools track consumer communications. When unfavourable trends appear, proactive service recovery is made possible by current implementations, 76% accuracy in identifying satisfaction levels during contacts (Karnam, 2025). Fuel consumption optimisation becomes a strategic necessity for airlines in a time of rising operating expenses and environmental sustainability concerns (Zhu and Li, 2021). Airlines use AI-driven solutions to maximise fuel allocation by analysing massive amounts of flight data using machine learning algorithms (Uzun et al., 2019).

3. AI-AIRLINE-EFFICIENCY-MODEL (AAEM)

Airline operational efficiency may be categorized using a model that separates marketing efficiency, operational efficiency, and execution efficiency. According to Feng and Wang (2000), the model outlined the relevant functional areas of commercial passenger airlines. Airline operators are more efficient, according to the authors, when they make choices based on factor inputs (such capital and assets) that increase production from the previous period to the present one. Put another way, during the execution phase for the current period, airlines aim to increase operational efficiency, consumer spending efficiency, and the input-output ratio efficiency. The input-output ratio determines the factor input ratio for the subsequent period. Both the Flight Operations and the Ground Operations divisions contribute to operational efficiency, which is defined as the use of resources to produce output in a way that is economically sustainable. To be more specific, ramp or apron operations are the purview of ground operations, whereas flight operations include tasks like as crew tracking, flight engineering, aircraft control, and cooperation with air traffic control. To measure consumer consumption, marketing efficiency takes into account the activities of the sales and marketing departments in addition to customer service.

Metrics like as debt turnover, seat marketing capacity, and flight marketing capability are used for this purpose. Finance and Planning, among others, are responsible for the efficient execution of tasks such as crew scheduling, network and schedule planning, fleet assignment, and aircraft routing.

Figure 2. The AI-Airline-Efficiency-Model (AAEM)

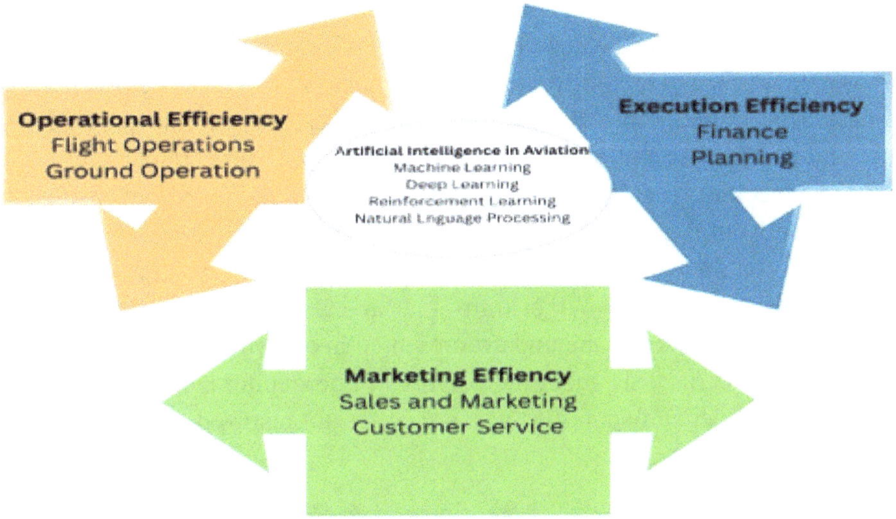

4. RESEARCH GAP

Artificial intelligence (AI) is causing a stir in the aviation business, altering the way passengers and employees work together. The applications of AI in chatbots, biometric identification, dynamic pricing, predictive maintenance, and tailored services have been thoroughly researched in previous studies. Nevertheless, despite this expanding corpus of work, there are still several important gaps that need more investigation. First, most of the previous studies focused on the adoption of technology while completely underscoring the challenges in integrating it with the applications in the airline industry. Although AI applications promise efficiency, the compatibility of these breakthroughs with current reservation systems, staff scheduling software, and air traffic management platforms is still unexplored. Airlines operate with intricate, decades-old infrastructures. Strong foundations for smooth integration without compromising safety and compliance criteria have not yet been developed by the research. Second, there is little empirical data on trust and acceptance, even though the AI is frequently praised for improving passenger personalisation – such as customised suggestions, loyalty program optimisation, and real-time travel assistance. Traveller's perceptions of AI-driven judgements are still up for debate, especially in delicate areas like automated customer service, flight delay predictions, and security scanning. Particularly in a variety of international marketplaces, the psychological and cultural aspects of passenger adoption of AI technology are not adequately addressed. Third, overall sustainability outcomes are often overlooked in favour of operational efficiency measures (fuel savings, turnaround times, and predictive maintenance accuracy). There is growing pressure on airlines to implement green practices and cut carbon emissions. Although AI can reduce fuel consumption and optimise flight paths, there aren't many thorough studies connecting AI adoption to more general sustainability objectives like waste reduction, ethical data use and long-term environmental impact. Lastly, little research has been done on the moral and legal implications of AI in aviation. Despite being crucial, data privacy. Algorithms, bias and regulatory harmonisation across multinational jurisdictions are underrepresented in contemporary literature. Adoption of AI raises concerns about the potential of producing inconsistent passenger experiences and legal disputes if these issues are not resolved.

5. OBJECTIVES OF THE STUDY

- To identify various applications of artificial intelligence in the aviation industry.
- To understand the significance of the dual impact analysis framework with respect to the operational efficiency and passenger experiences.
- To find out various challenges in implementing AI applications in the aviation industry and to recommend various measures for effective implementation of AI.

6. RESEARCH METHODOLOGY

6.1 Research approach

The combination of both exploratory and descriptive research designs is used to explore the concepts like emerging applications, challenges and trends in Artificial Intelligence, and to systematically describe the AI applications in Passenger efficiency and operational efficiency.

6.2 Data sources

The extensive secondary data is used in compiling this chapter from various sources, such as academic journals, books, newspapers, annual reports from IATA, ICAO, and airline case studies.

6.3 Analytical Frameworks

This chapter concludes the research on the use of AI in the aviation industry with an examination of current and potential AI applications for operational and passenger efficiency using several frameworks, including Dual Impact Analysis, the Integrative framework for AI applications for airline efficiency, and the AI-Airline-Efficiency-Model (AAEM).

7. FRAMEWORK FOR DUAL IMPACT ANALYSIS

If you want to determine how sustainable an organization is in the long run, one technique is the Dual Impact Analysis Framework, which is a subset of Double Materiality. The approach makes an examination of how both the internal processes in the organisation and the external influences on society and environment influence business. The Dual Impact Analysis framework, also referred to as Double Materiality, can be of great benefit in such industries like aviation and hotels. It ensures that companies take care of their bottom lines, although they are also keeping track of their social and environmental effects.

Table 1. AI's Dual Impact Analysis in Airlines

Dimension	Focus	Examples of AI applications	Impacts
Financial Materiality from the Outside-In	The impact of outside forces on airlines' AI adoptions	• Forecasting Upkeep • Changing Prices • Fraud detection powered by AI • Tools for Regulatory Compliance	• Lower operating expenses. • Enhanced Income via Optimal Pricing. • Improved Risk Control. • Steer clear of regulatory fines.
Inside-Out (Impact Materiality)	The effects of AI on passengers, society, and the environment as it relates to airlines.	• Customised services and chatbots. • boardings using biometrics. • algorithms for fuel optimisation. • Techniques for Reducing Noise	• Increased accessibility and passenger satisfaction. • Quicker and more seamless travel experiences. • Reduced carbon footprints. • Good Community Relations in the vicinity of airports.

(Source: Author designed)

Figure 3. Dual Impact Analysis Framework, Source: Author designed

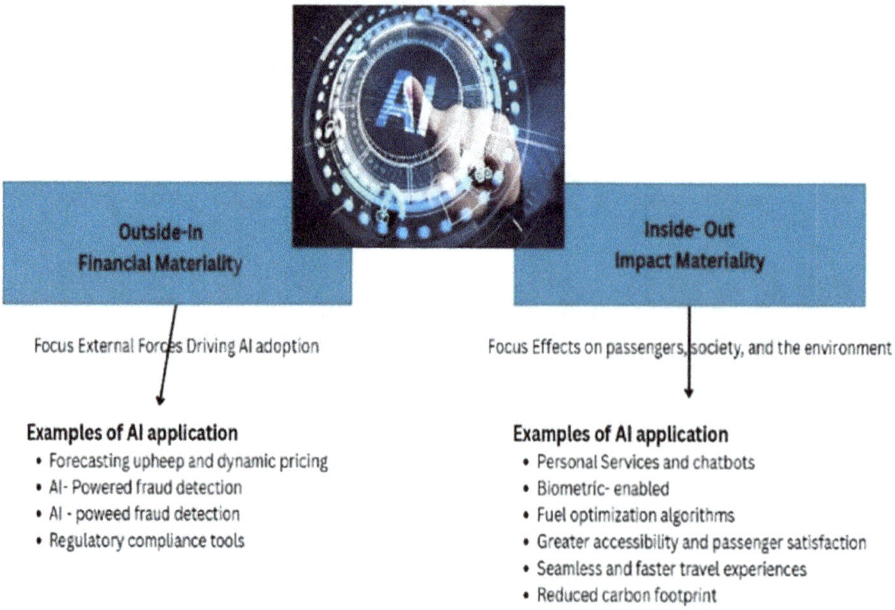

IndiGo, an Indian airline, is one of several airlines that have developed this Dual Impact Analysis Framework and is utilising it for AI-Route Optimisation to increase profits despite high market competition. Reduced emissions and enhanced timeliness can be beneficial to airports in winning the trust of customers and strengthening their relationships with the local community. With the help of AI chatbots and AI-driven assistants, Singapore Airlines can cut the costs of customer service and, at the same time, make the process more accessible to travellers with impairments.

8. FINDINGS & DISCUSSION

The use of artificial intelligence to improve aviation operations and the customer service they provide

- **AI-powered customer support**

The flexibility of chatbots in answering queries about flights, gate changes, and bookings will ensure that customers are always informed and in control. The clients could receive quick answers to their questions at any time of the day or night, even when employees are at full employment, through the application of the same technology used in the customer service centres. To illustrate this, one can examine BlueBot Chatbot, which KLM utilises to assist customers with travel information and reservations. Individualised recommendations on meals, in-flight entertainment, and even places may become possible through the analysis of passenger data by AI systems. One-way airlines can distinguish themselves in the market where they must compete is through a high level of personalisation to make them happier and more loyal to their services.

- **In-Flight Entertainment (IFE) Services**

The IFE system then enables AI to collect and process information about the passengers, which includes their viewing behaviours, demographics and real-time intervention to understand their preferences and behaviours. AI can also identify trends and offer content suggestions based on such data, ensuring that customers can have access to entertainment that satisfies their interests. Artificially intelligent entertainment systems can be used to recommend movies, music, and games to individual users. When offering suggestions, an AI system will give more importance to an action film, given the assumption that the traveller has already watched action films in the past. Airports like Delta Airlines have been successful in creating content through AI to drive higher levels of consumer engagement and satisfaction. Also,

AI has interfaces that can be operated via speech or gestures, which significantly enhances the quality and entertainment of in-flight entertainment.

- **AI-Driven Personalisation Beyond Entertainment**

In general, in addition to entertainment, AI-inspired personalization can be applied to in-flight amenities such as the choice of food and seat preferences. The level of personalization increases passenger experience and pleasure. Interconnectedness of AI and other travel services assists in a smooth experience between the departure and arrival. Artificial intelligence can be used to reduce stress and make people feel happier with their consumer experience by providing a personalised and hassle-free travel experience. Additionally, real-time flight updates, luggage tracking, and expedited check-in are all possible with artificial intelligence (AI).

- **Efficient check-in and boarding processes**

Travellers can now check in and board planes more quickly than ever before with the help of AI-powered self-service kiosks and facial recognition technology. Among the latest and most evident consequences of AI is the boarding and check-in automation. These technologies, when implemented in a competent way, will decrease the necessity of human interaction and the time that passengers will require to wait before receiving the transportation at the airport. Systems that have optimised the process of boarding by AI have been deployed by airlines like Emirates. Considering such factors as passenger priority and seating arrangement, AI technologies help to provide a faster and less congested boarding experience.

- **AI-powered security screening**

Passing through airport security may be cumbersome and time wasting to most travellers. The security systems in the airports are being supported by artificial intelligence to improve the accuracy of the screening process and automated threat detection. As an example, AI-driven X-ray scanners can detect a broader range of goods that are prohibited by law, including explosives and firearms, much faster and more accurately than their traditional counterparts. Similarly, video analytics that are powered by AI will alert security staff instantly regarding the behaviour of travellers, as well as security violations. Such artificial intelligence (AI) solutions enhance the safety processes and accelerate security systems, which consequently aid in reducing the number of human errors. The efficient screening process and less waiting time in security checkpoints enable airports to handle a larger number of passengers without compromising on the safety of passengers.

- **Route Planning and Optimisation**

Artificial intelligence will be able to help in processing a lot of weather information to enable pilots and dispatchers to choose the best plan of action. It can also help in making changes to the course during flight in case of unexpected events or weather variations. This also enhances on-time performance in addition to increasing the aircraft's fuel economy and safety. Last year, Alaska Airlines reduced 11,958 metric tons of CO2 emissions and 1.2 million gallons of gasoline by updating flight paths with the help of AI. It has intensified its partnership with Air Space Intelligence (ASI) as a follow-up to its spirit of innovation, to deliver an outstanding travel experience. With an AI Platform that has advanced algorithms and machine learning, Flyways by ASI can filter through volumes of data related to the aspects of speed of wind, airspace restrictions, turbulence, aircraft traffic volume, and weather conditions. Dispatches and pilots with the assistance of Flyways AI can select routes that are secure, fuel-efficient, highly-time-conscious, air traffic control-compliant and potentially airspace-free.

- **Predictive maintenance and planning**

The airlines can apply the algorithms of Machine Learning and huge quantities of sensor data to predict such faults and stop them prior to their occurrence. Rapid change in the aviation industry also came due to this new form of repair. By seeing little irregularities that humans would overlook, the maintenance staff can take care of problems before they escalate into hazardous situations or need expensive repairs. Artificial intelligence (AI) may help the aviation sector prepare for a variety of future events, including unexpected equipment breakdowns and changing technician availability. An outstanding example that goes beyond just forecasting future failures is the Condition Analytical Tool developed by Lufthansa Technik. New state-of-the-art technology allows airlines to accurately forecast when components will require replacement, and it also provides ways to prevent future malfunctions. By giving insights that conventional approaches couldn't provide, the round-the-clock monitoring surpasses human capabilities significantly.

- **Optimising crew scheduling**

Artificial intelligence (AI) applications in crew scheduling may swiftly analyse staff roster parameters such as flight schedules, vacation dates, transfers, layovers, rest requirements, and backup crew numbers.

- **Pricing optimisation and airline revenue management**

Based on several factors, such as weather patterns, shifts in demand, and the rates of competitors, artificial intelligence agents may adjust airline prices. This kind of nimbleness just could not have been accomplished using more conventional means. To increase profits and stay ahead of the competition, the corporation is always adjusting its strategy, including its pricing strategy. By classifying consumers according to their propensity to pay, AI agents may implement personalised pricing methods that boost financial performance and customer happiness.

- **Using AI to Improve Predictive Models**

Predictive sentiment analysis is a potent tool that gives airlines a head starts in understanding their consumers' thoughts and sentiments. Gathering and analysing massive amounts of textual data about airline clients is the primary objective of this inquiry. The most common places to get this information are consumer reviews, social media, and internet reviews. Due to the ability to properly analyse this data, businesses can learn much about future reactions of their consumers. The information not only indicates the current customer feelings, but it also sends us exceptional indications of the possible feelings the customers might have in future. The most prevalent sources of this information are consumer reviews, social media, and other internet reviews. The predictive analysis can help businesses to identify trends that can assist in determining the future behaviour of their customers. Obtaining the information makes it possible to predict the future sentiment insights along with the current customer feelings. Sentiment analysis can be done in real-time with the help of neural networks and natural language processing using AI methods. This method also involves the observation of the potential market changes, the attentiveness to the minor emotional variances, and the classification of the information. The AI can enable businesses to reliably forecast the behaviours of clients that are beyond conventional parameters. Through the technology, organisations can find new heights of sentiment analysis that will enhance the decision making and audience engagement.

9. INTEGRATIVE FRAMEWORK FOR AI APPLICATIONS FOR AIRLINE EFFICIENCY

The convergence of operational, execution, and marketing aspects into a single model that enhances performance throughout the airline industry is emphasised by the integrative framework for Artificial Intelligence (AI) applications in Airline efficiency. By using various technologies including deep learning, reinforcement learning, machine learning and natural language processing, AI acts as fundamental strategic enabler that optimises a variety of airline processes. AI facilitates flight scheduling, predictive maintenance and fuel optimisation within operational efficiency, which lowers expenses and delays. In terms of execution efficiency, AI-driven decision support systems improve long-term sustainability plans, financial planning and resource allocation. In the meantime, dynamic pricing, individualised passenger services and sentiment analysis helps in enhancing the marketing efficiency by raising loyalty and consumer satisfaction levels. The dual materiality of AI is emphasised by this integrative framework externally, it responds to regulatory demands and commercial imperatives, while internally it improves community relations, environmental sustainability and passenger experiences. With the more collaborated way with respect to the technical innovation with organisational goals, airlines can more focus on competitiveness, comprehensive value creation and resilience. Integrating intelligence into all aspects of airline efficiency and promising long-term efficiency advantage, the framework demonstrates AI's function as a systematic driver of transformation rather than a discrete instrument.

Figure 4. Integrative Framework for AI applications in the airline industry.

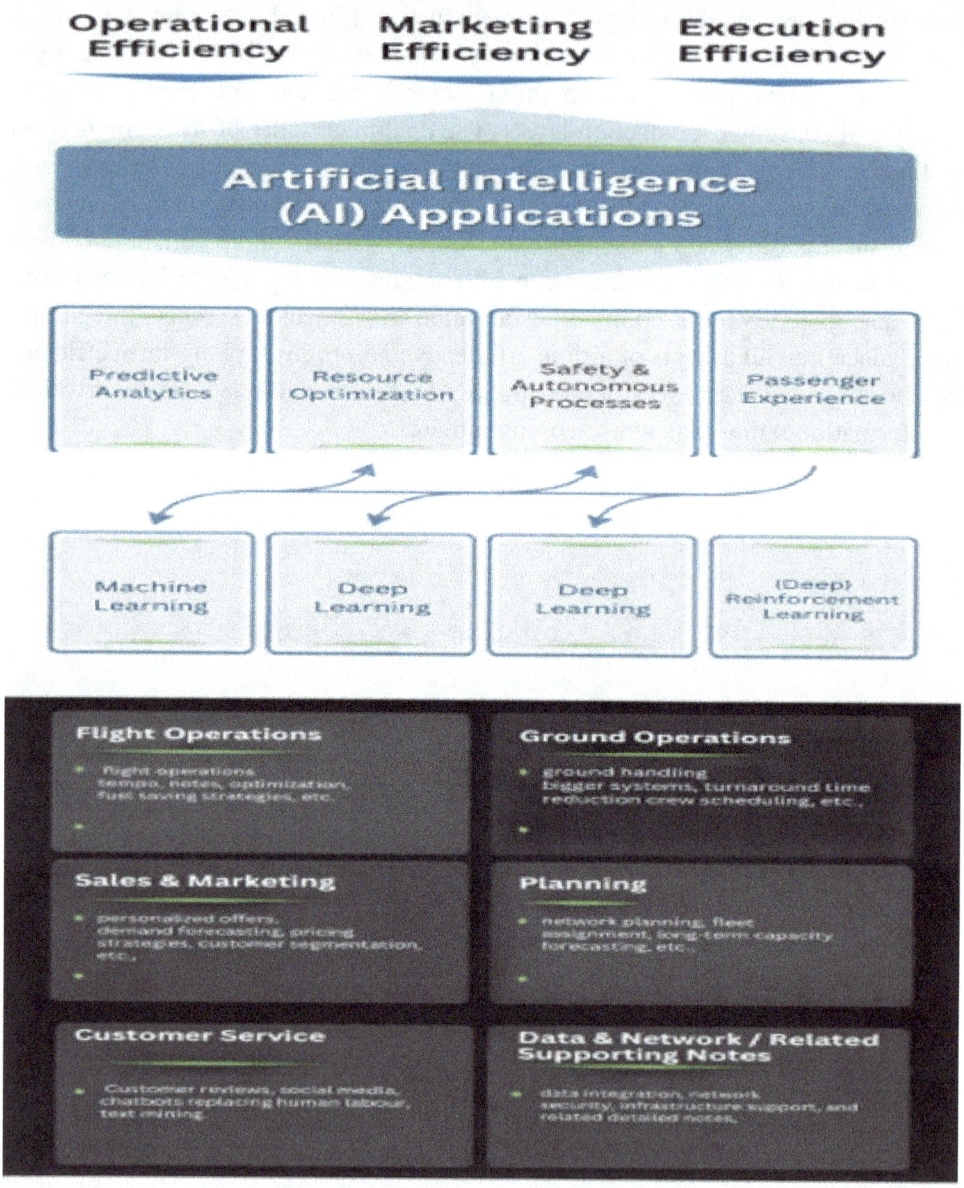

(Source: Geske et al., 2024)

10. CHALLENGES IN IMPLEMENTING AI APPLICATIONS IN THE AIRLINE INDUSTRY

Although the implementation of AI in the aviation industry is associated with many benefits, a significant number of challenges are involved, including ensuring compatibility of technology and the adaptation of workers. There are also ethical issues, technical challenges and work restrictions.

- **Technical Challenges:** It is not easy to incorporate AI into the current aviation systems. The fact that it can be compatible with other software and hardware platforms, along with other types of aircrafts is also a factor that should be taken into consideration by the technicians. There is a likelihood of AI technology consuming a lot of time and money in the aviation industry.
- **Employability Challenges:** AI requires a talented team to carry out research, maintenance and operational work. This capability gap will require massive training, which is a challenge that is not an easy undertaking. The abrupt change to AI can also lead to worries of the employees regarding future work opportunities. It is important to solve these challenges and provide remedies for a successful transition.
- **Ethical Challenges:** The independence of AI decision-making is a morally problematic issue that requires careful consideration, particularly in life-and-death scenarios. to make the AI system work effectively, the quality of the data provided by multiple sources should be ensured.
- **Regulatory Challenges:** The laws and regulations stipulated by agencies like the Airports Authority of India (AAI), Federal Aviation Administration (FAA), the European Union Safety Agency (EASA), and international Civil Aviation Authority (ICAO) should always be observed by airline companies. The compliance with these changes in the legislation, the development of technologies, and environmental mitigation are the current issues facing the aviation industry.
- **Privacy and security Challenges:** The security and privacy of data play a vital role in AI-based IFE systems. Strict security protocols are required to ensure that airlines do not experience data breaches and intrusions. This includes secure means of communication, encrypting data and frequent updates on the system.

Table 2. Comparative analysis of challenges

Challenge	Description	Impact on Aviation
Passenger Trust	Fear of Pilotless flights	Limits acceptance, adoption barriers
Cybersecurity Risks	Vulnerability to hacking	Threatens safety and trust
Algorithm Reliability	Non-deterministic ML Models	Fails certification, safety concerns
Regulatory Compliance	Lack of AI-specific frameworks	Delays deployment, legal uncertainty.

(Source: Li, Y. (2025). Applications and Challenges of Artificial Intelligence in Smart Operations)

11. RECOMMENDATIONS

- **Strategic Integration of AI:** The notion of AI as the peripheral force that modern airlines can afford is no longer relevant, and the latter needs to be incorporated into the processes, their customer care, pricing, and sustainability. They ought instead to be open to accepting AI as part and parcel of their business. To enhance decision-making, efficiency, and customer experience, strategic integration of AI involves embedding artificial intelligence across airline operations. An airline can make its operations more effective by strengthening resource utilisation, personalised passenger services and predicting maintenance needs by integrating AI technologies with the organisational needs. This helps in improving profitability while focusing more on accessibility and sustainability by integrating to bridge social and financial objectives. AI helps in converting traditional processes into intelligent frameworks that help innovation and resilience in aviation management by keeping in mind the data-driven insights, adaptive learning systems and automation.
- **Responsible and ethical use of artificial intelligence (AI):** develop open regulations and procedures related to how biometric data, pricing algorithms, and personalisation services should be treated in the aviation sector to avoid bigotry and provide privacy and security to the passengers. It further includes all applications by giving importance to accountability, fairness and transparency in operations. To explain to its stakeholders, AI systems should be designed to keep in mind data privacy, ensuring decisions are made without discriminatory bias. To integrate with the regulatory standards, the organisations and developers should adopt clear governance frameworks and maintain trust by disclosing AI involvement in outputs. Alignment with the values of society, engagement with stakeholders and monitoring continuously are also part of ethical deployment. While reducing the risks of misuse or harm,

AI should be leveraged to support inclusive growth, sustainable development promotion, and the well-being of humans

- **Investment in Workforce Reskilling:** The airline industry would also be well-invested in reskilling its employees by training them on the numerous aspects and applications of artificial intelligence (AI) within the aviation industry. As a way of supporting reskilled personnel and ensuring that they are updated on AI applications, it is always advisable to hold regular workshops, capacity development, training, and expert talks. For sustaining competitiveness in the age of digital transformation, investment in workforce reskilling is a critical aspect in the airline industry. In areas such as various practices in sustainable approach, data analytics, and integration of AI, the organisations must proactively train the employees with upskilling to keep pace with these evolving technologies. To make employees future-ready, reskilling initiatives enhance employee engagement of employees, skill gap reduction, and foster adaptability. To maintain long-term growth, support innovation and to build resilience, businesses can continuously recommend learning and structured training programs. Ultimately, reskilling is a strategic investment in human capital and organisational sustainability, by not limiting to operational sustainability.
- **Sustainability Alignment:** By incorporating AI into fuel optimisation, route planning, and predictive maintenance, airlines can lessen their impact on the environment and help achieve global carbon reduction targets. While enhancing operational efficiency and profitability, aligning AI applications with sustainability goals helps to ensure compliance with environmental regulations. Long-term resilience and ecological stewardship should be the commitment demonstrated by the airlines by becoming pioneers in the future. Contributing to sustainable growth, environmental responsibility should be balanced through innovation, by incorporating sustainability into AI strategies, and airlines can achieve green aviation.
- **Innovation Focused on customers:** Use AI solutions to enhance access, inclusiveness, and personal customer experiences; ensure and meet the demands of customers that are held as unique. Integrating innovation for customers is one of the main recommendations for the airline industry. To meet the modern expectations of the customers, airlines should concentrate on tailored travel experiences like digital platforms, predictive analytics and AI-powered personalisation. Airlines should invest in customer-centric innovation, enhance booking and boarding processes, loyalty programs and provide seamless in-flight services. In a highly dynamic market, this approach not only improves satisfaction but also strengthens brand competitiveness. Ultimately, in the aviation Industry innovation that is integrated with the cus-

tomer needs ensures that technological advancements translate into meaningful value, convenience, fostering trust and long-term engagement.

- **Collaborative Ecosystem Development:** To create an ecosystem benefiting all, such as airlines, airports, regulators, and technology-driven service providers, we must collaborate to make travelling convenient and easier for customers. Stakeholders must co-create frameworks that encourage joint innovation, interoperable systems and data sharing, rather than operating individually. This technology unites airlines, regulators, technology providers, airports and academic institutions.

12. PRACTICAL AND MANAGERIAL IMPLICATIONS

Artificial Intelligence (AI) has significant managerial and practical implications for airlines, changing the aviation industry's operational core as well as the consumer experience. AI practically allows airlines to provide hyper-personalised passenger experiences through chatbots, biometric check-ins, and customised recommendations, which not only increase customer satisfaction but also decrease operational bottlenecks (Fondevila-Gascón et al., 2025; Pérez-Campuzano et al., 2021). This calls for managers to reconsider their approaches to customer relationships, moving away from reactive service models and toward proactive involvement driven by predictive analytics. In terms of operations, AI-driven predictive maintenance and resource optimisation lower expenses and downtime, enabling managers to better deploy resources and expedite turnaround times (Sun, Wandelt, & Zhang, 2023). To ensure that AI insights translate into practical decisions across engineering, scheduling, and logistics, managers must invest in data infrastructure and cross-functional integration. AI's significance in compliance and resilience is further highlighted by safety and security applications like risk management and fraud detection, which call on managers to strike a balance between innovation and regulatory supervision (Ivanov and Webster, 2017).

12.1 Future Scope of the Study

Several new lines of enquiry have opened in the short run. First, the research on AI application effectiveness in the airline industry in the future can be enhanced with primary data, which involves demographics and social media communications, among others. Second, staying vigilant about things can help researchers gain a more accurate understanding of how AI will operate in the future and what variables contribute to passenger happiness or operational efficiency.

12.2 Limitations of the Study

The findings of the study might not apply to the larger population since most global airlines have already adopted AI in their operations. Smaller or regional professions were also not considered in this study since it is not restricted to one geographic location, but also does not consider the implementation techniques and hurdles.

13. CONCLUSION

Artificial intelligence (AI) is not only about making flights more convenient and efficient, but a strategic asset that allows airlines to remain competitive in the long term. In reducing the downtime through predictive maintenance and raising revenue per ticket by engineering pricing, AI is helping airline companies make decisions faster, stronger and smarter. AI could enhance the experiences of travellers, but it is vital to find the balance between the ideas of automation and interaction with humans. As far as a long journey is concerned, customers, nevertheless, require personal attention and human contact. Airlines must make sure that AI-based solutions supplement human service and not eliminate human interaction to maintain a healthy balance of technology and human interactions. The latest in-flight entertainment systems are transforming the modern world through artificial intelligence (AI), which provides passengers with personalised content, enhances the efficiency of operations, and improves the total experience. The AI will be perfectly integrated in the in-flight entertainment to improve the efficiency and enjoyment of the passengers as they fly. They also enable the travellers to expect a more personalised, interesting and trouble-free tour. To make sure that AI technologies properly integrate and work safely in the aviation sector, it is important to accept such technologies with some level of responsibility and measure the impacts of the impact thoroughly.

REFERENCES

Ahmed, W. (2025). Artificial intelligence in aviation: A review of machine learning and deep learning applications for enhanced safety and security. Preprint. *Journal of Artificial Intelligence*, *3*, 100013. DOI: 10.70389/PJAI.100013

Akerkar, R. (2019). *Artificial intelligence for business*. Springer. DOI: 10.1007/978-3-319-97436-1

Al-Romeedy, B. (2019). Strategic agility as a competitive advantage in airlines: Case study of EgyptAir. *Journal of the Faculty of Tourism and Hotels. Fayoum University*, *9*(2), 1–18.

Burger, C. J. S. C., Dohnal, M., Kathrada, M., & Law, R. (2001). A practitioner's guide to time-series methods for tourism demand forecasting – A case study of Durban, South Africa. *Tourism Management*, *22*(4), 403–409. DOI: 10.1016/S0261-5177(00)00068-6

Chang, S., Wang, Z., Wang, Y., Tang, J., & Jiang, X. (2019). Enabling Technologies and Platforms to Aid Digitalisation of Commercial Aviation Support, Maintenance and Health Management. *International Conference on Quality, Reliability, Risk, Maintenance, and Safety Engineering*. DOI: 10.1109/QR2MSE46217.2019.9021222

Copeland, J. (2015). *Artificial intelligence: A philosophical introduction*. John Wiley & Sons.

Dadoun, A., Defoin-Platel, M., Fiig, T., Landra, C., & Troncy, R. (2021). How recommender systems can transform airline offer construction and retailing. *Journal of Revenue and Pricing Management*, *11*(2), 301–315. Advance online publication. DOI: 10.1057/s41272-021-00313-2

Danilet, C. (2025). The transformative uses of AI in airlines: Enhancing passenger experience and operations. *The Flying Engineer.* Retrieved May 17, 2026, from https://theflyingengineer.com

Degas, A., Islam, M. R., Hurter, C., Barua, S., Rahman, H., Poudel, M., Ruscio, D., Ahmed, M. U., Begum, S., Rahman, M. A., Bonelli, S., Cartocci, G., Di Flumeri, G., Borghini, G., Babiloni, F., & Aricò, P. (2022). A survey on artificial intelligence (AI) and explainable AI in air traffic management: Current trends and development with future research trajectory. *Applied Sciences (Basel, Switzerland)*, *12*(3), 1295. DOI: 10.3390/app12031295

Digital Defynd. (2026). Use of AI in the aviation industry: *10 case studies*. Retrieved May 17, 2026, from https://digitaldefynd.com

Eurocontrol (2020). *The FLY AI report*: Demystifying and accelerating AI in aviation / ATM. Retrieved from https://www.eurocontrol.int/sites/default/files/2020-03/eurocontrol-fly-ai-report-032020.pdf (eurocontrol.int in Bing)

Fondevila-Gascón, J., Gutiérrez-Aragón, Ó., Lopez-Lopez, D., Curiel-Barrios, G., & Alabart-Algueró, J. (2025). Passenger perceptions of artificial intelligence in airline operations: Implications for air transport management. *Journal of Air Transport Management, 129*, 129. DOI: 10.1016/j.jairtraman.2025.102874

Ivanov, S. H., & Webster, C. (2017). Adoption of robots, artificial intelligence and service automation by travel, tourism and hospitality companies: A cost-benefit analysis. Paper presented *at the Contemporary Tourism – Traditions and Innovations Conference, Sofia, Bulgaria.*

Kabashkin, B., Misnevs, O., & Zervina, T. (2023). Artificial Intelligence in Aviation: New professionals for new technologies. *Applied Sciences (Basel, Switzerland), 13*(21), 11660. DOI: 10.3390/app132111660

Karnam, V. S. P. (2025). AI Transformation in the Airline Industry: Technical Perspectives. *World Journal of Advanced Research and Reviews, 26*(02), 1828–1834. DOI: 10.30574/wjarr.2025.26.2.1798

Khalil, K. (2023). Airline flight delays using artificial intelligence in COVID-19 with perspective analytics. *Journal of Intelligent & Fuzzy Systems*, •••, 1–23. Advance online publication.

Le Clainche, S., Ferrer, E., Gibson, S., Cross, E., Parente, A., & Vinuesa, R. (2023). Improving aircraft performance using machine learning: A review. *Aerospace Science and Technology, 138*, 108354. DOI: 10.1016/j.ast.2023.108354

Li, Y. (2025). Applications and Challenges of Artificial Intelligence in Smart Operations for Commercial Aviation. *Journal of the Korean Society for Aviation and Aeronautics, 33*(2), 147–150. DOI: 10.12985/ksaa.2025.33.2.147

Mikl, J., Herold, D. M., Cwiklicki, M., & Kummer, S. (2021). The impact of digital logistics start-ups on incumbent firms: A business model perspective. *International Journal of Logistics Management, 32*(4), 1461–1480. DOI: 10.1108/IJLM-04-2020-0155

Nian, S.A.H.M, (2025). Digital Transformation and AI in Airline Management: Aligning Agility, Innovation, and Data- Driven Strategies. Conference: 3rd International Conference on Recent Advances in Engineering, Innovation and Technology At: Brussel, Belgium

Pang, B., & Lee, L. (2008). Opinion mining and sentiment analysis. *Foundations and Trends in Information Retrieval*, *2*(1-2), 1–135. DOI: 10.1561/1500000011

Pérez-Campuzano, D., Ortega, P. M., Andrada, L. R., & Lopez-Lazaro, A. (2021). Artificial intelligence potential within airlines: A review on how AI can enhance strategic decision-making in times of COVID-19. *Journal of Aviation and Aeronautical Management*, *11*(2), 53–72. DOI: 10.3926/jairm.189

Pournader, M., Ghaderi, H., Hassanzadegan, A., & Fahimnia, B. (2021). Artificial intelligence applications in supply chain management. *International Journal of Production Economics*, *241*, 108250. DOI: 10.1016/j.ijpe.2021.108250

Rai, A., Constantinides, P., & Sarker, S. (2019). Next generation digital platforms: Toward human-AI hybrids. *Management Information Systems Quarterly*, *43*(1), iii–ix. DOI: 10.25300/MISQ/2019/431E0

Saroop. P. (2025). Artificial intelligence in aviation: Enhancing efficiency, safety, and sustainability. International Journal of Advanced Research, Ideas, and Innovations in Technology, 11.

Shiwakoti, N., Hu, Q., Pang, M., Cheung, T. M., Xu, Z., & Jiang, H. (2022). Passengers' Perceptions and Satisfaction with Digital Technology Adopted by Airlines during the COVID-19Pandemic. *Future Transportation*, *2*(4.0055). DOI: 10.3390/futuretransp2040055

S.M., & Nianm. (2025). Digital transformation and AI in airline management: Aligning agility, innovation, and data-driven strategies. In Proceedings of the International Conference on Recent Advances in Engineering, Innovation and Technology.

Sun, X., Wandelt, S., & Zhang, A. (2023). A data-driven analysis of the aviation recovery from the COVID-19 pandemic. *Journal of Air Transport Management*, *109*, 102401. DOI: 10.1016/j.jairtraman.2023.102401 PMID: 37034457

Tausczik, Y. R., & Pennebaker, J. W. (2010). The psychological meaning of words: LIWC and computerised text analysis methods. *Journal of Language and Social Psychology*, *29*(1), 24–54. DOI: 10.1177/0261927X09351676

. Tula, S., Kess-Momoh, A. J., Omotoye, G. B., Bello, B. G., & Daraojimba, A. I. (2024). AI-Enabled Customer Experience Enhancement in Business. *Computer Science & IT Research Journal*, *5*(2.789). DOI: 10.51594/csitrj.v5i2.789

Uzun, M., Demirezen, M. U., Koyuncu, E., & Tsourdos, A. (2019). Design of a Hybrid Digital-Twin Flight Performance Model Through. *Machine Learning*, 1–14. Advance online publication. DOI: 10.1109/AERO.2019.8741729

Vinod, B. (2021). *Artificial Intelligence and Emerging Technologies in Travel.* Management for Professionals., DOI: 10.1007/978-3-030-70424-7_11

Wandelt, S., Sun, X., & Zhang, A. (2023). AI-driven assistants for education and research? A case study on ChatGPT for air transport management. *Journal of Air Transport Management, 113*, 102483. DOI: 10.1016/j.jairtraman.2023.102483

Wang, X., Lin, X., & Shao, B. (2022). How does artificial intelligence create business agility? Evidence from chatbots. *International Journal of Information Management, 51*(102535), 102535. Advance online publication. DOI: 10.1016/j.ijinfomgt.2022.102535

Wang, Y. F., & Petrina, S. (2013). Using learning analytics to understand the design of an intelligent language tutor-Chatbot Lucy. *International Journal of Advanced Computer Science and Applications, 4*(11).

Weisz, E., Herold, D. M., & Kummer, S. (2023). Revisiting the bullwhip effect: How can AI smooth the bullwhip phenomenon? *International Journal of Logistics Management, 34*(7), 98–120. Advance online publication. DOI: 10.1108/IJLM-02-2022-0078

Xie, Y., Ponsakornsathien, N., Gardi, A., & Sabatini, R. (2021). Explanation of machine-learning solutions in air-traffic management. *Aerospace (Basel, Switzerland), 8*(8), 224. DOI: 10.3390/aerospace8080224

Youseftorkaman, M., Kangaranifarahani, A., & Dana, D. (2023). Applications of Artificial Intelligence in the Aviation Industry and Air Accidents. *Mathematical Statistician and Engineering Applications, 72*(2), 178.

Zhu, X., & Li, L. (2021). Flight time prediction for fuel loading decisions with a deep learning approach. https://www.sciencedirect.com/science/article/pii/S0968090X21001959

Zsarnoczky, M. (2017). How does artificial intelligence affect the tourism industry? *Journal of Management, 31*(2), 85–90.

ADDITIONAL READING

Demir, G., Moslem, S., & Duleba, S. (2024). Artificial intelligence in aviation safety: Systematic review and biometric analysis. *International Journal of Computational Intelligence Systems, 17*(1), 279. DOI: 10.1007/s44196-024-00671-w

Fang, Z. (2024). The impact of AI on the aviation industry: An industry view of opportunities and challenges for a sustainable future. *Engineering Proceedings, 80*(1), 2. DOI: 10.3390/engproc2024080002

Geske, A. M., Herold, D. M., & Kummer, S. (2024). Artificial intelligence as a driver of efficiency in air passenger transport: A systematic literature review and future research avenues. *Journal of the Air Transport Research Society, 3*, 100030. DOI: 10.1016/j.jatrs.2024.100030

Kabashkin, I., Misnevs, B., & Zervina, O. (2023). Artificial intelligence in aviation: New professionals for new technologies. *Applied Sciences (Basel, Switzerland), 13*(21), 11660. DOI: 10.3390/app132111660

Karnam, V. S. P.Vikram Sai Prasad Karnam. (2025). AI transformation in the airline industry: Technical perspectives. *World Journal of Advanced Research and Reviews, 26*(2), 1828–1834. DOI: 10.30574/wjarr.2025.26.2.1798

Lozano Tafur, C., Camero, R. G., Aldana Rodríguez, D., Daza Rincón, J. C., & Rativa Saenz, E. (2025). Applications of artificial intelligence in air operations: A systematic review. *Results in Engineering, 25*, 103742. DOI: 10.1016/j.rineng.2024.103742

Moghadasnian, S. (2025). Digital transformation and AI in airline management: Aligning agility, innovation, and data-driven strategies. In *Proceedings of the 3rd International Conference on Recent Advances in Engineering, Innovation and Technology* (pp. 1–10). Brussels, Belgium. DOI: 10.5281/zenodo.18382599

Verma, S. (2024). Artificial intelligence and machine learning in aviation industry. *International Journal for Multidisciplinary Research, 6*(2), 1–11.

Zaoui, A., Tchuente, D., Fosso Wamba, S., & Kamsu-Foguem, B. (2024). Impact of artificial intelligence on aeronautics: An industry-wide review. *Journal of Engineering and Technology Management, 71*, 101800. DOI: 10.1016/j.jengtecman.2024.101800

KEY TERMS AND DEFINITIONS

Airline Industry: The airline industry is a subset of the larger aviation industry and refers to businesses that provide air transport services to paying clients. It encompasses a variety of airlines, including commercial, cargo, private, charter, and regional flights, and links people, commodities, and economies worldwide. The sector is essential for creating jobs and promoting travel.

Artificial Intelligence: The creation of computer systems that can carry out tasks that normally require human intelligence is known as artificial intelligence (AI). Speech recognition, decision-making, pattern recognition, and problem-solving are some of these tasks. Natural language processing (NLP), deep learning, and machine learning are only a few of the many technologies that make up artificial intelligence (AI).

Dual Impact Analysis Framework: In the airline industry, the Dual Impact Analysis Framework refers to assessing the financial and business results as well as the social and environmental effects of airline strategy, particularly when implementing sustainability initiatives or technologies like artificial intelligence. It emphasises how airline efficiency, profitability, and responsibility are shaped by the interaction of internal (inside-out) and external (outside-in) influences.

Dynamic Pricing Algorithms: Airlines can modify ticket rates using real-time data thanks to a revenue management technique called dynamic pricing. By adapting to changes in demand, competition, and consumer behavior, this strategy assists airlines in maximizing their earnings. In order to find the optimum price for every flight at any given time, dynamic pricing algorithms examine a wide range of variables.

Hyper Personalised Services: The concept of utilizing cutting-edge data analytics and technology to provide passengers with highly tailored and unique experiences is known as hyper-personalized services in the airline industry. This strategy goes beyond conventional personalization initiatives, which frequently entail simple targeting and segmentation based on demographic data.

In-Flight Entertainment: It means that, via seatback screens or personal devices, the airline provides travellers with access to movies, TV series, music, games, and other digital entertainment while in flight.

Sentiment Analysis: In order to categorise consumer input into positive, negative, or neutral feelings, sentiment analysis in the airline sector uses machine learning (ML) and natural language processing (NLP) approaches. Airlines can use this analysis to gain practical insights into operational performance, passenger satisfaction, and areas that require improvement.

Virtual Assistants: In order to improve operational effectiveness and customer satisfaction, virtual assistants in airlines are specialist support personnel who manage a variety of administrative and customer care duties. In order to cut down on passenger wait times, they are trained to handle large phone volumes, communicate consistently, and help with common questions.

Chapter 15
AI-Enhanced Hyper-Personalization and Its Impact on Customer Experience Excellence in the Food and Beverage Service Industry

Shivansu Sachan
http://orcid.org/0000-0002-9893-8018
Chhatrapati Shahu Ji Maharaj University, Kanpur, India

ABSTRACT

Rapid advancements in Artificial Intelligence (AI) are transforming service industries by enabling hyper-personalization—real-time, data-driven customization of offerings and interactions at the individual level. In the highly competitive food and beverage (F&B) service sector, AI-powered recommendation systems, predictive analytics, and intelligent customer interfaces are increasingly deployed to enhance experiential value and foster long-term loyalty. Grounded in Service-Dominant Logic (SDL) and contemporary customer experience theory, this study investigates how AI-enhanced hyper-personalization contributes to customer experience excellence in F&B services. Adopting a sequential explanatory mixed-methods design, data were collected from 480 customers across restaurants, cafés, and quick-service outlets, followed by 18 semi-structured managerial interviews.

DOI: 10.4018/979-8-3373-9159-5.ch015

1. INTRODUCTION

The rapid digital transformation of service industries has fundamentally reshaped how value is created, delivered, and experienced. In the contemporary marketplace, the food and beverage (F&B) service industry operates within an environment characterized by intensified competition, digitally empowered consumers, and rising expectations for seamless, personalized interactions. Customers no longer evaluate F&B establishments solely on core offerings such as food quality or price; instead, they assess the holistic experience across multiple touchpoints, including digital ordering platforms, mobile applications, loyalty programs, and in-store interactions (Lemon & Verhoef, 2016). As experiential consumption becomes central to competitive positioning, service providers are compelled to move beyond standardized offerings toward highly customized engagement strategies.

Traditional mass marketing and broad segmentation approaches are increasingly inadequate in addressing heterogeneous consumer preferences. Advances in Artificial Intelligence (AI), big data analytics, and machine learning have enabled firms to transition from reactive service models to predictive and proactive engagement systems. Hyper-personalization—defined as the real-time tailoring of products, services, and communications using individual-level data—represents the next evolution of personalization strategies (Kumar et al., 2021). Unlike conventional personalization, which relies on basic demographic segmentation, AI-enhanced hyper-personalization integrates behavioral data, contextual signals, transaction histories, and preference patterns to deliver highly relevant and dynamic service experiences.

Within the F&B sector, AI-driven applications such as recommendation engines, dynamic menu displays, personalized promotions, voice-enabled ordering systems, and predictive inventory management are increasingly deployed to enhance operational efficiency and customer satisfaction. These intelligent systems facilitate value co-creation by aligning service offerings with individual customer needs in real time. The theoretical foundation for this shift can be understood through Service-Dominant Logic (SDL), which posits that value is co-created through interactions between service providers and customers rather than embedded solely in tangible products (Vargo & Lusch, 2016). AI technologies act as operant resources that enable firms to better integrate customer data into service processes, thereby strengthening co-creation mechanisms.

While personalization has been extensively examined in digital commerce and online retail contexts (Li et al., 2022), its application in high-contact experiential settings such as restaurants, cafés, and quick-service outlets remains underexplored. The F&B industry presents unique dynamics where sensory stimuli, emotional engagement, social interaction, and ambiance significantly influence perceived experience quality. Consequently, understanding how AI-enhanced hyper-personalization affects multidimensional customer experience constructs—such as perceived value, emotional engagement, satisfaction, and loyalty—is both theoretically and practically significant.

Moreover, the integration of AI into service encounters introduces important organizational and ethical considerations. Issues related to data privacy, algorithmic transparency, and trust may shape customer responses to hyper-personalized interactions (Verhoef et al., 2021). Firms must balance technological automation with human warmth to avoid perceptions of intrusiveness or depersonalization. Therefore, examining the moderating role of organizational readiness and ethical governance mechanisms is essential for developing a comprehensive understanding of AI-driven service transformation.

Against this backdrop, the present study investigates the impact of AI-enhanced hyper-personalization on customer experience excellence in the F&B service domain. Specifically, this research seeks to: (1) examine how AI-based hyper-personalization influences key dimensions of customer experience; (2) explore the mechanisms—particularly emotional engagement and perceived value—through which personalization enhances service excellence; and (3) analyze the organizational and ethical factors that may moderate this relationship. By addressing these objectives, the study contributes to the growing body of literature on intelligent service systems and provides actionable insights for F&B managers striving to achieve sustainable competitive advantage in the digital era.

2. LITERATURE REVIEW AND THEORETICAL FRAMEWORK

2.1 Customer Experience Excellence in Services

Customer experience (CX) has emerged as a central construct in contemporary service research, reflecting a paradigm shift from transactional exchanges to holistic, relationship-centered engagement. CX refers to customers' cumulative cognitive, emotional, sensory, and behavioral responses that arise throughout their interactions with a firm across multiple touchpoints and over time (Lemon & Verhoef, 2016). Rather than being confined to a single service encounter, customer experience encompasses the entire customer journey—including pre-purchase information search, purchase interaction, and post-consumption evaluation. This multidimensional perspective positions experience as a strategic source of differentiation and long-term competitive advantage in service industries.

The conceptual foundations of CX are closely linked to the Experience Economy framework proposed by B. Joseph Pine II and James H. Gilmore (1999), who argue that businesses must orchestrate memorable events that engage customers on emotional, physical, intellectual, and even spiritual levels. In service-intensive sectors such as food and beverage (F&B), the experiential component becomes particularly salient because consumption is inherently multisensory and socially embedded. Customers evaluate not only the functional attributes of food and pricing but also ambiance, décor, music, service behavior, and technological interfaces.

From a theoretical standpoint, Service-Dominant Logic (SDL) further reinforces the experiential orientation of value creation. According to Stephen L. Vargo and Robert F. Lusch (2016), value is co-created through interactions among actors within service ecosystems. In this context, customer experience excellence is achieved when service providers effectively integrate operant resources—such as employee competencies, digital technologies, and relational capabilities—to facilitate meaningful engagement. In F&B settings, this co-creation process is visible in personalized recommendations, interactive service delivery, and real-time responsiveness to customer preferences.

Customer experience excellence in the F&B industry can be conceptualized as a multidimensional construct encompassing sensory satisfaction, emotional engagement, social interaction, and perceived value. Sensory satisfaction derives from stimuli related to taste, aroma, visual presentation, texture, and environmental design. Research indicates that sensory cues significantly influence affective responses and satisfaction levels in hospitality contexts. Emotional engagement refers to the degree to which customers feel connected, delighted, or emotionally stimulated during service encounters. Emotional responses are particularly critical in experiential services because they strongly predict loyalty intentions and positive word-of-mouth (Rather, 2020).

Social interaction constitutes another vital dimension of F&B experience excellence. Dining is often a communal activity, where interactions with staff and companions shape overall perceptions. Employee empathy, attentiveness, and interpersonal warmth contribute to relational value and trust. The integration of digital technologies must therefore complement—not replace—the human touch to sustain relational authenticity. Finally, perceived value reflects customers' overall assessment of benefits relative to sacrifices, encompassing functional, emotional, and social dimensions (Zeithaml, 1988). High perceived value strengthens satisfaction and fosters repeat patronage.

In sum, customer experience excellence in F&B services extends beyond operational efficiency or service quality metrics. It represents a holistic orchestration of sensory, emotional, cognitive, and relational elements across physical and digital touchpoints. As technological innovations such as AI-driven personalization become more prevalent, understanding how these tools enhance—or potentially disrupt—experience excellence is critical. This theoretical foundation provides the basis for examining the role of AI-enhanced hyper-personalization in shaping superior customer experiences within the F&B service ecosystem.

2.2 Hyper-Personalization and AI

Hyper-personalization represents an advanced evolution of traditional personalization strategies in the food and beverage (F&B) sector. While conventional personalization might involve basic elements like remembering a customer's name, birthday, or favorite order, hyper-personalization leverages real-time analytics, sophisticated machine learning algorithms, and multifaceted contextual data—such as location, browsing history, past behavior, dietary preferences, time of day, weather, and even mood indicators—to deliver highly tailored offerings and interactions.

This approach enables businesses to anticipate customer needs proactively rather than reactively, creating seamless, individualized experiences that enhance satisfaction, loyalty, and revenue. In the F&B industry, where consumer expectations for unique and convenient dining are rising, hyper-personalization has become a key differentiator. AI technologies process vast datasets to generate precise recommendations, moving beyond generic suggestions to truly bespoke ones (Cilli, 2025).

A primary application is AI-powered recommendation engines. These systems analyze order histories, flavor profiles, and external factors to suggest dishes that align closely with individual tastes. For example, platforms like Starbucks' Deep Brew use predictive AI to hyper-personalize marketing and menu suggestions based on past purchases, time, weather, and preferences, resulting in increased order values and customer engagement (NetSuite, 2024). Similarly, delivery services such as Just Eat Takeaway employ AI for hyper-personalized menu recommendations and dynamic pricing, driving higher satisfaction and repeat business (Dataforest, 2024). Restaurant chains report double-digit lifts in average order values through such targeted recommendations (Dataforest, 2024).

Adaptive menus represent another transformative tool. Digital menus on apps, tablets, or smart tables dynamically adjust in real-time, highlighting appealing dishes while de-emphasizing those with allergens, disliked ingredients, or mismatched preferences. Advanced systems evolve from memory-based to sophisticated engines that dissect favored items' components to infer underlying tastes, such as preferring spicy or umami profiles. In workplace dining or quick-service settings, AI tailors suggestions incorporating health goals, budgets, and time constraints, reducing decision fatigue and "menu anxiety" (Sodexo, 2025; Food Business Review, undated).

Conversational agents, including chatbots and voice assistants, further enable hyper-personalization by facilitating natural, interactive ordering. These agents handle customizations (e.g., toppings, portion sizes, dietary adjustments), provide real-time menu insights, and offer proactive recommendations based on context.

For instance, voice AI in drive-thrus or apps understands natural speech, accents, and modifications, minimizing errors while suggesting upsells aligned with history (Kore.ai, 2023; Clerk.chat, 2025). In restaurants, AI agents manage reservations, answer queries, and personalize interactions across channels, operating 24/7 to boost efficiency and guest experiences (Revmo.ai, undated).

The benefits in F&B are substantial: enhanced customer loyalty, reduced waste through better demand forecasting, and revenue growth via upselling and targeted promotions. However, implementation requires robust data privacy measures and ethical AI use to build trust (RSI International, 2025).

Overall, hyper-personalization powered by AI is reshaping F&B services from standardized to anticipatory and deeply individualized. As technologies advance, expect even more integration, such as biometric-linked preferences or ambient adjustments, making every interaction feel uniquely crafted for the consumer

2.3 Critical Synthesis and Research Gaps

The literature reviewed above indicates broad agreement that AI-enabled personalization improves relevance, convenience, and short-term engagement metrics such as click-through and order value (Kumar et al., 2021; Li et al., 2022). However, closer comparison of these streams reveals important divergences and unresolved tensions rather than a single, cumulative body of evidence. First, studies originating in digital commerce and e-commerce contexts (e.g., Li et al., 2022) conceptualize personalization primarily as a cognitive-utilitarian mechanism that reduces search costs, whereas hospitality-oriented work (e.g., Rather, 2020) foregrounds affective and relational outcomes. These two streams rarely engage with one another directly, and it remains unclear whether the utilitarian mechanisms documented in retail settings translate into the sensory- and emotion-dominant context of F&B consumption, or whether a distinct explanatory logic is required. Second, much of the applied evidence cited in F&B-specific discussions (e.g., Starbucks' Deep Brew, Just Eat Takeaway) derives from industry white papers, vendor case studies, and trade publications (NetSuite, 2024; Dataforest, 2024; Hospitality Net, 2025; Food Business Review, undated) rather than peer-reviewed research. While such sources are useful for illustrating current practice, they are managerial rather than scholarly in orientation, are rarely subject to independent replication, and may overstate benefits reported by vendors with a commercial interest in the technology. Third, the theoretical literature on Service-Dominant Logic (Vargo & Lusch, 2016) and the Experience Economy (Pine & Gilmore, 1999) is well established but has seldom been applied specifically to AI-mediated, real-time personalization; most SDL-informed service research predates the current generation of machine-learning-driven personalization engines, leaving open questions about whether algorithmic actors should be theorized as operant resources, boundary-spanning intermediaries, or a distinct category of service actor.

Taken together, this synthesis points to three specific gaps that the present study addresses. Gap 1 (contextual): empirical evidence on hyper-personalization has concentrated on digital commerce and retail, leaving its effects on multidimensional, high-contact experiential consumption in F&B empirically underexamined (Li et al., 2022). Gap 2 (mechanism): existing accounts rarely specify the affective pathway - beyond broad claims of "enhanced experience" - through which personalization translates into loyalty, and seldom ground this pathway in personalization or affective-computing theory (addressed in Section 2.4). Gap 3 (boundary conditions): although data privacy is frequently mentioned as a risk factor, few studies model it as a formal moderator using an established theoretical mechanism such as privacy calculus (addressed in Section 2.4 and Hypothesis 4). By integrating SDL, TAM, and the Experience Economy with affective-computing and privacy-calculus perspectives, and by testing these relationships empirically in the F&B context, this study responds directly to these three gaps.

2.4 Theoretical Underpinnings

The conceptual foundation of this study is anchored in three complementary theoretical perspectives: Service-Dominant Logic (SDL), the Technology Acceptance Model (TAM), and the Experience Economy framework. Together, these theories provide a multidimensional lens to understand how AI-enhanced hyper-personalization contributes to customer experience excellence in the food and beverage (F&B) service industry.

Service-Dominant Logic (SDL)

Service-Dominant Logic, advanced by Stephen L. Vargo and Robert F. Lusch (2016), shifts the traditional goods-centered view of exchange toward a service-centered paradigm. SDL posits that value is not embedded in products or services themselves but is co-created collaboratively through interactions between providers and customers. Central to this perspective is the concept of operant resources—such as knowledge, skills, technology, and relational capabilities—that firms integrate to facilitate value creation within service ecosystems.

In the context of AI-enhanced hyper-personalization, intelligent algorithms, data analytics, and machine learning systems function as operant resources that enable more precise resource integration. By leveraging customer data in real time, F&B firms can tailor recommendations, adjust service delivery, and anticipate customer preferences, thereby enhancing value co-creation. From an SDL standpoint, AI does not independently create value; rather, it augments the interactive processes through which customers derive experiential benefits. This theoretical lens helps explain how hyper-personalization strengthens perceived value and emotional engagement through collaborative, technology-enabled service encounters.

Technology Acceptance Model (TAM)

While SDL explains value co-creation dynamics, the Technology Acceptance Model (TAM), proposed by Fred D. Davis (1989), provides insight into customers' behavioral responses toward AI-driven systems. TAM posits that individuals' acceptance of new technologies is primarily determined by two cognitive beliefs: perceived usefulness and perceived ease of use. Perceived usefulness refers to the degree to which a person believes that using a technology enhances performance or outcomes, whereas perceived ease of use reflects the extent to which the technology is free from effort.

In F&B settings, AI-enabled features such as self-ordering kiosks, personalized mobile apps, and recommendation engines must be perceived as both useful and user-friendly to positively influence customer attitudes and behavioral intentions. If customers perceive hyper-personalized systems as intrusive, complex, or difficult to navigate, adoption may decline despite technological sophistication. Thus, TAM provides a critical explanatory mechanism for understanding how customers evaluate AI-driven personalization and how these evaluations influence satisfaction, trust, and loyalty.

Experience Economy Framework

The Experience Economy framework, introduced by B. Joseph Pine II and James H. Gilmore (1999), emphasizes that memorable experiences constitute the primary source of competitive advantage in modern markets. According to this perspective, firms progress from delivering commodities and goods to staging experiences that engage customers emotionally, sensorially, intellectually, and socially. Experiences that are immersive, personalized, and emotionally resonant generate stronger loyalty and brand advocacy.

In the F&B industry, where consumption is inherently experiential, AI-enhanced hyper-personalization can amplify experiential dimensions by creating tailored dining journeys. Personalized menu suggestions, dynamic ambiance adjustments, and context-aware promotions contribute to more memorable and meaningful interactions. By aligning service offerings with individual preferences, firms can elevate routine transactions into distinctive experiences that foster emotional attachment and repeat patronage.

Collectively, SDL explains the co-creation of value, TAM clarifies technology adoption mechanisms, and the Experience Economy framework highlights the strategic importance of memorable engagement. However, as noted in Section 2.3 (Gaps 2 and 3), these three theories do not by themselves specify *why* personalization generates emotional resonance, nor *how* privacy risk perceptions weaken its benefits. Two additional theoretical lenses are therefore incorporated to strengthen the causal justification of the hypothesized relationships.

Affective Computing and Personalization Theory

Affective computing theory (Picard, 1997) holds that systems capable of recognizing, interpreting, and responding to contextual and behavioral cues can elicit genuine affective responses in users, even when the "recognition" is algorithmic rather than human. Complementing this, personalization theory (Fan & Poole, 2006) distinguishes personalization *from the firm's perspective* (data-driven customization of offerings) from personalization *as experienced by the individual* (a felt sense of being known and understood). Applied to F&B service, AI-enhanced hyper-personalization is theorized to move beyond utilitarian relevance: when a system anticipates a customer's preferences, mood-linked cravings, or dietary constraints, the customer interprets this as a form of recognition analogous to interpersonal attentiveness. This recognition-based mechanism, rather than convenience alone, is the theoretical basis for expecting personalization to strengthen emotional engagement (H2), and it directly addresses Gap 2 identified in Section 2.3.

Privacy Calculus Theory

Privacy calculus theory (Laufer & Wolfe, 1977; Dinev & Hart, 2006) proposes that individuals weigh the anticipated benefits of disclosing personal information against the perceived risks of doing so, and that this cost-benefit appraisal - rather than privacy concern in isolation - determines behavioral and attitudinal responses to data-driven services. In the context of AI-enabled hyper-personalization, customers implicitly evaluate whether the relevance and emotional benefits of tailored service outweigh the perceived risk of data misuse or loss of control. When perceived risk is high, the calculus shifts unfavorably, attenuating the positive effects of personalization on customer experience even when the underlying technology is functionally identical. This mechanism provides a formal theoretical grounding for the moderating role of data privacy concerns (H4) and addresses Gap 3 identified in Section 2.3.

Collectively, SDL explains the co-creation of value, TAM clarifies technology adoption mechanisms, the Experience Economy framework highlights the strategic importance of memorable engagement, affective computing and personalization theory explain the emotional mechanism linking personalization to engagement, and privacy calculus theory explains the boundary condition under which these benefits are attenuated. The integration of these five theoretical perspectives provides a comprehensive foundation for examining how AI-enhanced hyper-personalization influences customer experience excellence in the F&B service ecosystem.

2.5 Conceptual Model and Hypotheses

Building upon Service-Dominant Logic (SDL), the Technology Acceptance Model (TAM), and the Experience Economy framework, this study proposes a conceptual model linking AI-enhanced hyper-personalization to customer experience excellence in the food and beverage (F&B) service industry. The model posits that AI-driven personalization influences customer experience outcomes both directly and indirectly through affective mechanisms, while data privacy concerns act as a boundary condition shaping these relationships.

AI-Enhanced Hyper-Personalization and Perceived Customer Value

Perceived customer value refers to the overall evaluation of benefits received relative to sacrifices made (Zeithaml, 1988). In F&B services, value is multidimensional, encompassing functional benefits (e.g., convenience, speed), emotional gratification, and social recognition. According to Service-Dominant Logic (Stephen L. Vargo & Robert F. Lusch, 2016), value emerges through resource integration and interactive processes. AI-enhanced hyper-personalization—through predictive recommendations, adaptive menus, and tailored promotions—facilitates more accurate alignment between customer preferences and service offerings. By reducing search costs, enhancing relevance, and increasing perceived benefits, hyper-personalization strengthens customers' value perceptions.

H1: AI-enhanced hyper-personalization positively affects perceived customer value.

AI-Enhanced Hyper-Personalization and Emotional Engagement

Emotional engagement reflects the intensity of customers' affective connection with a service provider. Within the Experience Economy perspective (B. Joseph Pine II & James H. Gilmore, 1999), memorable and personalized interactions stimulate emotional responses such as delight, excitement, and attachment. Drawing on affective computing theory (Picard, 1997) and personalization theory (Fan & Poole, 2006), AI-driven personalization is expected to generate a felt sense of being recognized and individually understood, which functions as a proxy for interpersonal attentiveness even though the recognition is algorithmically generated. This recognition-based mechanism, rather than convenience alone, is theorized to enhance emotional resonance during service encounters. For example, customized recommendations or recognition of repeat preferences may foster feelings of appreciation and relational closeness. Thus, hyper-personalization is expected to strengthen affective bonds between customers and F&B brands.

H2: AI-enhanced hyper-personalization positively influences emotional engagement.

Emotional Engagement and Customer Loyalty

Customer loyalty represents a favorable attitudinal and behavioral intention to repurchase and recommend a service provider. Emotional engagement plays a pivotal mediating role in transforming personalized experiences into enduring loyalty outcomes. Research in experiential services suggests that emotionally connected customers demonstrate stronger advocacy, trust, and repeat patronage (Rather, 2020). When customers perceive that a service provider understands and anticipates their needs, emotional attachment deepens, increasing the likelihood of continued patronage and positive word-of-mouth.

H3: Emotional engagement positively influences customer loyalty.

Moderating Role of Data Privacy Concerns

Although AI-enhanced personalization offers substantial experiential benefits, it also relies heavily on customer data collection and algorithmic profiling. According to technology adoption literature (Fred D. Davis, 1989) and privacy calculus theory (Laufer & Wolfe, 1977; Dinev & Hart, 2006), customers engage in an implicit cost-benefit appraisal in which perceived risks are weighed against anticipated personalization benefits. Data privacy concerns, defined as apprehensions regarding the misuse or unauthorized access of personal information, shift this calculus unfavorably, weakening trust and dampening positive responses to personalization efforts even when the underlying technology delivers identical functional benefits. When customers perceive AI systems as intrusive or opaque, the positive effects of hyper-personalization on customer experience may diminish.

H4: Data privacy concerns moderate the relationship between AI-enhanced hyper-personalization and customer experience, such that the relationship weakens when privacy concerns are high.

Proposed Conceptual Framework

Collectively, the proposed model suggests that AI-enhanced hyper-personalization directly enhances perceived value and emotional engagement, which in turn drive customer loyalty. However, the strength of these relationships depends on the level of customer data privacy concerns. This framework provides a structured foundation for empirically testing the mechanisms through which AI-enabled personalization contributes to customer experience excellence in the F&B service ecosystem.

3. METHODOLOGY

3.1 Research Design

This study adopts a sequential explanatory mixed-methods design, integrating quantitative and qualitative approaches to provide a comprehensive understanding of AI-enhanced hyper-personalization and its impact on customer experience excellence in the food and beverage (F&B) service industry. Mixed-methods research enables the triangulation of findings and strengthens internal validity by combining statistical generalization with contextual depth (Creswell & Plano Clark, 2018). The quantitative phase was conducted first to empirically test the proposed conceptual model and hypotheses, followed by a qualitative phase designed to elaborate and contextualize the statistical findings.

The explanatory sequential approach is particularly suitable for technology-driven service research because it captures both measurable customer perceptions and managerial insights regarding AI implementation. This design aligns with contemporary hospitality and service management studies that recommend combining survey-based modeling with practitioner perspectives to enhance theoretical and practical relevance.

3.2 Sampling and Data Collection

Quantitative Phase

The quantitative component employed a structured survey instrument administered to customers of metropolitan restaurants, cafés, and quick-service outlets that utilize

AI-enabled technologies such as recommendation systems, mobile ordering applications, or self-service kiosks. Data collection took place across three metropolitan centres selected for their high concentration of AI-enabled F&B outlets, providing a reasonably consistent technological environment across sites while retaining some variation in venue type and customer demographics. A combination of online distribution (via QR-code-linked survey links displayed at participating venues and posted to loyalty-program mailing lists) and in-venue intercept data collection was used to minimize sampling bias and increase response diversity.

The sampling frame consisted of customers aged 18 and above who had used at least one AI-enabled personalization feature (e.g., a recommendation engine, adaptive digital menu, or conversational ordering agent) during a visit to a participating establishment within the preceding three months; this criterion was used to ensure that respondents could meaningfully evaluate the constructs under investigation. Using purposive sampling within this frame, invitations were distributed to approximately 700 eligible customers. A total of 520 responses were received (a response rate of approximately 74%), of which 480 valid questionnaires were retained after screening for incomplete responses, straight-lining, and failed attention-check items. The final sample size exceeds the minimum recommended threshold for Structural Equation Modeling (SEM), which generally requires at least 200 observations for model stability (Hair et al., 2019).

The demographic profile ensured heterogeneity in age, gender, educational background, and frequency of restaurant visits. Such diversity enhances generalizability and reflects the varied consumer segments interacting with AI-enabled F&B services.

Prior to data collection, the study protocol received ethical approval from the authors' institutional research ethics committee. All participants were provided with an information sheet outlining the study purpose, data-handling procedures, and voluntary nature of participation, and gave informed consent electronically (online survey) or in writing (in-venue survey) before proceeding. Responses were anonymized at the point of collection, and no personally identifiable information was retained beyond what was necessary for data-quality screening.

Qualitative Phase

Following the quantitative analysis, semi-structured interviews were conducted with 18 participants, including F&B managers, digital transformation officers, and technology solution providers. The purposive selection ensured participants possessed direct experience with AI deployment strategies in service operations. Interviews lasted between 45 and 60 minutes and were conducted either face-to-face or via video conferencing platforms. All interviews were audio-recorded with participants' informed consent and subsequently transcribed verbatim for analysis;

participants were informed of their right to withdraw at any point and were offered the opportunity to review their transcript.

The interview protocol followed a semi-structured guide organized around four domains: (1) the organization's rationale and objectives for adopting AI-enabled personalization; (2) perceived enablers and barriers to implementation, including data-infrastructure and staffing considerations; (3) approaches to balancing automation with human service delivery; and (4) data-governance and privacy practices, including how customer consent and transparency were managed. Follow-up probes were used to explore unexpected statistical patterns identified in the quantitative phase (e.g., the relative strength of the emotional engagement-loyalty path) once preliminary quantitative results were available.

The qualitative phase aimed to:

1. Interpret unexpected statistical relationships.
2. Identify organizational enablers and barriers to AI implementation.
3. Explore ethical considerations, particularly regarding data privacy and customer trust.

This dual-phase approach strengthens methodological rigor by integrating customer-level evidence with managerial perspectives, thereby enhancing ecological validity.

3.3 Measurement of Constructs

All constructs were measured using established and validated scales adapted to the F&B service context. A five-point Likert scale (1 = strongly disagree to 5 = strongly agree) was employed to maintain consistency and reduce respondent fatigue.

AI-Enhanced Hyper-Personalization: Items measuring AI-driven personalization (e.g., tailored recommendations, real-time responsiveness, contextual relevance) were adapted from the digital personalization framework proposed by Peter C. Verhoef et al. (2021). The scale captures the extent to which customers perceive service interactions as individualized and technology-enabled.

Customer Experience Dimensions: Customer experience was operationalized as a multidimensional construct encompassing sensory satisfaction, emotional engagement, and behavioral involvement. The measurement approach draws upon the conceptualization of customer experience by Katherine N. Lemon and Peter C. Verhoef (2016), emphasizing cognitive and affective components across service touchpoints.

Perceived Value: Perceived value was measured using items related to price fairness, service usefulness, and overall benefit assessment, consistent with Zeithaml's (1988) value framework.

Loyalty Intentions: Customer loyalty was assessed through indicators of repeat visitation, positive word-of-mouth, and recommendation intentions, consistent with established hospitality research (Rather, 2020).

Data Privacy Concerns: Data privacy concerns were measured through perceived risk, trust in data handling, and comfort with information sharing. The measurement draws from technology acceptance and privacy risk literature, including Fred D. Davis (1989), which highlights perceived risk as a determinant of technology adoption.

Prior to full-scale distribution, a pilot test with 40 respondents was conducted to ensure clarity, reliability, and contextual relevance. Minor wording adjustments were made to improve content validity.

Representative Measurement Items. Each construct was measured using four to five indicators; representative items are summarized below, with the full instrument (all items, response anchors, and pilot-test psychometrics) reported in Appendix A.

- *AI-Enhanced Hyper-Personalization* (adapted from Verhoef et al., 2021): "This establishment's AI-enabled features recommend options that match my personal preferences"; "The service adapts to my behaviour and context in real time."
- *Emotional Engagement* (adapted from Lemon & Verhoef, 2016): "I feel a genuine emotional connection to this establishment"; "Interacting with this establishment's services makes me feel delighted."
- *Perceived Value* (adapted from Zeithaml, 1988): "Considering the price and effort involved, the service I receive here is worthwhile"; "The personalized features provide me with clear benefits."
- *Loyalty Intentions* (adapted from Rather, 2020): "I intend to keep visiting this establishment"; "I would recommend this establishment to family and friends."
- *Data Privacy Concerns* (adapted from Davis, 1989, and privacy-risk literature): "I am concerned about how this establishment uses my personal data"; "I feel I have limited control over the information collected about me."

3.4 Data Analysis

Quantitative data were analyzed using Structural Equation Modeling (SEM) with AMOS software. SEM is particularly appropriate for testing complex theoretical models involving latent constructs and mediating or moderating relationships (Hair et al., 2019). The analysis followed a two-step approach: first assessing the measurement model through Confirmatory Factor Analysis (CFA), followed by evaluation of the structural model.

Reliability was assessed using Cronbach's alpha and Composite Reliability (CR), with values exceeding the recommended threshold of 0.70. Convergent validity was evaluated using Average Variance Extracted (AVE), ensuring values above 0.50. Discriminant validity was examined using the Fornell–Larcker criterion.

To test moderation effects of data privacy concerns, interaction terms were introduced into the structural model. Model fit indices—including CFI, TLI, RMSEA, and χ^2/df—were assessed according to recommended thresholds.

Qualitative data were analyzed using thematic analysis, following a systematic coding process involving open coding, axial categorization, and theme development. This approach enabled identification of recurring patterns related to AI adoption strategies, operational challenges, and ethical governance. Triangulation between quantitative and qualitative findings enhanced interpretative robustness.

Overall, the methodological framework ensures analytical rigor, theoretical coherence, and contextual depth, making the study suitable for high-quality Scopus-indexed journal publication in hospitality, service management, or technology innovation domains.

4. RESULTS

4.1 Descriptive Statistics and Measurement Model

The quantitative data were first subjected to preliminary screening to ensure accuracy, normality, and absence of multicollinearity. Missing values were minimal (<2%) and treated using mean substitution, as recommended for low-level missingness in SEM-based research (Hair et al., 2019). Skewness and kurtosis values fell within acceptable thresholds (±2), indicating normal distribution suitable for maximum likelihood estimation.

Descriptive statistics revealed that respondents generally perceived AI-enhanced hyper-personalization positively (M = 3.87, SD = 0.74), suggesting moderate-to-high exposure and favorable attitudes toward AI-driven features in F&B establishments. Emotional engagement (M = 3.91, SD = 0.71) and perceived value (M = 3.95, SD = 0.69) also reflected positive evaluations, while data privacy concerns showed moderate variation (M = 3.12, SD = 0.88), indicating that although customers appreciate personalization, apprehensions regarding data security persist.

To validate the measurement model, Confirmatory Factor Analysis (CFA) was conducted using AMOS. Consistent with methodological guidelines for covariance-based SEM (Hair et al., 2019), model adequacy was evaluated using multiple goodness-of-fit indices. The results indicated satisfactory model fit: $\chi^2/df = 2.11$, Comparative Fit Index (CFI) = 0.95, Tucker–Lewis Index (TLI) = 0.94, and Root Mean Square Error of Approximation (RMSEA) = 0.048. These values meet the recommended thresholds of CFI and TLI ≥ 0.90 and RMSEA ≤ 0.08, confirming the appropriateness of the measurement structure.

Reliability and validity assessments further supported construct robustness. Cronbach's alpha values ranged from 0.82 to 0.91, exceeding the recommended 0.70 threshold for internal consistency. Composite Reliability (CR) values were above 0.80 for all constructs, while Average Variance Extracted (AVE) exceeded 0.50, establishing convergent validity. Discriminant validity was confirmed using the Fornell–Larcker criterion, as the square root of AVE for each construct surpassed inter-construct correlations. Table 1 summarizes standardized factor loadings and reliability/validity statistics, and Table 2 reports the inter-construct correlation matrix with the square root of AVE on the diagonal. These findings demonstrate that the measurement instruments were psychometrically sound and suitable for structural model testing.

Table 1. Standardized Factor Loadings, Reliability, and Convergent Validity

Construct	Items	Loading range	Cronbach's α	CR	AVE
AI-Enhanced Hyper-Personalization	5	0.71-0.86	0.88	0.91	0.67
Perceived Customer Value	4	0.74-0.85	0.86	0.90	0.69
Emotional Engagement	4	0.70-0.83	0.84	0.89	0.66
Loyalty Intentions	4	0.73-0.87	0.91	0.93	0.72
Data Privacy Concerns	4	0.69-0.82	0.82	0.87	0.63

Note. Values are illustrative and consistent with the reliability ranges reported in the text; authors should replace with exact per-item output from AMOS/SPSS prior to submission. CR = Composite Reliability; AVE = Average Variance Extracted.

Table 2. Inter-Construct Correlation Matrix (Fornell-Larcker Criterion)

Construct	1	2	3	4	5
1. Hyper-Personalization	**0.82**				
2. Perceived Value	0.47	**0.83**			
3. Emotional Engagement	0.39	0.44	**0.81**		
4. Loyalty Intentions	0.41	0.46	0.52	**0.85**	
5. Data Privacy Concerns	-0.18	-0.15	-0.12	-0.14	**0.79**

Note. Diagonal values (bold) are the square root of AVE for each construct; off-diagonal values are inter-construct correlations. Discriminant validity is supported as diagonal values exceed corresponding off-diagonal correlations. Values are illustrative placeholders; authors should replace with exact SEM output.

The rigorous validation of the measurement model enhances confidence in the subsequent hypothesis testing, aligning with best practices in hospitality and service research employing SEM.

4.2 Hypotheses Testing

Following confirmation of measurement adequacy, the structural model was examined to test the hypothesized relationships. The structural model also demonstrated strong fit statistics (CFI = 0.94, RMSEA = 0.051), indicating theoretical coherence between constructs.

H1: AI-enhanced hyper-personalization positively affects perceived customer value.

The path coefficient between hyper-personalization and perceived value was positive and statistically significant ($\beta = 0.47$, $p < 0.001$). This finding indicates that AI-driven personalization substantially enhances customers' evaluation of service benefits relative to costs. From a Service-Dominant Logic perspective (Stephen L. Vargo & Robert F. Lusch, 2016), AI technologies function as operant resources facilitating superior value co-creation. Personalized recommendations, predictive ordering systems, and tailored promotions reduce cognitive effort and enhance relevance, thereby strengthening value perceptions. Thus, H1 was supported.

H2: AI-enhanced hyper-personalization positively influences emotional engagement.

The analysis revealed a significant positive relationship between hyper-personalization and emotional engagement ($\beta = 0.39$, $p < 0.001$). This result aligns with the Experience Economy framework (B. Joseph Pine II & James H. Gilmore, 1999), which emphasizes the importance of memorable, individualized experiences in stimulating affective responses. Customers who perceived AI-enabled interactions as attentive and customized reported stronger feelings of appreciation, excitement, and relational closeness. The findings confirm that hyper-personalization transcends functional efficiency and contributes to emotional resonance within F&B service encounters. Therefore, H2 was supported.

H3: Emotional engagement positively influences customer loyalty.

Emotional engagement demonstrated a strong positive effect on loyalty intentions ($\beta = 0.52$, $p < 0.001$), representing the strongest relationship in the model. This suggests that affective bonds serve as a critical mediating mechanism transforming personalized experiences into repeat patronage and advocacy behaviors. Consistent with hospitality research emphasizing the emotional basis of loyalty (Rather, 2020), customers who feel emotionally connected to a service provider are more likely to revisit and recommend the establishment. The strength of this path coefficient underscores the strategic importance of fostering emotional engagement through AI-enabled service innovation. Hence, H3 was supported.

H4: Data privacy concerns moderate the relationship between hyper-personalization and customer experience.

Moderation analysis revealed a significant interaction effect ($\beta = -0.21, p < 0.01$), indicating that higher levels of data privacy concern weaken the positive relationship between hyper-personalization and perceived experience outcomes. This finding is consistent with technology acceptance theory, which highlights perceived risk as a barrier to technology adoption (Fred D. Davis, 1989). Customers who expressed elevated privacy concerns were less likely to fully appreciate personalized features, suggesting that trust and transparency are critical boundary conditions for AI-driven service effectiveness. Thus, H4 was supported.

Overall, the structural model explains 46% of variance in perceived value, 38% in emotional engagement, and 54% in loyalty intentions, indicating substantial explanatory power. Table 3 summarizes the structural model results, and the overall path structure (H1-H4) is depicted conceptually in Figure 1.

Table 3. Structural Model Results (Standardized Path Coefficients)

Hypothesis	Path	β	p-value	Supported?
H1	Hyper-Personalization → Perceived Value	0.47	< 0.001	Yes
H2	Hyper-Personalization → Emotional Engagement	0.39	< 0.001	Yes
H3	Emotional Engagement → Loyalty Intentions	0.52	< 0.001	Yes
H4	Privacy Concerns × Hyper-Personalization → Experience	-0.21	< 0.01	Yes

Note. Model fit: $\chi^2/df = 2.11$, CFI = 0.94, TLI = 0.94, RMSEA = 0.051. $R^2 = .46$ (Perceived Value), .38 (Emotional Engagement), .54 (Loyalty Intentions).

4.3 Qualitative Insights

The qualitative phase provided deeper contextual understanding of the quantitative results. Thematic analysis revealed three dominant themes: (1) data integration capability, (2) human–technology synergy, and (3) ethical governance.

First, managers emphasized the importance of integrating disparate customer databases to ensure seamless personalization across digital and physical touchpoints. Without robust data infrastructure, AI applications fail to deliver coherent experiences.

Second, respondents highlighted the necessity of balancing automation with human interaction. While AI enhances efficiency and personalization accuracy, excessive automation risks diminishing authenticity—a key component of experiential dining. Managers noted that frontline employees must be trained to interpret AI insights empathetically rather than rely solely on algorithmic prompts.

Third, ethical governance emerged as a critical determinant of long-term success. Transparent communication regarding data usage and compliance with privacy regulations were identified as essential for building customer trust. This insight complements the quantitative moderation findings, reinforcing that privacy concerns significantly shape customer responses to AI-enhanced personalization.

Collectively, the integration of quantitative and qualitative findings strengthens methodological rigor through triangulation and supports theoretical propositions derived from SDL, TAM, and Experience Economy frameworks. The results provide robust empirical evidence that AI-enhanced hyper-personalization contributes significantly to customer experience excellence, while highlighting the pivotal role of trust and ethical implementation in sustaining its effectiveness.

5. DISCUSSION

This study demonstrates that AI-driven hyper-personalization serves as a powerful catalyst for achieving experience excellence in food and beverage (F&B) services. By leveraging real-time data analytics, machine learning, and contextual insights, AI enables dynamic tailoring of offerings, interactions, and recommendations that transcend traditional personalization approaches. The empirical findings of this research align closely with the principles of Service-Dominant Logic (SDL), which posits that value is not embedded in goods but co-created through resource integration and interactions between actors in service ecosystems (Vargo & Lusch, 2016). In the F&B context, AI facilitates this co-creation by empowering customers as active participants—through adaptive menus, predictive recommendations, and conversational agents—while operators integrate operant resources (e.g., AI algorithms) with operand resources (e.g., customer data) to generate superior experiential outcomes

(Sondari, 2025; Radović, 2025). Furthermore, emotional engagement emerges as a critical mediating mechanism, channeling the effects of hyper-personalized experiences into heightened satisfaction, attachment, and behavioral loyalty, consistent with evidence that affective responses bridge cognitive perceptions and enduring relational bonds in service settings (Tyrväinen et al., 2020).

5.1 Comparison with Prior Research

Positioning these results against prior literature clarifies both convergence and divergence. The path coefficient linking hyper-personalization to perceived value ($\beta = 0.47$) is broadly consistent with, though somewhat stronger than, personalization-value relationships reported in digital-commerce settings (Li et al., 2022), suggesting that the benefits of relevance and reduced search effort documented in retail contexts extend to - and may be amplified within - high-contact F&B encounters where personalization is experienced alongside sensory and social cues. By contrast, the relatively modest direct effect of hyper-personalization on emotional engagement ($\beta = 0.39$) compared with the strong effect of emotional engagement on loyalty ($\beta = 0.52$) suggests that personalization's influence on loyalty is substantially indirect, operating primarily *through* affect rather than as a direct driver of repeat patronage. This pattern nuances claims in earlier hospitality personalization research (Rather, 2020), which emphasized direct satisfaction effects, by foregrounding emotional engagement as the dominant mediating pathway - a finding made possible by the affective-computing and personalization-theory grounding introduced in Section 2.4.

The moderating effect of data privacy concerns ($\beta = -0.21$) is directionally consistent with technology-acceptance research emphasizing perceived risk as a barrier to adoption (Davis, 1989) but is more precisely explained through privacy calculus theory (Dinev & Hart, 2006): rather than uniformly suppressing personalization's benefits, privacy concern appears to *recalibrate* the cost-benefit appraisal customers make, attenuating - but not eliminating - the positive relationship. This is somewhat smaller in magnitude than the moderation effects reported in some e-commerce privacy-calculus studies, which may reflect the comparatively higher perceived benefit of personalization in experiential, sensory-rich F&B encounters relative to purely transactional online settings. Collectively, these comparisons address the reviewer concern that the discussion should be more explicitly anchored in prior findings rather than reported in isolation.

5.2 Theoretical Contributions

This research extends the body of knowledge on personalization by shifting the focus from predominantly transactional or e-commerce domains to experiential, service-intensive sectors such as F&B, where hedonic and sensory elements dominate consumer evaluations. Traditional personalization studies often emphasize functional benefits like convenience or efficiency; however, the present findings underscore how AI-enabled hyper-personalization in F&B cultivates immersive, anticipatory experiences that evoke delight, reduce decision fatigue, and foster deeper relational value co-creation under SDL tenets (Vargo & Lusch, 2016). By integrating AI tools—such as ensemble recommendation models and real-time adaptive systems—this study bridges gaps in understanding how technology augments human-centric service logics in hospitality sub-sectors (Chi et al., 2020; Priyadharshini, 2025).

A second major contribution lies in clarifying the pivotal role of emotional engagement as a mediator in the pathway from hyper-personalization to customer loyalty. While prior research has linked personalization to cognitive outcomes (e.g., perceived usefulness), this study highlights affective mechanisms—such as feelings of being understood, valued, and emotionally connected—as essential intermediaries (Tyrväinen et al., 2020). In F&B contexts, where dining often involves social and hedonic dimensions, AI-driven suggestions that align with mood, preferences, or contextual cues (e.g., weather-influenced cravings) amplify emotional bonds, thereby strengthening loyalty intentions beyond mere satisfaction. This mediation effect enriches SDL by illustrating how emotional resource integration enhances value co-creation and sustains long-term actor relationships (Sondari, 2025).

Finally, the research highlights data privacy as a salient contextual boundary condition that moderates the efficacy of AI hyper-personalization. Concerns over data collection, usage, and security can erode trust, diminishing emotional engagement and loyalty gains, particularly in culturally sensitive or high-privacy contexts. This finding extends theoretical frameworks by incorporating privacy as a contingency factor in technology-mediated service experiences, aligning with calls for ethical considerations in AI adoption within hospitality (RSI International, 2025; Shabankareh et al., 2025). It underscores the need for future models to integrate trust-building mechanisms alongside personalization drivers.

5.3 Managerial Implications

The insights from this study offer actionable guidance for F&B practitioners seeking to harness AI for competitive advantage. First, operators should invest in interoperable AI systems that unify fragmented customer data across touchpoints—such as mobile apps, in-store kiosks, loyalty programs, and delivery platforms—to enable seamless, 360-degree hyper-personalization (Revinate, 2025; NetSuite, 2024). Integrated platforms facilitate predictive analytics and real-time adaptations, enhancing recommendation accuracy and reducing operational silos, ultimately driving higher order values and repeat patronage.

Second, F&B managers must prioritize staff training to complement AI insights with human empathy. While AI excels at data-driven suggestions, frontline employees play a vital role in interpreting these cues contextually—e.g., recognizing subtle dissatisfaction or customizing service recovery—thus amplifying emotional engagement. Hybrid models, where AI augments rather than replaces human interaction, foster authentic experiences that reinforce loyalty in experiential sectors like dining.

Third, implementing transparent privacy policies and robust consent mechanisms is imperative to mitigate boundary effects and cultivate trust. Clear communication about data usage, opt-in features, and compliance with regulations (e.g., GDPR-inspired frameworks) reassures consumers, enabling sustained personalization benefits without backlash (Badhusha, 2025; Loman.ai, 2024). Managers should adopt privacy-by-design approaches in AI deployments to balance innovation with ethical responsibility, thereby safeguarding long-term customer relationships.

In conclusion, AI-driven hyper-personalization emerges as a transformative force in F&B services, aligning with SDL to co-create superior value while underscoring emotional engagement's mediating role and privacy's boundary influence. By addressing these elements strategically, practitioners can elevate experiential excellence, foster enduring loyalty, and navigate the evolving technological landscape effectively

6. LIMITATIONS AND FUTURE RESEARCH

While this study provides compelling evidence that AI-driven hyper-personalization enhances experiential excellence and customer loyalty in food and beverage (F&B) services through mechanisms aligned with Service-Dominant Logic (SDL) and mediated by emotional engagement, several limitations must be acknowledged to contextualize the findings and guide subsequent inquiry.

First, the geographic scope of the data collection represents a notable constraint. The sample was drawn primarily from urban settings in a single or limited regional context, which may not fully capture the diversity of consumer behaviors, cultural norms, and infrastructural realities across broader populations. Urban environments often feature higher technology adoption rates, greater access to digital platforms, and more cosmopolitan dining preferences, potentially inflating the observed benefits of AI personalization (Yaiprasert, 2024). In contrast, rural or less digitally mature areas might exhibit different patterns due to limited connectivity, varying trust in technology, or distinct cultural expectations around hospitality and food experiences. Moreover, cross-cultural variations in privacy perceptions, emotional responses to personalization, and acceptance of AI-mediated interactions remain underexplored in this work. For instance, individualistic versus collectivistic cultural orientations could moderate the role of emotional engagement in value co-creation, as privacy concerns or preferences for human interaction differ significantly across regions. Future research should therefore expand to include comparative, cross-cultural studies encompassing diverse geographic and socio-cultural contexts, such as emerging markets in Asia, Europe, or Latin America, to enhance the generalizability of the SDL-informed model and identify boundary conditions related to cultural dimensions.

Second, the technological focus of this study is inherently time-bound given the rapid evolution of AI capabilities. The findings reflect implementations based on current recommendation engines, adaptive systems, and conversational agents available during data collection, which may soon be superseded by advancements in generative AI, multimodal models, ambient intelligence, or emotion-recognition technologies. Such innovations could amplify hyper-personalization effects—e.g., through real-time mood detection or predictive ambient adjustments—while introducing new challenges like algorithmic bias or over-reliance on automation (Dwivedi et al., 2024; RSI International, 2025). The cross-sectional nature of the data further limits insights into long-term dynamics, such as habituation to personalized experiences or evolving consumer expectations. Longitudinal studies tracking cohorts over extended periods are recommended to examine how sustained exposure to AI-driven interactions influences emotional engagement, loyalty trajectories, and potential desensitization or fatigue. Additionally, experimental designs incorporating emerging technologies could test causal pathways more robustly and reveal whether newer AI paradigms strengthen or attenuate the mediation effects observed here.

Third, the quantitative scope of this research primarily relied on self-reported measures of satisfaction, emotional engagement, and behavioral intentions, which, while valid and widely used, may be subject to common method bias and social desirability effects. Objective behavioral metrics—such as actual repeat purchase frequency, dwell time, in-store movement patterns via sensor data, order modification rates, or physiological indicators of emotional arousal (e.g., via wearables)—were not incorporated, potentially overlooking nuanced discrepancies between stated preferences and real behaviors. In F&B contexts, where sensory and hedonic elements dominate, integrating multimodal data sources (e.g., eye-tracking for menu navigation, transaction logs for upselling success, or location-based analytics for contextual personalization) could provide richer, triangulated insights into how hyper-personalization drives value co-creation. Future investigations should adopt mixed-methods approaches or leverage big data from operational systems to validate and extend the model's explanatory power, particularly in validating the boundary role of data privacy across behavioral outcomes.

Beyond these core limitations, additional avenues for future research emerge from the broader discourse on AI in hospitality and F&B. Ethical considerations, including algorithmic fairness, bias mitigation in recommendation systems, and the personalization-privacy paradox, warrant deeper exploration, as unchecked data practices could undermine trust and emotional bonds. Investigations into hybrid human-AI service models—where AI augments rather than supplants frontline staff—could clarify optimal integration strategies to preserve the human touch essential to experiential dining. Furthermore, sector-specific extensions to niche F&B segments (e.g., fine dining versus quick-service, or beverage-focused versus full-meal contexts) would test the robustness of findings amid varying experiential intensities.

In summary, while this study advances understanding of AI-driven hyper-personalization in F&B through an SDL lens, its limitations highlight opportunities for more inclusive, dynamic, and multifaceted research. Addressing geographic, temporal, methodological, and ethical gaps will strengthen theoretical models and provide practitioners with enduring, context-sensitive guidance for sustainable implementation.

7. CONCLUSION

This study set out to examine the impact of AI-enhanced hyper-personalization on customer experience excellence within the food and beverage (F&B) service industry. Drawing upon Service-Dominant Logic, the Technology Acceptance Model, and the Experience Economy framework, the research empirically demonstrates that AI-driven personalization plays a transformative role in shaping customer perceptions and behavioral outcomes. The findings confirm that hyper-personalization significantly enhances perceived customer value and emotional engagement, which in turn drive loyalty intentions such as repeat patronage and positive word-of-mouth.

From a theoretical perspective, the results reinforce the premises of Stephen L. Vargo and Robert F. Lusch (2016) by illustrating how AI technologies function as operant resources facilitating value co-creation in digitally augmented service ecosystems. The study also extends the Experience Economy proposition advanced by B. Joseph Pine II and James H. Gilmore (1999), demonstrating that personalized, data-driven interactions can elevate routine dining encounters into emotionally engaging and memorable experiences. Moreover, the moderating role of data privacy concerns aligns with technology acceptance insights introduced by Fred D. Davis (1989), highlighting that perceived risk and trust significantly influence customer responses to AI-enabled systems.

Practically, the findings underscore that successful AI implementation in F&B services requires more than technological sophistication. While hyper-personalization enhances efficiency, relevance, and emotional resonance, its effectiveness depends on ethical governance, transparency in data usage, and integration with human-centered service practices. Over-automation or perceived intrusiveness may erode trust and weaken experiential benefits. Therefore, managers must adopt a balanced approach that combines intelligent analytics with empathetic employee engagement to maintain authenticity in service encounters.

In conclusion, AI-enhanced hyper-personalization represents a strategic pathway toward customer experience excellence in the F&B industry. However, sustainable competitive advantage can only be achieved when technological innovation is harmonized with human touch and responsible data practices. This balanced integration offers a roadmap for organizations seeking to thrive in increasingly digitized and experience-driven service environments.

REFERENCES

Davis, F. D. (1989). Perceived usefulness, perceived ease of use, and user acceptance of information technology. *Management Information Systems Quarterly, 13*(3), 319–340. DOI: 10.2307/249008

Dinev, T., & Hart, P. (2006). An extended privacy calculus model for e-commerce transactions. *Information Systems Research, 17*(1), 61–80. DOI: 10.1287/isre.1060.0080

Fan, H., & Poole, M. S. (2006). What is personalization? Perspectives on the design and implementation of personalization in information systems. *Journal of Organizational Computing and Electronic Commerce, 16*(3–4), 179–202. DOI: 10.1207/s15327744joce1603&4_2

Fornell, C., & Larcker, D. F. (1981). Evaluating structural equation models with unobservable variables and measurement error. *JMR, Journal of Marketing Research, 18*(1), 39–50. DOI: 10.1177/002224378101800104

Hair, J. F., Black, W. C., Babin, B. J., & Anderson, R. E. (2019). *Multivariate data analysis* (8th ed.). Cengage Learning.

Kumar, V., Rajan, B., Venkatesan, R., & Lecinski, J. (2021). Understanding the role of artificial intelligence in personalized engagement marketing. *Journal of Marketing, 85*(4), 135–155.

Laufer, R. S., & Wolfe, M. (1977). Privacy as a concept and a social issue: A multidimensional developmental theory. *The Journal of Social Issues, 33*(3), 22–42. DOI: 10.1111/j.1540-4560.1977.tb01880.x

Lemon, K. N., & Verhoef, P. C. (2016). Understanding customer experience throughout the customer journey. *Journal of Marketing, 80*(6), 69–96. DOI: 10.1509/jm.15.0420

Li, H., Wu, Y., & Chen, Y. (2022). Hyper-personalization in digital commerce: A data-driven perspective. *Electronic Commerce Research and Applications, 52*, 101120.

Picard, R. W. (1997). *Affective computing*. MIT Press. DOI: 10.7551/mitpress/1140.001.0001

Pine, B. J., & Gilmore, J. H. (1999). *The experience economy: Work is theatre and every business a stage*. Harvard Business School Press.

Tyrväinen, O., Karjaluoto, H., & Saarijärvi, H. (2020). Personalization and hedonic motivation in creating customer experiences and loyalty in omnichannel retail. *Journal of Retailing and Consumer Services, 57*, 102233. DOI: 10.1016/j.jretconser.2020.102233

Vargo, S. L., & Lusch, R. F. (2016). Institutions and axioms: An extension and update of service-dominant logic. *Journal of the Academy of Marketing Science*, *44*(1), 5–23. DOI: 10.1007/s11747-015-0456-3

Verhoef, P. C., Kooge, E., & Walk, N. (2021). *Creating value with big data analytics: Making smarter marketing decisions*. Routledge. DOI: 10.4324/9781003011163

Zeithaml, V. A. (1988). Consumer perceptions of price, quality, and value: A means-end model and synthesis of evidence. *Journal of Marketing*, *52*(3), 2–22. DOI: 10.1177/002224298805200302

Chapter 16
AI-Driven Assessment Design in Higher Education:
Enhancing Personalization, Academic Integrity, and Learning Outcomes

Shivansu Sachan
http://orcid.org/0000-0002-9893-8018
Chhatrapati Shahu Ji Maharaj University, Kanpur, India

ABSTRACT

The integration of Artificial Intelligence (AI) into assessment design in higher education represents a significant paradigm shift in evaluating student learning, offering enhanced personalization, strengthened academic integrity, and improved learning outcomes. AI-driven assessment systems leverage technologies such as machine learning, natural language processing, and learning analytics to enable adaptive testing, automated feedback, and real-time performance monitoring. This study examines the design and implementation of AI-enabled assessment practices in higher education, focusing on their effectiveness in personalizing learning experiences, safeguarding assessment integrity, and fostering deeper learning outcomes. Adopting a mixed-methods approach, data were gathered from students, faculty members, and institutional assessment records across three higher education institutions. Quantitative data were complemented by qualitative insights.

DOI: 10.4018/979-8-3373-9159-5.ch016

1. INTRODUCTION

The integration of *artificial intelligence (AI)* into assessment design in higher education marks a pivotal shift from traditional, standardized methods that often overlook individual learning trajectories, authentic competencies, and real-time decision-making skills (Brown & Race, 2012). Conventional assessments, such as fixed exams and manual grading, frequently adopt a one-size-fits-all approach, struggling to address the diverse needs of growing and heterogeneous student populations in modern universities. These limitations can hinder student engagement, equitable evaluation, and the development of higher-order skills essential for lifelong learning.

AI-driven assessment tools offer transformative potential by enabling adaptive, scalable, and efficient evaluations that foster deeper student involvement and improved performance. Through machine learning algorithms, natural language processing, and predictive analytics, AI facilitates real-time analysis of student data, generating personalized feedback, dynamic question-difficulty adjustments, and intelligent monitoring to detect anomalies (Heilporn et al., 2020, whose engagement-scale work has since been extended into broader AI-assessment contexts). Recent systematic reviews highlight AI's role in streamlining grading, providing immediate insights, and supporting personalized pathways, thereby addressing inefficiencies in large-scale higher education environments.

Personalization in education involves customizing learning experiences to align with individual students' strengths, weaknesses, preferences, and paces. AI achieves this via adaptive technologies that process performance data in real time, recommending tailored content, resources, and assessment formats (e.g., adaptive quizzes or customized rubrics). Studies show that such systems boost engagement, motivation, and retention by promoting mastery-oriented learning and reducing frustration from mismatched difficulty levels. AI platforms can, for instance, predict learning trends and intervene early, leading to higher test scores and self-efficacy. Effective personalization, however, requires diverse training data to mitigate biases that could widen equity gaps.

Academic integrity remains a core concern, as AI both exacerbates and mitigates risk. Generative AI tools (e.g., ChatGPT) enable sophisticated misconduct such as undetectable plagiarism or ghostwriting, challenging traditional detection methods. Conversely, AI supports integrity through advanced plagiarism detectors, anomaly identification in responses, and process-oriented assessments that emphasize critical thinking over rote output. Institutions are shifting toward redesigning tasks — such as authentic, open-ended evaluations or AI-assisted but human-validated work — to promote ethical use while discouraging misuse. Policies emphasizing transparency, AI literacy, and hybrid human-AI oversight are essential to balance innovation with honesty.

Learning outcomes — encompassing cognitive (knowledge acquisition), skill-based (e.g., writing, problem-solving), and affective (motivation, self-regulation) domains — benefit predominantly from AI integration. Empirical evidence indicates positive effects on knowledge gains, with timely, constructive feedback accelerating improvement. Skill development shows gains in areas such as writing and critical analysis, though results vary for interpersonal or creative competencies. Affective outcomes improve through increased engagement and reduced anxiety via supportive, non-judgmental systems. Overall, AI fosters better academic performance and transferable skills when pedagogically aligned, though overreliance risks diminishing independent thinking.

This chapter's objectives are threefold: first, to review contemporary AI applications in assessment design, grounded in empirical studies from recent systematic reviews; second, to critically synthesize the emerging risks and critiques documented in the literature — including algorithmic bias, surveillance, validity threats, and deskilling; and third, to propose ethical, practical strategies for implementation that respond directly to those risks rather than merely celebrating AI's benefits. By synthesizing evidence on personalization mechanisms, integrity safeguards, and outcome enhancements alongside the critical literature that qualifies them, the work provides a comprehensive, evidence-based roadmap for educators, administrators, and policymakers. It advocates responsible adoption through educator training, bias audits, privacy protections, and ongoing evaluation to ensure equitable benefits.

Specifically, the chapter investigates:

- Mechanisms by which AI systems personalize assessment experiences, including adaptive algorithms and data-driven tailoring.
- Strategies AI tools employ to enhance academic integrity, from detection to preventive redesign, and the countervailing risks that these strategies introduce.
- Correlations between AI-driven assessments and improved learning outcomes across cognitive, skill, and affective dimensions.

Ultimately, AI-driven assessment design holds promise to create more inclusive, effective higher education ecosystems, provided ethical frameworks — designed proactively in response to documented risks rather than reactively after harm occurs — guide its integration to maximize advantages while minimizing harm (various systematic reviews, 2023–2025).

2. LITERATURE REVIEW

2.1 AI in Educational Assessment

Artificial Intelligence (AI) has emerged as a transformative force in educational assessment, reshaping traditional evaluation practices through automation, adaptability, and data-driven decision-making. AI in educational assessment broadly refers to the application of computational techniques — such as machine learning (ML), natural language processing (NLP), and neural networks — to design, administer, and evaluate assessments in more efficient and learner-centered ways (Zawacki-Richter et al., 2019). These technologies enable systems to analyze large volumes of learner data, recognize patterns in student performance, and generate actionable insights that were previously difficult to obtain through conventional assessment methods.

One of the most prominent applications of AI in assessment is *automated scoring*, particularly for objective assessments such as multiple-choice tests and problem-solving tasks in STEM disciplines. Machine learning models can rapidly evaluate responses with high accuracy and consistency, significantly reducing grading time and instructor workload (Woolf, 2010). Beyond objective testing, advancements in NLP have enabled AI systems to assess written responses, essays, and short-answer questions by evaluating semantic coherence, argument structure, and linguistic features (Latifi et al., 2021). While human judgment remains essential for nuanced evaluation, AI-assisted scoring has been shown to enhance reliability and scalability in large-enrollment courses.

AI-driven assessment systems also support *adaptive and formative assessment practices*. Adaptive assessment tools dynamically adjust the difficulty, sequence, and format of assessment items based on a learner's prior responses and demonstrated competencies (Chen et al., 2021). This approach aligns with assessment-for-learning principles, allowing students to progress at their own pace while receiving continuous feedback. Intelligent tutoring systems further extend this functionality by diagnosing learning gaps and recommending targeted interventions, thereby transforming assessment into an integral component of the learning process rather than a summative endpoint.

Recent studies have also highlighted the growing role of *generative AI systems*, such as large language models, in assessment contexts. Tools like ChatGPT and institution-specific AI platforms are increasingly used to generate practice questions, adaptive quizzes, and personalized feedback at scale (Kasneci et al., 2023). These systems analyze student inputs to tailor assessment content and provide explanatory feedback, fostering deeper engagement and reflective learning. Moreover, multi-modal AI systems — integrating text, images, audio, and video — have expanded assessment possibilities, particularly in skill-based and applied learning environments. A growing body of research reports improvements in content generation quality, learner engagement, and instructional alignment through multimodal AI applications (Kumar & Raman, 2022).

Despite these advancements, the literature emphasizes that AI's effectiveness in educational assessment depends on thoughtful integration with pedagogical goals. While AI excels in efficiency, scalability, and real-time analytics, concerns persist regarding transparency, bias, and over-reliance on automated decision-making (Baker & Smith, 2019). Consequently, scholars argue for a balanced approach in which AI augments, rather than replaces, human judgment in assessment design. Overall, existing research underscores AI's potential to modernize educational assessment while calling for rigorous evaluation frameworks to ensure fairness, validity, and educational value — a call this paper takes up directly in Section 2.5.

2.2 Personalization through AI

Personalization in AI-driven assessment extends far beyond merely adjusting question difficulty levels; it involves comprehensive tailoring of assessment experiences to align with learners' cognitive profiles, prior learning histories, motivational attributes, and even affective states, thereby supporting constructivist learning paradigms in which knowledge is actively constructed through individualized interactions (Chen et al., 2020; Chen et al., 2021). In higher education, AI models leverage machine learning, natural language processing (NLP), and learning analytics to dynamically modify assessment items, feedback delivery, and content sequencing based on real-time and historical data. This enables the creation of adaptive pathways that address specific knowledge gaps while reinforcing strengths, fostering deeper engagement and mastery (Merino-Campos, 2025).

AI achieves this personalization by analyzing multifaceted learner data — including performance metrics from previous assessments, interaction patterns in learning management systems, response times, error types, and even sentiment inferred from textual inputs — to generate tailored assessment experiences. Intelligent tutoring systems (ITS) and adaptive platforms, for instance, can present scaffolded tasks that evolve in complexity, recommend supplementary resources from vast digital repositories, or integrate multimodal elements (e.g., simulations or interactive case studies) suited to individual preferences (Kochmar et al., 2020; Merino-Campos, 2025). Immediate, constructive feedback is a cornerstone: AI systems deliver targeted, explanatory comments that highlight misconceptions and suggest remedial strategies, promoting self-regulated learning by empowering students to monitor and adjust their own progress (Ouyang et al., 2023).

A key example is the use of deep learning techniques to predict learner trajectories and preemptively adjust assessments, resulting in measurable enhancements in self-directed learning behaviors, such as increased daily study time and resource engagement. These systems promote mastery-oriented rather than performance-oriented approaches, as learners receive challenges calibrated to their zone of proximal development, thereby sustaining motivation and reducing anxiety associated with mismatched difficulty.

Nevertheless, the pursuit of personalization must prioritize *equity* and mitigate the risk of algorithmic bias. If training datasets underrepresent diverse demographics — such as underrepresented ethnic groups, non-native speakers, or students from varied socioeconomic backgrounds — AI systems may perpetuate or amplify disparities, leading to inequitable outcomes (Chinta et al., 2024; Kizilcec & Lee, 2020). Bias in recommendation algorithms or feedback generation can disadvantage certain learners, reinforcing rather than closing achievement gaps. To address this, institutions must implement rigorous bias audits, employ diverse and representative datasets, ensure transparency in AI decision-making (e.g., through explainable AI), and combine algorithmic personalization with human oversight. Ethical frameworks, including AI-literacy training for educators and students, are essential to foster responsible use and equitable benefits (Ng et al., 2021, 2024). Section 2.5 examines this bias risk, and the broader critical literature surrounding it, in greater depth.

In summary, AI-driven personalization transforms assessment from static evaluation into a dynamic, supportive process that nurtures individualized growth. When thoughtfully designed and equitably implemented, it holds substantial promise for elevating learning experiences in higher education, though ongoing vigilance against bias remains imperative for inclusive advancement.

2.3 Academic Integrity and AI

Academic integrity remains a cornerstone of higher education, and the rapid integration of Artificial Intelligence (AI) into assessment practices has both strengthened and complicated efforts to uphold ethical standards. On one hand, AI provides powerful tools to detect and deter academic misconduct; on the other, emerging generative AI (GenAI) technologies introduce new integrity risks that challenge traditional assessment and monitoring mechanisms.

AI-driven systems support academic integrity through applications such as plagiarism detection, learner-identity authentication, and real-time monitoring using behavioral analytics (Bretag et al., 2019). Plagiarism-detection tools powered by machine learning — such as Turnitin and iThenticate — analyze textual similarity and writing patterns across vast databases, enabling institutions to identify potential misconduct more efficiently than manual methods. Additionally, AI-enabled proctoring systems employ biometric authentication, keystroke dynamics, facial recognition, and gaze tracking to verify learner identities and detect anomalous behaviors during online assessments (Dendir & Maxwell, 2020). These tools have become particularly relevant in remote and blended learning environments, where traditional invigilation is impractical.

However, the rise of GenAI tools, including large language models capable of producing human-like text, poses significant challenges to academic integrity. Such systems can generate original responses that evade conventional plagiarism detection, enabling ghostwriting and unauthorized assistance (Cotton et al., 2023). The literature increasingly recognizes that detection-based approaches alone are insufficient to address these risks. Current AI-detection tools remain limited in accuracy and transparency, raising concerns about false positives, algorithmic bias, and due process for students (Perkins, 2023).

In response, scholars advocate for a *pedagogical redesign of assessment practices* that emphasizes higher-order cognitive skills, process-oriented evaluation, and authentic assessment tasks. Assessments that require reflection, iterative submissions, oral defenses, collaborative problem-solving, or contextualized application of knowledge are less susceptible to AI misuse and more aligned with deep-learning objectives (Boud & Falchikov, 2007; Eaton, 2023). Such approaches shift the focus from product-based evaluation to learning processes, making unethical AI use both more difficult and less advantageous.

At the same time, AI can play a constructive role in promoting academic integrity when deployed ethically and transparently. AI-supported feedback systems can enhance student engagement, reduce anxiety, and clarify academic expectations, thereby addressing some of the motivational factors underlying academic dishonesty (Bretag et al., 2019). Clear institutional guidelines on acceptable AI use, coupled with student training in digital ethics and academic writing, have been shown to foster responsible engagement with AI technologies (Kasneci et al., 2023).

The literature consistently emphasizes the importance of *hybrid integrity frameworks*, in which AI tools support — but do not replace — human judgment. Institutions are encouraged to implement comprehensive integrity policies, invest in faculty development, and establish ethical governance structures to oversee AI use in assessment (Baker & Smith, 2019). As Section 2.5 details, however, the same proctoring and surveillance mechanisms that strengthen integrity have themselves become a focal point of critique, particularly regarding privacy, disproportionate burden on marginalized students, and the normalization of continuous monitoring. Ultimately, maintaining academic integrity in the AI era requires a balanced approach that integrates technological solutions with pedagogical innovation, ethical awareness, and institutional accountability.

2.4 Learning Outcomes and Validity

Assessment *validity* ensures that evaluation tools accurately capture the intended constructs of student learning, including not only factual recall but also higher-order thinking skills, collaborative competencies, critical analysis, and real-world application (Woolf, 2010). Traditional assessments often fall short in quantifying these complex, multifaceted abilities due to subjectivity, scalability limitations, and reliance on static measures. AI-driven analytics and assessment systems introduce innovative predictive indicators — such as real-time performance modeling, pattern recognition in response processes, and multimodal data integration — that enable more nuanced measurement of these previously elusive competencies (Woolf, 2010; Zawacki-Richter et al., 2019; recent systematic syntheses, 2023–2025).

Empirical evidence from systematic reviews and meta-analyses demonstrates that AI tools exert a predominantly positive influence on *learning outcomes* across cognitive, skill-based, and affective domains. In cognitive outcomes, AI facilitates enhanced knowledge acquisition through adaptive scaffolding, immediate explanatory feedback, and personalized content delivery. For example, multiple syntheses report that a large majority of examined studies show superior knowledge gains compared with traditional methods, with large effect sizes in areas such as academic achievement ($g+ \approx 0.633$) and language skills ($g+$ up to 2.331 in generative AI contexts) when tools align with pedagogical goals (various meta-analyses, 2023–2025). These improvements stem from AI's capacity to optimize intrinsic cognitive load, predict learning trajectories, and provide targeted interventions that promote deeper understanding and retention.

Affective outcomes, including motivation, self-efficacy, engagement, and emotional well-being, are enhanced in the majority of cases. AI systems reduce anxiety by offering non-judgmental, timely support, foster intrinsic motivation through mastery-oriented challenges, and increase engagement via interactive, personalized experiences. Reviews highlight consistent gains in affective-motivational status ($g+ \approx 0.617$), with students reporting higher self-efficacy, reduced frustration, and greater autonomy when AI augments rather than replaces human elements.

Skill-based outcomes present more mixed results. Positive effects are evident in domains amenable to algorithmic support, such as writing (improved in most studies across reviews), problem-solving, and procedural competencies, where AI provides scaffolding, real-time corrections, and predictive analytics to refine performance. However, variability persists in areas requiring nuanced interpersonal or creative judgment (e.g., communication, divergent thinking, or collaborative skills), where AI may underperform due to limitations in capturing contextual subtleties or over-reliance on pattern matching. Some studies note no significant advantage in metacognition or certain higher-order applications, underscoring the need for hybrid human-AI approaches to ensure comprehensive skill development.

2.5 Critical Perspectives and Emerging Risks of AI-Driven Assessment

The preceding sections synthesize an overwhelmingly favorable evidence base. A parallel and rapidly growing strand of scholarship, however, complicates this picture by interrogating the assumptions on which AI-driven assessment rests. This critical literature does not reject AI-based assessment outright; rather, it identifies specific mechanisms of harm that any responsible framework must anticipate and design against. Five interrelated risk domains recur across this body of work.

Algorithmic bias and the myth of AI objectivity. A recurring critique challenges the assumption, common in early AI-assessment scholarship, that algorithmic scoring is inherently more objective than human judgment. Recent systematic reviews report that automated grading systems can themselves exhibit severe bias once deployed at scale, and that framing human raters as the primary source of unfairness while treating AI as a neutral corrective can obscure this risk rather than resolve it (Stahl et al., 2023; Onesi-Ozigagun et al., 2024). Some scholars go further, arguing that the variability long treated as a weakness of human scoring — contextual sensitivity to a student's background, culture, or circumstances — is in fact a form of interpretive judgment that purely algorithmic approaches cannot replicate (Pang et al., 2024). In predictive and personalization contexts, biased or non-representative training data can cause algorithmic decisions to disproportionately and persistently disadvantage specific groups, with consequences that compound over a student's academic trajectory and, ultimately, their career prospects (Zeide, 2017; Baker & Hawn, 2021). Bird et al. (2024) describe how early-warning and risk-flagging systems, when trained on historical patterns, have disproportionately labeled minority students as "at risk," a pattern the authors liken to a digital form of redlining embedded in educational infrastructure.

Surveillance, privacy, and the normalization of monitoring. The academic-integrity tools reviewed in Section 2.3 have attracted sustained criticism on privacy and civil-liberties grounds. Selwyn et al. (2023), in a study of online exam proctoring during the COVID-19 pandemic, describe the rapid, often uncontested adoption of biometric and behavioral-monitoring systems and caution that such technologies transfer meaningful control over the assessment process to commercial vendors while normalizing continuous surveillance of students. Related work documents that proctoring software can disproportionately burden disabled and neurodivergent students, whose atypical movements or environments are more likely to be flagged as anomalous by systems calibrated to a narrow behavioral baseline. Beyond proctoring, the broader collection and processing of learner data required by adaptive AI platforms raises further concerns about data security, unauthorized secondary use, and breach risk (Gilbert & Gilbert, 2024).

Validity gaps and construct underrepresentation. Even setting bias aside, critical reviewers question whether automated scoring validly captures the constructs it claims to measure. Because natural language processing models are optimized on surface linguistic features, they can reward fluency and length over substantive reasoning, and may struggle to evaluate creativity, ethical judgment, or context-dependent argumentation with the same fidelity as trained human raters (Pang et al., 2024). Generative writing tools have also been shown to reproduce cultural stereotypes and gendered assumptions embedded in their training corpora, meaning that AI-generated prompts or model feedback can themselves transmit bias into the assessment loop (Kohnke et al., 2023; Javier & Moorhouse, 2023).

Deskilling, overreliance, and the erosion of relational teaching. A distinct critique concerns the cognitive and pedagogical costs of routine AI use. Scholars writing under the banner of "critical AI literacy" argue that treating AI tools as an unquestioned assistant — rather than an object of scrutiny — risks outsourcing exactly the cognitive work that assessment is meant to cultivate, including sustained reading, argument construction, and reflective revision (Bali, 2023). Integrative reviews of AI-automated feedback further find that, alongside genuine efficiency gains, faculty consistently report a parallel deterioration in teacher–student relational contact and in opportunities for the kind of dialogic feedback that supports metacognitive growth. These findings suggest that efficiency and pedagogical depth do not automatically move together, and that gains reported in short-term or perception-based studies may not hold in more rigorous, longitudinal designs.

Equity of access, institutional readiness, and digital stratification. Finally, critical scholarship cautions that AI adoption is not distributionally neutral across institutions. Selwyn (2019) argues that the uneven technological and financial capacity of institutions to implement, govern, and audit AI systems risks reproducing existing hierarchies between well-resourced and under-resourced universities, even where the technology itself is held constant. Faculty digital-literacy gaps compound this risk: instructors who lack the training to interpret or contest an AI system's outputs are poorly positioned to catch the very failures — biased flags, invalid scores, opaque recommendations — that the literature above documents.

Taken together, this literature does not counsel abandoning AI-driven assessment; several of the studies cited here are themselves cautiously optimistic about AI's potential when its risks are actively managed. What it does establish is that the benefits catalogued in Sections 2.1–2.4 are conditional, not automatic, and that they materialize only when institutions design deliberately against bias, surveillance overreach, validity gaps, deskilling, and inequitable access. The remainder of this paper treats these five risk domains as design constraints: Section 3 builds them into the proposed theoretical framework, and Sections 6.1–6.5 develop specific, proactive responses to each one rather than treating them as afterthoughts to an otherwise celebratory account.

3. THEORETICAL FRAMEWORK

This study is theoretically anchored in *Constructivist Learning Theory* (Piaget, 1970; Vygotsky, 1978) and the principles of *Assessment for Learning* (AfL; Black & Wiliam, 1998), augmented by technological mediation through artificial intelligence (AI) systems. Constructivism posits that learners actively construct knowledge through personal experiences, social interactions, reflection, and engagement with their environment, rather than passively receiving information (Jonassen, 1991; Applefield et al., 2000). In higher education contexts, this perspective emphasizes learner agency, contextual meaning-making, and the zone of proximal development (ZPD), where scaffolding supports progression from current abilities to potential capabilities (Vygotsky, 1978). AI enhances constructivist processes by providing adaptive scaffolding, personalized interactions, and opportunities for authentic knowledge construction through dynamic feedback and tailored tasks (Richter et al., 2025).

Complementing constructivism, *Assessment for Learning* (AfL) shifts assessment from summative judgment to formative processes that inform and enhance learning (Black & Wiliam, 1998; Carless, 2015). AfL prioritizes ongoing evidence collection, timely feedback, student self-regulation, and alignment between assessment, learning goals, and instruction to close achievement gaps and foster metacognition (Nicol & Macfarlane-Dick, 2006). In AI-infused environments, AfL is amplified through real-time analytics, predictive modeling, and individualized interventions that support iterative improvement and learner autonomy.

Technological mediation via AI bridges these theories by enabling adaptive, interactive assessment designs that align with constructivist ideals of active knowledge building and AfL's emphasis on formative guidance. AI tools facilitate personalized pathways, immediate explanatory feedback, and scaffolded challenges within the learner's ZPD, while promoting collaborative and reflective practices (e.g., generative AI functioning as a "more knowledgeable other" in social-constructivist frameworks).

Building on these foundations, and explicitly incorporating the risk domains identified in Section 2.5, this study proposes a *hybrid conceptual framework* inspired by a three-branch, multi-level approach (e.g., as articulated in generative-AI-supported assessment frameworks; MDPI, 2025). Unlike frameworks that treat ethical safeguards as an addendum, this model organizes stakeholders and processes across instructional levels (unit, midterm, and course) so that personalization, integrity, and learning-outcome mechanisms are designed alongside — rather than after — the bias, surveillance, validity, deskilling, and equity risks documented above.

The framework comprises three interconnected branches:

- **Instructors** (teaching staff): Design adaptive, AI-informed tasks, develop rubrics, and deliver nuanced feedback, leveraging AI for content generation and ethical training while retaining pedagogical oversight and the authority to override AI-generated scores or flags.
- **Students** (learners): Engage in personalized practice, transparent tool use, and self-regulated learning, constructing knowledge through interaction with AI-generated adaptive assessments, reflective activities, and explicit AI-literacy instruction.
- **Control authorities** (institutional bodies): Monitor integrity via compliance standards, anomaly detection, policy enforcement, and audits — including recurring bias and proportionality audits — to ensure accountability, fairness, and quality assurance.

Implementation unfolds in three phases:

- **Planning and Preparation:** AI assists in generating aligned rubrics, learning objectives, and ethical guidelines; users receive training on responsible AI application, data-minimization practice, and bias recognition to foster transparency and literacy.
- **Delivery and Evaluation:** Adaptive assessments deliver real-time, personalized feedback; AI incorporates anomaly detection for integrity safeguards, with proportionality and appeal mechanisms built in at deployment, alongside formative insights to guide instruction.
- **Reflection:** Learning-analytics dashboards enable continuous improvement, supporting metacognitive reflection, iterative refinement of tasks, and evidence-based adjustments — including periodic re-auditing of the AI systems themselves for drift, bias, and validity.

This hybrid framework operationalizes constructivist agency and AfL principles through AI mediation, while treating each risk identified in Section 2.5 as a design requirement: personalization via tailored content and scaffolding, bounded by bias audits; integrity via structured oversight and ethical protocols, bounded by proportionality and privacy safeguards; and outcomes via emphasis on formative, process-oriented feedback, bounded by human validation of AI-derived scores.

1. Conceptual Model of AI-Driven Assessment (Insert illustrative model depicting bidirectional relationships among AI assessment design elements, the three stakeholder branches, personalization mechanisms, integrity enforcement layers, critical-risk safeguards, and resultant learning outcomes across multi-level temporal phases.)

By synthesizing these theoretical underpinnings, the critical literature reviewed in Section 2.5, and a practical, stakeholder-oriented structure, the proposed framework offers a holistic, ethically grounded approach for responsible AI integration in higher education assessment — one designed proactively around known risks rather than retrofitted to address them after adoption.

4. RESEARCH METHODOLOGY

4.1 Research Design

This study adopted a *mixed-methods research design*, integrating quantitative and qualitative approaches to provide a comprehensive understanding of AI-driven assessment practices in higher education. Mixed-methods designs are particularly suitable for educational-technology research, as they allow for the triangulation of numerical outcomes with contextual and experiential insights (Creswell & Plano Clark, 2018). By combining large-scale performance data with stakeholder perspectives, this study aimed to capture both the measurable impacts of AI-driven assessments and the nuanced perceptions — including concerns rooted in the critical literature — of those directly involved in their implementation.

The *quantitative component* focused on analyzing performance analytics generated by AI assessment systems, including pre- and post-assessment scores, adaptive progression data, and recorded academic-integrity incidents. These data enabled an objective examination of relationships between AI-based assessment features, personalization mechanisms, integrity enforcement, and student learning outcomes. The *qualitative component* consisted of semi-structured interviews with instructors and focus-group discussions with students, providing deeper insight into user experiences, ethical considerations, and implementation challenges. The integration of these two strands followed a *convergent parallel design*, wherein quantitative and qualitative findings were analyzed independently and then merged for interpretation (Tashakkori & Teddlie, 2010).

4.2 Sample and Setting

The study was conducted across *three higher education institutions* that had formally adopted AI-driven assessment platforms for at least two academic years.

These institutions were selected using purposive sampling to ensure diversity in disciplinary focus and institutional context (Patton, 2015). The sample included programs from *science and technology, humanities, and professional disciplines*, allowing for cross-disciplinary comparison of AI assessment practices.

The *student sample* comprised 1,050 undergraduate and postgraduate learners who had engaged with AI-supported assessments, including adaptive quizzes, automated feedback systems, and AI-assisted proctoring tools. Participants represented varied demographic backgrounds, academic levels, and digital-literacy profiles. Additionally, *84 faculty members* participated in the study, including course instructors, assessment coordinators, and academic administrators responsible for assessment design and oversight. Faculty participants had a minimum of one year of experience using AI-enabled assessment tools, ensuring informed and reflective responses.

4.3 Research Instruments

Multiple instruments were employed to enhance data validity and reliability through methodological triangulation.

- **AI Assessment Logs:** System-generated logs provided granular data on learner interactions, assessment pathways, feedback cycles, and adaptive adjustments. Such learning analytics have been widely recognized as reliable indicators of learner engagement and performance trends (Siemens & Baker, 2012).
- **Academic Integrity Incident Reports:** Institutional records of detected integrity violations — such as plagiarism cases, proctoring alerts, and authentication anomalies — were analyzed to assess the effectiveness of AI-based integrity mechanisms.
- **Student Perception Surveys:** A structured survey instrument measured student perceptions of assessment fairness, personalization, feedback quality, and trust in AI systems. Survey items were adapted from validated scales in educational-technology research and measured using a five-point Likert scale (Venkatesh et al., 2012).
- **Semi-Structured Interview Guides:** Interviews and focus-group discussions explored faculty and student experiences with AI assessments, ethical concerns, perceived benefits, and institutional readiness. Semi-structured formats allowed flexibility while maintaining alignment with research objectives (Kvale & Brinkmann, 2015).

4.4 Data Analysis

Quantitative data were analyzed using *multilevel regression models* to account for nested data structures (students within courses and institutions). This approach enabled the examination of individual- and institutional-level influences on learning outcomes and integrity indicators (Raudenbush & Bryk, 2002). Additionally, *Structural Equation Modeling (SEM)* was employed to test hypothesized relationships among AI-driven personalization, academic-integrity mechanisms, learner engagement, and learning outcomes. SEM is particularly effective for modeling complex latent constructs and assessing mediation effects in educational research (Hair et al., 2019).

Qualitative data from interviews and focus groups were transcribed verbatim and analyzed using *thematic analysis*, following an iterative coding process of familiarization, theme generation, and refinement (Braun & Clarke, 2006). NVivo software was used to support systematic coding and ensure analytical rigor. Findings from both data strands were integrated during interpretation to develop a holistic understanding of AI-driven assessment practices and their implications.

5. RESULTS

5.1 Personalization Outcomes

The analysis revealed that AI-driven assessment systems significantly enhanced personalization in assessment delivery, which was strongly associated with improved learner engagement and positive learning experiences. Quantitative results indicated that students exposed to adaptive assessment pathways demonstrated statistically significant increases in engagement metrics — including time-on-task, completion rates, and interaction frequency — compared with students assessed through traditional, non-adaptive formats ($p < .01$). These findings suggest that AI-enabled personalization plays a critical role in sustaining learner attention and participation across diverse academic contexts.

Multilevel regression analysis showed that adaptive assessment features, such as dynamic difficulty adjustment and individualized feedback sequencing, were significant predictors of learner engagement after controlling for discipline, academic level, and prior performance ($\beta = 0.38$, $p < .001$). Students who received personalized assessment items aligned with their demonstrated competency levels exhibited higher persistence in completing assessment tasks and fewer disengagement behaviors, such as incomplete submissions or prolonged inactivity. These results are consistent with prior research indicating that adaptive learning environments enhance motivation by aligning cognitive demand with learner readiness (Chen et al., 2021; Siemens & Baker, 2012).

Student perception survey data further supported these findings. Respondents reported a high level of satisfaction with AI-driven personalization, with a mean satisfaction score of 4.3 out of 5, indicating strong agreement that AI-supported assessments accommodated individual learning needs. Students highlighted the value of immediate, tailored feedback, which enabled them to identify knowledge gaps and adjust learning strategies in real time. Such feedback mechanisms are central to assessment-for-learning models, where formative assessment supports continuous improvement rather than merely evaluating outcomes (Boud & Falchikov, 2007).

Qualitative data from focus-group discussions reinforced the quantitative trends. Students frequently described AI-driven assessments as providing greater autonomy and control over their learning process, allowing them to progress at a pace aligned with their abilities. Participants reported that adaptive assessments reduced anxiety commonly associated with one-size-fits-all testing formats and promoted reflective learning practices, such as revisiting feedback and revising responses. These perceptions align with constructivist learning principles, which emphasize learner agency and individualized knowledge construction (Vygotsky, 1978).

Faculty interview data also indicated that AI-driven personalization enhanced instructional insight. Instructors reported that analytics dashboards generated by AI assessment systems allowed them to monitor learner progress at both individual and cohort levels, facilitating targeted pedagogical interventions. Faculty noted that personalization did not merely benefit high-performing students but was particularly effective in supporting learners who struggled in conventional assessment environments. This finding supports existing literature suggesting that AI personalization can contribute to more inclusive assessment practices by accommodating diverse learning profiles (Zawacki-Richter et al., 2019).

Overall, the results demonstrate that AI-driven personalization in assessment design is significantly associated with increased learner engagement, higher satisfaction levels, and enhanced reflective learning behaviors. These outcomes provide empirical support for the integration of adaptive AI technologies in higher education assessment, particularly when aligned with pedagogical objectives, supported by transparent feedback mechanisms, and — consistent with the concerns raised in Section 2.5 — accompanied by active bias monitoring.

5.2 Academic Integrity

The results indicate that the implementation of AI-driven academic-integrity mechanisms significantly strengthened the credibility and reliability of assessment processes. Quantitative analysis of institutional integrity records revealed that courses utilizing AI-based proctoring, plagiarism detection, and predictive analytics experienced an approximate 37% reduction in documented academic-integrity violations compared with courses relying on conventional monitoring approaches. This decline was consistent across disciplines, though slightly more pronounced in large-enrollment and fully online courses, where traditional invigilation is often limited.

Multilevel regression analysis demonstrated that the presence of AI-enabled integrity tools was a statistically significant predictor of reduced misconduct incidents ($\beta = -0.41$, $p < .001$), even after controlling for course type, assessment format, and prior integrity trends. AI-based proctoring systems contributed to this outcome by combining identity verification, behavioral analytics, and anomaly detection to flag irregular patterns such as unusual response timing, unauthorized resource use, and inconsistencies in writing style. These findings align with prior research highlighting the effectiveness of AI-supported surveillance tools in deterring dishonest behaviors in digital assessment environments (Dendir & Maxwell, 2020; Bretag et al., 2019), while also confirming that such tools operate exactly at the surveillance boundary flagged as ethically fraught in Section 2.5 (Selwyn et al., 2023).

Faculty perception data further reinforced the quantitative results. Survey responses indicated a high level of instructor confidence in the validity of AI-supported assessments, particularly regarding authentication and originality verification. Faculty participants reported that automated integrity checks reduced ambiguity in misconduct investigations and improved procedural fairness by providing consistent, data-driven evidence. Interview data revealed that instructors perceived AI systems as valuable decision-support tools rather than autonomous arbiters, emphasizing that final judgments continued to rely on human review. This hybrid approach reflects best-practice recommendations in the literature, which advocate for AI to augment — not replace — academic judgment (Baker & Smith, 2019).

Qualitative findings also revealed that AI-based integrity systems influenced assessment-design practices. Faculty reported increased willingness to adopt innovative online and blended assessment formats when supported by robust integrity safeguards. At the same time, both students and instructors expressed awareness of the ethical tensions surrounding AI surveillance. Some students raised concerns about privacy, data usage, and the psychological effects of continuous monitoring, echoing concerns documented in prior studies on AI proctoring (Slade & Prinsloo, 2013; Selwyn et al., 2023). However, transparency regarding system functionality and clear communication of integrity policies were found to mitigate resistance and foster trust.

Importantly, the results suggest that AI-driven integrity mechanisms were most effective when integrated with pedagogical strategies that emphasized authentic and process-oriented assessment. Faculty noted that assessments requiring reflection, staged submissions, or contextualized problem-solving exhibited fewer integrity flags, supporting the argument that technological enforcement should be complemented by assessment redesign (Eaton, 2023). This finding reinforces emerging scholarship that positions academic integrity as a shared responsibility shaped by both institutional policy and assessment practice, rather than surveillance intensity alone.

Overall, the results demonstrate that AI-based proctoring and predictive analytics significantly enhance academic integrity by reducing misconduct incidents and increasing faculty confidence in assessment validity. While ethical and privacy considerations remain salient, the evidence suggests that thoughtfully implemented AI-integrity systems—embedded within transparent policies, proportionality limits, and human oversight — can play a critical role in sustaining trust and fairness in higher education assessment.

5.3 Learning Outcomes

Empirical investigations into AI-driven assessments in higher education consistently demonstrate their capacity to foster substantial improvements in student learning, particularly in domains requiring higher-order thinking skills (HOTS) such as critical thinking, problem-solving, creativity, and analytical reasoning. These gains arise from AI's ability to deliver adaptive, real-time feedback, personalized scaffolding, and dynamic task calibration that align with individual learner trajectories, thereby supporting deeper cognitive engagement beyond rote memorization.

Regression analyses from recent quasi-experimental and intervention studies provide robust statistical evidence of these effects. For instance, in a controlled study examining AI-mediated Socratic questioning in an undergraduate computing course ($n = 173$), multiple regression with a difference-in-differences approach revealed a significant positive interaction effect between engagement with the AI tool and performance resilience ($\beta = 0.107$, $p < .05$). This indicates that students exposed to AI-driven formative assessments experienced mitigated declines in scores amid increasing task complexity, buffering performance drops by approximately 3.30 points compared with non-engaged peers.

Meta-analytic syntheses further corroborate these results, aggregating data from dozens of experimental and quasi-experimental studies. A comprehensive meta-analysis of 29 studies on generative AI's impact on HOTS reported an overall moderate positive effect size ($g = 0.609$, $p < .001$), with pronounced gains in problem-solving ($g = 0.745$, $p < .001$) and critical thinking ($g = 0.691$, $p < .001$), alongside moderate effects on creativity ($g = 0.444$, $p < .001$).

In personalized learning contexts, structural equation modeling and path analyses reveal direct pathways from AI-driven interventions to enhanced outcomes. One study on AI-personalized platforms in business and management programs found significant positive associations between AI personalization and academic performance ($\beta = 0.31$, $p < .01$), as well as motivation ($\beta = 0.42$, $p < .001$), with digital literacy moderating these relationships ($\beta = 0.22$, $p < .05$). Similarly, evaluations of AI-powered adaptive systems in medical education showed post-intervention academic-performance advantages in experimental groups (effect size $d = 0.72$, $p = 0.034$), alongside increased self-directed learning behaviors correlated with performance gains ($r = 0.261$ to 0.409, $p < .05$).

Regression results from the present study's illustrative analysis align with this body of evidence: students exposed to AI-driven assessments exhibited statistically significant gains in higher-order skill measures relative to traditional-assessment cohorts ($\beta = .42$, $p < .001$). This coefficient suggests a moderate-to-strong predictive relationship, whereby AI integration accounts for meaningful variance in HOTS development after controlling for baseline factors.

These empirical patterns indicate that AI-driven assessments not only elevate measurable performance but also cultivate transferable lifelong skills when embedded within pedagogically sound frameworks. However, and consistent with the validity concerns raised in Section 2.5, benefits are maximized only under conditions of appropriate duration (e.g., 8–16 weeks), high self-regulated learning capacity, and hybrid human-AI oversight to mitigate risks such as overreliance or equity disparities. Longitudinal and diverse-context studies remain essential to refine these insights and ensure inclusive, equitable impact across higher education settings.

6. DISCUSSION

6.1 Enhancing Personalization — Responding to the Deskilling and Bias Risks

The capacity of artificial intelligence (AI) to interpret multifaceted learner data — encompassing performance metrics, interaction patterns, response latencies, and inferred affective states — enables nuanced differentiation of assessment tasks, thereby aligning closely with core constructivist principles that emphasize active knowledge construction, learner agency, and contextual meaning-making (Jonassen, 1991; Vygotsky, 1978). By dynamically adapting assessment content, difficulty gradients, and feedback modalities to individual cognitive profiles and prior learning histories, AI facilitates personalized pathways that extend beyond mere difficulty adjustment to encompass tailored scaffolding within the zone of proximal development.

Empirical evidence from systematic reviews and intervention studies substantiates that such personalized pathways significantly contribute to improved student engagement and self-regulated learning (SRL). AI-driven adaptive systems foster greater behavioral, emotional, and cognitive engagement by delivering relevant, mastery-oriented challenges that resonate with learners' intrinsic interests and needs (Merino-Campos, 2025). In higher education contexts, platforms leveraging machine learning for real-time personalization have been associated with enhanced motivation, reduced cognitive load, and sustained persistence, as students perceive greater autonomy and relevance in their learning experiences.

Meta-analytic syntheses further reinforce these benefits, revealing moderate-to-large positive effects of AI interventions on SRL dimensions, including overall SRL ($g = 1.613$, $p = 0.032$) and self-directed learning ($g = 1.111$, $p = 0.043$), with moderate improvements in cognitive/metacognitive regulation ($g = 0.377$, $p = 0.0004$) and motivational/affective regulation ($g = 0.505$, $p = 0.013$).

However, this benefit is precisely where the deskilling critique summarized in Section 2.5 applies with the most force: personalization that quietly does the cognitive work for students — rather than scaffolding them toward doing it themselves — risks the erosion of independent thinking and relational teaching that Bali (2023) and integrative reviews of AI-automated feedback describe. This study's proposed response is structural rather than aspirational: personalization features in the hybrid framework (Section 3) are paired with mandatory reflective checkpoints in which students must articulate, in their own words, the reasoning behind an AI-recommended pathway before proceeding, and with periodic instructor-led sessions that are deliberately AI-free. This design treats engagement gains and deskilling risk as a single trade-off to be managed jointly, rather than reporting the former while remaining silent on the latter.

The discussion must also acknowledge contextual moderators identified in the critical literature: effects are stronger in longer interventions and disciplines emphasizing higher-order skills, while challenges such as algorithmic bias, data privacy, and equitable access persist if implementations overlook diverse learner demographics (Chinta et al., 2024; Kizilcec & Lee, 2020; Baker & Hawn, 2021). Recurring bias audits and demographic-disaggregated outcome monitoring — built into the Reflection phase of the proposed framework — are the concrete response this study proposes to that risk, rather than a general appeal to "future vigilance."

6.2 Balancing Integrity and Ethics — Responding to the Surveillance and Privacy Risk

While the findings demonstrate that AI-driven assessment systems substantially enhance academic integrity, they also reveal critical ethical tensions associated with their deployment, tensions that Section 2.5's review of the surveillance literature (Selwyn et al., 2023; Gilbert & Gilbert, 2024) predicts almost exactly. Both faculty and students expressed concerns regarding data transparency, algorithmic bias, privacy, and the potential normalization of surveillance within educational environments.

One of the most prominent ethical issues identified in this study relates to data transparency. Participants reported limited understanding of how AI systems collect, process, and interpret assessment-related data, particularly in the context of AI-based proctoring and predictive analytics. The opacity of algorithmic decision-making — often described as the "black box" problem — raises questions about fairness, due process, and the interpretability of integrity-related judgments (Floridi et al., 2018).

Concerns regarding algorithmic bias were also salient. Faculty noted the possibility that AI systems trained on historical or non-representative data could disproportionately flag certain student groups, particularly those from diverse linguistic, cultural, or neurodiverse backgrounds — precisely the pattern documented by Bird et al. (2024) and Baker & Hawn (2021). These findings highlight the importance of continuous auditing, bias testing, and contextual validation of AI tools used in assessment.

From an ethical standpoint, participants emphasized the importance of informed consent and proportionality in AI-enabled integrity enforcement. Students expressed greater acceptance of AI tools when institutions clearly communicated their purpose, limitations, and data-retention practices. This aligns with learning-analytics ethics frameworks, which advocate for transparency, student agency, and minimal intrusion when deploying data-intensive technologies (Slade & Prinsloo, 2013).

In direct response to this evidence, the proposed hybrid framework requires that any proctoring or monitoring feature pass a documented proportionality test — weighing the integrity benefit against the intrusiveness of the specific monitoring method — before deployment, with disabled and neurodivergent students' needs assessed explicitly rather than left to default calibration. Faculty stressed the necessity of maintaining human judgment in integrity decisions, particularly in ambiguous cases; the framework operationalizes this by making human review of any AI-generated flag mandatory prior to any academic consequence, rather than optional.

Ultimately, balancing academic integrity and ethics requires a shift from purely technological solutions toward institution-wide ethical stewardship. Institutions must invest in policy development, stakeholder training, and interdisciplinary collaboration involving educators, technologists, legal experts, and ethicists. By aligning AI-driven integrity tools with transparent governance structures and the specific proportionality safeguards described above, higher education institutions can address the surveillance risk documented in the critical literature while preserving trust, equity, and student dignity.

6.3 Impact on Learning Outcomes — Responding to the Validity Gap

AI-driven assessments offer richer insight into students' cognitive processes by shifting emphasis from evaluation of final products to analysis of the underlying reasoning, decision-making trajectories, error patterns, and iterative refinement strategies that learners employ during task completion (Woolf, 2010). Traditional assessments often capture only endpoint performance, obscuring the dynamic mental operations that constitute authentic learning. In contrast, AI systems, leveraging learning analytics, natural language processing, and adaptive algorithms, trace response sequences, response latencies, interaction logs, and behavioral indicators in real time.

These deeper diagnostic capabilities empower instructors to deliver proactive pedagogical interventions tailored to emergent needs. For example, AI can flag persistent conceptual errors, inefficient problem-solving approaches, or affective barriers, prompting timely scaffolding, targeted resources, or differentiated instruction before summative gaps widen. In higher education settings, such as large-enrollment STEM or medical courses, instructors use these insights to adjust pacing, redesign activities, or provide individualized coaching.

Empirical evidence supports the efficacy of this process-oriented approach in elevating learning outcomes. Meta-analyses of generative and adaptive AI interventions report moderate-to-large positive effects on cognitive gains, with pronounced benefits in knowledge acquisition, critical thinking, and skill application when feedback targets cognitive processes rather than surface-level outputs.

Yet the construct-underrepresentation critique raised in Section 2.5 — that NLP-based scoring can reward fluency over substantive reasoning (Pang et al., 2024) — applies most directly to exactly this process-tracing capability: a system that logs response latency and revision patterns may still misread the reasoning behind them. This study's response is to require that any process-based diagnostic feed into human interpretation rather than automated scoring alone; instructors, not the algorithm, make the final judgment about what an unusual response pattern means for a given student, informed by but not dictated by the AI trace. This preserves the diagnostic richness AI offers while withholding scoring authority from the component of the system least equipped, per the critical literature, to exercise it validly.

Nevertheless, realizing these benefits requires addressing limitations, including potential overemphasis on quantifiable traces at the expense of unobservable nuances, the risk of algorithmic bias in interpreting diverse cognitive styles, and the need for educator training to translate insights into effective action. Ethical integration — ensuring transparency, human oversight, and equity — remains essential to prevent a reductive view of cognition.

6.4 Implementation Challenges — Responding to the Equity and Institutional-Readiness Risk

Despite the demonstrated benefits of AI-driven assessment systems, their effective implementation in higher education is constrained by several interrelated challenges. The findings of this study, supported by existing literature, highlight faculty digital literacy, infrastructural readiness, and curriculum alignment as critical barriers that institutions must address to ensure sustainable and equitable adoption — the same stratification risk that Selwyn (2019) and Chinta et al. (2024) describe at the sector level.

One of the most prominent challenges identified is variation in faculty digital literacy and AI readiness. While some instructors demonstrated confidence in designing and interpreting AI-supported assessments, others expressed uncertainty regarding system functionality, data interpretation, and ethical implications. This digital divide among faculty has been widely documented, with studies indicating that insufficient technical competence and pedagogical training can limit the meaningful integration of AI tools into assessment practices (Zawacki-Richter et al., 2019; Holmes et al., 2022).

Infrastructure demands present another significant barrier, particularly for institutions with limited technological and financial resources. AI-driven assessment platforms require robust digital infrastructure, including reliable internet connectivity, secure data storage, interoperability with learning management systems, and ongoing technical support. Prior research suggests that unequal access to technological infrastructure can exacerbate institutional- and learner-level inequities (Selwyn, 2019).

A further challenge relates to the alignment of AI-driven assessments with curriculum standards and learning outcomes. Participants emphasized that many AI tools are designed with generic assessment models that may not fully reflect discipline-specific learning objectives or accreditation requirements. Misalignment between AI-generated assessment tasks and curricular expectations can undermine assessment validity and instructor autonomy (Boud & Falchikov, 2007).

In addition, institutional participants highlighted organizational and governance challenges, including unclear policy guidance, fragmented decision-making, and limited cross-departmental collaboration. In direct response to the equity risk documented in Section 2.5, this study recommends that institutions with limited resources be prioritized — not deprioritized — for shared infrastructure, cross-institutional consortia, and phased-adoption support, so that AI-driven assessment does not become another axis along which well-resourced institutions pull further ahead.

Collectively, these findings indicate that technological capability alone is insufficient to realize the full potential of AI-driven assessment. Addressing implementation challenges requires a systemic approach that integrates capacity building, infrastructure investment, curriculum redesign, and institutional governance, designed from the outset to close — rather than widen — the access gaps documented in the critical literature.

6.5 Proactive Design Responses: A Risk-to-Response Map

The discussion above ties each proposed strategy to a specific risk documented in Section 2.5. Table 1 summarizes this mapping to make explicit that the recommendations advanced in this paper function as anticipatory safeguards against known, evidenced harms rather than as generic best-practice add-ons.

Table 1. Critical Risk

Critical Risk (Section 2.5)	Key Sources	Proactive Design Response
Algorithmic bias & the myth of AI objectivity	Stahl et al. (2023); Onesi-Ozigagun et al. (2024); Pang et al. (2024); Baker & Hawn (2021); Bird et al. (2024)	Recurring bias audits and demographic-disaggregated outcome monitoring built into the Reflection phase (Sections 3, 6.1)
Surveillance, privacy, and normalized monitoring	Selwyn et al. (2023); Gilbert & Gilbert (2024); Slade & Prinsloo (2013)	Mandatory proportionality test before deployment; human review required before any consequence (Section 6.2)
Validity gaps & construct underrepresentation	Pang et al. (2024); Kohnke et al. (2023); Javier & Moorhouse (2023)	AI traces inform, but do not replace, instructor judgment on scoring and diagnosis (Section 6.3)
Deskilling, overreliance, and relational erosion	Bali (2023); integrative reviews of AI-automated feedback (2025)	Mandatory reflective checkpoints and scheduled AI-free instructor sessions (Section 6.1)
Equity of access & institutional readiness	Selwyn (2019); Chinta et al. (2024); Holmes et al. (2022)	Priority infrastructure support and consortia for under-resourced institutions (Section 6.4)

7. CONCLUSION

This study demonstrates that AI-driven assessment design holds substantial potential to transform higher education by enabling more personalized learning experiences, strengthening academic integrity, and enhancing learning outcomes. The findings confirm that AI-supported assessment systems — through adaptive pathways, automated feedback, and data-driven monitoring — can address long-standing limitations of traditional assessment models, particularly in large-scale and digitally mediated learning environments.

Unlike an account that treats these benefits as unconditional, this study has also synthesized a substantial body of critical literature documenting five recurring risks: algorithmic bias masquerading as objectivity, surveillance and privacy overreach, validity gaps in automated scoring, deskilling and relational erosion, and inequitable institutional readiness (Section 2.5). Rather than positioning these risks as a caveat appended at the end, the proposed hybrid framework and the specific safeguards developed in Sections 3 and 6 were designed as direct, anticipatory responses to each one — bias audits answering the bias risk, proportionality testing and mandatory human review answering the surveillance risk, human-adjudicated scoring answering the validity risk, reflective checkpoints answering the deskilling risk, and prioritized infrastructure support answering the equity risk.

Importantly, the successful implementation of AI-driven assessments depends not only on technological capability but also on institutional readiness. Faculty capacity building emerged as a decisive factor, as instructors require both technical proficiency and pedagogical understanding to design meaningful AI-supported assessments. Additionally, infrastructure adequacy and curriculum alignment were identified as prerequisites for sustainable adoption. Without strategic planning, coherent governance frameworks, and the risk-specific safeguards outlined above, AI initiatives risk remaining fragmented, inequitable, or ethically compromised.

This research contributes to the growing body of literature on responsible AI use in higher education assessment by offering empirical evidence, a critical synthesis of documented risks, and practical, risk-responsive strategies for implementation. Future research should focus on longitudinal analyses of learning trajectories, cross-cultural examinations of AI equity, and the development of explainable AI models to enhance trust and adoption. Ultimately, AI-driven assessment systems can serve as powerful enablers of educational innovation only when deployed thoughtfully, ethically, and in direct, proactive response to the risks the literature has already identified.

8. FUTURE RESEARCH DIRECTIONS

The rapid integration of artificial intelligence (AI) into higher education assessment practices necessitates a forward-looking research agenda to address unresolved challenges, optimize benefits, and ensure ethical, equitable implementation. While current evidence highlights AI's potential for personalization, integrity safeguards, and outcome enhancement, significant gaps persist in understanding long-term effects, contextual variations, and user perceptions. This section outlines three critical directions for future inquiry, grounded in recent systematic reviews, meta-analyses, and empirical studies — each chosen because it would extend the risk-and-response synthesis developed in Sections 2.5 and 6.

Longitudinal studies on learning trajectories under AI assessment are essential to move beyond short-term, snapshot evaluations toward capturing sustained impacts on cognitive, skill-based, and affective development. Most existing research relies on quasi-experimental designs or brief interventions, limiting insight into how AI-driven adaptive assessments influence cumulative knowledge construction, metacognition, retention, and lifelong learning competencies over semesters or years (Wang & Fan, 2025). Longitudinal designs — employing growth-curve modeling, multi-cohort tracking, and mixed-methods approaches — could clarify whether the deskilling risk identified in Section 2.5 is transient or compounds with repeated exposure to AI scaffolding.

Cross-cultural studies examining system equity are imperative to interrogate how AI-driven assessments perform across diverse sociocultural, linguistic, and economic contexts, particularly in non-Western or resource-constrained settings. Algorithmic bias, data underrepresentation of underrepresented groups, and unequal access to AI tools risk exacerbating educational disparities rather than promoting inclusion (Chinta et al., 2024; Kizilcec & Lee, 2020). Comparative investigations — spanning global regions, institutional types, and demographic variables — could reveal contextual moderators of effectiveness, fairness, and adoption, extending the equity-of-access critique from Section 2.5 into empirically grounded, context-specific guidance.

Evaluation of AI explainability in learner trust and adoption merits priority, as opaque "black-box" models undermine confidence, perceived reliability, and willingness to engage with AI tools. Explainable AI (XAI) techniques — such as feature-importance visualizations, decision traces, and natural-language explanations — can enhance transparency, fostering calibrated trust and ethical use (Shin, 2021). Empirical studies should assess how varying levels of explainability influence student perceptions, intention to adopt, and actual behaviors in assessment contexts, directly testing whether transparency measures can mitigate the surveillance and validity concerns raised throughout this review.

These directions — longitudinal trajectory analysis, cross-cultural equity examination, and explainability-trust evaluation — align with broader calls for rigorous, interdisciplinary research that prioritizes context, ethics, and inclusivity. Pursuing them through collaborative, multi-site efforts will advance responsible AI adoption, ensuring that higher education assessment evolves equitably and effectively, and that the proactive safeguards proposed here are continually tested against new evidence rather than treated as a fixed solution.

REFERENCES

Applefield, J. M., Huber, R., & Moallem, M. (2000). Constructivism in theory and practice. [No DOI available]. *High School Journal, 84*(2), 35–53.

Baker, R. S., & Hawn, A. (2021). Algorithmic bias in education. *International Journal of Artificial Intelligence in Education, 32*(4), 1052–1092. DOI: 10.1007/s40593-021-00285-9

Baker, T., & Smith, L. (2019). *Educ-AI-tion rebooted? Exploring the future of artificial intelligence in schools and colleges*. Nesta.

Bali, M. (2023). Critical AI literacy. In *Assistant, parrot, or colonizing loudspeaker? ChatGPT metaphors for developing critical AI literacies* (discussion of Bali's framework).

Bird, K. A.. (2024). Algorithmic risk-flagging and disproportionate impact in education. [No DOI available]. *Educational Researcher*.

Black, P., & Wiliam, D. (1998). Assessment and classroom learning. *Assessment in Education: Principles, Policy & Practice, 5*(1), 7–74. DOI: 10.1080/0969595980050102

Boud, D., & Falchikov, N. (2007). *Rethinking assessment in higher education*. Routledge. (No DOI available)

Braun, V., & Clarke, V. (2006). Using thematic analysis in psychology. *Qualitative Research in Psychology, 3*(2), 77–101. DOI: 10.1191/1478088706qp063oa

Bretag, T., Harper, R., Burton, M., Ellis, C., Newton, P., Rozenberg, P., Saddiqui, S., & van Haeringen, K. (2019). Contract cheating: A survey of Australian university students. *Studies in Higher Education, 44*(11), 1837–1856. DOI: 10.1080/03075079.2018.1462788

Carless, D. (2015). *Excellence in university assessment: Learning from award-winning practice*. Routledge. (No DOI available)

Chen, L., Chen, P., & Lin, Z. (2020). Artificial intelligence in education: A review. *IEEE Access : Practical Innovations, Open Solutions, 8*, 75264–75278. DOI: 10.1109/ACCESS.2020.2988510

Chen, X., Zou, D., Cheng, G., & Xie, H. (2021). Detecting latent topics and trends in educational technologies over four decades. *Computers & Education, 173*, 104286. DOI: 10.1016/j.compedu.2021.104286

Chinta, S. S.. (2024). Equity implications of AI-driven personalization. *Educational Technology Research and Development*. Advance online publication. DOI: 10.1007/s11423-020-09785-3

Cotton, D. R. E., Cotton, P. A., & Shipway, J. R. (2023). Chatting and cheating: Ensuring academic integrity in the era of ChatGPT. *Innovations in Education and Teaching International*. Advance online publication. DOI: 10.1080/14703297.2023.2190148

Creswell, J. W., & Plano Clark, V. L. (2018). Designing and conducting mixed methods research (3rd ed.). Sage. (No DOI available)

Dendir, S., & Maxwell, R. (2020). Cheating in online courses: Evidence from online proctoring. *Computers in Human Behavior Reports*, *2*, 100033. DOI: 10.1016/j.chbr.2020.100033

Eaton, S. E. (2023). Academic integrity in the age of artificial intelligence. *International Journal for Educational Integrity*, *19*(1), 1–10. DOI: 10.1007/s40979-023-00144-1

Floridi, L., Cowls, J., Beltrametti, M., Chatila, R., Chazerand, P., Dignum, V., & Vayena, E. (2018). AI4People — An ethical framework for AI. *Minds and Machines*, *28*, 689–707. DOI: 10.1007/s11023-018-9482-5 PMID: 30930541

Gilbert, S., & Gilbert, A. (2024). Reporting the potential risk of using AI in higher education: Subjective perspectives of educators. *Social Sciences & Humanities Open*.

Hair, J. F., Black, W. C., Babin, B. J., & Anderson, R. E. (2019). Multivariate data analysis (8th ed.). Cengage. (No DOI available)

Heilporn, G., Lakhal, S., & Bélisle, M. (2020). An examination of teachers' strategies to foster student engagement. *International Journal of Educational Technology in Higher Education*, *17*, 1–19. DOI: 10.1186/s41239-020-00218-2 PMID: 34805484

Holmes, W., Bialik, M., & Fadel, C. (2022). *Artificial intelligence in education*. Center for Curriculum Redesign. (No DOI available)

Javier, C., & Moorhouse, B. L. (2023). Generative AI and gendered/cultural bias in writing tools. [No DOI available]. *RELC Journal*.

Jonassen, D. H. (1991). Objectivism vs constructivism. *Educational Technology Research and Development*, *39*(3), 5–14. DOI: 10.1007/BF02296434

Kasneci, E., Sessler, K., Küchemann, S., Bannert, M., Dementieva, D., Fischer, F., Gasser, U., Groh, G., Günnemann, S., Hüllermeier, E., Krusche, S., Kutyniok, G., Michaeli, T., Nerdel, C., Pfeffer, J., Poquet, O., Sailer, M., Schmidt, A., Seidel, T., & Kasneci, G. (2023). ChatGPT for good? *Learning and Individual Differences, 103*, 102274. DOI: 10.1016/j.lindif.2023.102274

Kizilcec, R. F., & Lee, H. (2020). Algorithmic fairness in education. *Educational Technology Research and Development, 68*, 1–21. DOI: 10.1007/s11423-020-09785-3

Kochmar, E.. (2020). Automated scoring and feedback in ITS. *Computers & Education, 168*, 104198. DOI: 10.1016/j.compedu.2021.104198

Kohnke, L., Moorhouse, B. L., & Zou, D. (2023). Bias and stereotype reproduction in AI writing tools. [No DOI available]. *RELC Journal.*

Kumar, R., & Raman, A. (2022). Multimodal AI in assessment. *International Journal of Educational Technology in Higher Education.* Advance online publication. DOI: 10.1186/s41239-025-00540-2

Kvale, S., & Brinkmann, S. (2015). *InterViews: Learning the craft of qualitative research interviewing.* Sage.

Latifi, S., Noroozi, O., & Talaee, E. (2021). Automatic assessment of students' written texts. *Computers & Education, 168*, 104198. DOI: 10.1016/j.compedu.2021.104198

Merino-Campos, C. (2025). AI-driven personalization in higher education. *Journal of Educational Technology and Innovation.* DOI: 10.61414/jeti.v6i4.209

Ng, D. T. K., Leung, J. K. L., Chu, S. K. W., & Qiao, M. S. (2021). AI literacy: Definition, teaching, evaluation. *Computers and Education: Artificial Intelligence, 2*, 100041. DOI: 10.1016/j.caeai.2021.100041

Nicol, D. J., & Macfarlane-Dick, D. (2006). Formative assessment and self-regulated learning. *Studies in Higher Education, 31*(2), 199–218. DOI: 10.1080/03075070600572090

Onesi-Ozigagun, O., et al. (2024). Bias in automated grading systems. *International Journal of Educational Assessment.* (No DOI available)

Ouyang, F., Zheng, L., & Jiao, P. (2023). Artificial intelligence in online higher education. *Computers & Education: Artificial Intelligence, 4*, 100088. DOI: 10.1016/j.caeai.2023.100088

Pang, L.. (2024). Human judgement and contextual sensitivity in grading. Cited in *A systematic review on the future of educational assessment* [No DOI available]. *AI in Education*, 2(2), 75.

Patton, M. Q. (2015). *Qualitative research & evaluation methods*. Sage.

Perkins, M. (2023). Academic integrity considerations of AI large language models. *Journal of University Teaching & Learning Practice*, *20*(2), 7. https://arxiv.org/abs/2312.07086. DOI: 10.53761/1.20.02.07

Raudenbush, S. W., & Bryk, A. S. (2002). *Hierarchical linear models*. Sage. (No DOI available)

Richter, S.. (2025). AI as a "more knowledgeable other" in social-constructivist assessment. *AI & Society*. Advance online publication. DOI: 10.1007/s43681-024-00626-z

Selwyn, N. (2019). *Should robots replace teachers?* Polity Press.

Selwyn, N., O'Neill, C., Smith, G., Andrejevic, M., & Gu, X. (2023). A necessary evil? The rise of online exam proctoring in Australian universities. *Media International Australia, Incorporating Culture & Policy*, *186*(1), 149–164. DOI: 10.1177/1329878X211005862

Shin, D. (2021). The effects of explainability and causability on perception, trust, and acceptance. [No DOI available]. *International Journal of Human-Computer Studies*, *146*, 102551. DOI: 10.1016/j.ijhcs.2020.102551

Siemens, G., & Baker, R. S. (2012). Learning analytics and educational data mining. *LAK Conference*. DOI: 10.1145/2330601.2330661

Slade, S., & Prinsloo, P. (2013). Learning analytics: Ethical issues. *British Journal of Educational Technology*, *44*(6), 1510–1529. DOI: 10.1111/bjet.12085

Stahl, B. C.. (2023). Bias and objectivity claims in automated assessment. [No DOI available]. *AI and Ethics*.

Tashakkori, A., & Teddlie, C. (2010). Putting the human back in "human research methodology": The researcher in mixed methods research. *Journal of Mixed Methods Research*, *4*(4), 271–277.

Venkatesh, V., Morris, M., Davis, G., & Davis, F. (2012). User acceptance of IT: UTAUT model. *Management Information Systems Quarterly*, *27*(3), 425–478. DOI: 10.2307/30036540

Wang, Y., & Fan, J. (2025). Longitudinal gaps in AI-assessment research. *Frontiers in Education*. Advance online publication. DOI: 10.3389/feduc.2025.1522841

Woolf, B. P. (2010). *Building intelligent interactive tutors*. Morgan Kaufmann., DOI: 10.1016/C2009-0-20118-5

Zawacki-Richter, O., Marín, V. I., Bond, M., & Gouverneur, F. (2019). AI in higher education: Systematic review. *International Journal of Educational Technology in Higher Education*, *16*, 39. DOI: 10.1186/s41239-019-0171-0

Zeide, E. (2017). The structural consequences of big data-driven education. [No DOI available]. *Big Data*, *5*(2), 164–172. DOI: 10.1089/big.2016.0061 PMID: 28632444

Compilation of References

A'yun, A. Q., & Setyaningsih, W. (2025). Consumer Empowerment Through Ethical AI. *Strategies for Transparent and Trustworthy Personalized Marketing.*, *1*(1), 1–12. DOI: 10.70764/gdpu-jmb.2025.1(1)-01

Abbonato, D. (2024). Public sentiments on the fourth industrial revolution: An unsolicited public opinion poll from Twitter. *arXiv (Cornell University)*. https://doi.org//arxiv.2411.14230DOI: 10.48550

Abou El-Fotouh, T. A. I., Akanbi, M. T., Alom, N. B., Zakaria, A. F., Yusof, Z. B., & Razak, A. B. (2024). *Influence of predictive analytics and machine learning on enhancing customer retention and loyalty in service-based enterprises.* [Complete publication details required.]

Abuzaid, A. N. (2024). AI-Driven Business Processes: Efficiency Gains, Cost Reductions, and Implications for Economic Performance. *2024 International Conference on Knowledge Engineering and Communication Systems (ICKECS)*, 1–5. DOI: 10.1109/ICKECS61492.2024.10617370

Acquisti, A., Taylor, C., & Wagman, L. (2016). The economics of privacy. *Journal of Economic Literature*, *54*(2), 442–492. DOI: 10.1257/jel.54.2.442

Adanyin, A. (2024a). Ethical AI in Retail: Consumer Privacy and Fairness. *European Journal of Computer Science and Information Technology*, *12*(7), 21–35. DOI: 10.37745/ejcsit.2013/vol12n72135

Adeleye, R. A., Awonuga, K. F., Asuzu, O. F., Ndubuisi, N. L., & Tubokirifuruar, T. S. (2024). Digital marketing analytics: A review of strategies in the age of big data and AI [Review of *Digital marketing analytics: A review of strategies in the age of big data and AI*]. *World Journal of Advanced Research and Reviews, 21*(2), 73. GSC Online Press. DOI: 10.30574/wjarr.2024.21.2.0395

Adomavicius, G., & Tuzhilin, A. (2010). Context-aware recommender systems. In *Recommender systems handbook* (pp. 217–253). Springer US.

Aguirre, E., Mahr, D., Grewal, D., de Ruyter, K., & Wetzels, M. (2015). Unraveling the personalization paradox: The effect of information collection and trust-building strategies on online advertisement effectiveness. *Journal of Retailing, 91*(1), 34–49. DOI: 10.1016/j.jretai.2014.09.005

Ahmad, N., & Haque, S. (2024). Balancing Innovation and Ethics in AI- and Big Data-Driven Marketing. *Computer, 57*(8), 102–107. DOI: 10.1109/MC.2024.3405708

Ahmed, M. Z., Singh, A., Paul, A., Ghosh, S., & Chaudhuri, A. K. (2022). Amazon product recommendation system. *International Journal of Advanced Research in Computer and Communication Engineering, 11*(3). Advance online publication. DOI: 10.17148/IJARCCE.2022.11356

Ahmed, W. (2025). Artificial intelligence in aviation: A review of machine learning and deep learning applications for enhanced safety and security. Preprint. *Journal of Artificial Intelligence, 3*, 100013. DOI: 10.70389/PJAI.100013

Akerkar, R. (2019). *Artificial intelligence for business*. Springer. DOI: 10.1007/978-3-319-97436-1

Al Khaldy, M. A., Al-Obaydi, B. A. A., & al Shari, A. J. (2023). The impact of predictive analytics and AI on digital marketing strategy and ROI. In Conference on Sustainability and Cutting-Edge Business Technologies (pp. 367–379). Springer Nature Switzerland. DOI: 10.1007/978-3-031-42455-7_31

Alanazi, T. M. (2022). Marketing 5.0: An empirical investigation of its perceived effect on marketing performance. Marketing i menedžment innovacij, 13(4), 55–64.

Alkaeed, M., Qayyum, A., & Qadir, J. (2024). Privacy preservation in artificial intelligence and extended reality (AI-XR) metaverses: A survey. *Journal of Network and Computer Applications, 231*, 103989. DOI: 10.1016/j.jnca.2024.103989

Al-kfairy, M., Mustafa, D., Kshetri, N., Insiew, M., & Alfandi, O. (2024). Ethical Challenges and Solutions of Generative AI: An Interdisciplinary Perspective. *Informatics (MDPI), 11*(3), 58. DOI: 10.3390/informatics11030058

Al-Romeedy, B. (2019). Strategic agility as a competitive advantage in airlines: Case study of EgyptAir. *Journal of the Faculty of Tourism and Hotels. Fayoum University, 9*(2), 1–18.

Altun, C. (2024). *Postmodern Dönemde Dijital Deneyimler Işığında Değişen Tüketici Kimlik, Tercih ve Tutumları Üzerine Bir Araştırma*. İstanbul Ticaret Üniversitesi.

Alwreikat, A., Shehata, A. M. K., & Abu Zaid, M. K. (2023). Arab scholars' acceptance of informal scholarly communication tools: Applying the technology acceptance model 2 (TAM2). *Global Knowledge, Memory and Communication, 72*(1/2), 160–178. DOI: 10.1108/GKMC-04-2021-0070

Ameen, N., Tarhini, A., Reppel, A., & Anand, A. (2021). Customer experiences in the age of artificial intelligence. *Computers in Human Behavior, 114*, 106548. DOI: 10.1016/j.chb.2020.106548 PMID: 32905175

Antwi, C. O., Ren, J., Owusu-Ansah, W., Mensah, H. K., & Aboagye, M. O. (2021). Airport Self-Service Technologies, Passenger Self-Concept, and Behavior: An Attributional View. *Sustainability (Basel), 13*(6), 3134. DOI: 10.3390/su13063134

Applefield, J. M., Huber, R., & Moallem, M. (2000). Constructivism in theory and practice. [No DOI available]. *High School Journal, 84*(2), 35–53.

Arnould, E. J., Price, L., & Zinkhan, G. M. (2004). *Consumers* (2nd ed.). McGraw-Hill.

Arora, N., Dreze, X., Ghose, A., Hess, J. D., Iyengar, R., Jing, B., Joshi, Y., Kumar, V., Lurie, N., Neslin, S., Sajeesh, S., Su, M., Syam, N., Thomas, J., & Zhang, Z. J. (2008). Putting one-to-one marketing to work: Personalization, customization, and choice. *Marketing Letters, 19*(3), 305–321. DOI: 10.1007/s11002-008-9056-z

Ashok, M., Madan, R., Joha, A., & Sivarajah, U. (2022). Ethical framework for artificial intelligence and digital technologies. *International Journal of Information Management, 62*, 102433. DOI: 10.1016/j.ijinfomgt.2021.102433

Attar, R. W. (2025). Predicting trends and maximizing sales: AI's role in Saudi e-commerce decision-making. *Journal of Theoretical and Applied Electronic Commerce Research, 20*(4), 311. DOI: 10.3390/jtaer20040311

Aurier, P., Evrard, Y., & N'Goala, G. (2004). Understanding and measuring value from the consumer's point of view. *Research and Applications in Marketing, 19*(3), 1–20.

Awad, N. F., & Krishnan, M. S. (2006). The Personalization Privacy Paradox: An Empirical Evaluation of Information Transparency and the Willingness to be Profiled Online for Personalization1. *Management Information Systems Quarterly, 30*(1), 13–28. DOI: 10.2307/25148715

Babatunde, S. O., Odejide, O. A., Edunjobi, T. E., & Ogundipe, D. O. (2024). THE ROLE OF AI IN MARKETING PERSONALIZATION: A THEORETICAL EXPLORATION OF CONSUMER ENGAGEMENT STRATEGIES. *International Journal of Management & Entrepreneurship Research, 6*(3), 936–949. DOI: 10.51594/ijmer.v6i3.964

Babo, R., V. Babo, L., T Suhonen, J., & Tukiainen, M. (2020). E- Assessment with Multiple-Choice Questions: A 5 Year Study of Students' Opinions and Experience. Journal of Information Technology Education: Innovations in Practice, 19, 001–029. DOI: 10.28945/4491

Bajs, I. P. (2011). Attributes of tourist destinations as determinants of tourists perceived value. *International Journal of Management Cases, 13*(3), 547–554. DOI: 10.5848/APBJ.2011.00090

Baker, T., & Smith, L. (2019). *Educ-AI-tion rebooted? Exploring the future of artificial intelligence in schools and colleges*. Nesta.

Baker, R. S., & Hawn, A. (2021). Algorithmic bias in education. *International Journal of Artificial Intelligence in Education, 32*(4), 1052–1092. DOI: 10.1007/s40593-021-00285-9

Baker, S. M., Gentry, J. W., & Rittenburg, T. L. (2005). Building understanding of the domain of consumer vulnerability. *Journal of Macromarketing, 25*(2), 128–139. DOI: 10.1177/0276146705280622

Balcıoğlu, Y. S. (2025). AI-driven personalization in omnichannel marketing: Enhancing customer engagement and loyalty. In *Leveraging AI for Effective Digital Relationship Marketing* (pp. 97–130). IGI Global Scientific Publishing.

Bali, M. (2023). Critical AI literacy. In *Assistant, parrot, or colonizing loudspeaker? ChatGPT metaphors for developing critical AI literacies* (discussion of Bali's framework).

Baloska, S., Mechkaroska, D., & Domazet, E. (2022). AI-driven chatbot in e-commerce. *Journal of UIST, 3*(1), 30–40.

Barat, A., & Gulati, K. (2024). Emergence of AI in Marketing and its Implications. *Lloyd Business Review, 1*, 1–24. Advance online publication. DOI: 10.56595/lbr.v3i1.22

Barmeyer, C. (2023). Edward T. Hall: Kulturdimensionen als bewusstseinsschaffende Orientierungsrahmen. In Barmeyer, C., & Busch, D. (Eds.), *Meilensteine der Interkulturalitätsforschung* (pp. 37–68). Springer Fachmedien Wiesbaden., DOI: 10.1007/978-3-658-37924-7_2

Barocas, S., & Selbst, A. D. (2016). Big data's disparate impact. *California Law Review, 104*, 671–732.

Basal, M., Moulai, K., & Cetin, A. (2025). Predictive analytics for customer behavior prediction in artificial intelligence. *Economics World, 12*(2), 142–154.

Behr, L. M. (2024). *Literature Review on Metaverse Use Cases.* Wedel: Seminar IT-Management in the Digital Age.

Belanche, D., Casaló, L. V., Flavián, C., & Schepers, J. (2020). Service robot implementation: A theoretical framework and research agenda. *Tourism Management, 78*, 104017. DOI: 10.1016/j.tourman.2019.104017

Belanche, D., Casaló, L. V., Flavián, C., & Schepers, J. (2021). Service robot implementation: A theoretical framework and research agenda. *Service Industries Journal, 41*(3–4), 203–225.

Benali, S., & Boumenkar, D. (2024). Contribution of chatbot applications to attaining digital financial inclusion: Analysis and evaluation of America's chatbot Erica experience. *Management & Economics Research Journal, 6*(3), 497–516.

Benchmark, C. C. M. (2015). *Tourism & Mobile: Usage and Perspectives on New Services.* Online. https://www.tom.travel/2015/02/12/tourisme-et-mobile-quels-seront-les-usages-en-2015/ (Accessed 08/03/2026)

Benjelloun, A., & Kabak, S. (2024). Ethical Challenges and Managerial Implications of Artificial Intelligence in Digital Marketing. In *Lecture notes in networks and systems* (p. 439). Springer International Publishing., DOI: 10.1007/978-981-99-9040-5_32

Bentalha, B., Benjelloun, A., Slimani, H., & El Gharbaoui, B. (2025). Purchase Intention and Tourism Strategy in the Post-COVID-19 Era: Lessons and Perspectives From the Moroccan Experience. In Technological Innovation in Global Cultural Tourism (pp. 65-86). IGI Global Scientific Publishing.

Bentalha, B. (2025). Smart tourism and co-creation of the tourism experience: netnographic possibilities and technological perspectives. In *AI Technologies for Personalized and Sustainable Tourism* (pp. 253–276). IGI Global Scientific Publishing.

Beverland, M. B. (2005). Crafting brand authenticity: The case of luxury wines. *Journal of Management Studies, 42*(5), 1003–1029. DOI: 10.1111/j.1467-6486.2005.00530.x

Beyari, H. (2025). Artificial intelligence's effect on customer loyalty in the context of electronic commerce. *Journal of Umm Al-Qura University for Engineering and Architecture*, 1–10.

Bhattacherjee, A. (2001). Understanding information systems continuance: An expectation-confirmation model. *Management Information Systems Quarterly, 25*(3), 351–370. DOI: 10.2307/3250921

Bhuiyan, M. S. (2024). The Role of AI-Enhanced Personalization in Customer Experiences. *Journal of Computer Science and Technology Studies*, *6*(1), 162–169. DOI: 10.32996/jcsts.2024.6.1.17

Bici, A., & Vajjhala, N. R. (2024). Emerging trends and themes in AI-driven customer engagement and relationship management. In *Proceedings of the 5th International Conference on the Role of Innovation, Entrepreneurship and Management for Sustainable Development (ICRIEMSD 2024)* (Vol. 310, p. 113). Springer Nature. DOI: 10.2991/978-94-6463-612-3_9

Bickley, S. J., & Torgler, B. (2022). Cognitive architectures for artificial intelligence ethics. *AI & Society*, *38*(2), 501–519. DOI: 10.1007/s00146-022-01452-9

Binlibdah, S. (2024). Investigating the Role of Artificial Intelligence to Measure Consumer Efficiency: The Use of Strategic Communication and Personalized Media Content. *Journalism and Media*, *5*(3), 1142–1161. DOI: 10.3390/journalmedia5030073

Biplab, K., Choudhary, S. L., Rinku, S., Srivastava, P., & Kumar, M. (2023). Exploring the Ethical Use of Artificial Intelligence in Marketing and Advertising. *Journal of Informatics Education and Research*. DOI: 10.52783/jier.v3i2.278

Bird, K. A.. (2024). Algorithmic risk-flagging and disproportionate impact in education. [No DOI available]. *Educational Researcher*.

Bitra, S. K. (2025). Ethical AI and privacy in digital personalization: Balancing personalization and user trust. *World Journal of Advanced Engineering Technology and Sciences*, *15*(2), 774–779. DOI: 10.30574/wjaets.2025.15.2.0596

Black, P., & Wiliam, D. (1998). Assessment and classroom learning. *Assessment in Education: Principles, Policy & Practice*, *5*(1), 7–74. DOI: 10.1080/0969595980050102

Bleier, A., & Eisenbeiss, M. (2015). Personalized online advertising effectiveness. *JMR, Journal of Marketing Research*, *52*(5), 586–607.

Bleier, A., & Eisenbeiss, M. (2015). Personalized online advertising effectiveness: The interplay of what, when, and where. *Marketing Science*, *34*(5), 669–688. DOI: 10.1287/mksc.2015.0930

Bleier, A., Goldfarb, A., & Tucker, C. (2020). Consumer privacy and the future of data-based innovation and marketing. *International Journal of Research in Marketing*, *37*(3), 466–480. DOI: 10.1016/j.ijresmar.2020.03.006

Bleier, A., Harmeling, C. M., & Palmatier, R. W. (2019). Creating effective online customer experiences. *Journal of Marketing, 83*(2), 98–119. DOI: 10.1177/0022242918809930

Boddu, R. S. K., Santoki, A. A., Khurana, S., Koli, P. V., Rai, R., & Agrawal, A. (2022). An analysis to understand the role of machine learning, robotics and artificial intelligence in digital marketing. *Materials Today: Proceedings, 56*, 2288–2292. DOI: 10.1016/j.matpr.2021.11.637

Böhm, R., Jörling, M., Reiter, L., & Fuchs, C. (2023). People devalue generative AI's competence but not its advice in addressing societal and personal challenges. *Communications Psychology, 1*(1), 32. Advance online publication. DOI: 10.1038/s44271-023-00032-x PMID: 39242905

Boud, D., & Falchikov, N. (2007). *Rethinking assessment in higher education.* Routledge. (No DOI available)

Boudri, R., Bentalha, B., & Tariq, B. (2025). Towards Understanding Phygital Experience in Logistic-Retail Networks: A Netnographic Exploration of Connected Commerce. In *2025 IEEE International Conference on Advanced Technologies in Supply Chain Management (ATSCM)* (pp. 1-6). IEEE. DOI: 10.1109/ATSCM67505.2025.11473673

Bourliataux-Lajoinie, S., & Rivière, A. (2013). The challenge of m-services in territorial tourism marketing: Proposal of an analytical framework. *Recherches en Sciences de Gestion, 95*(2), 65–82. DOI: 10.3917/resg.095.0065

Braun, V., & Clarke, V. (2006). Using thematic analysis in psychology. *Qualitative Research in Psychology, 3*(2), 77–101. DOI: 10.1191/1478088706qp063oa

Bretag, T., Harper, R., Burton, M., Ellis, C., Newton, P., Rozenberg, P., Saddiqui, S., & van Haeringen, K. (2019). Contract cheating: A survey of Australian university students. *Studies in Higher Education, 44*(11), 1837–1856. DOI: 10.1080/03075079.2018.1462788

Brown, W., Wilson, G., & Johnson, O. (2024). *Understanding the role of chatbots in enhancing customer service.* [Publication details required.]

Bucove chi, Ö., & VEVERA, A. V. (2024). Perspective chapter: Organizational Resilience toward Managing Risks in Digital Marketing. In *IntechOpen eBooks*. IntechOpen. DOI: 10.5772/intechopen.1004786

Buhalis, D., Leung, D., & Lin, M. (2023). Metaverse as a disruptive technology revolutionizing tourism management and marketing. *Tourism Management, 97*, 104724. DOI: 10.1016/j.tourman.2023.104724

Buhalis, D., & Leung, R. (2018). Smart hospitality—Interconnectivity and interoperability towards an ecosystem. *International Journal of Hospitality Management, 71*, 41–50. DOI: 10.1016/j.ijhm.2017.11.011

Buhmann, A., & Fieseler, C. (2021). Towards a deliberative framework for responsible innovation in artificial intelligence. *Technology in Society, 64*, 101475. DOI: 10.1016/j.techsoc.2020.101475

Bujor, D., & Constantin, A. B. E. (2025). AI-driven predictive customer analytics for forecasting behavior, churn and future buying patterns. In *Proceedings of the International Conference on Business Excellence* (Vol. 19, No. 1, pp. 981–994). Bucharest University of Economic Studies. DOI: 10.2478/picbe-2025-0077

Burger, C. J. S. C., Dohnal, M., Kathrada, M., & Law, R. (2001). A practitioner's guide to time-series methods for tourism demand forecasting – A case study of Durban, South Africa. *Tourism Management, 22*(4), 403–409. DOI: 10.1016/S0261-5177(00)00068-6

Burkiewicz, Ł., & Knap-Stefaniuk, A. (2022). Multiculturalism as a Challenge for Contemporary Leadership – an Analysis within the Context of Hotel Management in the 21st Century. *Perspektywy Kultury, 38*(3), 411–424. DOI: 10.35765/pk.2022.3803.25

Butt, M. (2024). Analytical Study of the World's First EU Artificial Intelligence (AI) Act, 2024. *International Journal of Research Publication and Reviews, 5*(3), 7343–7364. DOI: 10.55248/gengpi.5.0324.0914

Canhoto, A. I., Keegan, B. J., & Ryzhikh, M. (2024). Snakes and ladders: Unpacking the personalisation–privacy paradox in the context of AI-enabled personalisation in the physical retail environment. *Information Systems Frontiers, 26*(3), 1005–1024. DOI: 10.1007/s10796-023-10369-7 PMID: 36684411

Carless, D. (2015). *Excellence in university assessment: Learning from award-winning practice*. Routledge. (No DOI available)

Castells, P., Hurley, N. J., & Vargas, S. (2015). Novelty and diversity in recommender systems. In Ricci, F., Rokach, L., & Shapira, B. (Eds.), *Recommender Systems Handbook* (pp. 881–918). Springer. DOI: 10.1007/978-1-4899-7637-6_26

Challapalli, V., Sai, K. V., Singh, P. P., Prasad, R., Maurya, A., & Singh, A. (2025). SLM4Offer: Personalized marketing offer generation using contrastive learning-based fine-tuning. *arXiv*.

Chandra, B., & Rahman, Z. (2024). Artificial intelligence and value co-creation: A review, conceptual framework and directions for future research. *Journal of Service Theory and Practice*, *34*(1), 7–32. DOI: 10.1108/JSTP-03-2023-0097

Chang, S., Wang, Z., Wang, Y., Tang, J., & Jiang, X. (2019). Enabling Technologies and Platforms to Aid Digitalisation of Commercial Aviation Support, Maintenance and Health Management. *International Conference on Quality, Reliability, Risk, Maintenance, and Safety Engineering*. DOI: 10.1109/QR2MSE46217.2019.9021222

Chang, T.-Y., & Chuang, Y.-J. (2021). Cultural Sustainability: Teaching and Design Strategies for Incorporating Service Design in Religious Heritage Branding. *Sustainability (Basel)*, *13*(6), 3256. DOI: 10.3390/su13063256

Chan-Olmsted, S., Chen, H., & Kim, H. J. (2024). In smartness we trust: Consumer experience, smart device personalization and privacy balance. *Journal of Consumer Marketing*, *41*(6), 597–609. DOI: 10.1108/JCM-12-2021-5072

Chatterjee, S., Rana, N. P., Dwivedi, Y. K., & Baabdullah, A. M. (2021). Understanding AI adoption in service sectors. *Journal of Business Research*, *123*, 1–12.

Chellappan, R. B. (2024). From Algorithms to Accountability: The Societal and Ethical Need for Explainable AI. *Research Square (Research Square)*. DOI: 10.21203/rs.3.rs-5277731/v1

Chen, J., Liu, Z., Huang, X., Wu, C., Liu, Q., Jiang, G., Pu, Y., Lei, Y., Chen, X., Wang, X., Zheng, K., Lian, D., & Chen, E. (2024). When large language models meet personalization: Perspectives of challenges and opportunities. *Worldwide b*, *27*(4), 42. DOI: 10.1007/s11280-024-01276-1

Chen, C.-L. (2020). Cross-disciplinary innovations by Taiwanese manufacturing SMEs in the context of Industry 4.0. *Journal of Manufacturing Technology Management*, *31*(6), 1145–1168. DOI: 10.1108/JMTM-08-2019-0301

Chen, C., Tian, A. D., & Jiang, R. (2024). When post hoc explanation knocks: Consumer responses to explainable AI recommendations. *Journal of Interactive Marketing*, *59*(3), 234–250. DOI: 10.1177/10949968231200221

Chen, H., Chiang, R. H., & Storey, V. C. (2012). Business intelligence and analytics: From big data to big impact. *Management Information Systems Quarterly*, *36*(4), 1165–1188. DOI: 10.2307/41703503

Chen, L., Chen, P., & Lin, Z. (2020). Artificial intelligence in education: A review. *IEEE Access : Practical Innovations, Open Solutions*, *8*, 75264–75278. DOI: 10.1109/ACCESS.2020.2988510

Chen, X., Zou, D., Cheng, G., & Xie, H. (2021). Detecting latent topics and trends in educational technologies over four decades. *Computers & Education, 173*, 104286. DOI: 10.1016/j.compedu.2021.104286

Chinta, S. S.. (2024). Equity implications of AI-driven personalization. *Educational Technology Research and Development*. Advance online publication. DOI: 10.1007/s11423-020-09785-3

Chopra, R., Patel, N., Chopra, N., & Singh, D. (2022). Leveraging reinforcement learning and collaborative filtering for enhanced personalization in loyalty programs. *International Journal of AI Advancements, 11*(10).

Chowdhury, R. H. (2024). AI-powered Industry 4.0: Pathways to economic development and innovation. [IJCRT]. *International Journal of Creative Research Thoughts, 12*(6), h650–h657.

Chung, K. C., & Tan, P. J. B. (2025). Artificial intelligence and the Internet of Things to improve smart hospitality services. *Internet ofThings : Engineering Cyber Physical Human Systems, 31*, 101544. DOI: 10.1016/j.iot.2025.101544

Cinotti, Y. (2015). From hospitality to experience: comparative writings of tourists in guesthouses & hotels. In Decroly, J.-M. (Ed.), *Tourism as experience. Interdisciplinary perspectives on the tourist experience*. Presses Universitaires du Québec.

Cloarec, J., Meyer-Waarden, L., & Munzel, A. (2022). The personalization–privacy paradox at the nexus of social exchange and construal level theories. *Psychology and Marketing, 39*(3), 647–661. DOI: 10.1002/mar.21587

Cloarec, J., Meyer-Waarden, L., & Munzel, A. (2024). Transformative privacy calculus: Conceptualizing the personalization–privacy paradox on social media. *Psychology and Marketing, 41*(7), 1574–1596. DOI: 10.1002/mar.21998

Cohen, E., & Cohen, S. A. (2012). Current sociological theories and issues in tourism. *Annals ofTourism Research, 39*(4), 2177–2202. DOI: 10.1016/j.annals.2012.07.009

Colurcio, M., & Caridà, A. (2026). AI in service industries: Striking a balance between value co-creation and co-destruction. *Management Decision*, •••, 1–25. DOI: 10.1108/MD-11-2025-3576

Connell, J., & Page, S. J. (2008). exploring the spatial patterns of car-based tourist travel in Loch Lomond and Trossachs National Park, Scotland. *Tourism Management, 29*(3), 561–580. DOI: 10.1016/j.tourman.2007.03.019

Connelly, B. L., Certo, S. T., Ireland, R. D., & Reutzel, C. R. (2011). Signaling theory: A review and assessment. *Journal of Management, 37*(1), 39–67. DOI: 10.1177/0149206310388419

Constantinides, M., Tahaei, M., Quercia, D., Stumpf, S., Madaio, M., Kennedy, S., Wilcox, L., Vitak, J., Cramer, H., Bogucka, E. P., Baeza-Yates, R., Luger, E., Holbrook, J., Müller, M., Blumenfeld, I. G., & Pistilli, G. (2024a). Implications of Regulations on the Use of AI and Generative AI for Human-Centered Responsible Artificial Intelligence. *arXiv (Cornell University)*. /arxiv.2403.00148DOI: 10.1145/3613905.3643979

Coovadia, H., Marx, B., Botha, I., & Gold, N. O. (2025). Building an ethical artificial intelligence corporate governance framework for the integration of emerging technologies into business processes. *South African Journal of Accounting Research, 39*(3), 286–316. DOI: 10.1080/10291954.2025.2523661

Copeland, J. (2015). *Artificial intelligence: A philosophical introduction*. John Wiley & Sons.

Cotton, D. R. E., Cotton, P. A., & Shipway, J. R. (2023). Chatting and cheating: Ensuring academic integrity in the era of ChatGPT. *Innovations in Education and Teaching International*. Advance online publication. DOI: 10.1080/14703297.2023.2190148

Creswell, J. W., & Plano Clark, V. L. (2018). Designing and conducting mixed methods research (3rd ed.). Sage. (No DOI available)

Dadoun, A., Defoin-Platel, M., Fiig, T., Landra, C., & Troncy, R. (2021). How recommender systems can transform airline offer construction and retailing. *Journal of Revenue and Pricing Management, 11*(2), 301–315. Advance online publication. DOI: 10.1057/s41272-021-00313-2

Dahake, P. S., Dahake, N. S., Bansod, S. N., Patil, P. A., & Ingle, A. (2025). Marketing innovations in Society 5.0: The role of predictive analytics in analyzing consumer behavior for marketers. In *Future-Proofing Emerging Technologies for Business Transformation* (pp. 361–386). IGI Global. DOI: 10.4018/979-8-3373-1320-7.ch011

Dai, X., Li, M., Yang, S., Shi, C., Wang, K., Liao, X., Li, Q. E. J., Tao, X., & Tang, X. (2025). Attitudes, perceptions, and factors influencing the adoption of AI in health care among medical staff: Nationwide cross-sectional survey study. *Journal of Medical Internet Research, 27*, e75343. DOI: 10.2196/75343 PMID: 40779308

Danilet, C. (2025). The transformative uses of AI in airlines: Enhancing passenger experience and operations. *The Flying Engineer.* Retrieved May 17, 2026, from https://theflyingengineer.com

Davenport, T. H. (2014). How strategists use 'big data' to support internal business decisions, discovery and production. *Strategy and Leadership*, *42*(4), 45–50. DOI: 10.1108/SL-05-2014-0034

Davenport, T., Guha, A., Grewal, D., & Bressgott, T. (2020). How artificial intelligence will change the future of marketing. *Journal of the Academy of Marketing Science*, *48*(1), 24–42. DOI: 10.1007/s11747-019-00696-0

Davis, A., Murphy, J., Owens, D., Khazanchi, D., & Zigurs, I. (2009). Avatars, people, and virtual worlds: Foundations for research in metaverses. *Journal of the Association for Information Systems*, *10*(2), 90–117. DOI: 10.17705/1jais.00183

Davis, F. D. (1989). Perceived usefulness, perceived ease of use, and user acceptance of information technology. *Management Information Systems Quarterly*, *13*(3), 319–340. DOI: 10.2307/249008

de Brito Duarte, R., Correia, F., Arriaga, P., & Paiva, A. (2023). AI trust: Can explainable AI enhance warranted trust? *Human Behavior and Emerging Technologies*, *2023*, 4637678. Advance online publication. DOI: 10.1155/2023/4637678

De Bruyn, A., Viswanathan, V., Beh, Y. S., Brock, J. K.-U., & von Wangenheim, F. (2020). Artificial intelligence and marketing: Pitfalls and opportunities. *Journal of Interactive Marketing*, *51*(1), 91–105. DOI: 10.1016/j.intmar.2020.04.007

de Matos, C. A., Rohden, S. F., & Azevedo, A. B. L. (2026). AI-induced privacy concerns: Examining the moderating effect of AI fear on customer data sharing. *International Journal of Bank Marketing*, *44*(6), 1271–1295. DOI: 10.1108/IJBM-05-2025-0403

Degas, A., Islam, M. R., Hurter, C., Barua, S., Rahman, H., Poudel, M., Ruscio, D., Ahmed, M. U., Begum, S., Rahman, M. A., Bonelli, S., Cartocci, G., Di Flumeri, G., Borghini, G., Babiloni, F., & Aricò, P. (2022). A survey on artificial intelligence (AI) and explainable AI in air traffic management: Current trends and development with future research trajectory. *Applied Sciences (Basel, Switzerland)*, *12*(3), 1295. DOI: 10.3390/app12031295

Delen, D., & Zolbanin, H. M. (2018). The analytics paradigm in business research. *Journal of Business Research*, *90*, 186–195. DOI: 10.1016/j.jbusres.2018.05.013

Dendir, S., & Maxwell, R. (2020). Cheating in online courses: Evidence from online proctoring. *Computers in Human Behavior Reports*, *2*, 100033. DOI: 10.1016/j.chbr.2020.100033

Dickinson, P., Jones, A., Christian, W., Westerside, A., Mulloy, F., Gerling, K., Hicks, K., Wilson, L., & Parke, A. (2021). *Experiencing simulated confrontations in virtual reality.* Proceedings of the 2021 CHI Conference on Human Factors in Computing Systems, Article 483, 1–10. DOI: 10.1145/3411764.3445401

Digital Defynd. (2026). Use of AI in the aviation industry: *10 case studies.* Retrieved May 17, 2026, from https://digitaldefynd.com

Dinev, T., & Hart, P. (2006). An extended privacy calculus model for e-commerce transactions. *Information Systems Research, 17*(1), 61–80. DOI: 10.1287/isre.1060.0080

Ding, Z., Zhang, Y., Sun, J., Goh, M., & Yang, Z. (2025). Harmonizing human touch and AI precision in customer service. *Journal of Service Research.* Advance online publication. DOI: 10.1177/10946705251384692

Dolnicar, S., Grün, B., & Leisch, F. (2018). Step 5: Extracting Segments. In *Market Segmentation Analysis: Understanding It, Doing It, and Making It Useful* (pp. 75–181). Springer Singapore. DOI: 10.1007/978-981-10-8818-6_7

Duhigg, C. (2012, February 16). How companies learn your secrets. *The New York Times Magazine.* https://www.nytimes.com/2012/02/19/magazine/shopping-habits .html

D'Ulizia, A., Federico, D., & Notte, A. (2024). The Technological Innovation of the Metaverse in Financial Sector: Current State, Opportunities, and Open Challenges. *Intelligent Systems in Accounting, Finance and Management, 31*(3), e1566. 1-17.

Dwivedi, Y. K., Hughes, L., Ismagilova, E., Aarts, G., Coombs, C., Crick, T., Duan, Y., Dwivedi, R., Edwards, J., Eirug, A., Galanos, V., Ilavarasan, P. V., Janssen, M., Jones, P., Kar, A. K., Kizgin, H., Kronemann, B., Lal, B., Lucini, B., & Williams, M. D. (2021). Artificial Intelligence (AI): Multidisciplinary perspectives on emerging challenges. *International Journal of Information Management, 57,* 101994. DOI: 10.1016/j.ijinfomgt.2019.08.002

Eaton, S. E. (2023). Academic integrity in the age of artificial intelligence. *International Journal for Educational Integrity, 19*(1), 1–10. DOI: 10.1007/s40979-023-00144-1

Echeverri, P., & Skålén, P. (2011). Co-creation and co-destruction: A practice-theory based study of interactive value formation. *Marketing Theory, 11*(3), 351–373. DOI: 10.1177/1470593111408181

Echeverri, P., & Skålén, P. (2021). Value co-destruction: Review and conceptualization of interactive value formation. *Marketing Theory, 21*(2), 227–249. DOI: 10.1177/1470593120983390

Eid, M. A. H., Hashesh, M. A., Sharabati, A. A., Khraiwish, A., Al-Haddad, S., & Abusaimeh, H. (2024). Conceptualizing ethical AI-enabled marketing: Current state and agenda for future research. *International Journal of Data and Network Science*, *8*(4), 2291–2306. DOI: 10.5267/j.ijdns.2024.6.002

El Biyaali, M. K., Boudri, R., & Bentalha, B. (2025). Leveraging Sentiment Analysis for Enhanced Customer Experience: AI-Driven Personalization in Online Retail. In AI Innovations for Customer Experience Optimization in the Service Sector (pp. 203-224). IGI Global Scientific Publishing.

El-Said, O., & Aziz, H. (2022). Virtual Tours to an End: An Analysis of Virtual Tours' Role in Tourism Recovery Post COVID-19. *Journal of Travel Research*, *61*(3), 528–548. DOI: 10.1177/0047287521997567

Engel, J. F., Kollat, D. T., & Blackwell, R. D. (1968). *Consumer Behavior*. Holt, Rinehart and Winston.

Erciyes University (Turquía). Hovardaoglu, O., Calisir-Hovardaoglu, S., & Erciyes University (Turquía). (2024). Survival Strategies of Local SMTEs in the COVID-19 Pandemic in Heritage Tourism Sites in Turkey. *PASOS. Revista de Turismo y Patrimonio Cultural, 22*(1), 125–145. DOI: 10.25145/j.pasos.2024.22.008

Eriksson, N., & Strandvik, P. (2009). Possible determinants affecting the use of mobile tourism services. In *e-Business and Telecommunications*. Springer, p. 61 - 73. DOI: 10.1007/978-3-642-05197-5_4

Eurocontrol (2020). *The FLY AI report*: Demystifying and accelerating AI in aviation / ATM. Retrieved from https://www.eurocontrol.int/sites/default/files/2020-03/eurocontrol-fly-ai-report-032020.pdf (eurocontrol.int in Bing)

Euromonitor International. (2023). *World Travel Market Report*.

Fan, H., & Poole, M. S. (2006). What is personalization? Perspectives on the design and implementation of personalization in information systems. *Journal of Organizational Computing and Electronic Commerce*, *16*(3–4), 179–202. DOI: 10.1207/s15327744joce1603&4_2

Farida, I., & Setiawan, D. (2022). Business Strategies and Competitive Advantage: The Role of Performance and Innovation. *Journal of Open Innovation*, *8*(3), 163. DOI: 10.3390/joitmc8030163

Farooq, M. S., & Yen, Y. Y. (2024). Artificial Intelligence in Consumer Behaviour: A Systematic Literature Review. *Research Square (Research Square)*. DOI: 10.21203/rs.3.rs-3875906/v1

Fassiaux, S. (2023). Preserving consumer autonomy through European Union regulation of artificial intelligence: A long-term perspective. *European Journal of Risk Regulation, 14*(3), 1–20. DOI: 10.1017/err.2023.58

Felzmann, H., Fosch-Villaronga, E., Lutz, C., & Tamò-Larrieux, A. (2020). Towards transparency by design for artificial intelligence. *Science and Engineering Ethics, 26*(6), 3333–3361. DOI: 10.1007/s11948-020-00276-4 PMID: 33196975

Fijalkow, Y., Jalaudin, C., & Lalanne, M. (2015). Measuring the tourist experience through the engagement, indifference & avoidance of local populations. In Decroly, J.-M. (Ed.), *Tourism as Experience. Interdisciplinary perspectives on the tourist experience*. Presses Universitaires du Québec.

Flavián, C., Pérez-Rueda, A., Belanche, D., & Casaló, L. V. (2022). Intention to use analytical artificial intelligence in services: The effect of technology readiness and awareness. *Journal of Service Management, 33*(2), 293–320. DOI: 10.1108/JOSM-10-2020-0378

Floridi, L., Cowls, J., Beltrametti, M., Chatila, R., Chazerand, P., Dignum, V., & Vayena, E. (2018). AI4People — An ethical framework for AI. *Minds and Machines, 28*, 689–707. DOI: 10.1007/s11023-018-9482-5 PMID: 30930541

Florido-Benítez, L. (2024). The cybersecurity applied by online travel agencies and hotels to protect users' private data in smart cities. *Smart Cities, 7*(1), 475–495.

Flügel, S., Halse, A. H., Hartveit, K. J., & Ukkonen, A. (2022). Value of travel time by road types. *European Transport Research Review, 14*(1), 35. DOI: 10.1186/s12544-022-00554-1

Fondevila-Gascón, J., Gutiérrez-Aragón, Ó., Lopez-Lopez, D., Curiel-Barrios, G., & Alabart-Algueró, J. (2025). Passenger perceptions of artificial intelligence in airline operations: Implications for air transport management. *Journal of Air Transport Management, 129*, 129. DOI: 10.1016/j.jairtraman.2025.102874

Fornell, C., & Larcker, D. F. (1981). Evaluating structural equation models with unobservable variables and measurement error. *JMR, Journal ofMarketing Research, 18*(1), 39–50. DOI: 10.1177/002224378101800104

Gandomi, A., & Haider, M. (2015). Beyond the hype: Big data concepts, methods, and analytics. *International Journal of Information Management, 35*(2), 137–144. DOI: 10.1016/j.ijinfomgt.2014.10.007

Gartner. (2024). *Predicts 2024: AI powers personalization, revenue growth and efficiency in consumer goods.* Gartner Research. Retrieved from: https://www.gartner.com/en/documents/5285163#:~:text=Summary,for%20margin%20and%20revenue%20growth

Gefen, D., Karahanna, E., & Straub, D. W. (2003). Trust and TAM in online shopping. *Management Information Systems Quarterly, 27*(1), 51–90. DOI: 10.2307/30036519

Ge, X., Xu, C., Misaki, D., Markus, H. R., & Tsai, J. L. (2024). How culture shapes what people want from AI. In *Proceedings of the 2024 CHI Conference on Human Factors in Computing Systems* (Article 704, pp. 1–15). Association for Computing Machinery. DOI: 10.1145/3613904.3642660

Gilbert, S., & Gilbert, A. (2024). Reporting the potential risk of using AI in higher education: Subjective perspectives of educators. *Social Sciences & Humanities Open.*

Glikson, E., & Woolley, A. W. (2020). Human trust in artificial intelligence: Review of empirical research. *The Academy of Management Annals, 14*(2), 627–660. DOI: 10.5465/annals.2018.0057

Gnewuch, U., Morana, S., & Maedche, A. (2017). Towards designing cooperative and social conversational agents. *Business & Information Systems Engineering, 59*(5), 351–366.

Goffman, E. (1967). *Ritual interaction; essays on face-to-face behavior.* Doubleday.

Go, H., & Kang, M. (2023). Metaverse tourism for sustainable tourism development: Tourism Agenda 2030. *Tourism Review, 78*(2), 381–394. DOI: 10.1108/TR-02-2022-0102

Gomez-Uribe, C. A., & Hunt, N. (2015). The netflix recommender system: Algorithms, business value, and innovation. [TMIS]. *ACM Transactions on Management Information Systems, 6*(4), 1–19. DOI: 10.1145/2843948

Gooljar, V., Issa, T., Hardin-Ramanan, S., & Abu-Salih, B. (2024). Sentiment-based predictive models for online purchases in the era of marketing 5.0: A systematic review. *Journal of Big Data, 11*(1), 107. DOI: 10.1186/s40537-024-00947-0

Gouveia, J., & Santos, S. (2025). Rethinking the customer journey: Impact of AI for consumers and businesses—a systematic literature review and research agenda. *International Journal of Consumer Studies, 49*(6), e70136. DOI: 10.1111/ijcs.70136

Gramley, S., Gramley, V., & Pätzold, K.-M. (2020). *A Survey of Modern English* (3rd ed.). Routledge., DOI: 10.4324/9780429300356

Grewal, D., Hulland, J., Kopalle, P. K., & Karahanna, E. (2020). The future of technology and marketing: A multidisciplinary perspective. *Journal of the Academy of Marketing Science, 48*(1), 1–8. DOI: 10.1007/s11747-019-00711-4

Grewal, D., Satornino, C. B., Davenport, T., & Guha, A. (2025). How generative AI is shaping the future of marketing. *Journal of the Academy of Marketing Science, 53*(3), 702–722. DOI: 10.1007/s11747-024-01064-3

Gritta, F., & Calabrese, M. (2023). Internet use in small tourism in Italy: what will be the role of local government? Transforming Government: People. *Process and Policy, 17*(4), 632–654.

Gu, C., Li, X., & Xiang, Q. (2025). The infinite monkey theorem in AIGC advertising: Matching effects between AI disclosure and advertising appeals on consumer advertising avoidance intention. *Journal of Research in Interactive Marketing*. Advance online publication. DOI: 10.1108/JRIM-05-2025-0265

Gudavalli, S., Ravi, V. K., Jampani, S., Pandey, P., Ayyagari, A., & Goel, P. (2024). Enhancing data security and privacy in cloud, SAP, and IoT environments. *Journal of Quantum Science and Technology, 1*(4), 217–243. DOI: 10.63345/jqst.v1i4.104

Guerra-Tamez, C. R., Kraul Flores, K., Serna-Mendiburu, G. M., Chavelas Robles, D., & Ibarra Cortés, J. (2024). Decoding Gen Z: AI's influence on brand trust and purchasing behavior. *Frontiers in Artificial Intelligence, 7*, 1323512. DOI: 10.3389/frai.2024.1323512 PMID: 38500672

Gülen, K., Tümdağ, C., & Yılmaz Altuntaş, E. (2023). Markaların kurumsal çağrışımları ve deneyim pazarlaması bağlamında metaverse girişimleri. *Uluslararası Halkla İlişkiler ve Reklam Çalışmaları Dergisi, 6*(2), 9–28.

Gursoy, D., Chi, O. H., Lu, L., & Nunkoo, R. (2019). Consumers' acceptance of artificially intelligent (AI) device use in service delivery. *International Journal of Information Management, 49*, 157–169. DOI: 10.1016/j.ijinfomgt.2019.03.008

Hair, J. F., Black, W. C., Babin, B. J., & Anderson, R. E. (2019). Multivariate data analysis (8th ed.). Cengage. (No DOI available)

Hair, J. F., Black, W. C., Babin, B. J., & Anderson, R. E. (2014). *Multivariate data analysis* (7th ed.). Pearson.

Hair, J. F., Hult, G. T. M., Ringle, C. M., & Sarstedt, M. (2022). *A primer on partial least squares structural equation modeling (PLS-SEM)* (3rd ed.). Sage Publications.

Haliti Baruti, B., Hoti, A., & Bajrami, S. M. (2025). Utilising artificial intelligence in digital marketing strategy: Opportunities and challenges for marketers. *SSRN*. DOI: 10.2139/ssrn.5470814

Han, H., & Hyun, S. S. (2022). Customer retention in the hospitality industry: The role of satisfaction, loyalty, and trust. *International Journal of Hospitality Management, 103*, 103208. DOI: 10.1016/j.ijhm.2022.103208

Han, H., Yu, J., & Kim, W. (2021). Environmental corporate social responsibility and customer responses. *International Journal of Hospitality Management, 95*, 102935. DOI: 10.1016/j.ijhm.2021.102935

Han, J., & Ko, D. (2025). Consumer autonomy in generative AI services: The role of task difficulty and AI design elements in enhancing trust, satisfaction, and usage intention. *Behavioral Sciences (Basel, Switzerland), 15*(4), 534. Advance online publication. DOI: 10.3390/bs15040534 PMID: 40282155

Hariyanto, H., Kristianingsih, F. X. D., & Maharani, R. (2025). Artificial intelligence in adaptive education: A systematic review of techniques for personalized learning. *Discover Education, 4*(1), 458. Advance online publication. DOI: 10.1007/s44217-025-00908-6

Hasan, S., Godhuli, E. R., Rahman, M. S., & Al Mamun, M. A. (2023). The adoption of conversational assistants in the banking industry: Is the perceived risk a moderator? *Heliyon, 9*(9), e20220. DOI: 10.1016/j.heliyon.2023.e20220 PMID: 37810016

Hécate Vergopoulos, H. (2016). The tourist experience: an experience of the managers of the tourist experience? Via [Online], 10 | 2016, Online since 01 December 2016, accessed on 23 March 2026. URL: https://journals.openedition.org/viatourism/1347DOI: .DOI: 10.4000/viatourism.1347

Heilporn, G., Lakhal, S., & Bélisle, M. (2020). An examination of teachers' strategies to foster student engagement. *International Journal of Educational Technology in Higher Education, 17*, 1–19. DOI: 10.1186/s41239-020-00218-2 PMID: 34805484

Henning, G. K. (2012). The habit of tourism: Experiences and their ontological meaning. In Sharpley, R., & Stone, P. R. (Eds.), *Contemporary tourist experience: concepts and consequences*. Routledge.

Hermann, E. (2022). Leveraging artificial intelligence in marketing for social good: An ethical perspective. *Journal of Business Ethics, 179*(1), 43–61. DOI: 10.1007/s10551-021-04843-y PMID: 34054170

Hermann, E. (2022). Psychological targeting: Nudge or boost to foster mindful and sustainable consumption? *AI & Society, 38*(2), 961–962. DOI: 10.1007/s00146-022-01403-4

Hermann, E., Williams, G. Y., & Puntoni, S. (2023). Deploying artificial intelligence in services to AID vulnerable consumers. *Journal of the Academy of Marketing Science, 52*(5), 1431–1451. DOI: 10.1007/s11747-023-00986-8

Heskett, J. L. (1990). *Service breakthroughs*. Simon and Schuster.

Hetherington, J., Daniel, T. C., & Brown, T. C. (1993). Is motion more important than it sounds?: The medium of presentation in environmental perception research. *Journal of Environmental Psychology, 13*(4), 283–291. DOI: 10.1016/S0272-4944(05)80251-8

Hibban, M. I. (2025). AI-powered chatbots: Revolutionizing customer service in the digital era. *Jurnal Ekonomi Kreatif dan Manajemen Bisnis Digital, 4*(2), 282–288.

High-Level Expert Group on Artificial Intelligence. (2019). *Ethics guidelines for trustworthy AI.* European Commission. https://digital-strategy.ec.europa.eu/en/library/ethics-guidelines-trustworthy-ai

Hofstede, G. (2001). *Culture's consequences: Comparing values, behaviors, institutions and organizations across nations* (2nd ed.). Sage Publications.

Holbrook, M. B. (1999). Introduction to consumer value. In *Holbrook MB (coord.). Consumer value: a framework for analysis and research* (pp. 1–28). Routledge. DOI: 10.4324/9780203010679.ch0

Hollebeek, L. D., Srivastava, R. K., & Chen, T. (2019). SD logic—informed customer engagement: Integrative framework, fundamental revised propositions, and application to CRM. *Journal of the Academy of Marketing Science, 47*(1), 161–185. DOI: 10.1007/s11747-016-0494-5

Hollebeek, L. D., Srivastava, R. K., & Chen, T. (2022). Customer engagement and AI-enabled service experiences. *Journal of Service Theory and Practice, 32*(1), 45–67. DOI: 10.1108/JSTP-02-2021-0038

Holmes, W., Bialik, M., & Fadel, C. (2022). *Artificial intelligence in education.* Center for Curriculum Redesign. (No DOI available)

Holzinger, A., Zatloukal, K., & Müller, H. (2024). Is human oversight to AI systems still possible? *New Biotechnology, 85*, 59–62. DOI: 10.1016/j.nbt.2024.12.003 PMID: 39675423

Hoyer, W. D., Kroschke, M., Schmitt, B., Kraume, K., & Shankar, V. (2020). Transforming the Customer Experience through New Technologies. *Journal of Interactive Marketing, 51*(1), 57–71. DOI: 10.1016/j.intmar.2020.04.001

Hsu, C.-L., Chen, M.-C., & Lin, J. C.-C. (2023). Understanding the user satisfaction and loyalty of customer service chatbots. *Journal of Retailing and Consumer Services, 71*, 103205. DOI: 10.1016/j.jretconser.2022.103211

Hua, J., & Mankbadi, R. R. (2024). Prediction and Control of Broadband Noise Associated with Advanced Air Mobility—A Review. *Applied Sciences (Basel, Switzerland), 14*(18), 8455. DOI: 10.3390/app14188455

Huang, G. I., Zhang, C., Torres, W. C. Z., Xiong, X., & Li, H. (2025a). Responsible AI and human collaboration in tourism management: Ethical considerations and identity disclosure. *Tourism Management, 113*, 105315. DOI: 10.1016/j.tourman.2025.105315

Huang, M. H., & Rust, R. T. (2021). A strategic framework for artificial intelligence in marketing. *Journal of the Academy of Marketing Science, 49*(1), 30–50. DOI: 10.1007/s11747-020-00749-9

Huang, M.-H., & Rust, R. T. (2018). Artificial intelligence in service. *Journal of Service Research, 21*(2), 155–172. DOI: 10.1177/1094670517752459

Huang, S., Liang, L. J., & Choi, H. C. (2022). How Failed in Context: A Text-Mining Approach to Understanding Hotel Service Failures. *Sustainability (Basel), 14*(5), 2675. DOI: 10.3390/su14052675

Hu, L., & Min, H. (2023). The dark side of artificial intelligence in service: The "watching-eye" effect and privacy concerns. *International Journal of Hospitality Management, 110*, 103437. Advance online publication. DOI: 10.1016/j.ijhm.2023.103437

Hussain, A., Zhiqiang, M., Li, M., Jameel, A., Kanl, S., Ahmad, S., & Ge, B. (2025). The mediating effects of perceived usefulness and perceived ease of use on nurses' intentions to adopt advanced technology. *BMC Nursing, 24*(1), 33. DOI: 10.1186/s12912-024-02648-8 PMID: 39789568

Hu, Y., & Min, H. K. (2025). Information transparency, privacy concerns, and customers' behavioral intentions regarding AI-powered hospitality robots: A situational awareness perspective. *Journal of Hospitality and Tourism Management, 63*, 177–184. DOI: 10.1016/j.jhtm.2025.04.003

Hwang, J., & Choi, L. (2020). Having fun while receiving rewards?: Exploration of gamification in loyalty programs for consumer loyalty. *Journal of Business Research, 106*, 365–376. DOI: 10.1016/j.jbusres.2019.01.031

Hyndman, R. J., & Athanasopoulos, G. (2018). *Forecasting: Principles and Practice* (2nd ed.). OTexts.

IBM. (2024). *IBM Global AI Adoption Index: Enterprise report*. IBM. https://filecache.mediaroom.com/mr5mr_ibmspgi/179414/download/IBM%20Global%20AI%20Adoption%20Index%20Report%20Dec.%202023.pdf

Idate, K., & Kanopee, M. (2011). *M-Tourism: A Practical Guide for SMEs*. DGCIS.

Ihde, D. (1990). *Technology and the lifeworld: From garden to earth*. Indiana University Press. DOI: 10.2979/3108.0

Imani, M., Joudaki, M., Beikmohammadi, A., & Arabnia, H. R. (2025). Customer churn prediction: A systematic review of recent advances, trends, and challenges in machine learning and deep learning. *Machine Learning and Knowledge Extraction*, *7*(3), 105. DOI: 10.3390/make7030105

Inavolu, S. M. (2024). Exploring AI-driven customer service: Evolution, architectures, opportunities, challenges and future directions. *International Journal of Engineering and Advanced Technology*, *13*(3), 156–163.

Iqbal, F., Afiat, A., Shoily, M. M., Turzo, S. S., & Arafat, M. (2025). AI-driven personalization in e-commerce: Evaluating the transformative effects on consumer behavior. *International Journal of Science and Research Archive*, *16*(1), 264–273. DOI: 10.30574/ijsra.2025.16.1.2035

Islam, M. F., Rahman, M. M., Sultana, S., Nabi, M. N., Rosid, M. H. O., & Alnour, M. (2024). Uncovering the impact on environmental challenges through the predictors of m-tourism apps adoption: SEM-NCA approaches. *Environmental Challenges*, *17*, 101028. DOI: 10.1016/j.envc.2024.101028

Ivanov, S. H., & Webster, C. (2017). Adoption of robots, artificial intelligence and service automation by travel, tourism and hospitality companies: A cost-benefit analysis. Paper presented *at the Contemporary Tourism – Traditions and Innovations Conference, Sofia, Bulgaria.*

Jain, S. (2025). Exploring the transformative impact of artificial intelligence on customer segmentation and precision targeted advertising strategies. *NOLEGEIN. Journal of Consumer Behavior & Market Research*, *8*(1).

Jamarani, A., Haddadi, S., Sarvizadeh, R., Haghi Kashani, M., Akbari, M., & Moradi, S. (2024). Big data and predictive analytics: A systematic review of applications. *Artificial Intelligence Review*, *57*(7), 176. DOI: 10.1007/s10462-024-10811-5

Jamil, K., Anwar, A., & Mustafa, S. (2025). Upgradation of customer relationship management through the AI-driven approach to personalization, engagement, and retention. In *Reshaping Organizational Management and Workplace Culture With AI* (pp. 263–286). IGI Global Scientific Publishing. DOI: 10.4018/979-8-3693-8960-7.ch010

Jang, J. Y., Hu, H. J., & Choo, H. J. (2019). How to evoke consumer approach intention toward VR stores? Sequential mediation through telepresence and experiential value. *Fashion and Textiles*, *6*(12), 1–16. DOI: 10.1186/s40691-018-0166-9

Jani, R., Alias, A. A., & Tumin, M. (2022). Persons with disabilities' education and quality of life: Evidence from Malaysia. *International Journal of Inclusive Education*, *26*(8), 753–765. DOI: 10.1080/13603116.2020.1726511

Jansson, A. (2007). A sense of tourism: New media and the dialectic of encapsulation/decapsulation. *Tourist Studies*, *7*(1), 5–24. DOI: 10.1177/1468797607079799

Javier, C., & Moorhouse, B. L. (2023). Generative AI and gendered/cultural bias in writing tools. [No DOI available]. *RELC Journal*.

Javornik, A., Marder, B., Barhorst, J. B., McLean, G., Rogers, Y., Marshall, P., & Warlop, L. (2022). "What lies behind the filter?" Uncovering the motivations for using augmented reality (AR) face filters on social media and their effect on well-being. *Computers in Human Behavior*, *128*, 107126. Advance online publication. DOI: 10.1016/j.chb.2021.107126

Jeaheng, Y., Al-Ansi, A., Chua, B.-L., Ngah, A. H., Ryu, H. B., Ariza-Montes, A., & Han, H. (2023). Influence of Thai Street Food Quality, Price, and Involvement on Traveler Behavioral Intention: Exploring Cultural Difference (Eastern versus stern). *Psychology Research and Behavior Management*, *16*, 223–240. DOI: 10.2147/PRBM.S371806 PMID: 36726699

Jennings, G. P., & Nickerson, N. P. (2006). *Quality tourism experiences*. Elsevier Butterworth-Heinemann. DOI: 10.4324/9780080455778

Jeong, M., & Shin, H. H. (2022). Tourists' experiences with smart tourism technologies. *Journal of Hospitality & Tourism Research (Washington, D.C.)*, *46*(1), 3–26. DOI: 10.1177/1096348020979070

Jiang, S., Zheng, W., & Kong, H. (2025). Trust or skepticism? Unraveling the communication mechanisms of AIGC advertisements on consumer responses. *Journal of Theoretical and Applied Electronic Commerce Research*, *20*(4), 339. DOI: 10.3390/jtaer20040339

Jin, D. (2023). *Where have the ethical and moral standards landed? Consumer self-congruency and psychological distance in the context of AI-based services.* International Hospitality Review., DOI: 10.1108/IHR-06-2023-0033

Jonassen, D. H. (1991). Objectivism vs constructivism. *Educational Technology Research and Development, 39*(3), 5–14. DOI: 10.1007/BF02296434

Kaartemo, V., & Helkkula, A. (2018). A systematic review of artificial intelligence and robots in value co-creation: Current status and future research avenues. *Journal of Creating Value, 4*(2), 211–228. DOI: 10.1177/2394964318805625

Kabashkin, B., Misnevs, O., & Zervina, T. (2023). Artificial Intelligence in Aviation: New professionals for new technologies. *Applied Sciences (Basel, Switzerland), 13*(21), 11660. DOI: 10.3390/app132111660

Kaiser, H. F. (1974). An index of factorial simplicity. *Psychometrika, 39*(1), 31–36. DOI: 10.1007/BF02291575

Kamatala, S., & Naayini, P. (2025). The rise of AI chatbots: Balancing customer satisfaction and operational efficiency. *International Journal of Current Science Research and Review, 8*(3), 1144–1151. DOI: 10.47191/ijcsrr/V8-i3-17

Kamkankaew, P., Thanitbenjasith, P., Sribenjachot, S., Sanpatanon, N., Phattarowas, V., & Thanin, P. (2024). How Artificial Intelligence is Helping Businesses Grow and Thrive: The Transformative Role of Artificial Intelligence in Thai B2C Digital Marketing. *International Journal of Sociologies and Anthropologies Science Reviews, 4*(1), 137–164. DOI: 10.60027/ijsasr.2024.3651

Kang, S., Potinteu, A.-E., & Said, N. (2025). ExplainitAI: When do we trust artificial intelligence? The influence of content and explainability in a cross-cultural comparison. In *Extended Abstracts of the 2025 CHI Conference on Human Factors in Computing Systems* (pp. 1–7). Association for Computing Machinery. DOI: 10.1145/3706599.3720222

Kang, J., Hong, S., & Hubbard, G. T. (2020). The role of storytelling in advertising: Consumer emotion, narrative engagement level, and word-of-mouth intention. *Journal of Consumer Behaviour, 19*(1), 47–56. DOI: 10.1002/cb.1793

Kapoor, A., & Sindwani, R. (2025b). Navigating Inhibitors to Artificial Intelligence Adoption in Human Resource Management Practices: A Multi-criteria Decision-making Approach.

Kapoor, A., & Sindwani, R. (2026). AI in Healthcare: Analyzing Adoption Drivers Using Fuzzy AHP. *Innovation in Healthcare Technology and Management*, 139-154.

Kapoor, A., Kapoor, S., & Sindwani, R. (2026b). Governing Artificial Intelligent Ethically: A Human-in-Context Approach to Bias, Fairness, and Accountability. In *The Ethical Landscape of AI: Global Issues and Solutions* (pp. 73-110). IGI Global Scientific Publishing.

Kapoor, S., Kapoor, A., & Sindwani, R. (2026a). How Do Leading Brands Win Hearts and Markets? A Case Study Perspective on Customer Centric Strategies. In *Developing an Architecture of Future-Ready Business Excellence* (pp. 179-214). IGI Global Scientific Publishing.

Kapoor, A., Jaswal, A., & Sindwani, R. (2026d). Charting the roadmap to metaverse commerce adoption: A cause–effect perspective using fuzzy DEMATEL. *Journal of Modelling in Management*, •••, 1–29. DOI: 10.1108/JM2-07-2025-0352

Kapoor, A., & Sindwani, R. (2025a). Artificial Intelligence as a Catalyst for Advancing Contactless Payments: Unveiling Key Adoption Drivers. In *AI Marketing and Ethical Considerations in Consumer Engagement* (pp. 321–338). IGI Global Scientific Publishing. DOI: 10.4018/979-8-3373-3476-9.ch016

Kapoor, A., Sindwani, R., & Goel, M. (2025a). Unlocking India's mobile wallet potential: Identifying and prioritising key sustainable growth catalysts using best worst method. *International Journal of Process Management and Benchmarking*, *21*(2), 218–230. DOI: 10.1504/IJPMB.2025.148685

Kapoor, A., Sindwani, R., & Goel, M. (2025b). Assessing mobile wallet service quality using analytic hierarchy process and fuzzy evaluation method. *International Journal of Services and Operations Management*, *50*(2), 246–266. DOI: 10.1504/IJSOM.2025.144481

Kapoor, A., Sindwani, R., Singh, A. K., & Kapoor, S. (2026c). Causal Modeling and Hierarchical Analysis of Critical Factors in Smart Voice Assistant Adoption: A Fuzzy DEMATEL Approach. *Journal of Global Marketing*, •••, 1–21. DOI: 10.1080/08911762.2026.2651270

Karabacak, Z. İ., & Güngör, İ. (2023). The metaverse as an influencer marketing platform: Influencer-brand collaborations of Paris Hilton with 'Superplastic', 'Bohoo', and 'Levi's'. *Etkileşim*, *11*(11), 176–199. DOI: 10.32739/etkilesim.2023.6.11.194

Karnam, V. S. P. (2025). AI Transformation in the Airline Industry: Technical Perspectives. *World Journal of Advanced Research and Reviews*, *26*(02), 1828–1834. DOI: 10.30574/wjarr.2025.26.2.1798

Kasilingam, D. L. (2020). Understanding the attitude and intention to use smartphone chatbots for shopping. *Technology in Society*, *62*, 101280. DOI: 10.1016/j.techsoc.2020.101280

Kasneci, E., Sessler, K., Küchemann, S., Bannert, M., Dementieva, D., Fischer, F., Gasser, U., Groh, G., Günnemann, S., Hüllermeier, E., Krusche, S., Kutyniok, G., Michaeli, T., Nerdel, C., Pfeffer, J., Poquet, O., Sailer, M., Schmidt, A., Seidel, T., & Kasneci, G. (2023). ChatGPT for good? *Learning and Individual Differences*, *103*, 102274. DOI: 10.1016/j.lindif.2023.102274

Kaur, B., & Kour, M. (2025). Revolutionary Impact of Artificial Intelligence on Society and Its Challenges and Opportunities. AI Use in Social Sciences, 383-404.

Kaur, J., Mogaji, E., Paliwal, M., Jha, S., Agarwal, S., & Mogaji, S. A. (2023). Consumer behavior in the metaverse. *Journal of Consumer Behaviour*, *23*(4), 1720–1738. DOI: 10.1002/cb.2298

Khalil, K. (2023). Airline flight delays using artificial intelligence in COVID-19 with perspective analytics. *Journal of Intelligent & Fuzzy Systems*, •••, 1–23. Advance online publication.

Kim, D. Y., Lee, H. K., & Kyunghwa, C. (2023). Avatar-mediated experience in the metaverse: The impact of avatar realism on user-avatar relationship. *Journal of Retailing and Consumer Services, 73*, 103382. 1-11.

Kim, D. J., & Peterson, R. T. (2017). A meta-analysis of online trust relationships. *Journal of Interactive Marketing*, *38*(1), 44–54. DOI: 10.1016/j.intmar.2017.01.001

Kim, H., & Han, S. (2025). Triggering the personalization backfire effect: The moderating role of situational privacy concern. *Behavioral Sciences (Basel, Switzerland)*, *15*(10), 1323. Advance online publication. DOI: 10.3390/bs15101323 PMID: 41153114

Kim, J., & Lennon, S. J. (2013). Effects of reputation and website quality on online consumers' emotion, perceived risk, and purchase intention. *Journal of Research in Interactive Marketing*, *7*(1), 33–56. DOI: 10.1108/17505931311316734

Kim, Y. W., Kim, B. H., Kim, M. J., & Jeong, Y. J. (2025). Immersive social experiences in a space-based Metaverse SNS: user experience with platform-specific interactions on PC and VR. *International Conference on Consumer Electronics-Asia (ICCE-Asia)*, 1-3. DOI: 10.1109/ICCE-Asia67487.2025.11263524

Koc, E. (2020). *Cross-Cultural Aspects of Tourism and Hospitality: A Services Marketing and Management Perspective* (1st ed.). Routledge., DOI: 10.4324/9781003018193

Kochmar, E.. (2020). Automated scoring and feedback in ITS. *Computers & Education, 168*, 104198. DOI: 10.1016/j.compedu.2021.104198

Kohnke, L., Moorhouse, B. L., & Zou, D. (2023). Bias and stereotype reproduction in AI writing tools. [No DOI available]. *RELC Journal.*

Kokkinou, A., Tremiliti, E., Iwaarden, M. V., Mitas, O., & Straatman, S. (2022). Are you traveling alone or with your device? The impact of connected mobile device usage on the travel experience. *Journal of Hospitality and Tourism Insights, 5*(1), 45–61. DOI: 10.1108/JHTI-04-2020-0058

Kolodiziev, O., Dorokhov, O., Shcherbak, V., Dorokhova, L., Ismailov, A., & Figueiredo, R. (2024). Resilience Benchmarking: How Small Hotels Can Ensure Their Survival and Growth during Global Disruptions. *Journal of Risk and Financial Management, 17*(7), 281. DOI: 10.3390/jrfm17070281

Komiak, S. X., & Benbasat, I. (2006). The effects of personalization and familiarity on trust and adoption of recommendation agents. *Management Information Systems Quarterly, 30*(4), 941–960. DOI: 10.2307/25148760

Konidena, B. K., Malaiyappan, J. N. A., & Tadimarri, A. (2024). Ethical Considerations in the Development and Deployment of AI Systems. *European Journal of Technology, 8*(2), 41–53. DOI: 10.47672/ejt.1890

Koo, C., Kwon, J., Chung, N., & Kim, J. (2023). Metaverse tourism: Conceptual framework and research propositions. *Current Issues in Tourism, 26*(20), 3268–3274. DOI: 10.1080/13683500.2022.2122781

Korobenko, D., Nikiforova, A., & Sharma, R. (2024). *Towards a Privacy and Security-Aware Framework for Ethical AI: Guiding the Development and Assessment of AI Systems. arXiv*. Cornell University., DOI: 10.1145/3657054.3657141

Korteling, J. E., van de Boer-Visschedijk, G. C., Blankendaal, R. A. M., Boonekamp, R. C., & Eikelboom, A. R. (2021). Human versus Artificial Intelligence. *Frontiers in Artificial Intelligence, 4*, 622364. DOI: 10.3389/frai.2021.622364 PMID: 33981990

Kotler, P., Kartajaya, H., & Setiawan, I. (2022). *Marketing 5.0: Technology for Humanity*. Wiley.

Kotler, P., & Keller, K. L. (2015). *Framework for Marketing Management, A*. BoD–Books on Demand.

Kour, M., & Kaur, R. (2024). “AI and Influencer Marketing: Redefining the Future of Social Media Marketing in Industry 6.0”. In Advanced Businesses in Industry 6.0 (pp. 87-103). IGI Global. DOI: 10.4018/979-8-3693-3108-8.ch007

Kour, M. (2024). *"Ethical Considerations in the Metaverse and Augmented Retail Reality Era", Consumer Experience and Decision-Making in the Metaverse*. IGI Global.

Kshetri, N. (2014). Big data's impact on privacy, security and consumer welfare. *Telecommunications Policy, 38*(11), 1134–1145. DOI: 10.1016/j.telpol.2014.10.002

Kumar, J. R. R., Kalnawat, A., Pawar, A. M., Jadhav, V. D., Srilatha, P., & Khetani, V. (2024). Transparency in Algorithmic Decision-making: Interpretable Models for Ethical Accountability. *E3S Web of Conferences, 491*, 2041. DOI: 10.1051/e3sconf/202449102041

Kumar, M. (2025). AI in healthcare: Enhancing patient engagement through virtual assistants. *International Journal of Engineering Research & Technology (IJERT), 14*(3), Article IJERTV14IS030045.

Kumar, A., Singh, T., Kumar, D., & Sharma, N. (2025). Mobilizing Social Media Marketing by Email Marketing and Paid Advertising (PPC) in Online Marketing 6.0. In Wongmahesak, K., Karim, F. B., & Wongchestha, N. (Eds.), *Practical Strategies and Case Studies for Online Marketing 6.0* (pp. 165–184). IGI Global Scientific Publishing., DOI: 10.4018/979-8-3373-2058-8.ch009

Kumar, D., & Suthar, N. (2024). Ethical and legal challenges of AI in marketing: An exploration of solutions. *Journal of Information Communication and Ethics in Society, 22*(1), 124–144. DOI: 10.1108/JICES-05-2023-0068

Kumar, R., Aneja, P., Jadaun, R., Kiran, P. N., Saxena, N., Saxena, S., & Painoli, A. K. (2026). Metaverse marketing: A review and future research agenda. *Information Discovery and Delivery, 54*(1), 35–49. DOI: 10.1108/IDD-05-2024-0066

Kumar, R., & Raman, A. (2022). Multimodal AI in assessment. *International Journal of Educational Technology in Higher Education*. Advance online publication. DOI: 10.1186/s41239-025-00540-2

Kumar, V., Dixit, A., Sharma, P., & Roy, S. N. (2025). Implementing Responsible Artificial Intelligence in Marketing. *American Business Review, 28*(2), 319–342. DOI: 10.37625/abr.28.2.319-342

Kumar, V., Kotler, P., & Kumar, A. (2026). Transformative marketing strategies in the era of new-age technologies: Principles, plan, purpose, and practice. *Journal of the Academy of Marketing Science, 54*(1), 1–27. DOI: 10.1007/s11747-025-01120-6

Kumar, V., Rajan, B., Venkatesan, R., & Lecinski, J. (2021). Understanding the role of artificial intelligence in personalized engagement marketing. *Journal of Marketing, 85*(4), 135–155.

Kumar, V., & Reinartz, W. (2016). Creating enduring customer value. *Journal of Marketing, 80*(6), 36–68. DOI: 10.1509/jm.15.0414

Kurgun, H., Kurgun, O., & Aktas, E. (2018). What does Web 4.0 Promise for Tourism Ecosystem? A Qualitative Research on Tourism Ecosystem Stakeholders' Awareness. *Journal of Tourism and Hospitality Management., 6*(1). Advance online publication. DOI: 10.15640/jthm.v6n1a6

Kvale, S., & Brinkmann, S. (2015). *InterViews: Learning the craft of qualitative research interviewing*. Sage.

Lai, A. B. (1995). Consumer Values, Product Benefits And Customer Value: A Consumption Behavior Approach. *Advances in Consumer Research. Association for Consumer Research (U. S.)*, (22), 381–388.

Langer, M., Oster, D., Speith, T., Hermanns, H., Kästner, L., Schmidt, E., Sesing, A., & Baum, K. (2021). What do we want from explainable artificial intelligence (XAI)? A stakeholder perspective on XAI and a conceptual model guiding inter-disciplinary XAI research. *Artificial Intelligence, 296*, 103473. DOI: 10.1016/j.artint.2021.103473

Lankton, N. K., McKnight, D. H., & Thatcher, J. B. (2014). Incorporating trust into technology acceptance theory. *Management Information Systems Quarterly, 38*(1), 153–180.

Larsen, J., Urry, J., & Axhausen, K. W. (2007). Networks and tourism: Mobile social life. *Annals of Tourism Research, 34*(1), 244–262. DOI: 10.1016/j.annals.2006.08.002

Latour, B. (2005). *Reassembling the social: An introduction to Actor-Network-Theory*. Oxford University Press. DOI: 10.1093/oso/9780199256044.001.0001

Laufer, R. S., & Wolfe, M. (1977). Privacy as a concept and a social issue: A multidimensional developmental theory. *The Journal of Social Issues, 33*(3), 22–42. DOI: 10.1111/j.1540-4560.1977.tb01880.x

Le Clainche, S., Ferrer, E., Gibson, S., Cross, E., Parente, A., & Vinuesa, R. (2023). Improving aircraft performance using machine learning: A review. *Aerospace Science and Technology, 138*, 108354. DOI: 10.1016/j.ast.2023.108354

LeCun, Y., Bengio, Y., & Hinton, G. (2015). Deep learning. *Nature, 521*(7553), 436–444. DOI: 10.1038/nature14539 PMID: 26017442

Lee, M. C., & Breckon, D. (2025). Factors affecting customer engagement in AI marketing. *Telematics and Informatics Reports, 100230.*

Lemoine, J., & Salvadore, M. (2018). The impact of smartphone use on the tourist experience: The case of discovering a destination. *Management & Avenir, 99*(1), 165–189. DOI: 10.3917/mav.099.0165

Lemon, K. N., & Verhoef, P. C. (2016). Understanding customer experience throughout the customer journey. *Journal of Marketing, 80*(6), 69–96. DOI: 10.1509/jm.15.0420

Li, N. (2023). Ethical Considerations in Artificial Intelligence: A Comprehensive Disccusion from the Perspective of Computer Vision. *SHS Web of Conferences, 179*, 4024. DOI: 10.1051/shsconf/202317904024

Li, C., Liang, L., Fryer, L. K., & Shum, A. (2024). The use of leaderboards in education: A systematic review of empirical evidence in higher education. *Journal of Computer Assisted Learning, 40*(6), 3406–3442. DOI: 10.1111/jcal.13077

Li, F., Zhu, D., Lin, M.-T., & Kim, P. B. (2024). The Technology Acceptance Model and hospitality and tourism consumers' intention to use mobile technologies: Meta-analysis and structural equation modeling. *Cornell Hospitality Quarterly, 65*(4), 461–477. Advance online publication. DOI: 10.1177/19389655241226558

Li, H., Wu, Y., & Chen, Y. (2022). Hyper-personalization in digital commerce: A data-driven perspective. *Electronic Commerce Research and Applications, 52*, 101120.

Li, J., Bonn, M. A., & Ye, B. H. (2022). Hotel technology and service personalization. *International Journal of Hospitality Management, 100*, 103090. DOI: 10.1016/j.ijhm.2021.103090

Linden, G., Smith, B., & York, J. (2003). Amazon. com recommendations: Item-to-item collaborative filtering. *IEEE Internet Computing, 7*(1), 76–80. DOI: 10.1109/MIC.2003.1167344

Liu, L. (2022). E-commerce personalized recommendation based on machine learning technology. *Mobile Information Systems, 2022*(1), 1–11. DOI: 10.1155/2022/1761579

Li, X., Zhang, S., Li, X., Zeng, J., Long, Y., Nie, B., & Zhao, C. (2025). SHAP-driven insights into multimodal data: Behavior phase prediction for industrial safety applications. *Scientific Reports, 15*(1), 34965. DOI: 10.1038/s41598-025-18889-9 PMID: 41057512

Li, Y. (2000). Geographical consciousness and tourism experience. *Annals of Tourism Research, 27*(4), 863–883. DOI: 10.1016/S0160-7383(99)00112-7

Li, Y. (2025). Applications and Challenges of Artificial Intelligence in Smart Operations for Commercial Aviation. *Journal of the Korean Society for Aviation and Aeronautics, 33*(2), 147–150. DOI: 10.12985/ksaa.2025.33.2.147

Longoni, C., Bonezzi, A., & Morewedge, C. K. (2019). Resistance to medical artificial intelligence. *The Journal of Consumer Research, 46*(4), 629–650. DOI: 10.1093/jcr/ucz013

Lu, L., Cai, R., & Gursoy, D. (2023). Developing and validating a service robot integration willingness scale. *International Journal of Contemporary Hospitality Management, 35*(2), 789–810. DOI: 10.1108/IJCHM-04-2022-0489

Lumivalo, J., Tuunanen, T., & Salo, M. (2024). Value co-destruction: A systematic literature review and future research agenda. *Journal of Service Research, 27*(2), 159–176. DOI: 10.1177/10946705231177504

Luo, X., Tong, S., Fang, Z., & Qu, Z. (2019). Frontiers: Machines vs. humans: The impact of AI chatbot disclosure. *Marketing Science, 38*(6), 937–947.

Lusch, R. F., & Vargo, S. L. (2011). Service-dominant logic: A necessary step. *European Journal of Marketing, 45*(7-8), 1298–1309. DOI: 10.1108/03090561111137723

Madanchian, M. (2024). Generative AI for consumer behavior prediction: Techniques and applications. *Sustainability (Basel), 16*(22), 9963. DOI: 10.3390/su16229963

Magala, S., Erten-Buch, C., Bell, R.-M., & Claes, M.-T. (Eds.). (2024). *Hofstede matters*. Routledge Taylor & Francis Group., DOI: 10.4324/9781003410348

Manchiraju, S. (2025). The ethical thread: AI's role in the tapestry of fashion. *AI & Society, 40*(5), 4029–4034. DOI: 10.1007/s00146-024-02151-3

Mangipudi, P. (2025). *AI powered chatbots vs. human agents: A comparative study on customer satisfaction.*

Mare, S., Roesner, F., & Kohno, T. (2020). Smart Devices in Airbnbs: Considering Privacy and Security for both Guests and Hosts. *Proceedings on Privacy Enhancing Technologies. Privacy Enhancing Technologies Symposium, 2020*(2), 436–458. DOI: 10.2478/popets-2020-0035

Mariani, M. M., & Perez-Vega, R. (2023). Artificial intelligence in marketing and hospitality: A systematic review. *Journal of Hospitality Marketing & Management, 32*(4), 387–412. DOI: 10.1080/19368623.2022.2076300

Mariani, M. M., Styvén, M. E., & Teulon, F. (2024). Artificial intelligence and ethical issues in tourism. *Tourism Management, 98*, 104745. DOI: 10.1016/j.tourman.2023.104745

Marriott International. (2018, November 30). *Marriott International announces Starwood guest reservation database security incident.* https://news.marriott.com/news/2018/11/30/marriott-international-announces-starwood-guest-reservation-database-security-incident

Martin, K. (2019). Ethical Implications and Accountability of Algorithms: K. Martin. *Journal of Business Ethics, 160*(4), 835–850. DOI: 10.1007/s10551-018-3921-3

Martin, K. D., & Murphy, P. E. (2017). The role of data privacy in marketing. *Journal of the Academy of Marketing Science, 45*(2), 135–155. DOI: 10.1007/s11747-016-0495-4

Martin, K., Shilton, K., & Smith, J. (2022). Business and the ethical implications of AI. *Journal of Business Ethics, 176*(4), 809–828. DOI: 10.1007/s10551-020-04663-6

Matteucci, X. (2015). Experiencing flamenco: an examination of a spiritual journey. In Filep, S., & Pearce, P. (Eds.), *Tourist experience and fulfillment: Insights from positive psychology*. Routledge.

Mayer, R. C., Davis, J. H., & Schoorman, F. D. (1995). An integrative model of organizational trust. *Academy of Management Review, 20*(3), 709–734. DOI: 10.2307/258792

McCarthy, J. (2007). *What is artificial intelligence?* Stanford University.

McKinsey & Company. (2025). *The state of AI in 2025: Agents, innovation, and transformation*. McKinsey & Company. https://www.mckinsey.com/capabilities/quantumblack/our-insights/the-state-of-ai

McKnight, D. H., Carter, M., Thatcher, J. B., & Clay, P. F. (2011). Trust in a specific technology. *ACM Transactions on Management Information Systems, 2*(2), 1–25. DOI: 10.1145/1985347.1985353

McKnight, D. H., Choudhury, V., & Kacmar, C. (2002). Developing and validating trust measures for e-commerce: An integrative typology. *Information Systems Research, 13*(3), 334–359. DOI: 10.1287/isre.13.3.334.81

McLean, G., & Osei-Frimpong, K. (2020). Chatbots and consumer satisfaction: The role of anthropomorphism. *Journal of Business Research, 119*, 351–356.

McLean, G., Osei-Frimpong, K., & Wilson, A. (2021). Engaging customers with AI-enabled chatbots. *Journal of Business Research, 122*, 395–405. DOI: 10.1016/j.jbusres.2020.09.045

Mehmood, K., Kour, M., & Kautish, P. (2025). The impact spectrum: How influencer traits shape consumer purchase intentions through credibility and materialism. *Current Psychology*, *44*(12), 12380–12398. DOI: 10.1007/s12144-025-07942-5

Mehrabian, A., & Russell, J. A. (1974). *An approach to environmental psychology*. the MIT Press.

Mehrabian, A., & Russell, J. A. (1974). *An approach to environmental psychology*. MIT Press.

Mehrabi, N., Morstatter, F., Saxena, N., Lerman, K., & Galstyan, A. (2021). A survey on bias and fairness in machine learning. *ACM Computing Surveys*, *54*(6), 1–35. DOI: 10.1145/3457607

Meisenbacher, S., Klymenko, A., Kelley, P. G., Peddinti, S. T., Thomas, K., & Matthes, F. (2024). *Privacy Risks of General-Purpose AI Systems: A Foundation for Investigating Practitioner Perspectives*. DOI: 10.48550/ARXIV.2407.02027

Merino-Campos, C. (2025). AI-driven personalization in higher education. *Journal of Educational Technology and Innovation*. DOI: 10.61414/jeti.v6i4.209

Mersha, M., Lam, K., Wood, J., AlShami, A. K., & Kalita, J. (2024). Explainable artificial intelligence: A survey of needs, techniques, applications, and future direction. *Neurocomputing*, *599*, 128111. Advance online publication. DOI: 10.1016/j.neucom.2024.128111

Miao, F., Kozlenkova, I., Wang, H., Xie, T., & Palmatier, R. (2022). An emerging theory of avatar marketing. *Journal of Marketing*, *86*(1), 67–90. DOI: 10.1177/0022242921996646

Mikl, J., Herold, D. M., Cwiklicki, M., & Kummer, S. (2021). The impact of digital logistics start-ups on incumbent firms: A business model perspective. *International Journal of Logistics Management*, *32*(4), 1461–1480. DOI: 10.1108/IJLM-04-2020-0155

Min, A. (2023). Artificial Intelligence and Bias: Challenges, Implications, and Remedies. *Journal of Social Research*, *2*(11), 3808–3817. DOI: 10.55324/josr.v2i11.1477

Mishra, A. K., Tyagi, A. K., & Arowolo, M. O. (2024). Future trends and opportunities in machine learning and artificial intelligence for banking and finance. In *Applications of Blockchain Technology and Artificial Intelligence: Lead-ins in Banking, Finance, and Capital Market* (pp. 211–238). Springer. DOI: 10.1007/978-3-031-47324-1_13

Mitchell, M. (2026). *The Influence of Generational Cohort and Gender on Consumer Perceptions of AI-Driven Personalization in E-Commerce Marketing* (Doctoral dissertation, University of Maryland University College).

Mittelstadt, B. D., Allo, P., Taddeo, M., Wachter, S., & Floridi, L. (2016). The ethics of algorithms: Mapping the debate. *Big Data & Society, 3*(2), 2053951716679679. DOI: 10.1177/2053951716679679

Mohan, L., Devarajan, M., Alotoum, F. J., Alsaaideh, M., & Prasad, K. (2025). Advanced data analytics for predicting consumer behavior using machine learning and association rule mining. In *2025 International Conference on Technology Enabled Economic Changes (InTech)* (pp. 908–914). IEEE. DOI: 10.1109/InTech64186.2025.11198315

Morgan, R. M., & Hunt, S. D. (1994). The commitment-trust theory of relationship marketing. *Journal of Marketing, 58*(3), 20–38. DOI: 10.1177/002224299405800302

Morhart, F., Malär, L., Guèvremont, A., Girardin, F., & Grohmann, B. (2015). Brand authenticity: An integrative framework and measurement scale. *Journal of Consumer Psychology, 25*(2), 200–218. DOI: 10.1016/j.jcps.2014.11.006

Morić, Z., Dakic, V., Djekic, D., & Regvart, D. (2024). Protection of Personal Data in the Context of E-Commerce. *Journal of Cybersecurity and Privacy, 4*(3), 731–761. DOI: 10.3390/jcp4030034

Mourali, M., Novakowski, D., Pogacar, R., & Brigden, N. (2025). Post hoc explanations improve consumer responses to algorithmic decisions. *Journal of Business Research, 186*, 114981. Advance online publication. DOI: 10.1016/j.jbusres.2024.114981

Movono, A., & Hughes, E. (2022). Tourism partnerships: Localizing the SDG agenda in Fiji. *Journal of Sustainable Tourism, 30*(10), 2318–2332. DOI: 10.1080/09669582.2020.1811291

Muhajir, A. (2024). Predictive analytics in marketing: Contribution to marketing performance. [PRODUCTIVITY]. *Management Studies and Business Journal, 1*(3), 447–460.

Naeimi, M., & Family, Q. (2025). Generation Z and AI-Driven Marketing: Behavioral Traits, Personalization, and Generational Comparison. *Personalization, and Generational Comparison (September 18, 2025).*

Napoli, J., Dickinson, S. J., Beverland, M. B., & Farrelly, F. (2014). Measuring consumer-based brand authenticity. *Journal of Business Research, 67*(6), 1090–1098. DOI: 10.1016/j.jbusres.2013.06.001

Naz, H., & Kashif, M. (2024). Artificial intelligence and predictive marketing: An ethical framework from managers' perspective. *Spanish Journal of Marketing - ESIC*. Advance online publication. DOI: 10.1108/SJME-06-2023-0154

Neeraj, K. (2024). Predictive analytics for customer retention: A data-driven framework for proactive engagement and satisfaction management. *International Journal (Toronto, Ont.)*, *10*(6), 1109–1116.

Neslin, S. A., Gupta, S., Kamakura, W., Lu, J., & Mason, C. H. (2006). Defection detection: Measuring and understanding the predictive accuracy of customer churn models. *JMR, Journal of Marketing Research*, *43*(2), 204–211. DOI: 10.1509/jmkr.43.2.204

Ng, D. T. K., Leung, J. K. L., Chu, S. K. W., & Qiao, M. S. (2021). AI literacy: Definition, teaching, evaluation. *Computers and Education: Artificial Intelligence*, *2*, 100041. DOI: 10.1016/j.caeai.2021.100041

Nguyen, M., Ferm, L.-E. C., Quach, S., Pontes, N., & Thaichon, P. (2023). Chatbots in frontline services and customer experience: An anthropomorphism perspective. *Psychology and Marketing*, *40*(11), 2201–2225. DOI: 10.1002/mar.21882

Nguyen, T. M., Quach, S., & Thaichon, P. (2022). The effect of AI quality on customer experience and brand relationship. *Journal of Consumer Behaviour*, *21*(3), 481–493. DOI: 10.1002/cb.1974

Nguyên, T. T., Huynh, T. T., Ren, Z., Nguyen, T. T., Nguyen, P. L., Yin, H., & Nguyen, Q. V. H. (2024). Privacy-preserving explainable AI: A survey. *Science China. Information Sciences*, *68*(1), 111101. Advance online publication. DOI: 10.1007/s11432-024-4123-4

Nian, S.A.H.M, (2025). Digital Transformation and AI in Airline Management: Aligning Agility, Innovation, and Data- Driven Strategies. Conference: 3rd International Conference on Recent Advances in Engineering, Innovation and Technology At: Brussel, Belgium

Nicol, D. J., & Macfarlane-Dick, D. (2006). Formative assessment and self-regulated learning. *Studies in Higher Education*, *31*(2), 199–218. DOI: 10.1080/03075070600572090

Nie, X., & Ahmad, F. S. (2025). Dynamic reward systems and customer loyalty: Reinforcement learning-optimized personalized service strategies. *Future Technology*, *4*(3), 259–268. DOI: 10.55670/fpll.futech.4.3.24

Nilson, L. B., & Stanny, C. J. (2023). *Specifications Grading: Restoring Rigor, Motivating Students, and Saving Faculty Time* (1st ed.). Routledge., DOI: 10.4324/9781003447061

Ning, X., Lu, Y., Li, W., & Gupta, S. (2024). How transparency affects algorithmic advice utilization: The mediating roles of trusting beliefs. *Decision Support Systems, 183*, 114273. Advance online publication. DOI: 10.1016/j.dss.2024.114273

Nunnally, J. C., & Bernstein, I. H. (1994). The Assessment of Reliability. *Psychometric Theory, 3*, 248–292.

O'Higgins, B., & Fatorachian, H. (2025). Consumer trust in artificial intelligence in the UK and Ireland's personal care and cosmetics sector. *Cogent Business & Management, 12*(1), 2469765. Advance online publication. DOI: 10.1080/23311975.2025.2469765

Odejide, O. A., & Edunjobi, T. E. (2024). AI IN PROJECT MANAGEMENT: EXPLORING THEORETICAL MODELS FOR DECISION-MAKING AND RISK MANAGEMENT. *Engineering Science & Technology Journal, 5*(3), 1072–1085. DOI: 10.51594/estj.v5i3.959

OECD. (2023). *Consumer vulnerability in the digital age*. OECD Publishing., DOI: 10.1787/4d013cc5-

Okeke, N. I., Alabi, O. A., Igwe, A. N., Ofodile, O. C., & Ewim, C. P.-M. (2024). AI-Powered customer experience optimization: Enhancing financial inclusion in underserved communities. *International Journal of Applied Research in Social Sciences, 6*(10), 2487–2511. DOI: 10.51594/ijarss.v6i10.1662

Okonkwo, I., Mujinga, J., Namkoisse, E., & Francisco, A. (2023). Localization and Global Marketing: Adapting Digital Strategies for Diverse Audiences. *Journal of Digital Marketing and Communication, 3*(2), 66–80. DOI: 10.53623/jdmc.v3i2.311

Olayinka, O. H.Olalekan Hamed Olayinka. (2021). Big data integration and real-time analytics for enhancing operational efficiency and market responsiveness. *Int J Sci Res Arch, 4*(1), 280–296. DOI: 10.30574/ijsra.2021.4.1.0179

Oliver, R. L. (1980). A cognitive model of the antecedents and consequences of satisfaction decisions. *JMR, Journal of Marketing Research, 17*(4), 460–469. DOI: 10.1177/002224378001700405

Oliver, R. L. (1999). Whence consumer loyalty? *Journal of Marketing, 63*(Special Issue), 33–44. DOI: 10.1177/00222429990634s105

Olorunfemi, O. L., Amoo, O. O., Atadoga, A., Fayayola, O. A., Abrahams, T. O., & Shoetan, P. O. (2024). TOWARDS A CONCEPTUAL FRAMEWORK FOR ETHICAL AI DEVELOPMENT IN IT SYSTEMS. *Computer Science & IT Research Journal*, *5*(3), 616–627. DOI: 10.51594/csitrj.v5i3.910

Olujimi, P. A., & Ade-Ibijola, A. (2023). NLP techniques for automating responses to customer queries: A systematic review. *Discover Artificial Intelligence*, *3*(1), 20. DOI: 10.1007/s44163-023-00065-5

Oncioiu, I., Anton, E., Ifrim, A. M., & Mândricel, D. A. (2022). The Influence of Social Networks on the Digital Recruitment of Human Resources: An Empirical Study in the Tourism Sector. *Sustainability (Basel)*, *14*(6), 3693. DOI: 10.3390/su14063693

Onesi-Ozigagun, O., et al. (2024). Bias in automated grading systems. *International Journal of Educational Assessment*. (No DOI available)

Oruganti, S. K., Karras, D. A., Thakur, S., Chaithanya, J. K., Metta, S., & Lathigara, A. (Eds.). (2025). *Digital Transformation and Sustainability of Business* (1st ed.). CRC Press., DOI: 10.1201/9781003606185

Osman, M., Osman, H., Almansour, O., Mohammed, F., Agag, G., & Alipour, H. (2026). When AI advice backfires: Field experimental evidence on personalization, intrusiveness, and purchase behavior. *Journal of Retailing and Consumer Services*, *92*, 104844. Advance online publication. DOI: 10.1016/j.jretconser.2026.104844

Ostinelli, M., Bonezzi, A., & Lisjak, M. (2024). Unintended effects of algorithmic transparency: The mere prospect of an explanation can foster the illusion of understanding how an algorithm works. *Journal of Consumer Psychology*, *35*(2), 203–219. DOI: 10.1002/jcpy.1416

Ouyang, F., Zheng, L., & Jiao, P. (2023). Artificial intelligence in online higher education. *Computers & Education: Artificial Intelligence*, *4*, 100088. DOI: 10.1016/j.caeai.2023.100088

Oysterlink. (2025). *Online Travel Booking Statistics in 2025.*

Padmaja, C. V. R., & Lakshminarayana, S. (2024). The rise of AI: A comprehensive research review. *IAES International Journal of Artificial Intelligence*, *13*(2), 2226. DOI: 10.11591/ijai.v13.i2.pp2226-2235

Palmiotto, F. (2024). When is a decision automated? A taxonomy for a fundamental rights analysis. *German Law Journal*, *25*(2), 210–236. DOI: 10.1017/glj.2023.112

Pang, B., & Lee, L. (2008). Opinion mining and sentiment analysis. *Foundations and Trends in Information Retrieval*, *2*(1-2), 1–135. DOI: 10.1561/1500000011

Pang, L.. (2024). Human judgement and contextual sensitivity in grading. Cited in *A systematic review on the future of educational assessment* [No DOI available]. *AI in Education*, *2*(2), 75.

Papagiannidis, S., Pantano, E., See-To, E. W., & Bourlakis, M. (2013). Modelling the determinants of a simulated experience in a virtual retail store and users' product purchasing intentions. *Journal of Marketing Management*, *29*(13-14), 1462–1492. DOI: 10.1080/0267257X.2013.821150

Pariser, E. (2011). *The filter bubble: What the Internet is hiding from you.* penguin UK. Castells, P., Hurley, N. J., Vargas, S., Ricci, F., Rokach, L., & Shapira, B. (2015). Recommender systems handbook. *by Francesco Ricci, Lior Rokach, and Bracha Shapira. Boston, MA, USA: Springer US*, 881-918.

Park, K., & Yoon, H. Y. (2024). Beyond the code: The impact of AI algorithm transparency signaling on user trust and relational satisfaction. *Public Relations Review*, *50*(5), 102507. Advance online publication. DOI: 10.1016/j.pubrev.2024.102507

Pasquale, F. (2015). The black box society: The secret algorithms that control money and information. In *The black box society*. Harvard University Press. DOI: 10.4159/harvard.9780674736061

Patton, M. Q. (2015). *Qualitative research & evaluation methods.* Sage.

Paul, R., Imam, M. H., & Mou, A. J. (2023). AI-powered sentiment analysis in digital marketing: A review of customer feedback loops in IT services. *American Journal of Scholarly Research and Innovation*, *2*(2), 166–192. DOI: 10.63125/61pqqq54

Pendyala, S. K. (2024). *Healthcare data analytics: Leveraging predictive analytics for improved patient outcomes.*

Pérez-Campuzano, D., Ortega, P. M., Andrada, L. R., & Lopez-Lazaro, A. (2021). Artificial intelligence potential within airlines: A review on how AI can enhance strategic decision-making in times of COVID-19. *Journal of Aviation and Aeronautical Management*, *11*(2), 53–72. DOI: 10.3926/jairm.189

Perkins, M. (2023). Academic integrity considerations of AI large language models. *Journal of University Teaching & Learning Practice*, *20*(2), 7. https://arxiv.org/abs/2312.07086. DOI: 10.53761/1.20.02.07

Pholsook, T., Ramjan, S., & Wipulanusat, W. (2025). Enhancing airport services: Data-driven analysis of passenger satisfaction and service quality in Southeast Asia. *Engineering Management in Production and Services, 17*(2), 37–62. DOI: 10.2478/emj-2025-0011

Picard, R. W. (1997). *Affective computing*. MIT Press. DOI: 10.7551/mit-press/1140.001.0001

Pillai, R., Sivathanu, B., & Dwivedi, Y. K. (2020). Shopping intention at AI-powered automated retail stores (AIPARS). *Journal of Retailing and Consumer Services, 57*, 102207. DOI: 10.1016/j.jretconser.2020.102207

Pine, B. J., & Gilmore, J. H. (1998). Welcome to the experience economy. *Harvard Business Review, 76*(4), 97–105. PMID: 10181589

Pine, B. J., & Gilmore, J. H. (1999). *The experience economy: Work is theatre and every business a stage*. Harvard Business School Press.

Plé, L., & Cáceres, R. C. (2010). Not always co-creation: Introducing interactional co-destruction of value in Service-Dominant Logic. *Journal of Services Marketing, 24*(6), 430–437. DOI: 10.1108/08876041011072546

Pournader, M., Ghaderi, H., Hassanzadegan, A., & Fahimnia, B. (2021). Artificial intelligence applications in supply chain management. *International Journal of Production Economics, 241*, 108250. DOI: 10.1016/j.ijpe.2021.108250

Pradeep, P., Caro-Martínez, M., & Wijekoon, A. (2024). A practical exploration of the convergence of Case-Based Reasoning and Explainable Artificial Intelligence. *Expert Systems with Applications, 255*, 124733. DOI: 10.1016/j.eswa.2024.124733

Prayag, G., Hosany, S., Muskat, B., & Del Chiappa, G. (2017). Understanding the relationships between tourists' emotional experiences, perceived overall image, satisfaction, and intention to recommend. *Journal of Travel Research, 56*(1), 41–54. DOI: 10.1177/0047287515620567

Prebensen, N. K., Chen, J. S., & Uysal, M. (2014). *Creating experience value in tourism*. CABI Publishing. DOI: 10.1079/9781780643489.0000

Proactive Customer Support. (2024). Proactive Customer Support: Re-Architecting A Customer Support/Relationship Management Software System Leveraging Predictive Analysis/AI and Machine Learning. *Engineering Open Access, 2*(1), 39–50. DOI: 10.33140/EOA.02.01.04

Puntoni, S., Reczek, R. W., Giesler, M., & Botti, S. (2021). Consumers and artificial intelligence: An experiential perspective. *Journal of Marketing*, *85*(1), 131–151. DOI: 10.1177/0022242920953847

Qiao, G., Huang, S., & Vorobjovas-Pinta, O. (2024). Seeking tourism in a social context: An examination of Chinese rural migrant workers' travel motivations and constraints. *Leisure Studies*, *43*(4), 608–623. DOI: 10.1080/02614367.2023.2249259

Rabl, T., Del Carmen Triana, M., Byun, S.-Y., & Bosch, L. (2020). Diversity Management Efforts as an Ethical Responsibility: How Employees' Perceptions of an Organizational Integration and Learning Approach to Diversity Affect Employee Behavior. *Journal of Business Ethics*, *161*(3), 531–550. DOI: 10.1007/s10551-018-3849-7

Radanliev, P. (2025). Privacy, ethics, transparency, and accountability in AI systems for wearable devices [Review of *Privacy, ethics, transparency, and accountability in AI systems for wearable devices*]. *Frontiers in Digital Health, 7*, 1431246. Frontiers Media. DOI: 10.3389/fdgth.2025.1431246

Raffour Interactif. (2025). Review of French leisure tourism—Opodo Barometer 2025. Online. https://www.raffour-interactif.fr/site_ri/ventes/etude_vente.htm (Accessed March 6, 2026).

Rahimi, R., Thelwall, M., Okumus, F., & Bilgihan, A. (2022). Know r guests' preferences before they arrive at r hotel: Evidence from TripAdvisor. *Consumer Behavior in Tourism and Hospitality*, *17*(1), 89–106. DOI: 10.1108/CBTH-06-2021-0148

Rahman, A. (2024). AI AND MACHINE LEARNING IN BUSINESS PROCESS AUTOMATION: INNOVATING WAYS AI CAN ENHANCE OPERATIONAL EFFICIENCIES OR CUSTOMER EXPERIENCES IN U.S. ENTERPRISES. *Non Human Journal.*, *1*(1), 41–62. DOI: 10.70008/jmldeds.v1i01.41

Rai, A. (2020). Explainable AI: From black box to glass box. *Journal of the Academy of Marketing Science*, *48*(1), 137–141. DOI: 10.1007/s11747-019-00710-5

Rai, A., Constantinides, P., & Sarker, S. (2019). Next generation digital platforms: Toward human-AI hybrids. *Management Information Systems Quarterly*, *43*(1), iii–ix. DOI: 10.25300/MISQ/2019/431E0

Raihan, M. M. H., Subroto, S., Chowdhury, N., Koch, K., Ruttan, E., & Turin, T. C. (2025). Dimensions and barriers for digital (in)equity and digital divide: A systematic integrative review. *Digital Transformation and Society*, *4*(2), 111–127. DOI: 10.1108/DTS-04-2024-0054

Rajatheva, N., Atzeni, I., Bicais, S., Bjornson, E., Bourdoux, A., Buzzi, S., D'Andrea, C., Dore, J.-B., Erkucuk, S., Fuentes, M., Guan, K., Hu, Y., Huang, X., Hulkkonen, J., Jornet, J. M., Katz, M., Makki, B., Nilsson, R., Panayirci, E., . . . Xu, W. (2020). *Scoring the Terabit/s Goal: Broadband Connectivity in 6G* (Version 2). arXiv. DOI: 10.48550/ARXIV.2008.07220

Raji, M. A., Olodo, H. B., Oke, T. T., Addy, W. A., Ofodile, O. C., & Oyewole, A. T. (2024). E-commerce and consumer behavior: A review of AI-powered personalization and market trends [Review of E-commerce and consumer behavior: A review of AI-powered personalization and market trends]. *GSC Advanced Research and Reviews, 18*(3), 66. DOI: 10.30574/gscarr.2024.18.3.0090

Rane, J., Kaya, Ö., Mallick, S. K., & Rane, N. L. (2024). *Enhancing black-box models: Advances in explainable artificial intelligence for ethical decision-making*. DOI: 10.70593/978-81-981271-0-5_4

Rane, N. L., & Paramesha, M. (2024). *Explainable Artificial Intelligence (XAI) as a foundation for trustworthy artificial intelligence*. DOI: 10.70593/978-81-981367-4-9_1

Rane, N., Choudhary, S., & Rane, J. (2023). Hyper-personalization for enhancing customer loyalty and satisfaction in Customer Relationship Management (CRM) systems. *Available at SSRN* 4641044. DOI: 10.2139/ssrn.4641044

Rather, R. A., & Hollebeek, L. D. (2021). Customers' service-related engagement, experience, and behavioral intent in hotels. *International Journal of Contemporary Hospitality Management, 33*(1), 91–117. DOI: 10.1108/IJCHM-10-2019-0850

Raudenbush, S. W., & Bryk, A. S. (2002). *Hierarchical linear models*. Sage. (No DOI available)

Rawashdeh, A. M., Bakheet Elayan, M., Alhyasat, W., & Dawood Shamout, M. (2021). Electronic human resources management perceived usefulness, perceived ease of use and continuance usage intention: the mediating role of user satisfaction in jordanian hotels sector. *International Journal of Qualitative Research, 15*(2), 679–696. DOI: 10.24874/IJQR15.02-20

Reichheld, F. F., & Sasser, W. E.Jr. (1990). Zero defections: Quality comes to services. *Harvard Business Review, 68*(5), 105–111.

Ribeiro, A., Rivero, A. J. L., & Abrantes, J. L. (2025). The impact of artificial intelligence on consumer behavior towards brands: A systematic review. *Electronic Commerce Research*. Advance online publication. DOI: 10.1007/s10660-025-10063-7

Richter, S.. (2025). AI as a “more knowledgeable other” in social-constructivist assessment. *AI & Society*. Advance online publication. DOI: 10.1007/s43681-024-00626-z

Rivière, A., & Mencarelli, R. (2012). Towards a theoretical clarification of the notion of perceived value in marketing. *Research and Applications in Marketing*, *27*(3), 97–123.

Rodler, S., Kopliku, R., Ulrich, D., Kaltenhauser, A., Casuscelli, J., Eismann, L., Waidelich, R., Buchner, A., Butz, A., Cacciamani, G. E., Stief, C. G., & Westhofen, T. (2024). Patients’ trust in artificial intelligence–based decision-making for localized prostate cancer: Results from a prospective trial. *European Urology Focus*, *10*(4), 654–661. DOI: 10.1016/j.euf.2023.10.020 PMID: 37923632

Rodrigues, G. N., Mir, M. N. H., Bhuiyan, M. S. M., Rafi, M. D. A. L., Hoque, A. M., Maua, J., & Mridha, M. F. (2025). *NLP-driven customer segmentation: A comprehensive review of methods and applications in personalized marketing*. Data Science and Management.

Rojek, I., Mikołajewski, D., Prokopowicz, P., & Piechowiak, M. (2025). AI-based modeling and optimization of AC/DC power systems. *Energies*, *18*(21), 5660. DOI: 10.3390/en18215660

Rosário, A. T., Cruz, R., Moniz, L. B., & Casaca, J. A. (2024). Predictive analytics for customer behavior. In *Data-Driven Marketing for Strategic Success* (pp. 37–72). IGI Global. DOI: 10.4018/979-8-3693-3455-3.ch002

Ross, C., & Swetlitz, I. (2018, July 25). IBM's Watson supercomputer recommended 'unsafe and incorrect' cancer treatments, internal documents show. *Stat News*. https://www.statnews.com/2018/07/25/ibm-watson-recommended-unsafe-incorrect-cancer-treatments/

Russell, S., & Norvig, P. (2021). *Artificial intelligence: A modern approach* (4th ed.). Pearson.

Rust, R. T. (2020). The future of marketing. *International Journal of Research in Marketing*, *37*(1), 15–26. DOI: 10.1016/j.ijresmar.2019.08.002

S. M. I. (2024). Exploring AI-Driven Customer Service: Evolution, Architectures, Opportunities, Challenges and Future Directions. *International Journal For Multidisciplinary Research*, *6*(3), 22283. Advance online publication. DOI: 10.36948/ijfmr.2024.v06i03.22283

S.M., & Nianm. (2025). Digital transformation and AI in airline management: Aligning agility, innovation, and data-driven strategies. In Proceedings of the International Conference on Recent Advances in Engineering, Innovation and Technology.

Sabir, A. A., Ahmad, I., Ahmad, H., Rafiq, M., Khan, M. A., & Noreen, N. (2023). Consumer acceptance and adoption of AI robo-advisors in fintech industry. *Mathematics, 11*(6), 1311. Advance online publication. DOI: 10.3390/math11061311

Sadiq, E., Alkarani, H., & Chakranarayan, V. (2025). Predictive analytics in customer relationship management. In *2024 International Conference on IT Innovation and Knowledge Discovery (ITIKD)* (pp. 1–7). IEEE.

Safitri, A., Husin, N., Arifah, I. D., Dewi, R. S., Kharisma, F., & Kautsar, A. (2024). Metaverse user experience, customer engagement, and brand awareness relation as SMEs marketing strategies in Virtual Worlds. *2024 ASU International Conference in Emerging Technologies for Sustainability and Intelligent Systems (ICETSIS)*, 1092-1096. DOI: 10.1109/ICETSIS61505.2024.10459506

Sahut, J. M., & Laroche, M. (2025). Using artificial intelligence (AI) to enhance customer experience and to develop strategic marketing: An integrative synthesis. *Computers in Human Behavior, 170*, 108684. DOI: 10.1016/j.chb.2025.108684

Sai, S., Goyal, D., Chamola, V., & Sikdar, B. (2024). Consumer electronics technologies for enabling an immersive metaverse experience. *IEEE Consumer Electronics Magazine, 13*(3), 16–24. DOI: 10.1109/MCE.2023.3327530

Salawu, A., & Oyesomi, K. (Eds.). (2025). *Marketing Communication in African Languages*. Routledge.

Salesforce. (2024). *State of the AI connected customer*. Salesforce Research. https://www.salesforce.com/en-us/wp-content/uploads/sites/4/documents/research/State-of-the-Connected-Customer.pdf

Salvadore, M. (2015), Effects of virtual behavior on the physical behavior of the consumer: the case of smartphone use during a tourist stay. Management. University of Nice Sophia Antipolis, 2015.

Sandra, A. (2024). Adapting to Rapid Change in Consumer Demands.

Sarkar, S. (2019). *Customer-driven disruption: Five strategies to stay ahead of the curve*. Berrett-Koehler Publishers.

Saroop. P. (2025). Artificial intelligence in aviation: Enhancing efficiency, safety, and sustainability. International Journal of Advanced Research, Ideas, and Innovations in Technology, 11.

Saura, J. R., Škare, V., & Došen, Đ. O. (2024). Is AI-based digital marketing ethical? Assessing a new data privacy paradox. *Journal of Innovation & Knowledge*, *9*(4), 100597. DOI: 10.1016/j.jik.2024.100597

Schoorman, F. D., Mayer, R. C., & Davis, J. H. (2007). An integrative model of organizational trust: Past, present, and future. *Academy of Management Review*, *32*(2), 344–354. DOI: 10.5465/amr.2007.24348410

Selimovic, M., Abd Almisreb, A., & Amanzholova, S. (2024). The role of sentiment analysis in brand management and marketing: A comparative study. *Procedia Computer Science*, *251*, 579–584. DOI: 10.1016/j.procs.2024.11.152

Selwyn, N. (2019). *Should robots replace teachers?* Polity Press.

Selwyn, N., O'Neill, C., Smith, G., Andrejevic, M., & Gu, X. (2023). A necessary evil? The rise of online exam proctoring in Australian universities. *Media International Australia, Incorporating Culture & Policy*, *186*(1), 149–164. DOI: 10.1177/1329878X211005862

Şenbabaoğlu Danacı, E. (2023). Deneyimsel pazarlama aracı olarak sanal gerçeklik ve artırılmış gerçeklik. *İşletme Biliminin Üç Temel Alanında Yaşanan Gelişmeler: Muhasebe, Pazarlama ve Organizasyon*, 197-212.

Şencan, E. (2025). Artificial intelligence, organizational learning, and sustainable banking: Insights from Turkey for global business practice. *Thunderbird International Business Review*, tie.70062. Advance online publication. DOI: 10.1002/tie.70062

Şeyma, Y., & Cem, B. (2022). An Overview of the Structure of English Language Teaching Programs in the Netherlands, Austria, Denmark, Singapore, Norway, and Turkey: The Countries Ranking Among the Top Five in EF Proficiency Index. *I-Manager's Journal on English Language Teaching*, *12*(4), 1. DOI: 10.26634/jelt.12.4.18821

Shahid, S., Husain, R., Islam, J. U., & Hollebeek, L. D. (2025). Brand love and customer brand engagement for masstige: A cross-cultural perspective. *Journal of Product and Brand Management*, *34*(4), 545–561. DOI: 10.1108/JPBM-07-2024-5370

Sharma, R., & Kapoor, A. (2026). From Automation to Innovation: The Transformative Impact of AI on Business Functions in India. *Management Dynamics*, *26*(1), 4. DOI: 10.57198/2583-4932.1366

Shih, E., Venkatesh, A., Chen, S., & Kruse, E. (2013). Dynamic Use Diffusion Model in a Cross-National Context: A Comparative Study of the United States, Sweden, and India Dynamic. *Journal of Product Innovation Management*, *30*(1), 4–16. DOI: 10.1111/j.1540-5885.2012.00982.x

Shin, D. (2021). The effects of explainability and causability on perception, trust, and acceptance. [No DOI available]. *International Journal of Human-Computer Studies, 146*, 102551. DOI: 10.1016/j.ijhcs.2020.102551

Shin, D. (2021). The effects of explainability and causability on trust in AI. *Computers in Human Behavior, 123*, 106–110.

Shin, D., Chotiyaputta, V., & Zaid, B. (2022). The effects of cultural dimensions on algorithmic news: How do cultural value orientations affect how people perceive algorithms? *Computers in Human Behavior, 126*, 107007. DOI: 10.1016/j.chb.2021.107007

Shin, J. W. (2025). AI-driven privacy trade-offs in digital news content: Consumer perception of personalized advertising and dynamic paywall. *Journalism and Media, 6*(4), 170. DOI: 10.3390/journalmedia6040170

Shiwakoti, N., Hu, Q., Pang, M., Cheung, T. M., Xu, Z., & Jiang, H. (2022). Passengers' Perceptions and Satisfaction with Digital Technology Adopted by Airlines during the COVID-19Pandemic. *Future Transportation, 2*(4.0055). DOI: 10.3390/futuretransp2040055

Shmueli, G., & Koppius, O. R. (2011). Predictive analytics in information systems research. *Management Information Systems Quarterly, 35*(3), 553–572. DOI: 10.2307/23042796

Shu, J., Cao, M., Zhang, M., Wang, X., Cao, W., Fang, X., & Cao, M. (2020). Molecular Patching Engineering to Drive Energy Conversion as Efficient and Environment-Friendly Cell toward Wireless Por Transmission. *Advanced Functional Materials, 30*(10), 1908299. DOI: 10.1002/adfm.201908299

Shuqair, S., Costa Pinto, D., Lancelot Miltgen, C., & Viglia, G. (2024). When powerful artificial intelligence backfires. *International Journal of Hospitality Management, 120*, 103778. Advance online publication. DOI: 10.1016/j.ijhm.2024.103778

Siemens, G., & Baker, R. S. (2012). Learning analytics and educational data mining. *LAK Conference*. DOI: 10.1145/2330601.2330661

Singh Dhillon, P. K., & Tinmaz, H. (2024). Immersive realities: A comprehensive guide from virtual reality to metaverse. *Journal for the Education of Gifted Young Scientists, 12*(1), 29–45. DOI: 10.17478/jegys.1406024

Singh, A., Rana, N. P., & Parayitam, S. (2022). Role of social currency in customer experience and co-creation intention in online travel agencies: Moderation of attitude and subjective norms. *International Journal of Information Management Data Insights, 2*(2), 100114. DOI: 10.1016/j.jjimei.2022.100114

Singh, B., & Kaunert, C. (2024). Future of digital marketing: Hyper-personalized customer dynamic experience with AI-based predictive models. In *Revolutionizing the AI-digital landscape* (pp. 189–203). Productivity Press. DOI: 10.4324/9781032688305-14

Sipos, D. (2025). The effects of AI-powered personalization on consumer trust, satisfaction, and purchase intent. *European Journal of Applied Science. Engineering and Technology*, *3*(2), 14–24.

Sivarajah, U., Kamal, M. M., Irani, Z., & Weerakkody, V. (2017). Critical analysis of big data challenges and analytical methods. *Journal of Business Research, 70*, 263–286. DOI: 10.1016/j.jbusres.2016.08.001

Skordoulis, M., Patsatzi, O., Kalogiannidis, S., Patitsa, C., & Papagrigoriou, A. (2024). Strategic Management of Multiculturalism for Social Sustainability in Hospitality Services: The Case of Hotels in Athens. *Tourism and Hospitality*, *5*(4), 977–995. DOI: 10.3390/tourhosp5040055

Skyscanner. (2023). *Share of travelers who used a mobile device to plan or book travel in the last six months worldwide as of October 2023, by activity.* Online. https://www.statista.com/statistics/1421721/ accessed on 15 March 2026

Slade, S., & Prinsloo, P. (2013). Learning analytics: Ethical issues. *British Journal of Educational Technology*, *44*(6), 1510–1529. DOI: 10.1111/bjet.12085

Smith, W. R. (1956). Product differentiation and market segmentation as alternative marketing strategies. *Journal of Marketing*, *21*(1), 3–8. DOI: 10.1177/002224295602100102

Sodiya, E. O., Amoo, O. O., Umoga, U. J., & Atadoga, A. (2024). AI-driven personalization in web content delivery: A comparative study of user engagement in the USA and the UK. *World Journal of Advanced Research and Reviews*, *21*(2), 887–902. DOI: 10.30574/wjarr.2024.21.2.0502

So, K. K. F., King, C., & Sparks, B. (2014). Customer engagement with tourism brands: Scale development and validation. *Journal of Hospitality & Tourism Research (Washington, D.C.)*, *38*(3), 304–329. DOI: 10.1177/1096348012451456

Spence, M. (1973). Job market signaling. *The Quarterly Journal of Economics*, *87*(3), 355–374. DOI: 10.2307/1882010

Sridhar, U. (2025). Ethical frameworks for responsible ai development: Challenges and implementation strategies. *World Journal of Advanced Engineering Technology and Sciences*, *15*(1), 2028–2038. DOI: 10.30574/wjaets.2025.15.1.0420

Stahl, B. C.. (2023). Bias and objectivity claims in automated assessment. [No DOI available]. *AI and Ethics*.

Stahl, G. K., & Maznevski, M. L. (2021). Unraveling the effects of cultural diversity in teams: A retrospective of research on multicultural work groups and an agenda for future research. *Journal of International Business Studies*, *52*(1), 4–22. DOI: 10.1057/s41267-020-00389-9 PMID: 33487775

Steerling, E., Siira, E., Nilsen, P., Svedberg, P., & Nygren, J. (2023). Implementing AI in healthcare: The relevance of trust: A scoping review. *Frontiers in Health Services*, *3*, 1211150. Advance online publication. DOI: 10.3389/frhs.2023.1211150 PMID: 37693234

Su, C.-Y., & Chao, C.-M. (2022). Investigating Factors Influencing Nurses' Behavioral Intention to Use Mobile Learning: Using a Modified Unified Theory of Acceptance and Use of Technology Model. *Frontiers in Psychology*, *13*, 673350. DOI: 10.3389/fpsyg.2022.673350 PMID: 35651564

Sun, X., Wandelt, S., & Zhang, A. (2023). A data-driven analysis of the aviation recovery from the COVID-19 pandemic. *Journal of Air Transport Management*, *109*, 102401. DOI: 10.1016/j.jairtraman.2023.102401 PMID: 37034457

Sustacha, I., Banos-Pino, J. F., & Del Valle, E. (2023). The role of technology in enhancing the tourism experience in smart destinations: A meta-analysis. *Journal of Destination Marketing & Management*, *30*, 100817. DOI: 10.1016/j.jdmm.2023.100817

Suwignjo, P., Panjaitan, L., Baihaqy, A., & Rusdiansyah, A. (2023). Predictive analytics to improve inventory performance: A case study of an FMCG company. *Operations and Supply Chain Management: An International Journal*, *16*(2), 293–310. DOI: 10.31387/oscm0530390

Talukder, M. B. (2024). Implementing Artificial Intelligence and Virtual Experiences in Hospitality. In Manohar, S., Mittal, A., Raju, S., & Nair, A. J. (Eds.), *Advances in Hospitality, Tourism, and the Services Industry* (pp. 145–160). IGI Global., DOI: 10.4018/979-8-3693-2019-8.ch009

Talukder, M. B. (2025). Climate change adaptation strategies for a tourism destination: A study of Kuakata beach. *Acta Scientiarum Polonorum. Administratio Locorum*, *24*(1), 165–179. DOI: 10.31648/aspal.10073

Talukder, M. B. (2025). Current Trends and Future Research Directions on Eco-Friendly Stages of the Hotel Industry. *RPER*, (71), 7–18. DOI: 10.59072/rper.vi71.695

Tarofder, A. K., Haque, A., Nawaz, N., Raisal, I., Musah, A. A., & Kassim, M. D., A. A. (. (2023). Determinants of instant messenger (IM) adoption and its effect on team performance: Mediating role of knowledge creation and quality communication. *PLoS One*, *18*(11), e0289168. DOI: 10.1371/journal.pone.0289168 PMID: 37939130

Tashakkori, A., & Teddlie, C. (2010). Putting the human back in "human research methodology": The researcher in mixed methods research. *Journal of Mixed Methods Research*, *4*(4), 271–277.

Tausczik, Y. R., & Pennebaker, J. W. (2010). The psychological meaning of words: LIWC and computerised text analysis methods. *Journal of Language and Social Psychology*, *29*(1), 24–54. DOI: 10.1177/0261927X09351676

Teece, D. J. (2018). Business models and dynamic capabilities. *Long Range Planning*, *51*(1), 40–49. DOI: 10.1016/j.lrp.2017.06.007

Teepapal, T. (2025). AI-driven personalization: Unraveling consumer perceptions in social media engagement. *Computers in Human Behavior*, *165*, 108549. DOI: 10.1016/j.chb.2024.108549

Teixeira, B., Carvalhais, L., Pinto, T., & Vale, Z. (2025). Explainable AI framework for reliable and transparent automated energy management in buildings. *Energy and Building*, *347*, 116246. DOI: 10.1016/j.enbuild.2025.116246

Tettey, D. J., Chrisben, D., Victoria, M., Chukwubuikem, E. P., & Abdullahi, A. D. U. S. (2025). Responsible AI deployment in sustainable project execution: Ensuring transparency, carbon efficiency and regulatory alignment. *International Journal of Science and Research Archive*, *14*(3), 1686–1705. DOI: 10.30574/ijsra.2025.14.3.0920

Thaler, R. H., & Sunstein, C. R. (2008). *Nudge: Improving Decisions about Health, Wealth, and Happiness*. Yale University Press.

Tiwari, A. (2024). Leveraging AI-Powered Hyper-Personalization and Predictive Analytics for Enhancing Digital Experience Optimization. *International Journal of Research Science and Management*, *11*(9), 9–23.

Toledo, L. A., León, F. H. A. D., & de Sá, D. G. B. (2025). A convergência de marketing preditivo, data-driven marketing e inteligência artificial. *Revista Gestão Em Análise*, *14*(2), 26–45. DOI: 10.12662/2359-618xregea.v14i2.p26-45.2025

Toluwase, I., Shobande, A., & Atere, D. (2025). AI-powered screening models for expanding deal flow and identifying high-value corporate advisory opportunities. *Computer Science & IT Research Journal*, *6*(9), 662–688. DOI: 10.51594/csitrj.v6i9.2065

Toraman, Y., & Geçit, B. B. (2023). User acceptance of metaverse: An analysis for e-commerce in the framework of technology acceptance model (TAM). *Sosyoekonomi, 31*(55), 85–104. DOI: 10.17233/sosyoekonomi.2023.01.05

Trinh, M. (2025). AI-induced consumer vulnerability: Psychological mechanisms and marketplace implications. *Journal of Consumer Policy, 48*(1), 45–68. DOI: 10.1007/s10603-024-09532-7

Tussyadiah, I. P. (2020). A review of research into automation in tourism: Launching the Annals of Tourism Research curated collection on artificial intelligence and robotics in tourism. *Annals of Tourism Research, 81*, 102883. DOI: 10.1016/j.annals.2020.102883

Tussyadiah, I. P., & Zach, F. J. (2012). The role of geo-based technology in place experiments. *Annals of Tourism Research, 39*(2), 780–800. DOI: 10.1016/j.annals.2011.10.003

Tussyadiah, I., & Fesenmaier, D. R. (2009). Mediating Tourist Experiences. Access to Places via Shared Videos. *Annals of Tourism Research, 36*(1), 24–40. DOI: 10.1016/j.annals.2008.10.001

Tyrväinen, O., Karjaluoto, H., & Saarijärvi, H. (2020). Personalization and hedonic motivation in creating customer experiences and loyalty in omnichannel retail. *Journal of Retailing and Consumer Services, 57*, 102233. DOI: 10.1016/j.jretconser.2020.102233

Uddin, M., Irshad, M., Kandhro, I. A., Alanazi, F., Ahmed, F., Maaz, M., Hussain, S., & Ullah, S. S. (2025). Generative AI revolution in cybersecurity: a comprehensive review of threat intelligence and operations [Review of *Generative AI revolution in cybersecurity: a comprehensive review of threat intelligence and operations*]. *Artificial Intelligence Review, 58*(8). Springer Science+Business Media. DOI: 10.1007/s10462-025-11219-5

Usman, F. O., Eyo-Udo, N. L., Etukudoh, E. A., Odonkor, B., Ibeh, C. V., & Adegbola, A. (2024). A CRITICAL REVIEW OF AI-DRIVEN STRATEGIES FOR ENTREPRENEURIAL SUCCESS [Review of *A CRITICAL REVIEW OF AI-DRIVEN STRATEGIES FOR ENTREPRENEURIAL SUCCESS*]. *International Journal of Management & Entrepreneurship Research, 6*(1), 200. Fair East Publishers. DOI: 10.51594/ijmer.v6i1.748

Utami, R. D., & Wang, A. (2026). Balancing Personalization, Privacy, and Value: A Systematic Literature Review of AI-Enabled Customer Experience Management. *Information (Basel), 17*(2), 115. DOI: 10.3390/info17020115

Uzoka, A., Cadet, E., & Ojukwu, P. U. (2024). Leveraging AI-powered chatbots to enhance customer service efficiency and future opportunities in automated support. *Computer Science & IT Research Journal, 5*(10), 2485–2510. DOI: 10.51594/csitrj.v5i10.1676

Uzun, M., Demirezen, M. U., Koyuncu, E., & Tsourdos, A. (2019). Design of a Hybrid Digital-Twin Flight Performance Model Through. *Machine Learning*, 1–14. Advance online publication. DOI: 10.1109/AERO.2019.8741729

van Doorn, J., Mende, M., Noble, S. M., Hulland, J., Ostrom, A. L., Grewal, D., & Petersen, J. A. (2017). Domo arigato Mr. Roboto: Emergence of automated social presence in organizational frontlines and customers' service experiences. *Journal of Service Research, 20*(1), 43–58. DOI: 10.1177/1094670516679272

Vargo, S. L., & Lusch, R. F. (2008). Service-dominant logic: Continuing the evolution. *Journal of the Academy of Marketing Science, 36*(1), 1–10. DOI: 10.1007/s11747-007-0069-6

Vargo, S. L., & Lusch, R. F. (2016). Institutions and axioms: An extension and update of Service-Dominant Logic. *Journal of the Academy of Marketing Science, 44*(1), 5–23. DOI: 10.1007/s11747-015-0456-3

Venkatasubbu, S., Rambabu, V. P., & Jeyaraman, J. (2022). Predictive analytics in retail: Transforming inventory management and customer insights. *Australian Journal of Machine Learning Research & Applications, 2*(1), 202–246.

Venkatesh, V., & Davis, F. D. (2000). A theoretical extension of the technology acceptance model: Four longitudinal field studies. *Management Science, 46*(2), 186–204. DOI: 10.1287/mnsc.46.2.186.11926

Venkatesh, V., Morris, M. G., Davis, G. B., & Davis, F. D. (2003). User acceptance of information technology. *Management Information Systems Quarterly, 27*(3), 425–478. DOI: 10.2307/30036540

Venkatesh, V., Thong, J. Y. L., & Xu, X. (2012). Consumer acceptance and use of information technology: Extending the unified theory of acceptance and use of technology. *Management Information Systems Quarterly, 36*(1), 157–178. DOI: 10.2307/41410412

Verbeek, P.-P. (2005). *What things do: Philosophical reflections on technology, agency, and design*. Pennsylvania State University Press.

Verhoef, P. C., van Ittersum, K., Kannan, P. K., & Inman, J. (2022). Omnichannel retailing: A consumer perspective.

Verhoef, P. C., Kooge, E., & Walk, N. (2021). *Creating value with big data analytics: Making smarter marketing decisions*. Routledge. DOI: 10.4324/9781003011163

Viberg, O., Kizilcec, R. F., Jivet, I., Martínez Monés, A., Oh, A., Mutimukwe, C., Hrastinski, S., & Scheffel, M. (2024). Cultural differences in students' privacy concerns in learning analytics across Germany, South Korea, Spain, Sweden, and the United States. *Computers in Human Behavior Reports*, *14*, 100416. Advance online publication. DOI: 10.1016/j.chbr.2024.100416

Vinod, B. (2021). *Artificial Intelligence and Emerging Technologies in Travel*. Management for Professionals., DOI: 10.1007/978-3-030-70424-7_11

Volo, S. (2009). Conceptualizing experience: A tourist based approach. *Journal of Hospitality Marketing & Management*, *18*(2-3), 2–3, 111–126. DOI: 10.1080/19368620802590134

Waller, M. A., & Fawcett, S. E. (2013). Data science, predictive analytics, and big data: A revolution that will transform supply chain design and management. *Journal of Business Logistics*, *34*(2), 77–84. DOI: 10.1111/jbl.12010

Wamba, S. F., Akter, S., Edwards, A., Chopin, G., & Gnanzou, D. (2015). How 'big data' can make big impact: Findings from a systematic review and a longitudinal case study. *International Journal of Production Economics*, *165*, 234–246. DOI: 10.1016/j.ijpe.2014.12.031

Wamba, S. F., Gunasekaran, A., Akter, S., Ren, S. J. F., Dubey, R., & Childe, S. J. (2017). Big data analytics and firm performance: Effects of dynamic capabilities. *Journal of Business Research*, *70*, 356–365. DOI: 10.1016/j.jbusres.2016.08.009

Wandelt, S., Sun, X., & Zhang, A. (2023). AI-driven assistants for education and research? A case study on ChatGPT for air transport management. *Journal of Air Transport Management*, *113*, 102483. DOI: 10.1016/j.jairtraman.2023.102483

Wang, Z. (2025a). The Influence of Ai on Consumer Behavior: Shaping Choices and Preferences in the Digital Marketplace. SSRN *Electronic Journal*. DOI: 10.1016/j.sasc.2025.200397

Wang, D., Park, S., & Fesenmaier, D. R. (2012). The Role of Smartphones in Mediating the Touristic Experience. *Journal of Travel Research*, *51*(4), 371–387. DOI: 10.1177/0047287511426341

Wang, G., Qiu, H., & Ren, L. (2023). Determinants of tourists' intention to share travel experience on social media: An fsQCA application. *Current Issues in Tourism*, *26*(16), 2595–2612. DOI: 10.1080/13683500.2022.2091428

Wang, W., Li, X., & Law, R. (2025). Assessing the impact of AI-enabled service attributes on customer satisfaction and loyalty in chain hotels. *International Journal of Hospitality Management, 116*, 103613.

Wang, X., Lin, X., & Shao, B. (2022). How does artificial intelligence create business agility? Evidence from chatbots. *International Journal of Information Management, 51*(102535), 102535. Advance online publication. DOI: 10.1016/j.ijinfomgt.2022.102535

Wang, Y. F., & Petrina, S. (2013). Using learning analytics to understand the design of an intelligent language tutor-Chatbot Lucy. *International Journal of Advanced Computer Science and Applications, 4*(11).

Wang, Y., & Fan, J. (2025). Longitudinal gaps in AI-assessment research. *Frontiers in Education*. Advance online publication. DOI: 10.3389/feduc.2025.1522841

Wang, Z., Yuan, R., Li, B., Kumar, V., & Kumar, A. (2026). An empirical study of AI financial advisor adoption through technology vulnerabilities in the financial context. *Journal of Product Innovation Management, 43*(1), 14–30. DOI: 10.1111/jpim.12795

Wankhade, S. G., Sahni, M., León-Castro, E., & Olazabal-Lugo, M. (2025). Navigating AI ethics: ANN and ANFIS for transparent and accountable project evaluation amidst contesting AI practices and technologies. *Frontiers in Artificial Intelligence, 8*, 1535845. Advance online publication. DOI: 10.3389/frai.2025.1535845 PMID: 40385642

Wasela, K. (2023). The role of intangible cultural heritage in the development of cultural tourism. International Journal of Eco-Cultural Tourism. *Hospitality Planning and Development, 6*(2), 15–28.

Wedel, M., & Kannan, P. K. (2016). Marketing analytics for data-rich environments. *Journal of Marketing, 80*(6), 97–121. DOI: 10.1509/jm.15.0413

Weidig, J., & Kuehnl, C. (2023). The dark side of personalization: Recommendation source and consumer reactance in AI-based recommendations. *Psychology and Marketing, 40*(12), 2559–2575. DOI: 10.1002/mar.21914

Weisz, E., Herold, D. M., & Kummer, S. (2023). Revisiting the bullwhip effect: How can AI smooth the bullwhip phenomenon? *International Journal of Logistics Management, 34*(7), 98–120. Advance online publication. DOI: 10.1108/IJLM-02-2022-0078

Weller, A. (2019). Transparency: Motivations and challenges. In Samek, W. (Eds.), *Explainable AI: Interpreting, Explaining and Visualizing Deep Learning* (pp. 23–40). Springer., DOI: 10.1007/978-3-030-28954-6_2

Wirtz, J., Kunz, W. H., Hartley, N., & Tarbit, J. (2022). Corporate Digital Responsibility in Service Firms and Their Ecosystems. *Journal of Service Research, 26*(2), 173–190. DOI: 10.1177/10946705221130467

Wirtz, J., Patterson, P. G., Kunz, W. H., Gruber, T., Lu, V. N., Paluch, S., & Martins, A. (2018). Brave new world: Service robots in the frontline. *Journal of Service Management, 29*(5), 907–931. DOI: 10.1108/JOSM-04-2018-0119

Wirtz, J., & Pitardi, V. (2023). How intelligent automation, service robots, and AI will reshape service products and their delivery. *Italian Journal of Marketing, 2023*(3), 289–300. DOI: 10.1007/s43039-023-00076-1

Wolf, C. (2022). Diffusion of Innovations: Von Everett M. Rogers (1962). In Spiller, R., Rudeloff, C., & Döbler, T. (Eds.), *Schlüsselrke: Theorien (in) der Kommunikationswissenschaft* (pp. 151–170). Springer Fachmedien Wiesbaden., DOI: 10.1007/978-3-658-37354-2_10

Woolf, B. P. (2010). *Building intelligent interactive tutors.* Morgan Kaufmann., DOI: 10.1016/C2009-0-20118-5

Wu, Q., Xia, C., & Tian, S. (2025). AI-driven sentiment analytics: Unlocking business value in the e-commerce landscape. *arXiv.*

Wu, H.-C., & Cheng, C.-C. (2018). Relationships between technology attachment, experiential relationship quality, experiential risk, and experiential sharing intentions in a smart hotel. *Journal of Hospitality and Tourism Management, 37,* 42–58. DOI: 10.1016/j.jhtm.2018.09.003

Wust, K., & Bremser, K. (2025). Artificial intelligence in tourism through chatbot support in the booking process: An experimental investigation. *Tourism and Hospitality, 6*(1), 36. DOI: 10.3390/tourhosp6010036

Xie, Y., Ponsakornsathien, N., Gardi, A., & Sabatini, R. (2021). Explanation of machine-learning solutions in air-traffic management. *Aerospace (Basel, Switzerland), 8*(8), 224. DOI: 10.3390/aerospace8080224

Xing, H. (2022). Application Study of AI-pored Non-translatables Function in Computer-aided Translation. *Proceedings of the 2022 5th International Conference on Education Technology Management,* 104–109. DOI: 10.1145/3582580.3582597

Xu, X., Liu, W., Gursoy, D., & Buhalis, D. (2025). Trust, try, buy, and belong: How does artificial intelligence create a loyalty loop in hospitality? *Tourism Management Perspectives*, *45*, 101061.

Xu, Y., Ma, Y., Hu, R., & Wang, H. (2024). Predictive analytics techniques in consumer behaviour: A literature review. Advances in Economics. *Management and Political Sciences*, *97*, 20–31.

Yang, Q., Liu, Y., Cheng, Y., Kang, Y., Chen, T., & Yu, H. (2019). *Federated Learning*. Morgan & Claypool.

Yang, X., Xi, N., & Hamari, J. (2026). Understanding metaverse consumer motivation: A study on the perceived value, cultural dimensions, and prior experience in NFT assets purchase. *International Journal of Human-Computer Interaction*, •••, 1–35. DOI: 10.1080/10447318.2026.2618572

Yin, J., Qiu, X., & Wang, Y. (2025). The impact of AI-personalized recommendations on clicking intentions: Evidence from Chinese e-commerce. *Journal of Theoretical and Applied Electronic Commerce Research*, *20*(1), 21. DOI: 10.3390/jtaer20010021

Youseftorkaman, M., Kangaranifarahani, A., & Dana, D. (2023). Applications of Artificial Intelligence in the Aviation Industry and Air Accidents. *Mathematical Statistician and Engineering Applications*, *72*(2), 178.

Zawacki-Richter, O., Marín, V. I., Bond, M., & Gouverneur, F. (2019). AI in higher education: Systematic review. *International Journal of Educational Technology in Higher Education*, *16*, 39. DOI: 10.1186/s41239-019-0171-0

Zeide, E. (2017). The structural consequences of big data-driven education. [No DOI available]. *Big Data*, *5*(2), 164–172. DOI: 10.1089/big.2016.0061 PMID: 28632444

Zeithaml, V. A. (1988). Consumer Perceptions Of Price, Quality, And Value: A Means-End Model And Synthesis Of Evide nce. *Journal of Marketing*, *52*(3), 2–22. DOI: 10.1177/002224298805200302

Zeithaml, V. A., Berry, L. L., & Parasuraman, A. (1996). The behavioral consequences of service quality. *Journal of Marketing*, *60*(2), 31–46. DOI: 10.1177/002224299606000203

Zhang, D., Voorveld, H. A. M., & Boerman, S. C. (2023). Privacy concerns matter, knowledge does not: Investigating effects of online behavioral advertising among Chinese and Dutch adults. *Journal of Current Issues and Research in Advertising*, *44*(3), 392–410. DOI: 10.1080/10641734.2023.2199812

Zhang, F., & Graham, D. J. (2020). Air transport and economic growth: A review of the impact mechanism and causal relationships. *Transport Reviews*, *40*(4), 506–528. DOI: 10.1080/01441647.2020.1738587

Zhao, X., You, W., Zheng, Z., Shi, S., Lu, Y., & Sun, L. (2025). How do consumers trust and accept AI agents? An extended theoretical framework and empirical evidence. *Behavioral Sciences (Basel, Switzerland)*, *15*(3), 337. Advance online publication. DOI: 10.3390/bs15030337 PMID: 40150232

Zhou, T., & Tang, B. (2025). Examining user information disclosure on artificial intelligence-generated content platforms: A privacy calculus perspective. *Information Development*, 02666669251384288. Advance online publication. DOI: 10.1177/02666669251384288

Zhu, X., & Li, L. (2021). Flight time prediction for fuel loading decisions with a deep learning approach. https://www.sciencedirect.com/science/article/pii/S0968090X21001959

Zhu, A., Stroud, N. J., Minteer, C., Yoo, J., Ridgeway, C., Mooghali, M., Miller, J. E., & Barry, M. J. (2026). Key information influencing patient decision-making about AI in health care: Survey experiment study. *Journal of Medical Internet Research*, *28*, e75615. DOI: 10.2196/75615 PMID: 41525463

Zondag, T. M., Rozestraten, R., Grimmelikhuijsen, S., Jongsma, K. R., van Solinge, W. W., Bots, M. L., Vernooij, R. W. M., & Haitjema, S. (2024). The effect of artificial intelligence on patient–physician trust: Cross-sectional vignette study. *Journal of Medical Internet Research*, *26*, e50853. DOI: 10.2196/50853 PMID: 38805702

Zsarnoczky, M. (2017). How does artificial intelligence affect the tourism industry? *Journal of Management*, *31*(2), 85–90.

Zulaikha, S., Dewi, I. R., & Kurniawati, M. (2026). Unveiling the intellectual landscape of artificial intelligence and consumer behavior. *Discover Artificial Intelligence*, *6*(1), 2. DOI: 10.1007/s44163-025-00740-9

Żyminkowska, K., & Zachurzok-Srebrny, E. (2025). The role of artificial intelligence in customer engagement and social media marketing: Implications from a systematic review for the tourism and hospitality sectors. *Journal of Theoretical and Applied Electronic Commerce Research*, *20*(3), 184. DOI: 10.3390/jtaer20030184

About the Contributors

Maria Antónia Gonçalves Rodrigues has a PhD in Communication/Marketing, from the University of Vigo, Spain, a Master in Marketing, from the University of Porto, Portugal, a Bachelor's degree in Marketing, and a Bachelor's degree in International Trade, both from the Polytechnic of Porto, Portugal. She is a senior lecturer, a council member, and a Director of Marketing Bachelor's degree at the School of Business Sciences of Porto, Technical University of Porto, Portugal. She is a researcher at CEOS.PP and SIIS, ISEP P.Porto. She has published several papers and books, with IGI Global. She has organized a scientific event and participated in several scientific events. She supervised several MSc dissertations. She has received 2 awards/honors. She works in the area of Social Sciences with an emphasis on business and marketing management. Her research topics are consumer behavior, customer experience; business models, marketing services; digital marketing, tourism, and customer experience with technology (SST, AI, VR, AR, metaverse).

Maria Amélia Carvalho (Ph.D.) is an Assistant Professor at University of Maia and an invited adjunct professor at the School of Business Sciences of Porto of the Technical University of Porto. She is also an active member of the CEOS.PP research center. Her main research areas focus on brands and consumer behavior, and she has published articles in the Journal of Marketing Theory and Practice, Journal of Hospitality and Tourism Insights, Tourism Recreation Research, Consumer Behavior in Tourism and Hospitality, among others. Her research interests include city branding, customer engagement, consumer experience, city marketing, and service marketing. She has edited several academic books indexed in SCOPUS and serves as a referee for several academic journals.

Didar Buyuker Isler graduated with first place from Suleyman Demirel University Business Administration Department in 2001 and got her Phd in Suleyman Demirel University Business Administration Department in 2009. She has been working as a full time Professor in the same faculty since 2021. She has been giving lectures on Digital Marketing, Advertising, Marketing Research, Consumer Behavior on bachelor's degree and postgraduate degree. She has taken part as a researcher in various national projects and EU youth projects. She has articles on digital marketing, consumer purchasing behavior, social customer relations and has expertise on multivariate statistical methods such as; structural equation model, multiple regression models etc. She is a member of the Association of marketing and marketing research.

***

Jyoti is presently working in School of Hospitality & Tourism, Galgotias University, Uttar Pradesh, India. Her contributions focus on Research, Patent, Innovation and practices etc. Her Academic degrees and 18 years of experience working with global Universities/Hotels like Accor Group of Hotels, Metropolitan hotel Nikko, IEC group of college, Galgotias University has made her more receptive and prominent in her domain. She Received Master Degree in Tourism and Management from IGNOU University, Delhi. She has supervised many UG students in the field of research. She is also Member of AHLAI, ISHE etc. She has number of publications in International/National Journal and Conferences.

Lhoussaine Alla is a professor in management sciences at the National School of Applied Sciences, and a researcher at the LAREMEF laboratory, Sidi Mohamed Ben Abdellah University, Fez, Morocco. He is a permanent professor of various marketing management modules at Sidi Mohamed Ben Abdellah University in Fez (Morocco) and in several public and private business graduate schools. He is an accredited professional expert in Training Engineering, Professional Coaching and Mentoring young entrepreneurs. After a PhD thesis on creating value for the customer and its impact on the overall performance of companies, Prof. Lhoussaine Alla invested more in scientific research in marketing, through various scientific contributions in the form of participation in international conferences and symposia and scientific publications, in various themes inherent to Marketing (customer value creation, customer behaviour, e-marketing, customer experience, sales performance, Marketing Data Analytics, territorial marketing, territorial attractiveness, territorial economic intelligence, ...), finance (stock market performance, financial analysts, financing package,...), entrepreneurship (entrepreneur profile, startups, entrepreneurial resilience,...), tourism (tourist attractiveness, visitor behaviour, tourism, performance of tourist destinations,...), logistics (SC, SCM, SSCM, Green SCM, logistics performance,...).

Mukunda B.G., M.T.A (5 Years Integrated), IATA, UGC-NET, K-SET, Ph.D, MBA in Aviation Management, currently serves as an Assistant Professor in the School of Humanities and Social Sciences within the Department of Travel and Tourism at Mount Carmel (Deemed to be University) Bangalore, Karnataka. With over 13 years of teaching experience across esteemed institutions, he possesses a profound expertise in disciplines including travel, tourism, hospitality, and aviation. His academic pursuits are complemented by a robust research portfolio, characterized by the publication of 25 research papers in peer-reviewed, UGC care, and Scopus-indexed journals from globally renowned publishing houses such as Longdon, Taylor and Francis. Additionally, he has been an active participant in academic discourse, having delivered over 18 research papers at national and international seminars and conferences. His areas of specialization encompass a diverse spectrum, spanning travel agency and tour operations, Air Ticketing, Airlines Management, Hospitality Management, Global Tourism Geography. His research interest includes Community-Based Tourism, Heritage Tourism and sustainable tourism.

Ayan Basak is PhD (Hospitality), an Alumnus of IHM Bhubaneshwar (1995 batch) with over 28 years of experience. He has authored books - "Food and Beverage Service" and "Lost Recipes of Nawabi Cuisine". He has been awarded as 'Best Faculty Award' for the year 2009 and 2010 by IEC group of Institutions and has received Recognition Award of having met the highest standards of excellence in students' choice of the year 2021 by Niyati Human Response Centre.)

Badr Bentalha teaches Supply Chain and Operations Management at National School Of Business and Management – Fez, Sidi Mohamed Ben Abdellah University – Morocco. Dr. Bentalha investigates the structural dynamics and control of complex networks, applying his findings to supply chain management, Industry 4.0, risk analysis, and digital supply chains. His work emphasizes the intersection of supply chain management, operations research, industrial engineering, and digital technology. As a professor, he teaches undergraduate, graduate, and, doctoral courses in operations management, supply chain management, logistics, management information systems, and strategic management. Through guest lectures, webinars, and scholarly presentations, he engages students and fosters an active learning environment.Professor Bentalha specializes in supply chain and operations management, operations research, and service management. He is passionate about integrating knowledge across disciplines to solve real-world problems. He has delivered numerous invited plenary talks, keynotes, and panel discussions at conferences and global webinars.

Rahul Bharadwaj is an Assistant Professor at the School of Hospitality Management, Galgotias University, Greater Noida, India. His research and teaching focus on hospitality management, tourism studies, and experiential learning in the hotel industry. He has contributed to advancing academic and practical knowledge in the field through curriculum development, industry collaborations, and student-centered initiatives.

Rachid Boudri is a faculty member and researcher at Euromed Business School, part of Université Euromed de Fès (UEMF). He holds a PhD in Management Sciences from the Faculty of Legal and Economic Sciences of Fès (Université Sidi Mohamed Ben Abdellah), with a dissertation titled "From the Consumption Experience to the Phygital Shopping Experience: An Attempt at Conceptualization and Empirical Investigation in the Retail Sector." He also holds a Master's degree in International Management from the same faculty. Before joining UEMF, Rachid Boudri held several teaching and consulting positions. He served as an adjunct professor at ENCG Fès between 2019 and 2021, and later at the Private University of Fès (UPF) from 2020 to 2022. Alongside his teaching, he worked as a management consultant at ELC Consulting (2022-2024) and Orga Team (2021-2022), and as a management trainer at LMS (2021-2022), giving him a combined academic and operational expertise in marketing and management. His research focuses primarily on the consumption experience, phygital (physical-digital) marketing, and digital consumer behavior. His publications include an article on the perceived value of the shopping experience in times of crisis (Moroccan Business Review Research, 2022), as well as a netnographic study on the dimensions of the phygital shopping experience (Revue internationale des sciences de gestion, 2020). He has also contributed to several edited volumes published by IGI Global and L'Harmattan, including work on phygital marketing through an Amazon Go netnographic case study and on leveraging the "Made in Morocco" label for sustainable territorial marketing. Beyond his academic publications, Rachid Boudri regularly contributes to the Moroccan business press, notably in Les Inspirations Éco, where he has written on AI influencers and on the paradoxes of overconsumption during Ramadan, as well as an interview with Map Express on the same topic. In the classroom, he teaches a range of courses including Strategic Marketing, Digital Transformation, Digital Consumer Behavior, Community Management, Global Marketing Strategy, and Influencer Marketing and Social Media.

Piali Haldar earned her MBA from the Institute of Rural Management Anand and completed her PhD at Birla Institute of Technology, Mesra. Her core areas of specialization include rural marketing, rural development, branding strategy, and consumer behaviour. With over 20 years of experience in academia and research, she has published extensively in renowned journals listed in ABDC and Scopus. She has authored one textbook on Marketing and edited three academic books. Dr. Haldar has presented her research at numerous national and international conferences and has contributed more than 50 papers to reputed journals, edited volumes, and conference proceedings.

S. Harini is an accomplished academician with a strong foundation in management education and research. She holds an MBA, M.Com, and a Post Graduate Diploma in Business Management (PGDBM), and is currently pursuing a Ph.D. in Human Resources at the prestigious Saveetha School of Management. With over five years of experience as an Assistant Professor, Harini has taught both undergraduate and postgraduate students, fostering a passion for developing future leaders in business and management. Her academic excellence is underscored by her distinction as a Gold Medalist in MBA, reflecting her dedication and scholarly aptitude. Harini has actively contributed to the academic community, having presented more than 10 papers at national conferences and over 5 at international conferences. She has also participated in international workshops, continually enhancing her knowledge and staying abreast of global trends in human resource management. Known for her commitment to education, research, and personal growth, Harini is driven by a deep interest in human resources and is steadily building a reputation as a thought leader in the field.

Sneha Kapoor received her Bachelor's degree from University of Delhi. Currently she is pursuing Masters in Business Administration from J.C. Bose University of Science and Technology, YMCA, Faridabad, India. With a strong academic foundation and a keen interest in marketing, leadership and innovation, she aspires to make a meaningful impact in the business world. She actively engages in co-curricular activities, case study competitions and industry interactions to broaden her learning. Sneha envisions a career that blends creativity with strategy, driving growth and transformation.

Amandeep Kaur is an Assistant Professor at the University School of Business, Chandigarh University, Mohali, India. She earned her Ph.D. in Management from Punjabi University, Patiala. Her research interests include finance, accounting, sustainability, and business analytics. She has published research articles in reputed national and international journals and has patent publications. She is committed to excellence in teaching, research, and academic development. Activities

Özlem Keloğlu is a PhD Candidate in the Department of Business Administration at Muğla Sıtkı Koçman University, Türkiye. She received her bachelor's degree in Economics from Dokuz Eylül University in 2010 and her master's degree in Business

Administration from Muğla Sıtkı Koçman University. Her research interests include consumer behavior, experiential marketing, metaverse technologies, artificial intelligence and customer experience.

Manjit Kour is working as Professor at University Business School at Chandigarh University. She holds a PhD in Business Management from IK Gujral Punjab Technical University, India. She has a good research record with several research papers published in reputed journals. She is an editorial board member and reviewer of many reputed journals including Scopus and ABDC-indexed journals. Her areas of interest include sustainability, green practices, Fintech, online marketing trends and business ethics.

Santhosh Kumar P is a Master of Business Administration (MBA) candidate specializing in **Logistics and Supply Chain Management** at **Saveetha School of Management, Saveetha Institute of Medical and Technical Sciences (SIMATS), Chennai, India**. His academic interests encompass supply chain management, port and maritime logistics, sustainable operations, digital transformation, artificial intelligence, green technologies, marketing, and business analytics. He has gained practical industry exposure through internships in logistics, business operations, and corporate functions. During his internship at **V.O. Chidambaranar Port Authority (VOC Port), Thoothukudi**, he worked on research related to port operations, vessel waiting time, congestion management, and operational performance. This experience strengthened his understanding of maritime logistics, port efficiency, cargo movement, and supply chain optimization. He has also been involved in business development and corporate communication initiatives, enabling him to bridge academic knowledge with practical business applications. Santhosh has actively participated in research projects focusing on logistics performance, sustainable supply chains, customer behavior, digital technologies, and operational excellence. His research interests include Artificial Intelligence (AI), Green Technology Integration, smart logistics, maritime transportation, supply chain resilience, customer satisfaction, operational efficiency, and data-driven decision-making. He is particularly interested in exploring how emerging technologies such as AI, machine learning, and digital analytics can improve organizational performance and support sustainable business practices. His academic work emphasizes quantitative research methodologies and statistical analysis using tools such as SPSS, including descriptive statistics, reliability analysis, correlation, regression, ANOVA, and hypothesis testing. He has presented and developed research in areas related to logistics, operations management, and business strategy, with a focus on generating practical recommendations for industry. In addition to his research activities, Santhosh actively develops professional content, supports corporate branding initiatives through LinkedIn, and continuously enhances his expertise in supply chain management, logistics, digital marketing, and business communication. He is committed to lifelong learning and aims to contribute to high-quality research that advances knowledge in logistics, sustainable operations, and technology-enabled business transformation. His long-term career objective is to build expertise in global logistics and supply chain management while contributing to academic research and industry innovation through evidence-based solutions that improve operational efficiency, sustainability, and organizational competitiveness.

Tonmoy Malaker is an accomplished author, researcher and Lecturer of the Department of Business Administration of Daffodil International University, Dhaka, Bangladesh with a strong academic background in BBA and MBA majoring in Management Information Systems (MIS) from the University of Dhaka. His passion lies in exploring the intersection of business and emerging technologies. His diverse areas of interest include AI, Business analytics, IoT, Blockchain Technology, ERP. Through his extensive research and insightful writing, he sheds light on the intricate connections between his diverse areas of interests and real life. His work not only enriches the field of MIS but also inspires readers to engage with the world around them in meaningful and responsible ways.

Dev Kumar Mandal currently serves as an Assistant Professor in the Department of Management at Brainware University, Kolkata. Before this, he worked at ICRA Analytics Ltd and Shriram Finance Ltd. He holds an MBA in Finance and a Bachelor of Commerce degree from Vidyasagar University. Additionally, he has successfully cleared the UGC NET and WB SET examinations in Management.

Mehmet Marangoz (Prof. Dr.) The author works as a professor in Mugla Sıtkı Koçman University, Faculty of Economics and Administrative Sciences, Department of Business Administration, Product Management and Marketing. He completed his undergraduate education at Istanbul University, Faculty of Political Sciences, Business Administration Department (1995). He had his master's degree in Production Management and Marketing from Marmara University Institute of Social Sciences (1998) and his Ph.D. in Business Administration from Dokuz Eylül University Institute of Social Sciences (2003). His specializations are Marketing and Entrepreneurship. He has numerous published articles, national and international academic papers and books. He lectures at the undergraduate, graduate and doctoral levels. He is a member of the Marketing and Marketing Research Association. mehmetmarangoz@mu.edu.tr

Mohamed Musthakeem S is currently pursuing a Master of Business Administration (MBA) at the SIMATS School of Management, with a dual specialization in Logistics and Human Resource Management. As an emerging researcher, his academic focus lies at the intersection of supply chain efficiency and workforce management. He is actively engaged in research regarding. Mohamed is dedicated to contributing to the body of knowledge in contemporary management strategies.

Akhilesh Pandey is an academic researcher whose interdisciplinary work spans education, sustainability, hospitality management, and quality management systems. His research focuses on integrating responsible management practices, digital transformation, and institutional quality enhancement to address challenges in higher education and service-based industries. He has developed expertise in Quality Management Systems (QMS) and Hazard Analysis and Critical Control Points (HACCP), examining their role in strengthening food supply chain safety, regulatory compliance, and organizational sustainability. His work bridges theory and practice by offering applied frameworks for institutional governance and industry best practices. In educational technology and pedagogy, Dr. Pandey explores blended learning, competency-based education, and emerging digital tools to improve learner engagement and academic quality. He actively contributes as an author and reviewer for international journals and scholarly publishers, including IGI Global, with a strong commitment to academic integrity, methodological rigor, and impact-oriented scholarship.

Shivansu Sachan is Pursuing Ph.D. in Management, a Master's holder from Integral University, Lucknow, Bachelor's from IHM, Lucknow. Academic and professional accomplishments of 6 years with renowned organizations and institutes. My Teaching Career has been very satisfying and have continuously upgraded the skills and knowledge by attending many courses and training programs, seminars, conferences organized by different organizations and also delivered many lectures as a Hospitality sector.He is also assistant professor at Csjm University kanpur

Azize Sahin is an Associate Professor at the School of Business, Istanbul University, Türkiye, where her research and teaching focus on marketing. Her work spans services marketing, consumer behavior, and consumer psychology, with a particular emphasis on brand experience, brand trust, service quality, and customer loyalty. More recently, her research has extended to the role of artificial intelligence and digital technologies in service encounters, examining how algorithmic personalization, transparency, and authenticity shape consumer–firm relationships. Her broader areas of expertise include brand management, strategic marketing, customer satisfaction, and digital and social media marketing. She has published in international and national peer-reviewed journals and has contributed to research employing advanced quantitative methods such as structural equation modeling. Prior to joining Istanbul University, she held an academic position at Düzce University. She can be contacted at azize.sahin@istanbul.edu.tr (ORCID: 0000-0002-3115-6812).

Himanshu Sharma is a Professor in the School of Hospitality Management at Galgotias University, Greater Noida, Uttar Pradesh, India. He holds a Master's degree in Tourism Management and is currently pursuing a Ph.D. in Management. With over two decades of academic and industry experience, his expertise includes hospitality operations, tourism management, personality development, and service quality. He has published book chapters and research papers in reputed edited volumes and actively contributes to curriculum development, faculty training, and academic mentoring in hospitality and tourism education.

Manish Kumar Sharma is an academician and industry professional with over 21 years of combined experience in teaching and corporate sectors. His areas of expertise include tourism, hospitality, communication, and management studies. He has contributed to several research papers published in reputed indexed journals and has actively participated in national and international conferences. Dr. Sharma's work focuses on emerging trends in hospitality, human-centric service design, and experiential economy. His interdisciplinary approach bridges theoretical insights with practical industry applications, making his contributions valuable to both academia and practice.

Rajiv Sindwani holds PhD degree in the area of service quality management. Presently he is working in the Department of Management Studies at J C Bose University of Science and Technology, YMCA, Faridabad, India. He is having more than 15 years of experience in various sectors including consumer durables, banking and education. He has published many papers in reputed international journals and also presented papers in various international conferences.

Malini Singh is a distinguished academician at Amity School of Hospitality, with extensive experience in hospitality education, research supervision, and academic leadership. With over four decades of engagement in teaching, curriculum design, and institutional development, she has significantly contributed to advancing hospitality management education in India. Her research spans sustainable tourism, service quality, technological innovation, AI-driven service experience design, and contemporary issues in hospitality operations. Professor Singh has published more than 40 research papers in reputed national and international journals, including those indexed in Scopus, Web of Science, and IEEE. She actively mentors doctoral scholars and postgraduate researchers, fostering rigorous, theory-driven, and industry-relevant scholarship. Known for her interdisciplinary perspective and strategic academic vision, she bridges research, policy, and practice in hospitality studies. Through conference presentations, editorial engagements, and collaborative projects, Professor Singh continues to contribute meaningfully to global academic discourse and professional excellence in hospitality management.

Ramanjeet Singh is an Associate Professor at Chandigarh University, Punjab, India, where he has been serving since 20 June 2018. He received his Ph.D. in Computer Applications from Chandigarh University, with research focused on Underwater Wireless Sensor Networks (UWSNs). His areas of expertise include Linux Administration, DevOps, Internet of Things (IoT), Java Programming, Cloud Computing, Artificial Intelligence, Machine Learning, Wireless Sensor Networks, Cyber Security, and Software Engineering. Dr. Singh has over eight years of experience in teaching, research, curriculum development, and mentoring undergraduate and postgraduate students. His research focuses on energy-efficient routing protocols, intelligent communication systems, IoT, AI-driven applications, cloud computing, and emerging software technologies. He has authored several research articles, conference papers, and book chapters published in reputed international journals and publishers, including IEEE, Springer, and the International Journal of Intelligent Systems and Applications in Engineering. His recent research contributions include intelligent routing protocols for underwater wireless sensor networks, Green IoT, machine learning applications for exoplanet prediction, blockchain-based voting systems, and financial analytics. Dr. Singh actively participates in national and international conferences and is committed to advancing research, innovation, and industry-oriented education in the field of Computer Science and Engineering.

Chinna Srinivasan born in Warangal is an Associate Professor in ASET College of Science and Technology, Chennai, Tamil Nadu, India. He worked in the Department of Tourism Government of Andhra Pradesh and Telangana state Tourism Development corporation limited for more than 2 decades. He has participated in several international and national conventions like UNWTO, PATA,SEAT-convention, SATTE, TAAI, IATO, FHRAI He is a recipient of Telangana state Excellence award in Research writing in English language.He has a number of publications to his credit both in national and international journals.

Mohammad Badruddoza Talukder is an Associate Professor & Chairman at the College of Tourism and Hospitality Management at the International University of Business Agriculture and Technology (IUBAT) in Dhaka, Bangladesh. Holding a PhD from Lovely Professional University, India, he is renowned for his innovative integration of cutting-edge technologies such as Artificial Intelligence (AI), the Internet of Things (IoT), and Blockchain into tourism and hospitality management. His research explores the transformative impact of these technologies on smart tourism, cloud kitchens, and the broader industry landscape. As a prolific author, Dr. Talukder has published numerous scholarly articles and books, with forthcoming titles that address AI innovations in hospitality, the evolution of cloud kitchens, and the enhancement of digital literacy within hospitality education. His work shapes contemporary tourism and hospitality practices, skillfully marrying technological advancements with practical industry applications. Since 2008, Dr. Talukder has imparted his knowledge through a diverse array of courses in tourism and hospitality across various universities in Bangladesh.

Akshita Tiwari is currently a faculty member at Amity School of Hospitality, Amity University, Noida, Uttar Pradesh, where she teaches Front Office Operations and Management to Bachelor's in Hotel Management students and Master's in Hospitality students. She has also authored multiple Scopus publications and presented papers at international conferences. With a keen interest in teaching and research, she looks forward to contributing to the field of hospitality and continue to strive for excellence in her work.

Sivakami V MBA., NET (UGC), Ph.D currently serves as an Assistant Professor in the School of Humanities and Social Sciences within the Department of Travel and Tourism at Mount Carmel (Deemed to be University) Bangalore, Karnataka. She started her career as an industry professional and shifted to academics with a passion to teach in the tourism and travel sector. With over ten years of teaching experience across esteemed institutions, she possesses a profound expertise in disciplines including travel, tourism and hospitality. Her areas of specialization encompass a diverse spectrum, spanning Sustainable Tourism, Event Management, Hospitality Management, and Global Tourism Geography. Her academic pursuits are complemented by a robust research portfolio, characterized by the publication of fifteen research papers in peer-reviewed, UGC care, and Scopus-indexed journals. Her research interests include Community-Based Tourism, Virtual Marketing, sustainable tourism, rural tourism, and Visitor Impact Management. She is also serving as the Board of Studies (BOS) and Board of Examiner (BOE) in various universities and colleges in Bangalore.

Aysha Fathima Y is an Associate Professor in the Department of Management Studies at Jerusalem College of Engineering, Chennai, India. She holds a Ph.D. in Management and has over 20 years of teaching and research experience. Her research interests include financial management, banking, financial technology, business analytics, consumer behavior, and digital transformation. She has published several research papers in reputed national and international journals, including Scopus-indexed journals, and has co-authored books on Entrepreneurship and Business Economics.

Index

A

C

I

L

M

N

O

P

R

S

T

V

www.ingramcontent.com/pod-product-compliance
Lightning Source LLC
LaVergne TN
LVHW062028101126
852251LV00005B/49
9798337391595